THOMAS
AQUINAS

THOMAS AQUINAS

A HISTORICAL AND PHILOSOPHICAL PROFILE

PASQUALE PORRO

Translated by Joseph G. Trabbic
& Roger W. Nutt

THE CATHOLIC UNIVERSITY
OF AMERICA PRESS
Washington, D.C.

Originally published as *Tommaso d'Aquino: Un Profile storico-filosofico*
Copyright © 2012 by Carocci editore S.p.A., Roma

English translation Copyright © 2016
The Catholic University of America Press
The paper used in this publication meets the minimum requirements of
American National Standards for Information Science—Permanence of Paper
for Printed Library Materials, ANSI z39.48–1984.
∞

Design and typesetting by Kachergis Book Design

Library of Congress Cataloging-in-Publication Data
Porro, Pasquale.
[Tommaso d'Aquino. English]
Thomas Aquinas : a historical and philosophical profile /
Pasquale Porro ; translated by
Joseph G. Trabbic and Roger W. Nutt.
pages cm
Includes bibliographical references and index.
ISBN 978-0-8132-3010-8 (pbk : alk. paper)
1. Thomas, Aquinas, Saint, 1225?–1274. I. Title.
B765.T54P6713 2016
189'.4—dc23   2015032410

CONTENTS

TRANSLATORS' NOTE

Pasquale Porro writes in straightforward, clear Italian, which made our work much easier. In the Italian edition Porro uses existing Italian translations of Thomas (making occasional alterations) for quotations from Thomas's texts. In our translation of Porro we have used existing English translations of Thomas, when available, although we made several alterations to the ones we used to give a more literal rendering of the original or to fit with our word choices in surrounding text. See "Principal English Translations" in our bibliography for the translations we consulted. When there is no existing English translation of Thomas's text the rendering is, of course, our own. One issue we should comment on concerns the translation of the Italian terms *ente* and *essere* in English. In Porro's Italian text *ente* usually corresponds to Thomas's *ens*, and *essere* to his *esse*. Originally we considered distinguishing them by rendering *ente* as "a being/being" and *essere* as "existence. " In the end we settled on keeping *ente* as "a being/being" but translating *essere* mostly as "being" too. This decision is not unproblematic since in many cases we lose the clear linguistic distinction between *ente (ens)* and *essere (esse)*. But there are, arguably, good metaphysical and grammatical reasons for making this sacrifice. For Thomas, *esse*, in its most important metaphysical sense, is an act, that is, it is dynamic rather than static. This dynamic quality, we think, is better conveyed by "being" than by "existence" because the former, as a gerund, has the feel of an act whereas the latter lacks this sense. It is true that, according to this reasoning, we might have translated *essere* as "existing," "act of existing," "act of being," or (most literally) as "to be. " But these possibilities struck us in many instances as too awkward for a readable English text. Another reason for our decision is that *ens* is derived from *esse*. In English, "a being/being" is not derived from "existence. " So, translating *essere* as "existence" would not convey this fact of the relationship between the background Latin terms, whereas our rendering clearly indicates this relationship. Besides the metaphysical and grammatical reasons for our decision, previous translators have set a precedent: *inter alia,* Anton Pegis in his translation of the first book of the *Summa contra Gentiles* and Armand Maurer in his translation of the *De ente et essentia* (2nd revised edition). Both translations are currently the standard ones in English. Not everyone will agree with the approach we have taken, but we hope that the reasons for our decision will be seen to have merit. Another, related, issue concerns the translation of the Italian terms *esistere* and *esistenza*. Although these terms are often meant to correspond to some form of the Latin *esse*, we translated them respectively as "to exist/existing" and "existence" when "being" sounded strange in English.

We thank Sr. Albert Marie Surmanski, OP, for her generous help in proofreading. We thank Susan Needham for her meticulous copyediting, which improved the English of our translation and, in general, cleaned up the text. We thank our wives for their patience and support during the year that we worked on this book.

Joseph G. Trabbic
Roger W. Nutt

AUTHOR'S PREFACE

Writing a historical and *philosophical* profile of a thinker who did not think of himself as a philosopher and, in all probability, would not have accepted the title, might seem pointless if not exactly fiendish. The whole thing could seem still more paradoxical since Thomas Aquinas has been considered, starting at least with Leo XIII's encyclical *Aeterni Patris* (1879), the "prince" of Christian *philosophers*. It is, nevertheless, a fact that Thomas Aquinas by no means considered himself a philosopher. In his eyes, philosophy in general represented a time that was perhaps glorious but was now over, a period that began with the Greeks and ended with the Arabs—an experience to be spoken of in the past tense.

There are, however, four good reasons not to consider as arbitrary this attempt to dress Thomas in garments that are not his own.

The first is that, from the very beginning, in writing his own theological works Thomas always had the works of the philosophers in mind, works that indeed often constituted a large part of his citations. In a word, there is a reason why in a strictly theological work like his Commentary on Peter Lombard's *Sentences* (which was one of Thomas's very first writings) Aristotle is cited more than two thousand times, a number that is almost double that of the citations of Fathers of the Church like Augustine. And neither is it by chance that, to prepare some of the more delicate and important sections of his *Summa theologiae*, Thomas decided to write analytical commentaries on the works of Aristotle that would be the "scientific point of reference," as we would say today, for confronting specific topics (the *De anima* for the psychology section of the *Summa*, the *Nicomachean Ethics* for the practical questions developed in the second part).

The second reason is that Thomas never ceased to read and comment on the works of Aristotle and other philosophers, even up to the last months of his life. This is all the more noteworthy because Thomas did not teach in the faculty of arts (that is, the faculty that, at least in Paris, after the statutes of 1255, was transformed into a true philosophy faculty, although it retained the traditional name), but twice in the faculty of theology and then in theological *studia* of the Dominican order—institutional contexts in which commenting on Aristotle was not the primary task. So, Thomas commented on Aristotle not because he was obliged to but because he *chose* to do so. And the fact that many philosophical commentaries were concentrated in the last years of his life is especially significant. After much theological work had already been accomplished, Thomas continued to read and comment on works such as the *De caelo et mundo*, the *Meterologica*, and the *De generatione et corruptione*. Thomas's lively intellectual curiosity had led him over the course of his career to procure for himself not only everything of the Latin and Greek Fathers that was available but also all of the new translations of philosophical works. Once again it was not by chance that Thomas was the first to realize that the *Liber de causis*—a text in wide circulation but about whose origin quite disparate hypotheses had been formed—was, in reality, an Arab text based upon Proclus's *Elementatio theologica*—a discovery that was made possible by the fact that he had carefully read the Latin translation of the *Elementatio* produced at the time by William of Moerbeke and by his deep and broad knowledge of the philosophical vocabulary and translations.

The third reason is that Thomas himself clarified (above all in his Commentary on Boethius's *De Trinitate* and in the *Summa contra Gentiles*) the role that philosophy can continue to play within Christian theology, a role that we can reduce to three principal functions: (a) to demonstrate certain presuppositions or "preambles" of the faith accessible to natural reason, such as the existence and oneness of God; (b) to illustrate, through appropriate likenesses, certain truths of the faith that are otherwise hard to communicate and understand; (c) to refute rationally every possible argument against the faith. A good part of Thomas's output, in effect, aims at doing these three things, and this obviously justifies its broad use of philosophical argumentation.

The fourth reason is that, in defining his own professional occupation, Thomas adopted the term *sapiens* or "wise man." This is a term that, although it was certainly not unknown in the theological lexicon, and was, indeed, a fixture of it, nonetheless indicated (in the Aristotelian tradition in particular) the philosopher and the metaphysician. Thomas's *sapientia* is evidently theology founded on revelation (*sacra doctrina* or *theologia nostra*), but it retains many of the characteristics attributed by Aristotle to philosophy. Thus, even if what was said earlier is true, namely, that Thomas would perhaps never have accepted the title "philosopher," it is also true that when he describes what pertains to the task or function of the wise man (the *officium sapientis*), he employs the Aristotelian characterization of philosophical wisdom.

To these four reasons, we could add a fifth, and that is the fact that the very masters of the Paris faculty of arts (the "philosophers" of that period) considered Thomas, if not exactly as one of their number, as someone quite close to their interests. We will return to this in Chapter 6. If philosophy, for Thomas, belongs to a time that has come to a close because revelation has altered the situation, that time has not died or been forgotten: what it produced retains its vital function, and this to such a degree that Thomas never ceased to make use of it and to engage with it as long as he was intellectually active, that is, up to a few weeks before his death.

If we keep these reasons in mind, and we maintain the caution with which we started, the idea of writing a new *philosophical* profile of Thomas might prove (regardless of the outcome) not so improvident and desperate after all. The important thing is not to take it for granted that Thomas was a philosopher and that philosophy is, so to say, naturally and perfectly integrated in his theological reflection. As Thomas himself does not fail to acknowledge in the *Summa theologiae*, philosophy is and always will be something extrinsic to the realm of *sacra doctrina*. On the other hand, we should not succumb to the opposite error, viz., holding that *sacra doctrina*—the knowledge that Thomas considered himself to be serving—is something non-rational or non-scientific, as if human rationality were destined to explicate itself only in the realm of philosophy. In Thomas's view, theology too is a *science* (and a principally speculative science despite its practical implications) and it too develops rational arguments (as the entirety of Thomas's work demonstrates). The principles from which philosophy and theology begin are different. In the case of philosophy these are principles accessible to natural reason, and in the case of theology they are principles held by faith. But from start to finish the latter principles possess and maintain a scientific character. They do so from the start since, as Aristotle himself teaches, no science calls into question the existence of its own subject matter and principles, but proceeds from these to reach its own conclusions. And they continue to maintain their scientific character because the principles that *for us* are an article of faith are in reality evident (and thus epistemologically founded) in a superior science, that which God has of himself (and which the blessed have of God). The Aristotelian doctrine of the subalternation of the sciences, as we shall have ample opportunity to verify, is the true keystone of the whole edifice of theological science.

At this point two questions of method could be raised. The first regards the manner in which we might prove and distinguish the purely philosophical contents from the purely theological ones. While such a neat division is impossible, for the reasons just mentioned, we could employ a different criterion mentioned several times by Thomas himself. According to this criterion, there are truths of faith that are accessible to natural reason (everything that touches on God's existence and everything that has to do with his acting as a cause in the universe); these truths as such were already accessible to the philosophers and so we can and must take account of the arguments that they have developed in this respect. But how God is in himself—that is, everything that regards the divine *essence*—is inaccessible to natural reason and, therefore, to philosophy. In this case the discourse cannot but begin from revelation and what is held on faith. This means, for example, that the consideration of the Trinity and the Incarnation (questions that have to do with God in himself or his essence) belong exclusively to theology, and because of this, trinitarian theology and Christology shall be at the margins of our study—even if it would be naive to deny that both areas at any rate have interesting philosophical implications. Obviously, with regard to Thomas's philosophical commentaries, the question of philosophical pertinence does not arise.

The second question regards the thread to be followed in reconstructing the principal philosophical elements within Thomas's work. The classical and simplest solution would have been to adopt a purely systematic criterion, identifying certain major themes or aspects, including disciplinary ones (metaphysics, psychology, ethics, natural philosophy, etc.), and dedicating a chapter to each one. This approach runs the risk of misleading, because it reduces to a "system" what was not conceived as such. Moreover, this approach also carries with it the danger of reproducing in an artificial and somewhat stale way, not Thomas's thought, but the thought of "Thomism," that is, the way in which such thought has been interpreted and fixed by Renaissance commentators and above all by commentators of the nineteenth century and the first six or seven decades of the twentieth century. The great fame of Thomas Aquinas is undoubtedly linked to the fact that the Catholic Church chose him—by a decision that was fixed in *Aeterni Patris* but reaffirmed in more recent times too—as the most authoritative point of reference for Christian thought. This undisputed privilege has, nevertheless, sometimes produced an opposite effect, suggesting indeed an image of Thomism as an homogenous and rigid system—if not one that is also dogmatic and closed—without taking into account the effective context in which the different themes of Thomas's reflection were developed, or his interlocutors (usually read only *through* Thomas rather than vice-versa), or the unique intellectual vivacity of the Dominican master (which we have already mentioned)—a thinker who was, in fact, not at all dogmatic or conservative, as his own complicated and controverted legacy bears witness.

To distance ourselves from this tendency we have chosen instead to try to reconsider Thomas's thought in its very creation, retracing in chronological order the various phases of his output and seeking to show the continuity as much as the discontinuity, the subsequent reconsiderations, and the problematic twists and turns. But since a philosophical introduction must, in any event, be easy to consult and use (in the sense that the readers must be able to find what most interests them without too much difficulty), we have tried to highlight, in each of the works considered, the major themes, doing so with the awareness that this procedure exposes itself to two dangers: an inevitable margin of arbitrariness and a certain repetitiveness since Thomas often returns to the same themes in different works. The book's table of contents should make evident this attempt to bring and hold together the diachronic approach with the thematic and content-focused approach—or at least that is the hope.

In the great mass of secondary literature on Thomas we have privileged the more recent contributions, partly to be consistent with our announced intention to distance Thomas, to some extent, from Thomism.

Finally, I have the pleasure of dedicating this work, beyond its uncertain results, to two different people. The first is the Polish scholar Leszek Kuc, who, in fact, died more than twenty years ago. He was the first to guide me in a reading—that had very little of the dogmatic and conventional about it—of Thomas's texts. The second is the current president of the Leonine Commission, Adriano Oliva, OP, who has always honored me not only with indispensable information and advice but also with his profound and valuable friendship. I hope that the approach to Thomas's works that I attempt does not depart very far from their teaching nor disappoint others.

I would like to thank Lucrezia Iris Martone, Marienza Benedetto, and Francesco Marrone for their valuable collaboration in correcting the drafts. I feel obliged to specify that this work represents one of the products of the *Progetto COFIN/PRIN 2009: Filosofia e teologia nel Medioevo: modelli epistemologici e implicazioni antropologiche* (Bari Research Unit, Pasquale Porro, scientific director; Loris Sturlese, national coordinator).

Pasquale Porro

THOMAS
AQUINAS

1

STUDENT YEARS AND
BACCALAUREATE

—————•◦•◦•—————

We can determine the date of Thomas's birth only by calculating backwards from the date of his death (March 7, 1274), at which time, William of Tocco tells us in his *Ystoria sancti Thomae*—which was prepared in view of Thomas's canonization—he was forty-nine.[1] But this is an ambiguous claim because (and this too is on the basis of what Tocco himself later adds) it is not clear whether at the time of his death Thomas had completed forty-eight years (and so entered into his forty-ninth year) or was already forty-nine years old (and so had entered into his fiftieth year). Taking these oscillations into account, the year of his birth could have been 1225 or 1224 (here leaving aside the fact that other historians, for different reasons, do not exclude an earlier date, around 1220–21, nor a later one, and that is 1226).[2] The place of birth, Roccasecca, poses far fewer problems. It is located in the southern part of present-day Lazio, about half-

1. See William of Tocco, *Ystoria sancti Thomae de Aquino*, Studies and Texts 127, ed. C. Le Brun-Gouanvic (Toronto: Pontifical Institute of Mediaeval Studies, 1996), 205 (chap. 65). The most accurate reconstructions of the life and chronology of the work of Thomas, to which we make reference several times in the course of this volume, are: James Weisheipl, *Friar Thomas d'Aquino: His Life, Thought, and Work* (Washington, D.C.: The Catholic University of America Press, 1983); Simon Tugwell, "The Life and Works of Thomas Aquinas," in *Albert and Thomas: Selected Writings* (New York: Paulist Press, 1988), especially 201–67; and especially J.-P. Torrell, *Saint Thomas Aquinas*, vol. 1, *The Person and His Work*, trans. Robert Royal (Washington, D.C.: The Catholic University of America Press, 1996).

2. For the 1220–21 hypothesis, see G. Abate, "Intorno alla cronologia di San Tommaso," *Miscellanea Franciscana* 50 (1950): 231–47; C. J. Vansteenkiste in *Rassegna di Letteratura tomista* 24 (1991): 11–12. The same hypothesis was reaffirmed, or at least held not to be wholly false, by Adriano Oliva, OP, the current president of the Leonine Commission, in a critical edition of the works of St. Thomas: A. Oliva, *Les débuts de l'enseignement de Thomas d'Aquin et sa conception de la* Sacra Doctrina. *Avec l'édition du prologue de son Commentaire des* Sentences, Bibliothèque Thomiste 58, Librairie Philosophique (Paris: J. Vrin, 2006), especially 202n53, and 252–53n173. For the proposal regarding 1226, see Tugwell, "The Life and Works," 201.

way between Naples and Rome, and so on the border between what were then imperial lands (the Kingdom of Sicily under Frederick II) and papal territory. Thomas's family, a minor branch of the counts of Aquino, was aligned with the emperor, even though one of the older brothers eventually switched to the papal side and was condemned for treason. The last of many children, Thomas was for this reason excluded from the hereditary line and thus, from the time that he was small, an "oblate" entrusted by the family to the Abbey of Montecassino in view of an ecclesiastical career in the Benedictine order. Indeed, the family had a reasonable hope that one day he would become the abbot of that monastery. As an adolescent, perhaps around 1239, Thomas was sent to Naples to study. Here he probably had his first encounter with philosophy in general and with Aristotle in particular, thanks to the presence of capable teachers (among whom, according to Tocco's biography, were Peter of Ireland and a certain Martin, whose identity is not further specified) in the local *studium* founded by Frederick II in 1224.[3] But most importantly in Naples he had contact with two Dominican friars—in fact, the only two Dominican friars whom Frederick had not expelled from the kingdom (at the time the emperor was as much at odds with the mendicant orders as he was with the papacy). Thomas, as it seems, was immediately attracted by the order's ideals (especially the great importance attributed to intellectual formation and to the choice of voluntary poverty) and so much so that he received the Dominican habit in 1244. Thomas's entrance into the order, however, was firmly opposed by his family, who saw its plans for the Abbey of Montecassino upset. A mendicant order such as the Dominicans could not assure prestige or income. His mother went to Naples to try to dissuade him, but Thomas had already left, traveling with the master general of the order, John of Wildeshausen (also known as John the Teuton), in the direction of Rome and Bologna. The family decided then to intervene: two of Thomas's brothers—with the assistance, it seems, of Pier delle Vigne, who at

3. On the origins of the *Studium* in Naples see the recent outline by F. Delle Donne, "Per scientiarum haustum et seminarium doctrinarum: storia dello *Studium* di Napoli in età sveva," *Quaderni del Centro di Studi normanno-svevi* 3 (Bari: Adda, 2010). Since a large portion of the documents were lost, we do not have a sufficiently reliable and complete list of active teachers at the *studium* in Naples during the Swabian period. But see F. Torraca "Le Origini. L'età sveva," in *Storia della Università di Napoli, ed.* Torraca et al. (Naples: Ricciardi, 1924), 1–16. Doubts about the reliability of William of Tocco's information, in particular about whether Peter of Ireland was actually one of Thomas's teachers, were recently advanced by A. A. Robiglio in "'Neapolitan Gold': A Note on William of Tocco and Peter of Ireland," *Bulletin de Philosophie Médiévale* 44 (2002): 107–11. For the reply of M. Dunne, see "Concerning 'Neapolitan Gold': William of Tocco and Peter of Ireland: A Response to Andrea Robiglio," *Bulletin de Philosophie Médiévale* 45 (2003): 61–65. For Robiglio's rejoinder, see "'Et Petrus in insulam deportatur': Concerning Michael Dunne's Opinion on Peter of Ireland," *Bulletin de Philosophie Médiévale* 46 (2004): 191–94.

the time was a secretary and envoy of Frederick II—intercepted the friars and brought Thomas back to Roccasecca, where he was forced to remain for about a year. But, overcoming his family's resistance, Thomas was able to return to the order, first in Naples and then in Paris, where he was able to complete his philosophical studies (either at the faculty of arts or, more probably—according to the established custom of the mendicant orders—at the Dominican priory of Saint-Jacques) and start his theological studies under the guidance of Albert the Great, the Dominican master who was the architect of the plan to make the philosophy of Aristotle and his Arab interpreters available to Latin Christianity. In June of 1248 the order decided to start a *studium generale* (that is, an institute of higher learning) in Cologne. Its organization was entrusted to Albert the Great, who chose to take Thomas with him as an assistant. In this capacity Thomas was put in charge, among other things, of putting together his master's notes on Pseudo-Dionysius's *De divinis nominibus* and on Aristotle's *Nicomachean Ethics*, two works on which Thomas himself would comment some years later and that indisputably played a hugely important role in the course of his intellectual formation. It has long been maintained (beginning above all with the theses of Weisheipl) that Thomas gave "cursory" lectures (brief and essentially directed at the literal sense) on some books of the Bible, specifically Jeremiah, Lamentations, and (in part) Isaiah. But it appears, nevertheless, more probable that these biblical courses occurred after Thomas's return to Paris in 1251 or 1252.[4] In fact, at this time Thomas was sent back to Paris to assume the position of bachelor of the *Sentences* at the university, which meant that he was an assistant to a regent master and had the specific task of reading and commenting on the *Sentences* of Peter Lombard (a collection of opinions of Fathers of the Church, composed in the twelfth century and subsequently adopted in Paris as a basic theology textbook, about which we shall have more to say later). The first courses on the Bible are not of philosophical interest, inasmuch as they centered on a strictly literal interpretation of the texts. From the theological—or, at least, spiritual—perspective, *Super Isaiam* is partly an exception. We have this text in part thanks to a manuscript that has come down to us in the author's own hand (Vat. lat. 9850, 34–50) that presents a series of marginal annotations (which in the non-autograph part merge with the principal text). Such annotations, called *collationes*, are summary notes made by Thomas to prepare his lectures and to broaden his own exposition in other directions (referencing other biblical passages or the possible allegorical or moral meaning of

---

4. This has been suggested by Adriano Oliva with formidable argumentation in *Les débuts de l'enseignement*, 207–24.

the texts).[5] At any rate, it is a fact that in his biblical exegesis Thomas remained faithful to the principle of the priority of the literal sense.

DE PRINCIPIIS NATURAE: THE STRUCTURE
OF THE NATURAL WORLD

Two of the very first writings of Thomas from the period of his baccalaureate— *De principiis naturae* and *De ente et essentia*—offer us the best possible introduction to their author's philosophical vocabulary. Both opuscules were written more or less around 1255 at the request of his Dominican confreres (in the case of *De principiis naturae*, it was Brother Sylvester, who was perhaps another friar of Saint-Jacques). Indeed, it might be fitting to note from the beginning that roughly one-third (26 of about 90) of Thomas's works were written in response to requests from confreres, friends, superiors (even the pope himself), but also from sovereigns, countesses, and other laypersons. This fact alone gives the lie to the ill-informed belief that the Scholastic theologians were isolated researchers, removed from the social milieu and historical events of their own age.

As the title itself of the opuscule suggests, *De principiis naturae* (which could also date from 1252–53, if not to Thomas's stay in Paris prior to his sojourn in Cologne, when he would have completed his education in the faculty of arts, completely assimilating Aristotle's *Metaphysics* and *Physics*) also aims in particular at illustrating the principles that we can use to read the structure of natural reality. The point of departure is simple and evident: everything that we ordinarily observe in nature is subject to change. These changes are never a passage from absolute nothingness to being, but from being in a certain mode (viz., under a determinate *form*) to being in another mode (under *another form*). In other words, in the language of the Aristotelian lexicon already definitively in use, the whole of natural reality is marked by the passage from *being in potency* to *being in act*, that is, from that *which does not yet exist* as this determinate thing (but does always already exist as some other determinate thing) to that *which instead already exists* as this determinate thing. But being in its turn is twofold: we can distinguish *substantial being* from *accidental being*. Substantial being is the being proper to every substance as substance. For example, the being of man as man (the being, that is, of the substance "man," which is given by the substantial form of man). Accidental being is that proper to an accident that can inhere in a substance. For example, the being white of man (being

5. See P.-M. Gils, Les *"Collationes marginales* dans l'autographe du Commentaire de S. Thomas sur Isaïe," *Revue des Sciences Philosophiques et Théologiques* 42 (1958): 254–64; J.-P. Torrell and D. Bouthillier, "Quand saint Thomas méditait sur le prophète Isaïe," *Revue Thomiste* 90 (1990): 5–47.

white does not, in fact, define man as such, because whiteness does not enter
into the definition of the substance "man"). Being of the first sort (substantial
being) is absolute insofar as it does not depend on another (the Latin term
ab-solutus means precisely "free" or "loosed" from another). The second sort of
being (accidental being) is relative because it is added onto the first and cannot
obtain without it.

Every form supposes a substratum that can receive it, that is, a potential
substratum. This can be called "matter." Matter is, therefore, what can receive
different forms. But matter too is understood in different ways, depending on
whether it is referred to substantial or accidental being. If we are talking about
substantial being, then it is matter *from which*, and if we are talking about accidental being, then it is matter *in which*. Let us take the case of the substantial
being of man: the matter *from which* man has his origin as a substance is the
sperm and the menstrual blood (according to Scholastic biological assump-
tions); in the case of accidental being (being white), the matter is the man himself, or rather, that *in which* there can be whiteness. To be more precise, we can
call the matter of accidental being "subject," whereas only that which has the
potency to be substantial being can we call "material" in a proper sense. Let us,
with Thomas, clarify the difference: "subject" is what we call that which does
not receive its being from that which comes to it but already possesses a complete being (man, to keep with the previous example, does not receive his being
from the fact of being white or becoming white); "matter" in the strict sense
receives its being from that which comes to it (viz., from the substantial form),
since it has in itself an incomplete being. We can sum it up thus: matter in the
strict sense depends on the substantial form for its being; the accident depends
on the subject in which it inheres for its being.

If that from which a thing receives its being in act is the form (whether substantial or accidental), we can say that every form is act. At the level of natural
processes, then, there is in Thomas a strict correspondence, as there already is
in Aristotle, between potency and matter on the one hand, and act and form
on the other hand. But we shall see subsequently that, passing from the natural
plane to the metaphysical plane, this correspondence does not hold up.

Forms are always acquired through processes of *generation* (processes in
which something passes from potency to act). We can distinguish between generation in a proper sense (that through which something acquires a substantial form) and generation in a relative or accidental sense (that through which
something acquires an accidental form such as being white or black). When
a form cedes its place to another we speak of *corruption* and here too we can
speak of corruption in a proper sense (loss of the previous substantial form) and

in a relative or accidental sense (loss of an accidental form). All of the processes that are found in nature are thus processes of generation and corruption, or rather, passages from non-being to being and vice-versa: but "non-being" here must always be understood as being in potency, because nothing *is generated* from absolute non-being (from nothingness) or *corrupts* into nothing. In this sense, natural processes must not be confused with *creation*, which is the only true passage from absolute non-being (from nothingness) to being—a passage, however, not generally admitted by philosophers but only by revelation.

On the basis of what we have already seen, therefore, we can distinguish among three aspects: (a) *being in potency* (the fact that matter—that which is in potency—is disposed toward receiving a new form; (b) *privation*, a *not being in act* (the form that is presently lacking to matter but can be acquired); (c) *being in act*, the new *form* acquired by the matter, which just is the end point of every process of generation.

In this connection we will consider Thomas's own example of a copper statue (even if it is not the most felicitous example, since it regards not a natural thing but an artificial one). Before having the statue in act we will have some *matter* (the copper), which is in potency with respect to being a statue; we will have a *privation* (the fact that the copper as yet lacks the figure or shape that renders it a statue); finally, we will have a *form*, that is, in this case, the shape itself that makes a casting or block of copper a statue. Naturally, even before becoming a statue, the block of copper had in any case a substantial form (that which makes it copper rather than another metal or another thing). Matter is never found in nature entirely without a form (naked or prime matter, as absolutely potential, is only a mental concept). But a block of copper is not, in itself, a statue; to become such, it must take on a different form that it did not previously have.

We have thus identified the three fundamental principles already proposed by Aristotle: matter or substratum, privation, and form. It can be asked in what way matter and privation relate to each other. The two are identical from the perspective of the subject, but they can be conceptually distinguished: the block of copper that is in potency to being a statue is both the matter from which the statue will be drawn and that in which the form of the statue is not yet present. In a real sense, then, privation coincides with the matter, but it is distinguished from the latter to the extent that it is not considered a generic potency but as a determinate potency toward a determinate form. In the process of the generation of a statue, the copper must be considered as a privation of the form of the statue; when the statue exists, it will no longer be the privation of that form (even if potency or privation remains with respect to other possible forms, which would be acquired were the statue to be melted down and re-shaped or, for example, made into coins). So, let us note that if, at the beginning of the process of generation, matter and privation coincide, in the end the matter remains (organized under another determinate form), while privation (determinate privation) has disappeared, being absorbed by the new form.

Although substances change, that is, are generated and corrupted, acquiring different forms, forms themselves are not generated and corrupted. This thesis, which is also strictly Aristotelian, might seem to imply an equivocation. Did we not say that matter and form are the essential principles of generation and of every change? But precisely because they are principles, they are not subject to the same process. If matter is generated, we must admit a matter out of which the matter came, and so on to infinity, which is impossible; and if form is generated, we must admit that the form itself has a form to which it tends, and so on to infinity. On the contrary, only what results from these principles is generated and corrupted, namely, the composite of matter and form (the substance).

The three principles just distinguished (matter, privation, and form) are necessary but not sufficient to explain the process of generation. Something else is needed, because obviously the copper does not become a statue all by itself, for something else is needed to bring it from the state of potency and privation to that of being a statue in act. We will call this principle, this cause of change, the "motor cause" or "efficient cause" (the latter denomination was unknown to Aristotle, being introduced into the philosophical lexicon by the Arabs, by Avicenna in particular). And since everything that moves or acts does so in view of something, to the principle of movement or efficient cause there must correspond an end. Naturally, we need not posit here a goal consciously chosen, for all natural things, even those not provided with intelligence and freedom, act in view of their end. So, to the three principles distinguished above we must add the efficient cause and final cause.

We have altogether, therefore, five necessary conditions for understanding nature, a number that we arrive at by adding what Aristotle calls "principles" (matter, privation, and form) to what Aristotle calls "causes" (material, formal, agent, and final) and keeping in mind that the material and formal principles are identical with the material and formal causes. As Thomas observes, this is at least the subdivision found in the *Physics*, because in the *Metaphysics* Aristotle seems to regard extrinsic causes as "principles" properly speaking and intrinsic causes instead as "elements." The different language and lists proposed by Aristotle should not pose a problem, says Thomas. It should be sufficient to note that privation is a principle (because it is an intrinsic condition that makes it possible for us to understand the passage from a determined potency to a determined act), but is not a cause in the strict sense because it does not, in fact, contribute (as everything that is a cause does) to the being of the substance that is generated: privation is, indeed, what disappears in the process. On the other hand, agent and final cause are causes without a doubt, because they contribute to what is generated. But they are not principles in the strict sense, because they are mostly extrinsic and not intrinsic to what is generated.

Without pursuing the terminological issue further with Thomas, the fact remains that we now possess an adequate conceptual grid for reading the whole of natural reality. Every natural process presupposes (a) a substratum that persists under different forms (matter); (b) the potency or disposition to acquire a form that is presently absent (privation); (c) an agent that permits the passage from potency to act, that is, the acquisition of a new form (cause of the change or efficient cause); (d) the form itself that is acquired at the end of the process (formal cause); (e) the end in view of which the change comes about (final cause).[6]

There is a last question that we can ask ourselves. Are these conditions (principles and causes) identical in every process? They are not identical in a strict sense, because, for example, the conditions that define an individual (Socrates) belong only to that individual (Socrates's *matter* and *form* are *his* body and *his* soul and cannot be in any other individual). Nevertheless, the function that such principles and causes perform is common. In any being or process, there will generally be something that functions as matter, something that functions as privation, something that functions as form, something that functions as agent, and something that functions as end. But in the concrete, the matter of each individual is different from that of other individuals and so also for the other principles and causes. As we just said, these conditions offer a grid of the whole to read the real. But the way in which this grid is applied (or filled in) varies from case to case (even if nothing prevents certain conditions from being common to entire classes of individuals, viz., to a species or genus). The things that belong to different categories (substance and quality, for example) certainly cannot have principles that are really identical: in this case we can only speak of principles that are analogously common, of principles that perform the same function but that are, in fact, on each occasion, different. Here we encounter for the first time a term that is often considered fundamental in Thomas's lexicon, namely, *analogy*. We can understand what analogy is if we compare it with univocity and

6. It should be noted that, for most natural things, the end is identical with the form itself, and so the formal cause and final cause are only conceptually distinguished, while the efficient cause is identical with the thing generated only from the perspective of the species but, obviously, it is not identical with the thing generated as an individual.

equivocity. The three terms designate the various ways that the same word can be referred to different things. It is a matter of *univocity* when the same word is used to designate several things while having the same meaning in each case. It is a matter of *equivocity* (or homonymy) when the same word is used to designate several things while having a different meaning in each case. The word "dog" is used equivocally, for example, when it is applied to the animal with four legs and applied to the constellation *Canis Major* (the Great Dog). Following an already established tradition (but one that does not reflect Aristotle's use of the term), Thomas holds that there is *analogy* when the same word is used to designate different things that are, nevertheless, all related to some principal meaning. To use the celebrated example employed in *Metaphysics* IV (where Aristotle describes *pros hen* convergence—toward *one* principal meaning—of the many meanings of being, without, however, using the term "analogy"), the term "healthy" can be applied to the body (a *healthy* body), to diet (a *healthy* diet), to medicine (as procuring *health*), to urine (as a sign of *health*), and so on. These are different things, and the meanings are different, too (we go from what is healthy, to what procures health, to what is a sign of health), and yet all of these meanings are related to one principal concept, that of health. Now, Thomas specifies, an analogous relationship can be understood either (a) in reference *to one end*, as in the case in which something is "healthy" with respect to health; or (b) in the case of reference *to one agent*, as in the case of "medical" (another Aristotelian example), whether it is applied to the person who practices the art of medicine or to the instruments used by the art; or (c) in reference *to one subject*, as in the case of the different categories related to substance. In the case we are looking at, to say that the principles can be analogously common (or identical) is to say that, indeed, they perform the same function or they are in the same relationship (or proportion, which is the genuinely Aristotelian meaning of "analogy"), without their coinciding in being (even if Thomas grafts this purely proportional relationship onto one that is of a causal type, as, substance is the cause of all the other genera, so the principles of substance are the cause of all the other genera). Thomas can conclude his own personal compendium of the principles that support our understanding of the sensory or natural world—a compendium substantially put together by the integration of some basic concepts of Aristotle's *Physics* and *Metaphysics*—summing up the different forms of identity found respectively in individuals (numerical identity), in species (specific identity), *in* genera (generic identity), and *between* genera (analogical identity) thus:

Therefore, the form and matter of those things that are numerically the same are themselves likewise numerically the same, as are the form and matter of Tullius and Cicero.

The matter and form of those things that are specifically the same and numerically diverse are not the same numerically, but specifically, as the matter and form of Socrates and of Plato. Likewise, the matter and form of those things that are generically the same have principles that are generically the same, as the soul and body of an ass and a horse differ specifically but are the same generically; likewise, the principles of those things that agree only analogically or proportionally are the same only analogically or proportionally, because matter, form and privation or potency and act are the principles of substance and of the other genera. However, the matter, form and privation of substance and of quantity differ generically, but they agree according to proportion only, insofar as the matter of substance is to substance, in the nature of matter, as the matter of quantity is to quantity; still, just as substance is the cause of the others, so the principles of substance are the principles of all the others.

DE ENTE ET ESSENTIA
The Terms "Being" and "Essence" and the Essence of Composite Substances

De ente et essentia too was the product of a specific request. Thomas wrote it for his confreres and companions (*ad fratres et socios*) at the Dominican priory of Saint-Jacques in Paris when he was not yet a master (*nondum existens magister*), and so, as it seems, during the period of his baccalaureate. From the first lines of the text, Thomas explains the purpose of the work with great clarity:

- to define the fundamental terms "being" and "essence," which represent the first conceptions of our intellect;
- to outline the characteristics of essence in the different orders of the real (especially as it is found in composite substances, in simple or separate substances, and in accidents);
- to examine in what way, within each of these orders, essence is to be understood in relation to logical intentions, that is, in relation to universals (genera, species, differences).

Whereas *De principiis naturae* is dedicated to fundamental concepts that are indispensable for understanding natural reality, what Thomas proposes in the *De ente* is principally a lexical and metaphysical project, a project that deals with the connection between the logical and linguistic order and the real order. In what way, Thomas is asking, is the means by which we express the objective content of things—namely, essence—predicable of the things themselves?

Citing one of the best-known passages of Avicenna's *Metaphysics*—the text that more than any other constitutes the doctrinal point of reference for understanding the *De ente*—Thomas initiates his own treatment by observing that being and essence are the first concepts of our intellect.[7] A small mistake in the use of these concepts, therefore, runs the risk of compromising the entire ulterior development of knowledge. So, it is vital, first of all, to clarify what these terms express.

Being, Thomas first notes, can be understood in two ways: (a) as that which indicates the truth of a proposition, and (b) as that which is divided by the ten predicaments (the Aristotelian categories). The first way of understanding being is logical: "being" is said of whatever can be the object of an affirmative proposition. Understood thus, negations and privations are also beings. It is said, for example, that blindness *is* in the eye, even though, for the medievals, blindness represents only a privation of sight. The second way of understanding being, by contrast, points to real being, and only that which is a being in this sense has an essence. Consequently, "being" has a broader extension than the term "essence," or, as we could also say, being and essence are related to each other as concrete to abstract, or as composite to simple.

Essence indicates that through which and in which a being has its being (*per eam et in ea ens habet esse*). The two definitions are, thus, almost circular: a being is what possesses an essence, and essence is that through which and in which a being has its own being. In other words, essence is that which makes each thing be that determinate thing: that which makes a triangle be a triangle and nothing else, or makes a stone be a stone and nothing else. It is, in fact, only in virtue of its essence that each thing can be recognized and placed in a genus and species, and in that way be defined as that determinate thing. The essence is, hence, that which is expressed by the definition of the thing, and, for this reason, in the philosophical lexicon, essence is often also given the name "quiddity." (Every definition, in fact, answers the question *Quid est?* What is it?) Essence is, then, the foundation of the being (in the abovementioned sense according to which each being has its being in its essence and through its essence), of the knowability, and of the operations of each being.

Since the being that possesses essence is the being that is divided by the ten predicaments, essence itself must obviously be understood differently with respect to substances and with respect to accidents. Substances are for their part subdivided into two major classes: the class of those that are composed of matter and form, and the class of simple substances lacking matter. Because all of our knowledge has its origin in the senses—according to one of the ba-

7. On the presence of Avicenna across Thomas's work, the tabulation of citations made by C. Vansteenkiste remains fundamental, "Avicenna citaten bij S. Thomas," *Tijdschrift voor Filosofie* 15 (1953): 437–507.

sic convictions (of clear Aristotelian provenance) of Thomas's entire thought—composite substances are more accessible and evident to us than incorporeal substances, and so the essence of the former must be considered first, before we then pass on to the essence of the latter.

In *composite substances* essence does not coincide with the form alone (the Averroist thesis) or with matter alone, or with the link that binds the one to the other. It coincides, rather, with the composite itself: the essence is the union itself of matter and form (and, so, the very substance in its entirety). As we just saw, essence, in fact, expresses the definition of each thing; but every definition, if it is truly complete, contains neither the form alone nor the material alone, but the one and the other together.

Genus, Species, and Individuals

Finally, we consider the third of the three points listed earlier, which has to do with the way that the essence of composite substances must be understood in relation to genus, species, and specific difference. It will be necessary in the first place to recall what the terms "genus," "species," and "difference" (the so-called universals) mean. They represent three of the five predicaments posited by Porphyry, that is, the five ways that something can be predicated of a subject (the other two are "property" and "accident"). The genus is that which, when predicated of a subject together with the difference, tells us the essence; it can be predicated of many things and includes the subordinate species. From this vantage, the very same predicament can be the genus of a subordinate species and a species of a higher genus: "animal," for example, is genus with respect to "man," but it is "species" with respect to "body" ("animal" is equivalent, in fact, to "animate body"). Species—reciprocally—is that which is subordinated to a genus (in a more strict sense, it is that which cannot be the genus of any lower species; in the Scholastic lexicon, this is what is meant by the *species specialissima* or *infima*). Evidently, the relation between genus and species is not reversible: genus is predicated of species because it possesses a wider extension, but species cannot be predicated of genus.

The specific difference is, on the other hand, what permits us to distinguish between different species within the same genus, viz., to predicate the belonging of a thing to one species rather than another. For example, within the genus "animal," the difference "rational" separates the species "human" from other species. The union of genus and specific difference constitutes—as we have said—the definition. Man, to keep to the same example, is defined as "rational animal."

Within the same species, individuals are distinguished from each other, for Thomas, in virtue of the "designation" that they receive from quantitatively determined matter, and the latter is considered in its dimensional aspect (*materia signata*). By contrast, the matter that is part of a definition is matter only in a general sense: in the definition of man, for instance, matter is represented by flesh and bones in general. When we speak of the individual Socrates, however, we refer to this determinate flesh and these determinate bones that constitute his designated matter and differentiate Socrates from Plato within the species "human." The expression "designated matter" itself alludes to the possibility of indicating, even by a physical gesture, a concrete individual being: matter that is "designated," in fact, is matter that we can indicate (*signare* indeed means "to point out") concretely, and thus is localized according to the three dimensions of space, and is not matter taken in an absolute sense. Of course, Aristotle had already related the divisibility and multipliability of matter to its quantitative (continuous) nature, but it was above all Avicenna who took the next step, indicating in an explicit way that quantity itself—and, more precisely, extension— is the ultimate root of the possibility of individuation. The alternative that was developed in the Arab peripatetic tradition regarded the way of understanding the dimensions that made matter the principle of individuation: for Avicenna, it was a question of the effective, determinate, dimensions that in every body follow the general form of corporeity, permitting the divisions of specific forms. (Dimension is, then, intermediate, so to say, between the general form of corporeity and the substantial form proper to each single being.) For Averroes, on the contrary, dimension must be in the matter from the beginning, to account for the diversity and contrariety of forms (and so of their succeeding each other in generation and corruption). But it is just because of this that this sort of dimension—as he argues above all in *De substantia orbis*—cannot be determinate dimension (which obviously depends on the substantial form, and hence on the already formed, constituted, nature of each body), but must be "indeterminate" dimension (*interminatae* in the Latin). In other words, what is intended is the fact in general of having three dimensions ("tridimensionality absolutely considered" as it has been defined) and not the fact of having *these* determinate dimensions. Indeterminate dimension, therefore, represents in the Averroist doctrine the quantitative character that inheres in matter in an absolute sense *prior to* every substantial form (which leads to the difficult problem of how some accidents precede the substantial form itself) and that justifies the very possibility, for the form, of being subdivided so as to constitute many different substances within a single species.[8] It does not seem that, at the time of the

8. See S. Donati, "La dottrina delle dimensioni indeterminate in Egidio Romano," *Medioevo* 14 (1988): 149–233. See also Donati's "Materia e dimensioni tra XIII e XIV secolo: la dottrina delle dimensiones indeterminatae," *Quaestio* 7 (2007): 361–93.

composition of the *De ente,* Thomas was aware of the Averroist doctrine, which is mentioned for the first time in a passage from the Commentary on Book II of the *Sentences,* even if with some hesitation.[9] But in parallel to the rejection of the Avicennean doctrine of the *forma corporeitatis,* Averroes' view seems rather to be completely accepted beginning with the Commentary on Book IV (so much so that Thomas avails himself of it to explain transubstantiation and the resurrection) and above all by the Commentary on Boethius's *De Trinitate,* where it is explicitly observed that determinate dimension could not serve as the principle of individuation because, given its mutability, it would not be able to safeguard the numerical identity of the individual: from moment to moment the measure and the form of a thing's quantity are subject to change, and if the identity of an individual depended on such characteristics, nothing could remain numerically identical over the course of its existence. Extension, then, continues to be recognized as the principle of individuation in association with matter, but now it is extension considered under the aspect of indeterminate dimension. In the subsequent works there is never an explicit rejection of the Averroist doctrine, but the previous terminology seems to be carefully avoided, and, above all, Thomas is much more faithful to the Aristotelian doctrine that in a given being no accident can precede the substantial form. This fact has been interpreted as another turn of the wheel: on the one hand, as maintaining the position developed after the *De ente,* and, on the other hand, as an index of the simultaneous presence in Thomas of different models employed according to different requirements.[10] It is perhaps more prudent to say that Thomas's mature position consists in holding to the priority of dimensions over the purely apparent—or, better, purely *logical*—substantial form. In fact, because they are accidental, dimensions follow from the substantial form to the extent that it confers upon matter its character as a body, but they precede all the other determinations or perfections that the form confers on the substance (the fact of being a body of a determinate *species*).[11]

9. See *In II Sent.,* d. 3, q. 1, a. 4; but also d. 30, q. 2, a. 1.

10. For some bibliographic recommendations on this subject, see Tommaso d' Aquino, *L'ente e l'essenza,* ed. and trans. P. Porro (Milan: Bompiani, 2002), 50–53n27. In this chapter we take up some essential themes developed in the introduction of this edition.

11. See *Summa theologiae,* Ia, q. 76, a. 6, ad 2: "Dimensions of quantity are accidents consequent to the corporeity which belongs to the whole matter. Wherefore matter, once understood as corporeal and measurable, can be understood as distinct in its various parts, and as receptive of different forms according to the further degrees of perfection. For although *it is essentially the same form* which gives matter the various degrees of perfection, as we have said (ad 1), *yet it is considered as different when brought under the observation of reason*" (emphasis added). In the body of the same article Thomas defends in an unambiguous fashion the priority of the substantial form in relation to any accidents in effects: "it is impossible for any accidental disposition to come between the body and the soul, or

We can now return to our principal problem. Genus, difference, and species are abstracted respectively from the matter, from the form, and from the composite itself of composite substances, *but they do not coincide* with the matter, the form, and the composite. Here it is necessary not to confuse in any way the logical order with the real order. Let us take again the example of man: the genus ("animal") is abstracted from matter (the animate body), but it does not coincide with the body itself; the animate body as such is, in fact, a part of every existing man, whereas animality or "animal" as genus must be a whole, capable of including in itself different specifications (for instance, "rational" or "irrational"), and consequently not only the human species but also all the other animal species. Analogously, the difference ("rational") is taken from the form (the rational soul), but it does not coincide with it: the rational soul is, in fact, a part of the human composite (of *each* man), which in itself excludes matter, whereas rationality must be a whole capable of including within itself all the individuals of the human species (every human being, as such, is indeed rational)—individuals that are *de facto* endowed with matter. Finally, the species ("man" as "rational animal") is abstracted from the composite (man), but it does not coincide with it. We say, of course, in the definition that man is a rational animal but not that man is composed of "animal" and "rational." On the contrary, in the natural or real order, man is actually composed of soul and body. In the natural or real order, man is a third thing that differs as much from the soul as from the body, that is, from the two parts; in the logical order, "man" is instead a concept that results from the union of two other concepts ("animal" and "rational").

From what we have seen, it is clear that an essence can serve as a genus, species, and difference only when it is taken as a *whole* (from the standpoint of logic) and not as a *part* (from the standpoint of reality). In reality the parts are certainly not contained in each other. Rather, taken separately, the parts exclude each other. In a definition, however, one term by no means excludes another but is included in it and determines it. In sum, if in reality the body, as a part, is *not* the soul, in the definition, what corresponds to the body ("animal") cannot exclude what corresponds to the soul ("rational") but must actually implicitly contain it in itself as one of its possible specifications or determinations. But

---

between any substantial form whatever and its matter. The reason is because since matter is in potentiality to all manner of acts in a certain order, what is absolutely first among the acts must be understood as being first in matter. Now the first among all acts is existence. Therefore, it is impossible for matter to be apprehended as hot, or as having quantity, before it is actual. But matter has actual existence by the substantial form, which makes it to exist absolutely.... Wherefore *it is impossible for any accidental dispositions to pre-exist in matter before the substantial form* ... " (emphasis added).

this shows the untenability of the position of those who think of the essence as a separate reality in the Platonic sense. Since, in fact, the essence expresses the definition, to wit, the content of a thing, it is absurd to say that Socrates is something different and separate from Socrates himself.

It must be specified, nevertheless, that essence can be considered from at least three different perspectives. In the first place, according to the teaching of Avicenna (*Metaphysics*, V, 1–2), essence can be taken in an absolute sense, namely, inasmuch as in itself it is indifferent to existence or non-existence, to singularity or multiplicity. The objective content of an essence can, indeed, be considered in itself independently of its natural or mental existence. Taken in this way, no essence is in itself one or many: if it were one, it could not be common to many individuals, and if it were in itself many, it could not be entirely in one individual. In itself essence is nothing but essence (*essentia est essentia tantum*; Avicenna had said that *equinitas est equinitas tantum*, that is, "horseness [the essence of horse] is only horseness"). But, besides being considered in the absolute sense, essence can also be considered as it exists in the soul (as being endowed with mental existence) or in individual substances (as being endowed with real existence). In the latter case, it is likewise evident that essence cannot be regarded as predicable of many individuals, because, belonging to a particular individual, it cannot be common to many individuals. Only one possibility, then, remains: only essence as it exists in the soul (having mental existence) can serve as a universal, for it has already been stripped, by the operation of the intellect, of all individuating conditions and has a character of similarity or commonality with real existing individuals, from which it is drawn by abstraction. Here Thomas can conclude, this time citing Averroes explicitly, that it is the intellect that creates the universality in things; universals, in other words, exist only in the intellect. But Thomas is careful not to draw from this conclusion what Averroes believed to be inevitable, that is, that the unicity of the possible intellect is the foundation of the universality of the forms cognized. In Thomas's estimation, the universality does not, in fact, refer to the *subject* but to the *object* of thought. Put differently, human nature can be referred to all really existing individuals, not because it is thought by a single intellect common to all, but because the nature, once obtained through the same abstractive procedure, represents a similarity among all existing human beings. As such, humanity is always a particular concept that exists individually in each intellect. Its universality derives from the extension of its object, not from its intrinsic form. A statue that resembles many people—to use Thomas's example—has this feature in virtue of its similarity to them, but it does not for this reason cease to be singular. Universality, thus, is a product of the intellect, but it is not a characteristic of the intellect itself: it denotes, rather, the objective content and the referential capacity of the forms cognized. Every essence, then, is predicable as a universal not in itself nor insofar as it exists in natural reality, but only according to the being that it has in the intellect.

The Essence of Simple Substances and the Distinction between Being and Essence

All that we have considered so far only regards composite substances. In simple substances, which lack matter, things are quite different. Here it is a matter, first of all, of demonstrating the existence of simple substances different from God, and in this connection Thomas immediately distances himself from so-called "universal hylomorphism," viz., the doctrine according to which intelligences (angels) and souls are the result of a union of form with an incorporeal matter (the more or less direct origin of this thesis—which was quite prominent among Franciscans in the thirteenth century—is the *Fons Vitae* of Ibn Gabirola a Spanish Jewish philosopher of the eleventh century known to the Latins as Avicebron). Thomas's refutation of this thesis is principally based on the presupposition—to which he will often appeal in subsequent works as well—that the intellective capacity itself proper to angels and rational souls requires immateriality. All forms, in fact, are actually intelligible only to the extent that they are separated from matter, and this operation can be effected only by a faculty that is itself structurally immaterial. Hence, there are beings (intelligences in the Aristotelian and peripatetic cosmology, angels in the Judaeo-Christian tradition, and souls when they are temporarily separated from the body) lacking matter and so lacking form-matter composition.

Now, if the essence of composite substances is the composite itself, the essence of simple substances (in the absence of matter) is the *form alone*. And that permits us to recognize another important difference: if individuation depends in general on designated matter, and simple substances are absolutely without matter, then there is no plurality of individuals among these substances but only a plurality of species. In other words—according to a view also articulated many times by Thomas and condemned by Bishop Tempier in 1277[12]—each angel is its own species and there cannot be more than one angel in the same species. There not being anything within a species that could distinguish one angel from another, in incorporeal substances numerical unity, indeed, corresponds with unity of species. (That is not to say, as is sometimes erroneously thought, that each angel is not in itself an individual, but only that it is the only individual within its own species.)

12. See pp. 159–61.

There remains, nevertheless, the problem that, in any case, made universal hylomorphism popular with the Latins. If angels and souls are not composed of matter and form, what distinguishes their essence from the divine essence? For Thomas, prior yet to the composition of matter and form, there is a composition in creatures between essence (and in separate substances the form) and being (*esse*). This thesis too has its origin in Avicenna, even if Thomas takes his point of departure from a proposition of the pseudo-Aristotelian *Liber de causis* (in reality a reworking of the *Elementatio theologica* of the Neo-Platonic philosopher Proclus) that we will see again later: every intelligence has form and being.

To demonstrate the difference between being and essence (the *De ente* does not go beyond the expression *aliud est esse, aliud est essentia*), Thomas initially employs an argument based on the concept of essence (*intellectus essentiae*): whatever does not belong to the concept of an essence enters in some way from the outside the essence itself and is not a part of it, since one cannot have an adequate concept of an essence if the essence is considered without an integral part. But it is evident that being is not part of the concept of an essence. I can, in fact, have an adequate concept of the essence of man or of a phoenix without on this account knowing if the one or the other exists in reality, or at least without taking this last aspect into consideration. Being, thus, is not *in general* a part or a predicate of essence. And if I can conceive of an essence while mentally prescinding from its being, this means nothing else than that being is something different from essence and adds something to it. This conclusion is purely provisory (and, moreover, it is valid only in the logical order), because there could be a being whose essence or quiddity is inconceivable without being, to the extent that it is constituted by being itself. This is the crucial point for Thomas: if a being of this type exists, it cannot but be unique, for something can be multiplied only by some difference being added to it (as genus is divided by various species), or by designated matter (as a species is divided into various individuals), or because something, which can also exist in the pure and separated state, is received in different subjects; but that which is simply being, by its very definition, cannot be thought with the addition of a difference (because then it would already be "being" plus something else, namely, a determinate form), nor with the addition of matter (because then it would be "being" plus matter), nor received in several subjects (because then it would be "being" plus whatever would constitute these subjects). And if there is just one such being, then by necessity, with this one exception, in all other beings being and essence are distinct. The proof of the distinction between being and essence is thereby arrived at negatively or indirectly, showing that if they coincided, they could coincide in only one being—and that is enough to be able to conclude that in all other beings being and essence enter into composition with each other. But not only this: everything that is composed of essence and being evidently receives its being from another, because nothing can be the cause of itself; and since it is impossible—in an Aristotelian way—to proceed infinitely in the series of causes, it is necessary to stop at a first cause that is not caused by any other and is not self-caused but in which the essence is, precisely, its very being. And such a first cause is God.

As is obvious, the fulcrum of the whole argument is in the demonstration of the unicity of the being in which being and essence coincide. Said in other terms, we are justified in positing the composition of being and essence in all finite realities only if we are certain of the fact that there cannot exist but one being in which they coincide. In truth, we do not have immediate access to the essential content of all things, above all in what regards separate substances, but if we know with certainty that apart from one particular case (which is that of God) there cannot be other beings whose essence coincides with being, we will likewise be certain that all other things will be composite. It can be objected that the procedure adopted by Thomas appears somehow circular: Thomas deduces the necessity of the composition of being and essence in all creatures from the unicity of the case in which they coincide, that is, God; but it is exactly from the composition met with in all creatures that Thomas then demonstrates God's existence. In reality, Thomas carefully keeps the different phases of the argument separate. The first (which appeals to the *intellectus essentiae*) shows that whatever does not belong to the concept of an essence must be taken as something external to the essence itself; the second limits itself to showing that there could exist only one being in which essence and being coincide, regardless of whether this singular instance actually exists or not; we are, however, certain—at this point—that every other existing thing is composed, and since in every composite existence being is received from another, we can in the end conclude—in the third phase—that that one first being that was merely hypothesized also really exists.[13]

This last conclusion permits Thomas, furthermore, to clarify the way in which

---

13. This is the reconstruction of Wippel, with which we agree. See John Wippel, "Aquinas' Route to the Real Distinction: A Note on *De ente et essentia*, c. 4," *The Thomist* 43 (1979): 279–95 (reprinted in Wippel's *Metaphysical Themes in Aquinas* [Washington, D.C.: The Catholic University of America Press, 1984], 107–32). Owens disagrees on this point. According to him, Thomas actually held that a provisional recognition of being as a real nature is possible—to prove the reality of subsisting being—while it was possible later to posit a real diversity between essence and being in creatures. See J. Owens, "Stages and Distinction in *De ente*: A Rejoinder," *The Thomist* 45 (1981): 99–123, and "Aquinas' Distinction at *De ente et essentia* 4:119–123," *Mediaeval Studies* 48 (1986): 264–87. On this subject, see also S. MacDonald, "The *esse/essentia* Argument in Aquinas's *De ente et essentia*," *Journal of the History of Philosophy* 22 (1984): 157–72.

we are to understand the relationship between essence and being in creatures: if being is received from another, and, that is—in the final analysis—from God, what receives being will be in potency with respect to being itself, and being will function as act. The conceptual pair potency-act is, therefore, employed in a broader context than it was in Aristotle, with the result that a margin of potentiality is maintained even in created immaterial substances. God as well as the intelligences (along with separated souls) are without matter, but whereas God lacks all potentiality since he is subsistent being, the intelligences are in potency to the being that they receive from God. If, then, in composite substances, the matter is in potency to the form, and the latter is what gives being to the matter, in simple substances the form itself is in potency to being.

The distinction between being and essence returns in a great many places in Thomas's work, with arguments similar to the *De ente* argument or with different ones.[14] In Chapter 3, for example, we will examine the way that Thomas reproposes the question in the *Summa contra Gentiles*. The correct understanding of the nature of this distinction (Is it a real distinction? And in this case what exactly is meant by "real"?) is a problem that has tormented the entire history of Thomism from the end of the thirteenth century essentially to our own time. We have dealt with some parts of this long and complicated historical discussion elsewhere.[15] Here it will perhaps be sufficient to note that the debate about the way to understand the distinction between being and essence emerged, in fact, after Thomas's death and was initiated in the conflict between Giles of Rome, according to whom being and essence are different things (*res*), and Henry of Ghent, according to whom they are instead different intentions—*intentiones*—that is, aspects of the quidditative content of a thing that *can be considered separately* insofar as their meaning is different, but that *do not exist separately*. In the language of contemporary logic we would say that they are concepts with the same extension but a different intension. What is at stake in this debate is the contingency of the created universe. If essence and being are not really separate, according to Giles, every essence would always necessarily exist; but, according to Henry, if they are really different, each must in turn be composed of essence and existence, and so on *ad infinitum*—not forgetting that in this way creation would no longer be the positing in act of the created essence in its entirety but would be the acquisition of the form of being by a potential subject (namely, essence) that in some way preexists. Thomas is a stranger to this debate, not only for obvious chronological reasons but also because, as we will see later, creaturely contingency is not a topic that concerned

---

14. See the valuable study by John Wippel in *Metaphysical Themes in Aquinas*, 133–61.
15. See our comments in Tommaso d' Aquino, *L'ente e l'essenza*, 183–215.

him much—indeed, he even admits (for example in the *Summa contra Gentiles* and the *De potentia*) the being of formally necessary creatures (that is, *created*, but created with a *necessary nature*—Thomas obviously means, above all, intelligences or angels). Ultimately, the distinction seems to be used by Thomas not to indicate the radical contingency of things and the possibility of their annihilation (in Giles's terms, the real separability of essence and existence), but rather to indicate that, below the one subsistent being (God), being is always accompanied by a formal determinateness, an essential note, an objective content. The true novelty of Thomas's metaphysical thought, which we will try to follow to its final developments (in particular, to the Commentary on the *De causis*), is in its positing a radical caesura between what is being *and* form, viz., being determined by an essence (all of creation), and what is subsistent being alone, indeterminate and unobjectifiable. It is, in other words, a difference between what can be thought formally as an object (even if purely intelligible as in the case of the angels) and what, because of its unicity, removes itself in the most radical way from every form of objective determination.

Being and Essence in the Different Levels of Reality

At this point Thomas is ready to give a first answer to the questions posed at the beginning. To the three levels of reality (first cause, simple substances, composite substances), correspond three different ways of possessing an essence and of placing this in relation to logical intentions. On the first level is God, whose essence is simply identical with his being, so much so that some philosophers (the reference is still principally to Avicenna) have been driven to the point of denying that God possesses a quiddity in a strict sense: the objective content of God is, in fact, nothing other than his being. And if God does not have a quiddity (at least not as something distinct from his being), neither could he be contained in a genus (or in a predicament). It is actually on the basis of their essences, as we have seen, that things are distributed into diverse genera. God is, therefore, beyond every genus. But his existence should not for this reason be regarded as undifferentiated and universal. If such were held, it would lead to a formal pantheism (God as the being common to all things). God's being is not, therefore, the being of finite beings, precisely because pure being represents something different with respect to participated or formally determined being: God's being *is not determinable* whereas *common being is always, by its very definition, determinable*. In every creature being is, indeed, determined by its essence, whether the latter is form alone (in separate substances) or the union of matter and form (composite substances). In the same way, that fact that God is pure being does not exclude from him all the other attributes and perfections.

Put more simply, all the divine perfections are contained in a unified way within God's being itself. If this were not so, we would have to admit that there is some sort of multiplicity or composition in God.

In incorporeal substances—and we now come to the second level—being is different from essence and, because of this, is not pure but participated and limited according to the capacity of the nature itself that receives it. Hence, in Thomas's view, the being of such substances is not absolute. Their essence, however, is absolute (simple, independent) because it is not received by matter but is identical to the form itself. On account of this, as has been said, it is not possible at this level for there to exist several individuals of the same species.[16] Unlike God, all separate substances—inasmuch as they are endowed with a quiddity distinct from their being—are, nevertheless, contained within a genus and a species. The problem here, however, is that we do not have access to the constitutive differences of incorporeal substances, and because of this we are basically incapable of defining them.

We come finally to the third level, composite substances. Not only is their being limited and finite (since it is received in a distinct essence), but so is their essence (since it is received in a quantitatively determinate matter). Here we have a fundamental difference: in composite substances, the matter is in potency to the form that constitutes its actuality, and the whole composite is in turn in potency to being. In simple substances, it is rather the form itself (which exhausts the essence) that is in potency to being. So, in material substances we have a twofold composition and in separate substances only composition of essence and being. But this means that form itself *can no longer be considered as the ultimate actuality of a thing* (as it would be for Aristotle).

There is one more aspect that is worth considering, and it has to do with accidents. Thomas devotes the final chapter of the *De ente* to them. If essence is what is expressed through definition, it is necessary that accidents possess an essence in exactly the same way that they possess a definition. If, therefore, their definition is incomplete (in the sense that it must necessarily include reference to something else—namely, the subject in which they inhere—to be exhaustive), their essence will also be incomplete. So, if it is impossible to conceive of accidents without referring to their subject, it is likewise impossible for accidents to exist independently of their subject. Consequently, accidents are not part of the essence of a thing (as matter or form is) but are beings only in a relative sense and because of this possess an essence only in a relative sense (*secundum quid*).

---

16. The human soul is an exception since it is joined to the body. And yet the body, as Avicenna suggested, serves only as the origin of individuality, which the soul then preserves even after the corruption of the body itself.

At this point the hierarchy of reality can be considered complete. We have indicated how essence is to be understood in each of the orders (God, simple or separate substances, composite or material substances, accidents), what accounts for individuation (if it has a place), and how essence itself can possibly be predicated as a logical universal. We could put all of this into the form of the following schema:

1. God	essence is identical with being
	is not contained in any genus
	individuation is given by the unparticipatable character of his being
2. Separate substances	essence is different from being and identical with form
	specific differences are taken from the different degrees of perfection in receiving being, genus from the common character of immateriality
	several individuals do not exist within same species; every substance constitutes a species in itself (and is the only individual of its species)
3. Composite substances	essence is different from being and is identical with the material/form composite
	genus is taken from the matter, species from the form; so that the essence itself can be predicable, it must be understood as a whole (and not as a part) and only according to the being that it has in the intellect
	individuation has a place in virtue of quantitatively determined matter (*materia signata*)
4. Accidents	possess an incomplete and relative essence because the subject in which they inhere must always be placed in their definition
	can be regarded as genera and species only if taken in the abstract and not in the concrete (as with substances); genus is taken from the subject's mode of being, difference from the principles of the subject
	accidents that follow upon matter are individuals, those that follow upon form are proper to the genus or species

This schema outlines the metaphysical structure (divine simplicity; composition of essence and being in created beings; natural composition of matter and form in composite substances; composition of subject and accident) as much as the logical structure of reality. There is obviously a very close relationship between the two orders but, as we have noted, not perfect convertibility or identity. And it is for this reason that it is always necessary to know the precise way in which the essence of a being is to be understood in order to employ the essence as a predicament or universal.

THE COMMENTARY ON THE *SENTENCES*

Thomas's Approach to the *Sentences* of Peter Lombard

According to William of Tocco's *Ystoria*, toward the end of 1251 or the beginning of 1252 the master general of the Dominicans, John of Wildeshausen (John the Teuton, whom William actually confuses with John of Vercelli) asked Albert the Great to suggest to him someone to send to Paris as a bachelor to read (that is, comment on or explain in lectures) the *Sentences* of Peter Lombard. Albert proposed Thomas, who in Albert's eyes had the proper qualifications *in scientia et vita* (the two requisites for every person charged with teaching already to be found in the 1215 statutes of Robert de Courçon).[17] John—who also, as we have seen, knew Thomas well—hesitated, perhaps because of Thomas's youth. Albert then turned to Hugh of Saint-Cher, who was a cardinal at the time but had been a master of theology at Paris, and it seems that, thanks to the latter's intervention, Thomas was given the task of returning to Paris to lecture on the *Sentences* under the guidance of Master Elias Brunet de Bergerac, who held the chair reserved for non-French Dominicans (*schola extraneorum*). It is, nevertheless, likely that Thomas, as we saw, first gave cursory lectures on Isaiah and Jeremiah (toward the end of 1251 and 1252), and only afterward started on the lectures on the *Sentences*. Because these lectures required two academic years (which, at Paris, went from September to June, for a total of 100–130 days of lectures), they could reasonably be judged to have occurred either in 1252–54 or 1253–55. They could certainly not have gone beyond March of 1256, when Thomas obtained the *licentia docendi* and was then promoted to *magister*. As a *magister*, he obviously would no longer have had the task of commenting on the *Sentences*. Supposing, then, that Thomas finished his courses on the *Sentences* in June 1254 or June 1255, he would have continued to work at the side of his master until he received his *licentia* as a trained bachelor, while at the same time editing and publishing his commentary. It is necessary, in fact, to distinguish these two things: lecturing and publishing. In the Middle Ages, prior to the invention of the printing press, publishing meant that a text ceased to belong exclusively to the author and became public and available for copying. In the case of Thomas's Commentary on the *Sentences*, the text has not come down to

17. *Chartularium Universitatis Parisiensis* (hereafter CUP), vol. 1, ed. H. Denifle, E. Chatelain (Brussels: Culture et Civilisation, 1964), 79 (n. 20): *Nullus recipiatur Parisius ad lectiones sollempnes vel ad predicationis, nisi probate vite fuerit et scientie.*

us in the form of a *reportatio* (that is, as the record made by students or auditors present at lectures) but in the form of a *scriptum* (*Scriptum super Sententiis* is the correct Latin title of the work), that is, as a text already prepared for publication, something similar to what is called an *ordinatio*, an analogous type of commentary by certain fourteenth-century masters (Duns Scotus or Ockham, for example). It is not possible to indicate a definite date of publication, even though we know from references by Peter of Tarentaise and Annibaldo degli Annibaldi that Thomas's commentary was already in circulation around 1258 or 1259.[18]

Before looking at some aspects of the commentary, we should perhaps consider certain facts about Peter Lombard's *Sentences*. It is, as we have already observed, a collection of opinions (*sententiae*) on different theological questions taken from the Fathers of the Church. It was composed between 1155 and 1158. The extraordinary success of this text as a basic manual for theological training in medieval universities (its author receiving the title *magister Sententiarum*) is owed to the very way in which it was conceived. On the one hand, it permitted one to take up the study of theology—which only after the foundation of universities began to concern itself with its scientific status—following a possible systematic order of the material that was not merely an exposition of the Scriptures. On the other hand, through a review of the opinions presented, it permitted one to have the essentials of the doctrines of the Fathers (the *Sancti*, according to the Scholastic lexicon) constantly at one's fingertips in a form that lent itself to immediate didactic use.[19] Alexander of Hales may have been the first to introduce the *Sentences* into the university curriculum of the Paris faculty of theology in the 1220s (at least this is what Roger Bacon claims, not without a negative comment), and it is not unlikely that Alexander also introduced the division of the text (as we know it) into four books made up of "distinctions" rather than chapters. Reading and explaining the *Sentences* immediately became the pedagogical task of bachelors and not of masters. The fact that everyone had to do this to obtain the *licentia* explains the enormous quantity of commentaries on the *Sentences* that have come down to us, making

18. In fact, we also have an autograph of the Commentary up to the third book of the *Sentences* preserved in the manuscript Vat. Lat. 9851, which perhaps represents the first stage of text, which was later transformed by a revision (unknown to us) into what we possess today. Any hypothesis on the exact date of the publication, then, requires some caution, since the texts in circulation could be derived as much from the first redaction as from a later revision. On this topic, see P.-M. Gils, "Textes inédits de S. Thomas: Les premières rédactions du *Scriptum super Tertio Sententiarum*," *Revue des Sciences Philosophiques et Théologiques* 45 (1961): 201–28, and 46 (1962): 445–62 and 609–28.

19. The fact of having access to different (if not always opposed) opinions furnished the occasion to propose *quaestiones* that would be debated and resolved in the course itself.

it, together with the *Decretum* and after the Bible, the most commented on text in the whole Scholastic output.[20] It will be Thomas's *Summa theologiae* that will eventually replace the Lombard's *Sentences* as the basic pedagogical instrument for theological studies (but after a long transition and not without resistance, for it finally gained ascendancy only in the sixteenth century).

The Lombard's work is organized according to a typically Augustinian plan in which the distinction between things and signs (*res et signa*), which represent the material of Christian doctrine, is retained but overlaid with the distinction between *uti* and *frui*: there are things that we should enjoy (*quibus fruendum est*), others that we should make use of (*quibus utendum est*), and others that we should enjoy and use (*quae fruuntur et utuntur*). The Trinity is an object of enjoyment. The world and created things are objects of use. The beings that do the enjoying and using are angels and human beings. The treatment of all of these things (*res*) is then followed by a treatment of signs (*signa*). This schema runs through the development of the four books, which are devoted respectively to God as Trinity, God as creator (and so also to incorporeal and corporeal creatures—angels and human beings), the repairing of humanity (through grace, the Incarnation, the virtues and gifts of the Holy Spirit, and the commandments), *signa* (the sacraments), and final ends. The principal division of the work as a whole seems to be between the first three books, which treat of the *res*, and the last book, which treats instead of the *signa*.

But Thomas proposes a different schema in his commentary, one that hinges above all on the Neo-Platonic concepts of *exitus* and *reditus* (procession and return), borrowed from the *De causis*, Pseudo-Dionysius, and Avicenna and probably assimilated during his theological and philosophical apprenticeship with Albert the Great (although we can find something very similar in Alexander of Hales's Commentary on the *Sentences*). This fundamentally circular structure will also be the one that shapes more broadly the *Summa theologiae* (without, of course, the constraints of Peter Lombard's text). But it already informs his partitioning of the *Sentences* in his commentary, with a basic division being made between the first two books, which deal with the *exitus* (taking into account that Thomas explains the production of creation on the model of the inter-trinitarian procession: the generation of the Word is already in this sense

---

20. See the celebrated catalogue of F. Stegmuller, *Repertorium Commentariorum in Sententias Petri Lombardi*, 2 vols. (Wurzburg: F. Schoningh, 1947) and the supplement of V. Doucet, *Commentaires sur les Sentences. Supplément au Répertoire de M. Frédéric Stegmüller* (Quaracchi-Firenze: Typ. Collegii S. Bonaventurae, 1954), to which there are numerous other subsequent upgrading and integrating contributions. For a more recent treatment, see *Medieval Commentaries on the Sentences of Peter Lombard: Current Research*, vol. 1, ed. G. R. Evans (Leiden-Boston: Brill, 2002); *Medieval Commentaries on the Sentences of Peter Lombard*, vol. 2, ed. P. W. Rosemann (Leiden-Boston: Brill, 2010).

a form of "going forth," of *exitus*, from the principle) and the last two books, which treat of the *reditus* or return.[21] The prologue illustrates this different organization of the text with great clarity.[22] Beginning with the verse from Sirach, chosen as the exergue (24:40) and two verses from St. Paul's first Epistle to the Corinthians (1:24, 30), Thomas shows that through Wisdom (the Son): (a) the secrets of God have been manifested; (b) creatures have been produced; (c) they were restored after the fall; and (d) they were perfected, that is, led to their final end. The material of the four books of the *Sentences* is made to correspond to this: the first focuses on the manifestation of divine things; the second focuses on the production of creatures (but in parallel, as we said, to the trinitarian processions: the procession of creatures in time derives from the eternal processions of the Persons of the Trinity); the third deals with the work of restoration that Wisdom does; the fourth treats of the perfection that leads creatures to their end and maintains them in it (and because the achievement of the end cannot occur without an adequate preparation, in this book Thomas first discusses the sacraments and then the glory of the resurrection).

Closely tied to this reorganization of the *Sentences* is the decision—for that time still radical and innovative, however strange that view of it may seem to us—to make God himself the *subject* of theology rather than the *res* and the *signa* of the Augustinian tradition. This decision heralds the possibility of making theology itself a science in the proper sense according to the criteria of Aristotelian epistemology since it would have a well determined single subject.[23]

Finally, a third novel element,[24] which will be of particular interest to philosophical scholars, is the pervasive presence of philosophical references—especially quotations from Aristotle—in Thomas's Commentary. There are more than 2,000 quotes from the Greek philosopher (about 800 from the *Nicomachean Ethics*, about 300 from the *Metaphysics*, and about 250 in total from the *Physics* and the *De anima*), which is a striking fact if we consider that Thomas's task was to comment on a "textbook" that was a collection of texts from the Fathers and was strictly intended for theological education. Suffice it to note that

21. See P. Philippe, "Le plan des Sentences de Pierre Lombard d'après S. Thomas," *Bulletin Thomiste* 3 (1930–33): 131–54.

22. It should be noted that the prologue is the only part of the Commentary currently available in a critical edition. This is thanks to the exemplary work of Adriano Oliva. See his *Les débuts de l'enseignement*, pp. 303–40.

23. A "subject" is that which a science deals with. We will return to this point later in this chapter.

24. According to William of Tocco the originality of Thomas's commentary would have been immediately recognized by his contemporaries, even if Torrell—taking his cue from de Lubac and Gauthier—is right to maintain the dominance of the hagiographical intent that would have nudged Tocco to transfer what Thomas of Celano had written apropos Francis of Assisi to Aquinas. See Torrell, *Saint Thomas Aquinas*, vol. 1, *The Person and His Work*, 42.

there are only 1,000 quotations from Augustine (so half as many as from Aristotle) and about 500 from Pseudo-Dionysius, whom Thomas always thought of as an authentic Doctor of the Church.[25] The work, done under Albert's guidance (but perhaps already begun in Naples), here displays other obvious fruits. To cite only one example, a "strategic" reference to Aristotle already appears in what could be taken as the neuralgic point of the prologue: the relating of the processions of creatures to those of the Persons of the Trinity in which the former are made to depend on the latter. This dependence is, indeed, justified on the basis of the celebrated Aristotelian principle of causality of the maximum (*Metaphysics*, II, 2, 994a12–13), which, as it is opportune to begin to note, is one of the basic recurring principles in Thomas's thought (*semper enim id quod est primum est causa eorum que sunt post*).[26]

Theology and Philosophy: A First Sketch

We will focus our attention principally on the five articles that follow the prologue.[27] In these articles Thomas poses the following questions to himself: (a) Is *sacra doctrina* necessary?[28] In other words, is another science necessary beyond the natural sciences? (b) Is only one other science necessary or are many other sciences necessary? (c) Is sacred doctrine a practical or a speculative science and,

25. Ibid., 42

26. "It is always the case that what is first is the cause of what comes after" (*In I Sent.*, prol.). See A. Oliva, *Les débuts de l'enseignement*, 306.

27. Unlike the commentaries by authors of subsequent generations, Thomas's commentary retains expository sections (i.e., the *division textus* and the *expositio textus*, in other words, the subdivision and exposition of the text) but, as it is, consists mainly in a series of questions that follow the prologue and the distinctions of each of the four books of the Lombard. The questions are subdivided, in turn, into articles and smaller questions (*quaestiunculae*).

28. Thomas, in fact, does not here employ the term *theology*, but instead, as he does later in the first question of the *prima pars* of the *Summa theologiae*, uses the syntagm *sacra doctrina*. The exact meaning to ascribe to this expression (*sacra doctrina*) has been and continues to be much debated: according to Patfoort, Weisheipl, and Donneaud, *sacra doctrina*, as the knowledge of Sacred Scripture or of revelation, is something distinct from theology, understood, in the *Sentences* of the Lombard and Thomas's own *Summa*, as theoretical or practical knowledge. For Torrell, and even more for Oliva, the expression *sacra doctrina* must not be taken in a strict and univocal sense, such that it would be contrasted with *theology*. It should be understood, rather, as the entirety of what transmits, interprets, and reflects on divine teaching, so that it would include also the theological science practiced by Thomas. See J. Weisheipl, "The Meaning of *sacra doctrina* in the *Summa theologiae* Ia, q. 1," *The Thomist* 38 (1974): 49–80; A. Patfoort, "*Sacra doctrina*. Théologie et unité de la Iᵃ Pars," *Angelicum* 62 (1985): 306–15; J.-P. Torrell, "Le savoir théologique chez Saint Thomas," *Revue Thomiste* 96 (1996): 355–96; J. Donneaud, *Théologie et intelligence de la foi au XIIIème siècle* (Parole et Silence: Paris, 2006), especially 547–794 and 795–801; Oliva, *Les débuts de l'enseignement*, especially 279–87. See also Oliva's "Quelques éléments de la *doctrina theologie* selon Thomas d'Aquin," in *What Is Theology in the Middle Ages? Religious Cultures of Europe (11th–15th Centuries) as Reflected in Their Self-Understanding*, Archa verbi. Subsidia 1, ed. M. Olszewski (Munster: Aschendorff 2007), 167–93.

if it is the latter, is it correctly defined as science, wisdom, or understanding? (d) What is the subject of sacred doctrine? (e) In what way does sacred doctrine proceed? Each of these articles follows the classical format of the Scholastic *quaestio*, which we will find again in a great number of Thomas's principal works (from the various *Quaestiones disputatae* to the *Summa theologiae*). The *quaestio* begins with the posing of the question itself, and this is followed by a series of arguments in favor of a particular solution. Next there follow arguments for a contrary solution. After this comes the solution that Thomas himself adopts and, finally, come his replies to the initial arguments for a different solution, which is then rejected.

In regard to the first article in Thomas's Commentary (Is a science other than philosophy truly necessary?), his *solutio* rests on a more precise determination of the perfection or end of man, which is the contemplation of God. We should immediately point out an important element: this end is not simply revealed but is naturally knowable, given that the philosophers—and principally Aristotle—had already placed man's greatest happiness in the contemplation of divine things. In other words, that man's happiness should consist in the contemplation of the divine is not only a truth of faith but already a natural, philosophical truth. What marks the distinction between philosophy and theology on this matter is the way that contemplation is understood. There is, in fact, a form of contemplation that is had through creatures, and that is exactly proper to philosophical knowledge. Such knowledge, though is and remains imperfect, because it always seeks to reach the cause through the effects in a case in which the effects (which are finite) are in no way proportionate to the cause (which is infinite). It is a knowledge, therefore, that does lead to happiness but a partial happiness, or rather, a happiness *in via*, the kind that is accessible to us in the present state. But there is another form of contemplation in which God is seen immediately in his essence, and this contemplation is, for that reason, perfect. According to what is presupposed by faith, this is the contemplation that will be had *in patria*. And if this is the true *final* end, then it is necessary already in this life to concern ourselves with the most suitable means for achieving it. From what we have just seen, we can understand that these means cannot be found in natural knowledge alone, viz., in what we can glean from creatures. Thus, a knowledge directly inspired by God, namely theology founded on revelation, will be required. Thomas holds that we can draw two closely related conclusions from this: that this science—as directly ordained to the final end—has priority and command over all the other sciences and justifiably uses them as its servants.

So, here philosophy is identified with natural knowledge, whereas theology is identified with the knowledge that comes through divine inspiration, that is, from revelation. On the one hand, theology serves as a supplement for a defect of philosophy (*oportet aliquam aliam doctrinam … quae per revelationem procedat, et philosophiae defectum suppleat*), whereas, on the other hand, on account of the hierarchy of ends, theology is placed above philosophy. The fact is that, for Thomas, by himself man is able to reach only an imperfect good, but with the help of divine revelation he can reach a perfect good. It is worth noting that Thomas does not so much stress the impossibility of goodness or happiness in this life as he does, more positively, indicate that, unlike other creatures, man is destined to participate in the very glory of God. Thomas, then, insists not on the negative aspects of philosophical or natural knowledge but positively, on an exigency or openness toward which it points: what makes man needful of help from beyond the natural realm is not his limits (limits that would be found also in other things and in greater measure) but his finality or destiny itself, which transcends nature. It is not by chance that in this context there is not a strictly or exclusively theological reason behind Thomas's view but an Aristotelian principle as it was already reinterpreted and used by Averroes: everything that acquires a perfect good by much help and movement is more noble than what by itself or with less help acquires an imperfect good.[29] We, thus, begin to understand something of Thomas's attitude: in an eminently theological text, indeed, precisely at the point where he demonstrates the necessity of theology and its superiority vis-à-vis philosophy, Thomas paradoxically decides to make conspicuous use of Aristotle and philosophy.

But why should only *one* other science be necessary apart from philosophy? Why not hypothesize more? The oneness of the science that goes beyond philosophy (namely, theology) is deduced from the mode itself of divine knowing. The higher a form of knowledge is, the more one and unified it is, even if it extends to more things. The divine intellect, in fact, knows all things solely in virtue of itself, that is, God knows all that is other than himself simply by knowing himself as the cause of everything else. Since theological science draws its power from the light of divine inspiration, it too is one and not many. There are perhaps two further things to note in this connection. The first is that human theological knowledge is placed just below God's knowledge of himself. This *subalternation*[30] of our theology to a higher science, that is, God's knowledge of himself (and the knowledge that the blessed have of him) is an absolutely characteristic feature of Thomas's approach, which we will discuss a little later in

---

29. *De caelo*, II, 292a28–b4

30. This is a technical term derived from the Aristotelian epistemology of the *Posterior Analytics*.

this same chapter. The true theology is, therefore, in the first place, the knowledge that God has of himself; in a subordinate and dependent way (through the inspiration of the divine light, through revelation), it is the knowledge that, already in this life, we can have of the divine things. The second thing to note is the distinction that can be made here between theology (our theology) and metaphysics. Metaphysics too seems to present itself as a universal science (as Aristotle himself presents it in *Metaphysics*, VI, 1). Nevertheless, it considers all things insofar as they are beings, and the notion of being is not sufficient for a more determinate knowledge of things—for a knowledge that takes into account, for example, moral and natural realities. It is theology, rather, that can guarantee a knowledge of this type, to the extent that it is based on the divine light that gives both a general and particular access to each thing. The famous characteristic that Aristotle assigns to metaphysics (universal *because* it is first) becomes, in this way, an exclusive attribute of theology.

Analogy

It would also be worthwhile to reflect further on the reply to the second of the initial objections of the second article of the question of the prologue. According to the objection, a single science requires a single genus-subject. But theology treats of both God and creatures, and the two cannot belong to the same genus except equivocally. In his reply to the objection Thomas appeals to the doctrine of analogy, which we briefly touched on in the last part of our discussion of the *De principiis naturae*. Between creator and creatures there is neither complete univocity nor absolute equivocity but, indeed, a form of analogy. However, that analogy is carefully distinguished from the one established in the interpretation of Aristotle's *Metaphysics* in connection with the multiple meanings of being (notwithstanding the fact that Aristotle himself never spoke of the "analogy of being"). In this case it is not a matter of supposing that different terms participate in a different measure—according to a precise order of priority and posteriority—in something (in the way in which substance and the other categories or predicaments participate in the concept of being) but of recognizing that one of the terms of the analogical relationship depends on the other just as much with respect to being as with respect to the concept from which it takes its name. The creature is a being (that is, possesses being) only to the extent that it depends on God, and it can be called a "being" only to the extent that in this way it imitates the first being, namely, God:

The creator and the creature are reduced to unity not by a univocal commonality but by analogy. Now, such a commonality can be twofold. It can either be because certain things participate in something according to an order of priority and posteriority, as potency and act and substance and accident participate in the concept of being; or this commonality can be because a thing receives its being and its concept from another, and such is the analogy between creature and creator. In fact, the creature has being only insofar as it descends from the first being. Thus, it is called being only because it imitates the first being. And the same must be said of wisdom and everything else that is said of creatures.[31]

The analogy that Thomas employs here is not (to use the terminology that became standard only *after Thomas*) that of *proportionality* (as a relationship of relationships: *a* is to *b* as *c* is to *d*), as was the case in the *De principiis naturae*, but that of *attribution*, and not in the sense in which two things participate in a third thing (as substance and quantity both participate in the concept of being, even if according to a precise hierarchical order), but in the sense in which one of the two terms of the analogy depends on the other just as much ontologically as epistemologically. Yet here we must begin to confront the fact that Thomas never furnished a systematic and perfectly coherent treatise on analogy, even though the doctrine of the analogy of being was traditionally considered one of the cornerstones of his metaphysics. In another place in the Commentary, in d. 19, q. 5, a. 2, ad 1, we find a different and apparently more organic attempt at systematization (the one which Cajetan—one of the most celebrated renaissance commentators on Thomas—principally used to determine what he understood as Thomas's true position on the analogy of terms, establishing it as the genuine doctrine of the Thomist school):

Something is said according to analogy in three ways. It is said only according to concept (*intentio*) and not according to being, and this occurs when a concept is referred to several things according to the order of priority and posteriority, and, nevertheless has being only in one thing, as the concept of health refers to animal, urine, and diet in different ways according to an order of priority and posteriority but not according to a different being since the being of health is only in the animal. Or it is said according to being and not according to concept, and that happens when several things are made equal by the concept of something they have in common, something that is not common on account of the being of the same nature (*ratio*) in each, as all bodies are made equal by the concept of corporeality.... Or it is said according to the concept and according to being, and that occurs when [what is said analogously] is not made equal either in a common concept or in being, as when "being" is said of substance and accident; and in such things it is necessary that the common nature has some kind of being in the things about which one speaks but is in them according to the manner (*ratio*) of a greater or lesser perfection. And in this same way I say that truth and goodness and all such things

31. *In I Sent.* prol., q. 1, a. 2, ad 2.

are said analogously of God and creatures. Thus, it is necessary that all these things are, according to their proper being, in God and in creatures according to the manner of a greater and lesser perfection.

So, going with what has just been said, two or more things are said analogously: (a) when they are not univocal (viz., they differ) with respect to concept, which is applied to them in a hierarchical order (*per prius et posterius*), but do not have this same difference in being (that is, the difference in their being is not a hierarchical difference),[32] because the being to which the concept refers is found only in one of them;[33] (b) when they are univocal with respect to the concept ("corporeality" is said univocally of all bodies) but not with respect to being (ontologically speaking, the celestial bodies have nothing in common with sublunary bodies);[34] (c) when they are not completely univocal with respect to being or concept, even if the common nature on the basis of which they are named exists in each of them (obviously, because it is not univocal, it is a *different* being and is different according to a greater or lesser degree of perfection).[35]

There are, indeed, many things to note about this schema, but we will limit ourselves to just three points. In the first place, the example of health is clearly dissociated from that of being (in relation to substance and accident), contrary to the use to which Aristotle put it in Book IV of the *Metaphysics*. In the second place, we could ask ourselves if this really is—as Cajetan held—a tripartite form of analogy. In fact, the second case (that exemplified by the term "body") does not seem to presuppose an authentically analogous relationship, but only a strange combination of logical univocity (the logician uses the term "body" indifferently for celestial bodies and sublunary bodies, considering it a single genus anterior to the division introduced by the specifications "incorruptible" and "corruptible) and real equivocity (for the metaphysician, celestial bodies have nothing in common with sublunary bodies save for their sharing a merely logical genus). It has been proposed that what Thomas might have really intended here is a distinction between three forms of inequality rather than three forms of analogy: (a) an inequality according to intention or concept (as in the case of "healthy") but without the common nature (health) being truly present in all the things that are said to be "healthy"; (b) an inequality accord-

32. Translator's note: I have added this parenthetical remark to clarify the author's meaning.
33. In Cajetan's interpretation this is the "analogy of attribution," which is, in his judgment, only extrinsic. It is such that the nature to which the concept refers is only in the first term, that is, in the primary analogate.
34. Cajetan speaks here of the "analogy of inequality."
35. For Cajetan, this is the "analogy of proper proportionality," which obtains when a perfection is truly present in all of the subjects, but according to the measure proper to each.

ing to being between things of which a term is said univocally (as in the case of "body"); (c) an inequality according to both concept and being (as in the case of "being"), which suggests that in analogous naming sometimes there is an inequality (with respect to a lesser or greater degree of perfection) in being and sometimes there is not, and that in the real order this must never be confused with what is logical nor be simply superimposed upon it.[36] Nevertheless, against this possible interpretation is the fact that Thomas speaks explicitly of analogy (*aliquid dicitur secundum analogiam tripliciter*) and not of inequality (thus, analogy is principally understood here as that which moves away from univocity rather than toward it). In the third place, it cannot be denied that this text seems, in any case, to say something different from the previous one,[37] where the case of the analogical relationship between God and creature was carefully distinguished from that between substance and accident with respect to the concept of being. In that text, it was only in connection with the different categories that one could speak of a participation in some one thing (in a common nature) according to different degrees of perfection, while in the relationship between God and creatures analogy does not have to do with participation in some *tertium quid* (a common nature—in this case, being), but in the fact that the second imitated the first, which is, therefore, less perfect. In the Scholastic lexicon, we can distinguish in this regard between the analogy of *duorum ad tertium* (analogy of two or more things to another) and that of *unius ad alterum* (analogy of imitation), which seems, in fact, more suited to expressing the relationship between the creature and God—a relationship that, as the first of the two previous texts we have considered already attests, Thomas interprets both as an ontological dependence, and so in terms of *efficient causality* ("the creature has being only insofar as it descends from the first being"), and in terms of *formal or exemplary causality* to the extent that the divine essence is the form or exemplar that is imitated by all creaturely essences.

Later in the Commentary on Book I of the *Sentences*, in d. 35, q. 1, a. 4, Thomas returns to this problem in a still more explicit way:

Analogy is, nevertheless, of two types: one according to the conformity [of several things] to one thing, which conform to it according to an order of priority and posteriority, and this analogy cannot obtain between God and creature, just as univocity cannot obtain between them. The other analogy is that according to which a thing imitates another

---

36. See R. McInerny, *Aquinas and Analogy* (Washington, D.C.: The Catholic University of America Press, 1996). McInerny seems to base the proper interpretation of analogy in Thomas on a strictly ontological interpretation, and thus rather unilaterally, on the *modi significandi*.

37. *In I Sent.* prol., q. 1, a. 2, ad 2.

thing in the measure that this is possible but does not imitate it perfectly; and this is the analogy of the creature and God.

Thomas seems to return here to what was expressed in the question in the prologue of his Commentary, without taking into account what he had said in d. 19, q. 5, a. 2, ad 1. This oscillation between analogy of imitation and *analogy as conformity of two or more things to another* is probably an index of the fact that in the Commentary Thomas had not found a sufficiently stable and coherent position on the analogical relationship between creator and creature.[38] The evidence is given by the fact that in the questions of the *De veritate,* which were written not long after the Commentary (and which we will address in Chapter 2), Thomas effectively changes his view, abandoning both the analogy of imitation and that of the analogy of conformity to a common thing, and adopting more resolutely the analogy of proportionality. Thomas does not refer in the *De veritate* to being but again to knowledge (asking about the way that "knowledge" applies to God and to us). Nevertheless, the new position refers explicitly to all the divine names:

"Knowledge" is predicated neither entirely univocally nor yet purely equivocally of God's knowledge and ours. Instead, it is predicated analogously, or, in other words, according to a proportion. Since an agreement in proportion can happen in two ways, two kinds of community can be noted in analogy. There is a certain agreement between things having a proportion to each other from the fact that they have a determinate distance between each other or some other relation to each other, like the proportion which the number two has to unity in as far as it is the double of unity. Again, the agreement is occasionally noted not between two things which have a proportion between them, but rather between two related proportions—for example, six has something in common with four because six is two times three, just as four is two times two. The first type of agreement is one of proportion; the second, of proportionality. We find something predicated analogously of two realities according to the first type of agreement when one of them has a relation to the other, as when "being" is predicated of substance and accident because of the relation which accident has to substance, or as when "healthy" is predicated of urine and animal because urine has some relation to the health of an animal. Sometimes, however, a thing is predicated analogously according to the second type of agreement, as when "sight" is predicated of bodily sight and of the intellect because understanding is in the mind as sight is in the eye. In those terms predicated according to the first type of analogy, there must be some definite relation between the things having something in common analogously. Consequently, nothing can be predicated analogously of God and creature according to this type of analogy; for no

38. See J. Lonfat, "Archéologie de la notion d'analogie d'Aristote à saint Thomas d'Aquin," *Archives d' Histoire Doctrinale et Littéraire du Moyen Âge* 71 (2004): 35–107, especially 86–90.

creature has such a relation to God that it could determine the divine perfection. But in the other type of analogy, no definite relation is involved between the things which have something in common analogously, so there is no reason why some name cannot be predicated analogously of God and creature in this manner.[39]

It is worth noting how in this new systematization the relationship between animal and urine in the context of health and that of substance and accident with respect to being are no longer distinct from each other—as they were in d. 19 of the Commentary—but are placed together in the same class (agreement in proportion), and how any direct relationship between creator and creature is excluded in principle. One understands why, at least in this phase, Thomas prefers "agreement in proportionality"—to keep with the terminology of the passage quoted—to that of mere proportion. The latter in effect presupposes a *finite*, determined proportion that does not obtain between God and creature. From this point of view, it is certainly better to say that *God is to his knowledge* (or any other perfection of the same type) *as man is to his knowledge.*

We could, nevertheless, ask whether this proportionality actually makes sense, that is, whether the relationship between an absolutely simple essence like God's and its perfections (which are in no way really distinct from it) is truly identical to that between man (or any finite substance) and his qualities, which are, of course, not perfectly identical with his essence.[40]

Thomas must have asked the same question, since in some of his principal writings that followed (in the *Summa contra Gentiles*, the *Quaestiones disputatae de potentia*, and the *Summa theologiae*), he chose to go back over the ground he had already covered, trying even to resolve the initial ambiguity of the Commentary: analogy must be understood without further hesitation, as a relationship of *unius ad alterum*, and not as a relationship of *duorum ad tertium*. In this case too the relationship between God and creatures is considered from the perspectives of both formal causality and efficient causality, suggesting a complete integration of the two aspects: God, producing creatures, impresses upon them something of his perfections (on the basis of the principle according to which *omne agens agit sibi simile*, every agent produces something similar to itself).[41] We cite the most significant passage from the *Summa* on this topic:

Univocal predication is impossible between God and creatures.... Neither, on the other hand, are names applied to God and creatures in a purely equivocal sense, as some have said.... Therefore, it must be said that these names are said of God and creatures

39. *De veritate*, q. 2, a. 11.

40. See A. Patfoort, "La place de l'analogie dans la pensée de S. Thomas d'Aquin. Analogie, noms divins et 'perfections,'" *Revue des Sciences Philosophiques et Théologiques* 76 (1992): 235–54, especially 250.

41. *De potentia*, q. 7, a. 7; *Summa contra Gentiles*, I, cap. 34; *Summa theologiae* Ia, q. 13, a. 5.

in an analogous sense, that is, according to proportion. Now names are thus used in two ways: either according as many things are proportionate to one, thus, for example, "healthy" predicated of medicine and urine in relation and in proportion to health of a body, of which the first is the sign and the second the cause; or according as one thing is proportionate to another, thus "healthy" is said of medicine and animal, since medicine is the cause of health in the animal body. And in this way some things are said of God and creatures analogically, and not in a purely equivocal nor in a purely univocal sense. For we can name God only from creatures. Thus *whatever is said of God and creatures, is said according to the relation of a creature to God as its principle and cause, wherein all perfections of things pre-exist excellently.* Now this mode of commonality of idea is a mean between pure equivocation and simple univocation. For in analogies the idea is not, as it is in univocals, one and the same, yet it is not totally diverse as in equivocals; but a term which is thus used in a multiple sense signifies various proportions to some one thing; thus "healthy" applied to urine signifies the sign of animal health, and applied to medicine it signifies the cause of the same health.[42]

We could summarize the development we have seen in Thomas thus:

- In the Commentary on the *Sentences*, Thomas tries to describe the relationship between God and creatures by recourse to *analogy of imitation* (every creaturely perfection imitates the divine essence) and the *analogy of the conformity of many things to another thing.*

- In a second stage, in the *De veritate*, he adopts the *analogy of proportionality* (on the basis of which one could say that God is to his being as the creature is to its being).

- Finally, in the two *Summae* and in the *De potentia*, Thomas returns to analogy as *the relationship of one thing to another*,[43] describing this relationship as much in terms of formal causality (or imitation) as in terms of efficient causality.[44]

42. *Summa theologiae*, Ia, q. 13, a. 5. Emphasis added.

43. Above all, the *De potentia* illustrates very effectively the difference between the analogy that is made when two things agree with a third term and analogy that is made between two things in proportion to their reciprocal agreement. The second way alone can be applied to predications that are referred to God and creatures. Hence: "In the first way, there needs to be something prior to the two things, to which both of the two have a relation, such as substance to quantity and quality. In the second way, there does not, but it is necessary that one be prior to the other. And so, since there is nothing prior to God, and he is prior to a creature, the second, not the first, way of analogy is proper in predication about God." *De potentia*, q. 7, a. 7.

44. On these three phases see, above all, B. Montagnes, *The Doctrine of the Analogy of Being According to Thomas Aquinas*, Marquette Studies in Philosophy, trans. E. M. Macierowski (Milwaukee: Marquette University Press, 2004), especially chapters 1 and 2; E. J. Ashworth, *Les théories de l'analogie du XIIe au XVIe siècle* (Paris: Vrin, 2008), especially 37–43. Nevertheless, with respect to the God-creature analogy, it does not seem to us that one can speak of a real evolution in the importance that Thomas places on exemplar causality and efficient causality (first giving priority to the former, then to the

We will take up the thread of this discussion later when we look at how in his mature work Thomas deals with the problem of divine attributes or names. But there are three comments that can be made in light of what we have seen so far. In the first place, it is not only the case that Thomas never formulated a consistent and concise doctrine of *analogia entis,* but any purely systematic presentation of the matter is made problematic, if not impossible, by the fact that he changed his position on analogy several times. In the second place, the Renaissance attempts to systematize the doctrine of analogy, starting with Cajetan's work, perhaps do not represent the best schema for approaching Thomas. There is not a strict distinction in Thomas between the analogy of attribution and the analogy of proportionality, whereas the distinctions between proportion and proportionality, on the one hand, and the relationships of *unuius ad alterum* and *duorum ad tertium* (or several things of a common nature), on the other hand, play an important role. Finally, apart from the different perspectives that are adopted each time, what is truly at stake in this question clearly emerges from the very beginning, namely, finding the delicate balance in our discourse about God between two diametrically opposed demands: that of respecting the absolute transcendence of God and that of recognizing (positively) at least his causal role in relation to creatures. Thomas will continue dealing with this problem till his last writings, working through his Neo-Platonic inheritances and ultimately finding, precisely in a specific Neo-Platonic tradition, what to his eyes was the most satisfying solution.

The Scientific Status of Theology and the Theory of Subalternation

The third question of the prologue to the Commentary helps us to begin to determine the epistemological status of theology. First of all, we must ask whether theology is a speculative or a practical science. If theology is required for man's perfection, then evidently in this sense it regards his operations and, therefore, it must be understood as a practical science. However, from an Aristotelian point of view, the noblest science cannot but be speculative since it is an end in itself and is not ordered toward operation. In Thomas's judgment, theology possesses both characteristics since it brings man to his perfection, whether in that which concerns operation or in that which concerns contemplation. But since the ultimate end, as has been said, is the contemplation *in patria* of truth, theology

---

latter), since the latter is already explicitly referred to in q. 1, a. 2 of the prologue of the Commentary on the *Sentences*. See also J.-F. Courtine, *Inventio analogiae: Métaphysique et ontothéologie* (Paris: Vrin, 2005), 259–90.

is *principally* speculative. Ultimately, for Thomas, theology is more speculative than practical, and that marks a first point of difference from the views more widespread among Franciscans, for whom theology was, instead, eminently practical.

One could, nevertheless, ask whether theology could be considered science in the proper sense. In Aristotelian epistemology, every science starts from self-evident principles, principles known to all, whereas theology starts from what is believed, the object of faith, what as such is not accepted by everyone. But the articles of faith, replies Thomas, function here as first principles. They are grasped by those who believe on account of the light given by faith in the same way that the first principles of natural knowledge are naturally inherent in us on account of the light of the agent intellect. The articles of faith, moreover, are never in conflict with the first principles of natural knowledge, and thus theology proceeds from the former without rejecting the latter (*non respuens communia principia*). Such principles cannot be demonstrated by the science of which they are the principles (in conformity with one of the criteria of Aristotelian epistemology), but they can be defended from those who try to deny them. This first attempt to validate the scientificity of theology is, truth be told, a little weak. The articles of faith do not at all seem to have the obviousness necessary to be the principles of a science, nor does the parallel drawn with the natural light seem tenable.

But there is another approach offered by Thomas. It is based on the Aristotelian concept of *subalternation,* and it will be taken up and developed not only within the *Scriptum super Sententiis*[45] but also in subsequent works (especially in the Commentary on Boethius's *De Trinitate*).[46] Following what Aristotle says in the *Posterior Analytics*, one could, in fact, say that only the superior sciences start from self-evident principles, as, for example, is the case with geometry. But inferior sciences—that is, *subalternate* sciences—presuppose the conclusions demonstrated in superior sciences and use them as principles. One can speak, in this case, not of self-evident principles in the strict sense but of conclusions

45. *In III Sent.*, d. 24, a. 2, sol. 2, ad 3.

46. Actually, this second solution is missing from the third article of the prologue, both in the Piana edition (Rome 1570) and in the Parma edition (1856) of Thomas's Commentary on the *Sentences;* nor does it appear in the Italian translation of the work. Chenu has hypothesized that it can be treated as a later addition, originating from Thomas's Roman period. See M.-D. Chenu, *La théologie comme science au XIIIe siècle* (Paris: Vrin, 1969), 76n1. In the study that accompanies the critical edition of the prologue, Adriano Oliva demonstrates that it is a matter of a change that Thomas already made in Paris during his course on the *Sentences.* Thomas's aim was to tone down the parallelism between the infused light of faith and the light of the agent intellect that was present in the original redaction. See Oliva, *Les débuts de l'enseignement,* 139–44.

obtained from the superior science, which themselves are founded on self-evident principles. Thus, for example, the science of perspective, which concerns itself with visible lines, uses as principles what geometry—to which perspective is subordinated—demonstrates about lines as lines. Now, one science can be subalternate or inferior to another either by virtue of its subject or by virtue of its way of proceeding. And in this latter sense we can say that theology is inferior to the science that is directly in God inasmuch as what we know imperfectly he knows perfectly. The articles of faith, which theology takes as principles, can, therefore, be understood as conclusions infallibly proved in the superior science. From these principles theology subsequently proceeds to demonstrate their consequences. So, according to this model, our theology is a science because it is subalternate (or *quasi subalternata*, to use Thomas's own careful nuance) to the knowledge God has of himself.[47]

Subalternation thus permits Thomas to circumvent—with the aid of Aristotle himself—the strict requirements of the evidence of principles that Aristotelian epistemology prescribes for any science. In this way theology configures itself as that science which consists, on the one hand, in deducing conclusions from the principles believed by faith (but demonstrated with absolute certainty in divine science) and, on the other hand, in defending these same principles. As is obvious, even this solution has an intrinsic weakness, to wit, the idea that conclusions can be proved in a discursive way in divine science. It is not by accident that Henry of Ghent, the most important theologian in Paris in the generation immediately after Thomas, will bitterly state that "this position derives from *simple-mindedness and from ignorance* about the nature of subalternation ... because the knowledge of God and the blessed *is not discursive*, viz., it does not move, like ours does, from a first term to a last term through a middle term."[48] Whether or not we share Henry's criticism, it is still true that subalternation is the first sophisticated Scholastic attempt to establish theology as an authentic science, capable of answering the demands of the *Posterior Analytics* even at the price of bending God's own self-knowledge to these criteria.

This does not mean that theology, once constituted as a true science, must give up its traditional designation as *sapientia*, if this means the certain knowledge of causes. Indeed, it can claim the title of wisdom with more right than metaphysics, because it considers the supreme causes in themselves and not

47. Later Thomas will join to God's self-knowledge the knowledge enjoyed by the blessed who already see him and, therefore, possess evidence of the articles of faith. This knowledge possessed by the blessed will be regarded as subalternate science.

48. See Henry of Ghent, *Summa (Quaestiones ordinariae)*, a. VII, q. 5, ed. Badius, Paris 1520 (St. Bonaventure-Louvain-Paderborn: The Franciscan Institute–E. Nauwelaerts–F. Schoningh, 1953), vol. I, f. 53vE.

through creatures. Furthermore, though metaphysics was called "divine science" by philosophers only in reference to its subject, theology is divine not only by reason of its subject but also with respect to the way in which it proceeds and is received. One could object here too that the principles, since they are objects of faith, cannot be known with the same certainty that characterizes, for example, the natural principles from which the other sciences start. But this is not true, for the believer gives his assent more firmly to what he holds by faith than to the natural principles of reason themselves. We have, then, in theology, a well-defined itinerary: we begin with the articles of faith, which are held in an absolutely certain way through infused faith and which exceed reason's natural powers; reason itself, guided by faith, can, nevertheless, develop a gradual and better understanding of what is believed. In Thomas there appears here the famous verse of Isaiah, or more precisely the Isaiah of the *Septuagint* version, already amply employed by Augustine: *Nisi credideritis, non intelligetis*—"If you do not believe, you will not understand."

We must yet determine the subject of this science more precisely (in the fourth article of the prologue). It is necessary to clarify what is meant by *subjectum*. Once again, the background is constituted by the Aristotelian epistemology of the *Posterior Analytics* and by the interpretation of it by the Arab peripatetic tradition. "Subject" is understood here as that upon which the science itself focuses. It is what is presupposed in each science (either because it is evident in itself or because it is demonstrated by a superior science) and its properties (*passiones*) are shown by each science. The subject of physics, for example, is being as mobile, but this subject is nothing but the specification of the subject of a superior science—metaphysics—which has being as being as its subject. So, what is the subject of theology? Thomas must deal with some well-entrenched traditional answers to this question. There is the answer given by Hugh of St. Victor, according to whom the subject of theology is the work of restoration. There is also the answer that Peter Lombard himself gives in the prologue to the *Sentences*, namely, the things and signs of which Augustine spoke in the *De doctrina christiana*. Thomas for his part observes that the subject of a science can be understood in three ways. First, it can be understood as that which includes everything treated of in that science (and for this reason it is possible to speak of "things and signs" as the subject of theology). Second, it can be understood as that which is principally considered within a science, and in this case that would be God. Third, it can be understood as that which distinguishes a science from other sciences (on the basis of the principle of Aristotle's *De anima*, which holds that the division of the sciences follows the division of things: *secantur scientiae quemadmodum et res*), and following this idea some have said that the subject of theology is the truths of faith, because theology distinguishes itself from the other sciences precisely because it starts from the inspiration of faith. If we want to hold onto these three concerns of theology, then the subject of theology must be the divine being as known through inspiration. Everything that is considered by this science is reduced either to God, or to the things that come from God (that have God as their cause), or to those things that are ordered to God (that have God as their end).

The last article of the prologue (the fifth)—which regards theological method and the four senses of the exposition of Scripture (historical, moral, allegorical, and anagogic, that is, relative to the contemplation of the truth of things *in patria*)—allows Thomas to specify in what way it is possible to avail ourselves of argumentation in theological science. It is not for demonstrating the articles of faith, but can be used to defend the faith itself and to reach the truth about questions that can be posed beginning from the principles of the faith, according to the procedure that we have already discussed.

God and Being

Taking as his point of departure the famous Pauline verse according to which "the invisible perfections of God, that is, his eternal power and divinity, are contemplated and understood from the creation of the world through the works he has done" (Romans 1:20), Peter Lombard mentions in the third distinction of the *Sentences* four "reasons" by which people have or would have been able to know the creator: the impossibility that any creature could be the artificer of the whole of creation; the intrinsic mutability of all bodies and the soul itself, which necessarily points to something immutable; the fact that, if the spirit is superior to the body, we must posit as still more superior the artificer of spirits and bodies; the necessity of recognizing a primal beauty upon which the relative beauty of all bodies and souls depends. Thomas reorganizes these reasons according to the three "ways" of which Pseudo-Dionysius speaks: the way of *causality* (which is made to correspond to the Lombard's first reason), the way of *remotion* (the second reason), and the way of *eminence* (which is made to correspond to the third and fourth reasons since eminence itself can be understood according to being or according to knowledge). Apart from this resystematization, which attests to the early influence of Pseudo-Dionysius on Thomas (evidently due to the courses taken with Albert the Great), the text of the *Sentences* at this point offers the young Dominican Bachelor of Arts the possibility to highlight more generally the question of the knowability of existence of God.[49]

49. *In I Sent.*, d. 3, q. 1.

In the first article, Thomas explains that it is possible to know something of God, but not his essence, which exceeds the capacity of understanding. This is a key point, which we will come to see as a background theme to all of Thomas's thought: man can, through creatures, come to know the *existence* of God, not his *essence*. We will, however, see that on this question there is a slight, almost imperceptible, development. In this first phase Thomas insists above all on the incapacity of the created intellect to understand the divine essence; later, above all as an effect of a deeper reading of the *De causis*, he will also insist on an intrinsic aspect of the divine essence: God is beyond forms, he cannot be thought through them, and, therefore, he is not objectively thinkable.

Leaving aside, then, knowledge of the divine essence, can we hold that God's *existence* is *obvious*? In this case too, the Commentary of the *Sentences* substantially anticipates the position that Thomas will expound in the *Summa theologiae*. The knowledge of a thing can be considered either with regard to the thing in itself or in its relation to us. The background is, of course, the Aristotelian distinction between what is first and more evident in itself and what is first and most evident for us. In reference to God in himself, his existence is evident and intelligible in itself. In other words, it is not evident in a mediated way, through an abstractive procedure that moves from images that are delivered by the senses, as happens with our knowledge. God is, in sum, perfectly transparent, so to speak, to his intellect, with which he is identical (*ipse est per se intellectus*). In relation to us, God can be considered in two ways. (a) He can be considered according to his likeness and to what participates in him, and in this sense his existence is also immediately evident: nothing is known except through its proper truth, which has its exemplary cause in God (*quae est a Deo exemplata*), and it is immediately evident that truth exists. (b) He can be considered according to his individual reality (his "supposit," according to the technical Scholastic term), that is, considering him as a determinate incorporeal reality, and God's existence is simply not obvious in this way. And this is so much the case that some have denied God's existence. Let us reflect on this second case. Augustine is obviously a source for the first case: God is implicit in every particular truth, and the existence of truth as such is obvious. But this is still a generic determination. It is conceded that something like truth exists, but nothing is yet said about what this truth is like in itself. And here is where the possibility mentioned in the second case is rooted. God's existence, as a reality determined in his own nature, is not evident. In fact, the lack of its obviousness has led to the failure of some to recognize God's existence and to the denial of his existence by others. Thomas, following Aristotle (*Metaphysics*, I, 4 985b), cites in this regard those philosophers ("Democritus and others") who did not admit an agent cause, and, thus did not admit a productive cause of the universe. This occurs because what is evident to us is what we immediately perceive with our senses. If we observe whole and part, we immediately understand that the whole is greater than the part. However, sensible things do not permit us direct access to God. Through them we can reach God only in an indirect and discursive manner, through the recognition that everything is caused, that it depends on an agent cause, and that the first agent cause cannot be corporeal. And, of course, that at which we arrive by way of demonstration, beginning from effects, is not self-evident.

This question in Thomas's Commentary is also his first opportunity to deal with Anselmian argument, viz., with the demonstration offered by Anselm in the *Proslogion* (if God is that than which nothing greater can be thought, then he cannot exist only in the intellect, for otherwise it would be possible to think of something greater, something that exists also in reality outside the intellect). Thomas leagues himself here with the objections already expressed by Gaunilo in his *Liber pro insipiente*: after we have understood God (*postquam intelligimus Deum*), we can no longer think that it is God and that he cannot exist. In other words, the non-existence of God cannot be thought once we have really understood what God is. But we must, indeed, first understand this, and this means that, in an absolute sense, it is possible to think God as not existing, thinking that nothing of the sort—something than which nothing greater can be thought—exists at all. The whole Anselmian *ratio*, in effect, rests on a supposition, that is, that there exists something about which it is not possible to think of anything greater. We can see, above all with this conclusion, how Thomas insists not so much on the problem of the passage from the mental to the real, but on the more important of the objections formulated by Gaunilo: the Anselmian argument is in a certain way pleonastic (or question begging) because it presupposes that there exists something with respect to which we cannot demonstrate that there is anything greater (to wit, that such a concept is not empty or unfounded); and if I already know that it exists, and that it is such, it is evident that I cannot think of it as not existing. The absolute necessity of Anselm's argument is in this way reduced to mere hypothetical or conditional necessity: on the condition that there exists something than which nothing greater can be thought (on the condition that such a concept is not entirely arbitrary), it cannot be thought not to exist, but I must first grasp the concept of such a nature. In the *Summa theologiae*, as we will see, Thomas will insist on this aspect (the impossibility of having an essential knowledge of God); and this same concern—which cannot just be reduced to the simple objection to a gratuitous passage from the mental to the real—is the one that will move Henry of Ghent and Duns Scotus to postulate that the Anselmian argument works only if one prefixes to it a demonstration of the foundation of the initial concept, that is, a demonstration of the nature to which the necessary existence belongs.

In d. 3, q. 1, a. 3, Thomas can, therefore, return to specify that God can be known from creatures to the extent that every creature is nothing more than an imitation of God according to the limits and possibilities of its nature. And this justifies the adoption of the three ways mentioned earlier—the way of causality, of remotion, and of eminence—proposed by Pseudo-Dionysius and, according to Thomas, taken up again by Peter Lombard (with the doubling of the way of eminence, as we saw). To what does knowledge mediated by creatures lead us? Certainly not to the Trinity, for the knowledge of God from creatures leads us to be able to affirm—as we said—God's existence, but it does not lead us to any—or only a minimal (and this in a purely analogical form)—knowledge of God's essence, and certainly nothing distinct about the Persons of the Trinity. Consequently, "the philosophers knew nothing about this [that is, the Trinity] if not from revelation or from having heard it from others (*et ideo philosophi nihil de hoc sciverunt, nisi forte per revelationem vel auditum ab aliis*)." If we emphasize this aspect, it is first of all because it allows us, once again, to understand the reason why, according to Thomas, another science besides philosophy is necessary and, second, to note that Thomas, like the majority of his Scholastic colleagues, when he refers to the philosophers, almost always adopts the past tense (*sciverunt*) and does not do so purely fortuitously. For Thomas, "the philosophers" are the Greeks and the Arabs, and both belong to an experience that is now a thing of the past. There is no such thing as contemporary philosophers, there is no contemporary philosophy. In Thomas's view (and, as we have said, for the majority of his colleagues, even those of the faculty of arts), philosophy is a horizon that is essentially closed, already concluded, past, not a current option. Of course, philosophers did once exist and from them many useful doctrines can be appropriated, while others can be corrected or refuted, but philosophy as such (as *pure* philosophy) is something now obsolete, outdated. If we do not attend to this fact, there is a danger of creating confusion about the relationship between theology and philosophy in Thomas. This is why, as we announced at the beginning of this work, Thomas would never have understood himself as a philosopher, and also why in Thomas's eyes nothing existed that could be called a "Christian philosophy." Philosophy is an experience that has already passed into the archive, and precisely as such is serviceable in its *complete autonomy*, not because all of its conclusions are obsolete, but precisely because some are valid in themselves; they express what natural reason can reach. It is possible, in fact, to arrive at further conclusions (and here the Aristotelian epistemology of the *Posterior Analytics* remains the fundamental criterion) from new and different premises: those offered by revelation. It will not be a question of advancing philosophical discourse from within, but of making space for a new science that operates from different premises. In the history of humanity's scientific progress, as we will see, philosophy, without being abolished, is destined to make room for a new knowledge that has a subject that is different, at least in part, and, above all, uses entirely new premises. It cannot be stressed enough that this is the meaning of Thomas's *scientific* project (taking into account what *scientia* meant in the thirteenth century, namely, the model offered in the *Posterior Analytics*). This is not a matter of creating a synthesis between reason and philosophy, on the one hand, and faith and theology, on the other, as if reason stood wholly on the side of philosophy and faith wholly on the side of theology. The point is, rather, to construct a new *scientia* that must necessarily establish itself on philosophy, and hinges on it—even though it works rationally, as we have said, from different principles.

In d. 8, q. 1 Thomas returns explicitly to the problem of the relationship between God and being,[50] viz., to the problem of what today we would call "ontotheology" but which also implicates what Gilson, with a celebrated and felicitous expression, called the "metaphysics of Exodus" (the identification of the God of the Bible with pure being).[51] Already the first objection of a. 1 seems to clarify well the heart of the problem: being belongs to creatures too, not just to God, and so it does not seem that being is a property exclusive to God. But, on the other hand, indeed in Exodus (and Thomas invokes the interpretations of John Damascene and Moses Maimonides in support) God indicated that his proper name is *Qui est*, "He who is." Now, that this is the most appropriate name for God is, to Thomas's mind, indubitable, because such a name indicates the perfection of the divine being, emphasizes that we can reach him only to say *that he is*, and not *what he is*, and shows that being is the principle that pre-contains everything that follows. But a further reason for the preeminence of the name *Qui est* (a reason that derives still from a philosopher—Avicenna—and touches on the distinction between being and essence, which we already met

---

50. On this topic see, B. Bernardi, *Studio sul significato di esse forma essentia nel primo libro dello Scriptum in libros Sententiarum di San Tommaso d'Aquino* (New York: Peter Lang, 1984), 287–304.

51. See É. Gilson, *The Spirit of Mediaeval Philosophy*, trans. A. H. C. Downes (Notre Dame, Ind.: University of Notre Dame Press, 1991), 81n14.

in our analysis of the *De ente*) is the most important. In every existing thing, its quiddity (what it is, the determinate nature of the thing) and its being (that on the basis of which it is said to be in act) must be considered. The first aspect is indicated by the term *res*—"thing"—the second by the term *ens* or by the locution *qui est*. All created things are named not by the fact that they are, but on the basis of their quiddity, essence, or nature. Man is distinguished from the horse, the rock, or the triangle not by the fact that he exists but, indeed, by the fact of being a man and not a horse, a rock, or a triangle. In God, however, his being is his quiddity (*ipsum esse suum est sua quidditas*), and so it is only right that the most appropriate name for God should directly refer to being. God can be called "Being" or "He who is" because this is his most proper nature, and it is for exactly the same reason that a man is called a man. *The whatness of God (what he is) is his being*—which means that God does not have a whatness distinct from the fact of being, or, as we will better see, *God is not a thing but simply is*. The name "He who is" is, thus, not an affirmation, a thesis of positive theology; it is rather a thesis of negative theology, to the extent that it tells us that God is not thinkable as a thing, as an object. Thomas will draw the most explicit consequences of this in the later Commentary on the *De causis*, but this thesis is already met with here, as is evident in d. 8, q. 1, a. 1, ad 4: all names express a determinate and particular being ("wise" speaks of a certain being), but "He who is" expresses absolute being that is not determined by anything added to it, and for this reason John Damascene says that this name does not signify what God is, but "a certain infinite ocean of substance (*quodam pelagus substantiae infinitum*)," or, as Thomas glosses, almost something indeterminate (*quasi non determinatum*). God's identity with being is not *a positing* [*una posizione*]. It is, on the contrary, the outcome of a negative movement, a movement of remotion. First we eliminate from God all bodily aspects, then the intelligible ones such as goodness and wisdom (in the way in which they are found in creatures), and at the end there remains in our intellect only the fact that he is, and nothing more (*et tunc remanet tantum in intellectus nostro, quia est, et nihil amplius*). The last step, in fact, consists in removing being itself, as it is in creatures, from God. Divine being, then, because it is different from creaturely being, designates something totally inaccessible: our intellect cannot but remain in a kind of "darkness of ignorance," and this ignorance, as Dionysius says, is the best way for us to unite ourselves with God in this life. Thus, there is not in Thomas—despite what is claimed by twentieth-century Neo-Thomism—any rhetoric or fetishization of being. Being, rather, properly indicates the obscurity (*caligo*) in which God dwells.

But in the same article Thomas clarifies two other points. First, affirming that God is being does not mean that he is the being of all things (in a pantheistic sense), or, better put: God is the being of all things not in an essential sense but as the cause of all things. Nevertheless, further qualification is necessary, since cause and effect can relate univocally, equivocally, or analogically. Now, God is not a univocal cause, because nothing measures up univocally with God. But neither is he a purely equivocal cause, because then he would not truly be a cause (equivocal causality is such that cause and effect do not agree in name or in concept [*ratio*]). God is, therefore, an analogical cause—as we have already seen—which means that divine being produces creaturely being as an imperfect resemblance of itself.

Second, Thomas asks whether being is truly the first of the divine names. The competition is among four principal names: *ens, unum, bonum,* and *verum.* These are realities that will later be called transcendentals, and we will discuss them more extensively in Chapter 2. Now, there is no doubt that because of their commonalities these names must be held as first and having priority, but is it possible to establish a hierarchy among them? The comparison of these names can be made in three ways. (a) If the comparison is made according to the supposit (that is, the single individual), then they are convertible and are identical with each other (an individual man is being, one, good, and true). (b) If the comparison is made according to their concepts (their *intentiones*), then "being" has precedence over the others, because it is included in their concept but they are not included in its concept. "One" adds a negation to being, the fact of being undivided. "True" adds a relation to an exemplar cause or to a cognitive power, since a being is true inasmuch as it is the imitation of a divine exemplar or is known by an intellect. "Good" adds a relation to the end—a being is good in relation to its end. (c) If the comparison is made according to causality, good has the priority, for the final cause (toward which the good points, as we said) is the first among causes, since, as Avicenna had already taught, it is the causality of the causes of all other causes.[52]

Besides the influence of Avicenna, we also see in Thomas's Commentary on the *Sentences* the influence of Pseudo-Dionysius. It is here that we meet for the first time in Thomas the alternative between being and good as the most appropriate names of God, a topic that will return in the Commentary on Pseudo-Dionysius's *De divinis nominibus.* It is not by chance the Dionysius already appears in the first objection of d. 8, q. 1, a. 1, which argues for the priority of

---

52. See R. Wisnovsky, "Final and Efficient Causality in Avicenna's Cosmology and Theology," *Quaestio* 2 (2002): 97–123.

good over being. In his reply Thomas limits himself on this occasion to saying that the priority of good refers, as we have just seen, only to the order of causality. The option between two different and parallel Neo-Platonic traditions—one of which situates the Good beyond being, and the other which identifies God with pure being—is provisionally resolved here by distinguishing perspectives: one relative to concept (and to predication) and the other relative to the order of causes.

It is unnecessary to observe that the *Scriptum super Sententiis*, apart from the elements that we have commented on, contains other elements that are basic to Thomas's work as a whole. To cite only a few examples: the rejection of universal hylomorphism, the reduction of prime matter to pure potentiality, the defense of the unicity of substantial form in the human composite, the interpretation of the agent intellect and the possible intellect as two individual faculties. It is true that, at least until Capreolus (in the fifteenth century), Thomas's Commentary on the *Sentences* continued to be read and commented on more than the *Summa theologiae*.[53] But it is also true that the positions expressed by Thomas in the Commentary were not always maintained without change in successive works—the question of analogy, which we discussed, does not represent in this sense an isolated case.[54] Moreover, Thomas's contemporary disciples and readers were aware of this, as certain works circulated shortly after his death bear witness, above all, the *Articuli in quibus frater Thomas melius in Summa quam in*

---

53. See M.-D. Chenu, *Toward Understanding St. Thomas*, trans. A. M. Landry and Dominic Hughes (Chicago: Henry Regnery, 1964), 273: "In fact—and this observation is an important one for the history of Thomism—during two centuries, the Commentary on the *Sentences* remained the rule for the interpretation of Saint Thomas, since the professor, who was bound to the text of the Lombard by the university regulations, spontaneously referred to the *Sentences* and limited himself to a [mere] consultation of the *Summa*."

54. Another example to which we have already referred touches on the way in which dimension should be understood as that which makes the matter an actual principle of individuation. On this topic, in fact, an evolution within the Commentary on the *Sentences* itself could be mentioned: in the Commentary on the first book, which is probably anterior to *De ente*, Thomas notes that no accident can change the matter before it is determined by the substantial form, and such is, indeed, according to the thesis of Avicenna, the form of the corporeity, of which the matter can never be deprived (*In I Sent.*, d. 8, q. 5, a. 2.). But the language of "designation" is not yet employed. It only begins to appear in dd. 23 and 25 of the Commentary on Book I. This is what brought Roland-Gosselin to situate the composition of the *De ente* around the time of the composition of d. 25 of the Commentary on Book I. See M.-D. Roland-Gosselin, *Le De ente et essentia de S. Thomas d'Aquin, introduction, notes et etudes historiques* (Kain: Le Saulchoir, 1948), especially pp. xxvi–xxviii. As was said, in Book IV the Avicennian position seems to be completely replaced with the Averroist doctrine of indeterminate dimensions (*In IV Sent.*, d. 12, q. 1, a. 2–3 and d. 44, q. 1, a. 1, qla 3, ad 3). In Chapter 6 we consider another case of at least a partial rethinking of a position taken in the Commentary on the *Sentences*, namely, on the causes of predestination.

Scriptis, which was a list, composed around 1280 (and often revised afterward) of thirty-two points of divergence between positions expressed in the Commentary and the preferable ones adopted in the *Summa*.[55]

55. See R.-A. Gauthier, "Les *Articuli in quibus frater Thomas melius in Summa quam in Scriptis*," *Recherches de Théologie Ancienne et Médiévale* 19 (1952): 271–326. The principal amplification of the original list is the concordance, *Volens complecti*, which lists 42 articles and which, above all, is no more than an instrument aimed at guiding a reading of the Commentary on the *Sentences* that is integrated with the improvements of the *Summa*; this work aims to resolve all of the apparent contradictions in the principal works of St. Thomas. On this topic, one could refer also to the *De concordantiis in seipsum* (ascribed by some to the English Thomist Thomas of Sutton), which introduces a more sophisticated structure, modeled on the *Retractiones* of Augustine. The author imagines Thomas himself intervening, *ex parte post sui*, to clarify some apparently contradictory points in his writings.

2

THE FIRST PARIS REGENCY
(1256–59)

THE DEFENSE OF THE MENDICANT ORDERS:
CONTRA IMPUGNANTES DEI CULTUM
ET RELIGIONEM

The beginnings of Thomas's first teaching stint in Paris are marked by the conflict between the secular (diocesan) clergy and the mendicant orders that continued in successive phases throughout the whole second half of the thirteenth century.[1] The conflict developed on different levels, from the more general ecclesiological level (in connection with what we could call "ecclesiastical ideology") to the purely economic level. With respect to the conflict's first dimension, the universalism of the new mendicant orders, which answered externally only to the pope, deeply undermined the rigid hierarchical and territorial organization on which the Church had hitherto rested and which at the bottom level divided the territory into parishes, and at the next level gathered the parishes into dioceses under the leadership of a bishop, and placed the pope finally at the third and highest level. Every parish priest had full control of his area and his population of faithful—it was not, in fact, legal for a parishioner, for example, to go to confession in another parish without prior authorization. The fact that the Franciscans and Dominicans were permitted freely to preach and hear confessions obviously exploded this territorial organization and hierarchical order. Furthermore, it should be kept in mind that, following Pseudo-Dionysius the Areopagite, this structure was traditionally considered immutable, as an imitation of the celestial hierarchy and modeled on the primitive organization of the Church at time of Christ: the triad of pope–bishops–parish priests was understood to correspond to the triad of Christ–apostles–seventy-two dis-

---

1. For a detailed reconstruction, see Y. Congar, "Aspects ecclésiologiques de la querelle entre Mendiants et Séculiers dans la seconde moitié du XIIIe siècle et le début du XIVe," *Archives d' Histoire Doctrinale et Littéraire du Moyen Âge* 28 (1961): 35–161.

ciples. There was no room for other levels in this hierarchy except below the priests.[2]

With respect to the conflict's other dimension, as we have said, there were implications decidedly more material. The territorial control of the *cura animarum* provided income (rights for marriages, burials, etc.), which was suddenly in danger of being taken away from the parish priests in charge once the faithful were permitted to turn to the Dominican and Franciscan friars for the same rites and needs. Access to the same revenue sources was suddenly given over to different and more numerous parties, thus depriving the parishes and dioceses of a certain amount of funding.

Over the course of the thirteenth century the conflict developed, as we have said, in different ways. In the 1280s, for instance, the most controversial point was surely about the so-called privilege of confessions. But in the 1250s, in the period in which Thomas became a *magister* in Paris, the differences regarded the possibility of the mendicants teaching (occupying chairs) in the faculty of theology. The Dominicans entered the University of Paris in 1229, when, during a strike by the *magistri* (it should be said that strikes go back almost to the very foundation of the university), the bishop, William of Auvergne, attempted a renewal, so to say, of the professorate by calling on Roland of Cremona, a Dominican, to teach. Roland had been a bachelor of the *Sentences* of the secular master John of Saint-Giles and had just acquired the title of *magister*. Thus was born the first Dominican chair in theology but—to put it in the most charitable way possible—it was not born in the most hospitable environment, since the new academician came on the scene as a "scab," as we would say today. Already here we can perhaps grasp the reason for the concern of the other masters, who, until that time, had all belonged to the secular clergy. The mediaeval *universitas*, it is worthwhile to recall, was not a physical site but a corporation that enjoyed a certain autonomy sanctioned by privileges and immunities accorded to it by the civil and religious authorities. The members of this corporation, like those of any other medieval corporation, but to an even greater extent (given its greater degree of autonomy), answered in the first place to the organs of the corporation itself and followed their decisions. The mendicant friars had a vow of obedience external to the corporation and, thereby, threatened its internal unity (which was the essential guarantee of autonomy and self-government). The very fact that the first Dominican master did not participate in the strike but, in fact, obtained his chair because of the strike was a clear confirmation of this.

---

2. In Pseudo-Dionysius's ecclesiology monks were among those who needed to be perfected by the clergy and could certainly not assume the same functions.

The Dominicans and Franciscans certainly incarnated an ideal of the Church that was much more dynamic and modern (if we may use such terms), but the historical studies on Thomas, traditionally very favorable to the Dominicans (if not written by Dominicans themselves), cannot erase some objective causes of a quarrel that is mistakenly attributed only to the envy and malevolence of the seculars, as we still see claimed. In 1230 (when the long strike decreed the previous year was supposed to end), John of Saint-Giles became a Dominican, keeping his chair and, some years later, in 1236, another secular master, an Englishman called Alexander of Hales, decided to enter the Franciscan order, also keeping his chair by the decision of Bishop William of Auvergne. Thus, both of the principal mendicant orders had a foot in the University of Paris, and were destined in a short time to reach a position of absolute predominance (already by the end of the thirteenth century Henry of Ghent and Godfrey of Fontaines are the last two great exceptions).

We might find it astonishing that the secular masters should feel so threatened by the reservation of two academic chairs for Dominicans and one for Franciscans. But we must note the fact that the number of chairs in theology was limited, or, as we would say today, "programmed." At the beginning there were only eight, then in the 1250s there were twelve. The restriction of chairs to a particular group or groups diminished the possibility for other aspiring masters, and in this case also altered the former economic relationships (and it should also be observed that the Scholastic *magister* was the first professional intellectual known to the West).

In February of 1252 the seculars approved a statute that limited the chairs restricted to religious orders to just one each,[3] but without eliminating the second Dominican chair (the so-called chair "for foreigners," which Thomas would occupy). In March of 1253 the secular masters again went on strike to protest against the act of aggression toward four clerics and their lay servant by the city's night watch, an act of aggression that, in fact, violated the prerogatives of immunity and internal discipline of the university community. But even in this case the regulars, that is, the friars (Elias Brunet and Bonhomme le Breton for the Dominicans and Guillaume de Méliton for the Franciscans) continued to hold their courses. The seculars responded by decreeing their expulsion from the college of masters and promulgating new statutes that imposed an oath of fidelity on whoever wished to join the college. After a first intervention by the pope in June 1253 to reinstate the expelled professors, in February 1254 the seculars published a long document in which they reiterated their complaints, which were principally that

3. *CUP*, I, p. 226n200.

the Dominicans continued to have two chairs and that the regulars *de facto* violated the oath of fidelity of the corporation. It appears that the Franciscans (who still had only one chair) accepted the limitations, which permitted Bonaventure of Bagnoregio to begin teaching already in the 1253–54 academic year without being officially admitted to the *consortium magistrorum*. Disagreement also flared up on the theoretical or doctrinal front. In this arena the principal protagonist for the secular faction was William of Saint-Amour, who in 1255 published a very violent pamphlet against the mendicants entitled *De periculis novissorum temporum*, whose principle target was the Joachite theses taught by the Franciscan Gerard de Borgo San Donnino in his *Introductorius in Evangelium aeternum*.[4] The crisis began at the end of 1254 when Innocent IV, with the bull *Esti animarum* of November 21, revoked the privileges granted to the mendicant orders even in regard to preaching and confession. But Innocent IV died on December 7 and his successor Alexander IV immediately annulled the earlier bull with his *Nec insolitum*, and with *Quasi lignum vitae* of April 14, 1255, he broadened the privileges granted the friars, ordering the University of Paris to readmit the Dominican masters and suppressing the limit on the number of chairs. But this did nothing to calm the waters in Paris. The growing climate of hostility toward the friars obliged the authorities to the protect the Dominican priory of Saint-Jacques, and on the day of the inaugural lecture of the new Dominican master, Florent of Hesdin, King Louis IX had to send his archers—a real armed escort—so that the ceremony could take place without incident.

It was in this climate of not only verbal violence—the Friars Preachers had stones hurled at them on occasion—that Thomas received the *licentia docendi* to obtain his doctorate in theology—on the decision of the chancellor of the university, Aimeric of Veire—and, thus, to become a *magister*. Thomas probably was not of the requisite minimum age set down by the regulations[5] and probably did not personally ask for the *licentia*.[6] So, Thomas obtained his doc-

---

4. Translators' note: "Joachite theses" refers to theses of Joachim of Fiore, an Italian Cistercian abbot of the twelfth and thirteenth centuries. Certain of his doctrines were condemned by the Lateran Council of 1215 and by Alexander IV in 1256.

5. If we suppose that the year of his birth was 1224 or 1225 as is traditionally held, Thomas would have been thirty-one or thirty-two, whereas the age specified by the regulations of Robert of Courçon was thirty-five. For several internal problems on this point, see A. Oliva, *Les débuts de l'enseignement*, especially pp. 198–202. The fact that Thomas may not have met the age requirement could be a historiographical ambiguity bolstered by the aim of conferring an exceptional character on his career. In that case, however, the date of Thomas's birth would need to be moved back to 1220/1221 (see also p. 3n2 in this volume).

6. But the statutes specified that the chancellor might offer the license even in the absence of an explicit request by a candidate. Alexander IV would later compliment the chancellor on his timely decision to offer the *licentia* to Thomas.

torate in the spring of 1256 in the period between March and June 17, giving as his *principium* (the discourse given in the inaugural course or *inceptio*) a lesson on Psalm 103:13 (or Psalm 104:13 according to the numbering in the Hebrew version): "He who waters the hills from his high dwelling" (*Rigans montes de superioribus suis*). In his inaugural lecture Thomas concentrates on the problem of the communication of wisdom, on the fact that, just as God in general uses intermediaries and secondary causes (the Neo-Platonic framework is again easily noticed), so also for what regards wisdom he avails himself of doctors (the mountains mentioned in the Psalm), from whom the same wisdom streams down into the valleys, to the hearers.[7] June 17 can be reasonably fixed as the *terminus ante quem* of the period in question, because on that date a new, severe papal intervention occurred in which the four secular masters—among whom was William of Saint-Amour—who were most involved in the struggle against the regulars, were suspended from teaching. In his letter the pope explicitly mentions Thomas's inaugural lecture, confirming that it took place in less than ideal conditions or, better, a climate of real intimidation and threat:

As we well know, the masters and the students mentioned earlier have done nothing to maintain the concord that we have insisted upon with the edict *Quasi lignum vitae*. Instead they have opposed it, inciting everyone to continue the struggle. In the most shameful way they have hindered those who wanted to attend the lessons, the disputations, and the preaching of the friars, and particularly those who wanted to attend the inaugural discourse of our beloved son Friar Thomas Aquinas.[8]

The least that can be said is that the teaching career of the person who would become one of the principal Christian theologians (if not *the* principal one) did not begin in the best circumstances, and with the favor of all. But Thomas would have to wait almost a year to be admitted to the consortium of masters, an event that took place on August 12, 1257.[9] The months that followed the *inceptio* would, however, see the first great defeat for the seculars, at least in the sphere of ecclesiastical politics. William of Saint-Amour's *De periculis novissorum temporum* was seized by the king of France and was officially condemned by Alexander IV at Anagni on October 5, 1256. William himself was forced into exile, first in Rome and then in his native village.

It is probably in this period that we should situate Thomas's first interven-

7. On this subject perhaps another text could be mentioned, namely, the *Sermo secundus fratris Thome* which focuses on Baruch 4:1: *hic est liber mandatorum Dei*. Thomas could have delivered this on the occasion of the *resumptio*, which is the first day of classes after the *inceptio*.

8. *CUP*, I, p. 321n280.

9. All told, things went better for Thomas than for Bonaventure, who was admitted on the same day, but waited almost four years and, in the meantime, became the minister general of his order.

tion against the seculars, *Contra impugnantes Dei cultum et religionem* (*Against the adversaries of the worship of God and religion*). Thomas's biographers hypothesize that he examined William's *De periculus* during a provincial chapter in Anagni in 1256 (a meeting that some scholars doubt ever took place) and in a short time worked out a reply. In the opuscule Thomas demonstrates a knowledge of the papal condemnation of Gerard de Borgo San Donnino's *Introductorius in Evangelium aeternum* (October 23, 1256), but not yet of the condemnation of the *De periculis*. Hence, it must be assumed that the treatise was composed in Paris (without any evidence that Thomas had, indeed, traveled to Anangi) toward the end of the summer and the beginning of autumn of 1256. It is Thomas's first publication after having become a *magister*.

The work is made up of 26 chapters and is constructed according to the typical structure of the *quaestio*. Thomas first takes up the principal points of debate with his opponents: the compatibility of religious life with teaching, the coexistence of the friars and seculars in the college of teachers, the possibility of the friars preaching and hearing confessions, the rejection of manual labor, radical poverty to the point of renouncing communal goods, and mendicancy (cc. 2–7). There then follow Thomas's replies to a series of minor objections of the seculars (cc. 8–12), among which it is worthwhile to mention the accusations of excessive study (c. 11) and of overly sophisticated preaching (c. 12). Cc. 13–19 regard the accusations leveled by William of Saint-Amour touching on the friars' attempt to gain credit at the expense of the seculars by, for instance, trying to cater to the faithful (c. 17) or seeking the favor of the powerful (c. 19), and often not hesitating to have recourse to the courts (c. 15) to get sanctions imposed on their adversaries (c. 16). Finally, cc. 20–26 deal with the orchestration of gossip to defame the mendicants and especially the accusation of being false apostles (c. 22) and precursors of the Anti-Christ (cc. 24–25). Between the lines of the conflict one can read different conceptions of the role of the friars. For William the friars are (or, better, should be) substantially like the traditional monks, who live in solitude and, so, should not engage in public activities such as teaching. For Thomas, the friars are called to live in an urban context and they fully respond to the Aristotelian conception of man as an animal destined by nature to live in society.[10]

In light of our interests in this book it is particularly worth noting that when in the *Contra impugnantes* Thomas defends the decision of the friars to dedicate themselves to study, he references not only the Fathers but also Averroes, from whom he borrows the idea of philosophical chastity or ascesis:

10. See C. Roverselli, "Linee di antropologia nel *Contra impugnantes* di Tommaso d'Aquino," *Sapienza* 41 (1988): 429–45.

They are best capable of prosecuting their studies with success, who are least embarrassed by earthly ties.... The Commentator says in *Physics*, VII that chastity and the other virtues, whereby the concupiscence of the flesh is curbed, are special aids to the acquisition of speculative knowledge. Because religious above all subdue the concupiscence of the flesh by means of continence and abstinence, they are especially suited to study.[11]

It is significant that one of the central themes of so-called "Latin Averroism" appears explicitly here in defense of one of the prerogatives of the friars but without being a source of controversy.

The *Contra impugnantes* is without a doubt one of Thomas's more polemical writings, which he would follow up during his second Paris regency by the *De perfectione spiritualis vitae* and the *Contra retrahentes*. As a whole, these treatises, which do not have in themselves a strictly philosophical value, play an essential role in helping us correct a rather common error of perspective. However paradoxical it may seem to traditional philosophical historiography, Thomas was in an absolute sense more concerned by the attacks made against the mendicant orders by prelates and secular clergy than by the "theoretical" dangers connected, for example, with the spread of Averroist ideas in the faculty of arts.

THE *QUAESTIONES DISPUTATAE DE VERITATE*
The General Modes of Being

The *Quaestiones disputatae de veritate* comprise an ensemble of twenty-nine questions later divided into two-hundred fifty-three articles. The genre of disputed questions deserves perhaps some clarification.[12] *Disputare* disputing is one of the basic tasks of the Scholastic *magister*, together with those of *legere* (reading and explaining the texts for his courses) and *praedicare* preaching. Leaving the last activity aside, we can say that lectures and disputations constitute the double binary of medieval teaching. At Saint-Jacques, where Thomas held his courses (as we said, the medieval university was not a unified physical place, and the masters of the mendicant orders usually carried out their teaching activities in their respective priories), the masters' lectures normally took place in the early morning (followed by the lectures of the bachelors). The disputations were held in the afternoon. It is not easy to ascertain to what extent the writings of Thomas that have come down to us in the form of disputed questions reflect the disputations that were actually held in the school. They may also have been reworked

---

11. *Contra impugnantes*, 3, c. 4.

12. See B. C. Bazán, "Les questions disputées, principalement dans les facultés de théologie," in *Les questions disputées et les questions quodlibétiques dans la faculté de théologie, de droit et de médecine*, ed. B. C. Bazán, G. Fransen, J. F. Wippel, D. Jacquart (Turnhout: Brepols, 1985), 13–149.

to meet more directly the demands of publication. Nor is it easy to understand what part or unit of the published text might correspond to the actual development of a particular disputation. If an article seems, at times, too little, an entire question seems a bit too much.[13] Admitting, however, a certain independence between the actual disputation and the subsequent redaction, nothing prevents one from accepting the hypothesis of Carlos Bazán and Jean-Pierre Torrell[14] that the disputations unfolded without being strictly bound to one or another article, but followed, rather, the evolution of the discussion, and that when they were redacted the articles were reorganized and gathered into questions. On the other hand, nothing prevents one from thinking that some articles, while retaining the classical structure of the disputation (arguments *pro* and *contra*, *solutio*, replies to objections), were simply added according to the need for doctrinal completeness. In any event, if *Quaestiones disputatae de veritate*, as it seems, were disputed during the entire period of the first Paris regency (1256–59), an average of 80 articles per year results (whether they were a part of an actual dispute or were added during the redaction). We know, however, with certainty that their publication and the beginning of their circulation occurred not long after the actual disputations and redaction, since some of the questions of the *De veritate* were already cited by the Dominican encyclopedist Vincent of Beauvais before 1264–65.

The title of the collection is taken from the first question, but in reality the work deals with the true and knowledge only in the first part (qq. 1–20), while the second part (qq. 21–29) is dedicated to the good and the appetite that tends toward it. The true and the good are *transcendental* concepts, in the Scholastic sense of the term (that is, they transversally embrace all the categories without belonging specifically to any of them), and, thus, we could say that the *De veritate* is fundamentally a treatise on the transcendentals (even if Thomas himself does not adopt the term and instead uses the expression "general modes of being").[15]

The first question of the *De veritate*, in fact, permits us to clarify this point.

---

13. On this topic see, P. Mandonnet, "Chronologie des questions disputées de Saint Thomas d'Aquin," *Revue Thomiste* 23 (1918): 271n1, and "Introduction" in Thomas d' Aquin, *Quaestiones disputatae*, vol. 1 (Paris: Lethielleux, 1925), 12–17 (on the unity of each dispute and article); A. Dondaine, *Secrétaires de saint Thomas* (Rome: Editori di San Tommaso [Leonine Commission], 1956), especially 209–16 (on the unity of each dispute and the question).

14. See Bazán, *Les questions disputées*, esp. 70–85; J.-P. Torrell, *Saint Thomas Aquinas*, vol. 1, *The Person and His Work*, 59–66.

15. On the way in which Thomas develops his own doctrine of the general modes of being (the transcedentals), see, above all, J. A. Aertsen, *Medieval Philosophy and the Transcendentals. The Case of Thomas Aquinas*, Studien und Texte zur Geistesgeschichte des Mittelalters 52 (Leiden: Brill, 1996). See Chapters 6 and 7 for treatments of the true and the good. See also B. C. Bazán, "Thomas d'Aquin et les transcendantaux," *Revue de Sciences Philosophiques et Théologiques* 84 (2000): 93–104.

When we seek something, it is necessary to return to some first principle that is self-evident to the intellect so as not to drift off into the infinite. Now, according to Avicenna, what the intellect conceives of as first and most known is being.[16] Consequently, all other concepts represent determinations added to this first concept. Nevertheless, nothing can be added to being that is truly extraneous or external to it, because any nature—however it is understood—is already a being (and because of this, being is not a genus and is not restricted to a determinate category). When it is said, then, that the other concepts add something to being, it must not be understood that they add something that is not already being, but only that they express a *mode* of being that is not immediately expressed by the name "being" itself (*secundum hoc aliqua dicuntur addere super ens in quantum exprimunt modum ipsius entis qui nomine entis non exprimitur*). That happens in two ways: we can, in fact, refer to a *special mode* of being or to a mode that regards *every being as such*. In the first case, we have the highest genera of being, namely, the categories: substance, for example, does not add anything to being that is not already being, but expresses a certain mode of being and that is the fact of being *in itself* (whereas all the other categories need a subject in which to inhere—namely, substance—and express each of the other determinate *special modes* of being). In the second case, the mode expressed does not regard only some beings in distinction from others but is proper to every being either *in itself* or *in relation to another*. What is proper to every being in itself is, first of all, and in a positive sense, its *essence*, its being a determinate thing, its "whatness." The first mode proper to every being in itself is, therefore, what is expressed by the term *res*, "thing." In a negative sense, proper to every being is the fact of being undivided, which is expressed by the term *unum*, "one." Every being is one inasmuch as it is undivided (if a being were divided, indeed, it would not be *a* being, but several beings together). We must yet consider what accompanies every being *in relation to another*. We can distinguish in this respect between that which has to do with the division or distinction of one being from the others and that which has to do with a being's conformity to another. In the first case, every being, insofar as it is one and undivided in itself, is distinct from others, being *something determinate*, and this mode is expressed by the term *aliquid*, "something" (for Thomas, *aliquid* is something like *aliud quid*, "another thing," so something distinct, in itself). In the second case, the being must be considered in its relationship to the soul, because only the soul can be or become all things (as Aristotle teaches in Book III of the *De anima*), and so can conform to every being. The soul, however, has two powers: a cognitive power and a desiring

16. *Book of Healing*, I, 5 (Metaphysics).

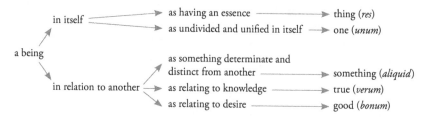

or appetitive power. The conformity of a being to the *vis cognitiva* of the soul is expressed by the term "true" and the conformity of a being with the appetitive power is expressed with the term "good." In other words, a being is true as known by the soul and good as desired or sought by the soul.

The schema of the *general modes* of being could be reconstructed in the way suggested by our diagram. The *De veritate* deals only with the last two modes in this schema.[17] And from what we have said we can already infer in what the true or the truth consists. It consists in the conformity or concordance of being with the intellect—a concordance that we find not by chance in the classical definition of truth (which Thomas, like others, attributes—but perhaps without any foundation—to the Jewish philosopher Isaac Israeli, who lived between the ninth and tenth centuries)[18] as *adaequatio rei et intellectus*, and which is the basis of all knowledge.

Truth and Falsity

Three aspects of truth are to be distinguished: (a) the ontological foundation (being); (b) the conformity to the soul (*adaequatio*); (c) the knowledge that is obtained by the intellect. *Formally*, however, truth coincides strictly with the second aspect, that is, with the conformity of being to the intellect. Thomas explains this point with precision in q. 1, a. 2 when he asks whether the true is principally in things or in the intellect, being guided again in this case by Aristotle (for whom the true and the false are more in the intellect than in things, or, better: they are in things but only inasmuch as they are known, composed

17. We should keep in mind that the *De ente* amply covered the first mode, and in part also the second and third. The relationship between "being" and "one" is also taken up in other works, especially in the *De potentia*.

18. See J. T. Muckle, "Isaak Israeli's Definition of Truth," *Archives d'Histoire Doctrinale et Littéraire du Moyen Âge* 8 (1933): 5–8. On the concept of truth in Aquinas, besides the work of Aertsen already cited, see J. F. Wippel, *Metaphysical Themes in Thomas Aquinas II*, Studies in Philosophy and the History of Philosophy 47 (Washington, D.C.: The Catholic University of America Press, 2007), 65–112; G. Schulz, Veritas est adaequatio intellectus et rei. *Untersuchungen zur Wahrheitslehre des Thomas von Aquin und zur Kritik Kants an einem überlieferten Wahrheitsbegriff*, Studien und Texte zur Geistesgeschichte des Mittelalters 36 (Leiden: Brill, 1993).

and divided by the intellect).[19] Thomas, then, has no doubts; the true is primarily found first of all in the intellect and secondarily in things (as a determination that is added to being, as we have said, to the extent that it relates to the intellect):

A thing is not called true, however, unless it conforms to an intellect. The true, therefore, is found secondarily in things and primarily in intellect.[20]

It should be said, however, that things relate not only to the human intellect but also to the divine intellect, and the nature of the relationship in the two cases is entirely different. The divine intellect relates to created things as a *practical intellect*, and not as purely speculative—it does not limit itself to knowing these beings but, in a more originary way, it produces them. In this sense we can say that things are *the measure of our intellect*, which must adequate (conform) itself to them, and does not produce them (save in the instance of human artifacts), but they are *measured by the divine intellect* (because it is God that gives them being). In other words (as Thomas states later in q. 1, a. 4), truth relates to the divine intellect as to its proper cause and relates to the human intellect as to an effect, insofar as the human intellect receives the science of things. A thing, thus, must be called true more in relation to the divine intellect than to the human intellect; and so, even if there were no human intellects, beings would still be true in relation to the divine intellect:

A natural thing, therefore, being placed between two intellects is called true insofar as it conforms to either. It is said to be true with respect to its conformity with the divine intellect insofar as it attains the end to which it was ordained by the divine intellect.... With respect to its conformity with a human intellect, a thing is said to be true insofar as it is such as to cause a true estimate about itself.... Truth is found especially in the first, rather than in the second, sense, for its reference to the divine intellect comes before its reference to a human intellect. Even if there were no human intellects, things could be said to be true because of their relation to the divine intellect.[21]

But if, absurdly, there were no intellects at all—neither human nor divine—but there were things, there would be nothing that was true, for, as we have said, a being is true only in relation to an intellect (practical or speculative).

To which operation of the intellect does the notion of truth more precisely relate? The intellect has, in fact, two fundamental operations, with which we

---

19. See Aristotle, *Metaphysics*, VI, 4, 1027b25–27. It also needs to be said that in the second book of the *Metaphysics* Aristotle himself held that things have truth inasmuch as they have being (a principle maintained by Thomas on many occasions).

20. *De veritate*, q. 1, a. 2.

21. *De veritate*, q. 1, a. 2.

will now begin to familiarize ourselves and which we will see again in connection with the determination of the subject of metaphysics in Thomas's Commentary on Boethius's *De Trinitate*. The one operation forms the quiddity (essence) of things and the other composes and divides. From what we have just seen, the true is not a property of things in themselves but of the intellect in relationship to things. The celebrated formula *veritas est adaequatio rei et intellectus* is, therefore, not understood by Thomas, as has sometimes been claimed, in the more naively realistic sense of a pure mirroring of the external state of things by the intellect, but in the sense that the intellect has the capacity to adequate itself to things, adding something to them that they do not already have. This is what happens in *judgment*, by which the intellect says that something is or is not. And this is the proper operation of the intellect composing and dividing. Truth, then, is primarily found in the composing and dividing of the intellect (*veritas per prius invenitur in compositione et divisione intellectus*).[22] Only secondarily is truth in the intellect when it forms the quiddity of things and definitions. A definition, indeed, is not said to be true in itself but only when it is correctly associated with what is defined, viz., to the extent that it is correctly composed. As the first operation of the intellect in itself, the formation of the quiddity is not properly the first locus of truth, because at this first stage the intellect itself does not have something of its own with which it could conform to the thing. We have, thus, a precise order, which still more clearly underscores truth's relative (to the intellect) nature than its ontological nature:

From our discussion, then, it is clear that the true is predicated, first of all, of composing and dividing by the intellect; second, of the definitions of things insofar as they imply a true or a false judgment. Third, the true may be predicated of things insofar as they are conformed with the divine intellect or insofar as, by their very nature, they can be conformed with the human intellect. Fourth, true or false may be predicated of man insofar as he chooses to express truth, or insofar as he gives a true or false impression of himself or of others by his words and actions.[23]

This allows us to respond to the question as to whether the truth, so conceived, is temporal or eternal. Evidently, everything depends upon which intellect we are talking about—the human or the divine. In the first case, truth is not eternal in the intellect or in things because neither the one nor the other is eternal. But if we are talking about the divine intellect—which, as we have said, is the extrinsic measure of all existing things—then truth is eternal. Further, in this regard Thomas explains that adequation does not presuppose that the two extremes

22. *De veritate*, q. 1, a. 3.
23. *De veritate*, q. 1, a. 3.

of the relationship are both in act. Just as our intellect can, in fact, conform to something (and in this way bring about a truth) that is not actually present inasmuch as it is past or future, so also, the divine intellect conceives from eternity the things that come into being in time, and this allows us to speak of eternal truths (as dependent on an eternal intellect) even in respect to temporal things. However, it must be observed in this connection that God does not have different acts of knowledge regarding different things, but knows all things through his one essence. For this reason eternal truth is one, despite the fact that it is differentiated in many temporal truths (q. 1, a. 5). Thomas distinguishes here between truth as an extrinsic measure (when something is called truth by virtue of its relationship to the first truth) and intrinsic truth that is found in changeable things themselves. Created things vary *in their participation* in the first truth, but the same first truth from which other things are called true never changes. But in what sense can we speak of a variable truth in regard to the *intrinsic* truth, inherent in things? Let us try to distinguish the different cases. If we consider the truth of the thing in relation to the divine intellect, then the truth of the thing constantly changes from one truth to another truth. Although the thing can change, it still remains the same being, even if according to a different form, and, therefore, remains true under another truth. However much it changes, it continues to conform to the divine intellect, remaining "true" in this way. If, instead, we consider the changing of things in relation to the human intellect, there can be change from one truth to another truth as well as change from truth to falsity. If, in fact, to the change of the thing there corresponds a change of the intellect, there would still be a form of adequation, and so truth, even if different from the preceding truth. But if the change of the thing is not accompanied by a change of the intellect, there would be, rather, falsity. As Thomas sums things up:

As is clear from what has been said about created things, truth is found both in things and in the intellect. In the intellect it is found according to the conformity which the intellect has with the things whose notions it has. In things truth is found according as they imitate the divine intellect, which is their measure—as art is the measure of all products of art—and also in another way, according as they can by their very nature bring about a true apprehension of themselves in the human intellect, which, as is said in the *Metaphysics*, X, is measured by things.[24]

We can, then, affirm that every truth is from God, since from God there derives both the being of things (which is convertible with their truth) and the activity by which the intellect conforms to things or to what they lack.

24. *De veritate*, q. 1, a. 8.

From what we have said, it is easy to conclude that "in comparison to the divine intellect nothing can be called false."[25] Because it is possible that there is not always an agreement of the human intellect with things, it is plain that, for man, some things can be false. The fact is that our intellect judges things according to their external appearance, because all of our knowledge originates from the senses. If, therefore, the thing appears differently from what it is—or put in more technical terms, if the sensible qualities of the thing indicate to us a nature that does not really belong to the thing—falsity results. But here too the same caveat we saw before applies. Just as truth is not primarily in things, neither is falsity. Falsity is always in the judgment of the intellect. We cannot fault things for appearing differently from what they really are, because things never necessarily lead us into error. The soul is never entirely passive with respect to things, and so it is able, at least in principle, to judge them correctly, instead of supinely accepting appearances. Thus, notes Thomas, "a thing is not said to be false because it always produces a false understanding of itself but because it is such as to generate this understanding through its appearances."[26] In an absolute sense, then, each thing is always true (it has as much truth as it does being); but accidentally, and in a relative sense, some things are called false in relation to our intellect.

This brief mention of the sensible qualities of things permits us to shift our discussion to the truth and falsity of sense knowledge. Truth, as Thomas understands it, is in the senses differently from how it is in the intellect, for it is in the senses in the measure that they judge things but it is not in them as known by them. Put differently, the senses judge correctly of things, with truth, but they do not know the truth whereby they judge, since the senses know that they sense but they do not know the nature or essence of their act and, hence, do not know their own truth. The intellect is able to return to itself and to know its own *activity* and its own *nature*; the senses know their own activity but not their own nature, because (as Thomas gleans from Avicenna) they always need a bodily organ and there is no bodily organ between the sensitive power and itself.

In q. 1, a. 11, Thomas adds important qualifications about the possible falsity of sense knowledge. The senses are intermediaries between things and the intellect, and so their falsity can be considered in relation to things or in relation to the intellect. In relation to the intellect, the senses can be considered in two ways: (a) insofar as they too are things—and in this respect there is never falsity,

25. *De veritate*, q. 1, a. 10.
26. *De veritate*, q. 1, a. 10.

given that the senses present themselves to the intellect in the way that they are disposed and cannot do otherwise (citing Augustine's *De vera religione*, Thomas points out that the senses "can only reveal to the soul how they are affected"); (b) insofar as they represent something else (*repraesentativum alterius*)—and in this respect the senses can be called false because they can generate a false cognition on the part of the intellect (even if not in a necessary way, as we have said, since the intellect is never purely passive and can always become aware of the distortion). In regard to things, the senses are true and false in the same way the intellect is, namely, not so much in the apprehension of the sensible realities (just as in the intellect true and false are not properly in the operation in which essences are grasped), but in judgment. Now, as regards the proper sensibles, judgment is natural, but as to common sensibles (such as figure, size, movement, rest, etc.) and accidental sensibles, judgment takes place through a comparison which brings into play one of the internal senses described by Avicenna, and, indeed, the principal among them, the *cogitativa*. The judgment about proper sensibles is always true (so long as there is no impediment in the organ or medium) but the judgment about common and accidental sensibles can be erroneous. In fact, there is a margin of error and falsity for the simple apprehension of a sensible thing, which depends more particularly on another internal sense, imagination. If, in general, it is true that the senses apprehend the thing as it is, the imagination mainly apprehends it as it is not. The imagination reproduces things as present even when they are no longer the object of the senses in act.

The first of the questions of the *De veritate* concludes with an interrogative about how it is possible for falsity to be in the intellect.[27] "Intellect," Thomas observes here, comes from *intus legere*, to read inside of things, to know what is most inward in a thing (*intima rei cognoscit*). In fact, the senses and the imagination grasp only the exterior accidents of a thing; only the intellect reaches the interior and essence of the thing. Now, in apprehending the essence of a thing—which is its adequate and proper object—the intellect can never err, just as the senses can never err in regard to proper sensibles. Falsity comes to be when the intellect composes or divides incorrectly, which happens in two ways: when it attributes the definition of one thing to another (taking, for instance, "rational, mortal animal" to be the definition, not of man, but of an ass), or when it joins together parts of a definition that it is impossible to join (as when it defines an ass as an "irrational, immortal animal," it not being possible for an irrational animal to be immortal): a definition is false when it implies a false judgment. Therefore, there is no falsity in the apprehension of essences and first

27. *De veritate*, q. 1, a. 12.

principles, while there can be falsity in reference to the complex of intellectual operations, which also include opinion and reasoning. But even in these, falsity can be avoided if the intellect always correctly carries out the reduction to first principles, about which it is impossible to be deceived.

God's Knowledge and Knowledge of Individuals

The second question of the *De veritate* deals with God's knowledge (*scientia*). We should perhaps reflect first of all on the term *scientia*. In the technical sense, "science" indicates certain and evident knowledge that is attained in virtue of a demonstrative argument (as Thomas will explain in his Commentary on the *Posterior Analytics*), that is, through reasoning. In this sense, science is properly the habit of conclusions and it is distinguished as much from understanding, which is the habit of first principles, as it is from wisdom, which includes not only the conclusions deduced from principles but also judgments about the same principles.[28] It is to this argumentative nature that reference is made when it is said with Aristotle that properly scientific knowledge is that which is obtained by knowing the cause or the why of something. In a broader sense "science" can stand for any certain and evident knowledge, even if it has not been reached through demonstration.

Can we speak, therefore, of science in God? We certainly cannot do this if by "science" we mean a disposition that is ulterior and additional to the essence (as is the case with the science of which we are capable), for then God would not be absolutely simple. Neither can we limit ourselves to saying that there is science in God only because he is its cause and brings it about in us—a thesis that Thomas seems to attribute, at least indirectly, to Origen and Augustine (and we should note here that this is one of his first disagreements with Augustine). In general, for Thomas, it cannot be said that something belongs to the cause only because it is found in the effects. If anything, the contrary must be said: God can bring about science in us because there is science in him. Neither can it be said that science is attributed to God only metaphorically, as when we read in the Scriptures that there is anger in God or similar things. Science is, rather, one of the divine attributes that is one with the divine essence and is distinguished from other attributes only in relation to our knowledge. And yet, as we will see more than once, the way that we represent such attributes is not completely false. It is, in fact, inevitable that our intellect form multiple concepts of the simple divine essence, which surpasses all our power of comprehension. It is a matter of imperfect, but not completely false, images.

---

28. *Summa theologiae*, Ia-IIae, q. 57, a. 2.

Before dealing more specifically with the question of divine knowledge, Thomas inserts an interesting metaphysical digression in which he explains that knowledge is a remedy for the imperfection in the various finite species that constitute the universe. Everything is, indeed, perfect according to the degree of perfection that belongs to its species and absolutely lacks what is the perfection of other species. Thus, everything, although perfect, is imperfect in relation to the overall perfection of the universe, which results from the convergence and sum of the different partial perfections. To compensate for this inevitable limitation (which, in the subsequent tradition will go under the name of *malum metaphysicum*) there is only one possibility, and that is that the perfections of some things can be found in a certain way in others, or at least in some of the others. And this is the perfection that only knowledge can secure, to the extent that the objects known are in the knowing subjects. We find ourselves before the most radical justification of the ideal of knowledge as the maximal perfection attainable by finite beings, a justification based on the Aristotelian assumption that the soul is in a way all things. And here is the fundamental intersection between the philosophical ideal and the Christian ideal:

The ultimate perfection which the soul can attain, therefore, is, according to the philosophers, to have in it the entire order and causes of the universe described. This they held to be the ultimate end of man. We, however, hold that it consists in the vision of God; for, as Gregory says: "What is there that they do not see who see him who sees all things?"[29]

The Greek and Arab philosophical ideal of pure intellectual felicity, in which the soul is able to possess the whole concatenation of causes that rule the universe (the Avicennian project of becoming an intelligible world in which the entire order of the universe is described), is, then, not abolished but, on the contrary, made concretely possible by Christian eschatology. The beatific vision permits what is not actually possible in this life. But let us pause for a moment over what it is possible for us to attain in this life. To know is to harbor the perfections of other things in ourselves. However, it is obvious that they cannot be in the one who knows in the way that they are in themselves, according to their determinate being. Instead, insofar as they are known, they are stripped of all the determinations that accompany them, and since the perfections (forms) of things are determined by matter, it follows that a thing is known to the extent that it is stripped of its materiality. And for this reason, as we already began to see in the *De ente*, it is inevitable that the knower is immaterial also, that is, that he receives these intelligible forms.[30] The capacity to know is, therefore,

29. *De veritate*, q. 2, a. 2.
30. In the post-Cartesian lexicon we would speak of the knower as the subject of knowledge. But

commensurate with the degree of the immateriality of the knower. Plants and other inferior realities cannot receive anything immaterial; they are deprived of knowledge. The senses receive the species of material things immaterially but not without the material conditions. The intellect receives the species stripped even of the material conditions. The same holds for the reality known: the more immaterial it is the more knowable it is. Consequently, God, who is supremely immaterial and lacks all potentiality, is in maximal possession of knowledge and is maximally knowable.

So, up to this point Thomas follows the philosophical line, and what he attributes to the revealed God is nothing more than the maximal intellectuality of the Aristotelian first mover according to its reinterpretation by Arab philosophers, Avicenna in particular (and it is no accident that this article concludes with another quotation from Avicenna supporting the connection between immateriality and intelligibility). But the absolute immutability and necessity of the God of the philosophers are not, as such, altogether descriptive of the God of Christian revelation. It is in his attempt to better determine the modality of God's knowledge that Thomas gradually distances himself from their position. The main question is, Does God know only himself, as is the case with Aristotle's first mover, or does he know things besides himself? If everything in nature is disposed toward an end—something that is evident for Thomas—and is not subject to chance, it cannot be doubted that it was disposed in an orderly way by its cause, and, thus, it cannot be denied that the divine intellect, which is the cause of the natural order, possesses knowledge of all natural things, and so of all the effects, which are, as we have seen, immaterially present in the cause.[31] It is, in fact, necessary that in this sense God have a determinate knowledge of the specific natures of particular things. But we can go further and ask whether God has knowledge of individuals. And here Thomas parts company with the Arab philosophers. Averroes, Thomas says, completely denied the knowledge of individuals by the first cause. And Avicenna conceded only that God had an indirect knowledge of individuals through knowledge of all the universal causes which produced the individuals.

The thesis attributed to Averroes is easy to refute because, with the desire to safeguard the maximal divine transcendence and simplicity, it makes God ignorant. On the other hand, against the Avicennian position (to which we will return later), the congregation of many universal causes could never produce a singular effect. There is no room, then, for doubt. "It must absolutely be con-

---

we must bear in mind that in the Scholastic lexicon, subjective being is what is present in the things themselves.

31. Here Thomas revises a proposition from the *De causis*: *intelligentia cognoscit id quod est sub se in quantum est causa ei.*

ceded that God knows all individuals, not only in the universal causes, but each one of them in its proper and singular nature."[32] Here Thomas makes use of the traditional comparison between God's science and the science of an artisan, a comparison that is justified by the fact that science is not predicated of God and man univocally or equivocally, but, as we already know, analogically according to the analogy of proportionality (God is to his science as man is to his science), which does not presuppose any real commonality between them.[33] Now, an artisan too knows all the things that he makes because he is their cause, but with a fundamental difference, namely, that every artisan is limited to making the form of his products, working on preexistent material. God, however, creates not only the form but also the matter, and since, as we also know, individuation depends on the matter, it can be concluded that God knows what he makes not only from a formal—and, therefore, universal—point of view, but he knows it in its singularity. It might seem strange that on the basis of this example Thomas denies that artisans have knowledge of individuals. Thomas's reasoning on this point is a little less obvious than it might seem. We are speaking here of the science that the artisan has before producing effects, and not of that which follows. Now, in Thomas's view, an architect, to do his work, must have the universal house in his mind, that is, he must know what is necessary to building a house. But the actual knowledge of individual houses he only acquires *a posteriori*, through the senses, and so through experience. It is not like this for God, who has science, and not simply experience, even of individuals.

It is worth reflecting briefly on this point, because it overturns what seems to be a natural conviction, viz., that human beings, in virtue of their bodiliness and senses, can know individuals, while God, because he is immaterial, can know only the universal. For Thomas, the contrary is true: God knows the individual and not only the universal. Human beings, however, do *not* directly know the individual. This will be clarified by Thomas later in the part of the *Summa theologiae* that treats of the mechanisms of human knowledge,[34] but in the meantime we can note the explanation Thomas suggests in the *De veritate*. The *similitudo* (likeness, representation) of things is in our intellect and in the divine intellect differently. The likeness that reaches our intellect is extracted from things through the senses, yet, although the senses perceive material beings, the matter itself, because of its potentiality, is unable to act on the soul. In consequence, the thing acts *on the senses* in virtue of its materiality but *on the soul* only in virtue of its formal aspect. So, in our intellect we have a *likeness* of

---

32. *De veritate*, q. 2, a. 5.
33. *De veritate*, q. 2, a. 11.
34. We will discuss it in Chapter 4 in the section on knowledge.

the form only, not of the matter, and, thus, we do not know things as individuals (that is, inasmuch as they are materially determinate), but only as universals. It might be said that we *sense* individuals and *intellectually know* the universal. The divine intellect, however, does not receive the likeness of things but produces things from the reasons or likenesses that it already eternally possesses: and since God already possesses a representation of the matter, he can immaterially know what is material, and so also individuals. The difference between the divine and the human intellects is situated entirely here. Both are obviously immaterial, and possess only immaterial representations, but the divine intellect possesses an immaterial representation of the material whereas the human intellect does not. As Thomas puts it:

Since the likeness of a thing existing in our intellect is received as separated from matter and all the conditions of matter, which are the principles of individuation, it follows that our intellect, of itself, does not know individuals but only universals. For every form as such is universal, unless it happens to be a subsistent form, which, from the very fact of its being subsistent, is incommunicable.[35]

Thomas allows man only a *per accidens* knowledge of individuals that is acquired in an indirect way. In fact, the only way for our intellect to remain in contact with individuals is by having a direct relationship with their sensible representations, that is, with the phantasms of them derived from the senses. But our intellect does not enjoy a perfect continuity or perfect transparency vis-à-vis the phantasms. Our knowledge always begins from the senses, which are in continuity with sensible things and, in its turn, our intellect is actualized by what it receives from the senses, which is the sensible species or phantasm, a sensible representation of the thing produced by the senses. So, just as the senses are in continuity with things, the intellect should be in continuity with the phantasms. We could express these relationships with this formula: things : senses :: phantasms : intellect. If this relationship were completely linear, many of the problems would be resolved. However, the fact is that, whereas the senses relate to sensible things as their proper object (from which they derive phantasms), the intellect does not relate to phantasms as its proper object but only as the *medium* from which it can abstract the intelligible species. To use the same example Thomas uses, the phantasm is like an image of the thing reflected in a mirror, and our intellect aims at the thing that is reflected more than at the reflection. This might appear to permit the intellect to remain in contact with the thing itself, but if we prescind from the mediation of the phantasm, the thing can be apprehended by the intellect only according to its formal aspect,

35. *De veritate*, q. 2, a. 6.

that is, in its universal aspect rather than as an individual. The only possibility for the intellect to have contact with individuals is, then, to return to attend to the phantasms through a sort of torsion or bending backward (*reflexio*), as when sight, in seeing an object reflected, turns in a first instance to the object itself but can return to attend to its image in a mirror. This movement back to the sensible image—this movement from the intellect back to the imagination—is, therefore, the only possibility for the human intellect to preserve a relationship—however indirect and minimal (through singular images)—with the actually existing singular realities:

Therefore, inasmuch as our intellect, through the likeness that it receives from the phantasm, turns back upon the phantasm from which it abstracts the species, the phantasm being a particular likeness, our intellect gets some kind of knowledge of the individual because of a certain continuity of the intellect with the imagination.[36]

As we have said, we will return to this topic in the *Summa*. But it should be noted here how the common notion that Thomas is a champion of realism must be drastically revised and qualified. Thomas aligns himself substantially with the moderate representationalism typical of a large segment of Scholasticism, of which he could, indeed, be easily pointed to as one of the more significant exponents. The myth of an ultrarealist Thomas is a late nineteenth- and twentieth-century invention that was used to oppose realism to post-Kantian and idealist representationalism. But to confuse the problems and alter the chronology of the history of ideas is often both a sterile and a misleading exercise.

At this point we can return to divine knowledge. Knowing the essence of each individual, God knows also all the common and proper accidents of each individual. Among these is time, within which every existing individual is really situated and on the basis of which it is said to exist now or not. So, God knows of every individual that it is or is not.[37] Moreover God knows the non-existent or non-beings. While our knowledge depends on the existence of objects, God's knowledge, being anterior to the existence of things, indifferently embraces all things whether they exist or not.[38] We must advert again here to the distinction between speculative knowledge (when something is known without the knowledge being immediately directed toward making something or doing something) and practical knowledge (when knowledge is directed toward making or doing something). In the case of human artifacts, practical knowledge always follows speculative knowledge and is, indeed, a kind of extension of the latter. God, on the other hand, possesses practical knowledge of those beings that he brings

---

36. *De veritate*, q. 2, a. 6.
38. *De veritate*, q. 2, a. 8.

37. *De veritate*, q. 2, a. 7.

about now, has brought about in the past, or will bring about in the future, along with a speculative knowledge of the beings that do not now exist, have not existed, and will not exist although are theoretically possible. From this there also stems the fact that, unlike human beings, God can know infinite things, because not only does he know those that have existed, exist now, or will exist, but also all those things (an infinity) that could have been or could be brought about. It could be objected that knowledge of the infinite appears logically impossible, for the infinite (according to Aristotle) cannot be "traversed"—it cannot be crossed and, thus, conceived. God, however, does not know in a successive way—one after the other—the infinite things that he could bring about (because, if it is a question of an infinite whole, that would be simply impossible); rather he knows them in a simultaneous and unified way (*simul et uno intuitu*). In this setting Thomas does not take a definite position on the issue of whether God can make an infinite number of things in act, because he seems inclined to concede that, at least in an accidental sense, an actual infinite is possible. If such a possibility be conceded, we must say that God is able to bring it about. But if with Averroes we take Aristotle's interdiction more strictly, admitting only a potential infinite and denying any actual infinite, then God cannot make infinite things, because it is not in God's nature to bring about what is contradictory. We notice here something else that we will encounter more widely in the *Questiones quodlibetales* and in the *De potentia*, viz., that for Thomas, as for almost all the medievals, the limit of divine omnipotence is set by the principle of non-contradiction, because what is impossible in itself is not possible for any agent—even the supreme and omnipotent agent. The real impossibility, therefore, is entirely on the side of the object and so does not touch the power or the capacities of the agent in any way.

In the catalogue of what is contained in God's knowledge we also find future contingents (events that are such for us to the extent that they could occur or not occur and so do not possess a determinate truth value) not as *future* (because God's knowledge is not temporally determined) but as *present*. The fact that God sees all events as present, nevertheless, does not change their modality (as Boethius already observed in the *Consolation of Philosophy*); it does not convert them from contingent events to necessary ones. The same thing is true for us in relation to present events. Our sight cannot help but see the contingent events that take place before us, but that does not prevent them from being in themselves contingent. Thomas himself uses this example:

Therefore, the fact that our sense of sight is never deceived when it sees contingents when they are present does not prevent the contingents themselves from happening contingently. In like manner, God infallibly knows all the contingents, whether they are present, past, or future to us; for they are not future to him, but he knows that they are when they are; and the fact of his knowing them does not prevent them from happening contingently.[39]

A further rejection of the so-called Greco-Arab necessitarianism can be found in q. 2, a. 14 of the *De veritate*. Thomas stresses that God's science is the cause of things whereas ours is caused by things. When, however, it is said that science is the cause of things, a clarification is in order, because the causation of divine science is not immediately operative and so there is no falling into emanationist necessitarianism. Between God's science and the things made there are, in fact, two intermediaries: one is the divine will, which decides what to bring into act, and the other is the system of secondary causes, because God does not immediately bring everything into being, but uses intermediate causes to bring about effects.

Finally, because God knows all individuals, he also knows their privations and contraries, and, therefore, also knows evil, without being its cause.[40] On the other hand, already in q. 1, a. 10, Thomas had opportunely explained that not all things relate to God as measured to measure, because some of them relate to him only as known to knower, and this is precisely the case with privations and negations, of which God is not the cause.

Ideas

The fact that God has science—something that we have seen is proved by the fact that the world is not constituted by chance or by necessity, but is the result of the action of a conscious agent who predetermines the end[41]—implies that he also possesses *ideas* or *forms*. Although often equivalent, "form" and "idea" do not always perfectly coincide for Thomas, since form can be understood in three distinct ways: (a) as that *from which* something is formed in the sense that, in general, effects proceed from the form of the agent; (b) as that *according to which* a thing is formed, in the sense in which the soul is the form of the human composite and the shape of the statue is the form of the bronze; (c) and, finally, as the model *of which* a thing is formed, that is, the exemplar in imitation of which something is made. It is only in this last sense that "form" and "idea" are equivalent in Thomas's usage, but on the condition that it is subsequently understood that this relationship is not accidental but intentional, deliberate, and conscious on the part of the agent. An idea is, thus, according to the definition proposed by Thomas, the form that something imitates according to the intention of an

39. *De veritate*, q. 2, a. 12.

40. *De veritate*, q. 2, a. 15.

41. It is worth noting that in this context Thomas appeals to the hermetic axiom—frequently adopted by Albert the Great—*opus naturae est opus intelligentiae*.

agent who predetermines (or proposes) an end (*Haec ergo videtur esse ratio ideae, quod idea sit forma quam aliquid imitatur ex intentione agentis qui praedeterminat sibi finem*). In other words, the ideas are the forms through which God intentionally produces creatures, letting himself be imitated in different ways.[42] This definition in itself excludes every sort of chance and necessity in the production of things, but also excludes the possibility that ideas could be posited outside the divine mind (after the manner of classical Platonism), because in this case God would not predetermine the end by himself but would be subjected to ends independent of him.

But what has been said permits us to explain more precisely the difference between Thomas's position and Avicenna's, which latter we have already mentioned and which excludes on God's part any immediate knowledge of multiplicity. Also for Avicenna, the first cause does not propose an end or intention outside of itself in producing things and does not bring them about unawares (that is, by blind necessity). But in knowing its goodness, Avicenna's first cause, unlike Thomas's, knows what streams forth from it in a universal way and not in its particulars, as we have seen. Because the first cause, as a necessary being, is absolutely one and unitary, even its first effect can only be one. If the contrary were true, we would have to admit a root of multiplicity already within it. What the first cause immediately produces, from the act by which it knows its own essence, is merely the first intelligence. The rest of creation depends on the first cause only indirectly, through intermediaries. The passage from the oneness and simplicity of God to the multiplicity of creation is justified by Avicenna on the ground that the first intelligence, unlike its cause, already has more things to think: thinking the first cause on which it depends, the first intelligence produces the intelligence immediately inferior to itself; thinking itself as possible in itself, it produces the first celestial sphere; finally, thinking itself as made necessary by its cause, it produces the soul of the celestial sphere. According to the Avicennian schema, this same mechanism repeats itself down to the tenth intelligence, which governs the sublunary world (the earth) and is the source of human souls and the natural forms of other things (and so this intelligence is called the "giver of forms"). In this system the ideas of things are

42. See L.-B. Geiger, "Les idées divines dans l'oeuvre de Saint Thomas," in *St. Thomas Aquinas, 1274-1974. Commemorative Studies*, ed. A. Maurer *et al.* (Toronto: Pontifical Institute of Mediaeval Studies, 1974), 175–209, which appears later in "Penser avec Thomas d'Aquin," *Études thomistes présentées par R. Imbach*, Paris: Editions Universitaires-Cerf, 2000), 63–110; V. Boland, *Ideas in God according to Saint Thomas Aquinas: Sources and Synthesis*, Studies in the History of Christian Thought 69 (Leiden: Brill, 1996); G. T. Doolan, *Aquinas on the Divine Ideas as Exemplar Causes* (Washington, D.C.: The Catholic University of America Press, 2008).

not placed directly in God but in the other celestial intelligences and especially in the last of these, the *dator formarum*. But in this way, Thomas observes, the distinction of things in our world would be ordered by secondary causes (which is what the tenth intelligence is), and only accidentally (because indirectly) by the first cause. With a move that is philosophically worthy of note, Thomas, thus, sets the original Neo-Platonic lesson of the *De causis* against its Avicennian revision. The causality of the first cause precedes the causality of the secondary causes and so it is impossible that something could be *per se* with respect to the secondary causes but accidental with respect to the first cause. It is necessary, then, to place a number of ideas—that is, the notions proper to individual things—in God.

But with this move does Thomas not run into the problem that Avicenna wanted at all costs to avoid, namely, putting plurality in God? For Thomas, it is the simple and unitary divine essence in itself that represents the idea of all things. There is plurality in created things because this unitary essence is imitable in different ways and different proportions. So, if we consider the divine essence, there is just one idea for all things, whereas there is a plurality of ideas if we consider the different relationships and the different proportions that creatures can have to it. There is no contradiction, nor is this a mere *ad hoc* expedient. What Thomas wishes to suggest is that the same simple and indivisible divine essence, considered together with the different relationships that creatable things can have with it, constitutes the idea of each thing and is the origin of a plurality of ideas (*ipsa divina essentia, cointellectis diversis proportionibus rerum ad eam, est idea uniuscuiusque rei: unde cum sint diversae rerum proportiones, necesse est plures ideas*).

The ideas, therefore, coincide with different *relationships of imitability* that creatures have with the divine essence. And since the imitability refers to the production of the creatures themselves, it seems natural to concede that the ideas belong more in the domain of practical science than in that of speculative science. In fact, Thomas concedes, if we take "idea" in a strict sense—the one we spoke of earlier—then it pertains principally to practical science (even if it retains a speculative valence with respect to those things that God *could* make, but *has decided not to make*, and that thus remain pure possibles); if we take "idea" instead in a more generic sense as the notion or likeness of a thing, without any causal implication, then it belongs to speculative science. This allows Thomas to respond to the question about whether prime matter has an idea in God,[43] a thesis that is manifestly opposed to the Platonic view, accord-

---

43. *De veritate*, q. 3, a. 5.

ing to which matter was to be understood as a co-cause *together with the ideas*. Now, it cannot be denied that God has the idea of matter in the sense we have just mentioned, viz., as a notion or likeness, because matter too is, in any case, caused by God, and he retains a likeness of whatever he causes. But if we take "idea" in a strict sense, it cannot be said that it has an idea in God that is distinct from that of form and of the composite. Since, indeed, "idea" in the strict sense regards the thing as it is producible in being, and matter never comes into being without form, it must be said that the whole composite corresponds to *a single idea* upon which the totality of the composite depends, in its form and in its matter.

It is different with evil. There is no idea of evil in God whether we consider him as a causal principle (because God cannot be the principle of evil) or we consider him as a likeness (because likeness always derives from form and evil does not have a form, as is evident in q. 3, a. 4). Instead, in God there are ideas of the things that do not, have not, and will not exist (on the condition that they are not impossible or contradictory in themselves, that is, they are *unrealized possibles*), ideas of accidents (even if they are conceived together with the idea of their subject), and ideas of individuals, since divine science—as we have seen—extends to the latter. The entirety of the distance between the original Platonic doctrine of the forms (known to the Scholastics, above all, through the Aristotelian objections) and Christian exemplarism can be perceived here.

Of course, this is not the only place where Thomas deals with the divine ideas. He already spoke about them in d. 36 of his Commentary on Book I of Peter Lombard's *Sentences,* and he will speak of them again in *Summa theologiae,* I, q. 15, for example. There is an anomaly, however, in Thomas's treatment of the divine ideas, and we find it in *Summa contra Gentiles,* I, c. 53, a text that we will examine with more care in the next chapter. Thomas revised it no fewer than three times between Paris and Rome. The revisions of this text are attested to in Thomas's own hand.[44] What is striking is that in the (for us) definitive redaction, Thomas seems to abandon the term *idea* in favor of *ratio*. It does not seem to be a definitive change, since in *Summa theologiae,* I, q. 15—a later text—Thomas returns to *idea*. But the strenuous reworking of the *Summa contra Gentiles* text is, at any rate, an index of the fact that Thomas did not feel completely at ease with the term, and it is not improbable that the systematic re-reading of Aristotle made him more suspicious of this very Platonic term (despite all of the modifications that we have noted). Still, other hypotheses can be proposed. More or less in the same period (which chronologically pre-

44. Vat. lat. 9850.

ceded the so-called Averroist crisis in Paris) Bonaventure, in his *Collationes in Hexaëmeron*, thundered against those who rejected the ideas. For the Franciscan master, this rejection inevitably led to the determinism and necessitarianism of the Greco-Arab peripatetic tradition. Obviously, Thomas shares the spirit of this thesis but is probably not disposed to follow it so radically to the letter, especially because, for Bonaventure, it is a criticism directed principally against Aristotle. Specifically in his epistemology and psychology, Thomas had always been close to Aristotle, and he is rather perplexed (and perhaps more and more perplexed) by the Augustinianism and Platonizing of the Franciscans in these fields.[45] Exemplarism in the strong sense is, on the other hand, linked at least implicitly to the doctrine of the plurality of forms, which, during this time, is a principal area of conflict for Thomas and the Franciscans. It is possible that Thomas saw it as less problematic and more appropriate to speak of *rationes* of imitability rather than directly of *ideae*, but not to the point that he would discard the term "idea" in his later work.

The Mind and Learning

The structure of the remaining questions of the *De veritate*, which, obviously, we cannot examine in detail, has already been noted. There is a section (q. 8– q. 20) that deals with knowledge. In particular, qq. 8–9 regard angelic knowledge, qq. 10–19 human knowledge, and q. 20 the knowledge of Christ's soul as human. With respect to human knowledge, Thomas is concerned to explain what "mind" means with great precision—not the *essence* of the human soul but its highest power, its intellective capacity (which comprises not only the intellect strictly understood but also the intellective or rational appetite, that is, the will).[46] He also takes up the typically Augustinian topic of the image of the Trinity in us, which, he points out, is a double image: a perfect image based on the *acts* of the soul, represented by memory, intelligence, and will, and one based on the *powers* of the soul, represented by the mind, knowledge, and love.[47] Finally, he reaffirms that our mind cannot know individuals except indirectly.[48] Above all, Thomas confirms here his fidelity to the Aristotelian epistemology to which we made reference earlier, refuting the Platonic thesis about the recollection of the ideal forms, the Avicennian thesis about the bestowal of intelligible forms by a separated intelligence (the *dator formarum* that

45. But, as we have already seen in part and as we will often see again in detail, in numerous other fields Thomas will superimpose many decidedly Platonic elements onto authentically Aristotelian theses. We must, however, patiently verify sources and influences case by case and avoid general labels.

46. *De veritate*, q. 10, a. 1.   47. *De veritate*, q. 10, a. 3.

48. *De veritate*, q. 10, a. 5.

we mentioned before),[49] and the substantially occasionalist thesis according to which the soul forms in itself its own content in the presence of external things, the latter serving merely as occasions for the soul to go about its work.[50] In the cognitive dynamic proposed by Thomas, which is entirely Aristotelian, there is a double relationship (in potency and in act) to sensible things. From the ontological point of view, it is evident that forms (as substantial forms) are in act in things and in potency in the soul. But from the point of view of intelligibility, forms are in potency in things and must be actualized by the intellect. In fact, what is intelligible in things (and in the sensible images derived from them) is only in potency and needs the intervention of something already in act—the agent intellect—to be actualized itself. But thinking is, ultimately, receiving these forms, which must be impressed on something that is potentially disposed to receive and think them (to become intentionally all things), and this is the potential or possible intellect. Thus, human knowledge always begins from what it draws from external things, even if it is also true that the intelligible species are properly a product of the soul itself since they are abstracted from sensible images.[51] Thomas will never abandon the basic aspects of this Aristotelian epistemology.

De veritate, q. 11, which reflects on the possibility of communicating science, that is, learning, is worth consideration and historically fortunate. We see here another instance of Thomas distancing himself from Augustine (for whom the only true teacher is the interior teacher, namely, Christ, who illumines the human mind from within) and Avicenna (again interpreted in light of the prominent role he gives to the *dator formarum*) and lining up with Aristotle. In Thomas's view, there exist in each of us the seeds of science, viz., the first conceptions of the intellect that can be drawn immediately from the species abstracted from sensible things thanks to the natural light of the agent intellect. Such conceptions can be simple and non-complex (principally those that we called transcendentals: being, one, etc.), or complex (propositional conceptions, that is, the first principles). Such principles contain virtually all the conclusions that can be drawn from them. Acquiring science means precisely developing knowledge beginning from the principles that the intellect grasps. It can be conceded to Plato, therefore, that science is already present potentially in each of us, as long

---

49. It is necessary, however, to observe that Thomas both radicalizes and partly misunderstands Avicennian psychology, overlooking the fact that it too is fundamentally based on an abstractive process. For one of the most correct reinterpretations of the psychology of Avicenna and of its reception in the Latin West, see D. N. Hasse, *Avicenna's De anima in the Latin West: The Formation of a Peripatetic Philosophy of the Soul 1160–1300*, Warburg Institute Studies and Texts (Turin: Nino Aragno, 2000).

50. This thesis is very close to the authentically Augustinian position.

51. *De veritate*, q. 10, a. 6.

as we clarify what type of potentiality we are dealing with here and the way that it gets actualized. Science preexists in each of us as an active, and not merely passive, potency. It is, in other words, something that is able by itself to bring about perfect act, as a sick person is able to get well by a natural power that is already in him, and not by something externally induced, even if this capacity to get well is partly facilitated by external aids (such as medicines, etc.). Thus it is for knowledge. When someone is able to gain knowledge by his natural capacity alone, we have what is called *discovery*. When this happens also because of external help (but on the basis of an internal power), we can then speak of *learning* in the strict sense. Ultimately, the teacher does not act differently from the physician. The latter helps his patient to reach health by himself, just as the former helps the student to gain knowledge. The teacher need do nothing else than lead the student to knowledge of that of which he is ignorant, following the same course that he would have taken had he done it by himself (or the course by which others have come to knowledge by themselves). The teacher must explain with the appropriate signs (words) the course that reason is able to follow on its own. Learning, then, is a kind of discovery guided from the outside that always relies on the natural reason itself of the disciple. If it were not this way, if the teacher did not entrust himself to the same principles that are present in him and in his student, the student would not truly acquire science. He would only *believe* in something or hold it to be true, he would not *understand* it. He would develop *faith* or *opinion*, not *science*. Thomas can also conclude this analysis with a concession to the traditional Augustinian thesis: since learning is always guided by the natural light of the agent intellect (by the light of the first principles), and this light has a divine origin (for God placed it in us), we can say that God is also our principal interior teacher. But we must not let ourselves be deceived by this formulation. In Thomas's judgment, the agent intellect is not God but a gift of God that belongs to all of us—it is the image of God in us. Knowing things by reason of such an image is something rather different from knowing them through God himself, as Thomas explains in a quodlibetal question debated in the same period in which the *De veritate* was composed:

We cannot know anything about the truth except on the basis of the first principles and in the light of the intellect, which cannot manifest the truth except inasmuch as they are a likeness of that first truth, since from it they have a certain immutability and infallibility. All truths are not seen in this life in the first truth according to its essence, given that neither is the first truth seen by us in this life in its essence. However, every truth is known in it on account of its image, that is, on account of the truth copied from it.[52]

---

52. *Quodlibet* X, q. 4, a. 1.

The development of knowledge, then, does not directly depend on divine instruction save, in a metaphorical and indirect sense, in the degree to which God has endowed us with the ability to discover and learn science. On the other hand, we must not forget the fact that Thomas is, for all intents and purposes, a *magister*, a university teacher, who is explicating his own precise, socially recognized function. As has been justly noted, if Augustinian pedagogy had been taken literally in the thirteenth century, the birth and the development of the university would have been entirely unthinkable (and science would probably have forever missed its crucial opportunity to take off in the West). The Augustinian position expressed an essential suspicion of purely human teaching, but the university structure demands just the opposite and presupposes the effective capacity of teachers with a solid formation (that is, publicly verifiable and sanctioned by regulations and documents) to instruct as much as an autonomous and critical capacity to learn on the part of students (who are called to exercise their natural reason and not to believe on authority by faith or hearsay). It is not by chance that Thomas, as we have seen, chose the topic of the communication of wisdom and of the role of teachers for his inaugural lecture as a *magister*. Moreover, in another quodlibetal question (debated during his second Paris regency) Thomas returned to this question with an unequivocal clarity:

A disputation in the schools has a specifically magisterial character because it is not aimed at removing error but at instructing the listeners so that they might be led to the understanding of the truth that they hold, and so it is necessary to use rational arguments that seek out the root of the truth and make known in what way what is said is true. Otherwise, if a master decides a question on mere authority, the listeners will doubtless be certain that things are as he says, but they will not acquire any science or understanding and they will go away empty.[53]

Thomas is not an inspired and isolated scholar. He is a teacher by profession, who understands the majority of his writings exactly in relation to this function (even if at times this aspect becomes secondary). Furthermore, he belongs to an order that makes study and teaching one of its central pillars. In the end, there is a danger of misunderstanding many of his writings and of his intellectual practice itself if we do not constantly keep before us his social role, that of a *magister* as much charged with public functions—in the realm of the Paris theology faculty, for example—as he is with the formation of the intellectual elite of his order, in Paris and in the other *studia* where he will be sent to teach.

---

53. *Quodlibet* IV, q. 9, a. 3.

The Good and the Will

De veritate, qq. 21–29 are devoted to the appetitive and volitional sphere and to the consideration of the general mode of being and the good. Whereas the true adds to being a relation to the intellect, the good adds to being a relationship to the end. In brief, a thing is good to the extent that it perfects something as the thing's end, or as leading the thing to its end (in this case Thomas speaks of the "useful"), or as what by its nature follows from the thing's end (in this case Thomas speaks of the "delectable"). Being and good are convertible with each other, which means that every being is good and every good is a being, or that every being tends toward its being as a good, and, on the other hand, every good includes the character of being. But in what relation does the good stand to the other general mode of being that we have discussed, namely, the true? In itself and in an absolute sense, the good follows on the true, but considering the realities that are perfected, the good precedes the true because it extends to a greater number of realities and is, itself, based directly on being, which, as we already know, precedes the true. We have also seen that every truth depends on the first truth. Can it also be said that every good depends on the first good? The answer is obvious, but we must clarify how this is so. It cannot be thought that God, the first good, enters into the intrinsic constitution of things, which would be to fall into a kind of formal pantheism. But, on the other hand, it cannot be a matter only of a purely extrinsic participation (in the Platonic sense, in which things would be good only by participation in a separated good). In reality, God acts not only as an exemplary cause, but also as an efficient cause, and in consequence imprints on every creature an intrinsic likeness of his own perfection. Therefore, it is true that things are good by participation, but they participate in the good because their being itself is good since it is *produced* by God: goodness, thus, is *intrinsic* to the creature, even if it always depends originally on the first good. So, things are good in themselves but without being essentially good.[54] As we will see, this will be the theme of Thomas's Commentary on Boethius's *De (h)ebdomadibus*.[55] Thomas also deals here with the famous Augustinian formula according to which the good consists in measure, species, and order. Measure indicates the being that each thing, as good, possesses (since everything receives being according to its proper measure). Species indicates the essence or nature specific to each thing. Finally, order indicates the capacity that every good possesses to perfect what is ordered to it.

---

54. *De veritate*, q. 21, a. 5.

55. The spelling adopted by the Leonine Commission omits the "h" and henceforth we will follow this convention.

The last element of the *De veritate* that we will take into consideration is its treatment of the will, or the intellectual or rational appetite, which is distinguished in man from the sensitive appetite. Unlike the latter, the will has the possibility of controlling its own inclination in such a way that it is not determined by another but by itself; this evidently presupposes knowledge of the end as much as it does knowledge of the actions that are the means to achieve it, operations that presuppose reason. In general, the will is free with respect to the object (there are different means to attain the good), to the act (because it could always will or not will), and to the end (because it can also tend toward that which only in appearance leads to the final end). Nevertheless, the will possesses a *natural* inclination to the good, and so it is necessarily directed (from the perspective of nature) toward beatitude, which represents the supreme good and the ultimate end. It is a question—it is well to emphasize this—precisely of a natural necessity and not of a constriction (as is proved by the fact that, in the present state, this necessity is always relative, since not everyone acts in such a way as to tend toward their end). In other words, the will cannot prescind from its natural inclination, but neither can it be constrained to will something. It should, nevertheless, be pointed out that freedom not to will the final end (that is, freedom for evil) holds only for this life. Only in this life is it possible to be mistaken about the ordering of intermediate ends to the final end. The blessed in the beatific vision are unable not to will the final end. When defect in intellectual judgment is gone, the will can never will evil.

This reference to judgment (the will can will evil only because of a defect of judgment) offers Thomas a first occasion to consider the relationship between intellect and will in more detail. They are distinct faculties, not only in respect to species but also in respect to genus, since the will is referred to the thing as it is in itself whereas the intellect regards the thing as it is grasped or known, as it is in the soul. On this distinction also depends a first answer to the particularly pressing question about which of the two faculties is the more noble. In general, the intellect is more noble because the thing as known is more noble than it is in itself. But this is obviously true only for the things that are inferior to the soul. With respect to what is superior to the soul, the will appears to be more noble because it leads to things as they are in themselves. Put more precisely: the dignity or nobility of the intellect is in having the excellence of the thing known in itself, while the nobility of the will is in its ordering itself toward what is more excellent than it. In an absolute sense, it is better to have the excellence of something else in oneself, and so—again in the absolute sense—the intellect is superior to the will. If we then attend to the realities themselves toward which the intellect and will are directed, there is no doubt that, with respect to material realities, the intellect is more noble, because such realities have a more excellent being in the intellect than they have in themselves. With respect to purely intelligible realities, it is instead evident that the mode of existence that they have in themselves is more excellent than the one they have in the intellect. Thus, the comparison of the intellect and the will can be conducted at three levels: (a) in an absolute sense the intellect is more noble; (b) with respect to material realities the intellect is more noble; (c) with respect to divine realities the will is more noble. To love God—Thomas seems to concede here—is more excellent than to know him, because the divine goodness has in itself a more excellent being than that of the knowing intellect.

There are at least two elements to notice here. The first is the obvious fidelity of Thomas to the Neo-Platonic principle (and in this particular case, Proclean) according to which everything that is inferior is pre-contained in a more excellent way in the knowledge of what is superior. Consequently, our intellect, which is on the frontier between the sensible and the intelligible, contains in itself at a higher level everything that is inferior to it, but it is ontologically and noetically subordinate to the superior intelligences. It is not by chance that Thomas singles out, once again, the *De causis*. When our intellect knows superior essences, the mode of being that they have in themselves is superior to the mode that they have in our intellect. The hierarchy of the intelligible order is one of the pillars of the whole of Thomas's thought, and we must never gloss over its importance for the sake of a presumed chemically pure Aristotelianism that is sometimes attributed to Thomas himself.

The other element worthy of note is that in this particular circumstance Thomas, although he acknowledges the absolute superiority of the intellect over the will, admits that loving God is superior to knowing him: a matter that will debated by Dominicans and Franciscans at length, and especially in the famous disputation between Meister Eckhart and Gonsalves of Spain at the beginning of the fourteenth century. We will, however, later see how the beatific vision, in which consists the maximal human felicity (and, thus, constitutes man's final end), is, indeed, an intellectual act for Thomas, in which love and the will play a completing and perfective role; we will thereby return to the topic of Thomas's so-called "intellectualism." In the meantime *De veritate*, q. 22 offers a further element in this regard for us to consider. Is it the intellect that moves the will or vice-versa? Thomas's answer is balanced in this case too. We can, in fact, say both that the intellect moves the will and that the will moves the intellect, because the intellect moves as *the end* (viz., it knows the end and proposes it to the will) and the will moves as an *efficient cause* since, as we have just seen, it ranges over things not as apprehended but in themselves: action and operation involve the things themselves and not concepts (as Thomas observes, it is ultimately fire as such that heats and not the concept of fire, or fire as apprehended by the intellect). The circularity that is established between the intellect and will reflects in this way the classic relationship between final cause and agent cause (or efficient cause): the end is first in intention (we would never act if an end were not proposed to us, and this is the task of the intellect), but last in execution (and this is the task of the will, which moves external things as well as the powers of the soul).

QUODLIBETA VII–XI
The Structure of Quodlibetal Questions

Between 1256 and 1259, as regent master, Thomas also had the opportunity to determine some quodlibetal questions. The *Quodlibeta* were, in fact, the prerogative of masters *actu regentes*. These were special disputations that took place only during two periods of the year (Advent and Lent), and were not restricted—as were the ordinary disputations—to the students of a particular course. Masters, bachelors, and students from different courses could participate (the concurrent lessons were normally suspended to give everyone the opportunity to attend) along with clerics and citizens from outside the university community. The distinct characteristic of the quodlibetal disputations is that the questions could be raised by any of the participants (*a quodlibet*) about any topic (*de quodlibet*). It is not surprising that these disputations always represented an extraordinary occasion of engagement and conflict between colleagues of the same faculty, reflecting as much the topics that were of interest in that period (from theological and philosophical questions in the strict sense to those that today we would call questions of applied ethics: economics, social issues, sexuality, etc.) as the events that had a major impact on the urban and civil fabric.[56] Some masters, above all the secular masters (in virtue of the greater continuity of their teaching), made it the principal outlet, or one of the principal outlets, of their own doctrines. Gerard of Abbeville, Henry of Ghent, and Godfrey of Fontaines were among those who approached the disputations in this way. The disputation had different parts: the actual disputation, in which the bachelors of a particular master played an important part; the master's *determinatio*, that is, the point in which the master, retracing the thread of the

---

56. On the quodlibetal disputes in the faculty of theology see, above all, J. F. Wippel, "Quodlibetal Questions, Chiefly in Theology Faculties," in *Les questions disputées*, ed. Bazán, Fransen, Wippel, Jacquart, 153–222; J. Hamesse, "Theological *Quaestiones Quodlibetales*," in *Theological* Quodlibeta *in the Middle Ages: The Thirteenth Century*, ed. C. Schabel, Brill's Companions to the Christian Tradition 1, (Leiden: Brill, 2006), 17–48.

whole debate, offered his solution to each question (usually the next day); and publication, which occurred (if it occurred) when the master had the time to review and rework the results of the disputations. This could take months, and some quodlibetal questions have come down to us as notes taken by those in attendance rather than as texts that were revised and published by the master. The hagiographic tendency that for a long time conditioned studies of Thomas's thought made him the inventor of the *Quodlibeta*, which is obviously false. It is true that Thomas produced work in this genre (alongside others: *summae*, *responsiones*, commentaries, opuscules, and ordinary disputed questions), with its advantages and its risks, disputing twelve *Quodlibeta*. These are important collections that present a view of Thomas that in certain aspects is different from the one we find in the more systematic writings.

The first thing to know in this regard is that the actual numbering of Thomas's quodlibetal disputes (definitively fixed after the edition of 1471) does not follow chronological order. The *Quodlibeta* numbered VII–XI, in reality, precede the others and were disputed between 1256 and 1259. The reason for this confusion is that the *Quodlibeta* disputed during the second Paris regency, between 1269 and 1271 (I–IV), were collected before the others in an *exemplar* (the official copy kept to ensure the circulation of his writings through the renting of individual booklets, the *peciae*) by a Parisian *stationarius* (the university "bookseller"). In fact, the *exemplar* in question appears on a "taxation" list—that is, a kind of official university price list—already from 1273–76. When a second *exemplar* was created (which appears in a taxation list from 1304), the *Quodlibeta* of the first regency were added (those now numbered VII–XI) but were placed after those that were already in circulation. Only *Quodlibet* XII is in the right place, chronologically speaking, because it is in fact the last *Quodlibet* that Thomas disputed, taking place during the Lenten session of 1272 (and this too is owed to a fortuitous circumstance). Let us leave aside for the moment the dating of the *Quodlibeta* of the second period to focus on those of the first. The most plausible chronology is the following:

Quodlibet VII: Lenten session 1256
Quodlibet VIII: Lenten session 1257
Quodlibet IX: Advent session 1257
Quodlibet X: Lenten or Advent session 1258
Quodlibet XI: Lenten session 1259

Already the first *Quodlibet*, the one numbered VII, presents some textual difficulties that give us an idea of the peculiar nature of this collection. The *Quodlibeta* are subdivided in questions, which are then subdivided in articles.

In the prologue, when Thomas presents and organizes the material, he does not mention q. 6, dedicated to the senses of Scripture, and q. 7, dedicated to manual labor. This could be interpreted in two different ways: these were independent questions that were later added (presumably by Thomas himself) to the *Quodlibet* while it was being redacted, or they were originally part of the quodlibetal disputation but Thomas chose to leave them out. The Leonine Commission editors, and R.-A. Gauthier in particular, incline toward the second hypothesis. Thomas decided to remove q. 7 on manual labor and develop it as a small treatise on its own (even though the tradition leaves it in the *Quodlibet*), and he neglected to present q. 6 in the prologue (unless he did not want to make it into an opuscule also). *Quodlibet* XI, for its part, seems incomplete, perhaps because of Thomas's return to Italy, which impeded its definitive revision for publication.

In the quodlibetal disputations it was the prerogative of the master to reorganize in a more orderly scheme the material of the different questions that were proposed. Thomas usually places the questions about God and separated substances first and those related to man after these. The tenor of the disputations is obviously heterogeneous. They do not have the same broad speculative range that distinguishes the *Quodlibeta* of Henry of Ghent, Godfrey of Fontaines, and Giles of Rome, in which very long *quaestiones* are dedicated to certain neuralgic points of their irrespective theological and metaphysical positions (Thomas's style is also more concise). On the other hand, his *Quodlibeta*, although they do not lack a casuistic element, do not strictly represent the privileged place in which Thomas addresses questions of a social character. Mostly, they develop themes of practical theology (especially those of the second series).[57]

Exemplarism and the Absolute Consideration of Essences

Among the various questions of the *Quodlibeta* of the first Paris regency, we select first of all one that is philosophically relevant and also bears a title that completely obscures its content. This is a good example of how an able and knowledgeable master can take advantage of any question proposed by an auditor—even an improbable one—to bend it toward his own didactic and scientific exigencies. The formulation of the question, or article,[58] runs thus: "Is the

---

57. For a general presentation of the principal arguments of Thomas's quodlibets, see L. Boyle, "The Quodlibets of St. Thomas and Pastoral Care," *The Thomist* 38 (1974): 232–56 (published later in *Facing History: A Different Thomas Aquinas* (Louvain: FIDEM, 2000), 13–35); and above all, K. White, "The *Quodlibeta* of Thomas Aquinas in the Context of His Work," in *Theological* Quodlibeta, ed. Schabel, 49–119.

58. *Quodlibet* VIII, q. 1, a. 1.

number six, according to which it is said that all creatures were made, creator or creature?"[59] The reference is to the six days of creation according to the account of Genesis, and in particular to Augustine's exegesis of the text in his *De Genesi ad litteram*,[60] but, in fact, the article is a useful occasion to take up again and revise the Avicennian doctrine (that we saw already in the *De ente et essentia*) about the indifference of essences. In Book V of the *Metaphysics* (also called the *Science of Divine Things*) of the *Book of Healing*, Avicenna distinguished between three different ways to consider an essence or nature: (a) according to the being it has in individuals; (b) according to the intelligible being it has in the intellect; (c) in an absolute sense, abstracting from both forms and existence (natural and mental) and considering solely in themselves the aspects that belong to such a nature and enter into its definition (the definition of "horse" prescinds from all reference to individual existing horses or to the universal concept of the horse, and so can be applied to either one). But what order, Thomas asks, is there among these different sorts of considerations? Two of them have a fixed order between them: in fact, the consideration of a thing according to its absolute nature always precedes that according to its being in individual realities. But the consideration of the essence or nature according to its intelligible being does not have an established place, because much depends on whether this being is *caused by things* (as happens in human science) or is *cause of things* (as in the case of God's science). In the first sense, this type of consideration follows the other two. In the second, it precedes them. If we divide the consideration of something according to its intelligible being, taking these two different cases into account, the result is a precise hierarchy:

Now, as the intellect of the artisan stands to the artifacts, so also the divine intellect stands to all creatures. For this reason, the first consideration of any caused nature is according to how it is found in the divine intellect; the second consideration is of the nature itself absolutely; the third is according to the being it has in the things themselves or in the angelic mind; the forth is according to the being it has in our intellect.[61]

The interest of this arrangement is in the fact that Avicenna left an essential point at least partly in ambiguity, that is, whether the absolute consideration of things is identical with the intelligible being they would enjoy in the divine intellect (in the case of Avicenna, this would be in a separate intelligence, the

59. See F. D. Wilhelmsen, "A Note: The Absolute Consideration of Nature in *Quaestiones Quodlibetales* VIII," *The New Scholasticism* 57 (1983): 352–61. And, especially, G. Pini, "*Absoluta consideratio naturae*: Tommaso d'Aquino e la dottrina avicenniana dell'essenza," *Documenti e studi sulla tradizione filosofica medievale* 15 (2004): 387–438.

60. IV, 7, 14.

61. *Quodlibet* VIII, q. 1, a. 1.

dator formarum, rather than in God himself), or whether, on the contrary, it is irreducible to any form of natural or mental existence (including its existence in the divine intellect). In fact, although Avicenna does not seem to raise this problem explicitly, a coherent interpretation of the doctrine of the indifference of essences would presuppose that the absolute consideration could not be made dependent upon a form of mental existence for the simple fact that the heart of the Avicennian doctrine foresees that the absolute does not imply a type of existence but that every nature can be thought apart from the kind of existence that accompanies it, despite being *always* accompanied by one kind of existence (natural or mental). But the problem raised by all of the Latin readers of Avicenna is that of knowing what constitutes a thing's purely quidditative nature in itself ("absolute"), its essential being—*esse essentiae*, according to the formulation of Henry of Ghent—the fact that a triangle is a triangle and a stone a stone. Does the quidditative constitution of essences consist in pure logical possibility (according to the solution proposed later by Dun Scotus, which will link the possibility of things to the fact that their content is not intrinsically contradictory), or does it depend instead on the fact that they are thought by a mind that is able to cause them, viz., posit them in being? Thomas will not go as far as Henry of Ghent's doctrine of the *esse essentiae* (according to which not only the existence but also the pure essential being of creatures is caused by God, and, more precisely, not by the divine will but by divine science), but holds an exemplarist position: the nature, insofar as it is thought by God, precedes its absolute consideration, its instantiation in individual realities, and the intelligible being that the same thing acquires from the human intellect after sense experience. Thus, a stone is first in the divine intellect; subsequently it can be considered absolutely solely in its definition and prescinding from any form of existence; then it can be regarded in the individual stones that exist in the world; and, finally, it can be considered in the concept of the stone formed by the human intellect from sense experience of these individual stones. This is the sense of the hierarchy we have just expounded; since the prior is always (once again in a Neo-Platonic way) cause of the posterior, the divine consideration is the cause of what belongs to the thing in its absolute consideration; the latter is the reason for that which is present in the existing individuals of the same nature (to Socrates belongs everything that is proper to man, because such properties belong to man as such); and, finally, the nature existing in individuals is the cause of the nature that exists in the human intellect. In Thomas's own terms:

In these things, then, what is prior is always the cause of what is posterior, and if what comes after is removed, what is prior remains, but the opposite is not true. From this it follows that what belongs to the nature according to the absolute consideration is the reason for it belonging to a certain nature according to the existence it has in the individual, and not vice-versa. In fact, Socrates is rational because man is rational, and not vice-versa. Because of this, supposing that Socrates and Plato do not exist, rationality would still belong to human nature. So also, in a similar way, the divine intellect is the reason for the nature considered in an absolute way or in individuals. And the same nature considered in the absolute sense or in individuals is the reason for [the presence of the concept of the nature in] the human intellect and in a certain sense the measure of the intellect.[62]

So, Thomas gives the impression of "re-Platonizing" a theory that Avicenna had elaborated precisely to bypass the Platonic and Neo-Platonic doctrine of universals (even though Avicenna himself had not rejected a form of exemplarism regarding the role of the intelligences). According to Giorgio Pini and Deborah Black, after *Quodlibet* VIII, and so beginning in the 1260s, Thomas seemed to want to avoid every direct reference to the distinction between the absolute consideration of essences and the two modes of their existence while maintaining the distinction between what accompanies the universal and the universal itself. This attitude is interpreted as the index of a transition from an "ontological" interpretation of essence in its absolute consideration, to its more strictly "gnoseological" interpretation, in which universality is attributed to the intellect, not to something neutral and indifferent, but to a concept abstracted from individuals, and, thus, to something that exists also in the intellect (Black, above all, insists on the fact that in Thomas what exists in the intellect is not the essence itself but its representation). It seems to us that it can be said that Thomas never really changed his mind on this topic, whether because, on the one hand, he never really embraced—not even in the *De ente*—a strictly ontological interpretation of "absolute" essence (as if essence were a constitutive element and, indeed, an actual part of the individual existents), or, on the other hand, because he never effectively identified the absolute consideration of an essence with the result of the same abstractive procedure by which the universal is obtained. In truth, we can say that Thomas's reworking of Avicenna's doctrine is just that, a reworking and not a betrayal of it.[63] This fact puts us again on our guard against a reading of

62. *Quodlibet* VIII, q. 1, a. 1.
63. See G. Pini, "*Absoluta consideratio naturae*: Tommaso d'Aquino e la dottrina avicenniana dell'essenza," *Documenti e studi sulla tradizione filosofica medievale* 15 (2004): 387–438; D. Black, "Mental Existence in Thomas Aquinas and Avicenna," *Mediaeval Studies* 61 (1999): 45–79. Gabriele Galluzzo, for his part, has suggested that, although Thomas is consistent in maintaining throughout his career the doctrine of the indifference of essences, there is at least one point of view from which the essence of a material substance can be interpreted as universal or common, that is, that relating to individuation. See G. Galluzzo, "Aquinas on Common Nature and Universals," *Recherches de Théologie et Philosophie Médiévales* 71 (2004): 131–71. In regard to the anti-Platonic significance of Avicenna's theory of the

Thomas that is both careless and widespread, a reading that portrays Thomas as a defender of pure Aristotelianism against the Neo-Platonic deviations introduced by Avicenna. In fact, like all "-isms," "Aristotelianism" and "Neo-Platonism" are labels that are empty in themselves unless we keep in mind the constant overlapping of the two traditions and of the actual and specific contexts in which particular theoretical solutions are adopted. It is not surprising, then, if at times Thomas appears nearer to Neo-Platonic positions than Aristotelian ones, and if he gives the impression of revising Avicenna in a Neo-Platonic way.

The Primacy of Species over Individuals

The *Quodlibeta* of this period often offer to Thomas the occasion to return to sharpen doctrinal points that we have already drawn attention to in the *De ente* and in the *De veritate*. For example, in the article immediately following the one we have been considering, Thomas reaffirms that the reasons of individual beings are present in God since, unlike what a human artisan can make, God is not limited to working on preexisting material but produces the material itself.[64] And since matter functions as the principle of individuation, it must be conceded that the exemplary forms of the divine intellect extend even to individuals. Nevertheless, Thomas explains here, in answer to the question posed in the article ("Do the reasons in the divine mind regard the things produced—creatures—primarily in their singularity or in their specific nature?"), that the divine ideas *first* regard the species and *then* the individuals. In fact, it is normal that every agent that acts for an end tends toward that which is most perfect, and there is no doubt that the nature of the species is what is most perfect in every individual. This is a claim that is entirely taken for granted in Greek philosophy (both Aristotelian and Neo-Platonic) but might be surprising in the context of Christian creationism. The superiority of the species lies in the fact that it lacks two imperfections present in every individual: one is related to matter, whose potentiality is perfected in the specific form and not in the individual form (no sublunary being, taken individually, is able perfectly to actualize the matter of its species); the other is related to the form of the genus, whose potentiality—genus functions almost as matter with respect to

---

indifference of essences, and for some further observations on the agreement between Thomas and Avicenna, see also P. Porro, "Antiplatonisme et néoplatonisme chez Avicenne (Ilāhiyyāt, livre VII)," in *Adorare caelestia, gubernare terrena*, ed. P. Arfè, I. Caiazzo, A. Sannino (Turnhout: Brepols, 2011), 113–45, and P. Porro, "Immateriality and Separation in Avicenna and Thomas Aquinas," in *The Arabic, Hebrew and Latin Reception of Avicenna's "Metaphysics,"* ed. A. Bertolacci and D. N. Hasse (Berlin: de Gruyter, 2012), 275–307.

64. *Quodlibet* VIII, q. 1, a. 2.

difference—is determined and actualized by the specific form. It is concluded that—for Aristotle and Avicenna as for Thomas the theologian—the structure of the universe rests on species more than on individuals, and especially on the most specific species, that is, species that do not admit other differences below them—in other words, they are not the genera of other species—but only individual differences. Referring explicitly to Avicenna, Thomas can, thus, claim that what is first in intention in nature is not the individual or the genus but the most specific species:

In fact, nature does not principally intend to generate Socrates, for if Socrates were destroyed, then the order and intention of nature would perish. It principally intends, rather, to generate man in Socrates. Similarly, it does not principally intend to generate animal [as a genus], for then its action would cease once it had arrived at the nature of animal.[65]

Since what is first in intention is last in execution, it is always true that the species is produced through the generation of individuals (as the species "man" is not created except inasmuch as this man is created). Nevertheless, it is true that both the lexicon and the fundamental structure of Greco-Arab philosophy are transported here into foreign territory, namely, that of creationism. These philosophical influences, however, are not a sort of residuum of which Thomas was not able to free himself. Until his last writings (the *De aeternitate mundi* is an optimal example), Thomas displays an unchanged preference for a metaphysical vision of the universe inspired mostly by the essential coordinates of the Aristotelian, Neo-Platonic, and Arab peripatetic traditions (overlapping the first two). Attention to singularity and to persons will be found in another area—in morals and the theology of grace. That Thomas's metaphysics gives absolute priority to existing individuals is for the most part an invention of twentieth-century Thomism.

The Passivity and Activity of the Soul

Quodlibet VIII, q. 2, a. 1 also permits Thomas better to clarify the soul's function in the cognitive process. There is no doubt that, as we have already partly seen, the soul receives the likenesses of things passively from the cause or agent—bearing in mind the fact that the agent (the thing) does not impress something of its own upon the senses but something like itself. The production of species (meaning by "species" here the representative image of the thing) does not derive from the matter or the substance of the thing of which it is a likeness, for otherwise the process would entail the impoverishment or dis-

---

65. *Quodlibet* VIII, q. 1, a. 2.

sipation of the subject; rather, species are generated by the potentiality of the receiving matter. In other words, the agent does not deposit the species in that which surrounds it, but produces it in the receiving subjects from their potentiality. Still, we must distinguish in general between sufficient causes or agents, able by themselves to impress their form in the patient, and insufficient agents, who, to achieve the same result, need another, concomitant cause. Analogously, in the patient, we must distinguish between what is in no way able to cooperate with the agent (like a stone when it is thrown up in the air) and what supports or cooperates with the action (like a stone when it is thrown to the ground—in this case the violent motion impressed by the agent is supported by the natural motion of the stone toward its natural place). On the basis of these distinctions, it can be said that external things relate to the powers of the soul in three different ways. In regard to the external senses, things relate as sufficient agents— the senses are passively received without cooperation (even though they can, then, judge what they receive). In regard to the imagination, things also relate as sufficient agents, but the imagination receives cooperatively, for it is able to form likenesses of things that it has not directly perceived, combining various images that it has received. In regard to the possible intellect, things relate as insufficient agents. It is true that sensible phantasms reach the intellect, but only as potentially intelligible. To be actualized, they require an intervention (of illumination) by another agent, and that is, of course, the agent intellect. It can, indeed, be said that the agent intellect is the principal agent that impresses the likenesses on the possible intellect, whereas the phantasms drawn from the senses function as instrumental agents. For its part, the possible intellect is a recipient that cooperates, since it is able to form the quiddity of a thing even when it is not actually perceived by the senses.

The Intellect and the Will in Beatitude

Quodlibet VIII, q. 9, a. 1 asks whether the beatitude of the saints is in the intellect before it is in the affections or vice-versa. The question allows us to return to a question on which we touched previously. Does beatitude principally regard the intellective or the affective sphere? In fact, according to the *Nicomachean Ethics*, happiness or beatitude is always first of all an act or activity (*energeia*), and not a habit. Nevertheless (and here Thomas integrates Aristotle and Augustine), it can be considered, in relation to the powers of the soul, not only as an act, but also as an object to enjoy. From this perspective, beatitude relates principally to the will. Beatitude is, in fact, the final end or highest good of man, and such things belong to the will (which, as we have seen, leads to things as they are in themselves). But, as an act, beatitude consists primarily and substantially in an act of the intellect, because when we want to pursue an external end, the act by which we can reach it is, for us, the internal or interior end. Now, we reach God in the first place through an act of the intellect, and so the same vision of God that is an act of the intellect, is substantially and primarily our beatitude. Because this operation is maximally perfect, it brings about maximum pleasure, which serves for its part to complete and adorn the operation itself. For this reason, the pleasure that pertains to the affective sphere (and, thus, the sphere of the will), formally completes beatitude. To sum up, if beatitude is considered as an *object*, it belongs to the will; if it is considered as an *act*, it belongs principally and primarily to the intellect while its completion belongs to the will.

In strictly Aristotelian terms (identifying happiness properly as an act), the relative—and not absolute—superiority of the intellect to the will must be conceded. In fact, here we find another fundamental philosophical development. Otherworldly beatitude is substantially conceived by Thomas along the lines of the intellectual felicity described by Aristotle (in Book X of the *Nicomachean Ethics*) as the ultimate end of man *in this life*. But Thomas's account goes further. He also recovers, through Augustine, what Aristotle excluded, that is, that happiness can also be considered an object and that there is a univocal and supreme good toward which we must tend.[66] In the *Summa theologiae* Thomas will make more precise this dynamic between the intellect and the will, distinguishing more carefully between what is enjoyed—the divine essence as object of the beatific vision—and that through which it is enjoyed—the act of the intellect.

The Actual Infinite

In *Quodlibet* IX q. 1, a. 1, Thomas deals with the problem of the actual infinite, a topic that we already briefly encountered in the *De veritate*. In this instance Thomas again affirms his basic thesis, viz., when we say that God cannot do something, it is not because of a defect of his power but because of an impossibility that we find in the thing itself as something made[67] or as a determinate thing.[68] Some claim, Thomas says, that God cannot make an infinite in act,

---

66. In Aristotle's eyes, the homonymy of the good, the positing of a single and "objective" good, is a residue of Platonism from which he wished to free himself. For the overall coordinates of the problem in the thirteenth century see J. Costa, "Il problema dell'omonimia del bene in alcuni commenti scolastici all'*Etica Nicomachea*," *Documenti e studi sulla tradizione filosofica medievale* 17 (2006): 157–230.

67. In this sense it is, for example, impossible for God to make a creature that conserves itself in existence by itself as made, because a thing that is made, as such, needs not only a maker but a conserver.

68. God cannot make a horse rational. True, there are rational creatures, but a horse cannot be, since, according to its definition, it is irrational.

since that is repugnant to the things made as such. It is against the notion of a creature to be equal to the creator, and if a creature were infinite, it would equal the infinity of the creator. Nevertheless, Thomas observes, that does not yet show anything, for nothing prevents what is infinite in a single way from surpassing what is infinite in several ways. A hypothetical infinite body would always be material and would in any event belong to one species. Therefore, however infinite it would be in dimension, it would be metaphysically finite and determinate as confined within a given species. God, however, would not have this form of finitude, because he lacks specific or formal determination (only in God, as we have already seen, essence does not limit being but coincides with it).

It is necessary, then, to attend to the impossibility that is rooted in the thing itself as something determinate. The hypothesis that Thomas first considers in this regard is one attributed to al-Ghazālī. However, it should be noted that what Thomas takes to be the *Metaphysics* of al-Ghazālī is in reality a compendium of Avicennian metaphysics (*Aims of the Philosophers*) prepared by al-Ghazālī in view of its meticulous refutation (*Incoherence of the Philosophers*). It is an interesting fact of the textual tradition that only the first part made it into Latin, making al-Ghazālī not an opponent but a proponent of philosophy (and of Avicenna in particular). According to al-Ghazālī (but we can well say, according to Avicenna), an actual infinite is not admissible in an essentially ordered series—in those series in which the order of the parts is essential, which do not obtain if just one element is missing—but is admissible in an accidentally ordered series in which the number of elements needed is not in itself essential. If a knife maker wants to make a knife, he will need at least one hammer, but if this hammer accidentally breaks, he will need another, and eventually even an infinite number, without the number of hammers used itself influencing the result. Since, therefore, an actual infinity of accidental causes would be theoretically possible, God would be able to bring it about. But he could not bring about an actual infinite of essential causes, because in that case the effect would in no way be produced since the infinite cannot be traversed. In other words, since every element in an essentially ordered series is necessary, if it were infinite, it would never lead to an effect.

As will be recalled, in the *De veritate* Thomas, without taking a definite position, does not seem to reject this solution. But in *Quodlibet* IX his preference is clearly for Averroes's view, according to whom the actual infinite is impossible both *per se* and *per accidens*, whereas in an Aristotelian way a potential infinite is possible *per accidens*. The reason for this preference is that in nature nothing exists in act without specific determinations. I can, for example, conceive of animal in general without specifying whether it is rational or not, but in reality, there is no animal that exists that is neither rational nor irrational. Analogously, every quantity in act is always specified by a certain termination whether of a numerical (every discrete reality in act corresponds to a determinate number) or an extensive nature (every continuous reality existing in act presents determinate dimensions). But a hypothetical actual infinite would precisely lack this determination. It would be in act but indeterminate, and this is contradictory. Infinite being is repugnant to being in act, just as being rational is repugnant to a horse. And since, as we have seen, God cannot do what implies a contradiction, he cannot make it the case that there be a being infinite in act.

So, with respect to this treatment that is practically contemporary with the *De veritate*, Thomas maintains (as he will consistently do in the rest of his writings) the principle of non-contradiction as the limit of divine power, but he opts more decisively for the position of Averroes in holding that the actual infinite is contradictory and is not hypothetically possible, at least accidentally.

THE COMMENTARY ON BOETHIUS'S *DE TRINITATE*
The Structure and Dating of the Commentary

Thomas commented on two of five theological opuscules attributed to Boethius: the *De Trinitate* and the *De ebdomadibus*, that is, the two texts that define in the Latin West—over a period of time that stretches from the Carolingian age to the twelfth century—the realm itself of speculative philosophy prior to the gradual introduction and affirmation of Aristotle's *Metaphysics* along with Avicenna's. In the thirteenth century, Boethius's opuscules, while continuing to be widely cited, lost the absolutely central position they had enjoyed previously. Thus, Thomas's decision to comment on them was, in his time, almost an exception.

Thomas's Commentary on the *De Trinitate* is carried out (on the model of the *Scriptum* on Peter Lombard's *Sentences*) on two levels: on the one hand, there is the literal exposition and, on the other hand, there is a series of questions that examine in more detail the problems raised by the text he is commenting on. The exposition of the *De Trinitate* is, moreover, incomplete: Thomas limits himself to commenting on the prooemium, the first chapter, and a part of the second chapter. From each of these three sections two questions follow, each of which is divided into four articles, for a total of six questions and twenty-four articles. It is hard to determine whether this shape of the texts reflects the development of a course of lectures or rather is a writing that

Thomas composed apart from any public occasion. It is true that, in at least one circumstance (in the literal exposition of the second chapter of Boethius's opuscule), Thomas refers to one of the questions of his Commentary with the term *disputatio*. This could just be a generic use relative to the literary form of the work. But if it is meant in the more technical and restricted sense, there is the difficult problem of ascertaining when Thomas would have held a cycle of lessons and disputations on the *De Trinitate*—a difficulty that immediately refers us to the question of the exact dating of the text. There is more or less agreement in attributing the composition of the Commentary to the later phase of Thomas's first teaching stint in Paris—thus, at the latest, between 1256 and 1259.[69] But not enough is known to be able to narrow the margin of approximation. In his introduction to the critical edition of the Commentary on the *De Trinitate*, P.-M. Gils maintains that none of the arguments of internal criticism comparing the Commentary and the *Summa contra Gentiles* (begun in 1259) are probative, since the latter was revised several times. He gives weight instead to codicological and paleographical evidence, also because from this point of view the Commentary on the *De Trinitate* is a particularly fortunate case. A good half of the text (from the *responsio* of q. 3, a. 2 to the conclusion) is available in Thomas's autograph, preserved in the Vat. lat. 9850 manuscript (ff. 90ra–103vb). On the basis of a comparison with the autograph fragments of the Commentary on the *Sentences* (1252–56) preserved in the same manuscript and the *Summa contra Gentiles*, Gils proposes the hypothesis that the redaction of the Commentary on the *De Trinitate* occurred prior but very close to the redaction of the *Summa contra Gentiles*. Ultimately, it must be situated between 1257 and 1259, before the beginning of the *Summa contra Gentiles* and after the redaction of the Commentary on the *Sentences* and the *De ente et essentia*, and more or less contemporary with the drafting of the *De veritate*.

It has also been suggested that the composition of the Commentary on the *De Trinitate* could be situated in the period between the reception of the *licentia docendi* (spring of 1256) and the beginning of teaching as a regent master and the admission into the *consortium magistrorum*.[70] If this were the case, the

---

69. As Chenu has demonstrated, at least one passage from Thomas's Commentary on the *De Trinitate* of Boethius (q. 2, a. 2, ad 7) was made use of by his student Annibaldo degli Annibaldi in his own commentary on the *Sentences* (*In I Sent.*, q. 1, a. 1, ad 2). It is usually thought that the redaction of this latter text was already finished in 1260. In this way a *terminus ante quem* can be sufficiently certain for Thomas's commentary. See M.-D. Chenu, "La date du commentaire de s. Thomas sur le De Trinitate de Boèce," *Revue des Sciences Philosophiques et Théologiques* 30 (1941–42): 432–34.

70. See, for example, S. Neumann, *Gegenstand und Methode der theoretischen Wissenschaften nach Thomas von Aquin auf Grund der* Expositio super librum Boethii De Trinitate (Münster: Aschendorff, 1965), 3–9.

Commentary could be considered either a personal undertaking in view of the redaction of his first systematic theological works (as Thomas would some years later work on the *Nicomachean Ethics* in view of the drafting of the "moral" part of the *Summa theologiae*) or a course held at the Dominican priory of Saint-Jacques. But the drafting of the Commentary could probably have been begun later and continued after Thomas started his teaching. In any case, we cannot rule out the possibility that Thomas decided to deal with Boethius's *De Trinitate* precisely to begin to pose the problem—closely connected with his new role—of the scientific status of theology. Boethius's text would have presented itself to him, in that sense, as the terrain in which to handle questions about God's knowability, the sort of exposition proper to theological discourse, the relation between rational inquiry and faith (and so between philosophy and revelation), and the distinction between theology (in its twofold meaning as doctrine of the faith and scientific discourse about the first substances) and the other speculative sciences.[71]

The Knowability of God

The above-listed topics are precisely those through which the Commentary on the *De Trinitate* winds its way. Already in the prologue, constructed around Wisdom 6:22 (6:24 in the Vulgate), Thomas introduces an important clarification. It is proper to philosophers, he says, who proceed according to the order of natural knowledge, to place the science of creatures before that of God and, thus, they place physics before metaphysics (a term that we must understand—for the moment—as designating the science of separate substances as well as the science of being as such), while the theologian proceeds in the opposite direction, moving from what is more known in itself (God and the separated substances) to what is better known to us (creatures or sensible effects), inverting the terms of the classic Aristotelian distinction. It is, therefore, in God himself that the origin of theology must be situated. But it is exactly here that the first major problem arises. Can we really have a knowledge of God such that we are able, from this point, to initiate the whole plexus of divine science? The first group of articles (which constitute the first question and follow upon the Commentary's literal exposition) is dedicated to this problem.

More particularly, Thomas is confronting the exponents of the doctrine of

71. For a presentation of the themes of the Commentary , in addition to the volume by Neumann cited in the preceding note, see, at the very least, M. Grabmann, *Die theologische Erkenntnis- und Einleitungslehre des hl. Thomas von Aquin auf Grund seiner Schrift* In Boethium De Trinitate (Freiburg: Paulusverlag, 1948); D. C. Hall, *The Trinity: An Analysis of St. Thomas Aquinas'* Expositio *of the* De Trinitate *of Boethius*, Studien und Texte zur Geistesgeschichte des Mittelalters 33 (Leiden: Brill, 1992).

divine illumination (above all, quite probably, Gilbert of Tournai), that is, those who held that it is impossible for the human mind to acquire any truth (about created things but also, and above all, about divine things) without the intervention and help of the divine light. We already know, at least in part, Thomas's position on this. The light that we possess to render knowable things actually intelligible was already placed in us from the very beginning and is the agent intellect and is the active faculty or power of our soul. Of course, this does not mean that the natural operation of the intellect is completely outside of the influence of divine power. However, the divine action must be understood here in its more general aspect and so not according to its causal efficacy in creation but according to its conserving and ordering of the world. In other words, our mind already possesses that which allows it to know everything that is naturally knowable and it does not need the continual direct intervention of God, but it is in any case—precisely as a divine effect—located in the order that is predisposed and regulated, in its totality, by God himself. The meaning of Thomas's distancing himself from the Neo-Augustinian and Franciscan illuminationist epistemology is, in effect, entirely here. To deny man the possibility of knowing (at least) some intelligible truths through his own agent intellect implies, in the final analysis, denying the value itself of his essence—rationality—as it was constituted by God.

Nevertheless, the efficacity of the agent intellect, just like that of all other created powers, is always limited. It permits us to know all those principles that are naturally knowable and everything that we can draw from them, but not that which exceeds our natural capacities, such as future contingents or the truths of faith themselves. Only in the latter case does our mind require an added divine light, that of faith itself. But where exactly does the line of demarcation pass between what can be known naturally (rationally) and that which can only be an object of faith? Does the human mind have, for example, the natural capacity to come to knowledge of separate substances, and to God himself? In general, something can be known through its own form or through a similar form (as a cause, for instance, can be known through its effects). The knowledge that is acquired through a form arises in different ways: through the form itself of the one knowing (as in the case of God, who knows himself through his own essence, which is also true—with certain limitations—for separate substances or angels); or through the form that is derived by abstraction from the objects known, in the manner that our intellect knows natural realities; or, finally, through the form that the knowable reality itself impresses on our cognitive faculty, in the way that—in the Avicennian system (as Thomas interprets it)—the *dator formarum* operates. None of these alternatives, however, is applicable in the case of our knowledge of God. We do not know other things through our essence, nor can God impress his form in us—in the Avicennian way we just mentioned—since an infinite form cannot in any way be received in a finite intellect, nor can we know the divine essence through abstraction, since our agent intellect is able only to abstract intelligible truths from phantasms (that is, from images) that are presented to it by the senses. Indeed, all our knowledge begins in the senses, and our intellect relates to sensible images—as Thomas observes, quoting Aristotle—with the same naturalness by which sight relates to colors. There remains, then, only one possibility for us, that of knowing God by other forms, namely, by the forms of his effects. Now, effects convey an adequate knowledge of the essence of the cause only when they are equal or in any case proportionate to the cause itself. But this is not how things stand in the relationship between creatures and the creator, for God infinitely surpasses any creature. The knowledge that we can glean from effects permits us to come to recognize the existence of God, but it does not permit us—at least in our present condition—to know his *essence* (which is the object of the beatific vision). We can, in other words, come to know *that God is*, but not *what he is*.[72]

The relationship between effects and their cause can, for its part, be considered from three points of view: (a) in relation to the efficaciousness of the cause itself; (b) in relation to the aspect by virtue of which a determinate likeness persists in the effects; (c) in relation to the aspect that distances the effects themselves from their cause. To each of these perspectives there corresponds one of the three ways to God indicated by Pseudo-Dionysius the Areopagite:[73] the *way of causality*, in which God is recognized as the cause of all creatures; the *way of eminence*, in which God is recognized as that which surpasses all that which is positively knowable in creatures; the *way of remotion*, in which God is recognized through the negation of everything that belongs to creatures. It is in this framework that the function of the *lumen fidei*—of the light that faith can add to natural knowledge—must be evaluated. It does not allow us to see God in his essence—which is impossible in this life—but only to understand through the way of remotion or negation, that God is beyond and above everything that we can naturally understand. In this way the nature that Thomas will attribute to theology is already intrinsically anticipated in outline. It proceeds in an affirmative way with respect to what regards the existence of God and the other

72. On this topic see, J. F. Wippel, "Quidditative Knowledge of God according to Thomas Aquinas," in *Graceful Reason: Essays in Ancient and Medieval Philosophy Presented to Joseph Owens, CSSR, on the Occasion of His 75th Birthday*, ed. L. Gerson (Toronto: Pontifical Institute of Mediaeval Studies, 1983), 273–99 (published later in Wippel's *Metaphysical Themes*, 215–41).

73. See pp. 198–202 below.

properties that are naturally demonstrable but in a negative way with respect to what regards the divine essence.

On the basis of this distinction, it is already easier to deal with the other two problems raised in the last two articles of this question. In q. 1, a. 3 Thomas rejects the doctrine (given prominence after Thomas's death by Henry of Ghent but already circulating in Franciscan quarters) according to which God is the first object known by our mind. According to what we have already seen, in Thomas's view (as in Aristotle's), our knowledge always has its origin in the senses and is derived from sensible objects and this to such an extent that the activity of the agent intellect always presupposes the availability of sensible images (phantasms) upon which it can exercise its abstractive capacity. In q. 1, a. 4 Thomas denies that our mind is naturally able to come to knowledge of the Trinity. The brevity of the *responsio* of this last article should not surprise us. If we can know of God only what is indicated by his effects, and these are limited to manifesting God's causal efficacy (which is not threefold but one), we can conclude without hesitation that the Trinity cannot in any way be rationally demonstrated. In other words, we can reach it only by faith and not by the intellect.

Faith and Reason

After indicating the range of our cognitive powers in relation to divine things, Thomas goes on to deal in q. 2 with the problems connected to the manifestation of these divine things. These problems circle around one primary question: In what way is it permitted to speak of God and of what belongs to faith? The key topic in the background has to do to with the reconciliation between rational inquiry and the demands of faith. It has already been said that certain truths cannot in any way be grasped by reason and so remain exclusively accessible to faith. But how must we comport ourselves vis-à-vis those truths of faith that we can also grasp by the efforts of reason? Does not the possibility of rationally demonstrating some articles of faith not perhaps empty faith itself of meaning or merit?

Since, in Thomas's estimation, man's destiny lies in his seeking—with everything he possesses—to conform to God as far as possible, using reason to examine questions about the divine within the limits set by the finitude of human nature is not only not inappropriate, it is a kind of duty. What is important—as is clearly affirmed in the first article of q. 2—is not to go to the opposite extreme, in the presumption of being able by reason perfectly to give an account of what is incomprehensible by its nature. Here too Thomas draws from the classic model of the right order between faith and reason condensed in the formula of Isaiah 7:9 (according the *Vetus Latina*): *nisi credideritis non intelligetis*. It is not necessary to believe in what has already been demonstrated (making faith follow after reason), but, on the contrary, in seeking and understanding it is necessary to proceed on the ground of what is believed. It is possible, therefore, to speak properly of divine *science,* as long as it is understood that in this science faith is the point of departure.

On the other hand, both the light of faith and that of reason are given us by God. So, if one were to be in irreparable contradiction with the other, God himself would be the author of contradiction and of falsity. When in philosophy we encounter something that is contrary to the dictates of faith, the fault cannot be that of philosophy itself but must be the fault of philosophy's misuse or of an error in inquiry. Ultimately, if it is used correctly, reason cannot but confirm what is already shown in faith and raise it to a higher level. Moreover, although it is true that what is an object of faith cannot be rationally demonstrated, it is likewise true that it cannot be rationally refuted.

The somewhat singular aspect of this position is that faith and reason come to define two domains whose effective connection often eludes us (since reason cannot finally demonstrate or refute what faith proposes). However, we believe that the light of reason is also given us by God and that God himself cannot deceive us, proposing conflicting conclusions to us through different channels. But what role does reason have within the divine science founded upon faith? This question (raised in q. 2, a. 3) is not about the relationship between the theology of the philosophers and the science of faith, but about the legitimacy of the use of philosophical arguments in the science of faith. In this case too the answer is positive. Philosophy can, indeed, be used in divine science (or *sacra doctrina,* as it is called here) for three purposes: (a) to demonstrate certain preambles or presuppositions of the faith itself, such as the existence and oneness of God; (b) to illustrate, by way of similitudes, some truths of faith otherwise hard to express; (c) to refute what is opposed to the faith, showing its falsity or irrelevance.

The important thing, as has already been said, is that philosophy not pretend to bring within its domain what belongs to faith. Yet it should be noted how Thomas's treatment seems to create a kind of circularity between philosophy and the science of faith (or, if you will, between reason and faith itself), inasmuch as he says, on the one hand, that reason must not precede faith, but must proceed, in its research, from what has been established by faith, and, on the other hand, that philosophy can, nevertheless, demonstrate certain indispensable presuppositions of faith. This circularity is ultimately founded on the one already implied in the Aristotelian principle according to which what is most evident in itself is not what is most evident for us and vice-versa.

In fact, faith—as Thomas specifies in q. 3, which follows upon the literal exposition of the first chapter of the *De Trinitate*—has something in common with science, namely, that its objects are certain and stable, and something in common with opinion, namely, that its objects are not evident, as *is* the case with those of science. Now, the lack of evidence can derive from the things themselves or from a defect in our understanding. The first case regards those singular and contingent events about which we have a faith (in the weaker sense of the term) based on the testimony of others. The second case regards divine things, which, although evident in themselves, are not evident to the human intellect, because of this intellect's limits. It is for this reason that in our knowledge we must proceed from what is more evident to us to what is more evident in itself. But if we look to the real order of things, what is less knowable in itself necessarily depends upon what is more knowable in itself. To put this in other terms: sensible substances depend—even for their ultimate intelligibility—on divine realities in the same way as an effect depends upon its cause. Consequently, we cannot have perfect knowledge of sensible things unless we already have some form of knowledge (however minimal and confused) of that on which they depend, that is, on divine realities. And precisely here faith—which permits us to have a kind of certainty about something that is not evident—intervenes. In this regard Thomas notes that the same thing can be encountered in the common order of learning in the sciences. Metaphysics, which focuses on the first principles, is studied after all the other sciences. Nevertheless, the latter presuppose some things that have their perfect demonstration only in the former.

From the beginning, then, faith directs man toward his ultimate destiny—the knowledge of God. And in this way the (at least apparent) circularity between faith and reason seems to be resolved. Faith offers reason the point of departure so that reason can proceed on its journey from effects to cause and in this way demonstrate some presuppositions necessary to faith itself. But reason remains always aware of the fact that, in this life, it cannot lead us to the perfect knowledge of divine realities. All of this applies, in the end, to those who intend to dedicate themselves to divine science. For everyone else, faith by itself is the easiest and surest path. This means, finally (as Thomas shows, appealing to Moses Maimonides), that we can hold by faith even those things for which it is possible to have a rational demonstration.

The Division of the Speculative Sciences: Abstraction and Separation

Boethius's thesis according to which the unity of the Trinity is founded on the absence of difference between the divine persons offers a starting point in q. 4

for a series of articles about the cause of plurality and the principle of individuation. This is an important juncture, because Thomas returns here to an issue—individuation—that he already considered in the Commentary on the *Sentences* and the *De ente et essentia*, but on which he obviously is continuing to reflect, as is witnessed to by his gradual acceptance of the Averroist doctrine of indeterminate dimensions. Since we have dealt with this topic earlier,[74] we can move on to a look at qq. 5 and 6 of the Commentary on the *De Trinitate*, which treat of the divisions of speculative philosophy and the method of proceeding in each.

Citing Avicenna, Thomas preliminarily notes that speculative philosophy has consideration of the truth as its aim, whereas practical philosophy aims at action, orienting its knowledge in this direction. And since the subject matter of a science is always proportioned to its end, the subject matter of the practical sciences consists in what we ourselves can accomplish and that is in some way in our power. The subject matter of the speculative sciences, on the other hand, consists in what does not depend on us, that is, in external objects.

For this reason, the division of the sciences within speculative philosophy must be drawn from the objects that these sciences study. Such objects should, nevertheless, not be considered in general but rather under the determinate aspect that brings them into the focus of the sciences in question. In other words, the division of the speculative sciences can be drawn from the diversity of objects only on the basis of the aspect by which they offer themselves to speculation, only to the extent that they—to use Thomas's own language—are "speculables" (*speculabilia*). What, then, are the characteristics of speculables, that is, what makes them speculables? The two things that make something speculable, in Thomas's view, are immateriality (which is the characteristic of the intellect itself) and necessity (which is the characteristic of science). And since that is necessary which is free of change, we can say more simply still that the basic characteristics of the speculables are immateriality and immutability. The division of speculables is derived from their respective degrees of immateriality and immutability, that is, on the basis of their greater or lesser proximity to matter and motion. The division of the sciences must be made to correspond to this division of speculables. On this point Thomas recovers the schema already developed by Aristotle and Boethius. In the first place there are objects that depend on matter and motion (they cannot be dissociated from it) as much for their being as for their being understood. These objects define the domain of physics or natural philosophy. Then there are objects that depend on matter for being but not for being understood, and these constitute the

74. See pp. 14–19 above.

domain of mathematics. Finally, there are objects that do not depend on matter or motion for their being or for being understood, even if we can subsequently distinguish within this group between those objects that are such as never to exist in matter and motion (God and the separate substances) and those that are such as to be able to exist without matter and motion even if sometimes they are found there; these sorts of objects would be substance, being, act, potency. The unified domain defined by these two subclasses of objects can be called be various names. It can be called *theology* or *divine science* to the extent that God is its principle object. It can be called *metaphysics* (or "beyond physics," as Thomas says here) since, in the order of learning, this science necessarily comes after physics (if it is true that our knowledge always begins with sensible things). Lastly, it can be called *first philosophy* because, in fact, all the other sciences receive their principles from it and, thus, in itself (even if not according to our consideration) it precedes all the other sciences.[75]

The articles that complete q. 5 provide a kind of case-by-case verification of this tripartite division of speculative philosophy. For example, it hardly seems plausible that physics concentrates on what exists in matter and motion, if it is true that every science as such must always deal with what is stable and permanent. This is a problem, at least in appearance, of no small account, if it is the case that because of it—as Thomas observes, following Aristotle—Plato was forced to introduce the doctrine of the ideas. But this problem can easily be avoided by keeping in mind the distinctions made by Aristotle in *Metaphysics* VII: what continually changes in the physical world is not the form of things but the composite itself. The forms and essential reasons of things are not generated or corrupted, and since they are immune to change, they can be the object of science and of definition. It must be said, therefore, that natural science does concern itself with things that exist in matter and motion, but through a consideration of their forms, which are unchanging and immaterial—or, to put it in other terms, and to be more precise—it considers them without designated matter but not without common matter, the concept of the form depending on the latter. When the natural scientist considers man, for instance, he attends to the form apart from the determinate flesh and bones that are in each individual (and which are mutable in themselves), but he does not prescind from flesh and bones in an absolute sense, which are the common matter that enter into the essential concept of man. So, natural philosophy does not proceed by abstracting the form from

75. See J. F. Wippel, "The Title 'First Philosophy' according to Thomas Aquinas and His Different Justifications for the Same," *The Review of Metaphysics* 27 (1974): 585–600 (published later in Wippel's *Metaphysical Themes in Thomas Aquinas*, 55–67).

matter in an absolute sense but by abstracting the universal (as common matter) from the particular.

In regard to mathematics, however, the principal difficulty that could be raised about the constitution of its field of inquiry is in the asymmetry that it presupposes between reality and understanding.[76] Mathematics, in fact, according to what we expounded earlier, considers without matter and motion what in reality never exists apart from matter and motion. Hence, we could say that it succeeds least in the task of all science, to wit, giving an account of how things are.

The problem offers to Thomas the occasion to distinguish with greater accuracy the different forms of abstraction and separation.[77] First of all, we must recall what we have already met with in the *De veritate*, that is, that our intellect possesses two quite distinct operations: one in which it knows—simply and undividedly—the essence of each thing, and the other in which through composition and division it formulates a positive or negative proposition about its objects. The first operation (the simple act of apprehending something) grasps the nature or quiddity of things. The second operation has to do with their being, which (at least in composite beings) results from the union of different principles. If we attend to this second operation, it is, indeed, neither permissible nor possible to abstract from (divide) what is joined in reality. This is possible in the first operation but only if the two terms do not depend on each other essentially, as a letter can be conceived apart from the syllable, but not vice-versa, and "animal" can be conceived without "foot" but not vice-versa.

To distinguish these various possibilities terminologically, Thomas reserves the term "separation" (*separatio*) for the composing and dividing operation of the intellect that grasps what is actually separated in reality, and the term "ab-

76. Also on this topic see, G. Schulz, "Die Struktur mathematischer Urteile nach Thomas von Aquin, *Expositio super librum Boethii De Trinitate*, q. 5 a. 3 und q. 6 a. 1," in *Scientia und ars in Hoch- und Spätmittelalter*, ed. I. Craemer-Ruegenberg and A. Speer, Miscellanea Mediaevalia 22 (Berlin: de Gruyter, 1994), 354–65.

77. The literature on this question is copious. In addition to the contributions cited successively in nn. 81, 84–85, see, at least, J.-D. Robert, "La métaphysique, science distincte de toute autre discipline philosophique, selon saint Thomas d'Aquin," *Divus Thomas* 50 (1947): 206–22; M. V. Leroy, "Le savoir spéculatif," *Revue Thomiste* 48 (1948): 236–339; "*Abstractio et separatio* d'après un texte controversé de saint Thomas," *Revue Thomiste* 48 (1948): 328–339; G. Van Riet, "La théorie thomiste de l'abstraction," *Revue Philosophique de Louvain* 50 (1952): 353–93; P. Merlan, "Abstraction and Metaphysics in St. Thomas' *Summa*," *Journal of the History of Ideas* 14 (1953): 284–91; W. Kane, "Abstraction and the Distinction of the Sciences," *The Thomist* 17 (1954): 43–68; F. A. Cunningham, "A Theory of Abstraction in St. Thomas," *The Modern Schoolman* 35 (1958): 249–70; R. Schmidt, "L'emploi de la séparation en métaphysique," *Revue Philosophique de Louvain* 58 (1960): 373–93; L. Oeing-Hanhoff, "Wesen und Formen der Abstraktion nach Thomas von Aquin," *Philosophisches Jahrbuch* 71 (1963): 14–137; J. Owens, "Metaphysical Separation in Aquinas," *Mediaeval Studies* 34 (1972): 212–18.

straction" for the operation by which simple apprehension distinguishes what is united in reality. But abstraction can take place in two ways: (a) insofar as the whole is drawn from the parts (and this is the abstraction of the universal from particulars that we have already seen in natural science); (b) insofar as the form is isolated from matter in an absolute way, which is possible only when the first does not depend on the second. So, to return to the specific case of mathematics, it is doubtless true that accidents cannot be separated from the substance, since they essentially depend on it as form on matter, but it is also true that quantity (that on which the mathematician focuses) precedes all the other accidents that make matter sensible, and by virtue of this it can be considered independently of them. In sum, quantity does not depend on sensible matter but on intelligible matter, and this justifies the fact that mathematics can consider its own objects, which in external reality are always found in matter and motion (both from which mathematics prescinds).

At this point the framework of the kinds of separation and abstraction can be regarded as established and can be summarized as follows:

1. The distinction that takes place according to the composing and dividing of the intellect and which consists in the *separation* of what is really disjoined in being, is proper to metaphysics, because it refers only to what is really separate in its being.

2. The distinction that takes place according to the operation that grasps the quiddity of things and that consists in the *abstraction of forms* (precisely of quantitative properties) *from sensible matter* is proper to mathematics.

3. The distinction that likewise takes place according to the operation that grasps the quiddity of things, but which consists in the *abstraction of the universal from the particular*, is proper to physics or natural science.

It remains for us to determine the exact contours of the field of objects considered by divine science, which is also—at first glance—the least homogenous field, containing objects of different natures. Now, every science deals with a determinate genus (*genus subjectum*) whose principles it investigates. But principles are of two types: some are such as to be natures complete in themselves and at the same time to function as principles. Others are not complete natures in themselves and function only as principles (as oneness is the principle of number or point the principle of line). Principles of the second type cannot be considered in a science by themselves but are considered in the sciences that study those things of which these are principles (there is no science of oneness, but the science itself of number also takes account of oneness).

The principles common to all beings, Thomas observes, are also those that are maximally complete in themselves. Such principles can be considered from two perspectives: in themselves and as principles common to other things. And it is on this basis that the dualistic nature of divine science can be understood. There is a science in which divine things are not the subject matter but are the principles of the subject matter, and this is the theology of the philosophers, or metaphysics, whose subject is being, substance, potency and act, etc. There is also a theology in which divine things *are* the subject matter, and this is the theology of Sacred Scripture. The principles that function as subject matter are, in the one case as in the other, really separate from matter and motion, but in a different way, as we have already noted. God and separate substances (the subject matter of the theology of Sacred Scripture) can never—by their nature—be in matter and motion. Being, substance, and the other things of this sort (the subject matter of the theology of metaphysics) do not include matter and motion in their proper concept, and yet they can sometimes exist in matter and motion.

The Modes of the Speculative Sciences and the Twofold Process of Resolution

The first and very dense article of q. 6 is constructed around Boethius's claim that in natural philosophy we must proceed *rationabiliter*, in mathematics *disciplinabiliter*, and in divine science *intellectualiter*. Each of these adverbs indicates the mode (*modus*) of proceeding—the method, we might say, if this term were not weighed down by a certain anachronism—proper to each of the sciences mentioned. The exact translation of *disciplinabiliter* could create some embarrassment, since in the term there is the sense of *disciplina* as the Latin correlate of the Greek *mathesis* and *episteme*[78] together with the sense of *disciplina* as learning.[79] In his Commentary Thomas seems to superimpose the two senses quite casually: mathematics is the science that more than any other meets the criteria of learning (it is, in fact, the easiest to learn) and proper scientificity (it is the most certain of all sciences). Moreover, it should be noted that while the other two terms make reference, if not to two distinct faculties (since, for Thomas, intellect and reason are not distinct), at least to two distinct operations of the soul, the mode assigned to mathematics does not appear to refer to any determinate cognitive function or habit.

In any event, Thomas does not interpret the Boethian schema in a rigid way. In other words, each way of proceeding must be considered not as exclu-

---

78. In his translation of the *Isagoge* Boethius himself uses *disciplina* for *episteme*.

79. This sense of *disciplina* was perhaps more predominant in Thomas's time. See M.-D. Chenu, "Notes de lexicographie philosophique médiévale: Disciplina," *Revue des Sciences Philosophiques et Théologiques* 25 (1936): 686–92.

sive of the science to which it is assigned but only as particularly suitable to it. For example, physics is not the only science to adopt a rational mode of proceeding, but it is that science which corresponds most to the internal dynamic itself of our reason. In fact, it is proper to reason to move from sensible realities to intelligible ones and to proceed discursively (and not by a simple intuitive act) from one thing to another, and the natural sciences principally do their work in these modes.

With regard to mathematics, it is, for Thomas—as we have already partly suggested—the science that is capable of the greatest certainty. It is more certain than natural science, because it abstracts from matter and motion, in which there is always an element of instability and contingency. But it is also more certain than divine science, since it considers things that are not as far removed from the senses and imagination.

It is proper to metaphysics to proceed intellectually, that is, in a way that conforms to the intellect. Now, what distinguishes the intellect is its ability to grasp a plurality of terms or objects in a single act, which is exactly the opposite of what reasoning does. This means that, on the one hand, rational consideration terminates in intellectual consideration according to the *way of resolution*, since reason itself reduces a plurality of things to the unity of principles, and, on the other hand, intellectual consideration is inversely the principle of the rational consideration according to the *way of composition*, since it grasps as a unity what reason embraces as a multiplicity.[80] Every process of resolution of reason, in all the sciences, terminates in the divine science. But this process can take place in two distinct ways: (a) It can unfold through a consideration of extrinsic causes—and taking this route the ultimate term is the supreme cause, viz., God. (b) It can unfold through a consideration of intrinsic causes, proceeding from particular intentions to universal ones—and in this case the ultimate term of the resolution is the set of properties common to beings that constitute the subject of theology as metaphysics.

The Commentary on the *De Trinitate*, thus, contains Thomas's most rigorous response to the problem of the apparent duality of the object of Aristotelian metaphysics, which is, on the one hand—as is well-known—the science of being as being, and on the other hand, the science of the supreme being—the

---

80. On the meaning of the *via resolutionis* and of the *via compositionis*, see E. Dolan, "Resolution and Composition in Speculative and Practical Discourse," *Laval Théologique et Philosophique* 6 (1950) 9–62; J. A. Aertsen, "Method and Metaphysics. The *via resolutionis* in Thomas Aquinas," in *Knowledge and the Sciences in Medieval Philosophy. Proceedings of the Eighth International Congress of Medieval Philosophy*, vol. III, ed. R. Tyorinoja, A. Inkeri Lehtinen, and D. Føllesdall (Helsinki: Annals of the Finnish Society for Missiology and Ecumenics, 1990), 3–12; M. Tavuzzi, "Aquinas on Resolution in Metaphysics," *The Thomist* 55 (1991): 199–227.

immobile and supersensible substance. Both ways of understanding metaphysics are acceptable for Thomas, but he does not see them as merely juxtaposed. In the strict sense, metaphysics has being as being as its subject matter but concerns itself with God and separate substances to the extent that they are the principles of being in general. The double polarity of the field of metaphysics, however, has its ultimate justification in the twofold path of resolution by which reason proceeds toward principles: in the order of efficient causality it leads to God; in the order of mental intentions it leads to the consideration of being in general and its properties. Thomas's attempt to (re-) constitute the realm of Aristotelian metaphysics in a unified way has its basis, not simply in the hierarchic subordination of the ontological and theological components, but in the double movement of knowledge that aims at the same sphere from two different but parallel perspectives.

There is also a twofold movement that makes it the case that metaphysics constitutes the origin and goal of all our knowledge (as if it were in some way—circularly—before and after itself).[81] It is meta-physics, and therefore the goal of knowledge, since in the process of resolution it comes after every science. It is first philosophy, and so the origin of every science, since it precedes every other science in the process of composition.

The last article of q. 6 (and the last of the Commentary) deals with the role of the speculative sciences with respect to the possibility of directly contemplating the form of the separate substances. In fact, there is no such possibility for the speculative sciences, since in them too our knowledge always proceeds from phantasms (that is, from sensible images), without which the light of the agent intellect is incapable of exercising its abstractive power. Although the interruption of the work at this point is in all probability accidental, the Commentary on the *De Trinitate* ends exactly where it had begun: the defense of the naturalness of the agent intellect as an intrinsic principle of knowledge.

Metaphysics and Theology

The Commentary on the *De Trinitate* of Boethius is perhaps the most significant of Thomas's texts regarding the issues related to the scientific status of theology and metaphysics. It is also worth noting that, in the development of

81. And, in fact, in a. 1, q. 5, ad 9, Thomas takes great care to avoid what could be viewed as a type of circular vision between metaphysics and inferior sciences (especially physics). The analysis of J. F. Wippel on this point is very penetrating: "Thomas Aquinas and Avicenna on the Relationship between First Philosophy and the Other Theoretical Sciences: A Note on Thomas's Commentary on Boethius's *De Trinitate*, Q. 5, article 1, ad 9," *The Thomist* 37 (1973): 133–54 (published later in *Metaphysical Themes in Thomas Aquinas*, 37–53).

the text, Thomas passes from the classical threefold division of the speculative sciences fixed by Aristotle and Boethius to a fourfold division by the dividing of divine science into the two disciplines of which we just spoke: theology founded on revelation (which has God and separate substances for its subject matter) and the "theology of the philosophers" or metaphysics (whose subject matter is being as being). One of the fundamental aims of the Commentary seems, in effect, to be that of making a space for a new science within the traditional division of the sciences. This new science is Christian theology explicitly conceived as a *speculative science* alongside and, indeed, surpassing the philosophical sciences. There are at least three things to observe about this schema.

First, if Christian theology is likewise a science, and if it conforms for this reason to the criteria of the Aristotelian epistemology of the *Posterior Analytics*, where do we find evidence of its principles? Here Thomas reaffirms and sharpens the doctrine of subalternation that he had already articulated in the Commentary on the *Sentences*:

Even in those sciences handed down to us by human tradition, there are certain principles in some of them which are not universally known, but which presuppose truths derived from a higher science, just as in subordinate sciences certain things taken from superior sciences are assumed and believed to be true; and truths of this kind are not evident in themselves except in the higher sciences. This is the case with the articles of faith, for they are principles of that science leading to knowledge of divine things, since those truths which are evident in themselves in the knowledge which God has of himself, are presupposed in our science; and he is believed as the one manifesting these truths to us through his messengers, even as the doctor believes from the word of the natural philosopher.[82]

We hold the principles of theology, therefore, by faith, but they are evident in a higher, subalternating, science, namely, the knowledge that God has of himself. In other words, the science of which the divine intellect is the first principle is the same science that we have access to by faith.:

Intellect is always the first principle of any science but not always the proximate principle; rather, it is often faith which is the proximate principle of a science, as is evident in the case of the subalternate sciences, since their conclusions proceed, on the one hand, from faith in what is accepted from a superior science as from a proximate principle, and, on the other hand, from the intellect of those who possess a superior science—superior because they possess an intellectual certitude of these things that are simply believed by subalternate sciences—as from a first principle.[83]

82. *In Boeth. De Trin.*, q. 2, a. 2, ad 5.
83. *In Boeth. De Trin.*, q. 2, a. 2, ad 7.

Second, how should we more exactly understand the function of the operation that founds divine science, viz., separation? As we have said, we have the good fortune of having at our disposal at least a part of Thomas's autograph of the Commentary on the *De Trinitate* (in Vat. lat. 9850). On some points the manuscript shows traces of successive redactions. The most significant of these redactions regard precisely q. 5, a. 3 and, more particularly, the doctrine of the abstraction-separation couplet. The redacting shows how Thomas seemed to admit, at first, *three* degrees of abstraction corresponding to each of the speculative sciences but then, in what we consider the definitive version, settles on *two* forms of abstraction (the abstraction of the universal from the particular, which is proper to physics, and the abstraction of form from matter, which is proper to mathematics) and an operation of the intellect composing and dividing (*separatio*), which is exclusively proper to metaphysics or *scientia divina*. In a celebrated article that first appeared in 1947,[84] in which the corrections that Thomas made to his text were first given the attention they deserved, L.-B. Geiger tried to stress adequately the importance of this turn, of the decision to make *separatio* the cornerstone of metaphysics. Without this intellectual operation, metaphysics could not distinguish itself from the other speculative sciences and could not secure its subject matter. Now, *separatio* consists in a negative judgment, in the judgment that being is *not* necessarily or in itself material. Nevertheless, according to Geiger, this negative judgment actually implicitly presupposes a positive judgment, to wit, that there are *in fact immaterial beings*. So that being can function as the subject matter of metaphysics, it is always necessary, in short, first to demonstrate the existence of separate substances and, above all, God. Metaphysics, then, although it deals with being as being, has an expressly theological origin.

More recently, and from different perspectives, John Wippel[85] and Jan Aertsen[86] have proposed a different interpretation. Without questioning the distinction between the *separatio* proper to metaphysics and the degrees of abstraction

84. See L.-B. Geiger, "Abstraction et séparation d'après S. Thomas *In De Trinitate* q. 5, a. 3," *Revue des Sciences Philosophiques et Theologiques* 31 (1947): 3–40. For further bibliographic recommendations and a panorama of the question, see "Metafisica e teologia nella divisione delle scienze speculative del *Super Boetium De Trinitate*," in Tommaso d' Aquino, *Commenti a Boezio (Super Boetium De Trinitate. Expositio libri Boetii De ebdomadibus)*, P. Porro, ed. and trans. (Milan: Bompiani, 2007), 467–526. We also refer to this edition for many of the topics that we address here.

85. See J. F. Wippel, "Metaphysics and *separatio* according to Thomas Aquinas," *The Review of Metaphysics* 31 (1978): 431–70 (published later in *Metaphysical Themes in Thomas Aquinas*, 69–104).

86. See J. A. Aertsen, "Was heißt Metaphysik bei Thomas von Aquin?" in *Scientia und ars in Hoch- und Spätmittelalter*, ed. I. Craemer-Ruegenberg and A. Speer, Miscellanea Mediaevalia 22 (Berlin: de Gruyter, 1994), 217–39; and Aertsen's *Medieval Philosophy and the Transcendentals*, especially 113–58.

proper to the other sciences, Wippel and Aertsen contest the idea that, in order to constitute itself as a science in itself, metaphysics must first come to admit the existence of immaterial beings. Put differently, it is not its immateriality or transmateriality that permits us to identify the subject matter of metaphysics but—as Aertsen, above all, emphasizes—its transcendentality (which Geiger was careful, moreover, not to deny). Metaphysics has as its subject matter those common and universal principles (and, in the first place, *ens commune*) in which all of our knowledge terminates, from the perspective of predication. But substances that are immaterial in themselves—and, first of all, God—are that in which all our knowledge in the order of extrinsic causality terminates (as we have seen). The latter, then—and in conformity with what Thomas himself explicitly writes—function in metaphysics as principles (causes) of the subject matter and not as the actual subject matter. In this way the ontological component (understood in a transcendentalist fashion) of metaphysics seems to precede the theological component. In truth, the double movement of resolution postulated by Thomas seems also to legitimize the hypothesis of a sort of parallelism (as we noted earlier) between the two principles: the resolution according to intrinsic causes terminates in the *subject matter* of metaphysics in the strict sense, whereas the resolution according to efficient causality terminates in the *principles of the subject matter* of metaphysics—and these principles constitute, in turn, the subject matter of the theology founded on revelation.

Third, and lastly, it cannot fail to be noted how the whole of Thomas's discourse on metaphysics is indebted to the Avicennian position from which it draws both the fundamental thesis about the determination of the subject matter proper to metaphysics and the key to this determination, that is, the two different understandings of immateriality.[87] This influence is decisive, since it makes it possible to keep faith with Aristotle's requirement in *Metaphysics* VI that metaphysics must always occupy itself with what is separate, while definitively resolving the Aristotelian oscillation over the subject matter of first philosophy. In sum, it is true that the subject matter is only being and its properties (and not separate substances), but it is also true that being itself can be said to be immaterial (separate) since it precedes the distinction between material and immaterial and so does not require matter in its definition. Despite this basic debt, there is also a basic difference. The distinction between the two different classes of immaterial beings does not lead, for Avicenna, to any effective

87. See J. F. Wippel, "The Latin Avicenna as a Source for Thomas Aquinas's Metaphysics," *Freiburger Zeitschrift für Philosophie und Theologie* 37 (1990): 51–90 (published later in *Metaphysical Themes in Thomas Aquinas II*, 31–64); P. Porro, "Tommaso d'Aquino, Avicenna e la struttura della metafisica," in *Tommaso d'Aquino e l'oggetto della metafisica*, ed. S. L. Brock (Rome: Armando, 2004), 65–87.

scission within the unitary field of *scientia divina*. This discipline, rather, moves gradually, within its own sphere, from that which can be grasped *not on the condition of being material* to that which can be grasped *only on the condition of not being material* or, as we might otherwise put it: from that which is abstracted from matter to that which is actually separate from matter (or differently still: from that which is *eidetically* separate to that which is *ontologically* separate). This is possible because Avicenna considers being as being as the subject matter of metaphysics *prior* to the division between cause and effect, or between God and creature. Thus, for Avicenna, God is not the absolute cause of the subject matter of first philosophy, but is instead *a part of the subject matter* (being as being) that is the cause of *another part of the same subject matter* (caused being). For Thomas, however, God enters into metaphysics as principle and *total cause* of the subject matter, which, as *ens commune,* is created being.[88] The result is, at first blush, paradoxical: admitting two distinct sciences that both deal with what is separate from matter (and, therefore, referring both to *separatio*), Thomas divides what was united in Avicenna (the science of being as the one *scientia divina* that comes to demonstrate God on the basis of what is neutrally or negatively immaterial, that is, from being as being), and reunites by the same operation (separation) what, for Avicenna, should be rigorously distinguished, so as not to fall into the Platonic error of postulating an ontological separation every time a separation is made at the level of consideration (an eidetic separation). But this difference between Thomas and Avicenna becomes perhaps more intelligible if we recall the fundamental aim of this move of Thomas, one which is entirely foreign to Avicenna: to legitimize the scientific constitution of theology in the strict sense, viz., theology based on revelation.[89]

88. This thesis was reiterated by Thomas, not only in the preface of his Commentary on the *Metaphysics*, but also on many other occasions: see, for example, *In librum Beati Dionysii De divinis nominibus expositio*, V, l. 2, *De potentia*, q. 7, a. 2, ad 4, and *ST*, Ia-IIae, q. 66, a. 5, ad 4.

89. See P. Porro, "Astrazione e separazione: Tommaso d'Aquino e la tradizione greco-araba," in Tommaso d'Aquino, *Commenti a Boezio*, 527–80.

3

THE RETURN TO ITALY

The Project of the *Summa contra Gentiles* and
the Writings of the Orvieto Period

THE CHAPTER OF VALENCIENNES
AND THE RETURN TO ITALY

Thomas's first period of teaching in Paris concluded more or less as it began: in a climate of conflict and intimidation. On April 6, 1259, Palm Sunday, while he was preaching before the university community, he was interrupted and publicly insulted by the beadle of the Picard nation, Guillot, who began provocatively to read aloud from William of Saint-Amour's treatise against the friars. On this occasion too Alexander IV was forced to intervene, calling for the excommunication and dismissal of Guillot in a subsequent letter on June 26. These provisions do not seem to have been taken literally, since there is evidence that in 1267 the same Guillot was the beadle of the university itself (which would be a promotion) and still harbored a visceral aversion to the friars, so much so that he entered into polemics with the powerful Simon de Brion (the future Pope Martin IV).

In June of 1259, Thomas traveled to Valenciennes for the Dominican general chapter. The chapter was an important one, for during it decisions would be made for the organization of *studia* in the order. To study the question a commission was formed, probably at the direction of the master general, Humbert of Romans. The commission was constituted by the principal masters: Thomas, Albert the Great, Bonhomme le Breton, Florent of Hesdin (whose *inceptio*, as we noted earlier, was especially difficult), and Peter of Tarentaise (he would later became pope, taking the name Innocent V). The commission worked out a series of proposals that were approved and inserted in the acts of the chapter. This was not simply a practical reorganization of studies by the order (nor was it, as we have observed, the composing of an actual *ratio studiorum*—a *ratio studiorum* would have been a novelty not only for the Dominicans but also in general, at least if the technical sense of that term, as it is used in religious

116

orders, is meant) but a strategic decision of much wider import. The document composed by the commission and approved by the chapter claims the absolute centrality of study in the life of the Friars Preachers, reviving and formalizing a concern that was already quite present in their founder. All or almost all the other tasks were to be subordinated to study. Thus, the following recommendations were made. Lectors should not be assigned other duties that might prevent them from teaching fulltime. Religious functions were not to overlap with the lecture times in a way that would compromise the frequency of the latter. In each priory young men would be selected to be sent to the *studia generalia* for further intellectual formation. Even the oldest friars (the priors themselves included, if possible) could continue to receive ongoing formation, taking courses. No priory was to be without a lector (which was already a provision from the founding of the order), but if this were to occur, young men should be transferred to priories where courses were available. If priories did not have public courses (courses open even to people outside the order, as at Saint-Jacques), they would at least have simplified private courses based on simple textbooks that were necessary for preaching and confession.[1] At the principal *studia*, at least, each master should be assigned a bachelor. To monitor the situation, strict provisions were made for "visitors" who were charged with verifying the frequency of courses—sanctioning the friars who did not attend them—and ascertaining the quality of the teaching imparted and the progress of the students, making sure that there were sufficient teachers for each province.

Perhaps the most interesting aspect of these decisions regards the importing of the study of the arts (philosophy). It was recommended that the young men should have an adequate basic formation in the arts (even if this meant sending them to another priory). The importance and novelty of this decision can be seen from two perspectives, an institutional one and an ideological-doctrinal one. In connection with the first aspect, it will perhaps not be idle to recall that the standard university *curriculum* foresaw that the higher faculties (law, medicine, but also theology) could be entered after study in the faculty of arts, which meant that, at least in general, the possibility of acquiring the doctorate in theology had a period of teaching in the faculty of arts as a prerequisite. This norm was clearly in place at Oxford from 1253. The candidate for teaching in theology must already have occupied the position of regent master in arts, even if not at the same university.[2] The occasion on which this statute was adopted

1. Two such textbooks would be Petrus Comestor's *Historia ecclesiastica* and Raymond of Peñafort's *Summa de causibus*.

2. See S. Gibson, ed., *Statuta antiqua Universitatis Oxoniensis*, (Oxford: Clarendon Press, 1931),

was the presentation of a Franciscan as a candidate for teaching in theology who had not previously been in a faculty of arts. In Paris a requirement of this type was foreseen for seculars but not for regulars, and this obviously added another reason for tension to the ones we saw in the last chapter. We can imagine what would happen nowadays if there were competition for a teaching position in which certain qualifications were expected of some candidates but not others. The fact is that the mendicant orders had developed a structure of higher education parallel to the university, aiming from the beginning only at theological formation. With respect to the Dominicans, for example, the original provisions (as we will see momentarily) expressly prohibited the study of other disciplines. The study of theology itself occurred, then, in a kind of hybrid system of priory and university education, as was the case, indeed, at Saint-Jacques, where the friars studied at the priory *studium,* which, in addition, was open to secular clergy and the laity. It was not unusual for the friars' schools to host university events (religious functions, inaugural ceremonies, etc.) and particular didactic activities. But the friars at places like Saint-Jacques followed an autonomous program that was principally directed toward forming a body of lectors, that is, the education of *lectores* for the order's schools, and only a restricted number (of genuine excellence) of true *magistri* for university chairs. From a formal point of view, the pursuants of the two titles—*lector* and *magister*—followed different paths. The appointment of a *lector* was something internal to the order in which the university administration was evidently not involved. The appointment of a *magister* was, however, a public matter subject to the procedures, didactic tests, and formalities dictated by the university statutes. But there were always exceptions. As we have said, the friars were not required to study or teach in the faculty of arts before teaching in the faculty of theology, and the attendance of classes along with teaching experience in the priories substituted for the comparable activities in university structures. So, a Dominican friar could become a *magister* in theology having attended courses in his *studium generale* and without having gone through the normal cycle of studies in the faculty of arts.

But it is precisely the transformation of this faculty in the course of the first half of the thirteenth century that created difficulties that the chapter of Valenciennes was trying to deal with. Originally the faculty of arts sought to impart basic instruction in the area of the late antique system of liberal arts

49 (ll. 17–20): "nullus in eadem universitate incipiat in theologia nisi prius rexerit in artibus in aliqua universitate." See also A. Maierù, "Formazione culturale e tecniche d'insegnamento nelle scuole degli Ordini mendicanti," in *Studio e studia: le scuole degli ordini mendicanti tra XIII e XIV secolo. Atti del XXIX Convegno internazionale. Assisi, 11–13 ottobre 2001* (Spoleto: CISAM, 2002), 3–31, especially 10.

(from which it takes its name), with particular weight given to the *trivium*, that is, to the arts of language (above all grammar and dialectic, the *Logica vetus*). But gradually the faculty evolved into a faculty of philosophy focusing on the systematic study of Aristotelian texts despite repeated prohibitions of the teaching of these texts in 1210, 1215, and 1231. Precisely at the time that Thomas was preparing to become a *magister* of theology in 1255, the Parisian faculty of arts set down the reading of all Aristotle's texts as a requirement, including those thought to be the most difficult or dangerous (the *libri naturales*, principally the *Physics* and the *Metaphysics*). The fact that the Dominicans were not in the faculty of arts, thus, suddenly had completely new implications. What they missed out on was no longer a basic education in grammar and logic, which was evidently something they could acquire in their priories, but a knowledge of the principal philosophical texts that were then available. We can understand, then, why masters such as Albert the Great and Thomas, who had already achieved an impressive command of Aristotelian and Arab philosophy on their own, were concerned with the formation of their young confreres.

We now turn to the second perspective of which we spoke earlier, the ideological-doctrinal perspective. In the Dominicans' constitutions the study of the books of the pagans and the philosophers and the study of the secular sciences and liberal arts were explicitly prohibited.[3] Of course there was something very traditional and formulaic in this rule,[4] but it had a different weight in an order that made study one of its priorities. The study of philosophy was again proscribed by the general chapter of Paris in 1243. From the acts of the chapter of the Roman province we can conclude, however, that—parallel to what was occurring in the Parisian faculty of arts before 1255—the friars were permitted to keep logic and moral philosophy texts, but all the other texts of secular science had to be immediately returned to the prior (although lectors were exempted from this norm). Restrictions of this sort would be reasserted—at least in some provinces—even after Valenciennes,[5] but that does not diminish the

3. See H. Denifle, "Die Constitutionen des Predigerordens in der Redaction Raimunds von Peñafort," *Archiv für Literatur- und Kirchengeschichte des Mittelalters* 5 (1889): 530–64, especially 562 (*De studentibus*): "In libris gentilium et phylosophorum non studeant, et si ad horam inspiciant. Seculares scientias non addiscant, nec artes quas liberals vocant, nisi aliquando circa aliquos magister ordinis vel capitulum generale voluerit aliter dispensare, sed tantum libros theologicos tam iuvenes quam alii legant."

4. See G. G. Meersseman, "'*In libris gentilium non studeant.*' L'étude des classiques interdite aux clercs au moyen âge?" *Italia medievale e umanistica* 1 (1958): 1–13; M. M. Mulchahey, "*First the Bow Is Bent in Study*": *Dominican Education before 1350*, Studies and Texts 132 (Toronto: Pontifical Institute of Mediaeval Studies, 1998).

5. For the circumstances of these prohibitions and restrictions, see L. Bianchi, "Ordini mendicanti e controllo 'ideologico': il caso delle province domenicane," in *Studio e* studia, 303–38.

importance of the decisions made by the chapter, which ratified the victory of the line of Albert and Thomas. Their case (not to take anything away from the other members of the commission), as should be stressed once more, was truly exceptional. Both had attained a knowledge of Aristotle, Avicenna, and the other "Arabs" that was quite unusual— especially since this learning had not in any way, formally or institutionally, been required of them. Albert had already conducted his personal battles—even within the order—against the "ignorant who wish in every way to fight the use of philosophy," "the brute animals who blaspheme against what they do not know."[6] Thomas, without the same polemical violence, shares the same conviction. If we do not take account of this cultural strategy, we will perhaps not be able to understand why Thomas continued into the last years of his life to read and comment on Aristotle.

From this perspective, the decisions of the chapter of Valenciennes were not destined to modify only the studies within the Dominican order. In general they renewed and safeguarded an essential link between theology and philosophy that was in danger of being irretrievably lost because of the practice of exempting the friars from studying and teaching in the faculty of arts. What was up until that point basically a personal decision of Albert and Thomas, thus, went on to become one of the characteristic traits of the subsequent history of the whole of Western culture.

THE *SUMMA CONTRA GENTILES*
The Purpose of the Work: The Truth of Faith and the Truth of Reason

After the chapter of Valenciennes, there is a little gap in Thomas's biography that scholars have tried to fill in various ways. The policy of the order (reinforced by the decisions of the chapter of Valenciennes) was to rotate regent masters as much as possible, and it was foreseen that Thomas would leave his chair to his bachelor William of Alton in the 1259–60 academic year. Without going into the merits of the different hypotheses that have been advanced, it seems possible that Thomas would have stayed in Paris for some time after the 1258–59 academic year before departing for Italy in the autumn of 1259 or, at the latest, the start of 1260. In the absence of precise documentary indications, it is also possible that Thomas went to Naples, to what was, for all intents and purposes, his home priory (his presence in the city seems, at any rate, attested to by the provincial

6. Albert the Great, *Commentarii in Epistolas B. Dionysii Areopagitae*, Alberti Magni Opera Omnia 14, A. Borgnet, ed. (Paris: Vives, 1892), 910: "quidam qui nesciunt, omnibus modis volunt impugnare usum philosophiae, et maxime in praedicatoribus, ubi nullus eis resistit, tamquam bruta animalia blasphemantes in iis quae ignorant."

chapter of September 1260). In this period Thomas took up some duties within the order without doing any teaching before September 1261, when he was assigned to teach at the priory of Orvieto. The usual reason given for this apparent inactivity—rather surprising considering Thomas's character—is that he took this time to work on an imposing project that he had already begun in Paris, viz., the *Summa contra Gentiles*. In the absence of plausible alternatives, we can content ourselves with this hypothesis. Paleographic evidence makes it, in any case, certain that the drafting of the work began in Paris.[7] As R.-A. Gauthier has shown, the first part of the text is written on the same parchment and with the same kind of ink that was used for the *Super Boethium De Trinitate*. Beginning with folio 15 different parchment is used, and already near folio 14 the ink that is used is very different, which leads us to suppose a similarly significant change in place and context. But, as with the *Super Boethium De Trinitate*, the autograph tells us even more. We see that Thomas subjected the text to a series of revisions that sometimes (as in the case of Book I, c. 53, which we spoke of earlier) reflect hesitations, reconsiderations, improvements. These successive interventions by the author make a chronology of the text rather difficult. The first 53 chapters of the book were composed in Paris (and so it seems during 1259). Having arrived in Italy, Thomas completely revised this part of the work (as we saw and will see, profound alterations are made to c. 53) and continued drafting it over the next four or five years (thus, after the transfer to Orvieto but before the move to Rome). It is, in fact, quite possible that the fourth and last book was completed between 1264 and 1265, but nothing prevents us from hypothesizing, as P.-M. Gils suggests, that Thomas made further small corrections to the whole work during his second teaching stint in Paris.

The best way to approach the text is probably to put aside for the moment the title that we use for it today (*Summa contra Gentiles*)—attested to by an *exemplar* that most probably dates from 1272, but that is misleading—to return to the one that is usually found at the beginning of the manuscripts: *Liber de veritate catholicae fidei contra errores infidelium*. The title that is more commonly used today effectively and inevitably suggests the idea of an apologetical or heresiological work or, at least, one aimed at missionary activity or proselytism, which has caused the most disparate interpretations. According to one of the most established interpretations (which appears to have its origin in Peter Marsilio's *Chronicle of the King of Aragon, James I*), the text was written by Thomas at the request of Raymond of Peñafort, who needed a good textbook as a resource for his doctrinal debates with Muslims in Spain. To this was then added the conviction that Averroes was the

---

7. As we have noted, we have Thomas's autograph of *Summa contra Gentiles*, I, c. 13–III, c. 120.

main polemical target of the text, and this without considering that Averroes had practically no influence in thirteenth-century Spain or that no Muslim would ever have dreamed of using Averroes as a shield in a hypothetical debate with a Christian! Averroes does appear in the *Liber* among supporters of erroneous doctrines (in particular about the intellect) but along with many others. The fact of the matter is that the interlocutors addressed by Thomas are not just pagans (the *gentiles*) or Muslims, because the work is not directed against a particular religion, philosophical sect, or heresy, and it does not propose to consider specific errors, as Thomas himself tries to make clear in his presentation of it:

But it is difficult to proceed against individual errors, and this for two reasons. First, because the sacrilegious remarks of those who have erred are not so well known to us that we may use what they say as the basis of proceeding to a refutation of their errors.... Second, it is difficult because some of them, such as the Mohammedans and the pagans, do not, as we do, accept the authority of the Scripture with which we are able to argue against the Jews by means of the Old Testament and against heretics by means of the New Testament. But the Mohammedans and the pagans do not accept of these. We must, therefore, have recourse to natural reason, to which all are forced to give their assent but which is defective in divine matters.[8]

We note in passing a fundamental principle of Thomas, reiterated also on other occasions. When faced with a particular interlocutor, he keeps only to those authorities that the interlocutor also accepts. Were he not to take this tack, obviously there could be no debate.[9] But returning to the motivations behind the present work, we can specify that the first and immediate objective is not that of refuting particular errors but that of considering the truths of the Christian faith and how it excludes certain errors on its own: "While we are investigating certain truths, we will also show what errors are excluded by it and we will likewise show how the truth that we come to know by demonstration is in accord with the Christian religion."[10] It is no accident that Thomas has chosen

8. *Summa contra Gentiles*, I, c. 2.
9. See also *Quodlibet* IV, q. 9, a. 3: "Some disputation is ordered to removing doubt about whether something is such [*an ita sit*]: in this type of disputation, theology ought to use chiefly the authorities which the ones with whom it is disputed receive. For example, if one disputes with the Jews, the authorities of the Old Testament must be exhibited; if one disputes with the Manicheans, who look down on the Old Testament, only the authorities of the New Testament must be used; if one disputes with schismatics who accept the Old and New Testament, but not the doctrine of our saints, as is the case with the Greeks, one must dispute from the authorities of the Old and New Testaments and those doctors whom they accept. If, however, the disputants do not accept any authority, they must be convinced by appealing to natural reasons" This type of disputation is aimed, negatively, at removing errors and, positively, at teaching the listeners to understand the truth that they believe. In the latter case it uses rational arguments only.
10. *Summa contra Gentiles*, I, c. 2.

Proverbs 8:7 as his epigraph, which follows the same order: "My mouth shall proclaim truth, and wickedness is horror for my lips."

The work is not conceived in the first place *against* someone, as the customary title suggests (although this is the secondary purpose) but as a meditation upon truth and its pursuit—that is, the pursuit of wisdom. That the pursuit of the latter in search of truth is followed or accompanied by the refutation of error is something natural:

It belongs to one and the same task, however, both to pursue one of two contraries and to oppose the other. Medicine, for example, seeks to effect health and to eliminate illness. Hence, just as it belongs to the wise man to meditate especially on the truth belonging to the first principle and to teach it to others, so it belongs to him to refute the opposing falsehood.[11]

The connection between wisdom and truth is the first thing that Thomas would like to show. Wise men—as Aristotle shows in many places—are those who rightly order things (they have a ruling or architectonic function) because they know the end. The person is wise in an absolute sense (and not only in a particular field) who turns his attention to the end of the whole universe. Now, the ultimate end is, of course, that pursued by the first cause, which (precisely because it acts in view of an end) is an intelligent cause. And since what relates to an intellect (as we saw at the beginning of the *Quaestiones de veritate*) is called "true," it is deduced that truth is the ultimate end of the universe and that wisdom has precisely as its principle aim the consideration of truth. Thus, the title of Thomas's work—as it is attested to by most of the manuscript tradition, and as Thomas might have originally designated it—is perfectly explained.

The fundamental theme of the *Liber*, then, is that of communicating wisdom and the role of the wise Christian (it is not by chance that the work opens with a chapter devoted to the task of the wise man).[12] This is, indeed, the subtle thread that connects most of Thomas's output, and it was chosen by Thomas himself as the topic of his *inceptio*: divine wisdom uses intermediaries—wise men—to spread itself out into all Christians. Finding oneself in this condition (being a mountain down which wisdom streams, according to the image chosen for the *inceptio*) is certainly a privilege, but also a terrible responsibility, which Thomas always felt personally and deeply and that he often thematized in his writings. All of his frenetic literary activity, carried out at a pace that for

11. *Summa contra Gentiles*, I, c. 1.

12. On the overall structure and foundational themes of the *Summa contra Gentiles*, see R.-A. Gauthier, *Introduction à Saint Thomas d'Aquin, Somme contre les Gentils* (Paris: Editions Universitaires, 1993); N. Kretzmann, *The Metaphysics of Theism: Aquinas's Natural Theology in* Summa contra Gentiles I (Oxford: Clarendon Press, 1997).

us today is simply inconceivable, is justified by an awareness of this charge. And this is what Thomas himself says (concealing himself behind a quotation from Hilary of Poitiers' *De Trinitate*) in perhaps one of the best-known passages of the *Liber,* if not his entire *corpus*:

Trusting in divine mercy in embarking upon the work of a wise man, even though this surpasses my powers, I have set myself the task of making known, as far as my limited powers will allow, the truth that the Catholic faith professes, and of setting aside the errors that are opposed to it. To use the words of Hilary: "I am aware that I owe this to God as the chief duty of my life, that my every word and sense may speak of him."[13]

Yet, there are two different types of truth about God. There are some truths that can be reached by natural reason, such as the existence of God himself, and other truths that exceed the capacity of human reason entirely, such as the Trinity and, in general, everything touching on the divine essence. This distinction is already well known to us. Thomas introduced it in the Commentary on the *Sentences* and he would always be faithful to it. The consideration that justifies it is well known to us too: our knowledge has its origin in the senses and so can arrive only at what can be attested to by sensible things. Now, sensible effects show us the existence of a cause (of their cause), but they cannot tell us anything about the intrinsic nature of this cause. Quoting the famous adage of *Metaphysics* II, Thomas asserts that our intellect relates to primary principles in the way that the eye of the bat does to the sun.[14] Nevertheless, in the other contexts Thomas does not adopt the dangerous syntagm *duplex veritas*. This distinction between two different truths is worth attentive consideration, above all in light of the fact that, in the writings of the second Parisian regency, and especially in *De unitate intellectus,* Thomas reproves his adversaries (certain masters of the faculty of arts) for speaking as if there were two different truths—one for faith and another for reason—coining the anathema then taken up by Bishop Tempier in the prologue to the celebrated condemnation of 1277. The first thing to note in this respect is that naturally this duality involves only our way of knowing God, and not God himself. ("I spoke of a twofold divine truth, not in reference to God, who is truth one and simple, but in reference to our knowledge, which in knowing the things of God, relates to it in different ways.")[15] The second thing to note is that the distinction is not strictly between truths of faith and truths of reason, of truths accessible to reason and

---

13. *Summa contra Gentiles,* I, c. 2.

14. On the use of this Aristotelian example by Thomas (in juxtaposition to the more "optimistic" interpretation of Albert the Great), see C. Steel, *Der Adler und die Nachteule: Thomas und Albert über die Möglichkeit der Metaphysik,* Lectio Albertina 4 (Münster: Aschendorff, 2001).

15. *Summa contra Gentiles,* I, c. 9.

truths inaccessible to it. We might ask ourselves at this point why truths that are knowable by reason alone are presented to us as objects of faith. Thomas offers three principal reasons for this (I, c. 4). If these truths were left to rational inquiry alone, then: (a) only a few would come to know about God, since the majority of humanity (because of physical disposition, family or civic commitments, or mere laziness)[16] would not have the means to attain it scientifically; (b) the few who would be able to reach it would only be able to do so after much time and great effort, since rational knowledge of divine things presupposes (among other things) a lengthy philosophical apprenticeship; (c) many of the truths attained would not be free from doubt, given the weakness of human reason, which often lets itself be conditioned by the imagination and, therefore, falls into falsehood and error. (Naturally, Thomas does not mean here to suggest that a well-conducted rational demonstration could yield a false conclusion, but that sometimes we can take what are actually probable or sophistical arguments as true demonstrations.)

That faith extends even to places that reason can reach by itself is, then, a divine gift that reduces the margin of doubt and error, but beyond that, it heads off philosophical elitism (of the kind that is found the *De summo bono* of Boethius of Dacia, one of the celebrated masters of the faculty of arts):

For this reason divine mercy salubriously provides that it should instruct us to hold by faith even those truths that human reason is able to investigate. In this way, everyone would easily be able to have a share in the knowledge of God, and this without uncertainty and error.[17]

With regard to the truths that transcend reason, it is obvious why they are objects of faith. Still, they have a beneficial effect on reason itself, both because they put the brakes on presumption and because, reinforcing the absolute transcendence and unknowability of the divine nature, they suggest to reason the one true way of knowing the divine essence, the negative way. Obliquely quoting Pseudo-Dionysius and Maimonides, Thomas can, in fact, state that "we only truly know God when we believe him to be beyond what man can think about him."[18]

---

16. It is interesting to note how these limitations (which, moreover, Thomas could have drawn—with some modification—from Maimonides) are later, at least in part, echoed by Dante in the opening of his *Convivio*: all men, as Aristotle states, desire by nature to know, but some do not succeed in reaching the perfection of their rational being because of impediments that are internal (bodily difficulty, unruly passions) or external (family and civil obligations, "laziness" in failing to leave a place that affords no opportunity for study).

17. *Summa contra Gentiles*, I, c. 4.

18. *Summa contra Gentiles*, I, c. 5.

On the other hand, Thomas explicitly denies, as it is sometimes assumed, that there can be a real conflict between the truth of faith and the truth of reason (falsehood is what is opposed to truth), for both derive, in the final analysis, from the same author, God, who communicates the truths of faith through revelation and has placed in our nature the possibility of certain knowledge founded on the first principles. If there are conflicts, they are only apparent, in the sense that what conflicts with the truth of faith could never be a real rational demonstration but, as we have already said, only a probable (dialectical) argument or a sophistical one. It is exactly here that we have the point of difference with the authentically Averroist position (expounded in the *Decisive Treatise*).[19] For Averroes too, as is known, there can be no real conflict between revelation and philosophy (scientific demonstration). However, the solution of apparent conflicts can occur only by taking the scientific demonstration as certain and proposing an interpretation of the sacred text that differs from its pure literal sense. As Thomas sees it, it is not the interpretation of the revealed text that must be adapted to the rational conclusion. The alleged rational demonstration, in the case of conflict, is in reality only a pseudo-demonstration, not the conclusion of apodictic or scientific syllogism; it is, rather, a purely probable or dialectical syllogism if not a pure sophism. Neither Averroes nor Thomas believes in a double truth. But, for the philosopher of Cordoba, the resolution of an apparent conflict requires hermeneutic work on the truths of faith, that is, on the revealed text (and passing from a proximate or literal translation, addressed to the vulgar, to an allegorical interpretation, reserved for those with scientific knowledge). For Thomas, the resolution requires an effort of refinement with respect to the truths of reason, an unmasking of the dialectical nature of what, at first glance, appeared scientifically incontrovertible.

We are now in a position at this point to return to the effective purpose of the work. The task of the wise man will be to concern himself with both kinds of truth and to refute the errors of those who oppose themselves to these truths. As we can see, here Thomas is reconnecting with something of which he earlier spoke at the level of theory in the *Super Boethium De Trinitate*. In this text—which is his veritable methodological manifesto—Thomas declared, as we might recall, that philosophy can be used in divine science for three different purposes: (a) to demonstrate certain preambles or presuppositions of the faith itself, such as God's existence and oneness; (b) to illustrate, by way of similitudes, certain truths of faith that are otherwise hard to express; (c) to confute what is opposed to faith, denouncing its falsehood or irrelevance.

---

19. The Latins knew similar theses through Maimonides's *Guide for the Perplexed* but did not know Averroes's book firsthand.

The *Expositio de veritate catholicae fidei—Summa contra Gentiles*—is nothing but the attempt to develop this program in a complete way:

Therefore, *to make the first kind of divine truths known*, we must proceed through *demonstrative arguments*, by which our adversary may become convinced. However, since such arguments are not available for the second kind of divine truth, our intention should not be to convince our adversary by arguments: it should be *to answer his arguments against the truth*; for, as we have shown, natural reason cannot be contrary to the truth of faith. The sole way to overcome an adversary of divine truth is from the authority of Scripture—an authority divinely confirmed by miracles. For that which is above human reason we believe only because God has revealed it. Nevertheless, *there are certain likely arguments that should be brought forth in order to make divine truth known*. This should be done for the training and consolation of the faithful, and not with any idea of refuting those who are adversaries. For the very inadequacy of the arguments would rather strengthen them in their error, since they would imagine that our acceptance of the truth of faith was based on such weak arguments.[20]

Here we find the same three basic ideas: (a) that there are truths of faith demonstrable by reason;[21] (b) that there are indemonstrable truths of faith, which can, nevertheless, be expounded through probable arguments;[22] (c) that the arguments of adversaries of the Catholic faith can be refuted.

In the *Summa contra Gentiles* the task of the wise man can at times appear twofold (expounding truth and refuting error) and not threefold, but we must not let ourselves be deceived. Since the truths are of two types, the wise man must treat each in a distinct way, demonstrating the first type and illustrating (with probable reasons and arguments from authority) the second type. If there is a problem in the long passage quoted above, it has to do with using scriptural authority to convince adversaries about indemonstrable truths. If we consider the principle articulated earlier, it is ineffectual to have recourse to Scripture when dealing with those who do not believe in it. But at this level there are no alternatives. Reason can offer only probable reasons, which are of use only to those who already believe (to help them better understand what they already believe) and which it is preferable not to use with adversaries, so as not to weaken one's position. In this case, in short, the task of the wise man is above all

20. *Summa contra Gentiles*, I, c. 9. The italics are mine.

21. These are what the *Super Boethium De Trinitate* called *praeambua fidei*, the example of which is always God's existence.

22. In the *Super Boethium* Thomas spoke of similitudes and this is substantially the same thing that he is talking about in *Summa contra Gentiles*, I, c. 8: "Human reason, in knowing the truths of faith—which can only be evident to those who see the divine substance—can gather certain similitudes of it, which are yet not sufficient to demonstrate these truths nor to comprehend them intellectually."

negative: to demonstrate the non-necessity of his adversaries' arguments so as to show the possibility of the truths of faith.

Finally, there is another small point that can be noted in regard to this re-systematization of the relationships between reason and faith. If the *Summa contra Gentiles* (to continue with the usual title) is, as we have tried to show, nothing but the actualization of what Thomas spoke of in the Commentary on the *De Trinitate*, this allows us to clarify the age-old question about whether it is to be understood as a work of theology or philosophy. Now, the three points of the program expounded in the Commentary on the *De Trinitate* explicitly regard the use of philosophical arguments in *sacra doctrina*. And this is exactly what is at issue here. Insofar as it is an exposition of the Catholic faith, the *Contra Gentiles* is certainly a theological work. But since the wise man is called to illustrate this truth and to defend it in the three distinct ways we have been discussing, it is at the same time a work of philosophy—not in the abstract but precisely according to the criteria set out by Thomas himself in the Boethian opuscule. It should not surprise us, then, if a direct confrontation—both positive and negative—with numerous philosophical positions is developed in the *Contra Gentiles* (with, for example, the *falāsifa*, considered not as Muslims but as philosophers) or if just the first chapter contains more quotations from Aristotle than from Scripture (including the epigraph mentioned earlier).

The threefold task thus outlined determines the plan itself of the work. Again, this is indicated by Thomas:

This, then, is the manner of procedure we intend to follow. We will *first seek to make known that truth which faith professes and reason investigates*. This we will do by bringing forward both demonstrative and probable arguments, some of which were drawn from the books of the philosophers and of the saints, *through which truth is strengthened and its adversary overcome* [Books I–III]. Then, in order to follow a development from the more manifest to the less manifest, we will proceed *to make known that truth which surpasses reason* [Book IV], *answering the objections of its adversaries and setting forth the truth of faith by probable arguments and by authorities*, insofar as God gives us the ability. We are aiming, then, to set out following the path of reason and to inquire into what human reason can investigate about God. In this aim the first consideration that confronts us is of that which belongs to God in himself [Book I]. The second consideration concerns the coming forth of creatures from God [Book II]. The third concerns the ordering of creatures to God as to their end [Book III].[23]

This plan takes up again in part the plan of the Commentary on the *Sentences* and in part anticipates that of the *Summa theologiae*. Once again, it is based on the circular Neo-Platonic dynamic of *abiding* (Book I: God in himself but

23. *Summa contra Gentiles*, I, c. 9. The italics are mine.

considered only from the perspective of his existence and the attributes infer-
able on analogy with creatures), *procession* (Book II: the derivation of creatures
from God and the consideration of the different creaturely orders), and *return*
(Book III: the tending of creatures toward God as end and, correspondingly, the
role of divine government and providence). This structure is, however, applied
only to the truths of faith that are also accessible to reason. Book IV, seemingly
out of place, regards the truths of faith that transcend reason. But here too, we
can see a kind of spiraling circle. The first chapters (cc. 1–26) again deal with
God in himself, yet considered from a trinitarian perspective (inaccessible to
reason); next come the treatises on the Incarnation (cc. 27–55), the sacraments
(cc. 56–78), and eschatology (cc. 79–97), which model the return, no longer
considered from a natural and rationally knowable point of view but from the
point of view of the mystery of redemption and salvation. Precisely in this last
regard we can glimpse the principal difference from the *Summa theologiae*, in
which Thomas drops the spiral structure and places the treatise on the Trinity
(relative to God in himself) in the *prima pars*. But this makes sense if we see
that the *Summa theologiae* has a more strictly theological character, whereas the
Contra Gentiles—according to the interpretation that we have proposed—has
a hybrid character (theology *and* philosophy). So, it is essential with the latter
work to keep more clearly distinct the two kinds of truth differently conceived
by reason, even at the price of splitting up the two treatises on God in himself
into two books. Furthermore, it must be born in mind that the *tertia pars* of
the *Summa theologiae* was not completed by Thomas himself and so we must
refer to the *Contra Gentiles* for the most complete treatment of sacramental and
eschatological doctrine.

God's Existence: The First Elaboration of the Ways

After the methodological preface, which has been the focus of our attention
so far (I, cc.1–9), Book I deals directly with the question of God's existence
as the first truth of faith accessible to natural reason (cc. 10–13). In this case
too, Thomas displays an absolute consistency with what he has said since his
youthful Commentary on the *Sentences* and with what will again be affirmed
in the *Summa theologiae*: God's existence is not immediately evident for us, but
neither is it something that cannot be proved with rational arguments. These
two extremes, which we must avoid, in fact, touch each other, because, for opposite reasons, both imply the superfluousness of every possible demonstration
of God's existence. It is quite likely that Thomas was influenced in his thinking
about this false alternative by the beginning of Avicenna's *Metaphysics* (although
he does not refer to it explicitly), in which it is established that God's exis-

tence is neither taken for granted (since some people doubt it) nor impossible to prove (since philosophy is able to produce arguments about it). The further problem, for Thomas, is to deal with Anselm's contention in the *Proslogion* that God's existence is self-evident because it is impossible to think of God as not existing.[24] Let us recall the essentials of the initial chapters of the *Proslogion*. God is that than which nothing greater can be thought. This is a concept of God that everyone (including the foolish) can recognize that they have in their intellect. Existing in reality is something greater (better) than existing in the intellect alone. But if God existed only in the intellect and not in reality, he would no longer be that than which nothing greater can be thought. This, of course, would contradict what has already been admitted. To Thomas's mind, the way out is already explained in the Commentary on the *Sentences*: echoing (perhaps unwittingly) Gaunilo's objection to Anselm, Thomas reduces the presumed evidence of God to a purely psychological fact, that is, to a sort of habitual belief:

This opinion arises partly from the·custom by which from their earliest days people are brought up to hear and to call upon the name of God. Custom, and especially custom in a child, comes to have the force of nature. As a result, what the mind is steeped in from childhood it clings to very firmly, as something known naturally and self-evidently.[25]

One of the reasons for this belief is the confusion—which we already know—between what is self-evident in itself, or in an absolute sense, and what is self-evident for us. Now, God's existence is self-evident in itself because God's existence is identical with his being. But we do not have access to the divine essence, and so neither are we able to grasp the self-evidence of this identity. We are also already aware of Thomas's other perplexities. Let us note only the two principal ones (which also echo objections raised by Gaunilo). First, we do not know whether "that than which nothing greater can be thought" is an adequate name or concept for God. We do not know the divine essence and, therefore, we do not have an adequate concept of it.[26] Second, even admitting that with the name "God" we intend that than which nothing greater can be thought, we would not be forced to postulate its existence outside the intellect. In fact,

24. We should note that what we call Anselm's *argument* was not always considered a real argument by the Scholastics. Postulating evidence for the existence of God is not the same as demonstrating it in a technical sense.

25. *Summa contra Gentiles*, I, c. 11.

26. If we did possess such a concept, we would not need to prove God's existence. As Gaunilo observed, we know that a concept is true and adequate when we know that it corresponds to something that exists, but to be able to recognize such an adequation or correspondence we must already know the thing as existing.

we must posit the thing and its denomination (*ratio nominis*) in the same way (in the same sphere). Conceiving with the mind (and in the mind) what is professed by the name "God," allows us to conclude only that what is conceived exists in the mind. Hence, what Anselm proposes is simply a definition relative to the *quid nominis*, to the name "God." In other words, it gives us the meaning (a possible meaning) of the name "God," but does not regard the *quid rei*, the content itself of the thing. Thus, invoking the presence of a nominal definition in the intellect does not permit us to affirm the existence of something outside the intellect itself. (As will subsequently be said—but modifying the terms of the question at least in part—it is not possible to pass from the ideal order to the real order.)

On the other hand, we should not "despair," as Avicenna said, of demonstrating God's existence. That would contradict the art itself of demonstration, which usually proceeds from effects to cause. It contradicts the order itself of the sciences, for if God's existence were scientifically indemonstrable, there would be no science of supersensible substances and physics would be the supreme science. It contradicts what many philosophers have already discovered and, finally, contradicts the famous Pauline verse according to which the invisible perfections of God can be contemplated in his works (Rm. 1:20). There is one aspect, however, that is worth considering in this regard. In the Aristotelian epistemology of the *Posterior Analytics*, to be able to proceed to the demonstration of something's existence, we must begin from the meaning of the relevant term, viz., its definition. A term's meaning corresponds to the essence, but in the case of God, we know nothing of his essence. Thomas's answer to this problem is to point out that the arguments by which God's existence is demonstrated are not *propter quid* demonstrations—demonstrations that are based on the thing's essence and proceed from the cause to what follows from it—but *quia* demonstrations, which proceed from effects to causes. Consequently, *quia* demonstrations concerning God's existence need not take the divine *essence*, but an effect, as their middle term.[27] This procedure, nevertheless, allows us to have a definition of God in relation to the effect. The fact that effects indicate their causes is sufficient for the demonstrative procedure as long as we remember that it will tell us nothing of God's essence (or of the *mode* of his existence), but only that there *exists* a cause of the effects that we can identify in reality, a cause that we call God. Let us put this more clearly: we do not possess a definition of the divine essence, and so we know nothing of what is expressed by the

27. Were we to know the divine essence, we could truly demonstrate God's existence with absolute certainty by means of a *propter quid* demonstration.

term "God." Because of this we are barred from the preferable form of demonstration, which takes its bearings from the essence of the thing (*propter quid*) and deduces what follows from it. But we do have before our eyes effects that disclose, indeed, demand the existence of their cause, that is, the pure fact that (*quia*) it exists, without telling us anything about how it is in itself. Therefore, we can content ourselves with referring the name "God" to what is required as the cause of such effects, and everything that we can say about this cause will exclusively depend on what we can analogically—and so improperly—reconstruct from the effects. We can properly know the divine essence only in the beatific vision. In the present life we can know of it only what God himself has granted us to know through revelation. Ultimately, the term "God" that is used in our demonstrations derives from an *extrinsic denomination,* and its value is solely propaedeutic or provisory. It is a name that we use (and that the philosophers above all use) to indicate the cause of the world. But God, in his essence, is something quite different (something more) than the cause of the world. If we thought otherwise, we would fall into the absurd pretense of trying to grasp God's intrinsic essence from a purely extrinsic or external relation (creation, the fact of being the cause of the world).

We must keep this distinction firmly in mind, because it establishes a definite boundary between the "God of the philosophers" and the God of revelation and makes it impossible for us to take the first—which we can know with natural reason—as if he were the second *tout court.* With this delicate distinction we can better understand Thomas's skepticism about Anselm's proof (or, better, Anselm's position). Because the definition that we can we can obtain and possess with our intellect is nominal and extrinsic, it is insufficient to guarantee the real presence of the *definitum* defined outside our intellect unless this is leveraged by what already exists outside the intellect, by finite things and by the fact that they require a cause. Having demonstrated the necessity of the existence of a cause *a posteriori*, we can attribute the name "God" to it, but only—as we should again stress—in an extrinsic and provisory way. This is why—as we will see—the five ways of the *Summa theologiae* all conclude with the same formula: "and this [namely, the uncaused term of a causal series,] is whom all call God." "God" appears only at the end of Thomas's proofs, as the predicate and as the name for something about whose essence we know nothing.

It would seem natural to postpone our presentation of the five ways until we treat of the *Summa theologiae* itself. However, it might be useful to pause here to reflect on the similarities and differences between the ways of the *Contra Gentiles* and the five ways of the other *Summa.* The first thing we might note is that there are four ways in the *Contra Gentiles.* However, if we consider the doubling of the first way, it would be possible to posit five ways. The ways proposed in the *Contra Gentiles* regard the cause of motion, the efficient cause, the causality of the maximum, and the final cause. We will limit ourselves only to noting the common mechanism, which, moreover, is already well known. What we naturally (through our senses) ascertain requires a cause. This cause is either itself uncaused and, thus, the first cause, and in that case we would already arrive at what we sought to demonstrate, or it is caused by another. But the causal series cannot be infinite, because, in consistently Aristotelian terms (*Metaphysics*, II), the infinite destroys any causal order (at least if it is a question of an essential order rather than an accidental one). So, it is necessary to stop at a first cause, whom we call "God." This mechanism is first employed with respect to motion: whatever is moved is moved by another; the latter is either an unmoved mover, which is what we were looking for, or will itself be moved by another. We continue the search until—wanting to avoid an infinite series—we come to an unmoved mover, whom we can call God. The version of this argument in the *Summa contra Gentiles* is much longer than the one in the *Summa theologiae* since Thomas spends time analyzing the two Aristotelian principles on which the demonstration rests: (a) everything that is moved is moved by another; (b) in a series of moved movers we cannot go on to infinity. It is also lengthened by the fact that Thomas adds a second line of argument (as a *secunda via ex parte motus*) in defense of the same conclusion. Like the first argument, the second also is taken from Aristotle's *Physics* (VIII, 5) and is almost a mirror image of the first, for it aims at the same result by reducing the opposed thesis (that every mover is moved) to absurdity. This thesis cannot be true *either in an accidental or in an essential sense*. It cannot be true in an accidental sense, because in that case it would be contingent and it could, thus, also happen (being something equally contingent) that no mover is moved. But, remaining with the assumption, if a mover is not moved, it does not move another (since the initial hypothesis that was to be reduced to absurdity is that every mover is moved). It could happen, then, that nothing is moved, because if nothing actually moves, nothing is moved. But this hypothesis—that is, that in some moment there is no movement—is impossible in strictly Aristotelian terms. But, logically speaking, a false impossibility never follows from a false contingency. Hence, the starting hypothesis is not true in an accidental sense. We could show the same thing much more easily by observing that when two things are conjoined in an accidental way, either could exist without the other. If, therefore, the fact of moving and the fact of being moved are only accidentally conjoined, and movement can be in something without it being a mover, then something can be a mover without being moved.

But even if the initial hypothesis is assumed to be true in itself, we would still face an absurd consequence. In fact, it would be necessary that each mover be moved either by the same species of movement by which it moves another or by a different species of movement. The first possibility is absurd, for in the same way we would be forced to say that he who teaches is also he who is taught, or that he who heals is also he who is healed, etc. With regard to the second possibility, it is enough to observe that the species of movement are finite and so we can go on infinitely. We must arrive at a first unmoved mover, which is what we intended to demonstrate.

We see, therefore, that this second line of argument is identical to the first: a first term must be posited that is not moved by another. However, it could be objected that saying that something is not moved by another is not the same as saying that it is completely immobile, because it could also be moved by itself, which is what occurs with animate beings. But certainly in this case too there would always be an immobile part that moves another part, and so an unmoved mover. It could still be objected here that in animals the soul, which is the principle of movement, is itself moved. But, for Aristotle, this happens accidentally, because animals belong to the world of generation and corruption, and it is necessary that everything that moves by itself and is corruptible be reduced to what moves by itself and is eternal. This system of motion assures the perpetuity of the generation of corruptible beings. Finally, we could ask whether we must stop at the moving part of the first being that moves itself (the first movement, that is, the first heaven in movement) or, again following Aristotle, ascend still higher to another separate mover. Now, since everything that moves itself is moved by desire, it follows that even the moving of the first being that moves itself (in the hypothesis that we are considering, the first heaven) moves by the desire of something, and this desirable object will be superior in moving, because the object of desire is an unmoved mover, while the desirer is in some way a moved mover. As is evident, Thomas follows Aristotle more or less faithfully here in supposing a plurality of celestial movers, which are reduced to a first unmoved mover only insofar as he is an object of love and desire.

None of this section is reprised in the *Summa theologiae*, either because Thomas wanted to simplify or because it is too much bound up with the hypothesis of a plurality of movers. In any event, after having articulated the bipartite first way *ex parte motus*, Thomas feels the need in the *Contra Gentiles* to eliminate any perplexity about two other presuppositions typical of the Aristotelian position that are not perfectly compatible with the Christian position. One of these is the thesis about the animation of the heavens, which supports the hypothesis that the first being in motion (the first movement) moves itself, moves spontaneously. But, as Thomas observes, the question is, in fact, irrelevant, for if it is not conceded that the first movement (or the other celestial spheres) moves itself, it must immediately be admitted that it is moved by the first unmoved mover, and the conclusion aimed at is arrived at much sooner. The other presupposition must be dealt with more delicately. It is clear that Thomas is perfectly conscious that the Aristotelian proof *ex parte motus* rests on the assumption of the world's eternity. Precisely because motion is eternal, there is need of a first unmoved mover that is always in act. For Thomas, however, the difficulty can be reversed and transform itself into an *ad abundantiam* element in favor of the strength of the proof. With the hypothesis of the eternity of the world, God's existence appears less evident. If it is believed, as Christian faith teaches, that the world and motion have a beginning, it is obvious that a cause of their production must be posited, for nothing brings itself from potency to act, or from not being to being. This is, in any case, a good example of the way in which Thomas makes use of Aristotle. The whole argument *ex parte motus*, as we have seen, faithfully follows the Aristotelian path (whether of the *Physics* or of the *Metaphysics*), although it sacrifices the element on which Aristotle built his proof and on which everything seems ultimately to rest (the eternity of motion). But it is a sacrifice that must be understood in its proper measure. We will see that the eternity of the world is not a dramatic problem for Thomas, because creation can easily be maintained even if it is deprived of its temporal connotation. There is no contradiction between createdness and eternality, as Thomas will clearly say, and so the hypothesis of an eternal but created world must not be rejected *a priori*. It cannot be rationally demonstrated, but then neither can the Christian belief in a creation in time. The careful formula introduced at the end of the argument *ex parte motus* in the *Contra Gentiles* shows that this undecidability does not in any way compromise the validity of the argument itself. What Aristotle assigned to the eternal world holds equally—indeed more so—for a world created in time.

The other ways anticipate in order the second, fourth, and fifth ways of the *Summa theologiae*. We will, therefore, touch on them only briefly.

1. We cannot go on to infinity in efficient causes, and so it is necessary to come to a first cause, which we call God. Thomas takes this proof too from Aristotle, from *Metaphysics*, II. And yet some doubts can be raised about the actual presence of the idea of efficient causality in Aristotle, since Thomas is aware in other places—as was his master Albert the Great—that efficient causality in the strict sense is a discovery of Avicenna. It was Avicenna who first separated the cause of change of which Aristotle spoke, that is, a physical cause

(the cause of motion), from a metaphysical cause (the efficient cause that brings something into being).

2. Again in *Metaphysics*, II, Aristotle states that things have as much being as they do truth (on account of the convertibility of transcendentals, with which we are already acquainted). Now, there is something that is maximally true (*Metaphysics*, IV), on the basis of which we judge things to be more or less true, and therefore, because of the convertibility we discussed earlier, this thing will also maximally exist, and this is what we call God. In the *Summa theologiae* Thomas will reformulate the argument, making it rest more directly upon the delicate Aristotelian principle of the causality of the maximum.

3. The last way can be derived, according to Thomas, from John Damascene (but also from Averroes's commentary on *Physics*, II). Things, even discordant ones, seem to come together in a single order, and this is possible only if it is admitted that there is a higher arrangement of things by someone who has assigned to all things a tendency toward a determinate end. In the world it occurs that even contrary and discordant things concur in the realization of a single order, and not by chance but always or for the most part. We must concede, then, that someone exists who arranges and rules the world by his providence and whom we call God.

Summing up, we can say that there are five ways both in the *Contra Gentiles* and in the *Summa theologiae,* but the grids that are applied are not exactly the same. What is presented in the *Summa theologiae* as the first way is divided into two ways in the *Contra Gentiles.* Three of the ways are more or less the same. Only the third way of the *Summa theologiae* seems to be absent from the *Contra Gentiles.* We say "seems" because, in reality, it can be found in this text, only it is not in the place where we would expect to find it, that is, among the arguments for God's existence. Thomas uses it instead in a discussion of God's eternity (I, c. 15). This is the "modal" way formulated by Avicenna and adopted by Maimonides. We see that in the world things can be or not be, but that which is indifferent with respect to these two possibilities needs a cause in order for it to exist (otherwise, because it is indifferent, it would be unable by itself to bring itself into existence or determine itself in existence). But, once again, in the series of causes we cannot proceed to infinity. Thus, we must posit a necessary being that is the cause of possible beings. Is this necessary being necessary *in virtue of another* or *in itself?* If the latter, then we have already arrived at what we were looking for, namely, the existence of a necessary cause. If the former, all we need to show to get to where we want to go is that it is not possible for there to be an infinite series of beings whose necessity comes from another. Curiously, though, as we have noted, Thomas transposes this argument in another place, using it only to show that God is eternal (God is a being necessary through himself and everything that is necessary in this way is eternal). But the conclusion could be debated because Thomas seems here to stick to a purely temporal or statistical interpretation of modality and does not (more correctly) employ a counterfactual, in which the modality would be freed from any temporal reference. (What is necessary is the thing whose counterfactual is impossible in the same instant in which the counterfactual is considered). It is true that the counterfactual criterion will begin to impose itself only with Duns Scotus, but it is also true that Thomas seems to reject a merely *statistical* or "frequency" approach to modality in his Commentary on the *De Interpretatione*.[28] In the *Summa theologiae* this argument will be placed more correctly among the five ways. And in this case too the argument is of philosophical origin. So, we have three proofs taken from Aristotle (even if two of them—those taken more or less from *Metaphysics*, II—are not used by Aristotle himself as possible proofs for God's existence or for the existence of a first unmoved mover), one from Avicenna and Maimonides (although the debt is not expressly acknowledged), and one from John Damascene and Averroes. The only source that is not strictly philosophical, then, is Damascene. But if we return to what we said earlier—that is, that this work regards what can be known of God by natural reason—this preponderance of philosophical sources for proofs of God's existence is by no means strange. On the contrary, it is completely natural if not, in perspective of the work, almost necessary.

The Negative Way

Between the arguments for God's existence (I, c. 13) and what figures in the *Contra Gentiles* as a proof for divine eternity (I, c. 15)—but will be refashioned in the *Summa theologiae* as an argument for God's existence—Thomas inserts an essential chapter on the negative way as the best cognitive approach to God (I, c. 14). There is nothing random about Thomas's positioning of this text. As has been noted several times, God's existence is among those truths that can be known by natural reason, and we have seen how the arguments that Thomas uses are almost all taken exclusively from philosophers. Now a further step is being taken to consider the divine properties (but not the divine essence in itself). In this area too natural reason has a right to speak, because there are many properties that can be attributed to God analogically even apart from revelation (and we know that Thomas reserves Book IV for that which can be known only by revelation), but how this is done must be clarified from the start. It is not a

28. See pp. 322–29 below.

matter of positively saying what God is but of gradually making more precise what he is not. The passage is worth quoting:

We have shown that there exists a first being, whom we call God. We must, accordingly, now investigate the properties of this being. Now, in considering the divine substance, we should especially make use of the method of remotion. For, by its immensity, the divine substance surpasses every form that our intellect reaches. Thus we are unable to apprehend it by knowing what it is. Yet we are able to have some knowledge of it by knowing what it is not. Furthermore, we approach nearer to a knowledge of God according as through our intellect we are able to remove more and more things from him.[29]

To know a thing perfectly we must place it in its genus and individuate it by its constitutive differences, that is, the differences that distinguish one nature from the others within a genus. But in the case of God, both things are impossible. God, in fact, is not in a genus (we will see how Thomas understands this divine excess in an ever more radical way), nor does he possess constitutive differences. We can, however, make use of negative differences, gradually excluding a whole series of determinations so as progressively to restrict the field. Saying, for example, that God is not an accident, we distinguish him from all accidents, and saying that he is not a body, we distinguish him from all corporeal substances, and so on. In this way we can develop a more appropriate approach to the divine nature, recognizing it as different from all the other things that we know. But obviously such a knowledge could not, in principle, be perfect, because it does not touch on what God is in himself. This is, in effect, the program that Thomas tries to develop in Book I, progressively establishing that God is not mutable (cc. 15–17), or composite (cc. 18–22), and so is without accidents (c. 23), cannot be determined by substantial differences (c. 24), is not in a genus (c. 25), is not the formal being of things (c. 26, against the so-called formal pantheism of Amaury de Bene), nor, obviously, the form of a body (c. 27). Beginning with c. 28, Thomas, however, begins to draw the thread of these negative premises, moving on to a more direct examination of the properties that can be positively deduced, starting with perfections (c. 28). Not by chance there follows a methodological interlude (cc. 29–36) in which Thomas reprises the discussion of the likenesses of God that can be found in creatures and, consequently, the possibility of adopting in an appropriate way in reference to God, the names that can be taken from creatures themselves. As we know, Thomas rejects both the thesis of univocity and that of equivocity, preferring that of analogy. Here Thomas again takes up the distinction between the order of analogy in which several terms are said in reference to a single reality distinct from them (as the term "healthy" is said al-

29. *Summa contra Gentiles*, I, c. 14.

ways in reference to health whether it be of the living body or medicine, food, or urine) and the order of analogy in which two things are not referred to a third distinct thing, but to one of the two according to a precise order of priority and posteriority (*per prius et posterius*): "being" is said of substance and accident insofar as the latter is said in relation to the former and not because both substance and accident refer to some third thing distinct from them. The names that refer analogically to God and creatures—as we saw in Chapter 1 of our book—are *not* of the first sort (because in that case, as is evident, it would happen that God would be in relation to something prior and superior to him) but of the second. Still, it must be pointed out that in the order of priority and posteriority there can on occasion be a discrepancy between reality and knowledge. We can know first what in reality is later or posterior. This is precisely the case with the divine names. We come to knowledge of God through things, and inasmuch as the perfection signified by the terms is found first in God and then in creatures (since God is the cause of creatures and every perfection is in creatures only as caused by God), the signification itself, or better, the term itself is referred first to creatures and then to the creator. And this is the sense in which it is said that God is named from his effects. The rest of Book I develops the theology of the divine names, examining God's goodness (cc. 37–42), oneness (c. 42), infinity (c. 43), intelligence (cc. 44–71), will (cc. 72–87), free will (c. 88), passions and virtues (cc. 89–96),[30] life (cc. 97–99) and happiness (cc. 100–102). With all of this, the thing that we must keep most before our minds, with respect to the philosophical angle, is Thomas's decision—quite fundamentally Neo-Platonic—in regard to negative theology. Thomas's negative theology is filtered above all through Pseudo-Dionysius and Maimonides—an influence that there has at times been an attempt to minimize.[31] It is odd that common opinion finds it difficult to associate with Thomas the image of a proponent of negative theology. But Thomas himself always left very little doubt in this regard, and the declarations of his intentions should perhaps be taken seriously.[32] The equivocation comes from the fact that—as an effect of much later discussions (modern and not medieval

---

30. In fact, every effective passion must be excluded from God, even if there are passions that—although they cannot belong to God inasmuch as they are passions—do not imply in their specific content any incompatibility with the divine nature (joy and love, for instance).

31. On the presence of Maimonides in Thomas, see A. Wohlman, *Thomas d'Aquin et Maïmonide: Un dialogue exemplaire* (Paris: Cerf, 1988), and above all R. Imbach, "Alcune precisazioni sulla presenza di Maimonide in Tommaso d'Aquino," *Studi* 2 (1995): 48–63, and "'Ut ait Rabbi Moyses': Maimonidische Philosopheme bei Thomas von Aquin und Meister Eckhart," *Collectanea Franciscana* 60 (1990): 99–115 (now in *Quodlibeta: Ausgewählte Artikel/Articles choisis*, ed. F. Cheneval, T. Ricklin, C. Pottier, S. Maspoli, and M. Mosch (Freiburg-Switzerland: Universitatsverlag, Freiburg, 1996).

32. The most recent and complete discussion of this topic is T.-D. Humbrecht, *Théologie négative*

ones)—negative theology was removed from its original philosophical context (which was above all Proclean) and seen as mysticism or irrationalism. We must, however, attend to the fact that almost all of the great Scholastic masters opt for negative theology—and Thomas is certainly not the least of them—without ceding anything to irrationalism. The audacity of Scholasticism has nothing to do with what they will be scolded for in the debates during the Reformation— wanting to reduce faith and all knowledge of God to a completely rational system—but in the fact that we must not give up on reason once God's transcendence of human cognitive possibilities and the superiority of the negative way to the positive way are acknowledged. Thomas's great *Summae* must be read in this perspective. They do not pretend to systematize—or worse, to sum up—what God is, but they recognize the ultimate unknowability of the divine essence, without allowing this to become a kind of laziness or sacrifice of the intellect.

A Delicate Question at the Boundary between Psychology and Theology: The Change of Perspective regarding the Word

In the course of the *Summa contra Gentiles,* Thomas reaffirms many of the things that we have already considered in the *De veritate* concerning the divine knowledge and will, things we will limit ourselves here merely to restating. In regard to the intellect, Thomas reaffirms, for example, that God's knowledge includes individuals, non-existing things, future contingents, possibles, infinite things, and evil. Special mention should be made, however, of cc. 53–54, which underwent several redactions. Now c. 53, as we already suggested, is probably the last chapter that Thomas wrote in Paris before his return to Italy. He seems to have come back to this chapter in 1264, when he was working on c. 11 of Book IV.[33] The reason for these changes has to do not with the main content of the chapter—there is no doubt that, in Thomas's view, God's knowledge does not imply multiplicity in the divine essence—but with the way of relating the divine and human intellects, and in particular the function of what is con-

et noms divins chez Saint Thomas d'Aquin, Bibliotheque thomiste 57 (Paris: Vrin, 2005). Humbrecht, however, seems overly cautious in ascribing to Thomas a fundamental option for negative theology (perhaps since the latter phrase is understood in a specific way which includes also contemporary critical philosophy and Western metaphysics), preferring rather to speak of a propensity for the negative "way." However, we do agree that the expressions "negative theology" and "divine names" are closely connected, forming a hendiadys: as we have seen, Thomas's negative approach always implies a theology of the divine names.

33. On this topic, see L.-B. Geiger, "Les rédactions successives de Contra Gentiles I, 53 d'après l'autographe," in *Saint Thomas d'Aquin aujourd'hui*, Recherches de philosophie 6, ed. J. Y. Jolif, et al. (Paris: Desclée de Brouwer, 1963), 221–40.

ceived by the intellect at the conclusion of the cognitive act, viz., the word. In the final draft Thomas distinguishes more clearly—with respect to the human intellect—between the role of the intelligible species, obtained by abstraction from phantasms (sensible species), and that of the *intentio intellecta*, which the intellect produces to express the definition of the thing that is known. Both are representations or likenesses of the thing known, but the first, the intelligible species, functions as the *beginning* of the cognitive act, and the second (which permits the intellect to think of a thing even when the thing is absent) functions as the *terminus*.[34] But matters are different with the divine intellect, because it knows, not through the mediation of a species, but through its own essence, which is the *likeness* of all things. Consequently, what is conceived by the divine intellect too—that is, its word (although we should write "Word," as we will do henceforth)—is not merely a likeness of God but a likeness of all the things that are, in their turn, likenesses of the divine essence (it is, so to say, a representation of all possible representations). In other words, God intends everything through a single cognitive act (the very divine essence, which functions in God in the way that intelligible species function in us) and a single concept or cognitive terminus, his Word.[35] A passage of what appears to be the second draft merits careful attention, because in this case Thomas, in order to defend the absolute unicity and simplicity of the divine intellect—as was partly anticipated in the preceding chapter—explicitly abandons the doctrine of ideas:

A thing is not said to be thought because it is something through which the action of the intellect passes but because its likeness is in him who thinks. It is not necessary, therefore, in order for God to think a multiplicity, to posit intelligible forms that are almost divine thoughts—whether in the divine intellect itself, or subsisting apart, as Plato proposed, or in other intellects, as others proposed. Instead, for God to know a multiplicity, it is enough that God by his essence be like many things.[36]

Thomas does not limit himself here to disqualifying the Platonic solution or ones that would place the ideal content in another intelligence,[37] but he asks himself

34. It is no accident that Thomas defines *intentio intellecta* in *SCG* IV, c. II, whose redaction seems precisely contemporary with the final revision of Book I, c. 53: "Dico autem intentionem intellectam id quod intellectus in seipso concipit de re intellecta" (Leonine edition, vol. III, 265n3466).

35. See G. Pini, "Henry of Ghent's Doctrine of *Verbum* in Its Theological Context," in *Henry of Ghent and the Transformation of Scholastic Thought: Studies in Memory of Jos Decorte*, Ancient and Medieval Philosophy, Series 1, ed. G. Guldentops and C. Steel (Leuven: Leuven University Press, 2003), 307–26.

36. *SCG*, I, c. 53 (Leonine edition), *Appendix ad I et II librum Summae S. Thomae de Aquino contra Gentiles*, p. 21*a; in the Marietti edition this passage can be read in *Appendix II* of the second volume (*Tabula fragmentorum quae ad I et II librum pertinent*), p. 323b.

37. The latter solutions could be Neo-Platonic or Avicennian. They would be Neo-Platonic if the

whether a plurality of ideas in the same divine essence might compromise its simplicity. And this perhaps partly explains why in the next chapter (c. 54), which we already noted in our discussion of the *De veritate*, Thomas shows a reluctance to employ the term "idea," which appears only at the end and in reference to the Platonic doctrine.[38] If we look also in this case at the passages that are suppressed in the autograph, it is easy to see how the original draft continued to speak of the ideas as God's thoughts without mentioning the Word.[39] Thomas, as we already know, prefers in the subsequent redaction principally to use the term *rationes*, and to explain that these exemplary reasons are not so much originally distinct content (for the first and original content of God's knowledge remains his own essence) but distinct ways in which God knows himself to be differently imitable by different creatures:

The divine intellect, therefore, can comprehend in his essence that which is proper to each thing by understanding wherein the divine essence is being imitated and wherein each thing falls short of its perfection. Thus, by understanding his essence as imitable in the mode of life and not of knowledge, God has the proper form of a plant; and if he knows his essence as imitable in the mode of knowledge and not of intellect, God has the proper form of animal, and so forth. Thus, it is clear that, being absolutely perfect, the divine essence can be taken as the proper exemplar of individuals. Through it, therefore, God can have a proper knowledge of all things.[40]

Some years later, it would be Henry of Ghent (usually considered an adversary of Thomas) who would give a definitive shape to this doctrine, distinguishing in divine knowledge between a primary object—the divine essence in itself—and a secondary object—the divine essence as imitable by creatures—and then subdividing the secondary object (a) according to its unitary root, still in the divine essence, and (b) according to the perspective of the different forms of imitability, which coincide at this level with the multiple created essences. It will not escape our notice, in any case, how already in Thomas the insistence on the relationship of imitability and the reworking of the function of the Word almost completely eliminates the implicit danger in the doctrine of the ideas as it was reprised by Christian Neo-Platonism—the danger of compromising the

---

ideal content is referred to *noûs* and Avicennian if it is referred to the system of separate intelligences, and in particular the *dator formarum*.

38. *SCG*, I, c. 54. "This conclusion likewise saves to some extent the opinion of Plato and his doctrine of Ideas, according to which would be formed everything that is found among material things."

39. *SCG*, I, c. 54 (Leonine edition), *Appendix ad Ium et IIum librum Summae S. Thomae de Aquino contra Gentiles*, p. 21*b: "Ex his ... videri potest ... (qualiter) in divina mente omnium formae vel rationes ... esse possint absque aliqua intellectus divini compositione. Sunt enim in ea ut intellecta in intelligente."

40. *Summa contra Gentiles*, I, c. 54.

simplicity of God's knowledge and essence (a danger, as it is fitting to note, that is foreign to pagan Neo-Platonism to the extent that it situated the exemplars outside the One). Distinguishing in general between the roles of the intelligible species (which informs the intellect, making thought possible) and of the concept or word (which is known and, therefore, is the object of thought), Thomas can already, in sum, isolate two distinct levels: (a) that of the divine essence in itself, which functions almost as a species, is identical with the divine intellect, and is absolutely simple, and (b) that of the essence as known (= Word), in which the multiplicity of *rationes ideales*, as possible relationships of imitability, is rooted.

However, this adjustment is not determined only—according to what we have already seen—by the desire to avoid the Platonizing language of "ideas." It also reflects a substantial modification that, over the years, Thomas brought about in his doctrine of the Word. We find ourselves here before one of the issues in his work on which Thomas radically changed his mind. The problem is actually theological in nature, but it inevitably encroaches on the theory of knowledge. The doctrine of the Word is an Augustinian legacy. In *De Trinitate*, XV Augustine posits the generation of the Son as parallel to the process of thought. When we think of something we produce an interior word, which, of course, is to be distinguished from the word that we utter. The spoken word *signifies* the interior word, which belongs to the domain of mental language. When Thomas deals with this doctrine for the first time in Book I of his Commentary on the *Sentences*, he tries (like other masters of that period) to adapt the Augustinian schema to the psychology and gnoseology derived from Aristotle. The basic difficulty is that the Augustinian theory of the *verbum* invests the intellect with an active role (the intellect generates the word), whereas the Aristotelian theory assigns to the intellect a primarily passive role in relation to its contents, in line with what occurs at the sensible level. (Aristotle taught, in effect, that thinking is in some way undergoing or enduring.) Moreover, in the Augustinian sense the *verbum* is the product of the mind and differs from it. In Aristotle the process of thinking does not produce anything different from thinking (for thinking is an intentional assimilation in which the intellect itself becomes all things), but receives something, and that is typical of any act of intellection. Precisely this difference might create problems at a theological level: for Augustine, it is obvious that only the Son can be defined as the *Verbum*, and it is a term that, thus, has a sense that is personal and not essential (inasmuch as it is referred only to the generation of the second person of the Trinity by the Father). But if the *verbum* is understood to be produced in any act of intellection, then the term would have an essential sense, because the other persons of the Trinity, and not only the Father, know and conceive themselves and the others.

This exact problem was presented when Thomas commented on Book I of the *Sentences*: the *verbum* is the *notitia* or concept that is generated in the mind when it thinks something. But since in the mind there are two elements—the intelligible species impressed on the possible intellect and the act of intellection—the *verbum* will be the one or the other (Thomas, in that text, does not further specify). Nevertheless, these are elements that are present whenever an act of knowledge occurs. Why, then, is it only the generation of the Son that is the origin of the Word? Why do the Son and the Holy Spirit not also produce a word when they know themselves? From here arises the question about whether the word is meant personally or essentially, which brings to the fore the contrast between *verbum* understood in an Augustinian way as something that is produced, and *verbum* understood as synonymous with intelligible *species* or with any act of intellection, as something that is not *produced* in the strict sense, which does not differ from the intellect, and because of this is found in each one of its acts.

Thomas tries to resolve the problem by distinguishing between the personal and essential senses. In the personal sense *Verbum* indicates a real relation with regard to the one who produces it, and this acceptation applies only to the Son. In the essential sense *verbum* indicates a mere relation of reason between the one who produces it and the product, and in this sense it is also said in reference to the acts by which the Son and the Holy Spirit know themselves. Hence, only the Father produces a *Verbum*, which really differs from himself, while the essential sense substantially coincides with the valence that the word assumes in the human process of knowing. Put differently, in the Commentary on the *Sentences*, the principal sense of *verbum* seems to be, at least implicitly, the essential sense, whereas the personal sense is more of an exception, a unique case. But already in *De veritate*, q. 4, Thomas changes his way of understanding *verbum*, moving closer to Augustinian psychology: *verbum* is a concept that is produced, it is what the intellect thinks, and it is something distinct from the intellect itself. So, in regard to the divine persons as well, *Verbum* is what is known, something produced and distinct. The Son himself and the Holy Spirit do not produce something different and, therefore, do not produce a word. *Contra Gentiles*, I, c. 53, with the consequences that trail behind it, reflects this transformation. As we have seen, *verbum* is made to coincide with the *intentio intellecta*, and so with what is known in the mind, and it is something different both from the intelligible species and from the act of intellection. Furthermore, the intellect produces a *verbum* both in the first operation—simple apprehension (in this case, *verbum* is the definition that expresses the things known)—and in the second operation—the intellect composing and dividing (in this case, *verbum* is the mental proposition that is composition or division).

Apart from epistemological motivations, quite evident in the background is the theological worry about having admitted an essential sense of *verbum* alongside the personal sense, and having subordinated the second to the first (with the danger of making the generation of the Son by the Father an essential operation rather than a personal one). In the *Summa theologiae* Thomas will ultimately explain that it is true that the *verbum* is a product but that there is a difference between *dicere* and *intelligere*. Only the Son is said by the Father, whereas the Son and the Spirit think themselves without, thus, producing a distinct *verbum*.

It can be debated whether this resystematization truly resolves the problem of how we can reconcile the fact that every act of intellection terminates in a *verbum* with the fact that, in the trinitarian sphere, only the operation of the Father generates the Word. But at least the relationship between the two cases is reversed vis-à-vis the Commentary on the *Sentences*. The case of generation is in accord with what commonly occurs in human knowing (or better, human knowing reflects what occurs in the generation of the Son), while the operations of the Son and the Holy Spirit become the exceptions since they do not produce a word. In this way Thomas avoids making generation an essential operation (in which the Son would then be generated not only by the Father but also by the Holy Spirit and himself) and not a personal one, which would hardly be an orthodox position. It is not by accident that the thesis according to which the word is essentially said in the Trinity was solemnly anathematized in Paris by the masters of theology between 1271 and 1272 during the *inceptio* of Cantor of Perona. This is reported by Roger Marston in one of his questions, and he adds that his master—the Franciscan John Peckham—and Thomas Aquinas were present at the disputation.[41] This event has often been misinterpreted (sometimes because at that time Peckham had begun his anti-Thomist campaign), with it being suggested that Peckham had been the accuser and Thomas among the accused. This reconstruction is, strictly speaking, inexact since Thomas was present at the disputation as one of the masters who promulgated the condemnation and not as one of the condemned. Nevertheless, it is undeniable that—the repeated Neo-Thomist protestations to the contrary notwithstanding—the condemnation struck a doctrine that Thomas himself had defended in the past, indeed, a doctrine of which he was perhaps the most

---

41. See Rogerus Marston, "Quaestiones de emanatione aeterna, q. 6," in *Quaestiones disputatae De emanatione aeterna, De statu naturae lapsae, et De anima*, Bibliotheca Franciscana Scholastica Medii Aevi 7 (Florence: Quaracchi, 1932), 116–17.

authoritative expositor. This episode is, therefore, instructive in many ways. It helps us to understand at least some of the reasons why in the later 1250s and mid-1260s Thomas revised cc. 53 and 54 several times. It also introduces us to the climate of Thomas's second Parisian regency. Finally, it shows us that Thomas himself was not always perceived by his contemporaries as a champion of orthodoxy and that his philosophical attitude—including in theology—was not always measured, conciliatory, and irenic.

The Existence of Formally Necessary Creatures

We will also limit ourselves to considering just a few elements of the treatment of the divine will in the *Contra Gentiles*. God's will is his essence itself (I, c. 73). God principally wills himself, his essence itself. Willing himself, God wills other things with the same act. God also wills things that are not now existing. God wills his own being and goodness by necessity but does not will other things with the same necessity. Here we find a topic that we will rediscover in the questions of the *De potentia*, and that is it that in God there is a fundamental asymmetry—essential to Christian creationism—between knowledge and will. God *knows with necessity* all things but does not *will by necessity* all things (or, as Thomas will say in the *De potentia*, God is omniscient but not omnivolent). The reason for this asymmetry is that knowledge requires that the *subject* have a determinate disposition, whereas will requires that the *thing willed* (the *object*) have a determinate disposition. In fact, a thing is willed either because it is the end or because it is ordered to the end. Now, divine perfection entails that God have a disposition such that all things be known by him, whereas goodness does not entail the existence of other things as if these things were an end to which the divine will would be subordinated. Thus, God knows all things that can or would be ordained in some way to his essence, but does not will all things that can or would be ordained to his goodness (I, c. 81).

This allows Thomas to explain that the divine will, although immutable, does not take away contingency from things by making them inevitably necessary. The explanation is very simple: *some things maintain their contingency because God wills them to be contingent.* The efficaciousness of the divine will makes it so that not only does what God wills exist, but also it exists in the way God wills it. In other words, it is the very perfection of the universe that demands that contingent things exist, for otherwise there would not be in the universe all of the grades of being. Furthermore, the divine causality is explicated through the system of secondary causes, which are mutable. So, even though the remote cause is necessary, if the proximate cause is contingent, the effects too will be contingent. In fine, God wills the things not by absolute necessity but by a hypothetical or conditional necessity. *If* God wills something, it will necessarily come about. This is the classical Boethian model. To use the same example that Thomas uses in this context, if Socrates runs, it is necessary that he runs, but this does not mean that it is intrinsically necessary that he runs. Similarly, *if and only if* God wills something, it will necessarily come about, but the intrinsic contingency of the thing will not thereby be compromised.

It should be noted how this attempt at a modal explanation brings Thomas near to Avicenna (things contingent in themselves are made necessary by the relationship with their cause), while the real point is that contingency is preserved in the world by the simple fact that God wills it thus. We can, therefore, underscore a fundamental aspect, and that is that in Thomas's thought the contingency of the world—despite the rhetoric expended on this point by the majority of twentieth-century Neo-Thomists—is little more than a false problem. For Thomas, it is fundamental to make it clear that *God does not act by necessity*. But that God's effects are in themselves either necessary or contingent is, all told, of little importance. Surprising as it may seem, Thomas sees no contradiction in principle between the creaturely condition and necessary existence. In other words, intrinsically necessary creatures are thinkable, and, indeed, as Thomas himself forcefully states:

Although all things depend on the will of God as first cause, who is subject to no necessity in his operation except on the supposition of his intention, nevertheless absolute necessity is not on this account excluded from things, so as to compel us to say that all things are contingent.[42]

We would have an entirely false image of Thomas's universe if we did not take account of the fact that certain necessary beings *other than* God exist in it, placed there by God himself. The list of these beings is quickly drawn up. It first contains those beings that lack the potentiality of matter, either because they are completely without matter (as in the case of angels) or because the matter is perfectly actualized by the substantial form such that it is not subject to any corruption but only to change of place, that is, locomotion (as in the case of celestial bodies). The most philosophically interesting aspect of this position is that the necessity of these beings is, to be sure, willed by God but, nevertheless, pertains to their own nature. In the angels and in the celestial bodies there is no potentiality to non-being, which is the same as saying that they are intrinsically necessary. To be more explicit: certain creatures in Thomas's universe (the most noble according to the peripatetic tradition), once created do not at all tend toward non-being. Of course, God retains in principle the possibility of reducing

42. *Summa contra Gentiles*, II, c. 30.

them to nothing, but this possibility of annihilation is not to be understood in a passive sense (it does not pertain to these creatures in themselves, since they are necessary in a simple and absolute sense), but only as an active power on the side of God. Because this interpretation is often the object of disagreement, it is perhaps preferable to let Thomas speak for himself: he, with characteristic foresight, replied to an objection of this sort.

Those things in which there is no possibility of not being exist of necessity in the full and absolute sense. Now, some things are so created by God that there is in their nature a potentiality to non-being; and this results from the fact that the matter present in them is in potentiality with respect to another form. On the other hand, neither immaterial things, nor things whose matter is not receptive of another form, have potentiality to non-being, so that their being is absolutely and simply necessary. Now, if it be said that whatever is from nothing of itself tends toward nothing, so that in all creatures there is the power not to be—this clearly does not follow. For created things are said to tend to nothing in the same way in which they are from nothing, namely, not otherwise than according to the power of their efficient cause. In this sense, then, the power not to be does not exist in created things. But in the creator there is the power to give them being, or to cease pouring forth being into them, for he produces things not by a necessity of his nature, but by his will, as we have shown.[43]

From the strictly philosophical point of view, we could draw attention to at least four implications, at different levels, of this position.

First—at the most elementary and least specialized level—we can make a clean sweep of the common view that the whole of Scholastic thought is pervaded by the idea of the precariousness of creaturely being. In truth, this holds only for some theologians, mainly those of an Augustinian bent. For many others, and certainly for Thomas, the created world is quite solid and stable and even includes within it intrinsically necessary creatures.

Second, it would be possible to cast more than one doubt on a certain standard interpretation proposed by twentieth-century Thomists, according to which the distinction between being and essence and Thomas's emphasis on the act of being served him to underscore creaturely contingency—as a result of

---

43. *Summa contra Gentiles*, II, c. 30. Thomas returns to the same principle in c. 55 in a discussion of the incorruptibility of intellectual substances: "Now, intellectual substances could not begin to be except by the potency of the first agent, since, as we have shown, they are not made out of a matter that could have existed antecedently to them. Hence, there is no potency with respect to their non-being except in the first agent, inasmuch as it lies within his power not to pour being into them. But nothing can be said to be corruptible with respect to this potency alone; and for two reasons: because things are said to be necessary and contingent according to a potentiality that is in them, and not according to the power of God, as we have already shown, and also because God, who is the Author of nature, does not take from things that which is proper to their natures; and we have just shown that it is proper to intellectual natures to exist forever, and that is why God will not take this property from them."

creatio ex nihilo—with respect to divine necessity. Now, as we have already seen, and as we will briefly return to later, the distinction between being and essence is introduced by Thomas above all in regard to simple creatures, and if it is likewise undeniable that their being is considered necessary on account of their nature itself, it is legitimate to suspect that Thomas uses the distinction between being and essence for other reasons, ones that have little to do with contingency. Indeed, to be more explicit: that the distinction between being and essence should have something to do with creaturely contingency is characteristic of the debate that developed after Thomas's death and is in particular a very precise theoretical decision of Giles of Rome.

Third, the existence of intrinsically necessary—or, to use Scholastic language, formally necessary—creatures, forces us to think that the difference between creator and creatures cannot be reduced to that between what is necessary and what is contingent, but must be located at another, more sophisticated level. Here we approach what is *the real heart of Thomistic metaphysics*, which we will address when we examine the Commentary on the *De causis*.

Fourth, this point—about necessary created beings—allows us to think with greater precision about the relationship between Thomas and Avicenna. We cannot rest content here with sublime pleasantries, which are often met with even in the most authoritative *theological* reconstructions of Thomas's thought. According to one such reconstruction, Thomas decisively distanced himself from the blind necessitarianism and emanationism of Avicenna. In fact, any careful reader of Avicenna—and Thomas was much more than careful—knows perfectly well that in Avicenna too the production of being by the first cause is anything but necessary and unconscious. The divide between the two thinkers lies elsewhere and consists in a rethinking of the bipartite structure that Avicenna placed at the basis of his theory of flow: everything, with the exception of the first cause, is possible in itself and necessary for another. This oxymoron (according to which everything is at the same time—but in different respects—both possible and necessary) Thomas casts off by holding on to the second part (things can very well be necessary *ex alio*) and dropping the first (things constituted by another as necessary in themselves are necessary and not possible). We will encounter this issue again in the *De potentia*. For now it will be sufficient to note how the disagreement with Avicenna consists not so much in the theoretical gesture with which it is normally identified—viz., the rejection of necessitarianism—as in another one that is certainly unexpected—in the rejection of the thesis of the intrinsic possibility of any being other than the first being.[44] For Thomas, the

44. It would be interesting to consider the influence exercised by Averroes here.

existence of creatures that are formally and intrinsically necessary is a demonstration of God's perfection:

It pertains to God's perfection to have placed his own likeness upon created things, excluding only beings incompatible with the nature of created being; for it belongs to the perfect agent to produce its like as far as possible. But to be simply necessary is not incompatible with the notion of created being; for nothing prevents a thing being necessary whose necessity nevertheless has a cause, as in the case of the conclusions of demonstrations. Hence, nothing prevents certain things being produced by God in such fashion that they exist in a simply necessary way; indeed, this attests to God's perfection.[45]

One might object that the admission of creatures that are formally necessary seems to nullify the validity of what will be the third way of the *Summa theologiae* and that we have seen in the *Contra Gentiles* as an argument in favor of divine eternity. But in the third way, as in the argument in the *Contra Gentiles* (I, c. 15), Thomas simply affirms that it is not possible to proceed to infinity in the series of causes that are necessary *ex alio*, and that it is therefore necessary to arrive at a first cause that is necessary in itself.

We must be careful: the production of things by God is by no means necessary (or, rather, it is only hypothetically or conditionally necessary), but this does not mean that God cannot choose to create beings that are formally and intrinsically necessary (necessary in their nature), and that such beings constitute, in effect, the apex of the hierarchy of creation. We cannot but conclude that Thomas still belongs to that horizon of thought (fundamentally Greco-Arab) for which necessity is in itself preferable to contingency. After the condemnation of 1277, Duns Scotus and Ockham will, in different ways, completely reverse this state of things, overturning the hierarchy: contingency will become synonymous with freedom, necessity with constriction, proper to things lacking will.

Creatures: The Points of View of the Philosopher and the Theologian

The discussion about formally necessary creatures has already introduced us to the heart of Book II of the *Contra Gentiles*. The passage from the Book I to II is effectively explained by Thomas in this way: knowing something also means knowing its *operations*, of which there are *intransitive* or immanent operations and *transitive* ones outwardly directed. In the *Contra Gentiles*, God's immanent operations (knowing, willing, loving) are dealt with in Book I. It remains for us

---

45. *Summa contra Gentiles*, II, c. 30. The rest of the chapter consists in a meticulous analysis of the forms of necessity that it is possible to find in nature in relation to different types of cause, from essential principles (matter and form) to the agent and final causes.

to consider the transitive operations, that is, those having to do with the production of things, their conservation, and their government by God (II, c. 1).[46] It is obvious to Thomas that this knowledge too is necessary for being instructed in the faith. Considering the products, we can also consider the art that produced them, namely, divine wisdom. This admiration causes reverence, because it is natural for us to suppose that the power of the artisan is superior to the power of the things produced. This awakens love for the creator, for if our soul is attracted by the goodness and beauty that are encountered in creatures, we can easily recognize that all goodness and beauty are gathered up and concentrated in him who is at their origin. Finally, it assures us of a certain likeness to divine perfection. If God, in fact, knows all things in knowing himself, and if faith leads us to know God, we can say that, with the aid of revelation, we can in some way arrive at knowing all creatures. We know, nevertheless, that the basic purposes of the *Summa contra Gentiles* are not only that of instructing, but also that of combating errors, and, in fact, errors about creatures distance us from faith because they can lead to an erroneous representation of God. Those who do not know creatures can have mistaken ideas about God, attributing to him what is proper to creatures—as in the case of those who identify God with some sort of body—or, on the contrary, attributing to creatures what is proper only to God—as in the case of those who attribute creation not to God but to other causes. Furthermore, in ignoring the nature of creation one inevitably questions the divine power, as in the case of those who admit two principles of reality, or of those who hold that things derive from God not by his willing them but by necessity, or of those who remove things from divine providence or deny that God can do something outside the ordained course of nature (that is, those who deny God's absolute power, something that becomes more common toward the end of the thirteenth century). Finally, if we do not know the ordering of the world, we can err about our own place in the universe, as in the case of those who maintain that the human will is subject to the stars, or think that the soul is mortal, or admit other things that derogate from the perfection of human nature. Taking his cue from Augustine, Thomas can, thus, claim the absolute necessity—not only for the philosopher but for the theologian as well—of having an adequate knowledge of the totality of creatures, that is, of the universe:

It is, therefore, evident that the opinion is false of those who asserted that it made no difference to the truth of the faith what anyone holds about creatures, so long as one thinks rightly about God, as Augustine tells us [in the *De anima et ejus origine*, IV, 4].

46. On the second book of the *Summa contra Gentiles* see N. Kretzmann, *The Metaphysics of Creation: Aquinas's Natural Theology in* Summa contra Gentiles *II* (Oxford: Clarendon Press, 2002).

For error concerning creatures, by subjecting them to causes other than God, spills over into false opinion about God, and takes human minds away from him to whom faith seeks to lead them.[47]

As is evident, this passage claims not merely the *right* but above all the *duty* of the theologian to concern himself with creatures. If we keep this point in mind, we can perhaps begin to understand why Thomas continued—indeed intensified—his study of Aristotelian texts until the last years of his life. It is at this point—the consideration of creatures—that the contact between the theologian and the philosopher, theology and philosophy, inevitably comes about. The difference in this case is not in the object but in the approach, as Thomas makes clear in the chapter that concludes this brief methodological introduction to Book II (c. 4). Philosophy concerns itself with creatures as they are in themselves, that is, according to the properties that belong to them by virtue of their nature. The believer (and the theologian) concern themselves with creatures insofar as they are referred to or ordered to God (as created by God and as subject to him). Precisely because of this difference, it can happen that the theologian does not occupy himself with all the details of natural knowledge but only those that are relevant to his perspective. But even when the philosopher and the believer find themselves considering creatures under the same aspect, they will, nevertheless, appeal to different principles, since it is proper to the philosopher to argue from proximate and immediate causes, whereas the believer always starts from the first cause. And exactly for this reason, the science of the believer has the right to adorn itself with the title of supreme wisdom and to subject philosophy to its service. This characteristic should not be understood in a merely negative sense. On the contrary, it means that wisdom or theology, as we have seen, has the right/duty to make use of what philosophy has established, and this is the program that Thomas himself concretely launches.

Finally—a point with which we are already familiar—philosophy and theology are distinguished by the different orders in their way of proceeding. Philosophy begins from creatures, which constitute the first object of consideration, to arrive in the end at their first and remote cause—God. The doctrine of the faith begins instead from God (in the measure that it, in any case, considers creatures not in themselves but in their relation to God) and considers creatures only subsequently. This reproduces the order of God's knowledge itself, which knows all other things in knowing itself, as we saw earlier. And this ultimately justifies the structure itself of the *Contra Gentiles*: the consideration of creatures follows what is expounded about God in himself in Book I.

47. *Summa contra Gentiles*, II, c. 3.

In Thomas's treatment of creatures, we will limit ourselves, as always, to bringing out only certain aspects. While we will have more to say later on the question of the eternity of the world (II, cc. 31–38),[48] we can already begin noting that in the *Contra Gentiles* Thomas adopts the position that he will hold in the *De aeternitate mundi*: there are no cogent arguments to demonstrate that the world is eternal, but neither are their absolutely necessary reasons that demonstrate—as the Franciscan masters, for example, pretend—that the world is not eternal. In regard to the first aspect, it might be interesting to recall how Thomas reconciles the existence of formally necessary creatures (which, as we saw a moment ago, he accepts) with their non-necessary eternity. Here Thomas affirms that the necessity that we observe in creatures (II, c. 36), is a necessity of order (*necessitas ordinis*) and has to do with the nature of the thing once it is posited in existence, but does not relate to that thing's coming into existence (which, as we have seen, is the fruit of a non-necessary decision by God). To say it with Thomas, and with his usual clarity:

> Although the substance of the heaven has necessity with respect to being, in virtue of the fact that it lacks potentiality to non-being, this necessity nevertheless is consequent upon its substance. Hence, once its substance has been established in being, this necessity entails the impossibility of not being; but if we consider the production of its very substance, it does not entail the impossibility of the heaven's not being at all.[49]

In Thomas's estimation, the non-necessity of the eternity of the world is justified at the same level. Since the world is produced by God not by necessity but by a free decision of the divine will (even if some creatures are then constituted as intrinsically necessary), we are not obliged to admit that the world always existed. This formulation deserves attention. It is always expressed negatively or cautiously or in the form of a litotes: "It is not necessary to admit that the world always existed." "It is not absolutely necessary that the creature exist. So, neither is it necessary that it always have existed." "It is not necessary that the creature always have existed." "From the fact that God is eternal, it does not follow that it is necessary that he create from eternity." "Nothing obliges us to think that creatures have always existed." On the other hand, Thomas's explicitly declared intention from the beginning is only that of "demonstrating that

---

48. On the importance of this question in the thirteenth century see L. Bianchi, *L'errore di Aristotele. La polemica contro l'eternità del mondo nel xiii secolo*, Pubblicazioni della Facoltà di Lettere e Filosofia—Universita di Milano 104 (Florence: La Nuova Italia, 1984); R. C. Dales, *Medieval Discussions of the Eternity of the World*, Brill's Studies in Intellectual History 18 (Leiden: Brill, 1990); J. B. M. Wissink, ed., *The Eternity of the World in the Thought of Thomas Aquinas and His Contemporaries*, Studien und Texte zur Geistesgeschichte des Mittelalters 27 (Leiden: Brill, 1990).

49. *Summa contra Gentiles*, II, c. 36.

it is not necessary that creatures should exist from eternity," and the conclusion does not at all go beyond this quite limited intention: "Thus, it appears evident that nothing prevents us from admitting that the world did not always exist, as the Catholic faith teaches" (II, c. 37). We should not ask Thomas for more than he intends to offer us: there are no cogent reasons that show the necessity of the world's eternity, which remains, at any rate, theoretically possible, that is, a hypothesis that is in principle legitimate, even if not at all necessary. In cc. 36–37 we have nothing other than the principal arguments for proving the eternity of the world (taken from God's nature, from the things produced, and from the process itself of production), along with the refutation of their presumed apodictic value. But the eternity of the world is not, for Thomas, an impossible or irrational hypothesis; rather, it is just indemonstrable and, since the Mosaic books and the tradition of their interpretation suggest a temporal beginning to the world, we must hold this latter thesis, but only on faith and not because it is more plausible. With this we anticipate the essentials of the *De aeternitate mundi*, which make Thomas a truly avant-garde theologian of his time. The eternity of the world was by no means a scandal, even if the philosophical reasons used to demonstrate it are not conclusive. In sum, the possible eternity of the world did not very much trouble Thomas, who on this point was almost closer to the masters of the Paris faculty of arts than to his colleagues in the faculty of theology, although—and this is the decisive point of difference with the masters of arts—this conclusion is not presented as a philosophical *truth* in the strict sense, for in that case there would be a possible conflict of competencies between the two groups, a possible conflict between competing truths. The most interesting aspect—which should not be minimized in any way—is that Thomas absolutely does not try to demonstrate, or even make more plausible, the theological thesis of the temporality of creation. As proof of this, we see that c. 38 is expressly dedicated to refuting the arguments proposed by his fellow theologians (especially the Franciscans) on behalf of creation in time. Thomas plays the role here of devil's advocate, as it were, putting himself in the shoes of those who defend the eternity of the world:

Now, these arguments, although they have probability, lack absolute and necessary conclusiveness. Hence it is sufficient to deal with them quite briefly, lest the Catholic faith might appear to be founded on ineffectual reasonings, and not, as it is, on the most solid teaching of God. It would seem fitting, then, to state how these arguments are countered by the proponents of the doctrine of the world's eternity.

There is something more in this attitude than a simple application of the principle of charity or benevolence with respect to Aristotle (especially given that

Thomas hesitated to attribute to the philosopher complete allegiance to the thesis of the world's eternity) or the acceptance of the exegetical model deployed by Moses Maimonides. Thomas the theologian is not the champion of the irenic conciliation of theology and philosophy—as is often thought to be the case—but a thinker who is particularly sensitive to the limits of the two spheres. Thomas certainly does not say that theology can demonstrate the opposite of what the philosophers claimed to demonstrate. The exercise of reason, in cases like this, consists precisely in avoiding conflicts of competencies, raising doubts about the apodictic pretenses of philosophy as well as of certain approaches in theology. We have in this way a double refutation, a double *pars destruens*, which is followed not by a true *pars construens* but only by the acceptance of a truth of faith, which reason can neither demonstrate nor refute. Finally, we can add that Thomas is simply not bothered by the thesis of the eternity of the world, because even if it is accepted, purely hypothetically, that some creatures are eternal like God, the fulcrum of his metaphysical position remains untouched. As we said, and as we will continue to try to understand, for Thomas, the difference between God and creatures is located at a higher level than that supposed by the traditional opposition between the necessary and the contingent, or between the eternal and the temporal. Let us be clear: these points of difference between God and creatures are not denied by Thomas; he just does not see them as decisive or essential.

Being and Essence Again

The topic of the intrinsic (or formal) necessity of the incorruptibility of certain substances brings us back to the topic of the distinction between being and essence. The *Contra Gentiles* contains in II, cc. 52–54 the most significant treatment of being and essence after that of *De ente*. As in that youthful text, in this one too the context is separate substances, that is, of angels or intelligences (the formulation that is used—which is more philosophical than theological—is that of "intellectual substances"). After having reaffirmed the immateriality of these substances, and rejecting again the doctrine of Avicebron (and in part that of the Franciscans) of universal hylomorphism, Thomas explains that in this case we are dealing not with forms that exist in matter but with forms that subsist in themselves or subsistent forms (c. 51). A thing that subsists is one that has the capacity to exist in itself without being mixed together with something else. But if separate substances are also simple and subsistent, are they not in this regard on a par with the divine nature? To grasp the difference it will be sufficient to attend to what subsists in the one case and in the other. Intelligences are subsistent *forms*, forms that do not depend on matter for their existence. God is subsistent *being*, being that absolutely does not depend on anything else. Put differently, the fact that intelligences lack form-matter composition does not mean that they are absolutely simple: their being is not perfectly identical with what they are (to return to the terminology with which we are already familiar, their *esse* is not identical with their *quod est*.) The arguments proposed to support this conclusion take up again and develop the ones we already saw in the *De ente* and are largely based on the unicity of subsistent being and on the concept of participation. We will summarize them briefly.

1. Being as such does not admit of differences but is distinguished only by what is added to it. The being of a stone is distinguished from the being of man not by reason of being itself but by reason of the fact that it belongs to different natures. So, if in God, as we have seen, being and essence coincide, there cannot be any other being that can be identical with its very being, and for this reason it is necessary that in every other substance, the substance itself be distinct from its being.

2. A genus without specific differences is indivisible. If being, therefore, were a genus, subsistent separate being could not but be one. But being, as we already know, is not a genus, because it is situated above every genus. There is all the more reason, then, that subsistent being could not but be one.

3. It is impossible that there be two beings that are wholly infinite and numerically distinct. It would not be possible to find something in each of the two infinite beings that could distinguish the one from the other. But subsistent being is infinite in the sense that it is not limited by any other principle. Thus, it is impossible that there be more than one subsistent being.

4. Only what belongs to or is applied to being as such can belong to or be applied to subsistent being. Being-caused-by-another cannot belong to being as such; otherwise every being would be caused and we would go on to infinity—which is what has already been excluded. So, subsistent being is not caused. From this we can inversely deduce that every caused being will not be subsistent and will be different from being itself.

5. Still more directly, we can note that in every caused reality being is received from another; otherwise we would not be dealing with a caused reality. But what a thing receives from another cannot be identified with that thing's substance.

6. Since every agent acts insofar as it is in act, the first agent cause must be in act to the maximal degree, indeed, it must be pure actuality, and not something that receives an act. Hence, the first agent cause will be the most perfect act, and such an act is being, which is the terminus of any change and potency. Consequently, only God, since he is the first agent cause, will be pure act of being, while in everything else being will be in some way received and mixed with potency.

7. Finally, if being belongs to God by his very essence, it can belong to everything else only by participation. But what belongs to a thing by participation cannot be identical with the essence itself of that thing. It is, then, impossible that the essence of anything other than God be its very being.

We find at the end of these arguments one of the most celebrated passages that led Étienne Gilson to coin the felicitous term "metaphysics of Exodus" to designate not only Thomas's thought but Scholastic thought in general:

This is why in Exodus [3:14] "He who is" is given as the proper name of God, for in him alone is essence nothing other than his being.[50]

That in God alone being and essence are identical is evidently not a thesis that is unique to Thomas. On the contrary, it is a *locus communis* for all Scholastic thinkers (and begins with Augustine, at least in the Latin world). What becomes more difficult is determining what kind of distinction must be admitted between the two principles in all other beings. In this respect we can again stress what we have already noted, namely, that the distinction between being and essence does not seem to have the scope in Thomas of marking the contingency of created beings. This is especially suggested by the fact that the distinction is introduced precisely in connection with those beings that Thomas himself did not hesitate to define as formally necessary. It is clear, nevertheless, that through this distinction there passes the metaphysical caesura between creator and creature (between the creator and the most noble creatures, those lacking matter). What is at stake—and will fully emerge in the late Commentary on the *De causis*—is a radical restructuring of the way of conceiving the metaphysical difference between the first cause and its effects, a difference that *has to do not so much with the potentiality of matter as with the potentiality of form*. Before getting to this point let us consider the other elements that Thomas reproposes here, following the path taken in the *De ente*.

1. In the first place, the composition of being and essence can be interpreted as a particular case of the composition of act and potency.

2. Nevertheless, this composition can in no way be assimilated to that between matter and form, which is the most common type of composition (and, it should be pointed out, the only kind known to Aristotle) between potency and act. Why this should be so is soon clarified: on the one hand, matter, as we know, is not the substance or essence of a thing but a part of it. On the other

---

50. *Summa contra Gentiles*, II, c. 52. (Translator's note: The Latin text has *substantia* rather than *essentia* and so the literal translation would be "substance" instead of "essence." The term rendered here as "being" is *esse*. The Italian translation that Porro uses renders *esse* as *esistenza*.)

hand, being is the act, not of matter only (as form is), but of the whole substance. Moreover, the form itself must not be confused with being, since being
actualizes the essence composed of matter and form (in the case of corporeal
substances) or the essence that is identical with the form (in the case of separate
substances). As already in the *De ente*, we find here the most striking novelty vis-
à-vis Aristotelian metaphysics: form is not the ultimate actuality of a thing. In
relation to being, form is in potency ("being itself stands as act to form"). *Quo
est* and *quod est* do not have a fixed meaning, but a variable functional value. In
the case of composed substances, *quod est* is the substance itself (composed of
matter and form) of which the form is the *quo est* (because every substance has
being through its form). Being constitutes a further actuality by virtue of which
the whole substance is called a "being." Yet in separate substances the form itself
(with which the substance or essence is identical) is the *quod est*, while being
functions as *quo est*. So, here we once again have the hierarchical structure that
we found in the *De ente*. (a) At the lowest level, corporeal substances admit of a
twofold composition between potency and act: one between form and matter,
which constitute the essence, and the other between the essence itself and being.
(b) At the next level up, separate substances admit of only one type of composition, that between form itself (which functions here as the potential substrate)
and being. (c) Only in God is there no type of composition just as there is no
type of potentiality.

It is easily deduced that composition between being and essence has a vast-
er field of application (with God as the only exception) than does that between
matter and form (which is not in any of the separate substances). Naturally, what
we already observed with respect to the *De ente* holds here as well, that is, that act
and potency end up developing the Aristotelian technical meaning in a still more
markedly functional sense, making it more variable in reference to that to which
it is in each case applied. In general, potency comes, thus, to signify everything
that receives and is perfected, and act, everything that is received and perfects:

It is therefore clear that the composition of act and potentiality has greater extension
than that of form and matter. Thus, matter and form divide natural substance, while
potentiality and act divide common being. Accordingly, whatever follows upon potentiality and act, as such, is common to both material and immaterial created substances,
as to receive and to be received, to perfect and to be perfected. Yet all that is proper to
matter and form as such, as to be generated and to be corrupted, and the like, is proper
to material substances, and in no way belongs to immaterial created substances.[51]

---

51. *Summa contra Gentiles*, II, c. 54. It is typical, especially among Neo-Thomists, to define the
first composition (that between being and essence) as "metaphysical" and the second composition

Once again we should stress the connection between the incorruptibility of immaterial created substances and the composition of being and essence, which, therefore, indicates a defect of simplicity and not of contingency or corruptibility.[52]

A Condemned Thesis: The Impossibility of a Numerical Multiplicity of Angels in the Same Species

It is a shame that we are unable to examine Thomas's whole treatment of separate substances or the entirety of his angelology, which is extremely fascinating and presents not a few interesting philosophical implications.[53] We should, however, address at least one of the theses expounded with great decisiveness in the *Contra Gentiles*, to wit, that there are not several separate substances within one species (II, c. 93), that each separate substance constitutes its own species. Before reflecting on its implications (also from the point of view of the history of its influence), it will be useful to recall the way that Thomas justifies such a theoretical decision. The first is a direct consequence of what we have just seen: separate substances are subsistent forms, and since in them the quiddity is constituted by the form alone, they are subsistent quiddities. Let us remember that (as we have seen since the *De ente*) the quiddity of a thing is what is expressed by the definition and so *de facto* coincides with the species (the definition of the human essence—"rational animal"—is the definition of the species "man"). To say, then, that separate substances are subsistent quiddities is just to say that they are subsistent species, and, therefore, the separate substances are species in themselves, distinct and multiple. The second principal argument proposed by Thomas can also be easily imagined. We know that the division of a species

---

(that between form and matter) as "physical," but this is, in reality, an improper distinction, for in strictly Aristotelian terms the composition of matter and form is a metaphysical composition (Aristotle's first philosophy is, in fact, supposed to treat of constitutive functional principles of substance in general, and matter and form are among these). On the other hand, it is correct to say—just as the letter of Thomas's text does—that matter and form divide the material substance; or, rather, substance composed of matter and form is subject to generation and corruption.

52. If anything, the contrary is true, as the text shows in an unequivocal way.

53. Among the various contributions, especially in relation to the language and knowledge of the angels, see, at least, B. Faes de Mottoni, "*Enuntiatores divini silentii*: Tommaso d'Aquino e il linguaggio degli angeli," *Medioevo* 12 (1986): 199–228; "Tommaso d'Aquino e la conoscenza mattutina e vespertina degli angeli," *Medioevo* 18 (1992): 167–202; T. Suarez-Nani, *Les anges et la philosophie. Subjectivité et fonction cosmologique des substances séparées à la fin du XIIIème siècle*, Etudes de philosophie médiévale 82 (Paris: Vrin, 2002); *Connaissance et langage des anges selon Thomas d'Aquin et Gilles de Rome*, Etudes de philosophie médiévale 85 (Paris: Vrin, 2003); B. Roling, Locutio angelica: *Die Diskussion der Engelsprache als Antizipation einer Sprechakttheorie in Mittelalter und früher Neuzeit*, Studien und Texte zur Geistesgeschichte des Mittelalters 97 (Leiden: Brill, 2008), especially 79–102. Also, see p. 309n53 below.

into individuals depends on matter, but separated substances lack matter and so cannot admit of numerical division within a single species. The other three arguments appeal, in a different way, to the superiority of the species over the individual (a topic that we have already considered in *Quodlibet* VIII). First, the end of the multiplicity of individuals within the same species is that of conserving the nature of the species when the individuals themselves are corruptible. But because separate substances are incorruptible, a single individual is enough to preserve the continuation of the species.[54] Second, since the element that constitutes the species is superior to that which produces the differences of the individuals within the species itself, the perfection of the universe is guaranteed more by the multiplicity of species than by the multiplicity of individuals. Now, separate substances are the most noble beings within the universe itself and so it is fitting that specific difference belong to them more than numerical (or individual) difference. Finally, as a corollary to what we have already seen, it can be noted that separate substances are more perfect than the celestial bodies. But among the latter the individual is identical with the species, for each contains and exhausts the matter of that species and each by itself fulfills the proper function of that species. All the more reason that among separate substances there should be but one individual per species.

It is not hard to see in this thesis Thomas's great fidelity to the principles of Aristotle's cosmology and metaphysics (and those of the Arab peripatetic tradition).[55] This fidelity is not, however, without its dangers, since precisely this thesis was harshly condemned by Bishop Tempier on the occasion of the celebrated Parisian condemnation of March 7, 1277. We find this condemnation in two articles: *Quod Deus non potest multiplicare individua sub una specie sine materia;*[56] *Quod quia intelligentiae non habent materiam, Deus non posset facere plures eiusdem speciei.*[57] What Bishop Tempier feared—or what the masters who made up the commission of censors of the institution feared—obviously had to do with the sphere of divine omnipotence. Why could God not multiply—even in the absence of matter—separate substances within the same species? Does

54. It is not by chance that the celestial bodies, which, although they are material, are incorruptible, subsist as the only individuals of their respective species.

55. A thesis that Thomas maintained throughout his entire work. See, for example, *In II Sent.*, d. 3, q. 1, a. 4; d. 32, q. 2, a. 3; IV, d. 12, q. 1, a. 1, 3, ad 3; *De ente et essentia*, c. 5; *Quaestiones disputatae de anima*, q. 7; *De spiritualibus creaturis*, a. 8; *ST*, Ia, q. 50, a. 4; q. 76, a. 2, ad 1.

56. A. 96 in the numeration of *CUP*; a. 42 in the numeration of Mandonnet and Hissette.

57. A. 81/43. See R. Hissette, *Enquête sur les 219 articles condamnés à Paris le 7 mars 1277* (Paris: Publications Universitaires, 1977), 82–87; J. F. Wippel, "Thomas Aquinas and the Condemnation of 1277," *The Modern Schoolman* 72 (1995): 233–72, especially. 243–48; *La condamnation parisienne de 1277*, ed. D. Piché (Paris: Vrin, 1999), 104–5 and 108–9.

not the maintaining of the specific unity rather than the numeric unity of the separate substances also conserve the essentialistic and necessitarian structure of Greco-Arab cosmology? It has been justly observed that the theses held by Thomas are also found in the writings of the masters of arts, which were the explicit and direct target of Tempier's censure. But this does not change the substance of the condemnation. Even if Thomas was not the one directly aimed at (we must deal with the implication of Thomas in the condemnation of 1277 separately), his position, nonetheless, is the same as the one condemned and lines up perfectly with that of the masters of arts. However one wishes to play down the thing or conceal it, there is no doubt that, in Thomas's judgment, the separate substances occupy a strategic place in the hierarchy of the universe, and species are in general, as we have already seen, more important than individuals.

The Soul and the Formation of the Embryo

Before leaving the *Contra Gentiles*, we should touch on at least two topics that reappear throughout Thomas's work, to show how he already formed some firm basic convictions during the period in which he drafted the first *Summa*. The first conviction regards the doctrine of the soul, which occupies a large part of Book II (cc. 56–90) and which we will take up again later on several occasions. It is interesting to observe how the fundamental theses of Thomas's psychology are already perfectly delineated here. We will sum them up in outline.

1. The vegetative, sensitive, and intellectual souls are not three distinct souls in man. There is only one soul in man, the intellectual soul, and it presides over all the functions, even the inferior ones.

2. The rational human soul is directly the substantial form of the human composite without need of any other mediation (of the sensitive soul, for instance), or of other formal intermediaries.

3. If the rational human soul is the form of the body, it is not necessary to hypothesize, as did Averroes, that the possible intellect (the soul that thinks, the intellectual soul as such) is a substance separate from individuals and connects with them only through phantasms (that is, through the sensible images drawn from the external senses and elaborated by the cogitative power).

4. The thesis of the separateness of the possible intellect is, furthermore, foreign to Aristotle's intentions.

5. The "organistic" (for lack of a better term) theses of Alexander of Aphrodisias and Galen are refuted (along with every other interpretation that reduces the possible intellect itself to bodily harmony, to any bodily element, to any sense, or to the imagination). According to Alexander, the possible intellect is

what follows from the simple composition of the elements of the human body. According to Galen, the possible intellect coincides with temperament.

6. If the possible intellect is not separate, neither is it one for everyone (and connected to them by phantasms), as is again held by Averroes.

7. We must not, with Avicenna, deny the possibility of an intellectual memory, that is, the possibility of the retention of species in the possible intellect. For Thomas, Avicenna's position leads to the Platonic separation of the intelligibles and to the belief in a separate intelligence as the locus of the intelligibles.

8. Nor is the agent intellect separate (as Alexander of Aphrodisias and Avicenna maintained). Just like the possible intellect, it is a faculty of the soul (and, in Thomas's view, this is also the authentic Aristotelian position).

9. The human soul begins to exist with the body (it does not preexist the body but is created by God at the moment that the body is formed) but does not corrupt with the body.

Perhaps we should draw attention to the order in which Thomas expounds and links the individual aspects. The true point of departure and the authentic foundation of the whole structure is the thesis according to which *the human intellectual or rational soul is the unique and immediate form of the human composite*—a thesis that automatically puts Thomas into conflict with his Franciscan colleagues and will be the object of grave censures. This thesis is behind Thomas's rejection of the Averroist thesis of the separateness and oneness of the possible intellect and the agent intellect and the Avicennian thesis of the separateness of the agent intellect (in itself less problematic and "scandalous" than the former thesis).

We would like to look at a final point about the beginning of the soul, which Thomas discusses in cc. 83–84 and 86–89. Thomas's principal concern is as much the Platonizing hypothesis that the soul preexists the formation of the body as it is the hypothesis that the soul is transmitted through semen—an understandable concern, but one that leads Thomas to certain judgments that do not fail to leave many supporters of contemporary Catholic bioethics unhappy. According to Thomas, in fact, the soul is created as the form of the body only when the body is completely formed and not in the initial stages (that is, when it is an embryo). To be more explicit, for Thomas, the embryo lacks a soul (not only actually but also potentially),[58] and its development is instead determined

58. *Summa contra Gentiles*, II, chap. 89. "Another theory, likewise inadmissible, is stated as follows. From the moment of severance the soul is not present in the semen actually but virtually, because of the lack of organs; and yet this very power of the semen—itself a body potentially endowed with organs though actually without them—is, proportionately to the semen, a potential but not an actual soul.... Now, this theory would involve the consequence that numerically one and the

by the formative power of the semen (with which the soul is not identical). The development of the embryo is marked by a succession of stages in which the purely vegetative soul is the first to be generated. The latter is corrupted to cede its place to the sensitive and nutritive soul. Up to this stage the embryo is nothing more than a plant or an animal. Only in the last stage is the rational soul infused from outside (that is, directly created by God) and only at this point can we properly speak of a human being. Here too, to avoid distorting the text and misunderstandings, we will let Thomas speak for himself.

Therefore, the very same power which is separated, together with the semen, and is called the formative power, is not the soul, nor does it become the soul in the process of generation.... This formative power thus remains the same in the abovementioned vital spirit from the beginning of the body's formation until the end. The species of the subject formed, however, does not remain the same, since at first it possesses the form of semen, afterwards of blood, and so on, until at last it arrives at that wherein it finds its fulfilment. For, although the generation of simple bodies does not proceed in serial order, since each of them possesses a form related immediately to prime matter, a progressive order of generation must obtain in the generation of other bodies because of the many intermediate forms between the first elemental form and the ultimate form which is the object of the generative process.... That is why, in the generation of an animal and a man, wherein the most perfect type of form exists, there are many intermediate forms and generations—and, hence, corruptions, because the generation of one thing is the corruption of another. Thus, the vegetative soul, which is present first (when the embryo lives the life of a plant), perishes, and is succeeded by a more perfect soul, both nutritive and sensitive in character, and then the embryo lives an animal life. And when this passes away it is succeeded by the rational soul introduced from without, while the preceding souls existed in virtue of the semen.[59]

Taken in its strict and technical sense, this statement implies that there is a specific difference between the embryo and the developed fetus. So, for Thomas,

---

same power is at one time a purely vegetative soul, and afterwards a sensitive soul, the substantial form itself thus being perfected successively more and more. It would further follow both that the substantial form would be brought from potentiality to act, not all at once but in successive stages, and that generation is a continuous movement, just as alteration is. Now, all these consequences are impossible in nature. But that theory would entail a consequence still more incongruous, namely, the mortality of the rational soul. For nothing formal in character that accrues to a corruptible thing makes it incorruptible by nature; in that case, the corruptible would be changed into the incorruptible, which is impossible, since they differ in genus, as Aristotle says in *Metaphysics* X." It should be noted that Thomas bases himself solely on natural reasons here ("all these consequences are impossible in nature"), and that, precisely because of these reasons, he tries to avoid an unacceptable naturalistic deviation (in other words, interpreting the soul's entry into the embryo naturalistically leads to absurd results on the natural plane itself). We have here a particularly significant example of Thomas's method and attitude.

59. *Summa contra Gentiles*, II, c. 89.

we are dealing with different *species* that have different substantial forms. We will not enter into the contemporary debate in bioethics about the beginning of human life. If we have cited this example, it is only to show that a thirteenth century theologian cannot always be forced to incarnate in every circumstance what would eventually become the official position of the Church (a tack that is beneficial neither to the author under discussion nor to the institution).[60] However, it is helpful to understand Thomas's reasoning, which once again—and with absolute consistency—is guided by the thesis that the rational soul is the one form of the human composite. Man is always, and by definition, a rational animal, and where there is no rationality (where there is no rational soul, but a different principle), we cannot, strictly speaking, have humanity.

Philosophical Happiness and Otherworldly Beatitude

The last thing that we will consider in the *Contra Gentiles* regards the doctrine of happiness in Book III. Obviously, we could have looked into other issues (evil, for example, or the whole fourth book, which, as we have said, deals with topics that are missing from the *Summa theologiae*). But some of these issues fall outside the strictly philosophical domain and so are outside the framework that we have chosen, while others will be addressed when we take up later writings. Thomas organically develops the theme of man's ultimate felicity in the *Summa theologiae* also. But it will be worthwhile to cast a quick glance at it already here. Everything is based on the central assumption that God is the final end of all things, and all things tend toward that end, that is, to be like God. But things tend toward God in accordance with their nature, inasmuch as they participate in a determinate likeness to the divine essence. In the case of creatures endowed with intellects, then, it is natural that they tend toward God through their highest and most characteristic operation—intellectual knowing. There are many reasons that Thomas gives for this, but we will examine only a few that we think merit attention. It is, for instance, significant that Thomas completely appropriates Aristotle's idea about the primacy of speculative activity as an activity that is gratuitous, autonomous, and lovable for itself:

60. The best study available with respect to rigor, sobriety, and balance is, without doubt, that of F. Amerini, *Tommaso d'Aquino. Origine e fine della vita umana* (Pisa: ETS, 2009), from which it is fitting to quote at least one passage, drawn from his conlusions: "It seems to me that it can be said that, for Thomas, the best bioethical approach to the question of the origin of human life could be that synthesizable in the formula 'the gradual protection of human life.' Like every gradual protection, the protection of human life takes into account the interaction of other factors, circumstances, and contexts, which lie outside a strictly metaphysical or philosophical appraisal. This is the basic reason why the attempts of some Catholics and exponents of so-called 'analytic Thomism' to connect Thomas Aquinas with the present position of the Catholic Church on the topic of abortion, besides being philosophically and philologically unsatisfactory, are also substantially useless" (266–67).

[T]hat which is capable of being loved only for the sake of some other object exists for the sake of that other thing which is lovable simply on its own account. In fact, there is no point in going on without end in the working of natural appetite, since natural desire would then be futile, because it is impossible to get to the end of an endless series. Now, all practical sciences, arts, and powers are objects of love only because they are means to something else, for their purpose is not knowledge but operation. But the speculative sciences are lovable for their own sake, since their end is knowledge itself. Nor do we find any action in human affairs, except speculative thought, that is not directed to some other end.... So, the practical arts are ordered to the speculative ones, and likewise every human operation to intellectual speculation, as an end. Now, among all the sciences and arts which are thus subordinated, the ultimate end seems to belong to the one that commands the others and is architectonic in relation to them.... In fact, this is the way that first philosophy is related to the other speculative sciences—for all the others depend on it, in the sense that they take their principles from it—and also the position to be assumed against those who deny the principles. And this first philosophy is wholly ordered to knowing God as its ultimate end. That is why it is also called divine science. So, divine knowledge is the ultimate end of every act of human knowledge and every operation.[61]

In this passage there is no mention of the distinction between the theology of the philosophers and the theology of Scripture that we saw delineated in the *Super Boethium de Trinitate*. Reference is made directly to the divine science of the philosophers. In the *Nicomachean Ethics* Aristotle seems to privilege the activity itself (speculation itself, which, as act, is divine) over the object (knowledge of God). In a word, happiness is principally activity (*energeia*) and not an objective good. (Aristotle aims to steer away from the Platonic temptation of the objectivity and separateness of the good.) Thomas, as we will see, will pose the problem in the *Summa theologiae* and will resolve it by a distinction between the *finis cuius* and the *finis quo*. Let us note for the moment a fundamental datum: the desire to know God, as also a philosophical desire, is absolutely natural.

A second reason Thomas gives for regarding intellectual knowledge of God as man's final end comes from the hierarchy of human faculties and follows perfectly from Thomas's basic conviction (for which he will be criticized by many Franciscan masters and in part by Henry of Ghent) about the primacy of the intellect over the will. The intellect is the first mover in man, for it is what moves the appetitive part (the will), proposing to it an object to pursue. The intellectual appetite (the will) then moves the sensitive appetites (the irascible and the concupiscible appetites), which then move the bodily organs. Now, it is always the end of the first agent or mover that constitutes the final end of all the rest, just as the end of the general is the final end of all the soldiers

---

61. *Summa contra Gentiles*, III, c. 25.

he commands. Thus, the end of the intellect constitutes the end of all human actions. But the end of the intellect, as we well know, is the first truth, namely, God, and so—as the end of the intellect—God will also be the ultimate end of the whole man, of all his actions and all his desires. We would perhaps lose the essence of Thomas's theology if we did not pay appropriate attention to this. Man's ultimate goal—that which constitutes his happiness or beatitude— is to *know* God. It is precisely this primacy of the intellect and knowledge that makes Thomas's theology a project that is by no means troubled by continuity with the Greek and Arab philosophical tradition, and determines that Thomas would always continue to concern himself with the texts of the philosophers. On this point there is a definite division between the Dominican and Franciscan traditions, a division that manifests itself in all its breadth in the subsequent debate at the beginning of the fourteenth century between Meister Eckhart and Gonsalves of Spain. We should again stress this: at least on this point Eckhart is not terribly far from Thomas and, indeed, does nothing but emphasize—with his own metaphysics of the intellect—a teaching that is already present in his Dominican predecessor and that is subsequently strengthened by the contributions of Proclus, Avicenna, and Averroes.

To show this it will be sufficient to quote what Thomas himself says in *Contra Gentiles*, III, c. 26 immediately after having drawn his main conclusion (viz., that man's beatitude is in knowing God). Someone might hold that human felicity does not consist in an act of the intellect but in an act of the will, for example, in loving God, Thomas observes. But he frankly asserts that it can clearly be demonstrated that this is impossible. Thomas offers nine arguments in support of the firm position that he takes. These arguments express the heart of Thomas's "intellectualism." We will present only some of them. First, we already said that each thing tends toward the final end, toward God, in the way that is proper to it. But it is not appetite or desire that is proper to the rational creature, because even those creatures that completely lack knowledge have a kind of appetite. It is true that the appetite differs in the various orders of beings, but this diversification always depends on knowledge. If the will, as an *intellectual* appetite, is proper to man and to other intellectual creatures, this is because of the intellect and not because of the appetite or will in itself. What characterizes intellectual creatures is the intellect itself, and it follows from this that "beatitude or happiness consists substantially and chiefly in an act of the intellect rather than in an act of the will" (III, c. 26). Moreover, says Thomas, it is possible even to desire and love false goods, for the will is unable by itself to discern the true and the false, which is the paramount task of the intellect. Further still, it is possible to love or desire what is not yet possessed while the operation whereby we effectively attain God is cognitive. Naturally, Thomas in no way excludes enjoyment or love from the sphere of human happiness. But these are concomitant elements and are not what defines beatitude itself. Let us be clear: our final end, Thomas holds, is not to love God but to know him. Love, like enjoyment, necessarily follows as a consequence of knowledge.

Putting the matter in such terms, it is easy to exclude everything that does not constitute or offer human happiness. The list does not present any surprises: happiness does not consist in pleasures of the flesh (III, c. 27), honors (c. 28), glory (c. 29), wealth (c. 30), worldly power (c. 31), bodily goods (c. 32), sensible goods (c. 33), acts of moral virtue—which are directed to determinate ends and that are not exclusive to rational natures (c. 34), prudence (c. 35), or art (c. 36). Induction leads us to the same result: "man's ultimate felicity consists in the contemplation of truth." The characteristics of this contemplation are again those that Aristotle attributes to it in the *Nicomachean Ethics*. Contemplation alone is specifically human, in the sense that no other animal participates in it, and so it is unique to the human essence. It is an end in itself, not being subordinated to any other purpose, and is, therefore divine, since it brings us near to the separate substances and to God himself. Contemplation is self-sufficient, in the sense that to engage in it we have no need of external aids or things (c. 37).

But greater precision is needed in ascertaining the nature of this knowledge. Thomas first rejects the idea that happiness consists in the natural knowledge of God possessed by the majority of people, precisely because such knowledge is generic and confused, while we are talking about ultimate or perfect happiness. Neither is it a matter of the knowledge that can be had by demonstration, because, as we have seen, such knowledge is limited with respect to the divine realities and admits more of negations than affirmations. Nor can it be a matter of the knowledge had by faith, because this knowledge is inferior to the authentic act of intellectual knowledge (the authentic act of the intellect consists in *understanding* its proper object, not in *believing* in it) and because the will plays a decisive role in it, whereas we have already said that beatitude cannot principally pertain to the sphere of the will. The real challenge comes with the philosophical ideal, according to which happiness consists in the conjunction, that is, the *copulatio*, in this life, with separated substances by way of speculation. This is the celebrated *fiducia philosophantium* described by Albert the Great. As Thomas expounds and synthesizes it, achieving perfect continuity with the intelligences is one way of attaining the final end—knowledge of the first cause. Every separated substance, in fact, in knowing its own essence knows not only what is inferior to it but also what is superior to it, and even more its proper cause. Consequently, any inferior intellect, such as the human intellect, that knows the essence of a separate substance could have a vision of God superior to that which it can have by itself by faith or demonstration. But is it possible to know separate substances in this life? Is there a basis for the hope of the philosophers? Everything depends on the basic assumption of Aristotelian gnoseology, namely, on the fact that all human intellectual knowledge presupposes sensible images, phantasms:

Therefore, if any of us could achieve the understanding of separate substances through the intellectual knowledge which is from phantasms, then it would be possible for someone in this life to understand separate substances themselves. Consequently, by seeing these separate substances one will participate in that mode of knowledge whereby the separate substance, while understanding itself, understands God. But, if one cannot in any way attain to the understanding of separate substances through the knowledge which depends on phantasms, then it will not be possible for man in the present state of life to achieve the aforesaid mode of divine knowledge.[62]

Thomas presents three positions that maintain the possibility of achieving knowledge of God through knowledge of separate substances. He attributes them to Avempace (separate substances are reached through the abstraction of the quiddities through the knowledge of what *possesses* a quiddity), Alexander of Aphrodisias (we know the separate substances when the agent intellect becomes the form of our habitual intellect, that is, through the intelligible species impressed on the possible intellect), and above all Averroes, whose doctrine Thomas sees as an essential correction of Alexander's doctrine to the extent that it makes the possible intellect a separate substance rather than a corruptible disposition. The agent intellect connects with it as the form of the intelligible species—derived from phantasms—that are thought by the potential or possible intellect. So, when speculative objects are in us only in potency, the agent intellect is united to us potentially. When the speculative objects are in us partly in potency and partly in act, then the agent intellect is united to us partly in potency and partly in act, and we are on the way to perfect conjunction. The more that the things known are actual, the more perfect is our union with the agent intellect (through the possible intellect). This increase occurs through study, which allows us to set aside errors, and through mutual assistance that we give each other in the speculative sciences. When everything that is potentially intelligible becomes actually intelligible, then the agent intellect unites with us as form. Through this conjunction we are able to understand separate substances as we are able to understand the principles of speculative thought. And, for Averroes, this is man's ultimate felicity, in which he becomes in some way like

62. *Summa contra Gentiles*, III, c. 41.

God. Now, we will not consider Thomas's refutation of this doctrine, which we have already seen in part and which we will encounter again, but limit ourselves to noting that Thomas denies that the possible intellect and agent intellect are separate substances. He observes how in Averroes it is not possible to say that man understands or thinks, since the whole process of thought unfolds in the separate substances. And he also indicates that, in Averroes's view, the agent intellect as form does not unite to us—as both Albert and Thomas held (the rational soul is from the beginning the only immediate form of the human composite)but only to the phantasms. What is more interesting in this text is Thomas's criticism of the "philosophers" (which will not reappear in the *De unitate*). They have placed the ideal of happiness too high, where few—indeed, no one—can reach:

Indeed, a thing is futile which exists for an end which it cannot attain. So, since the end of man is felicity, to which his natural desire tends, it is not possible for the felicity of man to be placed in something that man cannot achieve. Otherwise, it would follow that man is a futile being, and his natural desire would be incapable of fulfillment, which is impossible. Now, it is clear from what has been said that man cannot understand separate substances on the basis of the foregoing opinions. So, man's felicity is not located in such knowledge of separate substances.[63]

In fact, the agent intellect could be united to us only if the habitual intellect were completely developed (according to Alexander's doctrine) or if all the intelligible species were already in act (according to Averroes's doctrine)—two practically impossible conditions, or, on the most optimistic of hypotheses, attainable by only a few:

Even granting that such a conjunction of man with the agent intellect were possible as they describe it, it is plain that such perfection comes to very few men; so much so that not even they, nor anyone else, however diligent and expert in speculative sciences, have dared to claim such perfection for themselves. On the contrary, they all state that many things are unknown to them, as does Aristotle.... Now, felicity is a definite common good, which many men can attain, "unless they are defective," as Aristotle puts it. And this is also true of every natural end in any species, that the members of this species do attain it, in most cases. Therefore, it is not possible for man's ultimate felicity to consist in the aforesaid conjunction.[64]

On this occasion too, Aristotle differs from the peripatetic tradition. The ideal of speculative happiness sketched in Book X of the *Nicomachean Ethics* is not, in Thomas's view, the same as the doctrine of conjunction, since the possible

63. *Summa contra Gentiles*, III, c. 44.
64. *Summa contra Gentiles*, III, c. 44.

intellect and the agent intellect are not separate substances in Aristotle (at least not in Thomas's Aristotle).[65]

It remains, then, to determine in what way it is possible for man to attain happiness, that is, knowledge of separate substances and, even more (as final end), of God himself. To accomplish this last step, which we already know coincides with the doctrine of the beatific vision, Thomas takes his bearings from a philosophical position, from the argument of Themistius, according to which separate substances are more intelligible in themselves than material substances. The latter, in fact, to become intelligible, must be made actually intelligible by the agent intellect, while the former are intelligible in themselves. If, therefore, our intellect understands material things, all the more should it understand those things that are more intelligible in themselves. Everything depends, once again, on the way that the nature of the possible intellect is understood. It is obvious that in Averroes's doctrine the possible intellect, because it is a separate substance, always has knowledge of the other separate substances. But this is only of minimal relevance to man's situation, since the subject of thought, on this hypothesis, is the one and separate possible intellect and not the individual, and since the conjunction with the agent intellect is realized only when the phantasms are reduced from potentially intelligible to actually intelligible in the possible intellect. In other words, one of the inconveniences of Averroes's doctrine is that it must give an account of the fact that—even if we think through a separate substance (the possible intellect)—it is by no means easy to unite with the other separate substances. If, however, we hold that the possible intellect is bound to the body, then it must be granted that it cannot achieve any knowledge without the mediation of sensible images or phantasms. If this is how things stand, then although it is true that separate substances are more intelligible in themselves, they are not so for us, because our intellect is, so to say, calibrated for knowing sensible realities rather than separate ones. As we already observed earlier, this is the meaning of the celebrated Aristotelian adage that states that our intellect is related to the maximally intelligible realities, like

65. The speculative happiness of Aristotle, which is obtained by means of the exercise of speculative knowledge, thus, must not, for Thomas, be conflated with the ideal of the effective union with the agent intellect as an external form (and not of the human composite, but of the habitual intellect or of the phantasms). Moreover, this implies that the happiness of which Aristotle speaks has, from the very beginning, a more relative and limited importance than Averroes (and Alexander) suggests: "For these and like reasons, Alexander and Averroes claimed that man's ultimate felicity does not consist in the human knowledge which comes through the speculative sciences, but through a connection with a separate substance, which they believed to be possible for man in this life. But, since Aristotle says that there is no other knowledge for man in this life than through the speculative sciences, he maintained that man does not achieve perfect felicity, but only a limited kind."

the eyes of the bat are to the sun.[66] This example can also be interpreted differently. For Averroes, it indicates only a difficulty, not an impossibility, because if such substances were unintelligible, their existence as maximally intelligible would be pointless. For Thomas, on the contrary, Aristotle's example indicates an effective impossibility: if the possible intellect is truly joined to the body, it can never, in any way, understand separate substances. But this does not tell us everything, for our intellect is, indeed, joined to the sensible body during our earthly life, but it is incorruptible in itself and independent of matter. The Aristotelian interdict—to which Thomas remains so faithful against the *fiducia philosophantium*—applies only so long as the intellect is united to the mortal body. When the soul is separated from it, it can know separate substances directly.

What holds for separate substances in general holds still more for God. With this we arrive at the end of the journey: man's felicity—the knowledge of God—is in the vision that he enjoys *in patria*, at the conclusion of earthly life (c. 47). Let us allow Thomas himself to take stock:

> If, then, ultimate human felicity does not consist in the knowledge of God, whereby he is known in general by all, or most, men, by a sort of confused appraisal, and again, if it does not consist in the knowledge of God which is known by way of demonstration in the speculative sciences, nor in the cognition of God whereby he is known through faith ...; and if it is not possible in this life to reach a higher knowledge of God so as to know him through his essence, or even in such a way that, when the other separate substances are known, God might be known through the knowledge of them, as if from a closer vantage point, as we showed; and if it is necessary to identify ultimate felicity with some sort of knowledge of God, as we proved above; then it is not possible for man's ultimate felicity to come in this life.[67]

There is nothing original or surprising in this conclusion, as is plain. It would perhaps be worthwhile to underscore again the difference between this Christian ideal—according to which complete happiness is impossible in this life—and that of the "philosophers," and also that of the masters of arts of Thomas's time. A certain simplification should be avoided: none of the masters of arts (the so-called "Averroists") ever denied that complete happiness can be had only beyond this world (as is easy to verify by also checking the veritable "manifesto" of the arts masters, Boethius of Dacia's *De summo bono*). The difference is in the way of conceiving earthly happiness. The masters of arts' conception of happiness is too much based on possible human merits and so obscures the indispensable action of grace. Moreover, it is a conception that is too elitist and so

---

66. See p. 124n14 above.
67. *Summa contra Gentiles*, III, c. 48.

excludes the more simple folk. Finally, it is too difficult to achieve even for the few men of wisdom to whom it is promised and, thus weakens the hope itself that they place in the exercise of philosophy. Philosophical felicity—in the extreme form of *copulatio* with the separate substances or in the moderate form of Aristotelian speculation—is so elevated and inaccessible that it can only cause, Thomas thinks, disillusion and the very opposite of felicity:

> On this point there is abundant evidence of how even the brilliant minds of these men suffered from the narrowness of their viewpoint, from which narrow attitudes we shall be freed if we grant, in accord with the foregoing proofs, that man can reach true felicity after this life, when man's soul is existing immortally; in which state the soul will understand in the way that separate substances understand.[68]

THE OTHER WRITINGS OF THE ORVIETO PERIOD
The Commentary on Job

The cultural politics of the order that were established at Valenciennes, which we considered at the beginning of the present chapter, and which Thomas himself promoted, made it quite unlikely that a *magister*, once he had obtained his *licentia*, should remain inactive for a long period. Certainly Thomas did not lack other responsibilities in the order. On his return to Italy (on the occasion, it seems, of the provincial chapter in Naples in 1260, which we mentioned earlier), he was appointed the preacher general, which, among other things, obliged him to take part in all of the provincial chapters. But, without a doubt, his more natural destination was that of *lector* in one of the order's priories, and this is precisely what happened when, in September of 1261, Thomas was assigned as lector at the priory of Orvieto. At that time Orvieto was the site of the papal curia (even if, to be more exact, Urban IV only established himself there in 1262), to which a *studium* was annexed, but it should immediately be noted that Thomas was charged to teach, not at this institution (something that the Dominicans themselves could not have decided), but at the Dominican priory of this city. But Thomas would have had the possibility during this period (he remained in Orvieto until 1265) of visiting the curia and the library attached to it and to meet the various figures connected with it. Thomas's occasional writings composed during these years at the request of the pope or the prelates of the curia are a witness to this. What might appear surprising is that the new position is, if considered externally and in relation to the brief but significant career in Paris that Thomas already had behind him, quite modest. Not only did the priory at Orvieto not have a *studium generale*, but Thomas's students were,

---

68. *Summa contra Gentiles*, III, c. 48.

in fact, *fratres communes*, that is, friars who had not been chosen, on the basis of their abilities, to pursue studies in a provincial or general *studium*. It would be similar to—not forgetting the different context—a university professor with an already very brilliant and promising résumé suddenly being moved to a school for students of an advanced age with a less than advanced intellectual capacity.[69] Still, one of the objectives of the Valenciennes "reform," if we may call it that, was that of raising the cultural level of all the members of the order, equally promoting formation in excellence and an ordinary formation and making it so that all of the friars—even those who could not ascend to the highest levels of the formation program—had the possibility of increasing and updating their knowledge at least in relation to the two principal tasks of every Dominican: preaching and hearing confessions. The rotation of the masters was a practice adopted with the aim of making the studies undertaken by the leading Dominican intellectuals bear fruit throughout the order and to bring different areas of competence to different places.[70] Thus, although we do not have any document that tells us how Thomas reacted to his new duties, we can imagine that he happily welcomed them, since they answered to one of the exigencies that he himself had highlighted at Valenciennes.[71]

It is probable—as we will see—that it was precisely the necessity of dealing with the textbooks that were already circulating in the order for the basic formation of the friars (and principally aimed at casuistry) that gradually moved Thomas to develop a project for a new theological manual—the *Summa theologiae*. But the time in Orvieto was mostly dedicated to the drafting of the larger part of the *Contra Gentiles* (Books II–IV were probably composed during this period). Other writings of a more strictly theological character were produced too. First of all, some important works of scriptural exegesis: the *Super Job* (presumably during 1263–65) and the first part of the *Catena aurea in quatuor Evangelia* (the part on the Gospel of Matthew was completed between 1263 and 1264; the parts related to the other three Gospels would be finished in Rome between 1265 and 1268). The Commentary on the Book of Job (perhaps a result of lectures on the book for the friars of the priory) is considered one of the most beautiful

69. The fact that the priory was in a city that at the moment was the site of the Roman curia does not adorn it with any special prestige, and certainly does not make up the great difference in education that existed between the Parisian students and those of a simple priory school.

70. As an aside, we might mention that this practice could perhaps be worth introducing into the currently stagnant Italian university system.

71. As his biographers tell us, the only thing during his whole life that Thomas did not much care for was having to do a lot of traveling. And if we consider the many changes of place that he had to endure in a short time—not only because of his responsibilities as a *magister* and *lector* but also to participate in various chapters—it is not difficult to form an idea of the sacrifices that he had to make.

of the biblical commentaries composed by Thomas,[72] even if the observations on these commentaries that we already made in general in the first chapter—that is, that literal exegesis is always the central concern—also apply to it. Thomas himself makes this clear at the end of his prologue, declaring that he will not occupy himself with the context nor with the author, recommending Gregory the Great's commentary for a spiritual interpretation.[73] Thomas develops his whole reading around the concept of providence, as he himself states in the prologue, which is, as often happens in these cases, the part of the work that is of most philosophical interest—indeed, if it is too much to pretend that there is a complete philosophical anthropology in this commentary (as has been suggested), it is undoubtedly significant that the literal exposition of a biblical book is introduced from the perspective of an explicitly philosophical concern. Following the Aristotelian principle of the progress of knowledge (which he will present with great effectiveness in *Summa theologiae*, I, q. 44, a. 2), Thomas observes that the conquest of truth takes place in stages and that it is understandable that the ancients committed errors on account of their imperfect knowledge. Among these errors there is that of having attributed everything to fortune and to chance, as did the ancient natural philosophers (the Ionian physicists), who admitted only a material principle, and later Democritus and Empedocles. The subsequent philosophers, however, arrived at a demonstration that the world is ruled by providence, at least in what regards the natural world, in which it is impossible not to notice a certain regularity. There remains, then, the problem of the domain of human actions, which does not seem to possess the same regularity:

This doubt was fed especially because there is no sure order apparent in human events. For good things do not always befall the good nor evil things the wicked. On the other hand, evil things do not always befall the good nor good things the wicked, but good and evil indifferently befall both the good and the wicked.[74]

It was precisely this absence of order that led people to believe that human events were governed by chance—except to the extent that they are ruled by

72. See J.-P. Torrell, *Saint Thomas Aquinas*, vol. 1, *The Person and His Work*, 120.

73. *Expositio super Iob ad litteram*, prol.: "Now it is not our present intention to discuss the time in which Job lived or his parentage, even the authorship of this book, whether in fact Job himself wrote it about himself as if speaking of another or someone else related these incidents about him. For we intend briefly as far as we are able, having trust in divine help, to expound according to the literal sense that book which is entitled *Blessed Job*. Blessed Pope Gregory has already disclosed to us its mysteries so subtly and clearly that there seems no need to add anything further to them." On Thomas's biblical commentaries, see the panoramic view of E. Stump, "Biblical Commentary and Philosophy," in *The Cambridge Companion to Aquinas*, ed. N. Kretzmann and E. Stump (Cambridge: Cambridge University Press, 1993), 252–68.

74. *Expositio super Job ad litteram*, prol.

human prudence and planning—or by a fate determined by the heavens. But, to Thomas's mind, these views are the most dangerous ones for the human race. Eliminating providence entails denying all respect and fear of God, and, thus, any reason for man to seek the good and avoid evil. This is why the first concern of the sacred authors was immediately to eliminate this understanding from the human mind, and, in Thomas's eyes, this explains the location of the Book of Job, which immediately follows the books of the prophets. "The whole intention" of the Book of Job "is to show that human affairs are ruled by divine providence using probable arguments."[75] This is a theme that Thomas will develop in parallel, during those same years, in Book III of the *Contra Gentiles*.[76] And in this sense the careful formula that Thomas introduces in expounding the book's intention is also significant. Following the model suggested by the *Contra Gentiles*, Thomas says that in Job too providence is spoken of with only probable reasons and not strictly demonstrative ones. From this point of view, Thomas's approach, based on a precise distinction between what reason can demonstrate and what it can indicate only as probable and defend from errors, is always absolutely consistent.[77]

Catena aurea

The *Catena* seems to have been written in response to a specific request by Pope Urban IV. It is a continuous exposition (whence the name *Catena*), verse by

75. *Expositio super Job ad litteram*, prol. On the connection between providence and the human condition, and more generally on the anthropological implications of the *Expositio super Job*, see M. F. Manzanedo, "La antropología filosófica en el commentario tomista al libro de Job," *Angelicum* 62 (1985): 419–71; "La antropología teológica en el commentario tomista al libro de Job," *Angelicum* 64 (1987): 301–31; E. Stump, "Aquinas on the Suffering of Job," in *The Evidential Argument from Evil*, ed. D. Howard-Snyder (Bloomington: Indiana University Press, 1996), 49–68; D. Chardonnens, *L'homme sous le regard de la Providence. Providence de Dieu et condition humaine selon l'*Exposition littérale sur le Livre de Job *de Thomas d'Aquin*, Bibliothèque thomiste 50 (Paris: Vrin, 1997).

76. This is one of the elements in favor of the dating proposed for the work.

77. There are, perhaps, two small notes, by way of addition, on some philosophical aspects, so to speak, of the *Expositio super Job*. The first is that in this period too Thomas reaffirms much of what we saw in the *Summa contra Gentiles* on the subject of the fact that the ensoulment of the fetus (and therefore the true and proper homanization of the embryo) takes place only after the distinction of the organs and the full organization of the body (c. 10; Thomas insists here, however, more explicitly on the protection of life within and outside the womb). The second thing to note is that, reflecting on the limits of human justice in c. 10, Thomas justifies, albeit as an exception, the torture of someone who has been unjustly accused, a justification based on the inevitably limited nature of human knowledge and justice. Not all of the scholastic masters, however, granted this same assumption (Henry of Ghent is one example). On this topic see P. Porro, "Individual Rights and Common Good: Henry of Ghent and the Scholastic Origins of Human Rights," in *The European Image of God and Man. A Contribution to the Debate on Human Rights*, ed. H.-C. Gunther and A. A. Robiglio (Leiden: Brill, 2010), 245–58.

verse, of the four Gospels, accompanied by a system of glosses taken from the Fathers, following the model of the *Glossa ordinaria* composed by the School of Laon in the twelfth century and widely used by the masters of theology in Paris in their scriptural commentaries. It is more than probable that Thomas drew on compilations already in existence and that he was helped by some secretaries in the undertaking. Nevertheless, as has been rightly emphasized, the number of the patristic sources used is, in any event, impressive, and, what is more, increases as the work progresses, a testimony to the fact that Thomas systematically continued to seek out and read the works of the Fathers (especially the Greek Fathers). Evidence of this is found in the fact that, in introducing the exposition of the Gospel of Mark (that is, in the dedication of it to Annibaldo degli Annibaldi), Thomas himself says that he had some material translated that was not yet available in Latin. We will never sufficiently marvel at the man's incredible intellectual curiosity. He is not content to peddle in the province what he has already learned between Naples, Cologne, and Paris (something that he could easily have done), but continues to procure, to read, and to comment on—with method and passion—the majority of theological and philosophical texts available (the curia's library in Orvieto could assure him certain advantages in this sense). We will return to examine the philosophical texts later. Here it is fitting to recall that the justly accepted image of Thomas as a dogmatic theologian and a reader of philosophy should not be allowed to eclipse his great interest in Greek patristic thought. In the *Catena*, 57 Greek Fathers are quoted (compared to 22 Latin Fathers), some of whom were practically unknown in the West before Thomas's use of them.[78] John Chrysostom seemed to have an absolute importance for Thomas. According to the famous anecdote of his principal biographers,[79] answering the innocently mischievous question of one

78. See J.-P. Torrell, *Saint Thomas Aquinas*, vol. 1, *The Person and His Work*, 139. On Thomas and the Fathers, see C. G. Geenen, "Saint Thomas et les Pères," in *Dictionnaire de théologie catholique*, vol. XV/1, ed. A. Vacant, J.-E. Mangenot, and E. Amann (Paris: Letouzey et Ane, 1946), coll. 738–61; L.-J. Bataillon, "Saint Thomas et les Pères. De la Catena à la Tertia pars," in *Ordo sapientiae et amoris: Image et message de saint Thomas d'Aquin à travers les récentes études historiques herméneutiques et doctrinales. Hommage au Professeur Jean-Pierre Torrell op à l'occasion de son 65e anniversaire*, Studia Friburgensia 78, ed. C. J. Pinto de Oliveira (Fribourg: Éditions Universitaires de Fribourg, 1993), 15–36.

79. Guillelmus of Tocco, *Ystoria sancti Thomae de Aquino*, Studies and Texts 127, ed. C. Le Brun-Gouanvic (Toronto: Pontifical Institute of Mediaeval Studies, 1996), 172 (Chapter 42); J. Weisheipl, *Friar Thomas d'Aquino: His Life, Thought, and Work* (Washington, D.C.: The Catholic University of America Press, 1983). The version reported by Bartholomew of Capua (logothete of the King of Naples and authoritative witness of the first process of canonization) is slightly different: the student suggests to Thomas that, if he was able to possess the city of Paris, he would be able to sell it back to the king of France to build a new convent for the brothers, and to this point Thomas replies that he would prefer instead the commentary of Chrysostom on Matthew. See A. A. Robiglio, *La sopravvivenza*

of his Parisian students, he is supposed to have said that he would have preferred to possess all of John Chrysostom's homilies on the Gospel of Matthew than to possess the whole city of Paris. The text of Chrysostom from which Thomas quotes most often (in fact, the most quoted text in the entire *Catena*), however, is, oddly enough, the *Opus imperfectum in Matthaeum*, which is apocryphal. But this obviously takes nothing away from the special reverence that Thomas had for Chrysostom and, indeed, confirms it.[80] While the limits that we have set to our introduction to Thomas's thought do not permit us to reflect further on the *Catena* (and we would not, at any rate, have the competence to do so), we must observe that this work occupies a very important place in Thomas's overall output, as the tradition itself makes clear.

Expositio super primam et secundam Decretalem

At Orvieto, Thomas would have been able to begin working on the epistles of Paul. But since it is more likely that he did this during his time in Rome (and it is still a subject of debate, as we will see, whether he also worked on them in Naples between 1272 and 1273), we will return to it later.[81]

In the general ambit of exegetical works we could include the *Expositio super primam et secundam decretalem*. The texts on which Thomas comments are not from the Scriptures but two documents of the fourth Lateran Council of 1215. The first, *Firmiter*, is a profession of faith, and the second, *Damnamus*, is the council's condemnation of the trinitarian opuscule of Joachim of Fiore in which Peter Lombard's teaching on the Trinity is criticized. In other words, Thomas is commenting on the first title (subdivided into two chapters: *Firmiter* and *Damnamus*) in the first book of the *Decretals*. There is discord in the catalogues over the dedication of the work. It is variously reported as being dedicated to the *archidiaconum tridentinum, cundentinum,* and *tudertinum.* The third, which is attested to by Bartholomew of Capua, among others, seems the most plausible. In this case the dedicatee would be Giffredus or Goffredus of Anagni, the *socius* of the Dominican master Adenulfus of Anagni and archdeacon of Todi from 1260. There is uncertainty about the date of the work. It could possibly have been composed between 1261 and 1269 and so, in theory, even after Thomas's sojourn in Orvieto. Certainly Thomas drafted the Office of Corpus Christi while he was

---

e la gloria: Appunti sulla formazione della prima scuola tomista (sec. XIV), Sacra doctrina. Bibliotheca 53 (Bologna: ESD, 2008), especially 80–82.

80. Although it would not have been possible for Thomas to doubt the writing's authenticity, he did notice some of its differences with respect to the authentic homilies translated by Burgundio of Pisa and made an effort to moderate certain formulations dangerously close to Arianism.

81. See the section in Chapter 4 on the commentaries on the epistles of Paul.

in Orvieto. With this work the problem is not the date but the authorship.[82] But many doubts that have been raised about this have been dealt with, and we recommend Jean-Pierre Torrell's treatment of the state of the question.[83]

De emptione et venditione ad tempus

There are other writings of the Orvieto period, composed at the request of confreres and prelates with whom Thomas presumably came into contact in the papal curia.

In this group we can first mention *De emptione et venditione ad tempus*, written around 1262, which responds to a question posed by James of Viterbo, lector of the convent of Florence (and not to be confused with the important Augustinian master of the later thirteenth century, who was a student and successor to Giles of Rome). The same question was posed to Marinus of Eboli, the chaplain of Urban IV and archbishop-elect of Capua (even if, as it seems, he initially rejected the appointment). Thomas says that he had discussed the question with Marinus and with Cardinal Hugh of Saint-Cher, who had also been a master in Paris. James appears to have placed before Marinus and Thomas four very specific cases, which are not reported in their original formulation but the general idea is sufficiently clear: it is a matter of the deferment of payments. It is likely that the question arose out of the practice of deferring payment on goods for three months in commercial transactions. From the start Thomas's position is unequivocal. This practice is driven solely by the common interest of the merchants, but it cannot in any way justify an increase in price, for in this situation that would be usury. If, therefore, the merchants sell their goods within the limits of their value, deferment is not a problem. But if they charge more because of the delay in payment, they would be engaged in usury since, in a way that is analogous to those who lend on interest, they are "selling time." On this last point Thomas is so radical as to hold that even those who return what they have borrowed before the set time so as to earn a reduction in their payment are guilty of usury. This person too exploits time. Nevertheless, if the creditor accepts an amount that is lower than what was lent (lower not with respect to the interest—which he never has a right to ask—but with respect to the absolute amount), he is not guilty of usury, because he simply gives up something that he is owed. Analogously, those merchants are not guilty of usury who sell goods at a lower price if the payment is made upfront. So, if in determining the final price merchants can rightly ask for all the costs that they have incurred (in

---

82. It is certain that it was composed before August 11, 1264, that is, before the bull *Transiturus de hoc mundo*, with which Urban IV instituted the feast of Corpus Christi and also promulgated its office.

83. See Torrell, *Saint Thomas Aquinas*, vol. 1, *The Person and His Work*, 129–36.

transporting the goods, for example), any type of increase in the price or interest on account of time would, for Thomas, constitute an inexcusable form of usury.

De articulis fidei et ecclesiae sacramentis

The *De articulis fidei et ecclesiae sacramentis* is more difficult to date. It should be situated between 1261 and 1265, although some Dominican scholars, such as R.-A. Gauthier and Dalmazio Mongillo, suggest that it was composed between 1265 and 1268, while Thomas was in Rome. The opuscule was written at the request of Leonard, Alexander IV's chaplain and the archbishop of Palermo from 1261 to 1270, whom Thomas may have met at the papal curia. Thomas's introduction gives us to understand that his interlocutor had asked him to set down in writing a concise treatment of what belongs to faith and to the sacraments and the doubts that could be raised about them. Thomas preemptively observes that if he had wished to satisfy this request fully, he should have tried to synthesize all the material of theology, but that this would have had questionable results. Thus, Thomas opts for a kind of brief catalogue of the articles of faith, the sacraments, and the errors that have been committed (and that should be avoided) in regard to each of them. With respect to the division of the material, Thomas adopts an approach that is different from the one (usually circular) he uses in the great theological works. The whole of the Christian faith relates to the divinity and the humanity of Christ and so the chief articles of faith are subdivided in the first part into these two areas (following a process that is similar to the one already used by Philip the Chancellor in his *Summa de bono*, as the editors of the Leonine Commission note). The sacraments are dealt with in the second part with the essential traits of each noted (matter, form, ministers, and effects). From a philosophical point of view, the aspect that is perhaps most interesting is that the positions of the *philosophi* sometimes appear alongside those of classical heresies (mostly drawn from Augustine's *De haeresibus*) in the list of errors. In connection with the divine oneness, for example, Thomas recalls the position of the Epicureans, who denied divine knowledge and providence of human affairs, and that of "some pagan philosophers" (*quorundam gentilium philosophorum*) who limit the divine power to the natural course of events (it is possible that Thomas is implicitly aiming at Avicenna here). In regard to creation, the theses of Plato, Anaxagoras, and Aristotle are cited as erroneous, the first two as contrary to *creatio ex nihilo* (because of the assumption of a preexisting matter), and the third as contrary to creation in time.[84] In other

---

84. The *De articulus fidei*, therefore, is among the texts in which Thomas generously concedes that Aristotle held that God produces the world even though he understood this production as atemporal.

contexts, with regard to the denial of free will and the resurrection of the body, Thomas seems rather to deal with more recent (if not exactly contemporary) heretical positions (*error est quorundam modernorum hereticorum*), probably, that is, with those of the Cathars.

Contra errores Graecorum

The *Contra errores Graecorum* was composed between 1263 and 1264 at the request or prayer of Urban IV (*ad preces papae Urbani*). If it were possible to invent or denominate *a posteriori* a new literary genre—that of the "theology of equivocations"—the *Contra errores Graecorum* would be a small masterpiece of this genre. The work consists, in effect, in the examination (which is what the pope requested) of a compilation of texts of the Greek Fathers, the *Liber de fide Trinitatis*, probably put together by Nicholas of Durazzo, who became bishop of Cotrone (present day Crotone) in 1254. From what Thomas expressly says in the introduction, it would seem that he became aware of the text only when the pope drew his attention to it, with the request to evaluate it critically. But actually Thomas appears to have made use of it previously, in the *Contra impugnantes*, for instance. Nicholas of Durazzo composed a first draft of his opuscule in Greek at the request of the Byzantine emperor Theodore Laskaris. Thomas would have been able to consult a Latin translation, perhaps by the author himself, when he wrote the *Contra impugnantes*. Subsequently, around 1262, at the request of the new emperor, Michael Palaeologus, Nicholas returned to the work. A copy of this revision reached Urban IV, who then passed it on to Thomas. The whole episode is inscribed in the consultations between Urban IV and Michael Palaeologus about the relationship between the Roman and the Eastern Church. The book of Nicholas (who seems to have been perfectly bilingual) is nothing other than a dossier prepared for the Byzantine court to show the substantial unity of the Greek and Latin Fathers on topics that were at the center of the debate of those years. The collection is, then, already ideologically oriented or at least of a quite irenic tendency. Moreover, as the Leonine editors show, the use of the Greek sources is not always faithful or direct. Indeed, they are not only mixed together with an apparatus of glosses that often changes the original meaning but it can also be suspected that they were, on occasion, intentionally altered. Thomas, who obviously does not pose the question of the authenticity of the documentary material, takes the same route. Despite the title, we will not find in the text a list of the points of disagreement between the Greeks and Latins, but an interpretation of the Greek texts that is strongly marked by—as we would say today—the principle of hermeneutic charity. Thus, in the first part Thomas proposes to clarify all of the dubious or suspect expressions in the compiled Greek texts so that their apparent ambiguity—caused by the inevitable imprecisions of language and above all by the translation—not be the source of error. Or, to put it more exactly: this is what Thomas *takes* himself to be doing, for in reality he is principally addressing not the actual texts of the Greek Fathers but the glosses that accompany them and that might mostly derive from the Latin compiler! Also in the second part, Thomas proposes to reinterpret the same *auctoritates* of the Greek Fathers in a more systematic theological framework (to show how they contribute to teaching and defending the truth of the Catholic faith). But in this case too he focuses exclusively not on what is in the Greek texts but on what was added to them with the intention of smoothing over their differences with the views of the Latin Fathers. The result is somewhat bizarre, as we have said, because Thomas's analysis does not, in the end, directly confront the Greek sources, but generously reinterprets what a Latin commentator—who also wished to be generous but who, in fact, caused confusion—added to them. In this way it is concluded that it is possible to justify from the writings of the Greek Fathers the procession of the Holy Spirit from the Son, the primacy of the Roman pontiff, and the existence of purgatory. We can imagine, in any case, Thomas's difficulty. On the one hand, he had an authentic reverence for the Greek Fathers, and, on the other hand—prevented, like most of the masters of the time, from reading them in the original—he had to deal with incomplete and not always trustworthy translations. In regard to the *Catena*, we already recalled how Thomas sought or commissioned new translations of the Greek texts; and this same concern, as we know, will likewise guide him in his pursuit of new translations of philosophical texts. So, it is not by chance that in the introduction to the *Contra errores Graecorum*, apart from particular conclusions, Thomas explicitly reflects on the interpretive problems caused by a more or less technical language and by the method employed in the translation. Let us remember that Thomas's first intention is to eliminate as far as possible the apparent ambiguities in the texts (presumed to be) from the Greek Fathers. Now, these ambiguities depend, in Thomas's view, essentially on two factors. First, the theological language becomes more technical and precise when specific errors or heresies have to be refuted. Hence, it is inevitable that those who wrote about divine oneness before the spread of the Arian heresy used formulations that were much less careful and circumscriptive than those who had to confront Arianism or who wrote in later times. The other example that Thomas uses in this connection is perhaps more significant because it concerns the evolution of the language of an individual author, namely, Augustine. When the young Augustine faces the Manicheans, his main concern is with defending free will, and it is natural that some expressions emphasize this. When he later faces the Pelagians, his main concern is with defending the role of grace, and it is natural that the formulations about the free will are more precise and restrained (so much so that the Pelagians themselves used Augustine's earlier writings for their own ends). In general, the Scholastic masters are conscious of employing a language that is more and more technical and professional. Thomas tries in this context to offer an historical explanation of the phenomenon:

It is, therefore, no wonder if, after the appearance of various errors, modern teachers of the faith speak more cautiously and more selectively so as to steer clear of any kind of heresy. Hence, if there are found some points in statements of the ancient Fathers not expressed with the caution moderns find appropriate to observe, their statements are not to be ridiculed or rejected; on the other hand neither are they to be overextended, but reverently interpreted.[85]

The second factor is the difficulty inherent in any translation. There are, in fact, many expressions that are correct in Greek but that do not "sound" right in Latin, and it is because of this that the same truth of faith is expressed in different terms by the Latins and by the Greeks. The Greeks say, for example, that the Father, Son, and Holy Spirit are three *hypostases*. Now, if *hypostasis* is rendered literally with *substantia*, then in Latin it must be said that the Father, Son, and Holy Spirit are three substances, which sounds quite wrong since in Latin *substantia* is often synonymous with essence, and the divine essence is one. The lesson that we can learn from this is that translators should not be strictly literal:

It is, therefore, the task of the good translator, when translating material dealing with the Catholic faith, to preserve the meaning, but to adapt the mode of expression so that it is in harmony with the idiom of the language into which he is translating.[86]

When anything that is said in a sophisticated way in Latin is explained in common parlance, the explanation will be inept if it is simply word for word. All the more, then, should we avoid this method when we are translating from one language to another. Thus, it is of little importance that Thomas was unable to distinguish in the text between what came from the Greek Fathers and what came from the Latin compiler. In any event, we see in Thomas a preoccupation with the intelligibility of the texts that would make him appreciate the translation work of William of Moerbeke with respect to philosophical texts.

---

85. *Contra errores Graecorum.*
86. *Contra errores Graecorum.*

De rationibus fidei

In the *De rationibus fidei* (which we can date to around 1265) Thomas responds to a request by a person who is identified only as the cantor of Antioch. Perhaps he is a missionary who finds himself having to face numerous adversaries of the Catholic faith. First among these adversaries are the "Saracens," who laugh at the idea that God could have generated a son and see the Trinity, the Incarnation, and the Eucharist as equally absurd. But alongside these errors that regard the *fides christiana* (which consists principally in the mysteries of the Trinity and the Incarnation), there are others that have to do with the *spes christiana*, which also principally regards two aspects: what awaits us after death and the divine aid with which we can in this life merit future beatitude. The Greeks and the Armenians, for example, do not accept purgatory and deny that souls receive rewards and recompenses before the final judgment and the reunification with the body. The Muslims (but not only them), again, hold to a fatalism and deny free will as well as human merit. The unknown cantor asks explicitly for moral and philosophical arguments that can be accepted by the Muslims. As we already know, it is completely useless to argue only from *auctoritates* that our opponents do not accept. But it must nevertheless be emphasized (especially in our times, when it is very easily forgotten) that, for Thomas and most thirteenth-century theologians, engagement with Islam can and must occur on rational and philosophical ground. Nevertheless, as Thomas himself is concerned immediately to stress once more, the place of reason must be qualified and restricted. It is impossible to demonstrate the truths of the Catholic faith. But it *is* possible to show that the faith itself cannot in any way be rationally refuted or falsified. Reason, as we have learned to recognize, has an indirect or negative function. It serves only to show that what is believed by faith is not, in principle, false or impossible. This initial clarification by Thomas (which in the actual division of the text is the second chapter) is undoubtedly, even if redundant, the most philosophically interesting part of the work:

First of all, I wish to warn you that in disputations with unbelievers about articles of the faith, you should not try to prove the faith by necessary reasons. This would belittle the sublimity of the faith, whose truth exceeds not only human minds but also those of angels; we believe in them only because they are revealed by God. Yet whatever comes from the supreme truth cannot be false, and what is not false cannot be repudiated by any necessary reason. Just as our faith cannot be proved by necessary reasons, because it exceeds the human mind, so because of its truth it cannot be refuted by any necessary reason. So, any Christian disputing about the articles of the faith should not try to prove the faith, but defend the faith ... so that reason can show that what the Catholic faith holds is not false.

Here we have the same program that is articulated in the *Contra Gentiles*, and this is a point in favor of the strict chronological link between the two writings such that the drafting of the *De rationibus fidei* can be dated to around 1265. But it should be noted that on this aspect of the relationship between faith and reason Thomas never changed his position.

4

THE YEARS IN ROME
AND THE CONSTRUCTION OF
THE *SUMMA THEOLOGIAE*

———•◦•———

THE FOUNDATION OF THE *STUDIUM* IN ROME
AND THE PROBLEM OF THE *ALIA LECTURA*

In September 1265, the provincial chapter at Anagni directed Thomas ("for the remission of your sins") to transfer to Rome to found a new *studium*. Unlike Orvieto, here Thomas would not be charged with teaching only the friars of one priory, since the new *studium* had the purpose of gathering together a select group of friars from the various priories of the Roman province (and Thomas would have been able to send friars back who were not capable of the work). Naturally, that does not mean that the *studium* in Rome was at the same level of importance as the *studia generalia* of Paris and Cologne (also because, despite what one might suppose, the city of Rome could certainly not compete in size or importance with the true medieval metropolises). Leonard Boyle has spoken in this regard of a "personal *studium*," that is, of a project strictly connected with the figure of Thomas, but perhaps we need to reflect on the meaning of this expression.[1] It is probable that Thomas, participating in the provincial chapters as preacher general, asked that the mandates of Valenciennes be more strictly adhered to, even in the Roman province, and it is just as probable that he was asked to ensure this personally. In fact, it is possible that at the new Roman *studium* at Santa Sabina, Thomas was the only teacher (at least we have no knowledge of other masters, lectors, or bachelors), and the whole thing seems to have ceased to exist with his departure for Paris after only three years.

However brief, this experience in any case occupies an important place in the intellectual itinerary of Thomas, because it coincides with the beginning of the construction of the *Summa theologiae*. As many have suggested, it was per-

---

1. L. E. Boyle, "The Setting of the *Summa theologiae* of Saint Thomas," in Boyle's *Facing History: A Different Thomas Aquinas* (Louvain-la-Neuve: FIDEM, 2000), 73.

haps an unhappiness with the textbooks (mostly aimed at casuistry and rather impoverished on the dogmatic front) being used in the formation of the friars that moved Thomas also in this case to make up for the lack himself. In a *studium* that was directly entrusted to his care, Thomas could have taken the opportunity to create a hefty textbook structured in accordance with his own needs.

But this decision would have had to develop gradually. We know that during this period Thomas also began to revise his Commentary on the *Sentences* to use for his own teaching, following the Parisian custom. This is reported by Tolomeo of Lucca,[2] but for some time seemed to lack supporting evidence, that is, until the discovery in the Oxford manuscript, Lincoln College, Lat. 95 (a manuscript of Italian provenance, it should be noted), next to the text of the Parisian commentary on Book I of the *Sentences* (copied by hand A), some texts in the form of articles transcribed by a different hand (hand B) in the guard folios and in the margins of the principal text; these added texts were in turn corrected and integrated by a third hand (hand C) and refer principally to distinctions 1–18 and 23–24 of Book I of the *Sentences*. In some of these passages—and this is the decisive point—there appears an explicit reference to an *alia lectura fratris Thome* ("the other lecture [on the *Sentences*] of Friar Thomas"). This discovery provoked a complex and subtle debate among scholars of Thomas and the editors of the Leonine Commission about the meaning and value of this reference and about the authenticity of the additional articles contained in the manuscript. Hyacinthe Dondaine, who was the first to produce an edition of some of these passages, was rather cautious about attributing authorship to Thomas and declared that the text did not seem to contribute in any way toward the question of the existence of a second Commentary on the *Sentences*.[3] Some years later, Boyle proposed rethinking the syntagm *alia lectura*. He suggested that with this expression the author of the additional texts did not intend to refer to a new exposition started by Thomas in Rome but to the one composed in Paris. In other words, for a student or confrere who attended the lectures on the *Sentences* in Rome (or in some way found himself in Italy), the *alia lectura* would not have been the one he was attending (or was reading), but the one already completed in Paris at the beginning of the 1250s. The additional texts of the Oxford manuscript would, therefore, reflect the attempt, on the part of this unknown student or *lector*, to integrate in a copy of the Pa-

---

2. See Tolomeo of Lucca, *Historia ecclesiastica nova*, XXIII (15), in A. Dondaine, "Les 'Opuscula fratris Thomae' chez Ptolémée de Lucques," *Archivum Fratrum Praedicatorum* 31 (1961): 155. "Scripsit etiam eo tempore quo fuit Rome ..., iam magister existens, primum super Sententias, quem ego vidi Luce sed inde substractus nusquam ulterius vidi."

3. See H.-F. Dondaine, "*Alia lectura fratris Thome?* (Super I Sent.)," *Mediaeval Studies* 42 (1980): 308–36.

risian Commentary on the *Sentences* (the principal text of the Lincoln College manuscript, set down by A) some elements taken from the lectures given by Thomas in Italy (the text written by B). These additions would, in sum, derive indirectly from Thomas and more directly from a scholar-copyist (Boyle proposes the name of the Dominican Jacopo di Rinuccio da Castelbuono, who was one of the possessors of the codex now conserved at Lincoln College) who had been able to hear Thomas's teaching on the *Sentences* in Italy or had been able to procure himself a copy.[4] Mark F. Johnson subsequently furnished a list of all the identifiable articles in the Lincoln College manuscript, fixing the number at 94 (to which some notes of the reporter should be added) and aligning himself substantially with the opinion of Boyle.[5] All of these passages or articles were then collected in a critical edition by Boyle and John Boyle (the coincidence of surnames is merely chance), who stuck to the same position: the additional text of the Oxford codex reflects Thomas's new *lectura romana,* while the references to the *alia lectura* refer to the previous Parisian commentary.[6] Recently, the current president of the Leonine Commission, Adriano Oliva, directly reexamining the Oxford manuscript, was able to confirm that the third hand in the codex (C) is very probably that of Thomas's *socius continuus,* that is, his secretary and friend Reginald of Piperno (present-day Priverno in southern Lazio). If this is true, then we could develop the prudent hypothesis proposed by Oliva, to wit, that the passages in question are to be attributed not directly to Thomas but to an unknown commentator who, preparing his own course on the *Sentences* in Italy, made reference to another exposition and other texts of Thomas.[7] We might hypothesize that this commentator was Reginald himself, who, in view of his own exposition of the *Sentences,* prepared a manuscript drawing on the course Thomas had held in Italy.[8] Other scholars, such as Robert Wielockx,

4. See L. E. Boyle, "*Alia lectura fratris Thome,*" *Mediaeval Studies* 45 (1983): 418–29 (published later in *Facing History,* 93–106); See also E. Panella, "Jacopo di Rinuccio da Castelbuono op testimone dell'*alia lectura fratris Thome,*" *Memorie domenicane* 19 (1988): 369–85.

5. See M. F. Johnson, "*Alia lectura fratris Thome:* A List of the New Texts Found in Lincoln College, Oxford, Ms. Lat. 95," *Recherches de Théologie Ancienne et Médiévale* 57 (1990): 34–61.

6. See, Thomas Aquinas, *Lectura romana in primum Sententiarum Petri Lombardi,* ed. L. E. Boyle and J. F. Boyle, Studies and Texts 152 (Toronto: Pontifical Institute of Mediaeval Studies, 2006).

7. See A. Oliva, "La questione dell'*alia lectura* di Tommaso d'Aquino. A proposito dell'edizione delle note marginali del ms. Oxford, Lincoln College Lat. 95," *Quaestio* 6 (2006): 516–21. Despite the Italian title, Oliva's article is in French. He expresses some reservations about the edition cited in the preceding note, preferring the hypothesis that the passages attributed to Thomas are actually the work of another cleric, probably a Dominican friar, who was preparing for his own comments on the *Sentences* by integrating the Parisian Commentary of Thomas with other texts (also drawn from later work of Thomas—the *Compendium theologiae,* for instance) which might have been useful for this purpose.

8. See Oliva, "L'enseignement des Sentences dans les Studia dominicains italiens au XIIIe siècle:

however, continue to maintain that the passages as a whole more directly re-produce Thomas's new commentary and that there is no need to admit the me-diation of another commentator.[9] Both Oliva and Wielockx hold that Boyle's suggested reinterpretation of the expression *alia lectura* has been surpassed and is no longer tenable. The *alia lectura* to which the additional texts refer (in a more or less direct way, and on this point the problem still awaits a definitive solution) is the Italian and not the Parisian one. It is undeniable that on certain topics—among which are the subalternation of theological science and the re-lationship between theology and philosophy—the "Roman" commentary (with all the caution that such a formulation requires) seems less precise than the one published in Paris while not manifesting any real or dramatic doctrinal diver-gence. The gaps could stem from the fact that we are, in any case, dealing with a *reportatio* here (and, moreover, in a very compressed form, since the tran-scriber used only the margins and the guard folios of the Oxford manuscript) or from the fact that, on some points (as with the one on the *Verbum* that we already know well), Thomas effectively modified his judgment in the course of the years.

At any rate, if Thomas actually cultivated a project of taking up again and re-vising his earlier Commentary on the *Sentences*, it was almost immediately aban-doned to make room for the drafting of the *Summa*. It is with the *prima pars* of the latter that we will occupy ourselves in this chapter (together with the other writings of the Roman period) and in the next chapter we will attend to the *secunda pars*. (We will deal only briefly with the *tertia pars*, which is incomplete and is of less interest from a strictly speculative point of view.)

COMMENTARIES ON THE EPISTLES OF PAUL

Before focusing on the works of greater philosophical relevance, we wish to say a word about some the exegetical writings that we mentioned earlier, namely, the exposition of the epistles of Paul. The *corpus* of the commentaries or courses of Thomas on the epistles of Paul (*Expositio et lectura super Epistolas Pauli Apostoli*) appears to be divided into two distinct blocks, the one comprising the Epistle to the Romans and 1 Corinthians 1–10, the other starting from the remaining chapters of 1 Corinthians and going to the Epistle to the Hebrews. It has been

---

l'*Alia lectura* de Thomas d'Aquin et le *Scriptum* de Bombolognus de Bologne," in *Philosophy and The-ology in the Studia of the Religious Orders and at the Papal Court*, Rencontres de Philosophie Médiévale 15, ed. K. Emery Jr. and W. J. Courtenay (Turnhout: Brepols, 2012), 49–73. Oliva holds that it cannot, in fact, be denied that Thomas could have held a course on the *Sentences* also at Orvieto, and accord-ingly that the identification of the *alia lectura* with the *lectura romana* ought not be taken for granted.

9. Translator's note: Porro's comments on Wielockx draw from private correspondence.

suggested that this second block—which comes down to us in a *reportatio* of Reginald of Piperno (even if we have Hebrews 1–7 and 1 Corinthians 11–13 in two different editions)—precedes the first chronologically and is to be situated in the Italian period between the two sojourns in Paris, perhaps in Orvieto or more probably in Rome, where they could have been the object of teaching in the new *studium*. The first block has traditionally been situated in Thomas's stay in Naples (1272–73), where it is believed that Thomas could have revised and corrected Romans 1–8, since at least one of the principal witnesses to this text—Naples, Bibl. Naz. VIII.A.17—shows signs of minor redactions that are not in Thomas's hand but probably reflect his corrections nonetheless. Part of the exposition of 1 Corinthians (from 7:10 through chapter 10) is thought to be an interpolation. It is a text of Peter of Tarentaise, used to replace Thomas's original text, which was lost quite early on. This is also the thesis of Torrell, who, on the basis of what had already been suggested by Mandonnet (with a small discrepancy in the chronology), holds that Thomas taught/commented on the entire Pauline *corpus* in Rome but that the first part was neglected in the textual tradition and eventually disappeared because it was replaced by the Commentary (revised and corrected at least in part) subsequently undertaken in Naples. The transitional part between the two blocks—the Commentary on 1 Corinthians 7:10 through chapter 10—would have been the text of Peter of Tarentaise. In a recent reconsideration of the problem, Wielockx contends that, contrary to the countless hypotheses that have been advanced, the construction of the critical edition (by Gilles de Grandpré) already makes three points clear: (a) there is no proof that Thomas held courses on the Pauline *corpus* on two distinct occasions; (b) on the basis of the manuscript tradition it does not seem possible to distinguish between a manuscript redacted in part by the author and one circulated in the form of a *reportatio*;[10] (c) it is certain that Thomas made a quick revision of his course (limited to the Epistle to the Romans and up to the third lecture on the thirteenth chapter) through brief and quite sporadic annotations. But no precise date can be fixed with regard to the course, its revision, or its publication.[11]

10. Which means, as Grandpré also suggests, that the whole *corpus* could be a *reportatio* of Reginald of Piperno.

11. Although the text began to be circulated in Naples, this does not necessarily mean that it was published there. See R. Wielockx, "Au sujet du commentaire de Saint Thomas sur le 'Corpus Paulinum': critique littéraire," in *Doctor Communis: Saint Thomas's Interpretation on Saint Paul's Doctrines.* Proceedings of the IX Plenary Session, 19–21 June 2009 (Vatican City: The Pontifical Academy of St. Thomas Aquinas, 2009), 150–84. Regarding the expositive method (as it relates to the Epistle to the Romans), see T. Domanyi, *Der Römerbriefkommentar des Thomas von Aquin: Ein Beitrag zur Untersuchung seiner Auslegungsmethoden,* Basler und Berner Studien zur historischen und systematischen Theologie 39 (Bern: Lang, 1979).

We have briefly considered the events of the composition and transmission of these commentaries of Thomas only to offer an example of how complicated the situating of Thomas's works can be and to illustrate the difficulties that his editors face.[12] In this case too, the hope is that the critical Leonine edition can provide greater certainty with respect to the chronology and the relationship between the different editions.

RESPONSIO DE 108 ARTICULIS AD MAGISTRUM IOANNEM DE VERCELLIS

The mention of Peter of Tarentaise (who would later become Pope Innocent V) leads us immediately to comment on a text that Thomas composed at the request of John of Vercelli, who was the master general of the order between 1264 and 1283. He had solicited Thomas's opinion on 108 articles taken from Peter's Commentary on the *Sentences* that a reader had denounced as suspect.[13] While Thomas's attitude toward his powerful confrere (who, before becoming pope, was the head of the order in France) is generally charitable and he practically clears him of all suspicion, it is quite caustic in regard to his anonymous and over-zealous adversary, accusing him of bad faith for having initially manipulated some of the passages in question. This is not the only time that Thomas would be asked to respond to the requests of John of Vercelli. Two other writings of the second Parisian period will come into existence in the same way, testifying to the doctrinal authority that was attributed to Thomas in the order over his whole career.

SUPER LIBRUM DIONYSII DE DIVINIS NOMINIBUS
Causality and Transcendence: The Confrontation with Neo-Platonism

Of great philosophical interest is the Commentary on the *De divinis nominibus* of Pseudo-Dionysius (*Super librum Dionysii De divinis nominibus*), the unknown Christian author (perhaps Severian) of the fourth century who brilliantly pretended to be a contemporary of Paul, identifying himself as Dionysius, the convert made by the Apostle at the Areopagus in Athens.[14] For a long time there was hesitation about the period and place of Thomas's commentary and it was even hypothesized that it was composed in Orvieto. However, in one of

---

12. In Chapter 6 we will return to a topic that is particularly focused on the exposition of the Epistle to the Romans, namely, the causes of predestination.

13. Nothing is known of this reader, including whether he was a Dominican or an adversary of the order.

14. Cf. Acts 17:34.

the chapters, William of Moerbeke's translation of Aristotle's *Categories* is quoted at least twice. This translation was not completed until March 1266, when
Thomas would already have been in Rome.[15] The reasons for producing the
commentary are unclear. Was it the result of a lecture course given in Rome, or
was it a private venture destined for circulation but carried out because of doctrinal exigencies? Thomas would have been able to familiarize himself with texts
of Pseudo-Dionysius already from his time in Cologne, when he was charged
with transcribing Albert's course on the *De divinis nominibus*. At that time the
young Thomas was unable to grasp the doctrinal context adequately. Probably
influenced by Albert's syncretism, he speaks of Dionysius as a faithful follower
of Aristotle.[16] But when he decides to proceed with his own commentary on the
Divinis nominibus in Italy, Thomas is perfectly conscious of the Platonic (or,
as we would say today, Neo-Platonic) framework of the Dionysian *corpus*, and
we can suppose that if he had already become acquainted with the Latin version of Proclus's *Elementatio theologica* (completed by William of Moerbeke in
1268), he would even have suspected that behind the mask of Dionysius the Areopagite there was, in fact, quite likely hidden a Christian disciple of the same
Proclus.[17] As we will see, Thomas will be the first in the West (and precisely on
the basis of the just-mentioned Latin version of the *Elementatio theologica*) to
recognize the Proclean origin of the *Liber de causis*.

The Commentary on the *Divinis nominibus* is, in Thomas's view, a first important occasion to deal with the Platonic tradition.[18] The prologue itself to the
commentary offers a confirmation of this. After having presented the articulation of Pseudo-Dionysius's *corpus* according to the author's own indications,
Thomas explains that Pseudo-Dionysius adopts an obscure manner in his writing to shield the sacred and divine dogmas from the ridicule of unbelievers. This
obviously causes some difficulties, but apart from those owing to the laconic
style, Thomas concerns himself above all with those deriving from Pseudo-Dionysius's philosophical proclivities. The passage is worth quoting at length:

He frequently uses the Platonic style and manner of speaking, which is unfamiliar to
moderns. In fact, the Platonists, wishing to reduce all composite or material things to

15. See Torrell, *Saint Thomas Aquinas*, vol. 1, *The Person and His Work*, 127–29.
16. *In II Sent.* d. 14, q. 1, a. 2: "Dionysius follows Aristotle almost everywhere, as is evident from
a careful inspection of his books."
17. Hierotheos, of whom Dionysius often speaks, appears to be an avatar or alter-ego of Proclus.
18. On the relationship of Thomas with the "Platonists," see R. J. Henle, *Saint Thomas and Platonism: A Study of the "Plato" and "Platonici" Texts in the Writings of Saint Thomas* (Den Haag: Martinus Nijhoff, 1956); W. J. Hankey, "Aquinas and the Platonists," in *The Platonic Tradition in the Middle
Ages: A Doxographic Approach*, ed. S. Gersh and M. J. F. M. Hoenen (Berlin: de Gruyter, 2002),
279–324.

simple and abstract principles, admitted the separate species of things, affirming that "man" exists beyond matter as does "horse" and, in an analogous way, all the species of other material things. Thus, they said that this individual man is not identical with man but is called man because of his participation in the separate species.... Nor were the Platonists satisfied with considering this abstraction to be the ultimate species of natural things but applied it to the most common properties as well, such as good, one, being. This is because they admitted a first one, which is the essence itself of goodness, oneness, and being, which we call God, and from which all other things are called good, one, or being. For this reason they called this first reality the good itself, or the good in itself, or the principal good, or super-good, or also the good of all goods or also goodness, or essence, or substance, as is said of the separate species. Now, this theory of the Platonists, insofar as it regards the separate natural species, does not accord with the faith or with the truth. But, as regards the first principle of things, their thesis is most true and accords with the Christian faith.[19]

Clarity is something that Thomas never lacks. What he rejects in Platonism (in accord with the Christian faith but also with Aristotle) is the doctrine of separate forms. What he accepts is the doctrine of principles, especially according to its Neo-Platonic and Proclean reformulation (but he does not, in this place, thematize the possible conflict between this doctrine and the fundamental views of Aristotle). Put in this way, the confrontation with the Neo-Platonists seems to sort itself out quite easily. But things are complicated by the fact that Pseudo-Dionysius himself, although he insists quite firmly (unlike his pagan teachers) on divine monocausality,[20] and moderates the cyclical law of causation, never made a truly clean break with the Proclean laws of causality and participation. Hence, it is not surprising that some of Proclus's basic axioms should filter through to Thomas's own thought as well. It is enough to recall the thesis according to which every cause is present, inasmuch as it is participated, in its effects, whereas the latter are pre-contained in the causes in a more noble and eminent way;[21] or the principle according to which whatever is received (or participated) is received in the measure proper to the recipient.[22] Tensions arise, however, when it

19. *De divinis nominibus*, prologue.

20. Intending by "monocausality" the fact that only God is held as originating and primary cause of everything that follows.

21. Thomas perfectly recognizes the cyclical course of causality typical of Proclus's system, according to which all is in all, but according to the mode proper to each thing: the superior is present in the inferior by participation, whereas the inferior is present in the superior in a mode that is more excellent than it is in itself. See c. 4, l. 5: "According to the view of the Platonists, superior things are in inferior things by participation; inferior things, however, are in superior things, by a certain excellence, and, thus, all things are in all things. From the fact that all things are found in all things by a certain order, it follows that all things are ordered to the same end."

22. It is curious that some of Thomas's interpreters continue to present principles of this type as

is a question of minimizing the role of intermediate causes (the hypostases) to privilege divine monocausality, for at that point there must be found a different solution to the basic problem raised by Proclus (and resolved by him through the intermediaries). How can the absolute transcendence of the One (and/or God) and its just as absolute efficient causality be held together? If we unwaveringly hold that the One is beyond all discourse and thought, we cannot even say that it is the first cause of everything that follows. But if we stress that the causality of all the other causes depends on the causality of the One, we abandon the path of purely negative theology, that is, we break the silence that is appropriate to what is ineffable, and we end up stating something about it, at least that it is a cause. Here we have—at least in the way that it is treated by the Neo-Platonists —the basic dilemma of Plato's *Parmenides*. Must we say of the One that it is or that it is not? Or, to put it better: If the One is, how can the "many" be? But if the One is not, again, how can the "many" be? In the simplest terms, it can be said that Proclus (or at least the Proclus of the *Elementatio theologica*), along with Syrianus, attributes the negative hypothesis (understood as pure transcendence, as the One that is only One) to the One in itself, in its abiding (*monê*) and the positive hypothesis to the One considered in its relationship to others, to its turning outward or procession (*próodos*). Or better: Proclus attributes the negative hypothesis to the One and the positive hypothesis to the plurality of divine classes that have a positive and providential role vis-à-vis the world. All of the hypostases that come after the One depend on it for their causality (they do not lack "constitution" in an absolute sense), but they self-constitute in their specific form or determination (and in this sense are auto-hypostases or auto-hypostatic realities). The One is, thus, the first and supreme cause of what follows (and so every effect, even the most remote, carries in itself a trace of the One), but by superabundance, remains unaltered, untouched, unreachable in itself (according to the principle of *monê*), without any impoverishment or any effective compromise with the many. Because of this—and perhaps synthesizing too concisely a metaphysical system that is much more sophisticated—the dynamic of participation must be divided and analyzed in three different parts. Each relationship of participation presupposes: (a) a form that is unparticipated and unparticipatable and, therefore, absolutely transcendent; (b) a participatable form, which is

original features of his metaphysics. See c. 5, l. 1: "It should be considered that every form received in something is limited and fixed by the capacity of the one receiving." On the use of this complicated axiom in Thomas, see J. F. Wippel, "Thomas Aquinas and the Axiom 'What is Received Is Received according to the Mode of the Receiver,'" in *A Straight Path: Studies in Medieval Philosophy and Culture: Essays in Honor of Arthur Hyman*, ed. R. Link-Salinger et al. (Washington, D.C.: The Catholic University of America Press, 1998), 279–89 (published later in *Metaphysical Themes in Thomas Aquinas II*, 123–51.)

separate but participated in by inferior realities; (c) the participants themselves, in which the unitary form is multiplied.

The unparticipated or unparticipatable is, thus, the unity that precedes the many and is not mixed with them. The participatable (or participation as such according to the Proclean lexicon) is the unity present in the many. The individual participants are the many that are gathered into unity by the form that is participated.[23] In the Proclean universe this law governs the relationships, at every level, between the superior and inferior components, guaranteeing both the purity and transcendence of the superior hypostases and the consolidation of the universe itself. This consolidation consists in the fact that the effects derive from their causes and retain an essential similarity to them.[24] If we leave aside here the sphere of the enneads—that is, the first essential intermediaries through which the One, in itself absolutely unparticipated and unparticipatable, renders itself indirectly participatable—we can try to apply this dynamic to the first triad of forms that define the second hypostasis, the *Noûs*. We will have in the first place hypostatic, transcendent, and unparticipatable Being; then we will have Being as participatable participation; finally, we will have individual beings, which participate in Being. Things will be the same for the other two forms of this same triad, Life and Intelligence.

Pseudo-Dionysius, for his part, cannot admit with Proclus a class of inferior gods, and, because of this, with a particularly audacious gesture, he decides to transfer the distinction to God himself. He decides, that is, to make both unparticipatability and participatability coexist in God. More precisely, *transcendence* and *ineffability* (unparticipatability) pertain to God in his absolute *monè*, in his unknowable *essence* while the *divine names* (intelligible and symbolic) with which we refer to God pertain to his *causality*—his *próodos*—and so the creative and providential activity of God himself.

But this solution—destined to great fortune also with the whole Neo-Platonic tradition of Latin Christianity (from Erigena to Nicholas of Cusa)—

23. See Proclus, *Elementatio theologica*, prop. 24 (Greek text E. R. Dodds, ed., Oxford: Clarendon Press, 1963; Latin text of the Moerbeke translation: *Ancient and Medieval Philosophy*, I/15, ed. H. Boese [Leuven: Leuven University Press, 1987], 17); English translation, *Proclus' Elements of Theology*, trans. Thomas Taylor (Frome, England: The Prometheus Trust, 1998), 17: "The imparticipable, therefore, is the leader of things which are participated; but the latter are the leaders of the participants. For, in short, the imparticipable is one, prior to the many; but that which is participated in the many, is one and at the same time not one; and every thing which participates is not one, and at the same time one."

24. See especially Proclus, *Elementatio theologica*, prop. 23 (in Dodds, p. 26, 22–24 and Boese, p. 16); *Proclus' Elements of Theology*, p. 16: "*Every imparticipable gives subsistence from itself to things which are participated. And all participated hypostases are extended to imparticipable hyparxes.*" And from *Proclus' Elements of Theology*, prop. 24, p. 17: "Everything which participates is inferior to that which is participated; and that which is participated is inferior to that which is imparticipable."

does not completely eliminate every ambiguity. Do the names indicate the One-God only in his *ad extra* aspect, that is, as a cause of others, or something that is not properly still God, namely, the forms or exemplars, an ideal world interposed between God and sensible creatures? If, in fact, the names express the creative and providential work of God, they must be understood as general reasons of divine causality, and, therefore, the causes of inferior beings ("divine and good predeterminations and aims that determine and make beings"), and as the ultimate possible object of creaturely knowledge. But what is "named" in this way? Is it the first level of being below God (if God is beyond being) or God himself understood not as he is in himself but only as cause and explicated through what Byzantine theology calls the divine "energies"? The question is further complicated by the fact that the realm of names in Pseudo-Dionysius seems to include in some way what Proclus had distinguished as two different levels (the enneads, on the one hand, and the ideal forms of the *Noûs*, on the other) since One and Good (determinations that are anterior to the first Proclean triad of the *Noûs*) are names that, for Pseudo-Dionysius, do not belong to God in himself.

Thomas tries to deal carefully with this particularly problematic point, justifying Dionysius's hesitations, according to the interpretive hypothesis already offered in the prologue, on the basis of his adoption of Platonic language. Thus, when Dionysius speaks of being-in-itself or life-in-itself, we must in fact distinguish. In an ontological sense, such expressions designate God (who subsists independently) and nothing other than God. In a logical sense they simply indicate the quidditative content (today we would speak of the concept's "intension") to which every individual being or living thing refers (to keep with the examples given) without this content being really distinct from these individual realities:

But at this point we must examine the fact that here we speak of being-in-itself or life-in-itself or similar things. To do this we must understand that the Platonists—whom Dionysius follows very closely in this work—placed above all the things that participate by composition, realities separately existing in themselves, which are participated in by composite things. In the same way, above all individual men that participate in humanity, they placed a separately existing immaterial man through which all individual men are said to be by participation. And analogously they said that above all individual composite living things there exists a separate life, which they call life-in-itself, and through which all individual living things live. The same things also hold for wisdom-in-itself and being-in-itself. And they maintained that these separate principles are different from each other and from the first principle that they called the good-in-itself or the one-in-itself. Now Dionysius partly agrees with them and partly disagrees with them. He agrees with them in affirming that there is a separate life that exists in itself and a separate wisdom, being, and so on. But he disagrees with them in the fact that he does not say that these separate principles are different from each other, but that there is only one principle, which is God.... Thus, when we speak of life-in-itself, according to Dionysius, this can be understood in two ways. In the first way in the sense that "in-itself" implies a real distinction and separation, and thus life-in-itself is God himself; in a second way in the sense that "in-itself" implies only a logical distinction and separation, and so life-in-itself is that which exists in living things, which is not really but only logically distinguished from those living things.[25]

On closer inspection, we can perhaps see that Thomas seeks a way out of the problem of separation of forms by once again employing the Avicennian doctrine of the indifference of essences. A long passage from c. 11 is possibly more indicative of this:

Later ... he excludes an erroneous interpretation. To see this we must understand that the Platonists, who held that the ideas are separate from things, affirmed that all that is said abstractly subsists abstractly as a cause according to a certain order. Thus, they said that the first principle of things is goodness-in-itself and oneness-in-itself, and said that this first principle, which is essentially good and one, is the supreme God. Below the good they situated being, as we have already noted, and below being they situated life, and so forth with the other things. They thus held that below the supreme God there is a certain divine substance that is called being-in-itself, and below it another that is called life-in-itself. Now, wishing to exclude these theses, Dionysius affirms that what was said earlier—that is, that being-in-itself and life-in-itself above all draw existence from God—is not something erroneous but correct and has clear arguments [in its favor]. In fact, we do not say that being-in-itself is a divine or angelic substance that causes the existence of every being. He adds "angelic" because those whom the Platonists call the secondary gods we call angels. In fact, only divine supersubstantial being is the principle, the substance, and the cause by which all things exists.... Analogously, when we speak of life-in-itself, we do not intend some deity that would cause life that is not the life itself of the supreme God, who is the cause of all being and even of life-in-itself. And, to put it succinctly, we do not say that there are separate beings and substances that are principles of things and creators of them, which the Platonists called the gods and creators of existing things, as if they acted alone in the production of things.... Later ... Dionysius, following the truth, takes care of the error, and affirms that being-in-itself and life-in-itself can be said in two ways. According to the first way, they are said of God, who is the one supersubstantial principle and the cause of each thing. And God is called life-in-itself and being-in-itself because he does not live by participation in some life, nor does he exist through participation in some being. He is his own living and his own life, surpassing every being and every life that is participated by creatures, and he is the principle of the living and being of each thing. According to the second way, being-in-itself and life-in-itself are said of

25. *De divinis nominibus*, c. 5, l. 1.

certain powers and perfections granted to creatures to participate according to the providence of the one unparticipatable God. In fact, although God is the principle of these powers, he remains in himself unparticipatable and, consequently, is not participated. Nevertheless, his gifts are shared among creatures and are received in a partial way, for which reason it is said that creatures participate in them. And since they participate according to the mode proper to each participant, from this perspective it is said that the beings that participate in being are and are called by nature existing, and those that participate in life are called living, and those that participate in divinity are called gods, and the same holds for the other perfections. And because the unparticipated principle is the cause of the participations of the participants, God is the sustainer both of the participations and the participants. Now, in regard to the participants, they can be considered in three ways. First, they can be considered in themselves insofar as they prescind both from universality and from particularity, as is clearly the case when we speak of life-in-itself. Second, they can be considered in a general way, as when we speak of total or universal life. Third, they can be considered in a particular way, as when we speak of the life of this or that individual.[26]

When Thomas, following Dionysius, distinguishes "in the second way" between God as unparticipatable, participations, and participants, he does nothing other than repropose, quite exactly, the classical Proclean schema that we saw earlier. Everything turns on the ontological status of the second level, that of the participations. It is here that, once again, Avicenna's great lesson is useful (even if Avicenna is not explicitly mentioned), inasmuch as it is possible to apply to the participations the same threefold consideration that, for Avicenna, applies to every essence. They can be considered universally (and, thus, according to their being in the intellect), or in particular (according to the real being that they have in individuals), and, finally, in themselves, according to their quidditative content. But, as we already know, this "neutral" consideration does not apply to an autonomous being. Expressions such as being-in-itself and life-in-itself (when they do not signify God according to the first way of understanding) do not refer to separate subsisting forms but to the *intension* (that is, the meaning) of the two concepts "being" and "life," prescinding from their extension (natural or mental existence) that always inevitably accompanies them. The eidetic separation—to wit, the possibility of considering things in the pure quidditative content, prescinding from how they then exist—must not be confused with ontological separation—that is, with the existence of subsistent forms. Avicenna's anti-Platonic

26. *De divinis nominibus*, c. 11, l. 4. On the subject of the "error" of the Platonists, see, also, c. 5. Lect. 1: "Dionysius excludes the error of some Platonists who reduce universal effects to intelligible causes. And because they viewed the effect of the good to be most universal, they argued for its own cause to be goodness itself which emits goodness into all things, and under the good they placed another cause which gives life and so about other things, and in this way that called the principles gods."

strategy, therefore, remains a good antidote for Thomas against every excessive concession to Neo-Platonic realism, even when it is closer in some way.

The Good Beyond Being?

Beyond this confrontation over the basic framework, and over the separateness of forms (which, obviously, does not prevent Thomas from continuing to posit the exemplars in God himself), there is another small problem in dealing with the Neo-Platonists—especially with Proclus and his Christian "disciple"—that is perhaps worth attention. What we have in mind is the problem of the relationship between the One/Good and being. The Proclean One is notoriously beyond being since being is one of the inferior hypostatic realities that already introduces a form of limitedness/determination. In the first place, Thomas has no difficulty in following Pseudo-Dionysius's interpretation. To say that God (the One) *is not*, is doubtless correct—not, of course, in the sense that he does not exist, but in the sense that he exceeds and transcends being as we know it, the way that common things exist. God, in other words,

does not exist according to the common mode of existence, which is to say that he does not exist in the way of existing of any existing thing. And, nevertheless, he is the cause of the existing of each thing, communicating to each of them his own likeness such that he can be named by the names of creatures. It is for this reason that he is non-existent, not as if he were lacking with respect to existence but as he who exists above every substance.[27]

But Proclus actually meant to say much more than this, and that is that if being is a form (even if the first and most universal of forms), then it is always transcended by the One since the One is situated above every form. But Thomas's God, as we know, is pure being. In Thomas the absolute transcendence of the Proclean One with respect to being as such is transformed into the transcendence of common being or being in general, that is, created being. The Commentary on the *Divinis nominibus* is well-suited to complete what we began to see in the Commentary on the *De Trinitate* of Boethius, because here Thomas explicitly reflects on the relationship between God as pure being and common being. Here too it will be enough to read at least one passage from c. 5:

Common being itself is from the first being, which is God, which entails that common being relates to God differently than do other existing things in three ways. First, it relates differently by the fact that other existing things depend on common being, while God alone does not. On the contrary, common being depends on God, and for this reason he says that common being itself is from God since it depends on him, and God is not being,

27. *De divinis nominibus*, c. 1, l. 1.

that is, common being, since it depends on him. Second, it relates differently by the fact that all existing things are contained in common being, but God is not, and common being is rather contained in his power to the extent that divine power extends further with respect to the being of creatures. And this is what is affirmed when it is said that common being is in God himself as what is contained is in the container. But the converse is not true, that God is in being. Third, it relates differently by the fact that all other existing things participate in being but God does not. On the contrary, created being itself is a certain participation in God and a likeness of him. And this is what is affirmed when it is said that common being possesses God, that is, it possesses God as a participant of his likeness, while he does not possess being as a participation of being itself.[28]

Despite having explicitly stated in the prologue that he wished to follow the Platonists in regard to their doctrine of principles (but not in their doctrine of forms), Thomas does not seem at all disposed to concede to Proclus the superiority of the Good (the One) over being.[29] The roots of this decision could be seen as running quite deep, into the tradition of Middle Platonism and then into *Latin* Neo-Platonism, which, unlike Greek Neo-Platonism, chooses to identify the One and being. One thinks here of the decision already made by Augustine (*Deus idipsum esse, sincerum esse*, etc.), which corresponds to that (in Greek) made by the author of the Commentary on the *Parmenides* attributed to Porphyry. Pseudo-Dionysius, on the other hand, is a unique case in the East, precisely in his attempt to hold together, at the same supreme hypostatic level, the negative and positive hypotheses of the *Parmenides*: good will, thus, be superior to being, and yet being can at the same time be the first and most adequate divine name, because it is able to represent in the most appropriate way how the ineffable One is present in its procession (or better, in its providence, to keep with the language of Pseudo-Dionysius). But precisely because of this, Dionysius is not quite as far away from Proclus as Thomas is. Still—at least this is our conviction—Thomas's work on Dionysius has a profound influence

28. *De divinis nominibus*, c. 5, l. 2.

29. As usual, Thomas explains the Neo-Platonic doctrine with extreme accuracy. See, for example, c. 3, l. 1: "Accepting the term [Good as a name for God] in this way, it needs to be considered that the Platonists do not distinguish matter from privation, placing matter in the order of non-being, as Aristotle says in book I of the *Physics*. The causality of being, however, does not extend but to being. And so according to the Platonists the causality of being did not extend to prime matter, to which, nevertheless, the causality of the good extends. The sign of this is that matter most desires the good. Now it is proper of the effect that it be turned by desire to its cause. So therefore the good is a more universal and higher cause than being, since its causality extends to many things." See also in c. 5, l. 1: "After Dionysius treated the good in Chapter 4, here in Chapter 5 he turns to being, which he takes into consideration after the good, since the good, in a certain way, extends to many things, as the Plantonists say, for even not existing in act, which is being in potency, from that very fact has a relation to the good, possessing the nature of the good, but it participates in the causality of being when it becomes a being in act."

on how Thomas rethinks the identity between God and being. To be perfectly clear, this identity has a meaning for Thomas only in the key of negative theology, only in the negative approach that he privileges above every other approach to the divine in this life. We saw this decision take root in Thomas's earlier writings. In the Commentary on the *Divinis nominibus*—perhaps only to be consonant with text he is commenting on—this decision becomes especially radical and explicit. The negative way is by far preferable to the affirmative way, because God alone is above every created intellect and remains, for us, "incomprehensible" and "incontemplatable" in his essence "since our knowledge is bound to created realities inasmuch as they are connatural to us."[30] The same intelligible names that Pseudo-Dionysius treats of in his work, and that are taken from the intelligible perfections that proceed from God to creatures (such as "being," "living," etc.) are inadequate.[31] In the *De potentia*, which also belongs to Thomas's Roman period (and which we will examine shortly), Thomas returns to this theme at length.[32] In this latter text, Thomas explains the plurality of the divine names on the basis of the imperfection of human knowledge, on the one hand, and on the infinity of divine perfection, on the other hand. In short, it is not possible in the present life to express the divine nature in a single name: "The cause of difference or multiplicity in these expressions is on the part of the intellect, which is unable to compass the vision of that divine essence in itself, but sees it through many faulty likenesses thereof which are reflected by creatures as by a mirror. Whereof if it saw that very essence, it would not need to use many terms, nor would it need many concepts."[33] In regard to the inadequacy of the names, Thomas states that "it is impossible for anything to be predicated univocally of God and a creature: this is made plain as follows. Every effect of an univocal agent is adequate to the agent's power: and no creature, being finite, can be adequate to the power of the first agent, which is infinite. So it is impossible for a creature to receive a likeness to God univocally."[34] Is Moses Maimonides right, then? Should we concede that between God and creatures there is an absolute equivocity? This too is impossible, for absolute equivocity prevents us from talking about one thing in relation to another and what we say about God and creatures implies, in any case, a reciprocal reference. Furthermore, since all of our knowledge of God begins from creatures, if the relationship were

---

30. *De divinis nominibus*, c. 1, l. 1. 31. *De divinis nominibus*, c. 1, l. 3.
32. *De potentia*, q. 7, aa. 4–7. 33. *De potentia*, q. 7, a. 6.
34. *De potentia*, q. 7, a. 7. This inadequacy of the creature concerns not only the good ("since in God what is present in an immaterial and simple manner is in the creature materially and multiply"), but being itself: God is, in reality, his own being, and this is not true of any creature. Since being is the first of the predicaments, the lack of univocity is inevitably extended to others.

purely equivocal or nominal, we could not know anything about God, and all of the philosophers' arguments on the topic would be reduced to sophisms. Finally, in itself every relationship of cause and effect excludes a total equivocity. Faced with a choice between the two principal proponents of the negative way known to medieval Scholasticism—Pseudo-Dionysius and Maimonides—Thomas opts for the former. The negative way—to return to the Commentary on the *Divinis nominibus*—unfolds in degrees. If in a first moment the soul is awakened from its habitual condition and abandons the order of natural things, denying that God is material and sensible, it pushes itself subsequently to the intelligible names and to "divine thoughts" (the angelic orders) to reach God above every name, discourse, or science. This is the highest point that we can reach in this life, it is the maximal realizable union (the Neo-Platonic *hénōsis*), that is, knowing what God is not. "Thus, our union with God that is possible in this life is realized in the moment in which we reach the point of knowing that he is above the highest of creatures." Thus, within the *triplex via* by which, according to Dionysius, we can approach God—the way of causality (starting from effects), the way of eminence (attributing to God in a more eminent way the perfections that we meet in creatures), and the negative way—the last is posited as the preferable one:[35]

Thus, from the order of the universe, as from a certain way and order by means of the intellect, according to our ability, we ascend to God who surpasses all things. And we do this in three ways: with the first and principal way, from the privation of all things, insofar as nothing of what we see in the order of creatures is attributed to God or belongs to God; with the second way, from excellence, we remove from God perfections like life, wisdom, and so forth, not because they are lacking in God, but on account of the fact that God surpasses all the perfections of creatures, and the reason that we remove wisdom from God is that he surpasses all wisdom; with the third way, from the causality of all things, when we reflect that everything that is in creatures proceeds from God as their cause. Conequently, our knowledge of God comes about in the opposite way from how God knows himself. God knows creatures through his own essence, while we know God through creatures.[36]

35. On the utilization of Dionysius's *triplex via* by Thomas see, above all, M. B. Ewbank, "Diverse Orderings of Dionysius's *triplex via* by Saint Thomas Aquinas," *Mediaeval Studies* 52 (1990): 82–109; Fran O'Rourke, *Pseudo-Dionysius and the Metaphysics of Aquinas*, Studien und Texte zur Geistesgeschichte des Mittelalters 32 (Leiden: Brill, 1992). Humbrecht seems, instead, to hold that Thomas did not question the primacy of eminence, making it coincide directly with affirmative predication. In other words, Thomas does not—in light of the negation of affirmations or negations—make any precise distinction between the simple eminence that is the object of affirmative predication and eminence in the sense of the superlative theology of Dionysius (*Théologie négative et noms divins chez Saint Thomas d'Aquin*, Bibliothèque thomiste 57 [Paris: Vrin, 2005], especially 779).

36. *De divinis nominibus*, c. 7, l. 4. But in this itinerary man is not without guidance. Where

We can come back to the problem with which we began. How can we reconcile this absolute predilection for the *via negativa*, which respects the Proclean
axiom of the ineffability of the first principle, with the decision to continue to
identify God with being, following the Latin tradition? This contradiction, or
short-circuit, is more apparent than real and perhaps depends on a distorting
perspective with which a part of twentieth century Neo-Thomism emphasizes
Thomas's doctrine of being, transforming it into a philosophical thesis consistent with a framework of affirmative theology. However, we have already begun
to see that Thomas uses the identification of God with being not at all to say
what God is but to show his superiority with respect to every objective or formal determination. To say that in God his essence is resolved into his being is
to maintain a negative position; it means recognizing that divine being—insofar as it is unlimited, that is, not determined by a quidditative content—is
unrepresentable and unthinkable by us, ineffable according to the Neo-Platonic
doctrine. It is, thus, undoubtedly true that Thomas's God is not beyond being
in the manner of Proclus's One, and, nevertheless, like the latter, he is above
every form, every formal determination. Consequently, we see that the distance
between the two positions is considerably reduced when we bear in mind that,
for Thomas, being is no longer a form but indicates what is other than form,
other than essence. Pure being, then, will be what transcends every form, unlimited being. Thomas will be able to explicate this basic thesis completely in
the *De potentia* and, as we have already said, in the Commentary on the *De
causis*. And because the *De causis* is, as we know, nothing other than an Arab
reworking of certain propositions of Proclus's *Elementatio theologica*, before we
examine that text we can already anticipate here one of our conclusions. Thomas's doctrine of being (of God as being) is also, despite appearances, a reworking
of a Proclean theme, filtered through a creationist and monotheist resystematization to which it was submitted in Christian and Islamic environments respectively by Pseudo-Dionysius and the author of the *De causis*. The fact that the
names of both writers are unknown is in itself a fact worthy of note: some of the
epoch-making decisions in the history of ideas do not necessarily pass through
the most well known names.

---

reason cannot reach (if not precisely through negation) the help of Scripture always remains, even if
Scripture makes use principally of symbols and intelligible names: "The sense of the previous is that
we might stop scrutinizing divine things according to our reason, but rather we might cling to the
sacred Scriptures, in which the divine names are passed on to us, through which the gifts of God and
the principles of the gifts are manifest" (c. 1, l. 2). See also c. 1, l. 1: "From what is already said, the
principal conclusion can be inferred from the following: 'Therefore, the supersubstantial and hidden
deity, should not dare to be called or thought except as those things which are described to us in the
holy Scriptures'."

Beauty

A final aspect that perhaps merits attention in the Commentary on the *De divinis nominibus* is beauty. Even on this point it might be necessary to make a preliminary clarification. Despite the laudable efforts made on this front, speaking of a medieval aesthetics remains an anachronism. This does not mean that we cannot find in the Scholastics discussions (quite infrequent, to be sure) of the beautiful, which Jan Aertsen has not mistakenly called the "forgotten transcendental."[37] In Thomas one of these discussions is contained in c. 4 of the Commentary on the *Divinis nominibus* and is motivated by Pseudo-Dionysius's remarks on the beautiful as an intelligible name of God. So, we will not expect Thomas to depart very far from the text on which he is commenting. God is beautiful because he bestows beauty on all created beings according to the measure of each (beauty of the spirit is different from that of bodies and each body has its own beauty). But in what does such beauty consist? It consists in two fundamental elements: proportion or harmony (*consonantia*) and clarity (*claritas*). Each thing, in other words, is called beautiful to the extent that it has its own clarity (spiritual or corporeal) and is constituted according to its right proportion or correspondence. The latter is understood in two ways: according to the order of creatures to God (and it is no accident, says Thomas, that the Greek word for "beautiful"—*kalós*—derives from *kaléō*, "to call," because God calls all things to himself), and according to the reciprocal order among creatures. Here two we find the Neo-Platonic laws of causality and participation applied: superior realities are in inferior ones by participation, while inferior realities are in superior ones by a certain excellence, and everything is in everything. All things are found in others according to a certain order and everything, therefore, contributes to the same end.[38] Naturally, God transcends and exceeds this very dynamic. God is beautiful not merely according to a certain measure, or a certain aspect, or at a certain time, for he is absolutely beautiful.[39] Beauty is linked to causality: it is the principle of all things, it moves them and conserves them for the love of its own beauty. Like the good, beauty is also Platonically diffusive of itself: "In fact, since he possesses his own beauty, God wants to multiply it as far as possible, viz., through the communication of his own likeness."[40] Matter too, in this sense, participates in the beautiful and the good.

But what difference is there between these two terms? According to Thomas, it is purely a distinction of reason:

37. See, for example, J. A. Aertsen, *Medieval Philosophy and the Transcendentals: The Case of Thomas Aquinas*, Studien und Texte zur Geistesgeschichte des Mittelalters 52 (Leiden: Brill, 1996), 335–59.
38. *De divinis nominibus*, c. 4, l. 5   39. *De divinis nominibus*, c. 4, l. 5
40. *De divinis nominibus*, c. 4, l. 5.

Although the beautiful and the good are the same in respect to subject, since both splendor and harmony are contained in the concept of good, still they are logically distinct. The beautiful adds to the good a relation to the cognitive faculty that regards its being.[41]

Ultimately, for a thing to be judged "beautiful" it must be related to a cognitive faculty that recognizes its *claritas* and *consonantia*, and, hence that it in some way participates in the constitution of the beautiful itself. From this perspective we could say that in the logic of the transcendentals the beautiful seems to be more connected with the true than with the good, but this is a discussion that Thomas does not develop and that is foreign to Pseudo-Dionysius's text.

Little is said of the beautiful in the *Summa theologiae,* but in the two most significant passages (which both have to do with the good) there emerges the same tendency that we have encountered in the Commentary on the *Divinis nominibus.* The beautiful is a specification of the good (*quaedam boni species,* Cajetan will say in his commentary on the *Summa*) and adds to the latter a relation to apprehension or to the cognitive faculty. Thus, as the first of these passages explains, whereas the good has to do principally with the final cause, the beautiful principally regards the formal cause:

Beauty and goodness in a thing are identical fundamentally; for they are based upon the same thing, namely, the form; and consequently goodness is praised as beauty. But they differ logically, for goodness properly relates to the appetite (goodness being what all things desire); and therefore it has the aspect of an end (the appetite being a kind of movement towards a thing). On the other hand, beauty relates to the cognitive faculty; for beautiful things are those which please when seen. Hence beauty consists in due proportion; for the senses delight in things duly proportioned, as in what is after their own kind—because even sense is a sort of reason, just as is every cognitive faculty. Now since knowledge is by assimilation, and similarity relates to form, beauty properly belongs to the nature of a formal cause.[42]

We note here how the essential characteristic of the beautiful is identified with "proportion," which more directly takes the place of the *consonantia* and the *claritas* indicated in the Commentary on the *Divinis nominibus,* and how the discussion of the beautiful is situated in the first instance in the domain of sense

---

41. *De divinis nominibus,* c. 4, l. 5. Nevertheless there is some slippage with respect to Pseudo-Dionysius's complete identification of good and beauty. On this question, see J. A. Aertsen, "The Triad 'True-Good-Beautiful:' The Place of Beauty in the Middle Ages," in *Intellect et imagination dans la philosophie médiévale / Intellect and Imagination in Medieval Philosophy / Intelecto e imaginação na filosofia medieval. Actes du XIe Congrès International de Philosophie Médiévale de la Société Internationale pour l'Étude de la Philosophie Médiévale (SIEPM), Porto, du 26 au 31 août 2002,* vol. 1, Rencontres de Philosophie Médiévale 11, ed. M. C. Pacheco and J. F. Meirinhos (Turnhout: Brepols, 2006), 415–35, especially 424–25.

42. *Summa theologiae,* Ia, q. 5, a. 4, ad 1.

knowledge (and could not be otherwise if, in Thomas's view, all knowledge always has its origin in the senses). Those things are beautiful that please upon being seen (*pulchrum enim dicuntur quae via placent*). Analogously, in the second of the two passages mentioned earlier,[43] Thomas states again that the beautiful adds to the good a relationship to the cognitive faculty (*pulchrum addit supra bonum quendam ordinem ad vim cognoscitivam*), and so those things are called "good" that please the appetite, while those things are called "beautiful" that please apprehension (*id cuius ipsa apprehensio placet*).[44]

COMPENDIUM THEOLOGIAE

Written at the request of his friend and collaborator Reginald of Piperno, the *Compendium theologiae* was composed between 1265 and 1267, at least as regards the first part, having to do with faith (*De fide*). The second part, on hope (*De spe*), is suddenly interrupted at c. 10. Probably inspired by Augustine's *Enchiridion*, the *Compendium* was to be divided into three parts corresponding to the three theological virtues and organized according to the form of commentaries on the *Credo* (*De fide*), the *Pater noster* (*De spe*), and the commandments (*De caritate*). The plan of the work is clearly expounded by Thomas: the Word not only made himself small but also summed up the doctrine necessary for salvation in a manner to make it easily accessible to those "who are too occupied with work." This "brief" way is articulated by the theological virtues. Salvation consists in the knowledge of truth, which presupposes faith; in the orientation of the will toward the end, which presupposes hope; and in the observance of justice, which presupposes charity. This order is not only the one proposed by the Apostle but also corresponds to right reason:

Love cannot be rightly ordered unless the proper goal of our hope is established; nor can there be any hope if knowledge of the truth is lacking. Therefore the first thing necessary is faith, by which one may come to a knowledge of the truth. Secondly, hope is necessary, that one's intention may be fixed on the right end. Thirdly, love is necessary, that one's affections may be perfectly put in order.[45]

---

43. *Summa theologiae*, Ia-IIae, q. 27, a. 1, ad 3.

44. We will not engage the theme of evil here, since we will treat of it when we look at *Quaestiones disputatae de malo*. We will limit ourselves to recalling that in the *Divine Names* of Pseudo-Dionysius the section on evil relies very clearly on Proclus. As Thomas summarizes: "Evil is not, however, a specific type of existing thing, which, namely, is evil through its own essence, nor again is evil a completely non-existing thing, but evil is a thing that is partially good by the fact that it exists, and it is called evil since it is defective of something of being" (c. 4, l. 14). In this sense, evil has a merely accidental being and it does not have its own per se principle (c. 4, l. 12).

45. *Compendium theologiae*, c. 1.

After the prologue (c. 1), the *De fide* is composed of 245 chapters (cc. 2–246), which can be subdivided into two major parts: one on God (cc. 3–184; c. 2 expounds the order of arguments relative to faith) and the other on Christ's humanity (cc. 185–246), which traces a long arc from original sin to resurrection and glory. Of the second treatise, the *De spe*, as we have said, only ten chapters were completed, which deal with hope in general and begin to illustrate the *Pater noster* (up to the prayer's second petition: *Adveniat regnum tuum*). The most philosophically interesting part of the *Compendium* is undoubtedly cc. 3–36 of the *De fide*, in which Thomas summarizes the doctrine of God's oneness, and, therefore, everything about God that was (and is) philosophically accessible. The list is significant because it represents in a synthetic way elements that Thomas discusses at greater length in other works and it permits us a very precise idea of what we can know of God on the basis of philosophy and natural reason alone. By these we can know of God's existence (of the *Summa*'s five ways here only the first is given, the argument from motion); his necessity, eternity, immutability, simplicity (cc. 4–9); the identity of being and essence in God (cc. 10–11); the fact that God does not belong to any genus (cc. 12–13) and is not a species (c. 14); God's oneness (c. 15); his incorporeality (c. 16), omnipotence (c. 19), and infinity (c. 20); the fact that God contains every perfection in things in an eminent and unified way (cc. 21–22); the absence of accidents (c. 23); the fact that naming God with many names does not compromise his simplicity and the names are not purely univocal or equivocal (cc. 24–25 and 27); God's undefinability (c. 26); the fact that God is intelligent and is his own thinking (cc. 28–31) and possesses a will even if it is not distinct from his intellect and, so, is identical with his very essence (cc. 32–34).

All of these truths can be synthesized in the formula according to which God is one, simple, perfect, infinite, and possessing intelligence and will; and they can be still more briefly synthesized in the formula of the *Credo* in which belief is stated in a single, omnipotent God. But everything that represents the starting point of Christian faith was already reached by the philosophers, even if often in an imprecise way:

The truths about God thus far proposed have been subtly discussed by a number of pagan philosophers, although some of them erred concerning these matters. And those who propounded true doctrine in this respect were scarcely able to arrive at such truths even after long and painstaking investigation.[46]

From this juncture forward, we can proceed only with the assistance of faith:

---

46. *Compendium theologiae*, c. 36.

But there are other truths about God revealed to us in the teaching of the Christian religion, which they were not able to reach. These are truths about which we are instructed, in accord with the norm of Christian faith, in a way that transcends human perception.[47]

There is nothing new here with respect to what we have already seen previously. All of the truths about the Trinity and the Incarnation surpass natural reason. It should, however, be noted that in this case Thomas has "sinned by omission." In the *Compendium* he speaks regularly of creation, and many of the theses presented as belonging solely to the sphere of revelation—such as those regarding the faculty of the soul—are, in fact, defended elsewhere by Thomas *philosophically*. In conclusion we can say that the *Compendium* is a very useful resource for quickly checking what Thomas holds in almost any aspect of his theological doctrine but also for checking its basic philosophical implications.

QUAESTIONES DISPUTATAE DE POTENTIA
Divine Omnipotence and Its Limit: The Impossible

In Rome too Thomas drafts disputed questions; among them, those on power—the *Quaestiones disputatae de potentia*—deserve to be mentioned first. It would seem that they can be dated to 1265–66, before Thomas began work on the *Summa theologiae*.[48] The *De potentia* is made up of ten questions that include 83 articles. The first six questions deal more strictly with divine power and with the way that it is exhibited in the creation and conservation of the world. The last four questions are dedicated to topics of trinitarian theology.

It is obvious that power must be attributed to God and that this power is infinite, intending "infinite" here not in a *privative* sense—as what should have a limit but does not—but in a *negative* sense—as what in itself does not possess a limit or term. Put differently, God is infinite because he cannot be limited by anything. The infinity of divine power is such in an *extensive* sense and in an *intensive* sense, for it can never produce so many effects that it cannot produce more, but neither does it operate with such intensity that it cannot operate with more. But the fact that divine power is infinite, and, thus, unlimited, does not mean that it can really produce everything, even what is impossible. Responding directly to a question about whether things impossible in themselves are possible for God, in q. 3, a. 1, Thomas explains that something can be said to be "impossible" in three different ways: (a) in the sense that a given active

47. *Compendium theologiae*, c. 36.
48. He might also have worked on them at the same time. It is quite probable that Thomas held disputes on divine power to prepare better for the section on creation in the *prima pars* of the *Summa*.

power is insufficient to produce it; (b) in the sense that something else opposes itself to its production or offers resistance or is an impediment to the agent that could produce it; (c) in the sense that it could not be the object of any action or production.

That which is *by nature* impossible in the first two ways can be done by God. God's active power can never be held to be insufficient (first case) nor can something resist or oppose it as an impediment (second case). But what is impossible in the third way not even God can do. Every active power belongs to what is being in act (what is not a being or is only a being in potency can neither act nor produce anything), and since every cause produces something like itself (the other Neo-Platonic axiom that plays a fundamental role in Thomas),[49] it is evident that the action of every active potency, inasmuch as it is proper to a being in act, tends by itself toward a being or existing (*tende di per sé all'ente o all'essere*). The action of God too, who is the supreme being, can only direct itself toward a being, that is, toward what is or can be and not toward what *cannot* be. That which cannot be, on the other hand, is what implies a contradiction. So, God cannot do what implies a contradiction. "Hence, God cannot make it such that affirmation and negation are simultaneously true; nor make something of those things that imply a contradiction."[50]

As is plain, this impossibility indicates, not a defect in the active power of God, but the lack of a corresponding passive potency on the part of that which is impossible. "Nor is it said that he cannot do it because his power is lacking, but because the possible is lacking, which lacks precisely the character of the possible. Because of this some prefer to say that God can do it but it cannot done."[51]

Explaining that divine omnipotence extends to everything that possesses the *ratio entis*, viz., what does not imply a contradiction,[52] Thomas aligns himself

49. See J. F. Wippel, "Thomas Aquinas on Our Knowledge of God and the Axiom that Every Agent Produces Something like Itself," *Proceedings of the American Catholic Philosophical Association* 74 (2000), 81–101 (published later in *Metaphysical Themes in Thomas Aquinas II*, 152–71). On the historical background of the use of the axiom by Thomas, see also P. W. Rosemann, *Omne agens agit sibi simile: A "Repetition" of Scholastic Metaphysics* (Leuven: Leuven University Press, 1996). Rosemann seems to hold that Thomas considered the axiom as self-evident, or at least that he was not worried about justifying it, contrary to what Wippel shows.

50. *De potentia*, q. 1, a. 3.

51. *De potentia*, q. 1, a. 3.

52. This is very clear in *De potentia* q. 1, a. 7: "God's power, considered in itself, extends to all the objects that do not signify contradiction.... But God cannot do things that signify contradiction, which are indeed impossible as such. Therefore, we conclude that God's power extends to things that are possible as such. But there are things that do not signify contradiction. Therefore, we evidently call God "almighty" because he can do all the things that are possible as such."

with the standard position of medieval theologians, which will also be respected by those who in the fourteenth century will defend the prerogative of the *potentia Dei absoluta* (God's theoretical capacity to act outside the order that he has constituted). Divine omnipotence always has the principle of non-contradiction as its limit.[53] During the whole Middle Ages, only Peter Damian seems to have been driven to the point, in the eleventh century, of freeing divine power from the principle of non-contradiction and to have conceded that God can even intervene in the past, making it such, for example, that Rome never existed, or that a girl's lost virginity could be restored. But, for Thomas, it is clear that every modification of the past violates the principle of non-contradiction (the same event would both have happened and not have happened) and so is impossible in itself, independently of the power of the agent.

In q. 1, a. 5 Thomas asks whether God can do what he does not do and cease to do what he does do. Here Thomas confronts not just those philosophers who say that God acts only according to the necessity of his nature but also those theologians according to whom God can never act outside that order established by his justice and his wisdom. The latter is the error attributed to Peter Abelard, as Thomas does not fail to mention. The position of the philosophers can be refuted by noting that God is intellect and, as such, can choose and determine his own ends, whereas what acts by necessity of its nature cannot determine its own end. The error of the theologians proves a more delicate matter, above all for those who, like Thomas, follow Aristotle in holding that the intellect must always indicate to the will the end to pursue. The end of God's will is his goodness itself, and it is an end that God cannot not will. Creatures are not ordered to this end in an absolute way. Divine goodness is *actually* expressed with these creatures and this order, but it could also express itself with other creatures and with another order in the sense that God could achieve the same end with different means: with another ordering of the world, for example. This means that he could act in a different way from how he does act and so could make different things:

> This is the point on which they let themselves be deceived. They maintain that the order of creatures is adequate to the divine goodness, almost as if this goodness could not exist without it.[54]

Although omnipotence is a traditional attribute of God, the same cannot be said of omnivolence. It is up to the will to determine the activity of power and

53. See, in general, W. J. Courtenay, *Capacity and Volition: A History of the Distinction of Absolute and Ordained Power*, Quodlibet 8 (Bergamo: Lubrina, 1990). See 88–92 for the treatment of Thomas.

54. *De potentia*, q. 1, a. 5.

knowledge. All can be known and all done (in the sense spoken of earlier), but not all can be willed. The will can aim only at those things toward which power and knowledge direct it. God, then, is omniscient and omnipotent, but not omnivolent.

Creation As an Asymmetrical Relation

Divine power exercises itself primarily in the processes of generation and creation. The latter must be understood as the granting of being from nothing that is proper only to divine causality (all the other causes are limited to "informing" what has already been produced in being, and in this regard the influence of the *Liber de causis* on the *De potentia* is already evident).

In the strict sense creation is not really a change since according to the Aristotelian conception of continuous quantity, every instantaneous change is always the term of an antecedent motion (and, so, always implies the persistence of a primary substrate before and after it). But it is exactly this substrate that is lacking in the case of creation from nothing, even just from the point of view of temporal continuity between before and after:

> There is no common substrate actually or potentially existent. Again there is no continuous time, if we refer to the creation of the universe, since there was no time when there was no world. And yet we may find a common but purely imaginary substrate, insofar as we imagine one common time when there was no world and afterwards when the world had been brought into being.[55]

Although few have noted it, this is one of the points of Thomas's doctrine that will be objectively condemned, exactly three years after his death, by the censure of Bishop Tempier.[56]

But in what, precisely, does creation consist? We must distinguish in this regard between an active sense (God's producing) and a passive sense (the being produced of creatures). In the first sense, creation obviously indicates a divine action. But because action is identical with essence in God, it simply indicates God's essence itself considered together with a *relation* toward something else, namely, the created thing. It is a relation that, from God's perspective, is *purely of reason*, that is, conceptual. In the passive sense, creation is a new *relation*

---

55. *De potentia*, q. 3, a. 2.

56. It is article 217 in the original text of the condemnation: *Quod creatio non debet dici mutatio ad esse.—Error, si intelligatur de omni modo mutationis.* See R. Hissette, *Enquête sur les 219 articles condamnés à Paris le 7 mars 1277* (Louvain: Publications Universitaires; Paris: Publications Universitaires, 1977), 277–80 (a. 187). Hissette holds that it is unlikely that the target of Tempier is, in this case, Thomas, but he admits that Thomas explicitly proposes a thesis that is quite similar. See also *La condemnation parisienne de 1277*, ed. C. Lafleur and D. Piché (Paris: Vrin, 1999), 144–45.

(thus, it is not an undergoing, for example, because then it would presuppose an antecedent substrate), but in this case a *real relation* (all the more so because it is this relation that founds the reality of the creature). Hence, creation is the establishment of a double asymmetrical relationship: a conceptual relationship in God (active sense) and a real relation in creatures (passive sense). To explain this asymmetry Thomas has recourse in q. 7, a. 10 (in a discussion of the simplicity of the divine essence) to some examples that perhaps are not immediately perspicuous but are, in any case, effective. A coin, says Thomas, does not undergo any real change as a consequence of the variation of prices (for prices depend on human conventions), just as a man whose image is being made by an artist does not undergo any change as a result of the production of the image. In this sense, the man does not have a real relation with his image and the coin does not have a real relation with prices, since these relations are only logical relations. These examples are accompanied by other more suitable ones. If a man finds himself to the right or the left of a column, he is in a relation to the column that neither adds nor takes anything away from the column itself. In the same way, the acquisition of a science marks the emergence of a relationship between the mind and a thing, and although this relationship is real in the mind, it adds nothing to the thing itself (at least not in pre-Kantian terms). In fact, this distinction serves Thomas not only to deny the presence in God of any real relation that would compromise his absolute simplicity but also to make it clear that between God and creatures there exists a relationship not merely of likeness (based on dependence) but also one of diversity. Every effect certainly has a likeness to the cause from which it originates, but it must always distinguish itself from the cause if it is not its own cause. In this case also, Thomas ultimately makes use of a typically Neo-Platonic axiom—and one that is markedly Proclean—according to which there is always a relationship of identity and difference between cause and effect.

From what we have already seen we can easily conclude that God does not delegate any creative power to creatures (q. 3, a. 4), for creation properly so-called, that is, creation from nothing, requires an infinite power that only God possesses and can possess. God, rather, uses creatures as secondary causes to transform ulteriorly what he has created. In this way Thomas refutes the philosophical idea (of Avicennian provenance) of creation by intermediaries.[57] Creation is an act proper to God alone:

57. As might be recalled, in Avicenna the first cause produces only the first intelligence, and from the latter the emanative process takes place that leads to the production of the other intelligences, the celestial bodies and their souls, and, lastly, the sublunary world, which is the work of the tenth intelligence.

Now pure non-being is infinitely distant from being because non-being is further re-moved from any particular being than any other particular being is, however distant these may be. Consequently, none but an infinite power can produce being from non-being.[58]

Or, as Thomas says in the next question:

Being itself is the most common, first, and most intimate of all effects. Thus, it is an effect that it belongs to God alone to produce by his own power.[59]

If only God can create, then the opposite principle also holds, that is, that there cannot be anything that was not created by God. Being is what is common to all the beings of the world (which are distinct from each other by what they are, and not by being), and since creation is the establishment of being in general, there is nothing that is outside this domain. We, therefore, begin to distin-guish two quite determinate domains: that of *pure being*, which belongs to God alone and cannot be determined by any addition (only God is pure being and is nothing other than pure being), and that of *common being* (which is considered apart from everything that is added to it and, that is, from essential contents, but which does not in reality obtain apart from an essence),[60] which falls on the side of the whole of created being.

Being As the Actuality of Every Act and Perfection of Every Perfection

In the discussion about the identity of being and essence in God (q. 7, a. 2)—a thesis with which we are already well-acquainted—we find one of Thomas's most celebrated texts:

By "being" I understand the actuality of all acts and, because of this, the perfection of all perfections (*actualitas omnium actuum et perfectio omnium perfectionum*).[61]

This formulation was taken up by twentieth-century Neo-Thomists as the true key to Thomas's "system" considered as a "metaphysics of the act of being." Nev-ertheless, it is perhaps necessary to reflect on the meaning that we should attach to these kinds of expressions. First of all, the statement just quoted should be situated in its context. Thomas is replying to an argument according to which

---

58. *De potentia*, q. 3, a. 4.

59. *De potentia*, q. 3, a. 7.

60. See *De potentia*, q. 7, a. 2, ad 6: "We should say being in general is that to which nothing is added, although it does not belong to its nature that nothing can be added to it. But divine being is that to which nothing is added, and it belongs to its nature that nothing can be added to it." It is a question of a distinction borrowed from Avicenna's *Metaohysics*. See P. Porro, "Immateriality and Separation in Avicenna and Thomas Aquinas," in *The Arabic, Hebrew and Latin Reception of Avicenna's "Metaphysics,"* ed. D. N. Hasse and A. Bertolacci (Berlin: de Gruyter, 2012), 275–307.

61. *De potentia*, q. 7, a. 2, ad 9.

being should not be placed in God because it is, like prime matter, absolutely indeterminate and is, thus, in potency with respect to all possible determinations (beginning with predicamental determinations, that is, the categories). In his reply Thomas reverses the perspective. It is not being that is in potency to formal or essential determinations, he explains, but essence that is to be perfectly actualized by being:

By "being" I understand the maximal perfection. The proof of this is that act is always more perfect than potentiality. Now no designated form is understood to be in act unless it be supposed to have being.... Hence, it is clear that by "being" I understand the actuality of all acts and, because of this, the perfection of all perfections. Nor may we think that being, in this sense, can have anything added to it that is more formal and determines it as act determines potentiality: because being in this latter sense is essentially distinct from that to which it is added and whereby it is determined. But nothing that is outside the range of being can be added to being, for nothing is outside its range except non-being, which can be neither form nor matter. Hence, being is not determined by something else as potentiality by act but rather as act by potentiality.

Thomas explains, then, that if it is true that being is determined or limited by essence (by form in the case of simple substances and by form and matter in the case of composed substances), this must not be understood as if being itself were in potency in regard to such determinations but in the opposite sense. Potency is always determined by an act of something that is other than it, but nothing is truly other than being (save non-being), and so it is not in potency to any ulterior act. On the contrary, it is essence that is actualized by being. Now, the point of this discussion is not so much to insist on the primacy of being as the act in all created things (because, as we have seen, things are distinguished from each other not on the basis of being but on the basis of their nature or essence) as it is to mark the difference between the *singular* case of God, in which being is not limited by any form (or any material component) and, so, is pure and absolute, and that of all the other beings in which being is always determined by the fact of being-something, of at least having a form. If, therefore, understanding being as the actuality of every act and the perfection of every perfection unquestionably has a central place in Thomas's thought, it is always necessary to remember that its basic purpose is, first of all, to underscore and defend the identification of God and pure being, keeping at bay the suspicion that being brings with it a nimbus of potentiality with respect to all formal determination. And this is also the sense in which we must understand the celebrated comment on Exodus 3:14: "The expression 'He who is' belongs, above all, to God inasmuch as it does not determine any form for God but expresses his being in an indeterminate way."[62]

---

62. *De potentia*, q. 7, a. 5.

The Possibility of Annihilating Creatures

At least two further fundamental questions can be posed in connection with the topic of creation. Can what is different from God be eternal like God himself? Can any creature be necessary? In regard to the first question (q. 3, a. 14), it is necessary to distinguish the case of the generation of the Son (who is, of course, coeternal with the Father, since he is not distinct from him in essence) from that of creation properly understood (the production of things that are different from God in essence). Thomas expresses his basic conviction about the latter, which will find its clearest formulation in the opuscule *De aeternitate mundi*: not only does God not lack active power to produce from eternity an essence different from him, but there is no contradiction—in regard to the passive power of creatures—between the fact of existing eternally and deriving being from another. In short, it is not contradictory that something be created and exist eternally, because something, as Avicenna demonstrates, can be *eternally created*, that is, eternally dependent on another for its own being. And since, as we have seen, everything that is not contradictory is possible, the eternity of creation is, for Thomas, possible in principle. If this is not in fact the case, it is because the Catholic faith presupposes a temporal interpretation of creation. Creation in time is, therefore, not a rationally demonstrable truth but a truth of faith.

In q. 5 Thomas discusses the possibility of the annihilation of creatures (aa. 1–4), the possibility that, once created, things can be permitted to sink back into absolute nothingness. The most interesting aspect of this is, undoubtedly, the idea, insisted upon by Thomas in this context too, that there are creatures that are not subject to the possibility of total corruption, of falling back into nothingness. Already in the *Summa contra Gentiles*, as will be recalled,[63] Thomas conceded that although everything depends on God's will (and, thus, not on a necessary cause), the possibility of an absolute necessity in created things must not be excluded in such a way that we would have to admit that all things are contingent (II, c. 30). There are, in fact, things that necessarily exist in an absolute sense because they lack the possibility of not existing. Thomas returns to this point, above all, in *De potentia*, q. 5, a. 3. The possibility that is at issue here is obviously not that which depends on the power of the agent—for God could at any moment, even if only theoretically, let all creatures fall back into nothingness—but that which is present in the things produced themselves. Thomas reports two principal opinions about this last point. The first is that

---

63. See pp. 146–50 above.

of Avicenna, according to whom, apart from God, everything has in itself the possibility of being or not being. Because being is not a part of the essence of creatures, they are, in themselves, only possible (even if every effect is then necessary *ab alio*, that is, by reason of its cause). The second opinion is that of Averroes, who holds that at least some of the beings other than God do not present in their nature any potency not to be. If it were otherwise, there could not be sempiternal substances (such that, once created, they are not subject to *natural* corruption, as is the case with the intelligences and the heavens). This position is the one preferred by Thomas (*et haec positio videtur rationabilior*). It is solely on account of its materiality that a being is subject to the possibility of not being. So, in the case of subsistent pure forms (incorporeal substances) or of bodies whose matter is so proportioned to their form as not to be subject to contrariety (celestial bodies), every possibility of potentiality or tendency to non-being is excluded. In other words, only generable and corruptible substances are in potency to non-being (in the broad sense). All other substances are (formally) necessary, that is, by nature free from the possibility of not being (*Aliis vero rebus secundum suam naturam competit necessistas essendi, possibilitate non essendi ab earum natura sublata*). That does not mean such substances exist through themselves, that is, that they are uncreated or self-constituting. They are always *creatures*, but *already created in their necessary nature*. In sum, for Thomas, no creature is necessary *ex se* (this is true only of God), but some are necessary *ab alio* although not in the Avicennian sense.[64] Incorruptible creatures are not first possible in themselves and then rendered necessary by divine intervention (taking "first" and "then" not in a temporal but in a logical and metaphysical sense). They are directly created in their necessary nature, and precisely because of this—without contravening what Aristotle holds, as we have just seen—their creation could even be eternal. In a world as solid and stable as the one envisioned by Thomas, which is not drawn out by any preexisting possibility and does not constantly incline toward annihilation, the possible eternity of things—as we have already seen and as we will see again later—by no means appears to be a dangerous prospect to be neutralized at all costs.

The Role of Secondary Causes and Miracles

It should perhaps be clarified, however, that the fact that God creates without intermediaries does not entail that every activity of nature must be attributed directly to God in a manner such that natural agents do nothing from their

---

64. See P. Porro, "*Possibile ex se, necessarium ab alio*: Tommaso d'Aquino e Enrico di Gand," *Medioevo* 18 (1992): 231–73.

own capacities. This is the error of al-Ghazālī, according to whom it is not the fire that directly warms the object that is placed near it, but always and only God (even if, to respect the predetermined order of the world, God decided never to cause heat without the presence of fire, although the latter is not the true cause of heat). The confrontation with al-Ghazālī is, in fact, a confrontation with a radical occasionalism *ante litteram*. Thomas's position is also in this case inspired by what we could call a basic sane empiricism. "This position is, however, evidently in conflict with the senses."[65] It is clear, in fact, that man feels the heat of fire only if the fire produces a change in his sense organs. If the heat were produced not by the fire but by another agent (God), we would be deceived—which is impossible since, according to Aristotle, the senses are never deceived in judging the sensible things proper to them. Moreover, the "occasionalist" thesis, besides being counterintuitive, lacks economy and, therefore, is unreasonable. If natural things did not accomplish anything, the forms and capacities that nature had bestowed on them would be completely useless—"How pointless it would be for a knife that does not cut to be sharp,"[66] says Thomas. And further: "It would be just as useless to place wood in fire if God were to burn the wood even without fire."[67]

In the same question Thomas also takes a stand against Avicebron, who maintains that corporeal substances do not act (since matter is essentially passive) but, rather, a spiritual force that penetrates all bodies acts in them. The error here is, on the one hand, in identifying matter with corporeal substance (every corporeal substance is composed of matter and form and, so, acts through its form) and, on the other hand, in taking corporeal substance to be numerically one (corporeality in general, which is presupposed in Avicebron's universal hylomorphism), considering all distinctions between several substances to be purely accidental. Thomas can in this way stress that the fact that God acts in each natural thing must be understood not in the sense that the things themselves have no activity but in the sense that God acts *in and through* their activity without replacing or annihilating it: "God is the cause of every action in the sense that any agent cause is the instrument of the divine operating power."[68]

We can say, then, that God is the cause of the action of each thing since he confers on it the capacity to act (besides conserving it in its being and permitting it to actualize this capacity). After the initial creation, God delegates most of his causality to secondary causes, continuing to act through them. Perhaps one of the most characteristic features of Thomas's metaphysics is this profound

65. *De potentia*, q. 3, a. 7.
66. *De potentia*, q. 3, a. 7.
67. *De potentia*, q. 3, a. 7.
68. *De potentia*, q. 3, a. 7.

connection between the original dependence of all things on God and their ontological consistency, which permits them, once they are constituted, to act as causes in the proper sense and to produce determinate effects.[69] We should point out that the rational human soul (the form of the human composite) is an important exception in this order of natural causality in which God delegates the development of the world to secondary causes after creation. The human soul is not produced from or through natural agents, and it is not transmitted in generation through the seed but results from a direct creative act. Put differently, there is something that continues to be produced from nothing, directly by God, after the initial creation, namely, each single *rational* human soul.[70]

Beyond this structural exception, however, it should be observed that God always retains the capacity to act beyond created causes and independently of them. Because he does not act by necessity of nature or in a way bound to his *scientia* (as a universal cause of all beings through his intellect), God is cause of the being of natural realities, having a specific knowledge of each thing, and can intervene in particular effects outside the course of nature in relation to being, acting, or proper operations (making it so that fire does not burn, for instance). These divine interventions constitute miracles. Divine power can act *against particular nature* and *against universal nature insofar as it depends on the heavens, but never against nature as such*, that is, against nature in its still more universal and all-comprehending sense, as that which is identical with the divine ordering itself. Nevertheless, not all divine interventions are miracles. "Miracle" comes from "marvel," and two conditions are necessary for marveling: that the cause of what makes us marvel is hidden and that we expect to observe the contrary. Not everything that God does, therefore, is miraculous. A miracle in the strict sense is only what God works in what has a contrary disposition (a resistance that is overcome by the divine intervention). Therefore, a miracle has the characteristics of being difficult and unusual: *difficult* because it goes beyond the capacities of nature; *unusual* because it exceeds the capacities of our knowledge, or, as Thomas says, it appears to be beyond the hope of those who witness it. It certainly cannot be doubted that Thomas had a strong faith in miracles, but in general his cosmos is well-ordered and does not require constant and unexpected divine interventions. His biography too, apart from hagiographic modifications, is relatively lacking in miraculous events.[71]

69. On the theme of the causality of the creature (across the principal points of Thomas's work), see J. F. Wippel, "Thomas Aquinas on Creatures as Causes of *esse*," *International Philosophical Quarterly* 50 (2000) (*A Festschrift in Honor of W. Norris Clarke, SJ*): 197–213. (See also *Metaphysical Themes in Thomas Aquinas II*, 172–93.)

70. *De potentia*, q. 3, a. 9.

71. Among the miraculous events associated with the life of Thomas by his biographers and

Being, One, and Many

The last questions of the *De potentia* (qq. 8–10) are dedicated to the Trinitarian relations. Thomas returns here (q. 9, a. 2) to the Boethian definition of "person," viz., an "individual substance of a rational nature" (*nature rationalis individua substantia*), finding it adequate.[72] It is fitting that in regard to the rational nature (excluding, of course, both inanimate bodies and irrational animals) we give an appropriate name to the individual, whose characteristic it is properly and truly to act by itself (*proprie et vere per se agere*). To the objection that a separated soul can also be considered an individual of a rational nature, although it is not called a "person" (q. 9, a. 2, ad 14), Thomas replies with one of the cornerstones of his anthropology. The separated soul, he says, is a *part* of the rational nature (that is, of human nature) and *not the whole* of the rational human nature, and, hence, cannot be called a "person." The defense of the unity of the human composite is one of the most characteristic features of Thomas's entire thought.

In dealing with the question of how the numerical terms predicated of the divine persons are to be understood (that is, in a positive or negative sense, by remotion), Thomas discusses at length the convertibility of one with being and the distinction between oneness and multiplicity. First of all, the one that is convertible with being must not be confused with the one that belongs to the genus of quantity and that is the principle of number. The one that is convertible with being adds nothing to being itself save for the negation of division, that is, it adds a single negation—the fact of being undivided in itself—while multiplicity adds two negations—the fact of being undivided in itself and divided from others. Here a problem could be posed. If one is said by remotion of

---

hagiographers, some leave one a little perplexed. Consider, for example, the account of the lightning that killed a younger sister (and some horses) but did not harm Thomas, who was sleeping with the nurse. Thomas's mother, who held him more dear than his deceased sister, supposedly gave thanks to God for the outcome. See William of Tocco, *Ystoria sancti Thome de Aquino*, c. 3: "Mater uero, que de puero magis quam de filia erat sollicita,ad lectum in quo nutrix cum puero dormiebat tremebunda peruenit; que sanum ipsum cum nutrice inueniens, deo gratias reddidit qui paulatim in puero complere que promisere inchoabat." But the story of the sardines that were transformed into herring is more pleasant. When Thomas was at the end of his life at Maena and lacking an appetite, he responded to the pressing solicitations of his doctor by declaring that he might perhaps eat a little herring (which were not typically found in the Tyrrhenian Sea). At the market a basketful of sardines from Terracina were then transformed into herring before the eyes of the flabbergasted doctor (although it is not clear whether Thomas actually consumed them in the end ...). On the episode, recounted by Willam of Tocco (*Ystoria*, c. 56), see P. Porro, "Tra Napoli e la rive gauche: Tommaso d'Aquino," in *I viaggi dei filosofi*, ed. M. Bettetini and S. Poggi (Milan: Raffaello Cortina, 2010), 57–71.

72. Boethius, *Contra Eutychen et Nestorium*, 3, in Boethius, *The Theological Tractates*, Loeb Classical Library 74, trans. H. F. Stewart, E. K. Rand, and S. J. Tester (Cambridge, Mass.: Harvard University Press, 1973), 85.

multiplicity, it is necessary that the first must be opposed to the second as a privation is opposed to a habit or disposition. But every habit precedes negation as much according to nature as according to consideration (since a privation cannot be defined without reference to the corresponding habit). In consequence, multiplicity would have to precede that which is one as much by nature as in the order of knowledge. Thomas observes at this point (distancing himself from the solution that he could have borrowed from Aristotle—that of a simple anteriority of multiplicity only in the order of sense knowledge) that division is the cause of multiplicity and, as such, precedes multiplicity. One, however, being undivided in itself, is said in a privative way of division but is not so said of multiplicity. So, *division precedes oneness and oneness precedes multiplicity.* Thomas then suggests a precise order in which being is apprehended:

- *Being* is what first falls into the intellect
- The *negation of being* is then conceived.
- From this—and in a third step—there is *division* (if something is understood as being, and it is understood that it is *not* another being, it is likewise understood as *divided* from that being).
- Fourth, *oneness* is conceived to the extent that it is understood that this being is undivided in itself.
- Finally, *multiplicity* is conceived insofar as it is understood that one being is divided from another and that both are undivided in themselves. What is divided from another constitutes, in short, a multiplicity only if each is undivided in itself.

Thomas had already handled this question in the *Super Boethium De Trinitate* (q. 4, especially a. 1), but what is key here is above all the order in which the transcendentals are known. The convertibility between being and one is not, as it were, automatic, but passes through a negation, while the move from oneness to multiplicity requires a further negation. It is not perhaps by chance that the whole of Thomas's metaphysical thought seems to be founded on a series of logical operations of negation (as is Avicenna's thought).

THE *PRIMA PARS* OF THE *SUMMA THEOLOGIAE*

Plan and Structure of the *Summa*

The scope of the *Summa theologiae* is expounded with great clarity and concision by Thomas in the rather brief prologue to the work:

Because the doctor of Catholic truth ought not only to teach the proficient, but also to instruct beginners ... we purpose in this book to treat of whatever belongs to the Christian religion, in such a way as may tend to the instruction of beginners. We have considered that students in this doctrine have not seldom been hampered by what they have found written by other authors, partly on account of the multiplication of useless questions, articles, and arguments, partly also because those things that are needful for them to know are not taught according to the order of the subject matter, but according as the plan of the book might require, or the occasion of the argument offer, partly too because frequent repetition brought weariness and confusion to the minds of readers. Endeavoring to avoid these and other like faults, we shall try, by God's help, to set forth whatever is included in this sacred doctrine as briefly and clearly as the matter itself may allow.

Contrary to what might be thought, the *Summa* does not by any means answer, then, a desire to construct a system or to concentrate theological knowledge in an abstract form. It has, instead, an eminently didactic purpose. Thomas is not satisfied with the textbooks in use in the theological education of his young confreres (textbooks lacking order or focused merely on casuistry, that is, on the examination of pastoral and moral problems) and intends to propose an instrument that is more orderly, simple, and brief.[73] Of course, the last aim may cause us to smile, given that the *Summa* comprises 512 questions and 2669 articles across many hundreds of pages. But Thomas's statement should be taken seriously. The *Summa* is a simple compendium, effectively quite clear, and directed at an audience that is not yet educated and expert in theology. The work has a tripartite structure, typical of Thomas's theology, that occupies itself with the divine order (*prima pars*), the movement of the rational creature toward God (*secunda pars*), and Christ, who, taking on human nature, constitutes the way back to God (*tertia pars*). This threefold partition, with its circular form, brings readily to mind the circular conception of causality typical of Neo-Platonism, and of the Proclean tradition in particular. On the other hand, it is undeniable that this structure is in itself especially suited to express the essentials of Christian theology, taking account of the double movement of creation and redemption and of the double function of Christ as *alpha* and *omega*.[74] It should

73. For the context in which the project of the new *Summa* matured (Thomas's dissatisfaction with the existing manual, to which we have referred at the beginning of this chapter), see Boyle, "The Setting of the Summa theologiae," 65–91; A. Oliva, "La Somme de théologie de Thomas d'Aquin: Introduction historique et littéraire," *Chôra* 7–8 (2009–10): 217–53. For a general presentation of the structure of the *Summa*, see M.-D. Chenu, *Toward Understanding St. Thomas*, trans. A.-M. Landry, O.P., and D. Hughes, O.P. (Chicago: Henry Regnery Company, 1964), 298–322]; G. Lafont, *Structures et méthode dans la Somme théologique de saint Thomas d'Aquin* (Paris: Desclée de Brouwer, 1961); J.-P. Torrell, *Aquinas's Summa: Background, Structure, and Reception*, trans. Benedict M. Guevin, O.S.B. (Washington, D.C.: The Catholic University of America Press, 2005)]; *Aquinas's Summa Theologiae*, ed. B. Davies (Lanham, Md.: Rowman & Littlefield, 2005); *Thomas von Aquin: Die* Summa theologiae: *Werkinterpretationen*, ed. A. Speer (Berlin: de Gruyter, 2005).

74. Chenu, more than anyone, underscored the Neo-Platonic pattern (*exitus et reditus*) of the

be noted that, apart from the basic tripartite structure of the work as a whole, the *secunda pars* of the *Summa* is itself subdivided into two parts, traditionally called the *prima secundae* (the first of the second) and the *secunda secundae* (the second of the second). Each part of the *Summa* is composed of questions which are divided into articles constructed according to the schema of arguments *quod sic* and *contra*, *solutio*, and *ad argumenta*.

The 119 questions of the *prima pars*—the part composed during the stint in Rome (with qq. 1–74 presumably being drafted between October of 1265 and 1267 and qq. 75–119 between 1267 and 1268)—are grouped into three principal sections: one on God's existence, attributes, and operations (qq. 2–26); one on the persons of the Trinity, their processions, properties, and relations (qq. 27–43); and one on God as creator and ruler of the world (qq. 44–102). This last section could be further divided into various subsections related to: the order of the derivation of creatures from God (qq. 44–46; here Thomas once more observes—in q. 46, aa. 1 and 2—that it is not at all necessary that the world always existed but the fact that the world had a beginning in time is only the object of faith and not of demonstration or science); the origin of multiplicity and distinction and the presence of evil in the world (qq. 47–49); spiritual creatures (qq. 50–64); the totality of corporeal creatures, according to the biblical account of creation (qq. 65–74); man as a spiritual and corporeal creature (qq. 75–102; Thomas first reflects on the operations of the intellect and the will in qq. 75–89 and then on what it means for man to be created directly by God in his image in qq. 90–102); the divine providence and governance of the world (qq. 103–119).

The *Summa's* point of departure (q. 1, a. 1) is given by the question about whether, besides the traditional philosophical disciplines, another science might be necessary for man—theology founded on revelation, or in Thomas's terms, *sacra doctrina*. Here we find once again the position with which we are already familiar: man is directed toward an end (God) that exceeds the capacities of his reason. To be able to direct himself toward this end he must, however, know it in some way. And this is the meaning and scope of revelation. And even in regard to those things that we can know naturally, it is better to have revelation. The rational investigation of divine things is possible only for a few, demands much time and toil, and is never free from errors. On the other hand, sacred doctrine or theology is a science, however unique. Every science operates from

---

plan of the *Summa* (*Toward Understanding St. Thomas*, 304–18). For some clarifications on this subject, see Torrell, *Aquinas's* Summa, 17–62 (atop the tripartite division is placed another bipartite division between "theology" as the consideration of God in himself and "economy" as the consideration of the work of God in time and the history of salvation), and A. Speer, "Die *Summa theologiae* lesen—eine Einführung," in *Thomas von Aquin*, 1–28, especially 13–21.

specific principles. These principles can be evident in themselves by the natural light of the intellect (but this is not the case with theology) or they can be derived from a higher science in which they are demonstrated. And this is how it is with theology. It is based on principles known by the light of a higher science, which is the science that God has of himself and that the blessed have of God (q. 1, a. 2). So, in the *Summa theologiae* too Thomas applies to theology the Aristotelian model of the subalternation of the sciences elaborated in the *Posterior Analytics*. A strictly philosophical criterion is, thus, employed outside of philosophy and properly human knowledge (indeed, in a region inaccessible to philosophy) to define the scientificity of theology. In the same way—after having stated that "sacred doctrine" is more speculative than practical (q. 1, a. 4), that it is superior to all the other sciences whether speculative or practical (q. 1, a. 5), and that it alone is worthy of being called *sapientia* in an absolute sense (q. 1, a. 6)—Thomas reaffirms that God is the only true subject of this science (q. 1, a. 7)—a thesis that (as we already noted in regard to the Commentary on the *Sentences*) might appear obvious but that was not at all so prior to Thomas. Before Thomas, other subjects for theology were proposed and traditions of varying antiquity developed around them. Among these other subjects were the "things" and "signs" (*res et signa*) famously proposed by Augustine in *De doctrina christiana*; the union of Christ with the Church (the *Christus integer*), as suggested by Cassiodorus; and the restoration of human nature (the *opera restaurationis*) proposed by Hugh of Saint Victor in his *De sacramentis*. After Thomas, Giles of Rome—a master who was in many other ways close to Thomas's thought—held that God as such, God in the absolute sense, is not the subject of theology, but God as the "restorer and glorifier of human nature." Thomas, however, had no doubts on this score:

God is the subject of this science.... In sacred doctrine all things are treated of under the aspect of God either because they are God himself or because they refer to God as their beginning and end. Hence it follows that God is in very truth the object of this science.[75]

The Five Ways

The primary business of theology is to make God known. It is natural, therefore, that after the introductory question the first problem dealt with in the *Summa* has to do with God's existence. In this regard we can first of all ask whether God's existence is evident (q. 2, a. 1). Thomas, returning to the position he adopted in previous works, treats of the argument proposed by Anselm in the *Proslogion*:

75. *Summa theologiae*, Ia, q. 1, a. 7.

whoever understands what the name "God" means (that than which nothing greater can be thought) cannot but admit God's existence.

But, for Thomas, two different ways in which something may be self-evident must be distinguished. Something may be self-evident in itself and not for us, or self-evident in itself *and* for us. A proposition is self-evident in itself when the predicate is included in the notion of the subject, as in the example "Man is an animal." Now, "animal" (as a genus) is part of the definition and so of the notion itself of man. So, if the subject and predicate of a proposition are both known, the proposition in question will be evident to everyone, as is the case, for instance, with the proposition "The whole is greater than the part." This proposition is obvious to everyone since everyone knows the meanings of the terms "whole" and "part." But if the subject and predicate are not known to everyone, the proposition will remain self-evident (assuming that the predicate is contained in the subject) but it will not be evident to those who are ignorant about the subject and predicate.

The proposition "God exists" is of the last type. It is immediately evident in itself because the predicate not only is included in the subject but is identical with it, since God is his own being. But the proposition is not evident to us since we do not know God's essence and cannot, thus, claim to know the terms of the proposition. Since the proposition is not evident to us it must be demonstrated by other things that are more known to us (even if they are, paradoxically, less evident in themselves—Aristotle had already observed that our knowledge proceeds from what is more evident to us and less evident in itself to what is less evident to us and more evident in itself).

In this connection it is necessary also to distinguish between two types of demonstration. The one proceeds from knowledge of the cause (from what is more evident in itself), that is, from the "why," and for this reason is called a *propter quid* demonstration. The other demonstration begins from effects, and is called a *quia* demonstration. It begins from the recognition of a fact (the "that," *quia*) and passes to the cause. Of course, this type of demonstration starts from what is more known to us (to the extent that the effects are often more known to us than the causes) to arrive at what is more knowable in itself. This is how things stand for us with respect to God's existence, which, not being evident to us, can be demonstrated through the effects that we do know. As we already know, apart from revelation natural reason cannot demonstrate anything of the divine *essence*, although it can demonstrate its existence. The demonstration is in every case a *quia* demonstration that is limited to proving *a posteriori* the fact "that" God exists, and not a *propter quid* demonstration, which would be capable of proving God's existence *a priori*, that is, from its "why," its intrinsic cause, which would be God's essence, something that is unknown to us in natural terms.

It is in this context that Thomas proposes the famous five ways,[76] which in general begin from effects (they are *a posteriori*) and terminate with a complex proposition (*quia*) in which something (a first unmoved mover, a first efficient cause, an absolutely necessary being, a supremely perfect being, and an ordering cause of the universe) can be called "God." If four ways, as we will see, start from Aristotelian presuppositions (the impossibility of an infinite causal series and the assumption—expressed in *Metaphysics*, II—that the maximal term of a series is the cause of all the subsequent terms), one (the third) reproposes instead the "modal" argument elaborated by Avicenna and taken up by Maimonides. We can now look briefly at these arguments.

The first way—which is also the most evident in Thomas's view—is the one derived from motion; it very closely follows Aristotle's line of argument in *Metaphysics*, XII and *Physics*, VIII. Our senses make it perfectly evident to us that in this world some things are in motion. Now, according to a classical Aristotelian principle, everything that moves is moved by another. Every movement is, in fact, a passage from potency to act, and since nothing brings itself from potency to act, it is necessary that this passage be made possible by another being that is already in act (from a being capable of moving, a *moving* being). It is true that some beings seem capable of self-movement, that is, they seem to move themselves, but they are able to do so only on account of distinct parts that relate to each other as mover and moved. In animals (that is, in all beings that are endowed with a soul) it is the soul (which functions as form and act) that moves the body. If nothing, then, moves itself in a strict sense, we must grant that everything that moves is moved by another. The latter (that which moves) can also be moved in turn but always by another being in act that functions as a mover. It is obvious, however, that we cannot proceed in this way *ad infinitum*, for if the series of movers were infinite, there would never be a first mover, and if there is no first mover, all the subsequent movers would not receive motion. So, it is necessary to admit that

76. For a look at the five ways as a whole and as related to the arguments presented in Thomas's other works, see F. Van Steenberghen, *Le problème de l'existence de Dieu dans les écrits de S. Thomas d'Aquin,* Philosophes medievaux 23 (Louvain-la Neuve: Editions de l'Institut Supérieur de Philosophie, 1980); L. J. Elders, ed., Quinque sunt viae: *Actes du Symposium sur les 5 voies de la Somme theologique (Rolduc 1979),* Studi tomistici 9 (Vatican City: Libreria editrice vaticana, 1980); J. F. Wippel, *The Metaphysical Thought of Thomas Aquinas: From Finite Being to Uncreated Being,* Monographs of the Society for Medieval and Renaissance Philosophy 1 (Washington, D.C.: The Catholic University of America Press, 2000), in particular the third part, "From Finite Being to Uncreated Being," see especially 442–500 for the five ways.

there exists a first mover that is not moved by another and that all recognize as God. As can be noted, this way is Aristotelian not only in its general form but also in its fundamental presuppositions, namely, (a) that everything that is moved is moved by another (a principle that many Neo-Platonic philosophers, for example, would not have conceded); and (b) that it is not possible to proceed to infinity in the order of causes.

This last presupposition perhaps deserves some additional scrutiny, since it is present in the other ways too. For Aristotle, the infinite *per se* destroys every causal relationship, since it renders any order between cause and effects impossible. In the infinite it is not possible to specify a before and after, not even logically, and so it is impossible to distinguish an antecedent and a consequent, causes from effects. Furthermore, the ordered series of causes cannot be open. Where it is impossible to fix a first term, there can be no relationship of dependence and, therefore, there can be no subsequent terms (which would lack the principle on which they depend).

Thomas uses this same mechanism in the second way, which is based on the notion of efficient causality. The point of departure is again (as is always the case) given by sense observation (and because of this we are justified in speaking of *a posteriori* proofs). We see that in the sense world there is an order among efficient causes and that it is impossible that anything can be the efficient cause of itself, for then it would have to exist prior to itself, which is absurd. But it is also absurd that the order of efficient causes should stretch into infinity. In fact, in all the efficient causes concatenated in a series, the first is the cause of the one that follows and so on to the last cause, regardless of the number of intermediate causes. Now, if we eliminate the cause, we also eliminate the effect. Hence, if in the order of efficient causes, there is no first cause, there would be no intermediate causes and no ultimate cause. Since the infinite, by definition, has no end, to proceed to infinity in efficient causes is the same as eliminating the first efficient cause, and without it we would have neither the intermediate causes nor the ultimate effects. But we began with the fact that we observe with our senses effects produced by efficient causes. If the effects and intermediate causes exist, a first efficient cause must necessarily exist, which is not itself caused by another, and that all call God.

This way is, thus, nothing but a reproposal of the first way in which the notion of efficient cause replaces that of a moving cause. Indeed, in strictly Aristotelian terms, the two ways cannot really be distinct, since Aristotle poses in general a cause of motion without distinguishing between a moving cause and an efficient cause. But Thomas writes after Avicenna had already made a distinction between the two, separating what in Aristotle had been fundamentally united: the cause that produces movement (understood in a purely physical way) and the cause that produces substantial being (understood in a metaphysical way). From the point of view of the demonstrative mechanism and the conclusions, the framework of the proof does not change. It is necessary to posit a first term both to explain the motion that we perceive and to explain the production itself of things (the changes related to substantial being).

The mention of Avicenna introduces us to the third way, which is at least indirectly taken from the Persian philosopher (and from Maimonides, who develops a similar argument in the *Guide for the Perplexed*). This is a way that hinges on the so-called modalities, that is, notions of possibility and necessity (the modes of being are possible, necessary, and impossible). We see that some things can be and not be. Many things (actually, we could say everything that we observe with our senses) have a beginning and an end, that is, they are generated and corrupted. This is precisely the characteristic of what is possible or contingent—the fact of *not always existing* but of *existing only sometimes* (existing only at determinate moments). We must suppose that what has such a nature, in a certain moment did *not* exist (otherwise it would have *always existed*, which is what we have denied). If in general everything had such a nature, that is, if everything were contingent, *everything would at some moment have not existed*, and, therefore, at some point there would have been nothing at all. But if this were the case, there would be nothing existing now, because, as we know, nothing can bring itself from nothing into being, and everything that did not exist at some time can begin to exist only in virtue of something that already exists. So, if there were no being at all, nothing would have begun to exist and there would be nothing existing now, which is manifestly false. Therefore, all beings are not possible and contingent (capable of being and not being), and there must be at least one necessary being that is necessary in itself.[77] This necessary being, existing always, guarantees to contingent beings (those which sometimes are and sometimes are not) the possibility of coming into existence. And this being is the one that all call God.

The problem with this way is that, in our view, it is not immediately evident that, if everything were merely possible, at one time there would have had to have been nothing. To understand this logical move, we must keep in mind that according to the classical interpretation of modality that Thomas *at least in this instance* adopts:

---

77. Here Thomas admits—as does Avicenna—that some beings can be made necessary by another. But in this case too it is not possible to proceed to infinity and we must stop at a being that is necessary in itself.

* those things are *possible* that can exist and not exist, that is, they sometimes are and sometimes are not (and they do not have the reason for their being in them since, if they did, they would always exist);

* those things are *necessary* that exist and cannot not exist (and so they always exist);

* those things are *impossible* that do not exist and cannot exist (and so they never exist).

Now, if the possible always were, it would no longer be possible but would be necessary. But we see that the things in this world are possible because they begin to exist and cease to exist. Yet, if everything without exception were merely possible, there would be a point in time at which nothing at all existed. And since, as has been said, from absolute nothingness being cannot spontaneously come about, there would be nothing right now. But we see that many things now exist. The possibility of their existing must, then, be based on a being that always exists (God). It might be objected that perhaps it is not inevitable that all possible things not exist at the same time. We could think of a kind of continual succession of possible things. One would permit another to come into being and then go out of being, etc. However, even in this case we would have to come to a first possible thing that would have had to come into being from nothing.[78] And how would it have come to be from absolute nothingness? We must admit what has already been established, namely, that the possible cannot give itself existence but must depend on a necessary being, and if there is more than one necessary being (as is granted not only by Avicenna but Thomas himself, who, as we have seen, takes the angels to have received necessary existence from God), all must depend on a first being, as there can be no proceeding to infinity.

The fourth way (whose mechanism bears a similarity to the one proposed by Anselm) begins from the degrees of perfection that we see in things. It is obvious that things appear to us to be more or less perfect (more or less good, more or less true, more or less ontologically noble). But these different levels of perfection can obtain only in reference to a first and absolute term. In other words, we can judge a thing to be more or less perfect only in the measure that it more or less corresponds to supreme and absolute perfection. There must, then, exist something that is maximally perfect, maximally true, maximally good, maximally noble, and in consequence also maximally being, for, as Aristotle says in *Metaphysics*, XII things have as much truth as they have being. What is maximally true must maximally be. But Aristotle shows in the same place that what

78. If it had always existed, it would not be possible but necessary and would go on existing always, which is precisely what Thomas intends to demonstrate.

is the maximum in a genus is the cause of everything that belongs to that genus. Fire, for example, which is the maximum with respect to heat, is the cause of all heat (every hot thing will be so because it is directly or indirectly heated by fire). So, we must admit that there is a first term and cause of being, goodness, and any perfection whatsoever for all things, and this we call God.

The fifth way is derived from finality and the order itself (from governance, to use Thomas's term) of things. We see that in nature even those things that lack knowledge and consciousness (inanimate beings) seem to act in view of an end, as is evident from the fact that they always or for the most part act in the same way. Now, what is without intelligence obviously cannot tend toward an end by choice in a conscious way but only inasmuch as it is directed by an intelligent being, just as the arrow hits the target only because it is aimed at it by the archer. We must admit that there is an intelligent being that orders all natural beings to their end, and that it is what we call God. This is perhaps the simplest and most intuitive of the ways.[79] The regularity of the phenomena of nature presupposes an intelligent artificer, someone who has disposed nature itself not randomly but according to a precise order, which will assure its stability and conservation.

It could be objected, following Kant, that this argument suggests at most an architect of the world but not a true artificer, since the ordered disposition could have been conferred on preexisting material. But Thomas's arguments are less naive than presentations of them usually make them out to be, and they attempt to prove less than we think. It will be noted that each way concludes with "and this all call God" or a similar formula. Thomas is aware that his ways lead not to God as he is in himself (as we know, the divine essence is inaccessible to human reason) but to the cause of the effects that we observe in our world. In other words, the ways prove that there exists a first unmoved mover, a first efficient cause, a being necessary in itself, a maximum term in the hierarchy of being, and an ordering cause of the cosmos. These are all philosophical definitions, that is, definitions that lead to the divine as it is conceivable and demonstrable by reason and philosophy. To then maintain that this God of the philosophers is identical with the God of revelation is a further step and it is by no means taken for granted (for God in himself exceeds beyond measure what reason can demonstrate of him), and it is for this reason that at the end of each way Thomas is concerned to say that "this is what we call God." We are led commonly to use this name for something that in reality is not properly

79. It is not surprising that among the proofs of God's existence this is the one toward which Kant will be the most indulgent.

and completely defined as God. As has been noted, in the five ways, the name "God" always and only appears at the end, and never in the subject position but always in the predicate position. Thus, Thomas does not say, for example, "God is the unmoved mover" but "this is what we call God." This is a conscious decision and not one made by chance. Thomas does not propose actual demonstrations of God's being (demonstrations of the sort that we have called *propter quid* and that we have not employed in this case), but demonstrations that postulate in general the existence of a first cause in relation to the effects that we observe (*quia demonstrations*). We are certainly justified in using the name "God" to speak of this cause but with the understanding (and this is the point of the whole construction) that in himself God is quite other than this and cannot be reduced simply to the role of cause of the world. If it were not so, God's existence would not be absolute but would be bound up with the existence of the world itself. We can now perhaps better understand Thomas's criticism of the Anselmian argument (or any other *a priori* argument). Yes, God is his own being, and if we were able to demonstrate his being (which God is), we would have access to his essence. But this is precisely what is lacking:

"Being" (*esse*) can mean either of two things. It may mean the act of essence, or it may mean the composition of a proposition effected by the mind in joining a predicate to a subject. Taking "to be" in the first sense, we cannot understand God's being or his essence; but only in the second sense. We know that this proposition which we form about God when we say "God is," is true; and this we know from his effects.[80]

The five ways (as *quia* demonstrations) do not aim at proving, despite appearances, *that God is* (*che Dio è*), that is, *the being of God* (*l'essere di Dio*), but only the fact that (from effects) it can be affirmed that *there exists a first cause that we can in some way identify with God.*

Knowledge

As already noted, the itinerary of the *prima pars* of the *Summa* includes, after the question of God's existence, the consideration of God's essence (obviously on the basis of revelation), creation, the distinction of creatures, angels and human beings, and the image of God (qq. 75–102).[81] This last section is particularly interesting, because in it Thomas once again reprises and reproposes the

---

80. *Summa theologiae*, Ia, q. 3, a. 4, ad 2.

81. For a detailed analysis of the central part of this section, see R. Pasnau, *Thomas Aquinas on Human Nature: A Philosophical Study of Summa theologiae, 1a 75–89* (Cambridge: Cambridge University Press, 2002). For a classic study, in the English-speaking world, of Thomas's phsychology and epistemology, see A. Kenny, *Aquinas on Mind* (London: Routledge, 1993).

basic lines of his anthropology. Despite the strictly theological context, here too the philosophical tension and decision in favor of certain Aristotelian elements are perceptible. An exemplary case is that of human knowledge. We find here a reproposal of the Aristotelian noetic—with many decisive modifications— in the light of the Arab peripatetic tradition, especially that of Avicenna. All human knowledge, as Aristotle teaches, begins with the senses. The material furnished by the sense organs (external senses) is first reworked by the internal senses. Avicenna resystematized the few indications of Aristotle in the first three chapters of *De Anima*, III, distinguishing in his own *De Anima* (I, 5 and IV, 1) five internal senses that, as a whole, constitute what today we might call the neurophysiological basis of knowledge:

a. The *phantasy* or *common sense* (*fantasia vel sensus communis*), situated in the first brain cavity, is what receives and brings together the sensations conveyed by the organs of the external senses.

b. The *imagination* or *formative power* (*imaginatio, vis formans*), situated in the extremity of the anterior brain cavity, preserves the information conveyed by the external senses and organized by the common sense. It is a kind of sensible memory.

c. The *imaginative power*, or, in human beings, the *cogitative power* (*vis imaginativa* or *vis cogitans*), situated in the middle brain cavity, that is, the pineal gland, is the capacity to divide or break into parts the data prepared by the phantasy and stored in the imagination. To compare how these different functions operate we might imagine that we have a group of people before us. Our eyes do not see that there are human beings as such before us but only patches of color just as our ears only hear sounds. The phantasy or common sense organizes the different external sensations, obtaining different human figures. The imaginative power stores these figures. The cogitative power begins to associate or separate the figures, obtaining a first sufficiently abstract—but still sensible (and, so, individual and material) image of man.

The other two faculties are:

d. the *estimative power*. The estimative power (*vis aestimativa*), situated at the top of the middle brain cavity, which gathers not sensible forms but *intentions*, that is, those aspects of things that do not appear to the senses but that we immediately link to our utility or pleasure, or to our disadvantage and pain. It is thanks to the estimative power that the sheep immediately judges that the wolf is something dangerous to flee from and the lamb something to protect.

e. the *memorative power*. The memorative power (*vis memorialis et reminiscibilis, vis custoditiva*), situated in the posterior brain cavity, stores the intentions gathered by the estimative power (just as the imagination stores the data of the common sense).

Thomas, in turn, reorganizes the Avicennian system, positing just four internal senses (q. 78, a. 4):

a. The *common sense* draws all the perceptions of the senses together and permits the reflexivity of sense knowledge (common sense can perceive vision although vision cannot perceive its own act).

b. The *phantasy* or *imaginative power* receives all of the sensible forms perceived by the senses.

c. The *estimative power* collects the intentions (which are not perceived by the external senses).

d. Finally, *memory* stores the intentions collected by the estimative power.

With respect to the Avicennian schema, phantasy is disassociated from the common sense and assimilated to the sensible memory, and the latter is called the imaginative power and not imagination. But this change is understandable, since Avicenna himself had in part used them interchangeably (*et fortassis distinguunt inter imaginationem et imaginativam ad placitum; et non sumus de his qui hoc faciunt*).[82] Avicenna's cogitative power seems at first to be left out of this picture. It is, however, quite present in Thomas but with a change of function. Where in Avicenna the cogitative power is the other name for the imaginative power, in Thomas it is the name for what is called in other animals the *natural estimative power*. Said differently, the cogitative power here does not have the role of composing and dividing sensible images—in Thomas this is done by the phantasy or imaginative power; the cogitative power is, in Thomas, the capacity to arrive at intentions "through a kind of reasoning" (*per quandam collationem*) and not, as animals do, in an instinctive way (*quodam instinctu*). So, the cogitative power becomes the apex of sense knowledge, constituting *particular reason*:

Therefore, the power that in other animals is called the "natural estimative power," in man is called the "cogitative power," which by some sort of collation discovers these intentions. Hence, it is also called the "particular reason," to which physicians assign a certain particular organ, namely, the middle part of the head, for it compares individual intentions, just as the intellectual reason compares universal intentions.[83]

82. Avicenna Latinus, *Liber de anima seu sextus de naturalibus. IV–V*, IV, 1, Editions Orientalistes, S. Van Riet, ed. (Leiden: Brill, 1968), 5 (ll. 61–63). See C. Di Martino, Ratio particularis: *la doctrine des sens internes d'Avicenne à Thomas d'Aquin. Contribution à l'étude de la tradition arabo-latine de la psychologie d'Aristote*, Études de philosophie médiévale 94 (Paris: Vrin, 2008).

83. *Summa theologiae*, Ia, q. 78, a. 4.

It is worth noting that this reconfiguration of the function of the cogitative power brings Thomas closer to Averroes on this specific point than to Avicenna. In any event, the progressive elaboration of the sense data by the internal senses results in a sensible image or species that is already quite refined. This image—or *phantasm*, to use the Scholastic terminology—already lacks certain individual and accidental characteristics, but it is still an image, that is, a sensible representation and not an intelligible content (as is, for example, the definition "rational mortal animal"). The concept of man (arrived at by the passage from sensible to intelligible knowledge) presupposes that this image is stripped of *all* of its material characteristics, that it is no longer an image. This operation goes by the name of *abstraction*. It is made possible by the agent intellect, which, as Aristotle said, relates to sensible species or phantasms in the same way that sensible light relates to colors. In the dark, things have color but are only potentially perceivable as such. They can actually be perceived only when there is light. Analogously, sensible species are potentially intelligible but become actually so only by the light of the agent intellect. The status of this intellect was already the subject of differing interpretations among Aristotle's first commentators. Alexander of Aphrodisias hypothesized that it was external to the human soul and was identical with God. In the Arabic-speaking philosophical world, Avicenna identified it with the last (the tenth) of the celestial intelligences, which (as we have already seen) presides over the sublunary world, and Averroes too made it a separate substance. In the Latin-speaking world, some masters (especially the Franciscans) followed a similar path, making the agent intellect identical with God, that is, with that light that, already according to Augustine, enlightens every created intellect and is the font of all true knowledge. Thomas (as we have seen in part in our examination of the Commentary on Boethius's *De Trinitate*) rejects any interpretation of the agent intellect as a separate and transcendent faculty, holding instead that it is a light that naturally belongs to the human soul. It can also be called "divine," but in the sense that it has been given by God to every man. And because every man possesses it, it is unnecessary for God continually to intervene in human cognitive processes to enlighten our minds from without. The light shed by the agent intellect, as we have said, makes it so that sensible species pass from being potentially intelligible to being actually intelligible (by abstracting the intelligible species from the sensible species, eliminating all the residual material and accidental elements). The intelligible species in this state is impressed upon the intellective faculty of our soul, the possible or potential intellect. Let us leave aside for the moment Thomas's handling of the Averroist doctrine about the possible intellect also being a separate substance and the same for all humanity. The possible intellect is the actual faculty with which we think. The agent intellect is principally a condition (certainly necessary) of the intellectual process (that which assures the conditions of intelligibility), but thinking here fundamentally means receiving an intelligible species. Here too Thomas is faithful to Aristotle. Thinking (like sensing) is first of all an undergoing (in the sense of being in potency to something: q. 79, a. 2), a receiving. But Thomas goes beyond Aristotle (and his Arab interpreters) when he then attributes an *active* function to the intellect, taking his cue in this case more from the Augustinian tradition. This function consists essentially in the *production* of the mental word or concept or definition of the thing known,[84] and this coincides with the first operation of the intellect. The simple definition thus obtained (that is, the quidditative notion of the thing) can then be used by the intellect itself in the second operation to formulate propositions or judgments about the thing itself (q. 85, a. 2, ad 3).

It is not true, then, that, for Thomas, the possible intellect is always only passive. It is passive and receptive in the first phase of the cognitive process, in the sense that there can be nothing in the intellect that did not previously pass through the senses (that is, no concept is possible without images: to have intelligible species it is always necessary to be in possession of sensible images or phantasms from which they can be abstracted). Our intellect is, in short, from the very beginning oriented toward what comes from the senses and so toward natural and material reality:

It is proper to [the human intellect] to know a form existing individually in corporeal matter, but not as existing in this individual matter. But to know what is in individual matter, not as existing in such matter, is to abstract the form from individual matter which is represented by the phantasms. Therefore, we must say that our intellect understands material things by abstracting from the phantasms, and through material things thus considered we acquire some knowledge of immaterial things, just as, on the contrary, angels know material things through the immaterial.[85]

The proper object of our intellect is, thus, the essence of corporeal things (*quidditas rei materialis*), an essence that is abstracted from sensible images and known through intelligible species (which are the means and not the object of intellectual knowledge). Now, precisely because our intellect knows essences and knows them through an abstractive process, it properly knows what is universal and not the individual. This conclusion might appear surprising, since we have said that all knowledge begins from the senses and the senses always perceive

84. This is a topic that we touched upon in the section on ideas in Chapter 3.
85. *Summa theologiae*, Ia, q. 85, a. 1.

individual realities. But this is precisely the difference between sense knowledge and intellectual knowledge. The senses grasp the individual, the intellect
knows in an abstract and universal way, abstracting from everything individual
and material. Consequently, the intellect can know the individual only indirectly, through a kind of reversal that Thomas calls "reflection" (*reflexio*). From the
universal essence, which is its natural object, it can return to the act by which
it knew and thought it, that is, to the intelligible species, and from this to the
sensible image from which it was drawn (q. 86, a. 1).[86] In the same way, and only
through a complete process of reflection or "return" (*reditio completa*, an expression that also belongs to the Proclean tradition and that Thomas borrows in the
Commentary on the *De causis*), the soul can have full awareness of itself—it can
achieve self-knowledge (q. 87, a. 3). While the divine intellect is identical with
the essence itself of God, and the angelic intellect has as its first and immediate
object the essence itself of the angel, things are different for man. The human
essence is neither identical with the acts of intellection nor the first object of
the human intellect. The primary cognitive object of man, as we have said, "is
not his essence but some external thing, for this object is the nature of a material thing. And therefore that which is first known by the human intellect is
an object of this kind, and that which is known secondarily is the act by which
that object is known; and through the act the intellect itself is known."[87] The
human soul does, nevertheless, have a habitual knowledge of itself (*cognitio ha-
bitualis*)—since it is the ontological root of its own acts—a prereflective knowledge concomitant to every vital act with the possibility of "scientifically" arriving
at its own essence through an abstractive process.[88] The whole cognitive process
envisioned by Thomas is outlined in the diagram.

86. *Summa theologiae* Ia, q. 86, a. 1: "Our *intellect* cannot *know* the singular in material things
directly and primarily. The reason for this is that the principle of singularity in material things is *individual matter*.... But indirectly, and as it were by a kind of reflection, it can *know* the singular, because,
as we have said above, even after abstracting the intelligible *species*, the *intellect*, in order to understand,
needs to turn to the phantasms in which it understands the *species*, as is said in *De Anima*, III, 7. Therefore, the intellect understands the universal directly through the intelligible *species*, and indirectly the
singular represented by the phantasm."

87. *Summa theologiae*, Ia, q. 87, a. 3.

88. On all these modalities of reflexive knowledge, see the excellent contribution of F. X. Putallaz,
Le sens de la réflexion chez Thomas d'Aquin (Paris: Vrin, 1991). The most significant passage on the *reditio
completa* is, however, found not in the section of the first part of the *Summa theologiae* that we are considering, but in *De veritate* (q. 1, a. 9): "Although sense knows that it senses, it does not know its own
nature; consequently, it knows neither the nature of its act nor the proportion of this act to things....
The reason for this is that the most perfect beings, such as, for example, intellectual substances, return
to their essence with a complete return: knowing something external to themselves, in a certain sense
they go outside of themselves; but by knowing that they know, they are already beginning to return
to themselves, because the act of cognition mediates between the knower and the thing known. That

The knowing process

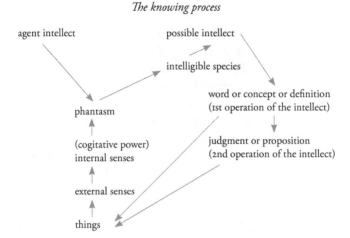

Every relation to the individual is, thus, inevitably mediated by images. Since we often hear of Thomistic "realism" in epistemology, it should be noted that Thomas is certainly not a representationalist in a strong sense, if by representationalism is meant the view that we know *only* our representations and not things. In Thomas's view, the intelligible species is only the medium through which we know things and only secondarily an object of knowledge in itself (q. 85, a. 2). But Thomas could be regarded as a moderate representationalist since he holds that the intellect grasps and knows its object not directly but through a series of indispensable mediations (the sensible and intelligible species). What the intellect ultimately knows is *never the thing as it exists in external reality* (for the simple fact that every existing thing is individual and the intellect cannot know the individual), *but the thing as intelligible*, to wit, insofar as it is conveyed by a species and as universal (and we should recall that, for Thomas, it is the intellect that creates universality).[89]

---

return is completed inasmuch as they know their own essences. Hence, it is said in the *De causis*: 'A being which is such as to know its own essence returns to it by a complete return'." Later the existence of an isolated disputed question, *Utrum anima coniuncta cognoscat seipsam per essentiam*, was discovered by Pelster in 1955 (in ms. Oxford, Bodl. Laud. Misc. 480) and published by Kennedy in 1977. See L. A. Kennedy, "The Soul's Knowledge of Itself: An Unpublished Work Attributed to St. Thomas Aquinas," *Vivarium* 15 (1977): 31–45. The authenticity of that question, though defended by the likes of A. Dondaine, Eschmann, and Weisheipl, appears, nevertheless, at least debatable: Putallaz himself observes (*Le sens de la réflexion*, 304–10) that it presents a theory of self-knowledge rather different from that normally presented by Thomas in the works that are certainly authentic.

89. It does not, therefore, follow that the intellect grasps something false, precisely because our intellect simply does not aim entirely at singular things, but their essence: "If, therefore, the intellect is said to be false when it understands a thing otherwise than as it is, that is so if the word 'otherwise'

DE REGNO: THE DUTIES OF A RULER

The treatise *De regno* is traditionally among the writings of the Roman period also. The work is dedicated to the king of Cyprus, whom, even to this day, it is not easy for us to identify. There are, indeed, at least three candidates: Henry I of Lusignan (1218–53), Hugh II of Lusignan (1253–67), and Hugh III of Antioch-Lusignan (1267–84). The fact that Thomas quotes William of Moerbeke's translation of Aristotle's *Politics* allows us to fix the *terminus post quem* of the *De regno* after 1260 and so to exclude Henry I.[90] The Leonine Commission editors (following an indication formulated by Échard) have suggested excluding Hugh III as well, supposing that it would have been difficult for Thomas, who was linked to the House of Anjou, to have dedicated a work to a rival of Charles of Anjou in the contest for the Kingdom of Jerusalem. So, the most probable addressee is Hugh II. His youth would have made fitting the composition of a *speculum principis* ("mirror of the prince")—a textbook of instruction for young people destined to rule—and his premature death would also have explained the interruption of work. The treatise is, in fact, incomplete if we do not consider the 62 chapters added by Tolomeo of Lucca. The authentic text of Thomas ends at Book II, c. 8 (according to the Leonine edition). Christoph Flüeler re-launched the discussion of the chronology, which had been considered established, proposing a later date of composition (1271–73—which would place it between Naples and Paris). But in that case the obvious addressee would be Hugh III.[91] Since the question is still far from settled, we will keep to the traditional dating, which is maintained by the present editors of the Leonine Commission.

The purpose of the treatise is to consider the origin of monarchy and the duties of the sovereign, following three parameters: the authority of Scripture, philosophical doctrine, and the example of the most illustrious princes. One problem for readers of the opuscule is that Thomas seems here to endorse theses that are different from those he holds in other writings. The most obvious

refers to the thing understood, for the intellect is false when it understands a thing otherwise than as it is, and so the intellect would be false if it abstracted the species of a stone from its matter in such a way as to regard the species as not existing in matter, as Plato held. But it is not so if the word 'otherwise' be taken as referring to the one who understands. For it is quite true that the mode of understanding, in one who understands, is not the same as the mode of a thing in existing, since the thing understood is immaterially in the one who understands, according to the mode of the intellect, and not materially, according to the mode of a material thing" (*Summa theologiae* Ia, q. 85, a. 1, ad 1).

90. However, at least one manuscript, namely, Vat. lat. 5088 (dating from the fourteenth century), names Henry as the addressee.

91. See C. Flüeler, *Rezeption und Interpretation der Aristotelischen Politica im späten Mittelalter*, Bochumer Studien zur Philosophie 19:1 (Amsterdam: Grüner, 1992), 23–29.

example is the fact that in the *De regno* Thomas goes in for absolute monarchy, whereas in other places he proposes a mixed regime in which the power is shared by the sovereign and an aristocracy elected by the citizens.[92] Another example—which we will consider further momentarily—is that Thomas seems (at least at first glance) to ignore the distinction between spiritual power and secular power, which he defends in other works. There have been numerous hypotheses advanced to explain these discrepancies. Thus, it has been suggested, for instance, that the particular circumstances of the Kingdom of Cyprus were a determining factor, or that Tolomeo revised some of Thomas's chapters (but we have no documentation or trace of these alleged revisions). At any rate, it should be emphasized that the *De regno* does not present itself so much as a treatise of political theory as, indeed, a *speculum principis*, which might justify certain concessions to this genre of writing.

But we cannot minimize the political import of this opuscule simply because we find it unsatisfactory or disappointing. The *De regno* opens with a brief but noteworthy discussion of the Aristotelian definition of man as a political animal. Man's political or social nature is owed not only to the necessities of survival (lacking natural defenses and adequate means, human beings can protect themselves only by joining together) but also to the peculiarly cumulative nature of human knowing and to the corresponding role of language (a topic that Thomas probably takes over from Avicenna's *De anima* but that he develops in a sufficiently original manner):

Other animals are endowed with a natural awareness of everything which is useful or harmful to them. For example, the sheep naturally judges the wolf to be an enemy. Some animals even have a natural awareness which enables them to recognize certain medicinal plants and other things as being necessary to their lives. Man, however, has a natural understanding of the things necessary to his life only in a general way, and it is by the use of reason that he passes from universal principles to an understanding of the particular things which are necessary to human life. But it is not possible for one man to apprehend all such things by reason. It is, therefore, necessary for man to live in a community, so that each man may devote his reason to some particular branch of learning: one to medicine, another to something else, another to something else again. And this is shown especially by the fact that only man has the capacity to use speech, by means of which one man can reveal all of his thoughts to another.[93]

The political community is *also* founded on language, since man is, absolutely speaking, the animal who is "most communicative" (*magis igitur homo est*

92. See J. M. Blythe, *Le gouvernement idéal et la constitution mixte au Moyen Âge*, Vestigia 32 (Fribourg-Paris: Academic Press–Cerf, 2005).

93. *De regno*, I, c. 1.

communicativus alteri quam quodcumque aliud animal quod gregale videtur). As such, man must enter into community and communities must be regulated, disciplined, and governed. The discussion of the Aristotelian forms of government (and their forms of degeneration) follows. Thomas, as we have just said, privileges monarchy, appealing for this move to experience and to three principal theoretical reasons: it is the better guarantee of peace, the better guarantee of unity in multiplicity, and the most natural form of government. At the opposite extreme, tyranny is the worst form of government ("as government by a king is the best, so government by a tyrant is the worst"). But, distancing himself from this speculative contraposition, Thomas observes that tyranny more often follows from rule by many persons than from monarchy:

The rule of many turns into tyranny more rather than less frequently than that of one. For when dissension arises under the rule of several persons, it often happens that one man rises superior to the others and usurps to himself sole dominion over the community. This can plainly be seen to have happened from time to time, for in almost every case government by many has ended in tyranny; and this appears very clearly in the example of the Roman republic.[94]

In the *De regno* the propensity for monarchy is, thus, joined with a strong suspicion of democracy. Regarding the measures against tyranny, Thomas observes that if the tyranny is not excessive, it is better to endure it for a time than to run the risk of falling into worse evils (such as making the tyrant more cruel or replacing him with a worse tyrant). If the tyranny is intolerable, "it has seemed to some that it would be an action consistent with virtue if the mightier people were to slay the tyrant, exposing themselves even to the peril of death in order to liberate the community" (I, c. 7). But Thomas does not share this view (which he takes to be out of step with the teaching of the apostles) and rejects the legitimacy of tyrannicide. The overthrow of the tyrant cannot be up to the initiative of a few but must be pursued through public authority. Finally, if recourse to other human authorities proves futile, the only path left is to entrust ourselves—rather fatalistically—to divine judgment.

Moving on to the other key topic of the treatise, Thomas says that all the actions of the ruler must tend toward the true good. In this context Thomas does not reject the traditional analogy between God and the prince. The prince rules over the people as the soul rules over the body and God over the world. Just as God creates and governs the world, the ruler must found and govern the realm. It is the second function that is to be stressed, since not all kings are the founders of the city or state they govern. The topic of *gubernatio*, in any case, provides

94. *De regno*, I, c. 6.

what is perhaps the most interesting part of the treatise, that is, a discussion of the Aristotelian question about whether true felicity resides in political life (and so in the pursuit of a secular, intraworldly end) or in contemplation (and so in pursuit, in the Christian sense, of the ultimate end of human nature—the contemplation of the divine essence). Thomas's answer is not without ambiguity, or rather, it is somewhat complex. The end of the community and of life together seems to be that of permitting the citizens to live according to virtue. (Human beings associate in order to live well together, being unable to do so in isolation, and living well is living virtuously.) Nevertheless, Thomas continues, living virtuously is ordered to an ulterior end, which is the enjoyment of God. If this is the ultimate end of every individual, it must be the ultimate end of the community. Therefore, the ultimate end of life in community is not living virtuously but to arrive at the enjoyment of God *through a virtuous life*. This is one of the points on which Thomas appears to depart from other works. In the Commentary on the *Sentences,* Thomas seems to affirm that both powers are equally fundamental inasmuch as both come from God:

Both spiritual and secular power descend from divine power. Thus, secular power is subject to spiritual power to the extent that it is subject to God, namely, in those things that regard the salvation of the soul. In such things it is necessary to obey the spiritual rather than the secular power. In the things that regard the civic good, it is necessary to obey the secular rather than the spiritual power.[95]

The double derivation from divine power sanctions and guarantees the autonomy of spiritual power and civil power. In the *De regno* it seems instead that the subordination of secular power to spiritual power is postulated even in what touches on the end of the secular power itself, since the enjoyment of God, as we have seen, is considered the ultimate end of the political community itself. Can a person (a prince or a ruler) lead his community to this eschatological goal? Or more radically: Is it possible to leave this final end to human efforts alone? For Thomas the theologian, the answer is obviously negative. Hence, guiding the community to the ultimate end cannot be the task of a purely human government. It is also the task of a divine government and is the office of Christ as the man-God. The exercise of this office on earth is entrusted to the vicars of Christ, and, thus, in the first place to the pope:

Because the enjoyment of divinity is an end which a person cannot attain through human virtue alone, but only through divine power ... it is not human but divine rule that will lead to this end. And government of this kind belongs only to that king who is not only man but also God, that is, to our Lord Jesus Christ, who by making us sons

95. *In II Sent.*, d. 44, q. 2, a. 3.

of God, has led us to the glory of heaven.... The administration of this kingdom, therefore, is not to earthly kings, but to priests—so that spiritual and earthly things may be kept distinct—and in particular to the supreme priest, the successor of Peter, the vicar of Christ, the Roman Pontiff, to whom all the kings of the Christian people should be subject, as if to the Lord Jesus Christ himself.[96]

Some commentators (especially Eschmann)[97] hold that this subordination is an obvious step backwards vis-à-vis the thesis of reciprocal autonomy maintained in the Commentary on the *Sentences,* and all the more so since in the *De regno* it is held that the person who has the responsibility to lead others to the final end is the one who must prescribe the means to the end. It is, for example, the captain of the ship who explains to the shipbuilder the best way to build the ship. Others (such as Leonard Boyle)[98] argue that precisely this example, if correctly interpreted, only reemphasizes the earlier thesis: the captain commands the builder with respect to what serves navigation as the ultimate end, but he does not instruct him in the finer details of his work, nor does he participate in building the ship himself. Going beyond the metaphor, the secular power is subject to papal power only with respect to what concerns the salvation of souls (the final end) but without prejudice to the secular power regarding all other spheres and all other ends. From this point of view, which, all told, seems plausible, even the *De regno* maintains a certain division of powers and ends. (Not by chance, the preceding passage states that the exercise of sovereignty regarding the final end is entrusted to priests and the pope precisely to keep spiritual things distinct from earthly ones—*ut a terrenis spiritualia essent discreta.*) Man's final end, as was said, is not in the power of man himself; it belongs to Christ and his vicar on earth, the pope.[99] And because all intermediary or anterior ends are subordinate to the final end, it is inevitable that all rulers will be subject to the pope relative to that end. This, however, does not preclude that the business of the ruler will be to concern himself with an end (virtuous living) that is secondary with respect to the final end but that is the most important of the community's earthly ends. This task of the ruler includes three

96. *De regno,* I, c. 15.

97. 47. See I. T. Eschmann, "St. Thomas Aquinas on the Two Powers," *Mediaeval Studies* 20 (1958): 177–205.

98. See L. E. Boyle, "The *De regno* and the Two Powers," in *Essays in Honour of Anton Charles Pegis,* ed. J. R. O'Donnell (Toronto: Pontifical Institute of Mediaeval Studies, 1974), 237–47 (also in Boyle's *Facing History,* 1–12).

99. Furthermore, it must be recalled that also in the sequence of the passage of the commentary on the second book of the *Sentences* first cited, contrary to what is maintained by Eschmann, Thomas attributed to the pope the possession of both the spiritual and secular power; from this point of view too the gap between the two writings does not seem very clear-cut.

specific duties: establishing a good life among his people; preserving this life by securing peace within the community and protecting it from external attacks; and promoting the betterment of the community.

Thomas then begins to discuss the *institutio* of the kingdom, that is, the choice of place for its foundation, proposing three criteria: wholesomeness of the air, availability of the means of subsistence, and pleasantness (since "a place where life is pleasant is not easily deserted nor will many inhabitants often flock to unpleasant places, for man cannot long endure a life without pleasure.")[100] But here the authentic part of the work breaks off, either because of the addressee's premature death (if we accept the hypothesis of the editors of the Leonine Commission) or because of other events in the last years of Thomas's life (if we accept the dating suggested by Flüeler).

THE *QUAESTIONES DISPUTATAE DE ANIMA:*
IS THE HUMAN SOUL A FORM OR A SUBSTANCE?

During his time in Rome, Thomas also held a disputation on a series of questions on the soul and published them—at least according to the chronology of Bernardo Bazán, who edited the text of the Leonine edition of these questions. From these questions we can gather that Thomas already knew William of Moerbeke's new Latin translation of Aristotle's *De anima*[101] (which was a revision of the previous translation by James of Venice), but he makes no mention— as he would later in his commentary on the Aristotelian text—of Themistius's paraphrase of it. Moreover, in these disputed questions he still attributes *De plantis* to Aristotle, which permits us to situate them before the Commentary on the *De sensu,* in which he will explicitly attribute that work instead to Theophrastus. Accordingly, Bazán's opinion is that the questions on the soul were not only disputed in Italy (perhaps between 1266 and 1267, after the *De potentia*) but published there too. It has at times been questioned whether the text stems from an actual disputation, but in Bazán's view the structure of the questions suggests ordinary disputations (that is, public disputations open not only to students but to all the members of the Dominican community) held weekly. The division of the work seems well thought out. Of the twenty-one articles, seven are on the essence of the soul, seven are on its conjunction with the body, and seven are on the soul in its state of separation.

As a whole, the *Quaestiones disputatae de anima* allow us to reconstruct some

100. *De regno,* II, c. 4.
101. Moreover, the date of Moerbeke's revision is not determinable with precision, save that two revisions of it are attested.

of the fundamental features of Thomas's anthropology, beginning from the conviction about the basic unity of the human composite—one of the characteristic features of Thomas's thought. It is truly difficult to find another Western thinker who is more radically anti-dualist than Thomas: man is not his soul, or is not primarily his soul, but is always the composite of soul and body. On this point Thomas—against any Platonizing temptation—remains faithful to Aristotelian hylomorphism. But a Christian theologian must always take account of the fact that the soul (in the period between death and the resurrection of the body) must be able to subsist on its own, that is, in a state of separation from the body. In the first series of articles, the question asked has to do with how it is possible for the soul to be at the same time the form of the body and *hoc aliquid* (the Latin expression that translates the *tode ti* of Aristotle), that is, something determinate, capable of subsisting on its own and as such endowed with a complete being in a determinate species of the genus of substance.[102] For Thomas, it is a matter here of avoiding two contrary errors: the error of those who deny the soul any autonomous subsistence and complete being, reducing it to the body's harmony (Empedocles as quoted by Aristotle) or temperament (Galen as quoted by Nemesius of Emesa), and the error of those who identify man completely with his soul (the Platonists), reducing its relationship to the body to one like that between a pilot and his ship (*sicut nauta ad navem*). The first error can easily be refuted by showing that the soul's operations (whether those of the vegetative or of the sensitive soul and more so those of the rational soul) exceed the elementary qualities of the body, something that would be impossible were the soul merely the harmony or temperament of the body. The second error, which is in a certain way more insidious, can be refuted by showing, first of all, that the soul is undoubtedly the form of the body (which is evident from the fact that the bodies in question are as they are only if they are alive, and they can receive life, as an act, from the soul alone) and then that

102. On this problem, see K. Bernath, Anima forma corporis: *Eine Untersuchung über die ontologischen Grundlagen der Anthropologie des Thomas von Aquin* (Bonn: Bouvier, 1969). For more recent commentary see B. C. Bazán, "The Human Soul: Form and Substance? Thomas Aquinas' Critique of Eclectic Aristotelianism," *Archives d'Histoire Doctrinale et Littéraire du Moyen Âge* 64 (1997): 95–126. According to Bazán, Thomas goes beyond the "eclectic" Aristotelianism of the masters of arts and of the theologians of the first half of the thirteenth century, who granted that the human soul could be at one time a substance *and* form. Another recent discussion of the topic is M. Lenzi's "Alberto e Tommaso sullo statuto dell'anima umana," *Archives d'Histoire Doctrinale et Littéraire du Moyen Âge* 74 (2007): 27–58. Lenzi argues that, in fact, Thomas is not so far from Albert and his predecessors and he understood the soul as a kind of frontier and subject to a twofold consideration. See also Lenzi's *Anima, forma e sostanza: filosofia e teologia nel dibattito antropologico del XIII secolo* (Spoleto: CISAM, 2011), especially 197–254, where the peculiar liminal position of the soul between the separate substances and the immanent forms is emphasized.

the union of the soul and body cannot be regarded as merely accidental (as is the case of the relationship of the pilot and the ship), for in that event the death of an individual could not be considered a process of substantial corruption, but only, Platonically, a process of the separation of the soul from the shell or vehicle to which it was accidentally conjoined. The being proper to the soul can be inferred from its operation, that is, by the way in which it knows. The measure in which the soul possesses an operation (that of the rational soul) that exceeds what is material elevates it above the body, on which it does not totally depend. But the extent to which immaterial knowledge in man has its origin in sense knowledge makes it clear that the soul's complete being (what constitutes the human species) depends on its union with the body. Thus, the soul is situated (according to one of the most ancient Neo-Platonic axioms, which Thomas probably borrows as much from Nemesius's *De natura hominis* as from the *Liber de causis*) on the frontier between corporeal and separate beings:

Consequently the human soul's mode of being can be known from its operation. For, inasmuch as the human soul has an operation transcending the material order, its being transcends the body and does not depend on the body. Indeed, inasmuch as the soul is naturally capable of acquiring immaterial knowledge from material things, evidently its species can be complete only when it is united to a body. For a thing's species is complete only if it has the things necessary for the proper operation of its species. Consequently, if the human soul, inasmuch as it is united as a form to the body, has an act of existing which transcends the body and does not depend on it, obviously the soul itself is established on the boundary line dividing corporeal from separate substances.[103]

In summary: man is not his soul but is always the union of soul and body. Nevertheless, the human soul, unlike the souls of other living things, possesses an operation—that of knowing what is intelligible and immaterial—that presupposes the body but that can be actualized apart from it. The possibility of the soul's separation is, therefore, founded on an operation, or better, on the specific operation of human nature, viz., intellectual knowing.

The other solutions that Thomas offers in the subsequent articles can also be understood on this ground. In a. 2—which asks whether the human soul is separate from the body in being—there is another occasion for a consideration of Avicenna. In Book III of the *De anima*, Aristotle posits that both the potential intellect and the productive or agent intellect are "separate." This is a claim that it is not easy to understand, since the term "separation" is ambiguous in the Aristotelian lexicon, usually designating the capacity to subsist or be conceived apart from another as well as—although in few instances and despite the

---

103. *Quaestiones disputatae de anima,* a. 1.

intention to oppose the Platonic understanding of "separation"—independence from matter. According to Thomas, Aristotle intended to say that the potential or possible intellect must be separate from sensible forms and so not have a corporeal organ, since if this were not the case, it would be determined according to the sensible nature of this organ. Aristotle, thus, intended to oppose those earlier philosophers who identified the intellect with the sense powers or in some way understood the intellect to be a form joined to the body in the way other material forms or powers are. But some, in arguing against this error, went too far in the other direction and fell into the opposite error (*Set hoc quidam fugientes, in contrarium dilabuntur errorem*). Thomas refers to Averroes and his doctrine of the unicity and separation of the potential intellect (the thesis that there is just one possible intellect—and ultimately one soul—for all humanity). Thomas thereby inscribes Averroes's thesis in a hyper-Platonizing tendency. The Commentator's error, in other words, is not (at least in this case) that of having radicalized the authentic Aristotelian position but of having transposed it into foreign terrain, that is, the terrain of Platonic separation:

They think that the possible intellect is devoid of every sensible nature and that it is not present in the body (*denudatum ab omni natura sensibili et impermixtum corpori*), because it is a certain substance which exists in separation from the body and is in potency to all intelligible forms.[104]

For Thomas, then, the possible intellect is a *vis* or power of the human soul that, however, does not have a corporeal organ and so transcends corporeal matter. Hence, the human soul has operations that both presuppose union with the body (the operations of the sensitive and vegetative powers) and transcend the body (with the limitation noted in the previous article) but that do not, on this account, assume a principle separate from the individual person.

The possible intellect is not a separate substance, nor is it one for all humanity (a. 3). We will return to this set of issues in the next chapter when we discuss the *De unitate intellectus*. In regard to the agent intellect, in the *Quaestiones disputatae de anima* Thomas stresses the necessity of acknowledging its existence (a. 4). If, in fact, the possible intellect is in potency with respect to intelligible things, it is necessary that these things themselves be able to "move" it, to actualize it. But the intelligible *per se* is not something that exists in nature (universals as such do not exist in nature). Consequently, there is a necessity for an agent intellect that "produces" the intelligible in act and makes it able to move the possible intellect. Now, "producing" the intelligible in act means nothing other than abstracting it from matter and material conditions, which

104. *Quaestiones disputatae de anima*, a. 2.

make things individuals (that is, make it such that forms are individuals in the particular things that exist). Were universals to exist in nature, as the Platonists held, there would be no need for the agent intellect. So, it is the Aristotelian refutation of the existence of ideas that postulates the necessity of the agent intellect. As Thomas adds, there are things that are intelligible in themselves (independently of the operation of the agent intellect), and these are the immaterial substances, but these are not immediately accessible to the human possible intellect, which can only ever know of their existence in some way (*aliqualiter*) through material and sensible things.

It can also be asked about the agent intellect whether it is one and separate (a. 5). It is ultimately Avicenna who identifies the agent intellect with the tenth intelligence, called by the Latins, as we know, the *dator formarum*. Now, Thomas thinks that this view is more reasonable than the one that claims the unicity of the possible intellect, since that which acts is often found separately from what it brings to act. It is for this reason that even some "Catholics" maintained that the agent intellect is separate, identifying it not with an intelligence but with God himself. Thomas is referring to the proponents (especially Franciscans) of what Gilson called "Avicennizing Augustinianism" that is, the combination of Augustinian illuminationism with Avicenna's theory of the *dator formarum*, which is identified with God. But, for Thomas, this position too is unacceptable. The relationship between superior substances and our souls can be considered to be similar to that between celestial bodies and inferior bodies. Now, not everything in our world is made to happen by the active universal principles of the celestial bodies, since the intervention of active particular principles is indispensable. The influence of celestial bodies, for example, can be sufficient to assure the spontaneous generation of the simplest living things (the maggots that are generated by the putrefaction of other living things) but not that of more complex living things in which the transmission of seed is needed and so the activity of active particular principles ("univocal" causes, that is, of the same species as what is produced). What is more perfect and complex in inferior substances is the intellectual operation. Therefore, it requires not only active universal principles (God's general illumination) but its own active principle, that is, the agent intellect. Avicenna's thesis presented a further problem. If the ultimate perfection and ultimate happiness of our species is in the performance of the most noble operation (intellectual knowledge, thinking), and this consists in the conjunction of the possible intellect with its active principle (the agent intellect), it would be the case that man's ultimate beatitude would not consist in union with God but would consist in union with an inferior separate substance—with a celestial intelligence. But if it is proper to the agent intellect to abstract the intelligible content from phantasms, we can apply to it what is true for the possible intellect: that we experience this abstractive capacity in ourselves (*Utramque autem harum operationum experimur in nobis ipsis, nam et nos intelligibilia recipimus et abstrahimus ea*). So, both the possible intellect and the agent intellect belong to the human soul. The former is the disposition to receive the intelligible species and the latter abstracts the intelligible species from phantasms.

The next step is that of rejecting the view that the soul is literally composed of matter and form (a. 6). Here we find again the rejection of Avicebron's universal hylomorphism. This is not a question of rejecting hylomorphism as such but of rightly understanding it. Hylomorphic composition regards man as a totality, as a substance, and consists in the fact that every man is composed of form (soul) and body (matter). Applying this distinction subsequently to the soul itself is a useless reduplication of hylomorphic composition within what is already an element of the fundamental hylomorphic composition of human nature. On the other hand, every hylomorphic composition constitutes a species, but the soul is not a species in itself. It is man, rather, that is a species, precisely because he is a composite of soul and body. Avicebron's approach to hylomorphism is, thus, for Thomas, another threat to the unity of the human composite. If the soul were, in turn, a composite of matter and form, it would already be something unitary in itself (a complete being in itself), and an explanation would be needed why it forms a further unity with the body. But denying the soul's hylomorphic composition does not mean denying that there is another composition within the soul between a principle of potentiality and a principle of actuality, that is (as we already know from the *De ente*), a composition of being and essence.

In the article that follows (a. 7) Thomas denies that human souls and angels belong to the same species, an error that is imputed particularly to Origen. The difference can be easily perceived if we simply consider that the human soul, unlike separate substances, derives intelligible species from sensible things. This occasion permits Thomas again to emphasize that a different degree of perfection in nature always carries with it a difference of species.

The middle articles (aa. 8–14), as we said, regard the soul in its state of conjunction with the body. Thomas first explains why the soul is joined to the human body rather than to another sort of body, such as a celestial body (a. 8). Because the human soul acquires knowledge by abstraction from sense knowledge, it is natural for it to be joined to a body possessing sense organs. In Thomas's view it is no accident that man has a brain proportionally superior to those of other living things, nor that he has an erect posture. Thomas denies that the soul is united to the body through some intermediary, through other forms (a. 9). Here we have an important issue for Thomas's engagement with the proponents of a plurality of substantial forms (the majority of Franciscan masters and others), and in this context Thomas once more stresses his unicity thesis: the soul is what gives being to the body, and since being is what is most intimate and immediate to each thing, it is necessary that the soul itself be conjoined with the body without any mediation. The pluralist error is always, for Thomas, an implicit form of Platonism to the extent that it assumes that the soul and the body are already substances in themselves (posing in this way the difficult and insurmountable problem of seeing how they can then be conjoined). The rational soul is, in Thomas's judgment, the only form of the human composite. The lower functions are not delegated to other principles (to other souls) but are in its charge, in the sense that what is more perfect takes up into itself what is less perfect. Said otherwise, the rational soul (as we have seen, among other places, in the *Summa contra Gentiles*) is not something that in man is added to other preexistent forms but is a principle that includes and absorbs the functions of the others in itself. We can say, then, that man is perfected by his one form according to different degrees of perfection: as a body, as an animate body, as a rational animal. It follows that the soul itself—as the only form of the human composite—is found in the whole body and in each of its parts. But this is a conclusion that is accompanied by two caveats: first, it is always necessary to remember that the soul is also capable of operations (thinking, but also willing) that transcend the body and do not require a bodily organ; second, it can be conceded that, although the soul is present in the whole body, the different parts of the body are proportioned differently to different operations of the soul.

Even if we deny that there are intermediate forms between the body and the soul, we can still ask whether the vegetative, sensitive, and rational soul form a single substance. To hypothesize that there are different souls present in man is again to fall into Platonism, that is, the denial of the unity of the human composite and the reduction of the soul-body relationship to that of a pilot and a ship. The Platonic doctrine itself implies that each individual is called "animal" inasmuch as it participates in the idea of animal and "man" inasmuch as it participates in the idea of man, and this is equivalent to making a real distinction between the sensitive soul—on the basis of which a man is called animal—and the rational soul—on the basis of which he is called man. But this is absurd, according to Thomas, from more than one point of view. First of all, if several things are predicated of the same subject according to different forms, the predication itself could not be accidental. Since, for example, "white" and "musical" are predicated of Socrates according to different forms, these must be accidental with respect to Socrates. But if this is how things stand, then the predication "man is an animal" would also be purely accidental, which is manifestly false. In the second place, from several existing things in act no one unified thing could result (at least if there is not something that holds the different things together). Thus, no man would ever be truly unified but would be a mere aggregate (for example, something animal + something rational). In the third place, were a distinct form for animal being to exist, it would already be something substantial, and so the rational soul would be added to something that was already complete and constituted. In that case the rational soul would be not a substantial form but an accidental one. It must be admitted, then, that in man there is but one soul, and it is rational, sensitive, and vegetative. The co-presence of these functions is guaranteed by the fact that a more perfect form (in this case a rational form) bestows upon matter everything that it could receive from less perfect forms, along with something more. The rational soul, thus, gives to the human composite everything that the vegetative soul gives to plants and everything that the sensitive soul gives to irrational animals, as well as something more that is proper only to man.

With the unicity of the human soul established, we can further ask whether it is identical with its powers (a. 12). Thomas's answer—in opposition to the one favored by many of the Franciscans—is negative. The soul is not strictly identical with its powers and faculties. Before we discuss Thomas's reasoning on this point, it would be helpful to consider the terms of the debate. For many of the Franciscan masters, the rational soul is not the only form of the human composite since, prior to the advent of the rational soul, the body is already in possession of other forms (for example, the form of corporeity, which—independently of the rational soul—organizes the matter as a determinate body with determinate dimensions). And the rational soul, they also maintain, is identical with its faculties. In Thomas's view, the rational soul is the only form of the human composite. It is united to the body without the mediation of any other form, as we just saw, and takes up the functions of the vegetative and sensitive souls into itself. But, for Thomas, the rational soul is not essentially identical with its powers; they are, rather, properties of the soul. This means that, as Thomas sees things, the soul is not the immediate principle of its operations but operates through accidental principles. In other words, it is accidental to the essence or substance of the soul actually to be understanding or sensing.[105]

---

105. Although here we might distinguish more carefully between the essence and substance of the soul, since the Franciscans would perhaps have conceded that powers are identical with the soul in substance but not in essence.

The idea behind Thomas's position is determined by the Aristotelian principle according to which the diversity of powers must be deduced from the diversity of corresponding acts. Now, precisely because the essence of the soul is one and unitary (it is one principle), it cannot immediately account for a plurality of actions, and it is precisely because of this that it is necessary to posit several powers or faculties corresponding to the diversity of actions. The thesis of the plurality and distinction of powers of the soul is not, therefore, in contradiction to the thesis of the unicity of the substantial form. It is, rather, an immediate consequence of it (if the soul is one, the diversity of its operations can be justified only on the basis of the presence of different powers and faculties). Thomas reflects at length here on the individuation and partition of different powers. We will limit ourselves only to the general conclusions. There are three levels of powers in the soul (corresponding to the vegetative, sensitive, and rational dimensions) and five genera of powers (nutritive, sensitive, intellective, appetitive, and motive, each of which includes more powers).[106]

The next article (a. 14) touches on the problem of the immortality of the human soul, which, in Thomas's estimation, can be demonstrated by it intellectual nature. Thinking, as we have seen, does not require a corporeal organ and is not in immediate relation with the body. So, the intellect is a form that is endowed with being. Now, forms (understood in an Aristotelian way) are incorruptible and so can be regarded as corrupted only in an accidental way when the composite of which they are the form is corrupted. For Thomas as for Aristotle, in other words, the composites are what are generated and corrupted, not the forms save *per accidens*. If, therefore, there exists a form endowed with being in itself, it will subsist as incorruptible. And this is, precisely, the case with the human soul. The capacity to think is, for Thomas, then, the fulcrum of the soul's immortality. And the proof is given by the fact that those who denied this either did not consider the soul to be a form, or did not distinguish thinking from sensing—hypothesizing, thus, a bodily organ for thinking—or, finally, took the intellect with which man thinks (the possible intellect) to be a separate substance, attributing immortality only to it. If these presuppositions are rejected, the immortality of the soul appears obvious. In support of his conclusion Thomas adds two further indications. First, what is incorruptible exists incorruptibly (that is, universally) in the intellect, and this testifies to the strict connection between intellective activity and immortality. Second, man possesses a natural desire for perpetuity.

106. See P. Künzle, *Das Verhältnis der Seele zu ihren Potenzen. Problemgeschichtliche Untersuchungen von Augustin bis und mit Thomas von Aquin* (Freiburg: Universitätsverlag, 1956). See also (especially in relation to *Summa theologiae*, Ia, q. 77) the observations of A. de Libera in *Archéologie du sujet*, vol. 1, *Naissance du sujet*, Bibliothèque d'histoire de la philosophie (Paris: Vrin, 2007), especially 303–11.

This desire is justified on the ground that man is able to think being in an absolute sense and not only *hic et nunc*. Knowing being in an absolute sense, beyond contingent determinations, it is natural that he too wishes to be, to exist, simply or in an absolute sense, at all times, and beyond contingent determinations. But a natural desire (that is, rooted in nature) cannot be in vain. Therefore, the intellectual human soul is incorruptible in itself.[107]

Once it is concluded that the soul is immortal (and, therefore, enjoys the possibility of subsisting apart from the body, although, as we must always note, for a limited time, namely, between death and the resurrection of the body) Thomas passes on to examine the characteristics proper to the separated soul, and, first of all, the capacity to know (a. 15). It might be objected that in the absence of sense organs, the separated soul can know nothing, and all the more so since here too Thomas insists that the senses are not an impediment to knowledge (according to the Platonic view), nor are they a simple disposition or preparation for acquiring intellectual knowledge from above (according to the Avicennian view), but they are that from which we naturally and inevitably acquire our knowledge. (It is not possible to think without phantasms, that is, without sensible images.) Now, for Thomas, our soul is an intellectual substance, even if it is infinitely weaker than God (who knows everything in knowing himself) and much weaker than separate substances (who know other things from intelligible species without the need to draw them from the senses). Without the aid of the senses, the intellectual knowledge proper to man would be confused and imperfect, and would not be such as to cover individual things. For this reason, as Thomas explicitly states, it is necessary for the soul to be united to the body:

The fact must be borne in mind that the soul, being lowest in the order of intellectual substances, participates in intellectual light or in intellectual nature, in the lowest and weakest measure.... Therefore, if the human soul, which is lowest in the order of intellectual substances and hence possesses the least intellectual power of them all, received forms abstractly and universally, as separate substances do, then it would have a most

107. It should perhaps be noted that this line of argumentation, however obviously debatable it is, is not in the first instance theological and so is not question-begging. Thomas is not saying that man aspires to *eternity*—which is proper only to God—for his soul is created by God. He is saying instead that man aspires to *perpetuity*, that is, not to be outside of time but to exist at every time, because he is able to think being as beyond every contingent determination and naturally to desire such being. On the problem of the immortality of the soul there also exists an isolated question attributed to Thomas reported in ms. Vat. lat. 781, published by Kennedy. See L. A. Kennedy, "A New Disputed Question of St. Thomas Aquinas on the Immortality of the Soul," *Archives d'Histoire Doctrinale et Littéraire du Moyen Âge* 45 (1978): 205–23. The authenticity of the question must nevertheless still be definitively established.

imperfect kind of knowledge: that of knowing things in the universal and indistinctly. Hence, in order that the soul's knowledge may be perfect in its kind and bear directly upon individuals, the soul must acquire a knowledge of truth from individual things. However, the light of the agent intellect is necessary in order that those things may be received in the soul and may exist there in a higher mode than that in which they exist materially. Hence, it was necessary that the soul be united to a body for the perfection of its intellectual operation.

However, this does not mean that when the soul is separated from the body, it will not be able to be directly influenced by separate substances and think on account of this influence, even without phantasms—something that is now impossible. But this holds only for those souls that through the beatific vision are able also to know directly in God all other things. So, the only exception that Thomas allows to the necessity that we gather our knowledge from the senses is theological, indeed, eschatological, and presupposes the intervention of grace. It is confirmed in general, then, that the knowledge that originates in the senses is not only inevitable but the best possible:

Therefore, when the soul will be separated completely from the body, it will be able to receive infused knowledge from superior substances more fully, because, thanks to such knowledge, it will be able to understand without a phantasm, which otherwise it cannot do. Nevertheless, an influx of this sort will not produce knowledge as perfect and as directly related to individuals as the knowledge which we acquire here below through the senses, though a much more perfect knowledge will be had in addition to this natural influx by those souls that will enjoy the influx of a supernatural light by which they will know all things most fully and will see God himself.[108]

All separated souls will retain, moreover, a determinate knowledge of the things apprehended in this life whose intelligible species they have stored up.[109]

The next article (a. 16) is of fundamental importance. At issue is whether the soul joined to the body is able to know separate substances. Thomas deals analytically here with the Greco-Arab peripatetic tradition, because Aristotle, although he had promised to treat of the question in Book III of the *De anima*, in fact, failed to do so. According to the first thesis rejected, the soul united to the body can achieve knowledge of separate substances not in the normal way that it knows other intelligible things, but through the agent intellect's contact (continuation, *continuatio*) with us. It is in this *continuatio* that ultimate hu-

---

108. *Quaestiones disputatae de anima*, a. 15.

109. Thomas, thus, admits with Albert the Great and against Avicenna, the possibility of an intellectual memory. On the other hand, it was precisely because of the impossibility of physiologically localizing an intellectual memory that Avicenna identified thought with accessing a separate intelligence that would be a stable site of intelligible species.

man happiness consists. Thomas distinguishes here between the thesis of Alexander of Aphrodisias (according to whom the possible intellect is individual and corruptible and the only sort of immortality possible for man is *to think immortal things*, that is, to connect with the separate agent intellect—identified with God—through the acquisition of intelligible speculative objects, through the exercise of science) and that of Averroes (for whom the possible intellect is incorruptible, one, and separate). With regard to the latter thesis, Thomas notes that it falls into two errors, which, furthermore, contradict each other: positing the agent intellect as separate (the separation of the possible intellect is no longer in question here) and explaining that knowledge is brought about by the agent intellect uniting to us as a form through the mediation of the possible intellect (to which we will in turn be united by phantasms). This last point merits attention. To act in virtue of a form, a thing must possess that form, it must be united to that form *in being*. But it is precisely this that Averroes denies, positing the agent intellect as separate. In Thomas's view it is, in sum, impossible "for a substance that is separate from another in being to act through the other substance."[110] It should not escape our attention that this criticism, although it is directed at Averroes, also strikes Thomas's one-time master, Albert the Great, who in his *De anima*, expressly held that the "hope of the philosophers" consists in the project of uniting with the agent intellect not only as a faculty of the soul or cause that produces intelligible species, but as a form. This "philosophical hope" is foreign to Thomas because in his eyes it is foreign to Aristotle. The agent intellect always belongs to us, and its function is to produce the intelligible species by abstracting from phantasms. The ideal of formal union with the agent intellect also presupposes that man already possesses another form, and this runs into all the problems of the thesis of the plurality of forms that Thomas has already pointed out.

With respect to Alexander, Thomas does not understand how the conjunction can take place by means of the acquisition of intelligible species. Something of the sort would be possible only if the intelligible speculative objects acquired by abstraction were able to equal the power and substance of the separate agent intellect, if, that is, the science we are able to acquire truly permitted us to identify with the supreme intellect. But Alexander's position contrasts with Aristotle's, since the former assumes that happiness is reserved to a few (those who succeed in uniting with the agent intellect through the exercise of the act of science), while the latter holds that happiness can be a common good. Alexander is also at odds with Aristotle because he confuses knowledge of

110. *Quaestiones disputatae de anima*, a. 16.

the most exalted intelligible things (separate substances) with knowledge of all intelligible things (the exercise of science as such). In brief, the ideal of union and continuation with the agent intellect is foreign to the intentions of Aristotle, who instead held that human happiness can be pursued through the principles of philosophy. It is, therefore, in this direction that we must inquire. There are, however, different opinions here, as Thomas already observed in the *Summa contra Gentiles*.[111] Some (and Thomas is probably referring here to Avempace—Ibn Bāǧǧa—whom he knew through Averroes) held that it is possible to know separate substances by perfecting the procedure of abstraction. Through abstraction the quiddity of a thing is grasped. But if we see that the quiddity thus abstracted is not yet pure but consists in knowledge of the thing *together with its quiddity*, we can abstract further. And because it is impossible to proceed to infinity in this process, we will eventually arrive at something that is only quiddity, and these are the separate substances. This path cannot be taken, Thomas thinks, because it does not take into consideration the fact that separate substances are of another genus than sensible substances and so the knowledge of the quiddities of the latter can never lead to the former. Another path must be taken, which Thomas ascribes to Pseudo-Dionysius, but that is actually a combination of Aristotelianism and Pseudo-Dionysian (and indirectly Proclean) Neo-Platonism. Our intellect is always ordered to phantasms (and so toward the images that we receive from the senses), and, hence, it is impossible to know the separate substances in themselves. But sense knowledge can still give us some clues. It does not allow us to know the *quid est* of separate substances (as we already know) but it at least allows us to know the *quia*, moving from effects to causes. It is a process that permits us perhaps more to know what such substances are *not* than to know effectively what they are. But this is exactly the knowledge that is possible for us in this life and so should not disappoint us. (Even of the celestial bodies we, in effect, know more of what they are not than of what they are.)

The question of whether separated souls can know separate substances—in this context, angels and devils—poses far fewer problems (a. 17). Although it is true that our knowledge always presupposes phantasms drawn from sense knowledge, it is also true that, as we have seen, in the state of separation a soul can be directly influenced by superior substances. In the state of separation, then, not only is it possible for the soul to intuit itself in some way (something that is not possible when it is joined to the body), but also it can know, even if imperfectly, something of superior substances from their influence on it. On

111. See pp. 164–72 above.

the other hand, as Thomas observes, "it does not seem credible that the souls of the damned do not know the devils whose society they share, and who are said to terrify the souls. Again, it seems even less likely that the souls of the good do not know the angels whose society they enjoy."[112] With respect to natural things, Thomas concedes (a. 18) that a separated soul can know in a universal way but cannot know individuals, at least as regards natural capacities. The souls of the blessed by grace are made similar to angels and so can know all of the individuals gathered in a species. In a. 20 Thomas adds, however, that the separated soul can know some individual realities, namely, those it knew when it was united to a body (otherwise it would have no memory of what it did in its earthly life), and even individuals connected to its new state. Were this not so, the souls of the damned could not know anything of the pains inflicted on them. We should bear firmly in mind that although superior substances know through universal forms the individuals related to those forms, the intellectual ability of souls in the state of separation always remains proportionate to the forms drawn from the things, and it is for this reason that the soul finds itself naturally conjoined to a body (as we saw in a. 15). The species that the separated soul receives by influx are sufficient for it to know all of the individuals within a species. Here the Neo-Platonic axiom applies according to which *omne receptum determinatur in recipiente secundum modum recipientis.* Thomas also notes that the sense powers are not retained in the separated soul, since they have the human composite and not the soul alone as their subject. With the body destroyed, the sense powers disappear too, even if they remain in the soul as in their principle or root.

The last article (a. 21) might appear rather bizarre to us but has a long history that stretches across the whole of medieval theology. The question posed has to do with whether, without a body or sense powers, a separated soul feel the flames of hell. Constrained by a long exegetical tradition (determined more by Gregory the Great than by Augustine) to reject any metaphorical interpretation of the fire of hell, Thomas (like many of his Scholastic colleagues) is obliged to find an *ad hoc* model to explain how a material agent can act on an immaterial substance. His solution is rather brilliant. The only action that a body can have on a soul (apart from the influence that the body joined to it in hylomorphic composition has, as in the case of the human body) is that of localizing and "confining" it (that is, making it so that the soul is detained in one place and is not at the same time present in another, that is, "confining" it to a particular place). The fire of hell does not play its punitive role by burning or heating the

---

112. *Quaestiones disputatae de anima,* a. 17.

soul, but by "detaining" it, acting as a prison and thereby frustrating its natural desire. The soul—which was born to be with God in beatific enjoyment—suffers by the fact of being subject to something inferior to it inasmuch as this thing is corporeal. In this way Thomas rejects any form of physical suffering in the soul caused by fire, replacing this with an internal sadness that afflicts the soul because it is held against its will. But he also maintains, in deference to orthodox doctrine, that the fire of hell is corporeal and its action real. This compromise, however sophisticated, will not please his adversaries. The Franciscan masters will bitterly reprove Thomas for an interpretation of the fire of hell that is not strictly realistic, feeling supported by Bishop Tempier's condemnation (in 1270 and 1277) of the thesis according to which the soul cannot suffer from the fire of hell. In 1277 Thomas was already dead. In regard to the condemnation of 1270, he should not have felt personally implicated, since in the *De unitate intellectus* he accuses his interlocutor (probably Siger of Brabant) of having the imprudence to discuss the fire of hell as a philosopher—which is neither more nor less than what he himself did in the *Quaestiones dispuatae de anima*. We begin to see the strange situation taking shape that would characterize Thomas's positions once he returned to Paris. He would deal quite critically with the Franciscan theologians, trying at the same time to distance himself from the positions of the masters of the faculty of arts. We will perhaps be able to discuss this further. The fact remains that the question about the fire of hell, although sinister, is one of the most fascinating in Scholastic disputes, even if it related to a temporary and substantially unnatural state—that of the soul separated from the body. Unlike Erigena or, in the Islamic world, Avicenna, no Scholastic master denied the action of the fire of hell after the resurrection of the body.

DE SPIRITUALIBUS CREATURIS

The disputations of the *Quaestiones disputatae de spiritualibus creaturis* also took place in Italy between November 1267 and September 1268. But unlike the *Quaestiones disputatae de anima*, they were published after Thomas's return to Paris. Some of the topics are the same as those in *Quaestiones disputatae de anima*. Avicebron's thesis of universal hylomorphism, for example, is dealt with in a. 1. Here it is discussed in reference to spiritual substances and not only the human soul. Considerations of the intellectual nature of these substances is behind Thomas's refutation. If they were endowed with matter, the intelligible forms received in them in the cognitive process would be individuated by the matter itself, making it difficult to explain the difference between the knower and the known. However, as Thomas once more states, "if we use the terms 'matter' and 'form' to mean any two things which are related to each other as potency and act, there is no difficulty in saying (so as to avoid a mere dispute about words) that matter and form exist in spiritual substances."[113] Thomas repeats here the essentials of what he had already said in his youthful *De ente*. God, who is unlimited act, is not limited by any generic or specific nature, but is identical with his being itself. But there can be only one subsistent being (in the same way in which it would be impossible to conceive of several separate whitenesses). Therefore, in everything that is other than God, "the nature of the thing which participates in being is one thing, and the participated being itself is another."[114] These two dimensions relate to each other as potency and act, or—as can also be granted—as matter and form, so long as these terms are understood as synonymous with potency and act.

In a. 2, which considers whether a spiritual substance can unite itself with a body, he emphasizes that the soul is both the form of the body and something determinate, capable of subsisting in itself, because it is endowed with an operation that is not linked to any bodily organ. In the questions that follow, Thomas rejects the hypothesis that the soul unites to the body through an intermediary (a. 3); argues that the soul is in each part of the body (a. 4); reaffirms the existence of spiritual substances not joined to a body (a. 5);[115] explains that spiritual substances are not necessarily the form of celestial bodies (a. 6);[116] and rejects the idea that a spiritual substance can be united to an ethereal body (a. 7).[117] Of particular importance is a. 8, in which Thomas once again proposes his thesis about angels differing from each other in species. In the absence of matter, as we know, there cannot be several distinct individuals in the same species. Thomas also develops another argument for this conclusion here, which he takes from the order of the universe. It must be admitted that those things in which there is order of themselves have a more perfect share in order than do those in which there is order only accidentally. Now, among several individuals of the same species there is only accidental order, but what differs by species has an essential order. Hence, just as each of the celestial bodies forms a species in

---

113. *Quaestiones disputatae de spiritualibus creaturis*, a. 1.

114. *Quaestiones disputatae de spiritualibus creaturis*, a. 1.

115. In this case Thomas's demonstration rests on the principle of fullness. The perfection of the universe requires that it does not lack a nature whose existence is possible.

116. Thomas does not exclude the hypothesis that the heavens are animate, although in a different way from earthly bodies, namely, since they have principles that govern them and are the cause of their movement. But he does admit the existence of other spiritual creatures that are entirely separate and not united to bodies, which are (in an Aristotelian and Avicennian way) the goal of the celestial movements.

117. This is a thesis of Augustinian origin, which reappears in a sense in Canto XXV of Dante's *Purgatorio*.

itself (one sun, one moon, etc.), so too each of the angels or intelligences constitutes a unique species. A third argument is taken from the perfection of the angelic nature itself. God, who is supremely perfect, lacks nothing that belongs to the totality of being. However, in the sublunary world it is necessary that there be a multitude of individuals in one species so that the specific nature—which cannot be eternally preserved in one individual—be preserved in many generable and corruptible individuals. But each celestial body is only one individual, because each contains all the characteristics of the species in itself and preserves them perpetually, not being subject to generation and corruption. All the more reason, then, that this should hold for angels too. We have already noted that this thesis is perhaps the point of Thomas's thought most directly targeted by Tempier's condemnation (leaving aside the unicity of the substantial form). Let us say again here that this thesis should not be misunderstood. Thomas is not saying that the angels are only natures, as if each angel were not an individual in itself. He is only saying that in each angelic species *there can be only one individual* (and in this sense each individual is a species in itself).[118]

In a. 9 Thomas again discusses the thesis of the unicity of the possible intellect, rejecting it for three principal reasons. First, if there were but one possible intellect, everyone would think the same thing. The Averroist response is that this would not happen, because the phantasms would be different in each individual (two individuals would think the same thing only if they had the same phantasms) but Thomas rejects this on the ground that it is not the phantasm that is actually thought but the intelligible universal species that is abstracted from it. Second, to Thomas's mind, in individuals of the same species it is impossible that what makes them a part of this species should be one. The principles of any species must be multiplied in the different individuals of that species. If what makes a man a man is the rational soul (or the possible intellect), it must belong to each individual and not be one and separate. Third, if the possible intellect were eternal and common to everyone, including those of past generations, it would no longer be capable of receiving the species abstracted from our phantasms because it would already have received all of them in the past. In other words, the possible or potential intellect would already be perfectly actualized by the phantasms received from all the previous generations

118. T. Suarez-Nani, for example, emphasizes the angel/species identification to the point of noting in it a new paradigm of subjectivity and the roots of the distinction between the "empirical I" and the "transcendental I." See her "Tommaso d'Aquino e l'angelologia: ipotesi sul suo significato storico e la sua rilevanza filosofica," in *Letture e interpretazioni di Tommaso d'Aquino oggi: cantieri aperti: Atti del Convegno internazionale di studio (Milano, 12–13 settembre 2005)*, Quaderni di Annali Chieresi, ed. A. Ghisalberti, A. Petagine, and R. Rizzello (Turin: Istituto di filosofia S. Tommaso d'Aquino, 2006), 11–30.

and so would no longer be, despite its name and function, "potential." On the other hand, it is absurd that what is superior (the possible intellect) should be actualized by what is inferior (the phantasms).[119] In any case, the Averroist thesis is, for Thomas, clearly contrary to the authentic Aristotelian doctrine. The line that Thomas will take in the *De unitate intellectus* is, thus, already developed, if only in summary form.

The last two articles take up points already dealt with in the *Quaestiones disputatae de anima*. In a. 10 Thomas argues for the thesis that the agent intellect is not one for everyone and is not a separate intelligence or God but is rather the natural light that is immediately impressed on each of us by God, thanks to which we are able to discern the true from the false and good from evil. In a. 11 Thomas argues for the distinction between the soul's faculties and its essence. It should be added that Thomas's interlocutors here on this issue are not "the philosophers" but theologians such as William of Auvergne and the Franciscan masters. Why does Thomas insist so much on this point? It is a matter of a position that permits him to maintain the assumption that there are operations of the soul that do not require a corporeal organ, even if the soul as a whole is the form of the body. If there were no distinction between the soul and its faculties, the intellect and will would not be distinct from the vegetative or sensitive functions. As we have already seen, the thesis of the unicity of the substantial form must not be confused with the thesis about the absolute unity and simplicity of the soul, and, indeed, requires that the powers of the soul be quite distinct from each other.

THE COMMENTARY ON THE *DE ANIMA*

With his Commentary on the *De anima* we enter into a new group of Thomas's writings, his commentaries on Aristotle, to which Thomas h dedicate himself in the second Paris regency and in his last years in Naples. The *De anima* is the exception, since it can be situated in his Roman period. We can establish the *terminus post quem* of the work's dating on the basis of the fact that in it Thomas demonstrates a knowledge of Themistius's paraphrase of the *De anima*, which William of Moerbeke completed on November 22, 1267, and William's new Latin translation of Aristotle's text (Thomas had used the old translation until now). The *terminus ante quem* can be determined on the basis of the fact that the entire Commentary on the *De anima* was published in Italy prior to Thomas's departure for Paris (even if for a time it was believed that only Book I was published in Italy and that the Commentary was finished in Paris). As Gauthier

---

119. Thomas seems to neglect here the role that the agent intellect also plays in Averroist psychology.

(who edited the text of the Leonine edition) suggests, the composition can be situated between September 1267 and November 1268. Here we can begin to note the first basic characteristic of Thomas's commentaries on Aristotle's works (which we will be able to discuss again in more detail in the next chapter) and that is that they are not the result of teaching activity, unlike the commentaries of the masters of the faculty of arts, whose institutional task it was to teach and explain Aristotle. Thomas decided to take up Aristotle's works and comment on them with great care, not only to make Aristotle more intelligible to others (as the publication shows us), but also, if not above all, to attain a still more perfect and certain mastery of them to assist him in the drafting of his theological works.[120] The decision to comment on the *De anima* might have been made, in this sense, in view of the drafting of the section of the *prima pars* of the *Summa theologiae* on the soul (qq. 75–89). But the technical and complex exegetical details would have been left out, of course, given that he wanted the *Summa* to be a more widely accessible textbook.

The point of departure of the Commentary on the *De anima* is already significant, to the extent that it forcefully reproposes knowing as the true perfection of man: "Hence, because science is the perfection of man, science is the good of man" (*cum igitur sciencia sit perfectio hominis in quantum homo, sciencia est bonum hominis*).[121] Following Aristotle's text, Thomas observes in the prologue that the science of the soul (understood as the science of what is common to all animate substances and not merely a study of the human soul) has two characteristics that give it its excellence among the speculative sciences: it rests on a basic certainty, since everyone can already experience in himself that he has a soul and that the soul is the source of life; and it concerns itself with what is more noble, since, among inferior creatures, the soul is the most noble.

The Commentary on the *De anima* is also the occasion for Thomas to return to an explicit engagement with Averroist psychology. Averroes's Great Commentary on the *De anima* was already becoming known in Paris in 1225, even if the reception had initially taken a peculiar form. Against Avicennian psychology (which taught the existence of a separate agent intellect), Averroes was taken as a proponent of the thesis that the agent intellect must be considered part of the individual soul. The situation began to change around 1250, when Albert

120. According to what R.-A. Gauthier writes in the Leonine edition of the Commentary on the *De anima*, the commentaries on Aristotle, which were "written to improve the instrument of theological reflections," are "an integral part of [Thomas's] work as a theologian, and this is especially true in the case of the commentary on the *De anima*" (Thomas de Aquino, *Sentencia libri de anima*, cura et studio fratrum praedicatorum, Rome-Paris: Commissio Leonina-Vrin, 1984, 289).

121. Commentary on the *De anima*, I, l. 1.

the Great indicated that, for Averroes, immortality could not be individual, and Robert Kilwardby and Bonaventure had explicitly identified and denounced in Averroes the thesis of the unicity of the potential intellect.[122] Thomas had for a long time thought of Averroes as a trustworthy and good commentator on Aristotle—an attitude that begins to change in the *Summa contra Gentiles* and definitively reverses itself during the second Paris regency and especially in the *De unitate intellectus*. But in the Commentary on the *De anima*, Thomas's attitude toward the Commentator is still "serene," to use Gauthier's expression. Thomas does not often reference Averroes and, above all, he does not do so unilaterally. There are, on the one hand, silent, undeclared appropriations (regarding, for example, the role of the cogitative power or the description of the reception of species in terms of *esse spirituale* or *esse intentionale*), and, on the other hand, a parting of ways on certain specific points (Thomas scolds Averroes, for instance, in a discussion of tangible qualities and the medium of touch, for not having known how to explain change of place, and elsewhere for having made common sensibles the object of the common sense). Criticism of the thesis of the unicity of the potential intellect is certainly not passed over but it essentially consists in what was already said on this front in the *Summa contra Gentiles* (II, cc. 59–79 and III, cc. 43–48) and developed in parallel, during the Roman period, in the *Compendium theologiae* (I, c. 85), the *Summa theologiae* (I, q. 76, aa. 1 and 2), and the *Quaestiones disputatae de spiritualis creaturibus* (aa. 2 and 9). Many other errors attributed to Averroes and denounced in other writings are not present here. Gauthier's hypothesis is that two moments of Thomas's anti-Averroism must be distinguished: the one coincides with the *Summa contra Gentiles,* while the other culminates in the *De unitate intellectus.* The Commentary on the *De anima* would be placed between the two and in it Thomas limits himself—so the hypothesis goes—almost to referring to what he had already said in the *Summa contra Gentiles* without pressing further into the engagement with Averroes (as he would eventually be constrained to do in Paris after having discovered that Averroism had proselytes). Thomas's "serenity" with respect to Averroes—still according to Gauthier's hypothesis—would be a reflection of the years of calm spent at Santa Sabina in Rome. It should, however, be pointed out that the overall judgment of Gauthier on the Commentary on the *De anima* is not particularly positive. He sees it as inferior to that attributed to

122. In the preface cited in n. 121, above (especially p. 222), Gauthier goes so far as to say that Latin Averroism is an "invention of the theologians" and that Averroes was not an "Averroist" insofar as the Averroism created by the theologians is not a "natural reading" of the Islamic thinker. *Salva reverentia*, and with all respect for Gauthier, it is a matter of an interpretation that is, at the very least, debatable.

Peter of Spain and to Albert's commentary, above all because Thomas alleged-
ly was unable to clarify what in Aristotle's text belonged to "eternal" philosophy. Thomas's commentary is for the most part "dead science."[123] Besides being
anachronistic and a little naive in distinguishing between "dead science" and
"eternal philosophy," Gauthier's judgment is perhaps lacking in generosity, neglecting what he himself so brilliantly established, namely, that the practice of
commentary, for Thomas, is above all an attentive and scrupulous propaedeutic
for the elaboration of his own work.

123. Thomae de Aquino, *Sentencia libri de anima*, cura et studio fratrum praedicatorum, 284.

5

THE SECOND PARIS REGENCY
(1268–72)

In 1268 Thomas was recalled to Paris for a second period of regency in one of the Dominican chairs in the faculty of theology. This return is often linked with the philosophical climate of those years, characterized by increasingly heated conflicts between the faculty of arts (by now transformed, for all intent and purpose, into a faculty of philosophy) and the faculty of theology, and by the spread in the former of "radical" Aristotelianism, as it has been called (that is, not subservient to the demands of the Christian faith), inspired above all by the commentaries on Averroes. In 1270 Bishop Tempier's first doctrinal intervention occurred, in which thirteen philosophical propositions were condemned, almost an anticipation of the more significant intervention of 1277, in which 219 propositions taught in the faculty of arts would be condemned. In fact, the real reason why the Dominican order needed Thomas to come back to Paris seems to have been, above all, the return of controversy between the secular clergy and the mendicant orders.

There are principally two works that testify to this task: the *De perfectionis spiritualis vitae* and the *Contra doctrinam retrahentium*. The first dates from 1269–70 and is a response to two works of the secular master Gerard of Abbeville: the *Contra adversarium perfectionis christianae*, published in the summer of 1269, and the *Quodlibet* XIV (its final chapters), disputed during the Advent term of 1269. Thomas proposes to clarify what is meant by perfection, how it is acquired, and what the state of perfection is, and he does this because "some, who are uninformed on the subject, have the pretense of speaking about the state of perfection." The perfection of the spiritual life consists essentially in charity and its two precepts: love of God and love of neighbor. The paths to perfection are the vows of poverty (the renunciation of temporal goods), chastity, and obedience

THE SECOND PARIS REGENCY | 263

(the renunciation not only of temporal goods but of our own will). These vows are typical of the mendicant orders (which Thomas discusses at length in the *secunda secundae* of the *Summa theologiae*) and drew the criticism of the secular clergy (above all in what regards poverty and obedience—to be truly meritorious an action must involve the will and not its negation). Thomas takes care not to question the preeminence of the episcopal office over the religious state but powerfully emphasizes the preeminence of the religious life over the clerical life. In other words, there is no doubt that bishops are above religious, but this does not hold for deacons, parish priests, archdeacons, and whoever else is charged with pastoral care. This intense confrontation with the ecclesiological arguments of the secular clergy occupies a large part of the treatise. A lot of space is dedicated in particular to the confutation of the thesis according to which, before taking religious vows, it is necessary to take much council (an attempt to check the proselytism of the mendicants). However, not only does Thomas defend the vows, he also defends the friars' preaching, hearing confessions, teaching, and everything that could be granted to them by pontifical or episcopal authority. The conclusion of the treatise is once more revealing not just of Thomas's attitude to conflict but that of every Scholastic master. Since truth is not itself if it does not resist refutation and contradiction, attempts to respond to the thesis advanced in the treatise are most welcome:

Should anyone desire to send me a reply, his words will be very welcome to me. For the surest way to elucidate truth and to confound error is by confuting the arguments brought against the truth. Solomon says, "Iron sharpens iron, so a man sharpens the countenance of a friend" (Prov. 27:17).[1]

The *Contra doctrinam* is later than the *De perfectione* and is either contemporary with or earlier than his *Quodlibet* IV (Easter 1272) and so can probably be dated to 1271. The complete title in English is *Against the doctrine of those who would prevent* (or *deter*) *entrance into the religious life*. In this case as well, the polemic against Gerard is evident. Gerard denounced the proselytism of the religious orders—their efforts to attract young men by underscoring the greater state of perfection of the religious life in comparison with the life of the diocesan or secular clergy—as illegitimate and dangerous. For Gerard and the seculars, it is desirable that young men exert themselves for a decent amount of time in the practice of the precepts, seeking counsel and reflecting carefully so as not to make a rash decision. Thomas's response is that with such arguments (to which is added one about the foolishness of renouncing ownership of goods) his ad-

---

1. *De perfectionis spiritualis vitae*, c. 30.

versaries prevent young men from pursuing the path of authentic perfection. Thomas also reaffirms the primacy of charity and stresses the importance of voluntary and mendicant poverty, not as a perfection in itself but as a way to perfection. The conclusion of this treatise is also worth citing:

This is all that occurs to me at present to write against the pernicious and erroneous teaching which deters some men from entering religious life. If anyone desires to contradict my words, let him not do so by chattering before boys but let him write and publish his writings, so that intelligent persons may judge what is true, and may be able to confute what is false by the authority of the truth.[2]

THE COMMENTARY ON THE GOSPEL OF JOHN:
A NEW ORDERING OF THE "MODES" OF ACHIEVING
KNOWLEDGE OF GOD

Naturally, also during his second regency Thomas, as a master of theology, continues to lecture on the Scriptures and publish exegetical writings. The Commentary on the Gospel of Matthew, recorded by Peter of Andria and Léger of Besançon, belongs to this period, probably being the object of a course in 1269–70. It seems harder to establish a more precise date for the Commentary on the Gospel of John (or, as it is perhaps more accurately called: the Course on the Gospel of John—the *Lectura super Ioannem*), recorded by Reginald of Piperno. Mandonnet suggests putting it between 1269 and 1271, Spicq between 1270 and 1271, and Torrell between 1270 and 1272.[3] It is uncertain whether Thomas revised Reginald's *reportatio*, although it seems unlikely. It is conceivable that in drafting the work Reginald amplified Thomas's text, possibly using the material already available in the *Catena aurea*. The text obviously belongs to the theological domain,[4] and it closes, significantly, with suggestive remarks on negative theology:

The words and deeds of Christ are also those of God. Thus, if one tried to write and tell of the nature of every one, he could not do so; indeed, the entire world could not do this. This is because even an infinite number of human words cannot equal one word of God. From the beginning of the Church, Christ has been written about, but this is still not equal to the subject. Indeed, even if the world lasted a hundred thousand years, and more books were written about Christ, his words and deeds could not be completely revealed: "Of making many books there is no end" (Eccl. 12:12); The works of God "are multiplied above number" (Ps. 50:5).[5]

---

2. *Contra doctrinam retrahentium*, c. 16.

3. J.-P. Torrell, *Saint Thomas Aquinas*, vol. 1, *The Person and His Work*, 198.

4. See *Reading John with Saint Thomas Aquinas: Theological Exegesis and Speculative Theology*, ed. M. Dauphinais and M. Levering (Washington, D.C.: The Catholic University of America Press, 2005).

5. *Super Evangelium S. Ioannem Lectura*, c. 21, l. 6.

It might be observed, incidentally, that this apophatic attitude, even about Christ, is probably at the origin of one of the accusations that are sometimes made against Thomas's theology, that of not being very Christocentric or of dedicating too little space to Christology. We will not enter into this theological question here, for our focus is philosophical, as we have indicated. But perhaps we will be permitted only to observe that if Thomas gives the impression of saying (relatively) little about Christ, it is to reaffirm his fully divine nature, and, thus, his absolute incomprehensibility and ineffability (infinite human words could never equal the one word of God).

From a philosophical point of view what is interesting is the reorganization of the proofs for God's existence with which the *Lectura* starts. Commenting on the verse of Isaiah chosen as the epigraph for his commentary (6:1–3: "I saw the Lord seated on a high and lofty throne, and the whole house was full of his majesty, and the things that were under him filled the temple"), Thomas sees in it four different forms of sublimity: authority ("I saw the Lord"), eternity ("seated"), dignity or nobility of nature ("on a high ... throne"), and incomprehensible truth ("and lofty"). Leaving aside questions about exegetical correctness, what is most important is that Thomas identifies the four forms of sublimity with the four modes "by which the early philosophers arrived at the knowledge of God."[6] These four modes reorganize the five ways of the *prima pars* of the *Summa theologiae* into a different order and number.[7] The first mode is that of authority, and it is for Thomas the most efficacious way. It is a modification of the teleological argument proposed in the fifth way of the *Summa*:

For we see the things in nature acting for an end, and attaining to ends which are both useful and certain. And since they lack intelligence, they are unable to direct themselves, but must be directed and moved by one directing them, one who possesses an intellect. Thus it is that the movement of the things of nature toward a certain end indicates the existence of something higher by which the things of nature are directed to an end and governed. And so, since the whole course of nature advances to an end in an orderly way and is directed, we have to posit something higher which directs and governs them as Lord. And this is God.[8]

The second mode is based on mutability. It does not correspond to the first way of the *Summa*—it is not based on the impossibility of an infinite regress of

6. *Super Evangelium S. Ioannem Lectura*, prologue.

7. For an accurate presentation of these "modes" see the annotated translation in Tommaso d'Aquino, *L'esistenza di Dio*, translation, introduction, and commentary by G. Zuanazzi (Brescia: La Scuola, 2003), 300–306. Fabro had already observed that the arguments in the *Super Evangelium S. Ioannem Lectura* could even be regarded as more mature than the five ways of the *Summa*. See C. Fabro, "Sviluppo, significato e valore della 'IV via,'" *Doctor Communis* 1–2 (1954): 71–109.

8. *Super Evangelium S. Ioannem Lectura*, prologue.

movers and on the necessity of positing a first unmoved mover—nor is it identical with the third way—since it does not appeal in a strict sense to the modal notions of contingency and necessity. It seems, rather, to be a particular case of the argumentative strategy based on the different degrees of perfection, which we find in the fourth way of the *Summa*:

Others came to a knowledge of God from his eternity. They saw that whatever was in things was changeable, and that the more noble something is in the grades of being, so much the less it has of mutability. For example, the lower bodies are mutable both as to their substance and to place, while the celestial bodies, which are more noble, are immutable in substance and change only with respect to place. We can clearly conclude from this that the first principle of all things, which is supreme and more noble, is changeless and eternal.[9]

This argument is, to tell the truth, a little truncated, not only because it lacks the concluding formula found in the *Summa* and in the other arguments of the Commentary on the Gospel of John (respectively: "and all call this God" and "and this is God"), but also because it seems to prove an attribute (eternity or immutability) rather than the existence of the first principle. The third mode is similar to the second, which appeals more explicitly to the Platonic concept of participation and the principle (which is actually Aristotelian) of the causality of the maximum:

Still others came to a knowledge of God from the dignity of God, and these were the Platonists. They noted that everything which is something by participation is reduced to what is the same thing by essence, as to the first and highest. Thus, all things which are fiery by participation are reduced to fire, which is such by its essence. And so, since all things which exist participate in being and are beings by participation, there must necessarily be, at the summit of all things, something which is being by its essence, that is, whose essence is its being. And this is God, who is the most sufficient, the most eminent, and the most perfect cause of the whole of being, from whom all things that are participate in being.[10]

We might note the affinity between this argument and the one proposed, nearly fifteen years earlier, in the *De ente et essentia*. Finally, the fourth mode is a kind of combination of the noological argument made by Augustine in Book II of the *De libero arbitrio* (even if Thomas expressly references another Neo-Platonic–Augustinian principle expounded, for example, in the *De civitate Dei*, according to which everything that is known is known according to the mode of the knower) and, again, the mechanism of the fourth way of the *Summa* based on

---

9. *Super Evangelium S. Ioannem Lectura*, prologue.
10. *Super Evangelium S. Ioannem Lectura*, prologue.

the degrees of perfection and the causality of the maximum. Here too the proof is a little truncated and runs the risk of (negatively) proving an attribute of God rather than his existence:

Yet others arrived at a knowledge of God from the incomprehensibility of truth. All the truth which our intellect is able to grasp is finite, since according to Augustine, "everything that is known is bounded by the comprehension of the one knowing," and if it is bounded, it is determined and particularized. Therefore, the first and supreme truth, which surpasses every intellect, must necessarily be incomprehensible and infinite. And this is God.

Thomas's argument runs more or less like this: if the truth that we are able to grasp is limited and partial, the supreme truth will be incomprehensible and infinite, and this is God. If this argument is not to remain an enthymeme (a partial or incomplete syllogism), it would be necessary to add at least one more premise, that is, that every partial truth points to an infinite truth (and so, if the first exists, the second must also exist). However much certain authoritative interpreters of Thomas—such as Cornelio Fabro—have judged this reformulation of the "ways" as more rich and mature than that in the *Summa*, it is necessary perhaps to admit that the exposition here is a little too bound to the schema suggested by the verse of Isaiah that Thomas employs as an epigraph and because of this is less perspicuous and less clear. In comparison, for example, to the *Summa*, the causal link here between the supreme cause and its effects is weak or too implicit. But the fact remains that natural reason (incarnated here by the "ancient philosophers") can prove the existence of a first principle to whom we can give the name God, holding, nevertheless, that the divine essence is beyond our understanding and every attempt at demonstration. We can demonstrate an intelligent principle of the cosmos that is eternal, incomprehensibly true, identical with its being and the cause of all other beings, but this does not yet tell us anything of what God is in himself. An infinite number of human words, as we read a moment ago in the conclusion of the commentary, could not do this.

QUAESTIONES DISPUTATAE DE MALO
Evil as a Privation

The *Quaestiones disputatae de malo* were disputed between 1269 and 1271 or between 1270 and 1271. The work is made up of 101 articles gathered together in 16 questions. The first question is on evil in general, qq. 2–3 are on sin and its causes, qq. 4–5 are on original sin and punishment, q. 6 is on human freedom, q. 7 is on venial sin, qq. 8–15 are on the capital vices, and q. 16 is on the devil.

The work begins with the classic question about whether evil can be considered something (q. 1). It is necessary to distinguish here—as it is for everything that has an accidental nature—between that which is the subject of evil and evil itself:

> Just as the color white is spoken of in two ways, so also is evil. For in one way when white is said, it can refer to that which is the subject of whiteness and in another way to the whiteness itself, namely the accident or quality itself. And likewise when evil is said, it can refer to that which is the subject of evil, and this is something, and in another way, it can refer to the evil itself, and this is not something but is the privation of some particular good.[11]

In the strict sense evil is interpreted, then, Neo-Platonically as a privation. If, in fact, the good has the characteristic of being appetible or desirable, it is evident that being in general is in some sense good, for everything generally desires its own preservation in being. In consequence, evil cannot belong to the domain of being or be anything in itself, although it is rooted in something that exists:

> Consequently, I say that evil is not something but that to which evil happens is something, inasmuch as evil deprives it of only some particular good. Thus, for instance, blindness itself is not something, but that to which blindness happens is something.[12]

The traditional Neo-Platonic position is, however, reread above all in the light of Avicenna.[13] Evil is not a privation in the generic sense but the *privation of a determinate good*, that is, the lack of a perfection in that which should possess it (to use a classic Avicennian example, the privation of sight is certainly an evil in a human being but not in a wall).

If evil is always rooted in an existing subject and everything that exists is good, as was said, must we conclude that evil is in the good? Thomas has no doubts on this point—"It must be said that evil cannot exist save in the good"—as long as the fact is kept in mind that evil is not something existing or "positive" in itself but only, again, the privation of a determinate perfection in that which, insofar as it exists, is good. In a corresponding way it is also necessary to distinguish the different things called good. First, the good of a thing is some perfection it has as when it is said—to use Thomas's own examples—the good of the eye is acuity of vision and the good of man is virtue. Second, the thing that possesses that perfection is good, that is, the composite of the subject

---

11. *Quaestiones disputatae de malo*, q. 1, a. 1.

12. *Quaestiones disputatae de malo*, q. 1, a. 1.

13. See C. Steel, "Avicenna and Thomas Aquinas on Evil," in *Avicenna and His Heritage: Acts of the International Colloquium, Leuven-Louvain-la-Neuve, September 8–September 11, 1999*, ed. J. Janssens and D. De Smet (Leuven: Leuven University Press, 2002), 171–96 (especially in reference to *In II Sent.*, d. 34, q. 1, a. 2, but also to the *De malo* itself).

with its perfection, like the healthy eye or the virtuous person. Finally, *the subject itself insofar as it is in potency to a determinate perfection* is good—consider the substance of the eye with respect to acuity of vision or the soul with respect to virtue. Now, if evil is nothing other than the absence or privation of a determinate or required perfection, it is rooted in the good in this last sense. Since privation exists only in the being that is in potency, it must be said that evil is in the good in the sense that the being in potency is a good. If we consider only the perfection, it is, as such, suppressed by evil, but if we consider the subject with its perfection, it undergoes a diminution of good because of evil (in the measure in which the perfection is suppressed and the subject remains, as in the example of the person who loses his sight).

With the mode in which evil is in the good established, it must be asked whether the good itself can be regarded as a cause of evil. Sticking with what we just considered, evil cannot have a cause in the strict sense, that is a *per se* cause. The good can be the cause of evil only in an accidental sense, which is the sole kind of cause that evil can have. This is evident for several reasons. First, if the good is what is appetible or desirable and evil is what is opposed to the good, it is obvious that evil cannot be desired and is located outside the intention of any cause. That which has a *per se* cause is always in the intention of that cause, it is always desired by its cause. When evil is pursued, it is done with a certain good in view ("for example, the adulterer sees enjoying a sensible pleasure as good and because of it commits adultery").[14] Second, every effect always has a likeness to its proper cause, and this is not the case with evil. Finally, every *per se* cause is always determinately ordered to its effect, and what happens according to a certain order is not evil, for evil consists precisely in the absence of order. Thus, evil does not have a *per se* cause. This evidently does not mean that evil does not have any cause at all. Since evil is not something in itself but something that inheres in a thing as a privation, it will not have a *per se* cause but only an accidental one.

The good, then, is not the *per se* cause of evil but only its accidental cause. In this connection, two aspects can be further distinguished. Good is the cause of evil either by defect or inasmuch as it acts accidentally. If we consider natural things, giving birth to a monster, for example, the cause will be defective semen (even if this deficiency is owed to the action of another principle that alters the semen), while the cause of the corruption of water (evaporation) is fire, which, however, does not act with the intention of corrupting water (and so is not the *per se cause* of its corruption), but acts only to propagate its own form.

14. *Quaestiones disputatae de malo*, q. 1, a. 3.

Hence, the fire is the cause of the corruption of the water only in an indirect or accidental sense. The same can be said in the context of voluntary acts. The will is the cause of evil either in an accidental sense (when it is directed toward something that is good under a certain aspect—such as pleasure in the case of adultery—but entails a privation of a greater good) or in a defective sense (when reason, in its choices, departs from the rule of reason and divine law in the same way that an artisan, for instance, errs and brings about something bad if, in executing a specific operation, he does not attend to the rule that should direct it). Naturally, not always keeping the rule of reason actually before our eyes is not an evil or a fault of the will. The fault arises when we do not consider this rule when we should, that is, in the decision that precedes or orients action. This conclusion allows us to consider what is perhaps Thomas's most concise definition of good and evil: the good is everything that conforms to a rule and measure, whereas evil is everything that is not regulated or measured.

In rational creatures it is necessary to distinguish the evil of fault (*malum culpae*) from the evil of punishment (*malum poenae*). The first consists in voluntarily doing a disordered action and the second in the privation of the form or habit that conduces to acting well. It is characteristic of the evil of punishment to be opposed to the will (not to be desired—as accidentally happens with the evil of fault), to be in relation to fault, and to be a passion more than an action. The two kinds of evil differ in three ways. The evil of fault is the evil itself of the action, whereas the evil of punishment is the evil of the agent. The evil of fault depends on the will, whereas the evil of punishment is opposed to the will. And, lastly, the evil of fault is in acting, whereas the evil of punishment is in undergoing. There is no doubt that the evil of fault is worse than that of punishment. That which makes us wicked is obviously fault and not punishment. (Thomas quotes Pseudo-Dionysius: "It is not evil to be punished but to deserve punishment.") Also, punishment has an aspect of correction that tends to compensate for fault, and so is certainly a lesser evil. "If a physician," says Thomas, "cuts off a hand to keep the body from perishing, it is evident that cutting the hand off is better than destroying the body."[15] In this respect, fault distances us from God but punishment is inflicted by God himself. Finally, if fault consists in operating or acting and punishment in undergoing, and if everything that operates in a wicked way is worse than what suffers evil (which does not make the sufferer himself wicked), it is clear that working evil is worse than suffering it and that fault is a worse evil than punishment.

---

15. *Quaestiones disputatae de malo*, q. 1, a. 5.

Sin and Responsibility: Ignorance and Weakness

After treating of evil in general Thomas takes into consideration sin understood as the violation of the rule and a deviation from the end. Sin consists in the interior act of the will and in exterior acts (q. 2, a. 3). There are sins in which the exterior acts are not evil in themselves, such as the alms given for reasons of vainglory (in this case the sin is principally in the will), and there are other exterior acts that are manifestly evil in themselves, as in the case of theft or murder. From the point of view of the completeness of sin, what is decisive is always the act of the will. Sins can be classified according to different species, and they possess varying degrees of gravity. All sins diminish the natural good, but without completely destroying it. Man—and not God or the devil—is always the cause of sin. The devil can only instigate evil by persuasion, but his instigation is never the real cause of sinful acts, nor are all sins committed in the wake of demonic instigation. Ignorance is a sin only when we ignore what *we should* know (in such a case it is also a sin of omission, because it derives from failure to inquire or to apply). An action not done voluntarily or whose voluntariness is impaired in some way excuses sin. The topic of ignorance, of course, suggests an engagement with Greek ethical philosophy. Thomas grants that we are at fault only when we have full consciousness of our acts, but he does not accept the immediate identification of ignorance with evil. Ignorance can be a fault, as we said, only when we should know our duties and the divine law.[16] The same engagement becomes even more evident in connection to the problem of weakness (*infirmitas*), that is, the incapacity to resist what we recognize as evil. Unlike ignorance, *infirmitas* implies the possibility of knowingly doing evil. Now, although he knows the rule of reason or the divine law, a man can act differently out of weakness when he is under the influence of a passion. Thomas takes a position here against Socratic intellectualism as conveyed by the *Nicomachean Ethics*:

Socrates, as Aristotle says in Book VII of the *Ethics*, considering the firmness and certitude of knowledge, held that knowledge cannot be overcome by passion, that is, that no one by reason of passion can do anything contrary to his knowledge; hence he called all

---

16. As for ignorance of what is revealed (and what the sin of infidelity is), Thomas points out in the *Super Romanos* that he who does not have the possibility of hearing the Christian message can be excused for his *infidelitas* but not for all the other sins: "Does this mean that those it had not reached, for example if they were raised in a jungle, have an excuse for their sin of unbelief? The answer is that . . . those who have not heard the Lord speaking either in person or through his disciples are excused from the sin of unbelief. However, they will not obtain God's blessing, namely, the removal of original sin or any sin added by leading an evil life; for these they are deservedly condemned."

virtues forms of scientific knowledge and he called all vices or sins forms of ignorance. From this it follows that no one having knowledge sins from weakness, which clearly is contrary to our everyday experience.[17]

The mechanism proposed by Thomas is simple. We can possess science in many ways, in a universal way and in a particular way, in habit and in act. In consequence, it is possible for us, while knowing something universally, or according to a habitual knowledge, to neglect this knowledge when we are moved by the passions (or also, more indirectly, on account of bodily changes introduced by the passions). In this way, even if we have a universal knowledge of what the good is, a particular judgment may be impeded, and this explains how it is possible to do evil deliberately.

For what regards original sin, Thomas aligns himself with some basic points of Augustinian theology. Original sin is transmitted biologically and is contracted at birth. On the one hand, Adam's sin, which distanced him from God, resulted in humanity's loss of original justice. On the other hand, the pursuit of a mutable good made it possible for inferior powers to free themselves from reason's rule. Because of this, no one's reason submits to God as a matter of course, nor do the sensible appetites (the irascible and concupiscible appetites) submit as a matter of course to reason. Original sin is responsible for the appearance of death and the other evils of this life. So, death is not something natural to man, or better: it is natural to the matter of the human composite (the organic body is composed of different elements and, thus, is subject to the contrariety of forms and thereby to corruption), but it is not natural to its form, the intellectual soul. Hence, according to Thomas, "death and dissolution are natural to man according to the necessity of matter, but according the nature of his form, immortality is proper to him."[18] Because of this double nature, death (corruption) always belongs to human destiny, but only in potency. In the prelapsarian state, that is, prior to original sin and the fall, God made it so that this potency, inherent in matter, should never be actualized. After the fall death became a *de facto* reality (death passed from a possibility to a reality). In general it remains true that immortality is natural while death and corruption are, for us, against nature (since the form, to which immortality belongs, expresses our nature better).

Although original sin introduced death into the human world, it is not such as to result in the loss of the beatific vision (otherwise no one could be saved, even though divine grace is always necessary for salvation) and it cannot be punished by the punishment of the senses (*poena sensi*), which is merited only by actual

---

17. *Quaestiones disputatae de malo*, q. 3, a. 9.
18. *Quaestiones disputatae de malo*, q. 5, a. 5.

sin. In a strict sense, those who die with only original sin (children who die before baptism or without it) do not even experience interior suffering from being deprived of eternal beatitude (which, in the theological lexicon, is the *poena damni*). These children have only a natural knowledge and not a supernatural knowledge, which would require baptism. On the basis of their natural knowledge, they know that man aspires to beatitude, but they do not know that this consists in the vision of God. Thus, not even knowing that they are deprived of this good, in their state they do not experience pain and do not suffer any punishment.

Will and Intellect

The topic of human responsibility for evil and sin leads Thomas to insert a question into the *De malo* that deals exclusively with human choice (*electio*). This is one of the privileged places for understanding not only Thomas's conception of freedom but even more his conception of the relationship between freedom and the intellect. The controversy over this became increasingly heated and finally exploded after the condemnation of 1277. The question can be simplified in these terms: Which faculty is superior and hierarchically more important, the will or the intellect? For the Franciscan masters in general (and for the most important secular master in Paris in the last quarter of the thirteenth century, Henry of Ghent), the will is absolutely free and capable of moving itself. It moves itself toward the object seen as good, choosing in an absolute way between the goods proposed by the intellect. For the masters of the faculty of arts nearest to the Aristotelian tradition (and for the other most prominent secular master in the faculty of theology after Thomas's death, Godfrey of Fontaines), it is always the object that determines the psychological acts (since, in strictly Aristotelian terms, everything that is moved is moved by another), and the object (identified as good and desirable) is known only through the intellect. In this way the will is unable not to follow the intellect's indications, being in some way necessitated (according to the view that is called "psychological determinism"). The remote origin of this conflict is primarily the opposition between Greek ethical intellectualism and the Christian doctrine of sin. For the "intellectualists," that is, the proponents of the primacy of the intellect, it is fundamentally the intellect that is responsible for erroneous ethical choices, directing the will toward what is mistakenly conceived as the good to be chosen. For the "voluntarists," the will is absolutely free to lead itself to what it holds to be preferable at that moment, choosing between the different options presented by the intellect (and in the end, within certain limits, *against* the intellect's indication). As we have said, this controversy exploded after Thomas's death, but it was already a topic of debate in the last years of his life.

For Thomas, freedom of will is not only an indispensable presupposition of faith, it is also an indispensable presupposition for morality in general. If everything is done out of necessity, no human action would have the least moral quality. That said, it is necessary to consider that an active principle exists in all things and that in man this principle takes the form of the intellect and the will. Now, in natural things it is possible to distinguish a form, which is a principle of action, and an inclination, which is an appetite that follows from the form and leads to action. In man, we can analogously distinguish the intellectual form, the form of the things known, and the inclination that relates man to that form, viz., the will or rational appetite. The difference between man and other natural things is in the fact that in the latter the form is always individualized by matter and so the corresponding inclination is always directed toward a determinate thing, whereas the form by which the human intellect knows things is universal and refers to a multiplicity of individual objects. Consequently, the will's inclination is not necessitated but relates to a plurality of possible objects. To use Thomas's own example, the architect who plans a house possesses a universal form of the house (what assures its subsistence generally and structurally), but the will chooses which model of house to bring into being. But a natural reality is oriented by its form toward something determinate (a stone tends naturally to the lowest place if not impeded by a violent action to the contrary). Irrational animals are halfway between inanimate things and man. They are endowed with knowledge but not intellectual knowledge (universal knowledge), only sense knowledge. The senses permit only knowledge of the individual, and the appetite that follows upon them is likewise individualized. Of course, animals know different forms, perceiving some as useful or pleasant and others as dangerous or unpleasant (on the basis of the internal sense that Avicenna calls "estimative" and that Thomas, as we have seen, calls in man the "cogitative" power),[19] and because of this are each time oriented toward something different, desiring one thing and fleeing another. But in each of these circumstances the appetite always moves toward one determinate option known through the senses. The rational human appetite, however, has the possibility of being directed toward many individual objects known through the universal form. This is not yet sufficient to show how the powers of the soul can begin to move. It is necessary in this respect to consider that any power is moved both by the subject and by the object. Sight, for example, is subjectively moved to have a better or more clear vision of its object, while it is objectively moved by different colors (that is, it changes according to

19. See the section in Chapter 4 on knowledge.

the presence of different colors). The first type of movement regards *the exercise of the act* (the fact of acting or not or of acting more or less efficaciously), and the second regards *the specification of the act,* since, in Aristotelian terms, every action is specified by its object. Now, among natural things, the exercise of the act depends on the agent, and, more precisely, on the end, for the agent acts in view of the end. The specification of the act depends on the form. But in the case of rational beings, if we consider the object that specifies the act, the first principle of movement is the intellect. From the objective point of view, it is the good as known that moves the will. Yet, *from the point of view of the exercise of the act, the principle of movement is the will,* to which the chief end belongs. In this sense, observes Thomas, it can well be said that the will moves itself and all other powers. This self-movement, however, has its origin in an external impulse (*instinctus*), so there is no infinite regress. To understand this point, we can adopt one of Thomas's examples. If I am sick and want to be healed, I move myself to take medicine (that is, my will leads me to take medicine). But to be able to take medicine, I must *know* which medicine is best in my case and, therefore, engage in practical deliberation (*consilium*) by comparing different medicines. The *consilium* is already an activity in itself and as such must depend on a principle, which can only be the will itself. And in general it is always the will that moves itself to bring about a *consilium,* that is, to compare and deliberate. To decide on this step I will need a prior *consilium* (If I want to be healed, should I decide to take medicine?), and this *consilium* must in turn depend on a prior act of the will. To escape from this vicious circle, it must be conceded that the first impulse derives from an external agent. Such an agent cannot be a celestial body, as some wished to claim, since an incorporeal power like the will cannot be directly subject to the action of a corporeal reality. Taking up a thesis from *De bona fortuna,* Thomas concludes that what first moves the will and the intellect is something above the will and the intellect, namely, God. God moves the will not in a necessary way but according to its nature, as something that can relate itself indifferently to many things.

Here we can establish a first basic point. *From the point of view of the exercise of the act* (that is, from the subjective point of view), *the will moves itself* (and as such is unconditioned), even if, absolutely speaking, the first impulse—that which gives it the capacity to move itself—comes from God.

The other aspect, the specification of the act, must now be considered. The object that moves the will in this case can only be the fitting good known (*bonum conveniens apprehensum*). The qualification "fitting" has its importance in this formula. To be able to move the will, the good must be known not in a universal way but in a particular way, because the *consilium* always regards particular cases. Obviously, if there were a good recognized as fitting in all possible cases, it alone would move the will in the necessary way. This good is, for man, beatitude, and it is for this reason that beatitude is the only good that the will is unable not to will and that it necessarily seeks. None of the other goods necessitate the will, because it can always consider different aspects of fittingness. What is a good for health, for example, is not a good for pleasure and vice-versa. In this regard different factors can come into play in the will's decision: the rational consideration of each aspect (as when the will chooses what is healthful as opposed to what is pleasant), the consideration of the different circumstances in which the particular good is presented, and the disposition itself of the agent (the will of those who are prone to anger is moved differently from that of those who are prone to calm). The disposition of the agent, above all, plays an important part because there are natural dispositions that regard natural goods that we all naturally perceive as fitting, such as existing, living, and knowing. In these cases we can say that the will follows such dispositions according to a kind of natural necessity even if not an absolute one.

Let us draw together the various strands of the whole discussion. From the perspective of the exercise of the act (the subjective point of view), the will is free because it moves itself. It is true that the first impulse (under the ontological aspect, so to speak) depends on God, but God puts the human will in motion (he posits it in being) not as something necessary but as something free, able to choose between different goods that are fitting in various ways. From the perspective of the specification of the act (the objective point of view), the will is free in general because it can choose on the basis of different sorts of fittingness, but there are some exceptions: it is absolutely necessitated in regard to the absolute good (no one cannot not will his own beatitude), and it is naturally necessitated with respect to some dispositions of the human species as such that are not unique to individuals (the desire to exist, live, and know).

Ultimately, for Thomas, there are few impediments to freedom of the will, and all of these impediments regard the specification of acts (the objects) and not the exercise of the act. The will can always choose between different options but cannot choose in what concerns its absolute beatitude, its subsistence, its survival, and its natural desire to know (because this is connatural to the specific essence of man).

On this basis it is difficult to make Thomas a pure or radical intellectualist like Siger of Brabant or, still more, Godfrey of Fontaines, who is quite close to Thomas on some points (so much so as to generate the impression of complete overlap). The Franciscans, and later Henry of Ghent, interpret Thomas as generally acknowledging the will's self-movement, refusing to maintain a rigid and restrictive interpretation of the Aristotelian postulate according to which everything that is moved is moved by another. If an extrinsic mover of the will exists, it is not so much in the object or in the good known as it is in the ontological cause itself of the will, that is, God. But all of that, as we have seen, regards the exercise of voluntary acts. From the point of view of specification, the will is at least in part conditioned by its objects, and, therefore, by the role of the intellect. For Thomas, this ambivalence turns on the presupposition (borrowed once again from Avicennian metaphysics) that the object of the will (the good) is first in the order of final causality whereas that of the object of the intellect (the true) is first in the order of formal causality, and this leads inevitably to a kind of reciprocal subordination. In fact,

even the good itself inasmuch as it is an apprehensible form, is contained under the true as a particular truth, and the true itself, inasmuch as it is the end of the intellectual operation, is contained under the good as a particular good.[20]

The intellect, as pursuit of the true, is moved by the will (and this perfectly corresponds to the freedom of exercise). But the particular goods chosen by the intellect come under the true and are, therefore, at least in part subordinated to the cognitive process of the intellect. In other words, although the will is what moves the intellect to operate (as is the case with every other power), it is true that in the case of the choice of a particular good, the will's operation must be preceded by the apprehension of the good itself, and so by an act of the intellect. If we were to adopt a label, we should say that Thomas is a very moderate intellectualist, who does not deny the self-movement of the will but rather recognizes that the will plays an essential role (as suggested by Aristotle) in the choice of particular goods, and, moreover, some objects presented by the intellect appear to the will as absolutely or naturally irresistible. What the later voluntarists (such as Henry of Ghent) criticize Thomas for is the very sharp distinction between the sphere of the exercise of the act and that of its specification. For someone like Henry, who is, in the final analysis, a very moderate voluntarist, the intellect is only a condition of the will's operation (a *sine qua non* cause), which is always absolutely free and so able to choose among the goods proposed by the intellect, even those presented as less good.

The Capital Sins and the Devil: A Small Treatise of Scholastic Demonology

After a question devoted to venial sin, the *De malo* offers a detailed treatment of the capital sins or vices. For Thomas, "capital" here means "principal"—each

20. *Quaestiones disputatae de malo*, q. 6, a. 1.

capital sin is a principle of other sins. These capital sins or vices are, in order, pride, vainglory, envy, acedia, anger, greed, gluttony, and lust. Pride has a special place because it is not only a particular sin but the root and queen of all the other sins (or, as Thomas says in *Summa theologiae*, I-II, q. 84, a. 3, it is the *initium omnis peccati*). It maximally manifests what is characteristic of every sin: breaking the rule of right reason. Every appetite, when it is directed toward a good naturally desired according to the rule of reason, is right and virtuous. If we depart from it by excess or defect, it is transformed into sin. The desire to know is, for example, entirely natural in man, and so pursuing the sciences according to what reason indicates is praiseworthy. To go beyond this is the sin of curiosity. Not to apply ourselves enough in the pursuit of knowledge is the sin of negligence. Among the things that man naturally desires is excellence. If this desire is pursued in keeping with the right rule, it is magnanimity. If we fail to pursue it, it becomes pusillanimity and if we go beyond the right measure, it becomes pride. To become proud, explains Thomas, "is to go beyond the proper measure in the desire for excellence."[21] Pride is the root of all sins not only because of the extension of its dominion but because it reveals the basic characteristic (at least in regard to effects) of all sins. Every sin always consists in refusing to submit to a superior rule, and, thus, implicitly contains an act of pride. With regard to acedia, Thomas describes it as an unjustified sadness over an interior good. Interior goods really are such and they can be considered evil only because they oppose the pleasures of the body. To be sad about such a good, then, is a specific sin. The condemnation of usury in the discussion of greed is important. We will find it elsewhere. Usury contradicts natural justice since it is based on something that does not exist. There are, in fact, some things that cannot be separated from the goods themselves, and money is among these. Money, therefore, is not something that can be sold itself but something that must be used to sell and buy other goods. In the case of gluttony and lust, it is perhaps worth noting that Thomas considers these to be mortal sins only in the measure that they contradict the final end or replace it (when these desires oppose the love of God and neighbor). If they do not do this, they are venial sins.

There is a small treatise on demonology in q. 16 in a pure Scholastic style, that is, absolutely rational.[22] Thomas first of all explains that devils do not pos-

---

21. *Quaestiones disputatae de malo*, q. 8, a. 2.

22. As J. B. Russell once observed, scholastic theology is certainly that which conceded the least to any form of superstitious or esoteric demonology. See Russell's *Lucifer: The Devil in the Middle Ages* (Ithaca: Cornell University Press, 1984). In direct reference to Thomas, for example, Russell writes: "Having already shown that an evil principle without God cannot exist, Thomas's logic leads him to a point where an evil being dependent upon God is also unnecessary to explain evil. Christian Scripture and tradition require belief in the Devil, but natural reason and logic do not" (202–3).

sess a body, not even an ethereal one (a thesis that Augustine did not reject, as is well known), and are wicked not by nature but by will since their will is not in conformity with divine wisdom. In an especially interesting article—even for reasons that are not strictly theological—Thomas says that the devil's sin is not in wanting to be equal to God (q. 16, a. 3). The devils, as intellectual creatures, knew perfectly well that they could not become equal to God, and no one desires what is impossible. Analogously, the devils knew well that identification with God would have entailed, from an ontological perspective, the suppression of their specific nature, and nothing desires what is contrary to the preservation of its species. On the other hand, if the nature of the devils was created good and from the beginning they had what belonged to their natural perfection, it must be granted that evil could root itself in them only in what concerns the supernatural order, in that perfection that they by no means already possessed but toward which they had a potency (and without potency, after all, there could be no evil). Thus, the sin of the fallen angels consisted in holding that they could pursue supernatural beatitude by their own power without the aid of divine grace:

Therefore the first sin of the devil is that in pursuing supernatural happiness, which consists in the full vision of God, he did not direct himself to God as desiring with the holy angels his final perfection through God's grace, but wanted to obtain it by virtue of his own nature—not, however, without God operating in nature, but without God bestowing grace.... The devil sinned not by desiring something evil but by desiring something good, namely, final happiness, but not according to the proper order, that is, not as a thing to be attained by the grace of God.[23]

For Thomas, then, the devil sinned not in regard to the end but in regard to the way of pursuing it, and in this line his sin was not to neglect God but to admit God's work only in the order of nature and not also, and above all, in the order of grace. Hence, at the origin of the fall of the angels is a sin of self-sufficiency— the illusion of being able to pursue happiness, or beatitude, *not without God but without grace*, that is, only naturally. If we consider the ideal of philosophical felicity formulated more or less during those same years by the faculty of arts in Paris, and by Boethius of Dacia in particular in his *De summo bono*—an ideal based on the self-sufficiency of philosophy in the purely natural sphere (only the philosopher does not sin, only he is naturally happy)—we can well say that the sin of the devils was, for Thomas, an essentially philosophical sin, or, inversely, that the "natural" autonomy pursued by the new philosophers of the faculty of arts in Paris was, in Thomas's eyes, a Luciferian temptation.

---

23. *Quaestiones disputatae de malo*, q. 16, a. 3.

This also explains why the devil was unable to sin in the first instant of creation. According to Thomas, spiritual creatures know in a successive way, that is, passing in time from one content to another (although they are subject to a different time than the cosmic time of our world). In the first moment, the devil knew what was natural and at that point could not sin. Only in a subsequent moment could he consider what was superior to nature and detach himself from that supernatural reality. This sin, as we said, is rooted in the supernatural order.

However, once the choice was made, it was immutable, since the intellect and will of purely spiritual creatures are, in themselves, beyond change after the initial decision. Because of this, the free will of the devils cannot return to the good and their intellect remains clouded by error and deception. Devils do not know the future except from present causes (more or less as we do). This does not allow them to foresee merely contingent events; they can foresee only those that, in relation to their causes, always occur or occur for the most part. (Ultimately they know the inclination of the causes—that is, what the causes normally produce—only in the light of their knowledge of the present conditions.) Neither do they know our hidden thoughts. They can perhaps infer them from external signs. They do not know what a person is actually thinking at a given moment, since what is actually thought depends on the will of individuals, and only God knows the acts of the human will since he is the cause. But the devils certainly know better than we do all the intelligible species by which things are intellectually known. Furthermore, they cannot transform the form of things in such a way as to deceive those who apprehend them. But they can affect the sensitive part of the soul, that is, the imagination, although that is the case mainly for the images of things that exist in nature; it is much more problematic with respect to images of nonexistent things. We can, in short, hold that the devils (like the angels) can work ("physiologically," as it were) on the humors of the human body and the impressions left by the changes of sensible things. Thus, they cannot directly deceive the human intellect, introducing such things as false intelligible species; rather, they can only modify sense images or the phantasms in which the intellective process originates, orienting it in an erroneous direction. We cannot know things about separate substances (devils included), because all human knowledge, as we already know, begins from phantasms, and there are no phantasms of spiritual creatures.

THE *SECUNDA PARS* OF THE *SUMMA THEOLOGIAE*
An Overview of the Second Part and
the Habits of Practical Action

One of Thomas's principal tasks in the course of the second Paris regency was the drafting of the massive second part of the *Summa theologiae*, which consists of an analysis of the end of rational creatures—beatitude—and the necessary means to pursue it. At the center of attention here is primarily the appetitive faculty or power that makes man, because he is free, the master of his acts.

To carry out his plan, Thomas first considers human action in general (in the first of his subdivisions, which we mentioned earlier, the *prima secundae*) and then in various particular contexts (*secunda secundae*).[24] Here is the general plan of the *prima secundae*, organized according to these core topics:

* an introductory section on beatitude or happiness (qq. 1–5) that retraces the treatment that we have already seen in the *Summa contra Gentiles*; beatitude consists in an act of the speculative intellect, in the vision of the divine essence (q. 3, a. 8); this is a *natural* desire that can be quenched only after death;

* voluntary acts and their moral qualities (qq. 6–11);

* the passions (qq. 22–48), that is, the movements of the sensitive power conditioned by the perception of the object (qq. 22–25). Thomas considers first the passions of the concupiscible or desiring part of the soul: love and hate (qq. 26–29), concupiscence and repugnance (q. 30), pleasure and sadness (qq. 31–239), and then the passions of the irascible part: hope and despair (q. 40), fear and daring (qq. 41–45), anger (qq. 46–48);

* the interior principles of human acts (qq. 48–89): the habits that can be good (virtues) or bad (vices) and that permit us to act; the gifts of the Holy Spirit (q. 68), the beatitudes (q. 69), and the fruits of the Holy Spirit (q. 70) also are treated here, obviously in a more strictly theological fashion;

---

24. For a systematic presentation (overly systematic, in fact) of Thomistic ethics, see W. Kluxen, *L'etica filosofica di Tommaso d'Aquino*, ed. C. Vigna (Milan: Vita e Pensiero, 2005) [original edition: *Philosophische Ethik bei Thomas von Aquin* (Hamburg: Felix Meiner, Hamburg 1963, 1998]). For a discussion of some epistemological aspects of Thomas approach to practical philosophy, see M. Lutz-Bachmann, "Praktisches Wissen und 'Praktische Wissenschaft': Zur Epistemologie der Moralphilosophie bei Thomas von Aquin," in *Handlung und Wissenschaft—Action and Science. Die Epistemologie der praktischen Wissenschaften im 13. und 14. Jahrhundert—The Epistemology of the Practical Sciences in the 13th and 14th Centurie*, ed. M. Lutz-Bachmann and A. Fidora (Berlin: Akademie Verlag, 2008), 89–96.

• the external principles of human action (qq. 90–114): the law (qq. 90–108) and grace (qq. 109–114).

The *secunda secundae* is itself further organized into two large subdivisions devoted respectively to particular virtues and vices (qq. 1–170) and different human states (qq. 171–189). In this case as well we can attempt to identify certain core topics:

• the theological virtues (qq. 1–46): faith (qq. 1–16), hope and fear (qq. 17–22), and charity (qq. 23–46);

• the cardinal virtues (prudence, justice, courage, and temperance). Much space is especially dedicated to prudence (qq. 47–56)—which, as we will see, has a fundamental role in rational action and, thus, supports all the other virtues—and to justice (qq. 57–122), under which Thomas treats of issues relating to property, usury, and just prices (qq. 77–78), piety (q. 101), gratitude (qq. 106–107), truth and lies (qq. 109–113), affability (q. 114), and generosity (qq. 117–119). Next is a discussion of courage (qq. 123–140)—with interesting questions on fear (q. 125) and magnanimity (q. 129). Then temperance is addressed (qq. 141–170) and considered in relation to: food (qq. 146–150), sensuality (qq. 151–154), connected virtues (such as clemency, modesty, and humility, qq. 155–165), the desire to know and curiosity (qq. 166–167);

• the difference states of life. This topic includes a group of questions on prophecy (qq. 171–174), the gifts of grace (qq. 175–178), the active and contemplative lives (qq. 179–182), and the different tasks and "states" in the Church (qq. 183–189).

Evidently, a detailed account of all this material cannot be given, but it is possible to try to select—in an inevitably arbitrary way—a few points to discuss that are more relevant from a philosophical point of view.

Whereas the *prima pars* of the *Summa* included an analysis of the human cognitive faculty, that is, the intellect, the second part, considered as a whole, is focused on the appetitive faculty, which is divided into the *sensitive appetite* (the faculty that has to do with the lower functions of the soul, that is, with the sensitive soul) and the *intellectual* or *rational appetite*, that is, *the will*. Now, we already know that every appetite moves toward its proper sensible or intelligible object. The quality of moral actions depends, therefore, precisely on *the way in which man disposes himself in view of his proper end*. And since man, insofar as he is rational, pursues his proper end not in a blind and unwitting way but in a willing and conscious way, his acts will have a moral value if they are *voluntary*. If we do something unconsciously or against our will, then, we do not do something that, in the strict sense, has any moral relevance. This being the case, Thomas is of the view that it is always necessary to look at the *intention* of acts, to the fact that the will must will the good for the good. But it is always the intellect that presents the good to the will and makes it know the good as such. In this context Thomas distinguishes between *synderesis*, which is the natural habit by which we grasp the most universal moral principles (the practical equivalent of the theoretical capacity immediately to grasp the first speculative principles),[25] and *conscience*, which has to do with the application of these principles in different contingent situations. The habit (or disposition) of the practical intellect that permits the formulation of correct judgments of conscience is *prudence*, which is in a sense the practical correlate of science. As is easy to see, this position depends heavily on Aristotelian ethics, including the basic idea that our moral choices are always the result of practical syllogisms that stem from prudence.

The Passions

Before more carefully examining the crucial role of prudence we should consider the sphere of the sensitive appetite, and the passions in particular.[26] This is a topic that Thomas already touched on in his Commentary on Book III of the *Sentences* (in connection with Christ's passions) and above all in *De veritate*, q. 26. We should not be surprised that in the *Summa* Thomas situates the treatment of the passions in a decidedly ethical context rather than in a reflection on the soul

25. On synderesis as a habit of the practical intellect, see *De Veritate*, q. 16, a. 1: "just as there is a natural habit of the human soul through which it knows principles of the speculative sciences, which we call understanding of principles, so too there is in the soul a natural habit of first principles of action, which are the universal principles of the natural law. This habit pertains to synderesis." And, *Summa theologiae* I, 79, a. 12: "Now the first speculative principles bestowed on us by nature do not belong to a special power, but to a special habit, which is called 'the understanding of principles,' as the Philosopher explains (Ethic. vi, 6). Wherefore the first practical principles, bestowed on us by nature, do not belong to a special power, but to a special natural habit, which we call 'synderesis.' Whence 'synderesis' is said to incite to good, and to murmur at evil, inasmuch as through first principles we proceed to discover, and judge of what we have discovered." For an incisive outline of the problem of the origins of the notion of "synderesis," see C. Trottmann, "La syndérèse: heureuse faute?" in *Mots médiévaux offerts à Ruedi Imbach*, Textes et etudes du Moyen Âge 57, ed. I. Atucha, D. Calma, C. Konig-Pralong, and I. Zavattero (Porto: FIDEM, 2011), 717–27.

26. See M. D. Jordan, "Aquinas's Construction of a Moral Account of the Passions," *Freiburger Zeitschrift für Philosophie und Theologie* 33 (1986): 71–97; A. Brungs, *Metaphysik der Sinnlichkeit: Das System der passiones animae bei Thomas von Aquin* (Halle an der Saale: Hallescher, 2002). See also S. Vecchio's brief but incisive introduction to the truly beautiful translation of the section of the *prima secundae* dedicated to the passions: Tommaso d'Aquino, *Le passioni dell'anima* [*dalla* Somma di teologia Ia-IIae, *questioni 22–48*], I biancospini 3, trans. S. Vecchio (Florence: Le Lettere, 2002), 5–18.

or psychology. Aristotle had already, in effect, placed an analysis of the passions in Book II of the *Nicomachean Ethics*, and the moral tone of the discussion of the passions (apart from its physiological or psychological—in the Aristotelian acceptation of the term—tone) was already an established feature of the treatments of the thirteenth century.[27] But the placement of the discussion of the passions in ethics should not mislead us either. Thomas remains faithful to Aristotle in insisting that the passions cannot be the direct object of moral evaluation but that they help to explain in what those voluntary dispositions are rooted that have a moral quality in the strict sense. The passions are, thus, situated on a terrain that is at the boundary between the natural movements of the soul (which, not being totally voluntary, are not morally qualifiable) and the voluntary ones, which belong to the domain of the rational appetite. So, the passions are *the movements of the sensible appetitive power*. From this point of view, the formula itself, "passions of the soul," should be used with caution. The soul is not the subject of the passions but only their site, and it is this inasmuch as it is joined to the body. According to Thomas, there is passion only where there is bodily change (Ia-IIae, q. 22, a. 3), and this change is found in the sensitive appetite. The two faculties of the sensitive appetite are, as we already know, the concupiscible and the irascible. The passions of the concupiscible faculty are related to good and evil as such, since they are the motive of pleasure or pain for the individual. *Love* is the passion related to the inclination or attitude or connaturality toward the good. If this good is not yet possessed, it produces *desire* or *concupiscence*. But when the appetite is quieted by the good acquired there is *pleasure* or *joy*. Speculatively, *hate* is the passion that relates to the repulsion of evil. *Flight* or *repugnance* (*abominatio*) is the passion that is related to an evil that has not yet been suffered. *Sorrow* or *sadness* is the passion that is related to an evil that has already been suffered (Ia-IIae, q. 23, a. 4). The passions that belong to the sphere of the irascible do not relate to good or evil as such but as "arduous," that is, difficult to achieve or avoid. *Hope* relates to a good that is hard to achieve and *despair* (the opposite of hope) relates to the renunciation of pursuing a good insofar as it is hard or difficult. *Fear* and *daring* are passions that relate to an evil that is hard to avoid. Insofar as the evil looms, it generates fear, and when we decide to face it this produces daring. If the difficult-to-avoid-evil has already been suffered, this gives rise to *anger*.[28] The principle that guides Thomas's classification is that the

27. Albert the Great is an example of this. His treatment of the passions in the *De bono* is the most significant antecedent to Thomas's treatment, as has been noted, but it must be added that Thomas's classifications and analyses are much more detailed and extensive.

28. "Anger is provoked by an evil that is hard to eliminate and is already present" (*Summa theologiae* Ia-IIae, q. 23, a. 3).

contrary nature of passions must be reduced to contrary movements, supposing that passions are themselves movements. In movements there are two types of contrariety: one pertaining to instantaneous movements (such as generation and corruption), which consists in the approach or withdrawal of the same thing, and the other pertaining to movements properly so-called (such as those of a qualitative sort), which consists in the contrariety of objects. Therefore, in the passions of the soul too we will find these two types of contrariety: one based on the contrary nature of the things (in this case good and evil) and the other based on the approach or withdrawal of the same thing. In the concupiscible passions, in which good and evil are considered in an absolute sense, there is only the contrariety about the objects themselves without reference to approaching or withdrawing—nothing can turn away from what it perceives as good nor turn toward what it perceives as evil (in an absolute sense). In fact, the concupiscible passions that relate to the good—like love, desire, joy—tend toward it, whereas those that relate to evil—like hatred, repugnance, and sadness—flee from *it*. In the irascible passions, good and evil are not considered in themselves but, as we have just seen, as "arduous," that is, as (relatively) difficult to pursue and avoid. Because of this we should here consider both of the forms of contrariety (but not anger, which relates to an evil that is already present or past from which it is no longer impossible to turn away—it is for this reason that anger is unique among the passions in that it has no contrary).[29] As Thomas explains:

Now the good which is difficult or arduous, considered as good, is of such a nature as to produce in us a tendency to it, which tendency pertains to the passion of "hope," whereas, considered as arduous or difficult, it makes us turn from it, and this pertains to the passion of "despair." In like manner the arduous evil, considered as an evil, has the aspect of something to be shunned, and this belongs to the passion of "fear." But it also contains a reason for tending to it, as attempting something arduous, whereby to escape being subject to evil, and this tendency is called "daring." Consequently, in the irascible passions we find contrariety in respect of good and evil, as between hope and fear, and also contrariety according to approach and withdrawal in respect of the same term, as between daring and fear.[30]

We have, then, a classification articulated that, although it is not exhaustive, includes eleven passions: six concupiscible (love, concupiscence or desire, pleasure or joy, hatred, and repugnance, and sadness) and five irascible (hope, despair, fear, daring, and anger). Thomas attempts to find a definition, cause, and effects of each of these passions.

29. *Summa theologiae* Ia-IIae, q. 23, a. 3.
30. *Summa theologiae* Ia-IIae, q. 23, a. 2.

As we said, none of the passions have a moral valence in themselves. They acquire it to the extent that they enter into relation with the higher sphere of voluntary acts, that is, with reason and the rational appetite. It is only in light of such acts that the passions cease to be morally neutral and become positive or negative, good or bad. In other words, in Thomas's view, the passions in themselves do not at all constitute an evil or something opposed to reason and the rational appetite; on the contrary, it is the use of these passions by the rational appetite that gives them a moral status (a status that Thomas develops at great length in the analysis of the virtues and vices that, as we have seen, takes up a large part of the *secunda secundae*). In q. 24, a. 1 he is particularly clear and explicit about this point:

We may consider the passions of the soul in two ways: first, in themselves; secondly, as being subject to the command of the reason and will. If, then, the passions be considered in themselves, to wit, as movements of the irrational appetite, there is no moral good or evil in them, since this depends on the reason.... If, however, they be considered as subject to the command of the reason and will, then moral good and evil are in them. The sensitive appetite is nearer than the outward members to the reason and will, and yet the movements and actions of the outward members are morally good or evil, since they are voluntary. Much more, therefore, may the passions, since they are voluntary, be called morally good or evil. And they are said to be voluntary, either from being commanded by the will, or from not being checked by the will.

As natural realities, Thomas explains in q. 24, a. 1, the passions are in no way specified by moral good and evil. It is only when there is "an element of voluntariness and the judgment of reason," and the relationship to customs is considered, that moral good and evil can determine the species of the passion.

Love seems to have special place among the passions, since "there is no passion of the soul that does not presuppose love."[31] All of the passions imply a movement toward something or a resting in something. And motion and rest always depend on a conformity or connaturality that is proper to love. We move toward what is connatural (and which we thereby love) and we rest in what is connatural (and which we thereby love). For this reason the most general definition of love is that it is "the principle of movement tending toward the end loved" (*principium motus tendentis in finem amatum*).[32] Since every agent acts for an end, and the end is the good that each person loves, it can be concluded in a general way that "every agent of any sort acts according to some love."[33] Love, therefore, is found at different levels. In inanimate things it indicates the

31. *Summa theologiae* Ia-IIae, q. 27, a. 4.   32. *Summa theologiae* Ia-IIae, q. 26, a. 1.
33. *Summa theologiae* Ia-IIae, q. 28, a. 6.

nature common to that which tends toward something and of that which constitutes the term of this tendency (for example, the nature common to stones and the earth that makes it such that the former tend toward the center of the latter). In irrational living things, love is found in the sensitive appetite. In man it is found in both the sensitive and the intellectual appetites. In these cases love always follows upon the knowledge of the subject, a knowledge that is necessary (in the sense of natural necessity) for irrational living things and free—following as it does upon free judgment—in living things endowed with reason. Sensible and intellectual love are both included in the sphere of love. The two aspects can be better distinguished terminologically by examining the meanings of *amor, dilectio,* and *caritas*:

Love has a wider signification than the others, since every dilection or charity is love, but not vice versa because dilection implies, in addition to love, a choice (*dilectionem*) made beforehand, as the very word denotes. Therefore, dilection is not in the concupiscible power, but only in the will, and only in the rational nature. Charity denotes, in addition to love, a certain perfection of love, since that which is loved is held to be of great price, as the word itself implies.[34]

In regard to friendship, it [love] indicates more of a habit than an act. But its deeper meaning can be gleaned from the Aristotelian definition of love as "willing the good of the other."[35] Love, thus, has two objects: the good that is willed for someone (another or oneself) and the person for whom the good is willed. In relation to the first aspect (the good willed) Thomas speaks of the love of concupiscence; in relation to the person he speaks of the love of friendship. But in this distinction there is also a difference of degree: "That which is loved with the love of friendship is loved simply and for itself, whereas that which is loved with the love of concupiscence, is loved not simply and for itself, but for something else."[36] There is no doubt, however, that love depends on knowledge (and in this Thomas remains an intellectualist, so to speak). If it is the good that causes love, it can be the object of an appetite only insofar as it is known. So, love always presupposes the knowledge of the good that is loved, knowledge that can be of different kinds: bodily sight is the principle of sensible love, whereas contemplation of the spiritual beautiful or good is the principle of spiritual love.

Of course, Thomas attributes a supreme value to love (*caritas*) of God. This thesis is joined (in an Augustinian manner) to the thesis about the primacy of the love of self, which is the form and root of love of all other things (Ia-IIae,

---

34. *Summa theologiae* Ia-IIae, q. 26, a. 3.   35. *Rhetoric,* IV, 1380b35.
36. *Summa theologiae* Ia-IIae, q. 26, a. 4.

q. 25, a. 4 and above all q. 26, a. 4). The two theses are interconnected rather than contradictory. This is because God is for man the highest good (if he were not, he should not be loved: IIa-IIae, q. 26, a. 13, ad 3). Loving God, man maximally loves himself, because he seeks the highest good for himself (*De virtutibus*, q. 2, a. 7, ad 10).

The Intrinsic Principles of Human Action: The Intellectual Virtues and the Key Role of Prudence

Following the analysis of the passions in the *prima secundae* is a group of questions about the intrinsic principles of human action (qq. 49–89). These principles are in general, on the one hand, the powers or faculties, and, on the other hand, the habits or dispositions. Since Thomas has already spoken of the powers in the *prima pars* of the *Summa,* the whole discussion here turns on habits. By habits Thomas means the specific qualities or inherent forms of a power that incline it toward doing certain acts (Ia-IIae, q. 54, a. 1). Said differently, these are dispositions to act in a particular way. The habits or dispositions that incline us toward good actions are the virtues, and those that incline us toward wicked actions or actual sin are vices. In the division of virtues Thomas follows the Aristotelian distinction between intellectual virtues—those that dispose the intellect toward the consideration of the true (Ia-IIae, q. 57, a. 2)—and moral virtues, to which Thomas adds the theological virtues.

Again following Aristotle, Thomas situates understanding (the habit of the first or self-evident principles), science (the habit that conduces toward the ultimate term of knowledge in a particular genus), and wisdom (the habit that conduces toward the ultimate term of knowledge in an absolute sense) among the intellectual virtues. To this list, art and prudence can be added. Art is an operative habit but it has something in common with the speculative habits, because it regards the manner of being of the thing produced and not how the human appetite relates to it. Thomas adds *euboulia* (the virtue of deliberating well), *synesis* (the ability to grasp the common principles in the order of the action to be done), and *gnome* (the ability to discern in particular cases) to prudence as secondary virtues. Prudence has a key role not only in the system of intellectual virtues but in the whole of Thomas's ethics. Whereas art is right reason with respect to what can be produced or realized (*recta ratio factibilium*), prudence is right reason with respect to what can be done, that is, action (*recta ratio agibilium*). Prudence, then, relates to human actions that consist in the use of or the unfolding of powers and habits as art relates to external production. The one and the other are the perfect reasoning about that to which they relate. Now, the perfection or rectitude of reason, in the practical domain, is given by the ends. Prudence, therefore, has the fundamental task of making it so that man is well-disposed toward his proper ends and that his appetite is rightly ordered in this regard. In this sense, there is no doubt that prudence is the most necessary virtue for man:

Prudence is a virtue most necessary for human life. For a good life consists in good deeds. Now in order to do good deeds, it matters not only what one does, but also how he does it, to wit, that he do it from right choice and not merely from impulse or passion. And, since choice is about things in reference to the end, rectitude of choice requires two things, namely, the due end, and something suitably ordained to that due end. Now man is suitably directed to his due end by a virtue which perfects the soul in the appetitive part, the object of which is the good and the end. And to that which is suitably ordained to the due end man needs to be rightly disposed by a habit in his reason, because *deliberation and choice, which are about things ordained to the end, are acts of the reason.* Consequently, an intellectual virtue is needed in reason, to perfect reason and to make it suitably affected towards things ordained to the end; and this virtue is prudence. Consequently, prudence is a virtue necessary to lead a good life.[37]

The *prudentia* of Thomas, thus, substantially contains the *phronesis* of Aristotle. Its role as an intellectual virtue is in deliberating about and choosing, not the end itself (which pertains to the appetitive part and the will), but the way to pursue it, that is (to use Aristotle's language rather than Thomas's), the most appropriate means to pursue it. But its key role is manifested also in its placement among the cardinal virtues. It is not by chance that Thomas returns to an even lengthier treatment of prudence as a determinate virtue in the *secunda secundae* and precisely in q. 47 (accompanied by the discussion of the parts of prudence in qq. 48–51). Here Thomas explains, first of all and explicitly, that prudence belongs directly to the cognitive power, and more precisely to reason, and not to the sensitive cognitive power, since prudence seeks to infer the future from past and present events, something which the senses cannot do (IIa-IIae, q. 47, a. 1). Thus, prudence *de facto* coincides with practical reason, that is, with reason that dictates the actions that must be done in view of an end (q. 47, a. 2). But precisely because of its eminently practical connotation, that is, because of its relation to operation and action (*applicatio ad opus*), prudence is also related to the will and so is counted among the properly moral virtues (as are the cardinal virtues). As Thomas explains further in q. 47, a. 5:

Now it belongs to prudence, as stated above, to apply right reason to action, and this is not done without a right appetite. Hence prudence has the nature of virtue not only as the other intellectual virtues have it, but also as the moral virtues have it, among which virtues it is counted.[38]

---

37. *Summa theologiae* Ia-IIae, q. 57, a. 5.
38. *Summa theologiae* IIa-IIae, q. 47, a. 4. See also *Summa theologiae* Ia-IIae, q. 58, a. 3, ad 1: "Pru-

What, more exactly, is the role of prudence? Just as in the domain of speculative reason we can distinguish between principles that are self-evident and
are grasped by the understanding (the habit of principles) and the conclusions
that are drawn from them through science, so also in the domain of practical
reason we can distinguish between ends that preexist and are naturally known
and what relates to them (*ea quae sunt ad finem*) and is determined by them.
Hence, the task of prudence is not that of indicating the ends to the other moral virtues but that of determining what relates to the end, that is, what serves
to pursue the end itself. Prudence is in this way the true motor of practical
reasoning. It seeks to apply the previously known universal principles (the ends)
to particular and contingent cases, deciding what must be done in view of those
ends in each determinate circumstance (q. 47, a. 6). As such (as *recta ratio agibilium*), prudence is characterized by three principal acts or operations: *consil-
iari, iudicare, praecipere*—investigating what is fitting in relation to the desired
end (*consilium*), judging the results of the preliminary investigation (*iudicium*),
and prescribing what should be done (*praeceptum*), that is, applying to action
or operation what was identified by *consilium* and *iudicium*. This articulation
helps us better to understand, from a different perspective, the hybrid nature
of prudence, which is intellectual and moral (and speculative and practical).
Consilium and *iudicium* belong more properly to speculative reason, whereas
praeceptum belongs to practical reason. But of the three, it is precisely the third
that most distinguishes the essence of prudence (q. 47, a. 8).

Thomas goes on to distinguish between prudence that superintends or is
ordered to the individual good and that which is ordered to the common good.
From here we can deduce the internal articulation of prudence. From the point
of view of its integral parts, it includes memory (which allows us to build up
a store of experiences about what should be done in particular cases), reason
(which presides in *consilium*), understanding (not in the sense of the intellectual power but in the sense of the correct grasp of a naturally known principle),
docility (the openness to learn from others what to do in different particular
circumstances), shrewdness (the ability to learn on our own the right way to
judge), foresight (the ability to foresee, within limits, future contingents based
on the past and the present), circumspection (the ability to take account of the
circumstances), and caution (necessary to distinguish good from evil in individual contingent operations). This is a traditional list, assembled using material from Macrobius, Cicero, and Aristotle. Alongside the integral parts, we

---

dence is essentially an intellectual virtue. But considered on the part of its matter, it has something in
common with the moral virtues, for it is right reason about things to be done, as stated above. It is in
this sense that it is reckoned with the moral virtues."

must also consider the subjective parts (the different species). Precisely because prudence is oriented not only toward the individual good but also toward the common good, it is necessary to include *"regnative" prudence* (proper to the sovereign in the care of public things), *political prudence* (proper to subjects who must conform to laws in each political community), *economic prudence* (for the needs of every family or *domus*—the latter being a political community that is an intermediary between the individual and the state), and *military prudence* (necessary for knowing how to repel attacks against the political community). The potential parts of prudence (powers of prudence analogous to the vegetative and sensitive powers, which are potential parts of the human soul) are already mentioned in the *prima secundae* and borrowed from Book IV of the *Nicomachean Ethics*: *euboulia* (which presides over the goodness of deliberation), *synesis* (which presides over right judgments about particular actions to be done), and *gnome* (which relates, beyond the common rules of judgment, to the highest principles, and so is a certain perspicacity of judgment).

We could ask, lastly, whether prudence, playing such an important role in human action, is innate in each man (IIa-IIae, q. 47, a. 15). As we have seen, it is for prudence to determine the contingent actions relating to ends. The latter are what is pre-known or naturally known. And, just as in the speculative realm, the conclusions, unlike the principles, are not naturally known but must be deduced, so also in the practical realm individual deliberations about particular actions must be conquered, as it were, by experience and learning. So, *prudence is not natural.* Nor could it be otherwise, because an exclusively natural inclination would be unable to deal with the infinite variety of particular cases that are presented in the life of each person. But it is true, nonetheless, that each person, as a rational animal, is called to have a rational response to the circumstances that he must face, and in this sense prudence (as something to be forged, constructed) belongs to each man (IIa-IIae, q. 47, a. 12). It is threatened not so much by forgetfulness—except in its more strictly speculative components—as by the passions, to the extent that these are not oriented and channeled by reason (q. 45, a. 16).

The Moral Virtues

In the *prima secundae* the treatment of the moral virtues follows that of the intellectual virtues. This is a propitious occasion to reconsider—from a different angle—the question of the relationship between the intellectual and appetitive spheres. Can it really be said that the moral virtues constitute a whole that is different from the whole constituted by the intellectual virtues? If Socrates was right—as Thomas notes, taking up again the topic developed in parallel in the

De malo—the distinction between the two would, indeed, be superfluous. If every error or sin were only a consequence of ignorance (a cognitive error), all of human action would depend solely on the intellectual virtues. But this is not how it is, as Thomas points out (Ia-IIae, q. 58, a. 2), because the appetitive part does not follow reason in a blind and necessary way (*ad nutum*) but can also oppose it (*cum aliqua contradictione*), as Aristotle himself recognizes when he admits that the regime by which the soul rules the body is "despotic" whereas the regime by which reason commands the appetitive part is "political" (in the sense that it is a regime that admits freedom and so the possibility of opposition and contradiction). The Socratic thesis, according to which there is no sin without ignorance, would be true if reason's rule were absolute even in particular actions that are the object of choice (*aliqualiter verum est quod Socrates dixit, quod scientia praesente, non peccatur: si tamen hoc extendatur usque ad usum rationis in particulari eligibili*). This nuance (*aliqualiter*) is, in fact, significant. Thomas would be disposed to concede (with Aristotle) a decided priority to the intellectual power even in the practical domain if it were not that, in the choice of actions for achieving an end, the will retained a possibility of dissent. There are two things to note on this score and that validate, in a sense, our earlier pronouncement on Thomas's moderate intellectualism. In theory, the appetitive part should not dissent from the intellectual part, and when that happens it is in the domain of particular and contingent choices. It remains true, then, that in Thomas's judgment no moral virtue is possible without intellectual virtue (or at least without the intellect, which grasps the principles, and without prudence, which deliberates, judges, and commands), while the intellectual virtues (with the obvious exception of prudence) by no means presuppose the moral virtues (Ia-IIae, q. 58, aa. 4–5). A little later Thomas asks still more explicitly which virtues—the moral or the intellectual—must be considered the most noble and preeminent (q. 66, a. 3). In an absolute sense the virtue that possesses the most noble object is the most noble, and there is no doubt that the object of reason is nobler than the object of appetite. Reason apprehends something universal, whereas appetite tends toward particular things. Thus, in an absolute sense the intellectual virtues, which perfect reason, are nobler than the moral virtues, which perfect the appetite. But if we consider the virtues in relation to act, the moral virtues are nobler, because the appetite moves all the other powers to act. This is, in appearance, a Solomonic solution, and all the more so since Thomas notes that the character of "virtue" in a strict sense (that is, of a disposition that inclines us to act) pertains perhaps more to the moral virtues than the intellectual virtues. But, considering the habits independently of action, and so in an absolute sense (*simpliciter*), there is no doubt that the intellectual virtues are superior. The line in the practical sphere that separates Thomas and the Franciscans (and Henry of Ghent) passes through here too.

The list of moral virtues does not end with the cardinal virtues. In the *prima secundae* he discusses others that relate to the passions (liberality, magnificence, magnanimity, *philotimia* or love of honor, meekness, affability, truth—understood here as sincerity, and *eutrapelia* or wittiness—the Aristotelian virtue of playfulness). But the whole treatment of particular virtues is postponed, as we know, until the *secunda secundae*. Thomas instead explains in the development of the *prima secundae* that all the moral virtues are connected to each other (above all because of the transversal role of prudence: Ia-IIae, q. 65, a. 1).

In regard to the theological virtues (faith, hope, and charity—which are also dealt with in the *Compendium theologiae* and the *Quaestiones disputatae de virtutibus*), they are directed toward a supernatural end (beatitude as vision of the divine essence) and so cannot be naturally acquired through learning or experience in the way that the moral virtues are, but are infused. The section on the intrinsic principles of human action concludes (after the questions on the gifts and fruits of the Holy Spirit and the beatitudes) with the analysis of vices and sins (Ia-IIae, qq. 71–89), which is largely the same as the analysis that we considered in the *De malo*.

The External Principles of Human Action: The Law

After the internal principles of human action have been considered, the external principles must be considered. Whereas the devil can be the external principle of the actions aimed at evil (although the responsibility for them rests entirely with the human will), God is the external principle of the actions aimed at the good, and in a twofold way: by teaching through the law and by the succor of grace. The law is that principle that externally guides or sustains human action in its orientation toward its proper end. The first distinctive feature of the law is its rational character, its belonging to the realm of reason:

Law is a rule and measure of acts, whereby man is induced to act or is restrained from acting, for *lex* [law] is derived from *ligare* [to bind], because it binds one to act. Now the rule and measure of human acts is reason, which is the first principle of human acts.... It belongs to reason to direct to the end, which is the first principle in all matters of action, according to the Philosopher.... Consequently, it follows that law is something pertaining to reason.[39]

The second basic feature of law is that it is oriented toward the common good. It could be objected that human laws, for example, regulate private relationships

---

39. *Summa theologiae* Ia-IIae, q. 90, a. 1.

too, but, for Thomas, any precept related to particular actions has the character of law only in the measure in which it is ordained to the common good. Summing up these two fundamental features, we can say that law is a rational ordering to the common good that is promulgated by those who have care of a community (*quaedam rationis ordinatio ad bonum commune ab eo qui curam communitatis habet promulgata*, Ia-IIae, q. 90, a. 4).

Laws, however, are of different types. In a descending hierarchical order we can distinguish the following:

1. First there is eternal law (*lex aeterna*), which is identical with the ordering of the universe as it is established in the divine mind. More precisely: just as divine wisdom is called *ars* or *exemplar* or *idea* since everything is created through it, it can also be called *lex* insofar as it moves everything toward its proper end. The eternal law is, then, nothing other than the reason of divine wisdom since it directs all acts and movements (Ia-IIae, q. 93, a. 1: *lex aeterna nihil aliud est quam ratio divinae sapientiae, secundum quod est directiva omnium actuum et motionum*). Thus, all the necessary and contingent things of the universe are subject to the eternal law, except for God, who is not subordinate to this law but is identical with it. As such, the eternal law is not accessible to anyone but the blessed, who see God in his essence. Yet, rational creatures can know this law indirectly, by reflection, to the extent that all knowledge of truth is a kind of participation in the eternal law (Ia-IIae, q. 93, a. 2).

2. Next, there is natural law (*lex naturalis*), which coincides with the eternal law itself as it is participated by the rational creature (*lex naturalis nihil aliud est quam participatio legis aeternae in rationali creatura*). In fact, everything in the universe is under the sign of the eternal law, for nothing escapes the divine order. But the rational creature finds himself in this order in a conscious way (that is, he can direct himself consciously toward his proper end) and so can grasp and assimilate this law. Man is, then, subject to the eternal law in a twofold manner: as a natural being, he is ruled by it just like all the other, irrational beings; as endowed with knowledge, he is subject to it in a different and special way. Indeed, in the strict sense we must speak of law only for rational creatures. For a particular ordinance to be called a law it must be known and followed as such. So, we are able to access the law of nature by our natural light and can employ practical reasoning and the habit of prudence to apply this law to particular cases.

3. Third is human law (*lex humana*), which is necessary since natural law and reason are not sufficient for regulating civil life. Human law is (or should be) always founded upon the *lex naturalis*. For Thomas too this is the case,

because he takes over from Aristotle the idea that man is a naturally political animal, who has the natural tendency to live in society. The purpose of human law is to apply to contingent circumstances what the natural law prescribes in general. This application can also be made by individuals through practical reasoning, but not everyone is able to do this and many do not want to. Human law adds coercion to what we should do rationally, establishing forms of retribution (punishments) for those who do not follow it. But Thomas does not hold that human laws should repeat the whole content of natural law. Since the purpose is to guarantee the minimal conditions for peaceful coexistence, it will be enough for human laws to prohibit the worst vices and crimes but not absolutely all vices. Similarly, human laws prescribe only the most important virtues and the exercise of all the virtues. Thomas is particularly explicit about this (even if a part of the subsequent tradition of Catholic thought often tried to make the sphere of morality identical with that of positive law):

Now human law is framed for a number of human beings, the majority of whom are not perfect in virtue. So, human laws do not forbid all vices, from which the virtuous abstain, but only the more grievous vices, from which it is possible for the majority to abstain, and chiefly those that are to the hurt of others, without the prohibition of which human society could not be maintained. Thus, human law prohibits murder, theft, and the like.[40]

It could also happen that the human lawmaker errs, promulgating unjust laws. That can occur in two ways: if the laws are contrary to the common good (because they are directed toward the interests of the lawmakers or are unjust in the distribution of obligations or are promulgated without the proper authority) or if they are contrary to the divine good (because they impose idolatry, for instance). In the first case the laws do not bind us in conscience so long as acting contrary to them does not provoke scandal or social unrest. In the second case, they must not be observed at all (Ia-IIae, q. 96, a. 4). Precisely because human law does not cover all possible situations, the lawmaker should aim at what can be useful to the common good in most situations. If the observance of the law proves destructive rather than useful to the common good in a particular case, the law should not be followed (Ia-IIae, q. 96, a. 5). The foregoing three kinds of law have a top-down relationship. Every law, to the extent that it participates in right reason, depends on the *lex aeterna*: the *lex naturalis* depends on it in a direct way and the *lex humana* depends on it through the *lex naturalis*. But a fourth kind of law—which inverts the descending order—must be added to these three.

40. *Summa theologiae* Ia-IIae, q. 96, a. 2.

4. Here we come to the divine law (*lex divina*), that is, the law positively promulgated by God and communicated through the Scriptures (Old and New Testaments). Why, in addition to the *lex aeterna* (and the *lex naturalis* by which rational creatures participate in it), was there a need, on God's part, to add a positive law? In fact, were man not ordered to an end that exceeded his natural powers, there would be no need of any legislation apart from the natural law and human law. But because man is ordained to eternal beatitude, which exceeds the capacity of his natural faculties, an aid (an external principle) to guide him to this end was necessary. To this it must be added that, in regard to contingent and particular things, human judgment is often uncertain and changing, producing different and sometimes conflicting laws. The divine law, then, has the purpose of helping man always to know—without the possibility of doubt—which actions he must do and which he must avoid. Again, human laws regard what it is possible to judge, namely, external actions, and not internal movements, which remain hidden. Nevertheless, the perfection of virtue requires that man conduct himself with rectitude in both cases. Internal actions are outside the sphere of human law but not that of divine law, which regulates them. Finally, human law cannot, as we already noted, punish or prohibit all possible evils, for if it did, many goods that are necessary for communal life would also be impeded. Divine law makes it the case that no evil fails to be prohibited or punished, including those sins tolerated by civil law. With respect to the twofold divine law (Old and New Testaments), Thomas is not too far from the preceding theological tradition: the old law has to do, above all, with the sensible and earthly good and the new with the intelligible and heavenly good, including the ordering of internal actions. Furthermore, from the point of view of authority and efficaciousness, the old law was based, above all, on fear and punishment, whereas the new is based on the love infused by Christ in human hearts.

The most philosophically interesting aspects of Thomas's treatment of law obviously regard natural law and how human law relates to it.[41] If every law is a form of rational ordering to the good, then there can be no wicked or unjust laws, which seems to be contradicted by experience. According to Thomas, everything depends on the way in which we understand the good toward which that law directs us. It can be the common good regulated according to divine

41. See especially A. J. Lisska, *Aquinas's Theory of Natural Law: An Analytic Reconstruction* (Oxford: Clarendon Press, 1996). More generally on the use of the Thomistic doctrine in the construction of a theory of natural right, see J. Finnis, *Natural Law and Natural Right* (Oxford: Clarendon Press, Oxford 1980/2011) and J. Porter, *Nature as Reason: A Thomistic Theory of the Natural Law* (Grand Rapids, Mich.: Eerdmans, 2005).

justice or a relative good that is, for example, only the personal good of the lawmaker himself (in the situation in which a law is promulgated only in the interest of those in authority). In the first case, there is no doubt that law makes everyone better, directing them toward what is truly good. In the second case it does not have the effect of making them good or better, because it directs them toward a relative good (the personal interests of the lawmaker, for instance). In sum, every law, by definition, directs us toward a good, but it does not thereby automatically make those who respect it good or better, since everything depends on the good that is assumed as the end.[42] Obviously, natural law is not always consciously considered by everyone or by all lawmakers, and in this sense it is a kind of habit. It can be reduced to a fundamental principle: do and pursue the good and avoid evil. All the other precepts of natural law are founded on this basic principle. Although we may think that everyone knows the natural law, this is not exactly the case. Even in the realm of speculative reason, the truth, although it is the same for everyone, is not known equally by everyone. The fact that the sum of the internal angles of a triangle equals 180 degrees is equally true for everyone, but it is not equally known by everyone. In the realm of practical reason things are still more complicated, since there is no one truth or kind of rectitude that is the same for everyone in an absolute sense, nor is it equally known by everyone. It is certainly true and right for everyone to act according to reason, but from this general principle it is possible to draw—and people do draw—different conclusions, on account of different contingent and particular cases. In brief, the rectitude and accessibility of the natural law hold only in the majority of cases, but not absolutely:

Consequently, we must say that the natural law, as to general principles, is the same for all men, both as to rectitude and as to knowledge. But as to certain matters of detail, which are conclusions, as it were, of those general principles, it is the same for all men in the majority of cases, both as to rectitude and as to knowledge; and yet in some few cases it may fail, both as to rectitude—by reason of certain obstacles (just as natures subject to generation and corruption fail in some few cases on account of some obstacle)—and as to knowledge—since in some men reason is perverted by passion, or evil habit, or an evil disposition of nature.[43]

At the end of the above quote Thomas is referring to the Germans, among whom, according to Julius Caesar, theft was not considered unjust. This limitation of the validity—or at least the knowability—of the natural law seems to stem from the fact that—for Thomas as for Aristotle—in the sphere of human

---

42. It is not paradoxical to use the term "good" even for what is, in fact, an evil. It is even possible to call someone a "good" thief if he operates in a way conducive to his purpose.

43. *Summa theologiae* Ia-IIae, q. 94, a. 4.

actions (the practical sphere) it is not possible to have the same certainty, universality, and necessity that we can have in the speculative sciences. The complexity of the countless particular cases makes it so that the *lex naturalis* has a real universal relevance only in what regards its first and most general principles (which can never really be eradicated from the human heart, as q. 94, a. 6 makes clear) but not in what regards the principles that can be concluded from them, which are valid only in the majority of cases. Everything else is subject to the variability of circumstances, in which external impediments enter in, as we have seen, but also—regarding the knowability—passions, habits, and natural dispositions. It can seem bizarre that knowledge of the natural law can be disturbed by dispositions that are otherwise natural. Thomas does not go into detail on this point, but we can hypothesize that, with Thomas as with Aristotle, nature can be considered as that which is most often but not always the case.

Can the natural law change? Thomas's answer is that it can change with respect to addition but not with respect to subtraction (Ia-IIae, q. 94, a. 5). If by change we mean the addition of other laws, this is obviously possible, for the divine law and human law (both forms of positive law) add many particular norms to the natural law. But if by "change" we mean the elimination of some of the norms of the natural law or dispensation from them, the natural law is completely immutable, at least with respect to its first principles. Because there is room for exceptions among the principles that are derived from natural law (in the sense that it is not absolutely the same for everyone or known by everyone), the criterion "for the most part" is valid here too. The natural law is invariable for the majority of cases, but it can vary in some particular case because of some impediment that renders some precepts impossible to observe. Correspondingly, human law will contain certain norms that are not merely positive but fully embody the natural law and certain additional norms that are valid only on the basis of the human law itself (Ia-IIae, q. 95, a. 2).

Human law is changeable in itself both in the domain of reason (human reason is perfected gradually and, therefore, historically) and because of the men themselves who are ruled by it, since their conditions also change (Ia-IIae, q. 97, a. 1). These same considerations also lead Thomas to admit that custom can sometimes have the force of law as well.

As is evident, the whole treatment of law is determined by the criterion of rationality, which, moreover, permeates the definition of law itself. But it is not an abstract rationality; rather, it is rationality modeled on the Aristotelian ideal of what can be right in the majority of cases and is alert to the fact that in human affairs it is impossible to attain certainty of a mathematical sort. Thus, if the whole normative structure rests on an eternal and immutable law, its mediation and effects at the level of the action of rational creatures must be conditioned by the multiplicity of situations and particular cases; the structure must adapt itself to them with a certain flexibility. It is not by chance, then, that God himself promulgated a positive law (the *lex divina*) to integrate with the *lex aeterna*, nor (even more so) that there should be human laws.

Right, Justice, and Just War

Thomas's distinct attention to particular cases justifies the expansiveness of the "second part of the second part" of the *Summa* (the *secunda secundae*), devoted to a meticulous analysis of virtues and vices, for, as he explicitly says in the prologue, "universal moral discourse is less useful, since actions are particulars." As we have already noted, this second part is further divided into two sections. The first section, which is the longest, consists in the analysis of individual virtues and vices. The second part deals with people's different conditions or "states" (*status*) and in it Thomas considers, for example, the distinction between the active and the contemplative life (to which is attached the examination of the differing situations of the clergy and religious orders).

Of course, we will not go through the whole detailed treatment of virtues and vices here but will restrict ourselves to comments on a few particular points. Linked to the topic of law is, for instance, the treatment of right and justice. For Thomas, justice is that virtue that orders our actions in relation to other people. Hence, the rectitude involved in justice not only has to do with he who acts but constitutes a relation to another according to a certain mode of equality. The equality in this context can be objective and natural—and in this case defines the sphere of natural right—or it can be established by public or private consent—and in these cases we have the sphere of positive right. Justice, in accord with the traditional definition, is understood as the will to give to each person his due, his right (IIa-IIae, q. 58, a. 1), or rather to give to each person what belongs to him (q. 58, a. 11). It always regards our relationship with others and, consequently, the external actions by which we relate to each other. Following Aristotle, Thomas divides justice into *commutative* and *distributive*. The first has to do with the relationship between parts, that is, between two private persons, whereas the second has to do with the relationship of the whole and the parts, that is, the distribution of what is common to individuals according to a criterion of proportionality (q. 61, a. 1). In the domain of moral virtues in the strict sense, justice is certainly the most noble and important virtue (q. 58, a. 12). It is no accident that whereas the other moral virtues are rooted in the sensitive appetite, justice is rooted in the rational appetite, namely, the will. It is indispensable to appeal to the rational appetite to grasp the just proportion in intersubjective relationships and to be able to give each person what belongs to him (q. 58, a. 4).

To the topic of justice we can connect that of just war (which Thomas actually discusses in an earlier question: q. 40). For a war to be considered just, three conditions must be met. (a) It must be waged by someone who has the authority, that is, someone who is charged with the care of the commonweal, that is, by princes. (b) The cause must be just, for whoever is attacked must be attacked because of some fault. (c) Those prosecuting the war must have the right intention, that is, pursuing good and avoiding evil.

This third condition is not the same as the second. Even if the cause is just, the prince can wage war with a less than honest intention (out of cruelty, the wish to do damage, or to dominate, according to some of the examples that Thomas takes from Augustine). Clerics and bishops cannot take part in conflicts, because military operations take away from the contemplation of God and because it does not belong to them to kill and shed blood (if necessary, like the martyrs, they should be prepared to shed their own blood as a witness to their faith). In war it is legitimate not to let your enemy know your plans, but it is never right to lie to or deceive your enemy, because agreements and the norms of war should always be respected.

Although Thomas does not hesitate to reject the possibility of clergy taking an active part in conflicts (so as to distance himself from the religious military orders), he does not go beyond the limits of his time in accepting the violent repression of heretics by the secular power (IIa-IIae, q. 11, a. 3). The question can be considered, first of all, on the part of the heretics themselves, who by their sin merit exclusion not only from the Christian community by excommunication but also from the whole world by death. If counterfeiters are condemned to death, there is no doubt heretics should be too, since they have committed a worse crime, or so the argument—which is not particularly brilliant or persuasive—goes. The question can also be considered on the part of the Church, which must be merciful toward those who err and must desire their conversion. These exigencies are legitimate, for the Church does not immediately condemn the heretics but makes two preliminary attempts at correction. If these are unsuccessful and there is no further hope of conversion, it is appropriate, in Thomas's view, for the Church to concern herself with the salvation of the others, separating the heretic from the rest of the Christian community by excommunication and handing him over to the judgment of the secular power so that he be eliminated from the world (*et ulterius relinquit eum iudicio saeculari a mundo exterminandum per mortem*).

Thomas's position on usury is just as clear but much less sinister. To loan money at interest is unequivocally a sin since, in fact, to charge interest on the sum loaned is either to sell the same thing twice or to sell a non-existent good. Thomas's argument is based on the distinction between things whose use coincides with their consumption and things whose use does not. In the case of wine, for instance, the use of the thing is identical with its consumption and so it cannot be calculated as a value that is independent of the thing itself. If I sell wine, it is normal for me to expect that it be consumed. So, I should not charge for the use of the wine on top of charging for the wine itself (or grain). In the case of other goods, property and its use can be distinct from each other. A house has one value in what concerns property and another in what concerns rent or use. Money, as Aristotle suggested in Book VI of the *Nicomachean Ethics* and Book I of the *Politics*, is in the first category of goods, those whose use coincides with their consumption. Money was invented to make commercial exchange possible but is not itself merchandise. For this reason, selling money means selling the same thing twice or selling a nonexistent good whose value is distinct from the value of the money itself. So, it is illegitimate, and whoever lends money at interest must return whatever interest was collected. The same holds for interest in the form of other goods besides money, unless it is a question of freely given gifts of gratitude or symbolic recompense. This is a position that Thomas takes in many other places.[44] It could always be objected that those who lend money ask for interest that is commensurate with risk and time. But this too is unacceptable because—as we have already seen in part in *De emptione et venditione ad tempus*, c. 3—time is not a good at our disposal such that we are able to sell it.

Many other vices in the dense forest of the *secunda secundae* offer Thomas occasions for inquiries worthy of interest. This is so for the question of irony, which occurs when a person pretends to be less than he is and is a sin when it opposes the truth (q. 113, a. 1); or the discussion of gluttony, which includes among its species the pursuit of food that is "too nicely prepared" (a kind of condemnation *ante litteram* of *nouvelle cuisine*: q. 148, a. 4); or the well-constructed subdivisions of the species of lust (q. 154). The treatment of *curiositas* (q. 167)—a vice that earned a forceful condemnation already in Augustine's time—merits some consideration. The curiosity that is in question here does not have to do with the knowledge of truth in itself (which is always positive, apart from certain particular and accidental cases, as when someone becomes proud about his

---

44. We find the same position, for example, in the *De malo*, as we already saw, and in his letter to the Countess of Flanders.

knowledge) but has to do with the appetite and desire to acquire knowledge. Now, this desire can be perverse (from the subjective point of view) in at least four cases: (a) when it leads us to turn away from study that is necessary toward study that is less useful; (b) when we desire to know something that it is not legitimate to investigate, as when people seek to know the future by asking demons (superstitious curiosity); (c) when we seek the truth about creatures without referring this knowledge to its due end, namely, knowledge of God; (d) when we desire to know a truth that exceeds our intelligence. The third case, above all, clearly inspired by Augustine (it is not by chance that Thomas himself quotes the *De vera religione*), could make us think of an absolute condemnation of the autonomy of purely natural or philosophical inquiry into the real. But, replying to the third objection, Thomas explains that the study of philosophy is legitimate and laudable (*licitum et laudabile*) because of the truth that the philosophers manage to grasp on account of what God has indirectly revealed to them. Thomas, thus, does not condemn philosophy as depraved curiosity. Had he thought otherwise, he would not have continued to study it until the very last years of his life and to make wide use of it (and if he had not engaged in this way with philosophy, the present book would not have much point). Nevertheless, as we already noted in the preface, Thomas does not see philosophy as an option that is still open and present. The age of philosophy came to a close with the Greeks (and, in part, with the Arabs). But philosophy is a precious resource for those among Christians who intend to dedicate their life to the *officium sapientis*, to the task of the wise man.

The Primacy of the Contemplative Life

The last part of the *secunda secundae* is dedicated to the analysis and comparison of the different states and conditions of life. Thomas, without hesitation (drawing heavily from Book X of the *Nicomachean Ethics*), proposes the primacy of the contemplative life (q. 182, a. 1), of that life that essentially consists in the consideration of the truth. This is another element of the intellectualism (in the restricted, moderate sense of the term that we have adopted) that marks the whole of Thomas's thought. The contemplative life pertains fundamentally (*quantum ad ipsam essentiam actionis*) to the intellect, even if the intention to devote ourselves to this life belongs to the will, and the consideration of the truth cannot be dissociated from the love and joy it produces (q. 180, a. 1). The moral virtues themselves, in the strict sense, do not essentially belong to contemplation, although they do contribute to disposing us toward it by correctly channeling the passions (aq. 180, a. 2). The contemplation that Thomas discusses is, obviously, that of divine truth. But the contemplation of the divine effects (the world) is indissolubly linked to it, for in the present state these effects are, for us, a privileged path to arrive at God. The contemplation of the divine essence constitutes, as by now we well know, the essence of eternal beatitude.

In this impassioned defense of the primacy of the contemplative life Thomas does not go much beyond the preceding theological tradition.[45] Still, two aspects are perhaps worthy of further attention. First, the defense of the contemplative life is also a defense of the prerogatives of the religious orders over those of the secular clergy (thus, we might almost say, self-interested), and it is not by chance that the comparison of these two states of life comes immediately afterward. Prelates (who are members of the secular clergy) are employed in the pastoral care of souls, and so are immersed in the affairs and activities of the world. The religious (especially the religious of the mendicant orders and, in Thomas's specific case, the Dominicans) can make contemplation not only their goal beyond this life but also their principal goal in the present, through detachment from worldly goods and activities. The second point to consider is of a more theoretical import. Contemplation too is an activity, but a strictly intellectual activity, which consists in the consideration of truth. For Thomas, we certainly cannot separate loving God from knowing God. But it is always the latter that has the priority and that implies the former (assuming it under itself). Thomas's universe is a rational one that must be studied and understood—within the limits of the possible—through what is most essential to man: his intellect.

It is not surprising, then, that Thomas's strenuous defense of the primacy of the contemplative life includes one exception with respect to worldly activity that is not irrelevant: teaching (q. 181, a. 3). In the Scholastic lexicon, teaching (*docere*) includes both the activity of study and research[46] and didactic activity in the strict sense. Teaching is, in sum, making others participants in our own doctrine. But this external activity assumes the possession of something—*doctrina*—that belongs to the contemplative life to the extent that it is the interior man who dedicates himself in this way to the consideration of intelligible truth and rejoices in it. In this regard there comes to mind the verse of Ecclesiasti-

45. We will have to wait for Henry of Ghent and Meister Eckhart to encounter Scholastic masters who are disposed to prefer Martha to Mary and, thus, the active life to the contemplative life (at least in some respects). On this question, see P. Porro, "La (parziale) rivincita di Marta: Vita attiva e vita contemplativa in Enrico di Gand," in *Vie active et vie contemplative au Moyen Âge et au seuil de la Renaissance*, Collection de l'École Française de Rome 423, ed. C. Trottmann (Rome: École Française de Rome, 2009), 155–72.

46. We must not forget that, to become a master of theology, more than twenty years of study and university formation (on average) were necessary, and that a *magister* continued to study and publish during his whole teaching career.

cus that Thomas chose as the epigraph for his commentary on Boethius's *De ebdomadibus*: "First run to your house and recollect yourself. There entertain yourself and develop your thoughts."

As we mentioned earlier, it is sufficiently probable that Thomas chose to comment on Aristotle's *Nicomachean Ethics* precisely to prepare himself adequately for drafting the *secunda pars* of the *Summa*, that is, the properly ethical part. This extremely scrupulous work on the *Nicomachean Ethics* took shape in two principal texts: the *Tabula libri Ethicorum* and the *Sententia libri Ethicorum*. The *Tabula* is a kind of very detailed analytical index of the topics dealt with in the *Nicomachean Ethics* that also takes account of the work already done on it by Albert the Great. It is a meticulous catalogue produced around 1270 that aims at completely mastering Aristotle's text and facilitating access to it. It is possible that Thomas prepared a series of lists that had to be revised and reordered by his secretaries and that he did not then have time or the possibility of preparing a definitive copy. On the other hand, since it was a work that was directed toward personal use (as we are led to believe), a final revision, while indispensable for a text meant to be published, would have been rather superfluous. The *Tabula* testifies in general to a characteristic of Thomas's method of work, which often made use of loose notes and gave secretaries the task of developing a unitary text, with Thomas usually intervening in the final draft (but not in this case, as is made evident by some duplicates and some doctrinally dubious passages).

The *Sententia* is the real commentary on the *Nicomachean Ethics*, composed between 1271 and 1272 in preparation for, or perhaps parallel to, the redaction of the *secunda pars*. The title that has come down to us, *Sententia*, indicates something that, at least in part, is different from an *expositio*, that is, a strictly literal commentary. Thomas proceeds (after having analytically outlined all of the pertinent material in the *Tabula*) by expounding the principal lines of the work without discussing individual textual passages. The prologue gives us some suggestions about the place of ethics in the edifice of knowledge, which confirms what we have already seen. Ethics is in its entirety under the sign of rationality. It is proper to reason to recognize the order of things. But that happens in different ways. There is an order that reason does not create but can know and consider. It is the order inherent in natural things. There is also an order that is created autonomously by reason, and this is the one that reason intuits between its own concepts and the sounds (uttered words) used to express these concepts. A third type of order is that determined by reason in the operations of the will. A fourth type of order is that produced by reason in external things when it produces artifacts. The first type of order defines the object of natural philosophy (understood in a broad sense and including the whole sphere of orders not produced by reason and studied by mathematics and metaphysics). The second type is proper to rational philosophy or logic. The third type—relating to voluntary actions—belongs to morality and the fourth to the mechanical arts. Moral philosophy, then, has the task of considering human actions as ordered among themselves and to an end and as arising from the will or rational appetite. All other human actions, if they are not voluntary, have no moral relevance. Summing up, we could say that the subject of moral philosophy is human action ordered to an end or also, more concretely, man as he acts voluntarily for an end.

Although we cannot enter into the specifics of Thomas's commentary, we should stress that it is hard to overestimate Thomas's debt to Aristotelian ethics. Many commentators, including recent ones, speak of Thomas baptizing and Christianizing Aristotelian ethics, introducing God where he is hardly mentioned. This is true but it is, frankly, little more than a truism, a banality, that philosophically explains very little. The reality is that the whole plot of the *secunda pars* of the *Summa* is situated in an Aristotelian framework. And this is the case not only for what regards the general description of moral action (and so the relationship between intellect and will and the role of prudence) but also for the extensive and detailed analysis itself of the virtues and vices. In effect, Thomas's original purpose in undertaking the *Summa* was to produce an alternative to the theological textbooks in use at the time and, above all, the casuistic ones (in which Christian morality was broken up into a myriad of more or less concrete cases, mostly for the use of confessors). He achieved the result by constructing a rational whole inspired by the fundamental principles of Aristotelian practical philosophy: the rationality of human action, the morally neutral role of the passions, the construction of an ethics founded on the virtues as habits or dispositions that incline us toward determinate acts. The confused mass of possible moral cases for the confessor to keep in mind gives way to an interpretive scheme that is extensive and analytical, to be sure, but that also has an intrinsic rational coherence. And although the Christian God takes the place of the divine things of which Aristotle speaks, it is also true that the final end itself of human action that the theologian Thomas posits—beatitude as intellectual contemplation of the divine essence—is largely borrowed from the speculative felicity proposed in Book X of the *Nicomachean Ethics*.

THE *QUAESTIONES DISPUTATAE DE VIRTUTIBUS* AND THE *QUAESTIONES DISPUTATAE DE UNIONE VERBI INCARNATI*

Another set of disputed questions is also linked to the *secunda pars*, namely, the *Quaestiones disputatae de virtutibus*, which can be dated to 1271–72 and thus as contemporaneous with the drafting of the *secunda secundae*. This is a collection 36 articles devoted, in order, to: fraternal correction, hope, and the cardinal virtues. The content, thus, mostly overlaps with the corresponding section of the *Summa*. On the other hand, as with the *De malo*, it is not hard to imagine what would have led Thomas to hold disputations (or to oversee their redaction and publication) at roughly the same time as the drafting of the *Summa*—a motivation similar to the one that still leads university professors today to offer courses on topics that they are concurrently researching and on which they plan to publish something. This not only saves time but forces them to go more deeply into the material and make it clearer to others.

There are major problems with trying to fix the dates of the *Quaestiones disputatae de unione Verbi incarnati*, which treats of the problem of the hypostatic union in Christ (that is, of the union between the divine nature and human nature). Thomas deals with this issue in the *tertia pars* of the *Summa* (above all in q. 17), which he could have started while he was still in Paris or after his return to Italy in 1272 to teach in Naples. If these disputed questions—like those on the soul, evil, and virtue—were also drafted shortly before or in parallel with the corresponding sections of the *Summa*, this work should be dated to the very end of the second Parisian regency or to the beginnings of the Neapolitan regency (as M. M. Mulchahey suggests).[47] But the problem is that Thomas does not hold exactly the same position in the *De unione Verbi* that he does in the *Summa*. In the *Summa* Thomas holds that there is one being in Christ for the two natures, but in the *De unione Verbi* he holds that each nature has its own being (the one principal and the other secondary). Using the same criterion to date this work as is used for the other three disputed questions just mentioned, therefore, seems problematic. It is hard to imagine that Thomas would have adopted different theses about the same question in texts composed at the same time. But there is another difficulty, one that Concetta Luna has recently pointed ed out. In the *reportatio* of his course on Book III of the *Sentences,* the young Giles of Rome already seems to cite Thomas's *De unione Verbi*. Now, Giles's

---

47. M. M. Mulchahey, *"First the Bow is Bent in Study": Dominican Education before 1350* (Studies and Texts 132) (Toronto: Pontifical Institute of Mediaeval Studies, 1998), 315–18.

reportatio can be dated either to 1269–71 or to 1270–72, and both possibilities seem incompatible with the dating of the *De unione Verbi* to the spring of 1272, right at the end of the second sojourn in Paris (toward which other elements of external criticism point) or at the beginning of the sojourn in Naples.[48] With respect to the doctrinal discrepancy (or internal criticism) just noted, it has been a topic of discussion for centuries, since it is not easy to ascertain which text reflects Thomas's authentic—or more mature—position. It should be observed, in any case, that the thesis Thomas defends in the *Summa* is the one that he maintained his whole career. The *De unione Verbi*, if it is not an indication of a change of mind in the last phase of Thomas's thought (which the external chronology does not clearly support), must still be considered an exception that is not easily harmonized with the rest of Thomas's work.

I *QUODLIBETA* I–VI AND XII

Clarifications on Human Action and Angelic Nature

Thomas held some quodlibetal disputations during the second Parisian regency as well. These are *Quodlibeta* I–VI and XII according to the current numeration.[49] The chronology of the *Quodlibeta* has not been definitively established and we can still hypothesize (on the basis, for example, of dates determined by Gauthier in the Leonine edition) that *Quodlibet* VI was disputed before *Quodlibeta* IV and V. *Quodlibet* XII is a reportatio that Thomas himself did not revise. Gauthier suggests the following chronology:

> *Quodlibet* I: Lent, 1269
> *Quodlibet* II: Advent, 1269
> *Quodlibet* III: Lent, 1270
> *Quodlibet* IV: Lent, 1271
> *Quodlibet* V: Advent, 1271
> *Quodlibet* VI: Advent, 1270
> *Quodlibet* XII: Lent, 1272

As is the case with quodlibetal disputations, the topics are quite varied, and it is not possible to offer a unified reconstruction of the whole. Many questions,

---

48. See Aegidius Romanus (Giles of Rome), *Reportatio Lecturae super libros I-IV Sententiarum. Reportatio Monacensis. Excerpta Godefridi de Fontibus* (Corpus Philosophorum Medii Aevi. Testi e studi 17), ed. C. Luna (Florence: SISMEL-Edizioni del Galluzzo, 2003). Overturning the hypothesis of Mulchahey (who, in fact, is cited as "Mulchaney"), Luna suggests that the *De unione* must be "situated at the beginning rather than at the end of the second stay in Paris" (23), and, therefore, prior to Thomas's *Quodlibet* IV (usually situated in the Lenten session of 1271).

49. On the numeration of the *Quodlibeta* see p. 87 above.

however, permit Thomas to restate or clarify positions (including philosophical ones) adopted elsewhere. Thus—to cite just a few examples—Thomas again discusses the unity of substantial form (*Quodlibet* I, q. 4);[50] the impossibility of demonstrating a temporal beginning of the world (*Quodlibet* III, q. 14, a. 2; *Quodlibet* XII, q. 5, a. 1); and the human intellect's inability to know individuals (*Quodlibet* XII, q. 7, a. 1). On three occasions Thomas again explains that the separated soul is subject to the action of fire, not as something hot, but because the soul's proper function is impeded (*Quodlibet* II, q. 7, a. 1; *Quodlibet* III, q. 10, a. 1; *Quodlibet* XII, q. 23, a. 2).[51]

In other areas Thomas proposes an interesting integration or clarification. In regard to human action, or the practical sphere, Thomas explains that conscience cannot be mistaken. We cannot, in fact, be deceived about first principles (just as in the speculative sphere we cannot be mistaken about first self-evident principles), although it is possible to be mistaken about more particular knowledge. Error in both speculative and practical reasoning is caused, then, by particular false premises and not by universal ones. To use Thomas's own example, the conscience of the heretic who undertakes never to swear errs because it holds that all swearing is contrary to the divine commandment (false particular premise) but does not err regarding the general principle (we should not do anything against the divine precepts) (*Quodlibet* III, q. 12, a. 1).

In the area of angelology Thomas again proposes the thesis according to which the angel is a composite of essence and being rather than of matter and form (*Quodlibet* II, q. 2, a. 1). Here Thomas is not afraid to return to the basic core of the Avicennian doctrine of the indifference of essences, observing that being is not an element in the definition of anything and so has an accidental characteristic: "Because everything that is outside a thing's essence may be called an accident; the being which pertains to the question 'Is it?' is an accident."[52] Then Thomas again notes that angels are in place through the application of their *virtus* (*contactus virtutis*), and so by their operations more than by their substance (a thesis condemned by Tempier; cf. *Quodlibet* I, q. 3, a. 1). Thus, on this view, an angel can pass from one point in space to another by deciding to pass freely through intermediary points or not (and so applying his *virtus* in a successive way only to the two extremes: *Quodlibet* I, q. 3, a. 2). Pre-

---

50. Thomas again says that there cannot be more than one substantial form in each being and that the rational soul—as the one form of the human composite—brings about the corruption of the previous forms.

51. The last article is missing in the *reportatio*.

52. This thesis is obviously Avicennian but, curiously, in this article Thomas appeals to Averroes, who usually is presented as an opponent of this thesis.

cisely because the movements of angels depend on their acts of understanding and willing and are not bound by corporeal extension, they are measured by a discrete time (made of instances that are really distinct from each other—an "atomic" time, so to speak) different from continuous time that measures all celestial and sublunary movements and that is the only time of which Aristotle spoke (*Quodlibet* II, q. 2, a. 1). It is necessary to explain here that Thomas acknowledges two distinct measures for the substantial being of angels and for their operations. The substantial existence of angels (but also that of celestial bodies) is measured by the *aevum* (sempiternity), a stable and simultaneous duration that distinguishes itself from divine eternity only because in God essence and being are identical, while in the angels they form a composite, and this composition (which implies, as we know, a form of potentiality) is sufficient to mark an ontological distance between two kinds of duration that are both supertemporal. The operations of angels (the acts of understanding and willing and *ad extra* operations in the physical world that depend on such acts) are measured by a discrete time (*tempus discretum, tempus angelorum*) that does not have the same nature as continuous cosmic time, which measures all the movements of sublunary beings. This is an "atomic" time made up of really distinct instants (since every angel can persist in a determinate operation as it pleases) and not infinitely divisible without ever resolving into instants, as is the case with the continuous cosmic time that Aristotle describes. To these different forms of duration Thomas subsequently adds "participated eternity" (*aeternitatis participata*), that is, the beatific vision, which is nothing other than a participation in divine eternity. However, this participated eternity is distinct from the *aevum* (and this is a point on which Thomas differs from all the other masters of the period) because the *aevum*, as we said, is absolutely stable, whereas participated eternity is subject to the variation linked to epektasis, which is the incremental beatitude of the vision of the divine essence.[53]

Obviously, the *Quodlibeta* are not the only place where Thomas reflects on angels. Ample treatments of them appear in both *Summae* and in the various disputed questions, and we have already mentioned some of these. It is worth pointing out that, for Thomas, angelology is a mixed or limit topic, since it not only pertains to theology (as is natural) but raises—directly or indirectly—many philosophical and scientific questions: those about the temporality of angelic op-

---

53. The reunification of the soul with the body after the final judgment is an example of this increase in beatitude. On all these non-Aristotelian forms of duration accepted by Thomas and, in diverse ways, by the other masters of the thirteenth and fourteenth centuries, see P. Porro, *Forme e modelli di durata nel pensiero medievale: L'aevum, il tempo discreto, la categoria "quando,"* Ancient and Medieval Philosophy, I/16 (Leuven: Leuven University Press, 1996), 367–68.

erations are already a good example, as are those—likewise fascinating—about the modality of the knowledge and language of the angels.[54] And it is no accident that Thomas also decided to devote a treatise to simple substances, the *De substantiis separatis*, programmatically divided in two parts: one on what the philosophers said about the intelligences and the other on what revelation says about angels. We will discuss this opuscule and the meaning of this partition at the end of this chapter.

THE FIGURE OF THE *MAGISTER* AND HIS PROFESSIONAL DEONTOLOGY

The questions on the duties (the "professional deontology" we might say) of the *magister* of theology are perhaps especially interesting. In *Quodlibet* I, q. 7, a. 2 it is asked whether a person should abandon the study of theology—even if he is suited to teach others—to dedicate himself to the salvation of souls. Thomas's response is based on the principle that he who directs the work (*architector*) has a more important role than those who are limited to carrying it out, that is, the manual laborers. He adds that "in the spiritual edifice" the manual laborers are they who dedicate themselves in particular to the care of souls, administering the sacraments or other such things. The principal builders, however, are the bishops and doctors of theology, who "research and teach the way that the others should procure the salvation of souls." Thus, "absolutely speaking, it is better to teach sacred doctrine—and more meritorious if done with good intentions—than to see to the salvation of this person or that person in particular," that is, so long as the concrete circumstances do not demand otherwise. This is an authoritative witness—but by no means an isolated one—of the acute professional self-consciousness that the Parisian masters of theology had developed in the second half of the thirteenth century, seeing themselves as the leaders of

54. Regarding the modality of angelic knowledge, see n. 133. On the question of language, in the Commentary on the *Sentences* Thomas applies to the angels the same division into phases that he applies to human language: in the first moment the *species concepita* remains in the intellect alone; then it is "ordered" by being manifested to others and, therefore, it becomes *verbum*, even if purely interior (*verbum cordis*); in the end it is manifested externally by means of signs that constitute a veritable *locutio* but which, in the case of the angels, are intelligible rather than physical (*In II Sent.*, d. 2, q. 2, a. 3). In q. 9 of the *Quaestiones de veritate* (*De communicatione scientiae angelicae*), especially in a. 4 (*Utrum unnus angelus alii loquatur*), Thomas holds that an angel employs language to manifest to the others a thought initially "reserved," reshaping the role of intelligible signs. What really matters is the intention which directs the manifestation (*ordo intentionis ad manifestandum*) and which allows the interior word to be conveyed to an interlocutor. In the *Summa theologiae* (Ia, q. 107, a. 1) the jettisoning of intelligible signs seems already a *fait accompli*: the language of the angels is best understood as a direct communication of the intelligible content (without the necessity of a semiotic mediation) founded on the intentionality of the speaker. In other words, each angel can manifest directly his own concepts,

Christianity.[55] To see this it is sufficient also to consider *Quodlibet*, III, q. 4, a. 1, which asks whether it is legitimate for someone to ask for the license to teach theology. Here the teaching chair is directly compared to the pontifical office. There are three differences between them. The first difference is that he who receives the teaching chair does not receive a form of eminence that he did not previously have but only the opportunity to communicate the science that he already possessed. The second difference is that the perfection of science, on the basis of which someone would obtain a teaching chair, is a perfection that regards man in himself, whereas the eminence of the pontifical office regards man in his relationship with others. The third difference is that the teaching chair makes us suitable through science, whereas the pontifical office makes us so through charity. Now, since desiring something that belongs to our perfection is not at all improper, but, on the contrary, praiseworthy, whereas seeking power over others is vile, there is nothing wrong with asking for the license to teach and, therefore, a university chair. Indeed, "communicating our science to others is praiseworthy and belongs to charity." The only danger to avoid in this case is presumption. But whereas we could never know whether we possess sufficient charity to be able to aspire to the episcopal or pontifical office, we can know with certainty whether we have the science required to teach. It is plausible that this question was raised to put a mendicant friar like Thomas—who had to distance himself from a more active life to focus on contemplation—in a difficult spot. But we have already seen how Thomas judges the activity of contemplation (and the fundamental precept of charity, which the mendicant orders took as the inspiration for their way of life) to be compatible with teaching.

In *Quodlibet* V, q. 12, a. 1 Thomas considers whether a doctor who has always preached and taught principally because of vainglory would receive the aureole if he repented on his deathbed. The aureole or nimbus, we should recall, was thought to be the distinct sign of doctors, that is, the fruit of doctrine. Thomas responds negatively. Repenting restores the rewards previously earned but it does not create new ones. Consequently, if someone never went about his teaching in a meritorious way, he could not regain what he never lost but simply never achieved.

The *magister*, for his part, should not appeal to *auctoritates*[56] but give rational arguments. A Scholastic disputation in the university,

---

but only to whom he intends to do so (to guarantee a minimal privacy . . .). On this question see the study cited already in n. 53 in Chapter 3.

55. See E. Marmursztejn, *L'autorité des maîtres: Scolastique, normes et société au XIII siècle* (Paris: Les Belles Lettres, 2007), especially Chapter 1.

56. This occurs with adversaries in theological disputes. In this context Thomas returns to what he

is not aimed at removing error but at instructing the listeners so that they might be led to the understanding of the truth that they hold, and so it is necessary to use rational arguments that seek out the root of the truth and make known in what way what is said is true. Otherwise, if a master decides a question on mere authority, the listeners will doubtless be certain that things are as he says but they will not acquire any science or understanding and they will go away empty.[57]

This is, of course, another fine defense of the role of rationality and of the function of teachers.

From the point of view of the auditors (the students) Thomas explains that no one can be excused, invoking simplicity or ignorance, if he follows the erroneous opinions of some master on some matter of faith and the rightness of customs. In all other areas there is no problem if the students follow different opinions expressed by different masters. If some master realizes that he has done damage by his teaching, he must immediately revoke what he has taught. That could actually happen in different ways. If the doctrine taught is false, evidently there is no doubt that the master must take it back. If the doctrine is true, the damage could come from two causes: either a doctrine is proposed that is so subtle that it misleads the simple or it is proposed in a confused and disorderly way that leaves the student similarly confused and perplexed. In these cases the master has the duty to try to explain himself more clearly.

THE COMMENTARIES ON ARISTOTLE
The Framework of the Commentaries

The commentaries on Aristotle's works constitute a fundamental part of Thomas's output. We have already looked at the Commentary on the *De Anima* and in this chapter at the *Sententia libri Ethicorum* and the *Tabula libri Ethicorum*. To these we must add other commentaries that substantially occupy Thomas's last years of activity. These are the commentaries composed during Thomas's second regency in Paris and his time in Naples. It is possible that his *Sentencia libri de sensu et sensato* was already begun in Rome and finished in Paris before 1270. The *Sententia* or *Expositio super Physicam* and the *Sententia super Meteora* both date from the second Parisian regency (1268–70), before 1270. The *Expositio libri Peryermenias*[58] (that is, the Commentary on the *De interpretatione*) can be situated between December 1270 and October 1271. The *Expositio libri Posteriorum* (that is, the Commentary on the *Posterior Analytics*), was begun at the same time

---

had proposed in the *De rationibus fidei*, namely, that authorities must be used who are accepted by the different interlocutors, or, in the absence of common *auctoriates*, natural reason must be appealed to.

57. *Quodlibet* IV, q. 9, a. 3.

58. Here we follow the spelling of this work adopted by the Leonine editors.

as the *Expositio libri Peryermenias* or immediately afterward and concluded in Naples, presumably before 1272. Thomas seems to have used James of Venice's translation of the *Posterior Analytics* for the first part of his commentary (I, cc. 1–26) and William of Moerbeke's for the rest (I, c. 27–II, c. 20). The *Sententia libri Politicorum* was undertaken in Paris, but it is hard to determine with precision the exact dates of its composition. The *Sententia libri Metaphysicae* also has an uncertain date. Since Thomas began to designate Book Lambda as Book XII after mid-1271, we can assume that the commentary on Books VII–XII follows that date, while the commentary on the earlier books was done between 1270 and 1271 (although Books II and III were subsequently corrected and revised). Nevertheless, it is possible that the work was completed in Naples. It is quite probable that the *Sententia super librum De caelo et mundo* and the *Sententia super libros De generatione et corruptione* belong to the Neapolitan period.

Not all of the commentaries are complete, and some of them were finished by Thomas's disciples. The *Sententia super Meteora* stops at Book II.[59] The *Expositio libri Peryermenias* stops at c. II, 2. The *Expositio libri Posteriorum* is complete even though, as we said, the first part used James of Venice's translation and the second, "Neapolitan," part used Moerbeke's. The *Sententia libri Politicorum* stops at Book III, c. 6.[60] The Commentary on the *De caelo et mundo* stops at the beginning of Book III. The Commentary on *De generatione et corruptione* stops at Book I, c. 5. The *Sententia libri Metaphysicae* does not go beyond Book XII. The complete commentaries are those on the *De anima*, the *De sensu et sensato* (which, as we will see, includes the Commentary on the *De memoria et reminiscentia*), the *Physica*, the *Posterior Analytics*, and the *Nicomachean Ethics*.

Two basic questions could be posed with respect to Thomas's intense work on Aristotle's texts; the one would be about the *how* and the other about the *why*. The first of these two is perhaps the simpler one. We will postpone responding to the other one until the end of our brief overview of Thomas's commentaries on Aristotle. If we consider the way in which Thomas deals with the reading and explanation of Aristotle's text, we cannot but observe that Thomas is an optimal commentator (often referred to in the glosses as the *Expositor*, to distinguish him from the *Commentator*, Averroes), respectful of the *intentio auctoris*, even when he explicitly says, as in a celebrated passage from the Commentary on the *De caelo*, that the point of philosophy consists not in knowing what people think or thought but in knowing how things truly are:

59. The Leonine edition of 1886 takes the commentary up to II, c. 5 to be authentic. But it seems that Thomas commented on all of Book II except for the last chapter. The commentary on c. 6, however, appears to have been lost.

60. In many editions the missing part is completed by the commentary of Peter of Auvergne.

Now, some claim that these poets and philosophers, and especially Plato, did not understand these matters in the way their words sound on the surface, but wished to conceal their wisdom under certain fables and enigmatic statements. Moreover, they claim that Aristotle's custom in many cases was not to object against their understanding, which was sound, but against their words, lest anyone should fall into error on account of their way of speaking. So says Simplicius in his commentary. But Alexander held that Plato and the other early philosophers understood the matter just as the words sound literally, and that Aristotle undertook to argue not only against their words but against their understanding as well. Whichever of these may be the case, it is of little concern to us, because the study of philosophy aims not at knowing what men think (*senserint*), but at what is the truth of things.[61]

Although he subordinates the attempt to identify the author's intention to the inquiry into truth (an approach that differs from the "professional" attitude of Siger of Brabant, for example), Thomas never goes so far as to neglect the first task by hastily Christianizing Aristotle (even if certain interpretations are benevolent)[62] or immediately using him for his own purposes.[63] It is not surprising that

61. *In libros De caelo et mundo*, I, l. 22, c. 10.

62. The example of "benevolent" interpretation that most often returns is the attempt (rooted, moreover, in a potentially ambiguous passage from *De substantia orbis* of Averroes) to make of Aristotle's prime mover, not only a cause of movement, but also the cause of the being of what ensues (*In De caelo*, I, l. 6 and l. 8; *In Phys.*, VIII, l. 3; *In Metaph.*, II, l. 2 and VI, l. 1). A good example of the contrary attitude can be found in the Commentary on the *Physics* (*In Phys.*, VIII, lect. 2,): "Indeed some, attempting in vain to show that Aristotle has not spoken contrary to faith, have said that Aristotle does not intend here to prove as a truth that motion is eternal, but to introduce arguments on both sides, as if for a point in doubt. But because of his method of procedure this appears to be nonsense." On the question of the cases in which Thomas distances himself from Aristotle, see M. D. Jordan, "Thomas Aquinas' Disclaimers in the Aristotelian Commentaries," in *Philosophy and the God of Abraham: Essays in Memory of J. A. Weisheipl, OP*, ed. R. J. Long (Toronto: Pontifical Institute of Mediaeval Studies, 1991), 99–112.

63. See J. Jenkins, "Expositions of the Text: Aquinas's Aristotelian Commentaries," *Medieval Philosophy and Theology* 5 (1996): 36–62. Jenkins proposes moving beyond the division between "historicists" (for whom the aim of the commentaries is only that of explaining Aristotle) and "appropriationists" (for whom the commentaries express, the opinions of Thomas), trying to identify the principles that would have guided Thomas's hermeneutical work. On the one hand, following Aristotle, there is the appeal to the dialectical method of the discussions of the *éndoxa* (common opinions and those of predecessors). On the other hand, there is the adherence to what in contemporary analytic debates is called "externalism" (according to the terminology adopted by, for example, Tyler Burge, Hilary Putnam, and Colin McGinn), which is the thesis that the meaning of the terms of a speaker or a linguistic community depends at least partially on the context or milieu ("semantic externalism") and the individuation of certain mental states depends at least in part on the context or milieu of the subject ("mental content externalism"). From this perspective, each interpretive approach aims not only to clarify what the speaker or writer has in mind, but also to construct the best possible theory about what is in his milieu. In the specific case of Thomas, therefore, the commentaries aim not only to explicate the authentic positions of Aristotle, considered in isolation, but *at the same time* to elaborate the best possible theory about those things discussed by Aristotle, or about the direction in which

in the contemporary analytic approaches to Aristotle's work Thomas's commentaries are often treated—in regard to discussions of specific points—as being on the same level as twentieth-century commentaries and interpretations. In sum, Thomas's effort to understand what Aristotle wrote is particularly scrupulous and meticulous; it is an effort that testifies to an impressive scientific seriousness. Not all of the commentaries were carried out in the same way. Leaving aside the case of the *Tabula*, which is not even a commentary in the strict sense, we could divide the others into two main types. The difference between them is signaled by the different titles chosen by the Leonine editors (but always based on the manuscript traditions): *sentencia* or *sententia* and *expositio*. *Sentencia* (or *sententia*) indicates a literal commentary—but not one that is intensely analytical—in which there dominates the exigency to reestablish (even by personal interpretive work) all of Aristotle's fundamental *doctrinal* points. *Expositio* indicates a more fastidious commentary in which there dominates the concern to make every passage in the text *fully intelligible*.[64] Thomas did not use the *quaestio* format in his commentaries on Aristotle or a mixed format (*expositio + quaestiones*), which he did use in the case of Boethius's *De Trinitate*. We can only suppose that with regard to the Aristotelian texts the primary concern was to take up again and develop Albert's project of making Aristotle perfectly comprehensible to the Latins. This is not to say that Thomas does not intervene in the first person and does not manifest his own opinion on many occasions. But he always does so from the perspective of a total engagement with what was presented (beginning at least from the new statutes of the faculty of arts in 1255) as the organic encyclopedia of scientific knowledge. For Thomas, commenting on Aristotle does not mean dealing with a particular philosopher (or with the philosopher *par excellence*) but with the "system of thought" (in the Foucaultian meaning of the term) that took shape around the middle of the thirteenth century.

---

the mind of Aristotle might have inclined. In this work of "externalist integration" (similar to the procedure by means of which he tries to understand a substance by starting with what the accidents allow him infer about it) Thomas would be left to be guided by both his metaphysical principles and the Christian faith.

64. The *sententia* is, in fact, one of the three levels of approach to a text in the same teaching process: "the grammatical explanation, word for word (the *littera*), the literal commentary or the paraphrase intended to extract the general sense and the nuance of the phrase (the *sensus*), and finally the in-depth and personal explanation of the professor concerning the passage commented on (the *sententia*)" (J. Hamesse, "Il modello della lettura nell'età della Scolastica," in *Storia della lettura*, ed. G. Cavallo and R. Chartier [Rome: Laterza, 2004], 104).

Thomas and the Commentatorial Tradition:
Natural Philosophy and Averroes

As evidence for what we have claimed, we should also remember the fact that Thomas paid particular attention to Aristotle's ancient and late ancient commentators, seeking to procure and read them as soon as they were made available in Latin (by William of Moerbeke above all): Alexander of Aphrodisias, Themistius, Simplicius (and, through this last commentator, all of the commentatorial material not yet available, including the Neo-Platonic commentaries). Again, this consideration of the work of the other commentators is not a display of erudition but a sign of the desire to engage with a stratified tradition that represented—except for theology—the entirety of scientific knowledge. We only need to read the prologue to the Commentary on the *De caelo* to see this. There Thomas notes that because Aristotle's text deals with different things, the ancient commentators were uncertain about the actual subject of this science. For Alexander of Aphrodisias, the subject is the universe, with all of its properties (the fact that it is finite, one, etc.). Others thought that the subject was the celestial body that moves in a circular motion as the title suggests (*De caelo* and not *De universo*), other bodies being discussed only in connection with it. Thomas explicitly cites the names of Iamblichus and Syrianus, which in all probability he found in Simplicius's commentary. Their thesis is regarded as having little plausibility, since the other bodies are treated of more extensively than the heavens.[65] Simplicius himself holds that Aristotle's intention was to deal principally with simple bodies and what they have in common according to their concept. The title of the work is *De caelo* because the heavens are the most important of the simple bodies, or so Simplicius maintains. But this thesis is hampered by the fact that Aristotle fails to discuss many things that pertain to simple bodies, which are considered only with respect to their lightness and heaviness. Thomas favors Alexander's interpretation: the *De caelo* treats of the universe and of simple bodies as parts. Simple bodies have their own order according to place. He does not speak about the other bodies (plants, animals, etc.) because each is ordered to a place, not in itself but through simple bodies (the elements). And, inversely, in the *De caelo* Aristotle speaks of the elements only insofar as they are parts of the universe (and so in reference to the lightness or heaviness that determines their natural place) and not in what regards the other properties or qualities (the fact of being hot or cold, etc.). As we can see, from the very beginning of the commentary Thomas engages with the whole

---

65. Iamblichus and Syrianus differ only with respect to the reason why Aristotle discusses these other bodies.

exegetical tradition that was available to him to discuss and determine the subject itself of the *De caelo*.

Thomas shows this same attentiveness in many other places in his commentaries. Another good example, among many, is the discussion about the place of the last sphere in the Commentary on the *Physics* (l. 7), in which Thomas reviews the whole peripatetic tradition from the Greeks to the Arabs. The problem in this text is the fact that, according to Aristotle, the last sphere moves but it is not in place, since it is his view that place is the limit of the containing body and the last sphere is not contained in any body. On the other hand, everything that moves must be in a place. Thomas singles out the solutions offered by Alexander (the last sphere is not in place in any manner and does not move according to place), Avicenna (the sphere moves according to position—*situs*—but not according to place), Avempace (rectilinear motion requires an external containing place but circular motion does not), Averroes (the last sphere is in place only *per accidens* in the sense that the center around which it revolves is in place), and Themistius (the last sphere is in place through its parts). Thomas adopts the last position (*In Phys.*, IV, l. 7).

Here as elsewhere, the reference to Averroes is worth noting, because Thomas's attitude toward the *Commentator* is never easy to ascertain. In many cases, when Thomas follows Averroes's solutions (or actual doctrinal proposals), he does so implicitly. But when it is a matter of disagreement, he signals this explicitly. This is especially evident in the Commentary on the *Physics*. Many aspects of this commentary are perfectly in line with Averroes's position. One example is the interpretation of time, which is taken as coinciding materially with movement but requiring the formal complement of the soul's activity of counting or measuring in order to exist. In many other places, however, Thomas does not fail to make known his dissent from Averroes:

1. Regarding the way Averroes justifies the possibility of movement in the void (Thomas contests not Aristotle's thesis but Averroes's defense of it, which is based on the proportionality between the mover and the mobile and the resistance of the mobile. Thomas calls Averroes's argumentation here "frivolous") (VI, l. 12).

2. Regarding the objection that Averroes raises about the possibility of assimilating the case of the movements of generation and corruption (that is, of movements according to the substance, which, being instantaneous, are neither temporal nor continuous) to the other forms of movement (VI, l. 5).

3. Regarding the way in which Averroes understands Aristotle's demonstration of the principle according to which everything that moves is moved by an-

other. (For Averroes, this is a *quia* demonstration, valid in a conditional sense, but for Thomas, it is a *propter quid* demonstration and, therefore, able truly to exhibit the reason why it is impossible for something moving to move itself [VII, l. 1].)

4. Regarding Averroes's interpretation, in Book VII, of the Aristotelian principle according to which there is no alteration of the first species of quality, whether this has to do with dispositions of the body or of the soul, including (with respect to the soul) virtues and vices. (Thomas scolds Averroes in an interesting way for not recognizing in this context Aristotle's usual procedure of never omitting what a conclusion principally depends on [VII, l. 5].)

5. Regarding Aristotle's discussion of the eternity of motion, which Averroes understands in a restricted way, that is, in reference only to the first movement. Thomas, on the contrary, understands it in reference to any movement. (Here too Thomas calls Averroes's arguments "frivolous" [VIII, l. 1].)

6. Regarding the principle according to which no finite magnitude possesses infinite power, which subtends the conclusion that an infinite movement can be produced only by an infinite power that does not possess magnitude or extension. In this case Averroes's position (according to which a power not possessing magnitude is neither finite nor infinite) is, in Thomas's judgment, both *contra intentionem Aristotelis et contra veritatem.* It is against Aristotle's intention because he had shown that a power that causes motion for an infinite time is infinite, and from this he later concludes that the power moving the heavens is not a power existing in a magnitude. And it is against the truth because every form is endowed with its own power (even if not in the order of extension) and such power can be finite or infinite (VIII, l. 21).

7. Regarding the incorruptibility of celestial bodies, which Averroes attributes to the fact that they are not endowed with a real hylomorphic composition. The form of celestial bodies (their soul, according to Averroes's interpretation) guarantees not their existence but only their capacity to move, and in this sense the celestial bodies are not in potency to non-being but only to place (to the fact of being able to find themselves in a different place). In this case also Averroes's solution *et veritati repugnat, et intentioni Aristoteli.* In reality, the celestial bodies are composed of matter and form like all other composite substances, but their matter is perfectly actualized by form, such that it is never in potency to another substantial form. And this is sufficient to guarantee their incorruptibility (VIII, l. 21).

The discussion in Book VIII about the sempiternity of motion merits a brief consideration, since Thomas is quite conscious of the fact that, basing himself on the Aristotelian text, Averroes introduces an explicit digression against the Christian doctrine of creation from nothing, taking his cue from the principle that whatever exists derives from some subject (for every change presupposes, in Aristotelian terms, a preceding subject) and the principle that everything derived from an opposite (as in the hypothesis of creation from nothing, being from nothing) must always root itself in the opposite subject and not in non-being in an absolute sense. The principal part of Thomas's answer is worth quoting:

But if one considers the matter rightly, he was deceived by a cause similar to the cause by which he claimed we are deceived, namely, by considering particular things. For it is clear that a particular active power presupposes the matter which a more universal agent produces, just as an artisan uses the matter which nature makes. From the fact, therefore, that every particular agent presupposes matter which it does not produce, one should not suppose that the first universal agent—which is active with respect to all being—should presuppose something not caused by it. Nor, moreover, is this in keeping with the intention of Aristotle, who in *Metaphysics* II proves that what is maximally true and maximally being is the cause of the being of all existing things. Hence the being which prime matter has—that is, a being in potency—is derived from the first principle of being, which is itself maximally being. Therefore, it is not necessary to presuppose for its action anything not produced by it. And because every motion needs a subject—as Aristotle proves here, and as is the truth of the matter—it follows that the universal production of being by God is neither motion nor change, but a certain simple coming forth. Consequently, "to be made" and "to make" are used in an equivocal sense when applied to this universal production of being and to other productions. Therefore, just as, if we should understand the production of things to be from God as eternal—as Aristotle supposed, and a number of the Platonists do—it is not necessary, indeed, it is impossible, that there have been a pre-existing but unproduced subject of this universal production, so also, in accord with the tenets of our faith, if we posit that he did not produce things eternally but produced them after they had not existed, it is not necessary to posit a subject for this universal production. It is evident, therefore, that what Aristotle proves here, namely, that every motion requires a mobile subject, is not against a tenet of our faith—for it has already been said that the universal production of things, whether or not it is understood as eternal, is neither a motion nor a change. For in order that there be motion or change, it is required that something be other now than it was previously, and, thus, there would be something previously existing, and, consequently, this would not be the universal production of things about which we are now speaking. Similarly, Averroes's statement that something is said to come to be accidentally from its opposite and *per se* from its subject is true in particular productions according to which this or that being comes to be, for instance, a man or a dog, but is not true in the universal production of being.[66]

66. *In libros Physicorum*, VIII, l. 2.

This passage displays quite well the complexity of levels on which Thomas operates as a commentator. At least in regard to the more delicate questions, Thomas attends to: (a) the *intentio auctoris,* that is, Aristotle's true position; (b) *veritas* itself, that is, how things actually are (an element that—as we saw in the Commentary on the *De caelo*—must prevail over the *intentio auctoris,* even though the *veritas* often coincides or can coincide with Aristotle's theses); (c) *fides,* that is, what is held by Christian doctrine founded on revelation.[67]

It is clear that (a) and (b) can or do very often coincide but not always, while (b) and (c) always coincide. Averroes's position can at times contradict all three levels: it can oppose Aristotle's intention, the truth, and what Christian faith suggests. What holds for Averroes evidently holds for all the other commentators or interpreters of Aristotle. But the engagement with Averroes is significant because it is also a confrontation between two different general interpretive strategies (*Expositor* vs. *Commentator*) and so over what is the best point of entry into Aristotle's text, and with it, the system of the sciences.

The Commentaries on the Works of Natural Philosophy

Since it is not possible here to examine each of the different interpretive positions that Thomas takes on the various points of the Aristotelian texts on which he comments, we will restrict our attention to the articulation of knowledge that the commentaries as a whole seem to suggest. This can be gleaned above all from the prologues that Thomas composed for the commentaries.[68]

What we said earlier about Thomas's relationship with the commentators of late antiquity and the Arabic-speaking commentators already permitted us to recall some of the more significant points of Thomas's Commentary on the *Physics.* We can add something about the way in which Thomas conceived the subdivision of natural philosophy (which is itself just one of the subdivisions of speculative philosophy) and the order of corresponding texts. The subject of natural philosophy is, for Thomas, as it is for Aristotle, mobile being. It is the strict business of the *Physics* to concern itself with what belongs to the realm of mobile being in general. The *De caelo* (which we have also discussed and precisely with respect to the debate about its subject) treats of those beings that engage only in local motion, namely, celestial bodies, and so interests itself in the structure of the universe. The *De generatione et corruptione* deals with substantial movement

67. See R. Imbach and A. Oliva, *La philosophie de Thomas d'Aquin: Repères* (Paris: Vrin, 2009), 138–39.

68. F. Cehevale and R. Imbach's approach to the prologues of Thomas's commentaries on Aristotle in *Prologe zu den Aristoteleskommentaren* (Frankfurt-Main: Klostermann, 1993) is magisterial.

(*motus ad formam*), that is, with the processes of generation and corruption together with the natural movements of the elements considered in general. The
same elements studied in regard to their particular transmutations are the subject
of the *Meteorologica* (or *Meteora*). The motion of mixed inanimate bodies is the
subject of the *De mineralibus* (which, in fact, is absent from the Aristotelian corpus strictly considered) and the motion of animate bodies is the subject of the *De
anima* and of the texts subsequent to it. To this quite simple schema of Aristotle's
texts of natural philosophy, which is drawn up in the prologue of the Commentary on the *Physics*, Thomas adds another in the prologue to the Commentary on
the *De caelo*, which is based on the parallel between natural processes and mental
or epistemological ones. Speculative reason, Thomas observes, follows a fourfold
order: that of proceeding from the general to the less general; that of proceeding
from the whole to the parts; that of proceeding from the simple to the composite;
and that in which we first consider what is principal (such as the heart and liver)
with respect to what is secondary (such as arteries and blood). This fourfold order
is also observed in the natural sciences. The *Physics*, which treats of mobile being
in general, considers what is common in nature. This is fittingly followed by the
De caelo, which considers the whole universe before its parts, since the simple
bodies (the elements) must be dealt with before the mixed ones and because the
celestial bodies are more noble and important than the others. How these different sections are harmonized with each other and what their respective subjects
are is determined in discussion with other commentators, as we saw before. The
prologue of the Commentary on the *De generatione et corruptione*, in reprising the
schema of the prologue to the Commentary on the *Physics*, explains why substantial movement is less important than local movement but more important than
the movements of alteration, growth, and diminishment. (The latter are processes
related to accidental forms, whereas the processes of generation and corruption
have to do with substantial forms.) The necessity of the *Meterologica* is justified
on the basis of the fact that the perfection accomplished in each science requires
that we do not stop at the universal but proceed at least to the species of the phenomena (but there is no science of individuals). In the *De generatione et corruptione* Aristotle expounds only the changes of the elements in general; the part related
to their specific changes is delegated to the *Meterologica*.

As far as the *De anima* goes (which we have already discussed), Thomas
has no doubts that psychology—as Aristotle has shown—belongs to the domain of natural philosophy, even if it then has much to offer also to ethics and
metaphysics.[69] Whereas the *De anima* concerns itself with the soul in itself, the

69. The route that will take the *scientia de anima* in the direction of metaphysics will arrive at its
destination, in fact, only in the Renaissance.

group of texts that is placed under the common title *Parva naturalia* concerns itself with the soul in relation to its link or application to the body (*secundum quamdam concretionem sive applicationem ad corpus*) but also with the soul in general. The consideration of the relationship of the body and soul in each living species belongs to the books on animals and plants. Among the texts of the *Parva naturalia*, Thomas is interested only in the *De sensu et sensato*, which focuses on the sensitive part of the soul and sensible things, and the *De memoria et reminiscentia*, which is considered to be a continuation of the *De sensu et sensato*. The two commentaries once more manifest the breadth of Thomas's scientific interests, which are not immediately directed toward theological use.

"Rational" Philosophy: The Commentaries on the *De interpretatione* and the *Posterior Analytics*

We have already seen in the Commentary on Boethius's *De Trinitate* a general division of philosophy based on the distinction proposed by Aristotle in Book VI of the *Metaphysics* and taken up again by Boethius himself. It was a classification within speculative knowledge, a classification of the speculative sciences: natural philosophy, mathematics, and first philosophy or metaphysics, to which Thomas adds *theologia nostra*, as we have seen. We have already discussed a possible subdivision within the speculative sciences, namely, in natural philosophy. But alongside of this, other fields must be taken into account, such as logic (rational philosophy) and practical philosophy. In regard to rational philosophy, its internal structure can be learned from the prologues to the commentaries on the *De interpretatione* and the *Posterior Analytics*. This schema is the same as the partition that Aristotle proposed for his logical writings. In the Commentary on the *De interpretatione* (dedicated to the provost of Louvain) Thomas starts from the claim that our intellect has three activities. We know the first two from the Commentary on Boethius's *De Trinitate*: the simple apprehension of indivisibles, by which the intellect grasps essences in themselves, and composing and dividing, by which the intellect forms judgments about the content apprehended. A third activity must be added to these two, an argumentative or "ratiocinative" one by which our intellect moves from things known to those not yet known. These three activities have a precise order among themselves. The first is ordered to the second, for there can be no composing or dividing except of what has been apprehended in a simple way. The second activity is ordered to the third, for once the truth is known by a judgment (truth, in Aristotle's view, always regards judgments and not the undivided apprehension of essences), we can go on to acquire certainties about what is not yet known. Aristotle's logical writings follow this partition: the *Categories* treat of the first operation of the intellect, the *De interpretatione* or *Perì hermēneías* the second, and the third is dealt with in the *Prior Analytics*, the *Posterior Analytics*, the *Topics*, the *Rhetoric*, the *Poetics*, and *On Sophistical Refutations*. Thomas illustrates a further organization of these works in the prologue to the Commentary on the *Posterior Analytics*. Here Thomas begins from the idea that reason, since it constitutes—together with art—what most characterizes the human race, is able to direct not only the actions of the inferior parts but its own actions. In other words, reason is able to engage in reasoning about its own operations. This capacity presupposes an art, which consists precisely in rational philosophy or logic, which has the acts itself of reason as its material. After having again listed the three fundamental operations or activities of the intellect already mentioned, Thomas appeals to the classic Aristotelian parallel between art and nature. In nature some things happen always and necessarily (since nature cannot fail in its act), others happen in the majority of cases, and still others happen rarely (when nature fails in what is proper to it, as in the case of giving birth to a monster). The same divisions obtain in the acts of reason: some processes lead to necessary conclusions, and the analytic part of logic is concerned with these since judgments resolve themselves into their principles (to analyze is to dissolve or break apart). The analytic part of logic is then divided into two parts: one that deals with the form of syllogisms (the *Prior Analytics*) and one that deals with their material (the *Posterior Analytics*). There is then a part of logic (the "inventive" part) that is concerned not with what is absolutely certain but with what is so in the majority of cases and thus is not the object of science in a strict sense but is the object of belief or opinion, what can be arrived at through probable or likely syllogisms (dialectic) rather than demonstrative (apodictic) ones. The *Topics* takes up such syllogisms. Now belief and opinion do not give rise to certainty but only incline us more to one thesis than to its contradictory, and so we enter into the realm of the *Rhetoric*. Sometimes, however, this inclination is produced not by true reasoning but by the estimative faculty (which we discussed in Chapter 4) through a representation. And this is what the *Poetics* deals with. "It is proper to the poet to induce toward something virtuous through an adequate representation" (*poetae est inducere ad aliquid virtuosum per aliquam decentem repraesentationem*). Finally, *On Sophistical Refutations* considers fallacies or errors in reasoning (parallel to the monstrous parts of nature). As we can see, Thomas is within the tradition that situates the *Rhetoric* and *Poetics*—and not only the writings of the *Organon*—in the domain of logic and rational philosophy.

There are passages in the commentaries on the *De interpretatione* and the *Posterior Analytics* that are worth noting. In the Commentary on the *De inter-*

pretatione, Thomas asks how it is possible to maintain the Aristotelian assumption that truth always consists in composition and division (and so in a complex judgment) and cede at the same that it can be predicated of simple things (in the sense in which, by the conversion of the transcendentals, we say that every being is true) or be referred to the divine intellect, which knows everything in an absolutely simple way, without the operations of composition and division. Thomas does not argue—as we first saw in the *De veritate*—that truth always has a relational valence, in the sense that it is always in relation to an intellect. Whatever is called true must be in relation to the intellect. But something can be in relation to the intellect in two different ways: (a) as the measure to the measured, as natural things relate to the human speculative intellect. In this case an understanding is true if it conforms to the thing, false if it does not; (b) as measured to the measure, as actions are produced (measured) by our practical intellect or artifacts are made by art. In fact, all the things of nature are measured by an intellect: God's. In this case all things are true in virtue of their form to the extent that the form corresponds to the divine plan. This is the principle that guarantees the convertibility of being and truth: every being is true since it relates, by its form, to the divine intellect. Even when we refer to the truth of something simple and individual ("This is true gold"), we implicitly refer to a relationship. In regard to the human intellect the gold is true or false in relation to the representation that it produces of itself. In regard to the divine intellect, it is true or false in relation to its form. True gold is that which possesses the form of gold, and false gold will always be true brass! In regard to the way that truth can be attributed subjectively to the divine intellect, it must be said that, for Thomas, as our intellect knows in an immaterial way what is in matter, so the divine intellect knows in a simple way what entails composition and division, without running afoul of the principle according to which truth always consists in a relation to the intellect (I, l. 3).

Thomas then follows Aristotle—and even more Boethius—in distinguishing between two different valences of the verb "to be," viz., the predicative use and the existential use (*secundum adiacens* and *tertium adiacens* in Boethius's terminology).[70] In the first place "is" (*est*) indicates what falls into the intellect

70. See A. Zimmermann, "'*Ipsum enim* [<est>] *nihil est*' (Aristoteles, *Peri hermeneias* I, c. 3): Thomas von Aquin und die Bedeutung der Kopula," in *Der Begriff der* repraesentatio *im Mittelalter. Stellvertretung, Symbol, Zeichen, Bild,* Miscellanea Mediaevalia 8, ed. A. Zimmermann (Berlin-New York: de Gruyter, 1971), 282–95; G. Klima, "Aquinas' Theory of the copula and the Analogy of Being," *Logical Analysis and History of Philosophy* 5 (2002): 159–76; J. A. Garcia Cuadrado, "Existence et vérité: nome et verbe dans l'*Expositio libri Peri hermeneias* de Thomas d'Aquin," *Revue Thomiste* 106 (2006): 355–92. On the more general history of the distinction between *secundum* and *tertium adiacens,* see

insofar as it is in act and is, thus, the actuality of something. Obviously, the actuality of a thing is its existence (*tertium adiacens*: "Socrates is"). Since, however, actuality refers to any form and so not only to that which confers substantial existence upon something but also to the various accidental forms, the copula also indicates everything that belongs to a determinate subject, that is, whatever can be predicated of it (*secundum adiacens*: "Socrates is white").

Finally, Chapter 9 of the *De interpretatione* forces Thomas to take a position on future contingents. In general Thomas does not depart from Aristotle on this point. Propositions about contingent future events—"Tomorrow there will be a naval battle," for example—escape from the principle of bivalence, that is, they do not have a determinate truth value. They are neither true nor false. But all propositions about the past and present always have a determinate truth value. They are always either true or false, as the principle of bivalence specifies. The proposition "Yesterday there was a naval battle" can be true or false depending on whether or not there really was a naval battle yesterday, but it is necessarily either true or false, and the same is the case for propositions about the present. In Christian theology, however, this is all complicated by the fact that many events that are future from our point of view are from God's point of view known atemporally and so in an eternal present. What does not have a determinate truth value for us does have one for the divine intellect. But does this not mean eliminating all of the contingency of this world, making everything come about by necessity? Here Thomas can avail himself of the strategy of Boethius (not only as employed in his own commentary on the *De interpretatione* but also and above all as employed in the *Consolatio*). The fact that God knows all things in the present does not alter their intrinsic modality. Suppose we were to observe an event from a window high above. If someone walks down the street, it would be impossible for me not to see him. But from the fact that I necessarily observe him now it does not follow that he necessarily had to walk down the street now. For the person walking, the decision to go down this street at some moment is, therefore, entirely free, even if an observer from above cannot but necessarily see him as present. Hence, the necessity by which God, in his eternal present, knows all human events is a hypothetical or conditional necessity, and not an absolute one bound to the condition of the divine knowledge. As Thomas writes:

God, however, is wholly outside the order of time, stationed as it were at the summit of eternity, which is wholly simultaneous, and to him the whole course of time is sub-

---

G. Nuchelmans, *Secundum/tertium adiacens* (Amsterdam: Koniglijke Akademie van Wetenschappen, 1992). See 18–19 for the treatment of Thomas.

jected in one simple intuition. For this reason, he sees in one glance everything that is effected in the evolution of time, and each thing as it is in itself, and it is not future to him in relation to his view as it is in the order of its causes alone (although he also sees the very order of the causes), but each of the things that are in whatever time is seen wholly eternally as the human eye sees Socrates sitting, not in its causes but in itself. Now from the fact that man sees Socrates sitting, the contingency of his sitting, which concerns the order of cause to effect, is not destroyed; yet the eye of man most certainly and infallibly sees Socrates sitting while he is sitting, since each thing as it is in itself is already determined. Hence it follows that God knows all things that take place in time most certainly and infallibly, and yet the things that happen in time neither are nor take place of necessity, but contingently.[71]

Thomas adds to this a line of argument used in other works (we will return to it shortly), namely, that the divine will has disposed some effects to be necessary (giving them necessary causes) and others contingent.[72] Since Thomas reprises an already solidified position, this is an opportune occasion to raise again the problem of determinism, which Thomas believes to be the greatest theoretical threat to the order of human coexistence and to all of the principles of practical philosophy. First of all (and still drawing on Boethius), Thomas explains the way in which the modal concepts of necessity, contingency, and impossibility are to be understood. Interestingly, (and contrary to what he himself seems to assume, for example, in the third way of the *Summa* [see pp. 226–27]), Thomas rejects a merely statistical-temporal or frequency interpretation according to which the necessary is what happens always, the impossible is what never happens, and the contingent is what sometimes happens and sometimes does not. Instead, with Boethius (who cites Philo), he considers necessity, impossibility, and contingency as intrinsic. Thomas says that this is also Aristotle's view. The necessary is what in its nature is determined only to exist. The possible or contingent is what is not determined in itself to exist or not exist, whether because of what regards the potentiality of matter (which is open to receive different forms, without being determined to one in particular) or because of what regards the active power (which can perform different acts—as is the case for the human will—without being determined to one in particular). To exclude the necessary in the realm of human events, it must be maintained that all actions

71. *In libros Perihermeneias expositio*, I, l. 14. On this question see J. Marenbon, *Le temps, l'éternité et la prescience de Boèce à Thomas d'Aquin* (Conferences Pierre Abelard) (Paris: Vrin, 2005), especially 117–62. Nevertheless, accordiing to Marenbon, divine a-temporality is not the authentic core of the solution that is commonly attributed to Boethius and Thomas. It is, rather, that Thomas develops two other ideas that are really Boethian: the fact that God knows all things as present and the principle according to which what is known is known according to the mode of the knower.

72. Some decades later Dun Scotus will say, rather, that everything that the divine will produces is produced contingently.

are contingent and not necessitated by external causes. This excludes fate as it is understood by the Stoics, namely, as a certain series or connection of causes. It also excludes the notion that all the affairs of the world (the sublunary world) are unfailingly brought about by the action of the celestial bodies, a kind of astral determinism. The celestial bodies, as bodies, can act only on other bodies and not on the human intellect and will, which are immaterial. On the basis of this same assumption, however, Thomas does grant that the celestial bodies can act on the sensitive part of our nature and, thus, indirectly exercise a certain influence on the intellect and will. In the *Summa theologiae* he stated even more expressly that only the wise, to the extent that they develop the rational part of their nature, are entirely immune to the influence of the stars (Ia, q. 115, a. 4, ad 3). There is a last form of determinism that must be rejected and it is the one that we had earlier called psychological determinism, that is, the idea that the will is necessitated by the representation of the good (the objects that each time are identified as good by the intellect). Thomas reaffirms what he had maintained in the *secunda pars*: just as the intellect cannot but assent to first indemonstrable principles, so also the will is necessitated by its ultimate end, happiness, and by the means by which we are indissolubly bound to it (existence, living, understanding). The will is in no way determined by any of the other intermediate ends proposed by the intellect. It might be worthwhile to recall here that psychological determinism was condemned by Bishop Tempier in December 1270. It is not surprising, then, that in a primarily logical context Thomas should take the opportunity to distance himself from every form of unilateral intellectualism, also clearing Aristotle himself of this charge, and precisely in the moment that he also defends the essential role of *consilium*, the capacity of practical reason to consider courses of action. "These things have been stated to save the roots of contingency"—that is, the freedom of *consilium* with regard to things in view of the end—"which Aristotle posits here, although they may seem to exceed the mode of logical matter."[73] Later in this chapter, precisely in regard to the Commentary on the *Metaphysics*, we will see how Thomas reproposes another form of *theological* determinism that is entirely foreign to the Aristotelian horizon.

The Commentary on the *Posterior Analytics*, however technical, also offers material of interest. Regarding demonstrations relating to what usually happens (*ut frequenter*) in the natural world, Thomas is, for example, very careful (unlike Grosseteste, and also despite that for which he has sometimes been criticized) to distinguish between rare but necessary celestial events (eclipses rarely occur

73. *In libros Perihermeneias expositio*, I, l. 14.

but they can be the object of necessary demonstrations) and what is normal in the sublunary world but can fail to happen because the corresponding causes are impeded in their activity. For events of this sort, Thomas—on the basis of what Albert the Great had also already suggested in part—proposes the model of an *ex suppositione finis* demonstration (which he develops and adopts in the Commentary on the *Physics*). If it is impossible to establish an absolutely necessary connection between cause and effect, then we must begin from the effect itself, which is the terminus of a natural process, and hold that, if it obtains (or when it does), it is possible to return by way of demonstration (even without absolute necessity) to the causes that make it possible. There is in this case not an *a priori* necessity but an *a posteriori* one, which is taken from the end and from the form. Thomas's example regards the growth of an olive tree. It is by no means necessary that an olive tree grow, for the seed could be lost or be impeded in its activity by other causes. But if an olive tree should grow, it is necessary that its cause exist, that is, the seed. This necessity, although inferior to absolute necessity, is nevertheless sufficient to give us valid scientific propositions in the sublunary world, in the world of *ut frequenter* events.[74] With respect to self-evident principles, Thomas follows the distinction proposed by Boethius in *De ebdomadibus*. These principles are the causes by which we obtain the conclusion, and they are immediate because they cannot be deduced from other principles. Their characteristic feature is in the fact that the predicate is included in the reason or definition of the subject. Some propositions are formed by terms truly known to all, such as the principle of identity or the axiom that "the whole is greater than the part." Other self-evident propositions are formed by terms that are known only to the specialists in a discipline. One example of propositions of this type is the axiom that "all right angles are equal," which is self-evident because the predicate is included in the subject, but it is not known to all, because some people do not immediately know the meaning of "right angle." Thomas seems to reserve the designation *dignitates* for propositions of the first type and *positiones* for propositions of the second type. Thomas's approach, as has been observed, thus reflects the penetration of the Euclidian model into the very heart of Aristotelian epistemology. Other original developments in Thomas's commentary regard the interpretation of the second mode of predication *per se* (in which the subject is cause of the predicate and, more precisely, its material cause) and the application to that mode of the distinction between abstract and concrete predication. In the first case the accident is defined in

74. See A. Corbini, *La teoria della scienza nel XIII secolo: I commenti agli Analitici secondi*, Unione accademica nazionale. Testi e studi 20 (Florence: SISMEL-Edizioni del Galluzzo, 2006), especially 42–47. For the other topics that we have mentioned, see 74–79 and 106–8.

general without reference to a determinate substrate, and the subject appears *in obliquo*, that is, indirectly (aquilinity is a curvature of a nose). In the second case the subject appears in the definition *in recto*—as the focal point—and functions almost as a genus (the aquiline is a curved nose).

The Commentary on the *Metaphysics:*
The Subject of First Philosophy

As with the other commentaries on Aristotle, so also with the Commentary on the *Metaphysics,* we will not be able to enter into detail about the different interpretive and doctrinal decisions in Thomas's meticulous exposition.[75] We can, however, begin by considering at least two points: the way in which Thomas interprets the structure of the Aristotelian text and the new discussion, in the prologue, about the subject itself of metaphysics as a science. With respect to the first point it is interesting to note—as has been ably shown—that Thomas interprets Book III (Beta) as the agenda or plan for the whole of the *Metaphysics.*[76] This reading of the text obviously rests upon a basic presupposition, to wit, that the *Metaphysics* as we know it can be considered an entirely unified work, despite not only the perplexities of contemporary interpreters but also the doubts raised by some later ancient and Arab interpreters about certain tensions that are hard to reconcile. For Thomas, the *Metaphysics* presents a fundamentally bipartite structure (I–VI and VII–XII) that is, nevertheless, organized and homogenous. The books of the first group must, in fact, be considered propaedeutic, whereas the books of the second group follow the classic articulation of Aristotelian epistemology and are concerned successively with the subject of the science, its properties, and principles (*subiectum, passiones subiecti, principia subiecti*). Books VII–IX (Zeta, Eta, Theta) have to do with the *subiectum;* Book X (Iota) with the *passiones subiecti* (one and many, etc.); Books XI–XII (Kappa and Lambda) with the *principia subiecti.*[77] The key to this ordering of the text is explained by Thomas in

75. On this question see J. C. Doig, *Aquinas on Metaphysics: A Historico-Doctrinal Study of the Commentary on the Metaphysics* (The Hague: Martinus Nijhoff, 1972); J. F. Wippel, "Thomas Aquinas' Commentary on Aristotle's Metaphysics," in *Uses and Abuses of the Classics: Western Interpretations of Greek Philosophy,* ed. J. J. E. Gracia and J. Yu (Aldershot-Burlington: Ashgate, 2004), 137–64 (published later in *Metaphysical Themes in Thomas Aquinas II,* 240–71). On the other hand, for a systematic (but sufficiently sober) presentation of the principal metaphysical themes within the entire opera of St. Thomas, see J. J. Kockelmans, *The Metaphysics of Aquinas: A Systematic Presentation* (Leuven: Bibliotheek van de Faculteit Godgeleerdheid, 2001).

76. See G. Galluzzo, "Aquinas on the Structure of Aristotle's Metaphysics," in *Documenti e studi sulla tradizione filosofica medievale* 15 (2004): 353–86; "Aquinas's Interpretation of Metaphysics Book Beta," *Quaestio* 5 (2005): 413–27. Galluzzo also very opportunely stresses that Thomas's reading of Aristotle's *Metaphysics*—contrary to what continues often to be maintained—is not at all oriented to book Lambda.

77. Thomas, as we have already noted, did not comment on the last two books.

Book III—the book of aporiae—which has its own internal subdivision. The first chapter presents the aporiae themselves in a general way. They are then explicitly formulated in the other five chapters. It is no accident, then, that Thomas, commenting on Book III, 2–6, specifies the places in the *Metaphysics* where the various aporiae are discussed and resolved. These places are almost all in the second part of the main division proposed by Thomas (Books VII–XII, Zeta–Lambda). Only Book IV (Gamma) presents a problem in this respect because, although it belongs to the first part (the "propaedeutic" part), it already offers the solution to some of the aporiae. Thomas gets around the problem by explaining that this book, together with Book VI (Epsilon), concerns only the preliminary aporiae that have to do with the science's way of proceeding and not with its contents, which are dealt with in Books VII–XII. Thus, as has been suggested, Aristotle's *Metaphysics* seems as a whole to assume the form of a genuine Scholastic *quaestio*, whose arguments *pro* and *contra* are posed in Book III, while the solutions are offered in Books IV and VII–XII. This type of approach shows the truly technical and disciplinary attitude with which Thomas goes about his Commentary on the *Metaphysics*, working independently of the questions that have been projected onto his text by his readers over the centuries.

The problem of the subject of metaphysics is discussed by Thomas in his prologue, which again takes up and integrates what he had already said in the Commentary on Boethius's *De Trinitate*. All the arts and sciences are directed toward a single end, an end that constitutes man's perfection, that is, happiness (*beatitudo*). When several things are ordained to a single thing, one of them rules and directs the others. So, since all the arts and sciences are ordained to a single thing, one of them must rule and direct the others. This science can rightly claim the name "wisdom" for itself if, as Aristotle says, it is proper to the wise man to order or direct (*sapientis est ordinare*). The Aristotelian example that Thomas adopts in this regard is that of the natural division between masters and slaves. Just as those who are especially endowed with an intellectual capacity subjugate those who are intellectually weak, in the same way the science that is maximally intellectual must naturally be the ruler of the others. How can we determine which science this is? If the sciences are divided according to their objects, the science that concerns itself with the maximally intelligible cannot but be the science that is maximally intellectual. But maximal intelligibility can be understood in three different ways. Maximal intelligibility can be understood first according to the order of knowledge, and in this sense the first causes are maximally intelligible, for through knowledge of them we acquire certainty. Therefore, the science that investigates first causes is maximally intellectual.

What is furthest from sense knowledge is also maximally intelligible. The sensible is always particular, while the intelligible is universal. Hence, the science that deals with maximally universal principles—being and everything that is immediately connected with it, such as the one and the many, potency and act, etc.—will be maximally intellectual.

Finally, whatever is most separate from matter will be maximally intelligible. This is not only what is abstracted from designated matter, that is, the matter that functions as the principle of individuation, as in the case of natural philosophy, but what is abstracted in general from all sensible matter, and not only according to consideration, as in the case of mathematics, but according to being. God and the other separate substances (the intelligences) are absolutely separated from matter according to being. The science that studies them will be maximally intellectual.

These three distinct perspectives on the maximally intelligible do not indicate three distinct sciences, each with its own distinct subject (first causes, being and its properties, and God and the other separate substances), but a single science, since the separate substances are identical with the first and universal causes of being. And because it belongs to one and the same science to consider the proper causes of any genus and the genus itself, it follows that one science inquires about separate substances and common being, whose common and universal causes are the separate substances.

Since it is necessary that every science have one determinate subject, as Aristotle himself prescribes in the *Posterior Analytics*, it must be said more precisely that *ens commune* is the only subject of this science. Every science seeks out the causes and properties of its subject. The causes themselves are not the subject but the end toward which the science tends. The difficulty that we already encountered in the Commentary on the *De Trinitate* returns here. How do we reconcile the choice of *ens commune* as the subject of metaphysics with the other Aristotelian postulate according to which first philosophy concerns itself with what is separate and, therefore, as it seems, immaterial? Thomas again proposes the model borrowed from Avicenna. The immaterial is not only what never exists in matter but also what can exist without matter, and this is the case for *ens commune*. The different names of the science are also explained on the basis of Avicenna. It is called "divine science" because it occupies itself with separate substances. It is called "metaphysics" because it occupies itself with what is beyond physical reality. It is called "first philosophy" because it occupies itself with the first causes of being.

As is easy to see, for instance, in the explanations of the different names of the science and the distinctions between the different types of immateriality, this prologue has some elements in common with the approach developed with more subtlety in the Commentary on the *De Trinitate*. But there are also some differences that perhaps are not irrelevant. The distinction between abstraction and separation is hardly mentioned (and is often ignored in the rest of the commentary) and is in no way connected to the two distinct operations of the intellect. Although some fundamental Avicennian themes are still present, the decisive point is left out, namely, the passage from the "transcendental" analysis of the concept of being to the analysis of divine being—an operation that is possible in Avicenna since being in general includes the divine (and so the divine itself is one of the properties, even if the most excellent, of being itself). On this last point, Thomas—because he makes it clear that *ens commune* is created and not divine—breaks with Avicenna. The prologue, thus, seems to mark a step back with regard to the Commentary on the *De Trinitate*. The sophisticated Avicennian effort to unify Aristotle's scattered indications about the subject of first philosophy seems to give way to a more traditional interpretation. If there is a text of Thomas that leaves itself open to Heidegger's accusation that Western metaphysics is essentially constituted as ontotheology (granted that this is, evidently, an accusation), it is precisely the prologue to the Commentary on the *Metaphysics*. Metaphysics, in the way that it is presented here, is ontotheology, because it concerns itself both with what is universal and with what is first, establishing the link between the two spheres with the bond of causality between the second and the first (*pace* those who minimize this connection to try to save Thomas from the Heideggerian anathema regarding ontotheology).[78] Finally, there is no reference in the prologue or in the rest of the commentary to doubleness of divine science, that is, to the exigency to create an epistemically adequate space for *theologia nostra* alongside of and above the theology of the philosophers. This particular absence could, however, be explained by the fact that here Thomas's principal intention is to explain Aristotle's *Metaphysics* and not to expand the discussion to include the problem of the relationship between this divine science and the one founded on revelation. Until the Leonine critical edition of Thomas's commentary finally becomes available, the text should be

78. See, above all, J.-L. Marion, "Saint Thomas d'Aquin et l'onto-théo-logie," *Revue Thomiste* 95 (1995): 31–66. This article is a kind of palinode—or, to use the terms selected by the author himself, a "retraction"—of what the author himself had previously written (above all in *God Without Being*: Hors-Texte, trans. Thomas Carlson [Chicago: The University of Chicago Press, 2012]). For some observations on this question (and on the alleged usefulness of making reference in medieval studies to Heidegger's "accusations" regarding ontotheology), see P. Porro, "Heidegger, la filosofia medievale, la medievistica contemporanea," *Quaestio* 1 (2001): 431–61; "Metafisica e teologia nella divisione delle scienze speculative del *Super Boetium De Trinitate*," in Tommaso d'Aquino, *Commenti a Boezio* (*Super Boetium De Trinitate. Expositio libri Boetii De ebdomadibus*), translation and introduction by P. Porro (Milan: Bompiani, 2007), 467–526.

read with extreme care. Since the critical edition will permit the substantial correction of the editions presently available, we can say that its publication will be the event desired most by all "philosophical" readers of Thomas.

The *triplex gradus causarum*:
Determinism, Fate, and Providence in the
Commentary on the *Metaphysics*

As we have already seen, the Commentary on the *Metaphysics* offers us the occasion to return to the problem of determinism. It is well known how the refutation that Aristotle proposes in many crucial points of his works has two fundamental bases. From the logical point of view, it rests on the inapplicability of the principle of bivalence to individual contingent future events, as is theorized and defended in *De interpretatione*, 9, which we have already discussed. From the, as it were, ontological-factual point of view, it rests on the presupposition that the space of this logical indeterminacy coincides with that of *katà symbebekós*, accidental causes. In *Metaphysics*, VI, 3—a text that is just as celebrated and controversial as *De interpretatione*, 9—Aristotle explains, in effect, that the determinate connection of causes can be interrupted by an accidental cause that is generated (and corrupted) without passing through a real process of generation, that is, from a cause that produces it without being brought about or deduced from a prior cause. Thus, if someone eats spicy food now—a person whom many subsequent commentators give the name Nicostratus—it is not necessary that he die a violent death shortly thereafter. It is obvious and *causally* determinate that whoever eats spicy food becomes thirsty, but leaving his house is not an event that depends on the previous event, that is, not through a real process of generation. Instead, it occurs spontaneously, as does the decision of the malefactors (never mentioned as such by Aristotle) to be on the street precisely at the time when Nicostratus walks by.

In his commentary Thomas reflects on this issue (VI, l. 3), reprising things that he had already said in the *Summa contra Gentiles* (and perhaps already in some *opuscula,* but the chronological relationship between them and the Commentary on the *Metaphysics* is difficult to determine), but now situating them in their natural context—that in which Aristotle speaks of accidental causes and the indeterminacy that is rooted in them—and, above all, discussing them in relation to the positions of the philosophers, including Aristotle in particular. Aristotle's anti-determinist strategy, while it legitimates chance and fortune as accidental causes, eliminates *de facto* both fate and providence, as Thomas cannot but point out. Aristotle had admitted the anteriority of *per se* causes with respect to accidental causes, but had then denied the absolute reduction of the latter to the former. If such a reduction were possible, determinism would *de facto* be ineluctable. Fate and providence both imply that everything happens according to a certain order. But what follows from an order is, for that reason, not accidental and so occurs either always or for the most part (*in maiori parte*). The determinism that Aristotle deals with in *De interpretatione*, 9, and in *Metaphysics* VI, 3, is rooted in the fact that if the causes of something are posited in the past or in the present, and the possibility of accidental causes is excluded, what will happen in the future is already predetermined—the death of the unfortunate Nicostratus, for example, who eats spicy food and leaves his house to quench his thirst. But in the case of fate and providence the essential causes are already posited in the past and in the present. In the first instance it is a matter of celestial bodies, whose action is unchanging, and in the second, God's eternal providence.

Thomas's attempt to circumvent Aristotle's argument depends on the hierarchical order of causes. The higher the cause, the more effects that are included in its causality. The order that exists among the effects that depend on a cause is coextensive with the causality of that cause. This means that the effects that depend on particular inferior causes do not have an order among themselves, even if at times they accidentally coincide. But these same effects, related back to a common superior cause, can manifest a kind of order. Thus it is accidental that a plant flowers at the same time as another, considering the *virtus* of each plant separately. But the coincidence is not accidental if the simultaneous flowering is related to the *virtus* of the heavenly bodies, which regulate the natural cycles of plants. Thomas introduces the celebrated doctrine of the *triplex gradus causarum*, derived from the ontological regions in which the Aristotelian cosmos is subdivided: there is an incorruptible immutable cause (God); there are some incorruptible but changing causes (the celestial bodies); and there are corruptible and changing causes (the generable and corruptible substances of the sublunary world). These last causes, as particular, are always *univocal*, inasmuch as they always produce their proper effects according to individual determinate species: fire always generates fire, a plant always generates a plant of the same type, and a human being always generates another human being.

The intermediate causes, those of the second level, are partly universal and partly particular. They are *particular* because they extend only to what is produced through movement. They are *universal* because they regard, not one species of mobile reality only, but everything that is alterable, generable, or corruptible. Everything that moves depends on the first motion.

The cause on the first level is universal only because its effect is properly being. So, *everything that is* is included within the causality and the order of the first cause.

If we consider only proximate and particular causes, it is undeniable that many things happen accidentally. This depends on three distinct factors: (a) competition or interference among several causes; (b) the weakness of the agent that is not able to realize the end that was posited; (c) the absence of a suitable disposition on the part of the matter.

If we go up one level, this contingency is largely reduced, since many of the things that appear accidental reveal that they are not. The competition of many accidental causes can, in fact, have a determinate celestial cause. Moreover, at this level, even the weaknesses of the agent can be substantially eliminated. But since celestial bodies act through movement, they always need matter, and they depend on its disposition. Although accidentality is reduced, it does not completely disappear. Up to this point Aristotle is right: if the effect is produced in the majority of cases (*ut in pluribus*), and not *semper*, it is obvious that there is a residual accidentality (*in paucioribus*). Another fundamental factor of indeterminacy resides in the fact that some sublunary beings, such as rational souls, are not directly subject to celestial bodies, even if, as we know, the soul is indirectly affected by the bodily changes influenced by celestial bodies and so inclined to act in certain ways. Beyond this inclination, it is, in any case, a fact that our deliberate actions cannot be directly connected with the actions of celestial bodies. That is sufficient for Thomas to reject, with Aristotle, the fatalism of astral determinism (as we already saw in the Commentary on the *De interpretatione*). But, ascending to the next level, we find nothing that escapes the divine order. This is true also for matter, since it too receives its being from the first cause. So, with respect to the first cause, *if everything is ordained, nothing is accidental*—which is to say that everything is subject to providence, as Thomas already amply explained in the *Summa contra Gentiles*.

Thus, whereas fate, as we have just seen, does not suppress or nullify accidentality or contingency because of the margin of indeterminacy that results from matter and from the free activity of rational beings, the case of providence, Thomas recognizes, is much more complicated (*maiorem habet difficultatem*). Providence does not deceive itself, nor does it have any intrinsic or extrinsic limitation, unlike celestial bodies. In short, it is impossible that something be disposed (*provisum*) by God and not come about, and this seems to imply that every effect of providence occurs by necessity. Now, for Thomas, not only does a cause produce an effect, it also produces all of its accidents. Nature, for example, does not limit itself to producing man, but it produces man with the specific property of being able to laugh. If God, therefore, is the cause of being as being, he is likewise the cause of the accidents that inhere in being as being, among which figure modalities like necessity and contingency. It belongs to providence, then, not only to produce a being, but to make it contingent or necessary, and this is what providence achieves by predisposing the intermediary causes, from which a certain effect will follow either necessarily or contingently.

It is true, therefore, that every effect that is subject to divine providence possesses a necessity, but always in the form of a hypothetical necessity. If it has been disposed by God, then it will happen (*si aliquid est a Deo provisum, hoc erit*). However, the same thing, in relation to proximate causes, is contingent, and, for Thomas, that is enough to say that not every effect is necessary. Some effects are necessary and some are contingent *secundum analogiam suae causae*. The effects resemble proximate causes and not remote ones, which they can never equal.

God has not only made it the case that something exists. He has also made it the case that it is necessary or contingent. The position of providence does not imply—as Aristotle hypothesized—an absolute necessity but a necessity in a composite sense. It is necessary that the effect be either contingent or necessary. Going well beyond Aristotle, Thomas speaks expressly in this context of the *lex necessitatis vel contigentiae* or the *ordo necessitatis vel contingentiae*, and, thus, of *lex necessaria* at least in the composite sense, which is in all the effects, even the contingent ones.

Obviously, there are more things that could be said on this topic. We will limit ourselves to two.

First, we could note that although Thomas, in defending the freedom of divine action, certainly breaks with the necessitarianism of the Greco-Arab tradition (as we have already seen beginning with the *De veritate*), it is true that he also demolishes Aristotle's anti-deterministic strategy to the point of being, from this perspective, even more deterministic than Aristotle himself. However surprising, this is clearly attested by the third lecture on Book VI, from the Commentary on the *Metaphysics*. Thomas proposes here, with the doctrine of the *triplex gradus causarum*, a model that is certainly sophisticated, that seeks to hold together the necessity of providence with the contingency of things, but that tries to maintain a delicate balance, the fruit of two theoretical moves. The first involves the extension of the Boethian model of hypothetical necessity, which we considered from the point of view of foreknowledge and from that of providence. The difference is easily seen. For Boethius the fact that God knows about a certain event beforehand does not influence its modal status. Thomas, however, does not limit himself to saying that God knows about an event beforehand but adds that he also predisposes it and predisposes its modal status. The second move is the reemployment of the distinction between the composite senses and divided sense that Aristotle had used anti-deterministically in *De interpretatione*, 9. The fact that tomorrow there will or will not be a naval battle is true in the composite sense, but in the divided sense neither of the two possible alternatives now (today) possesses a determinate truth value. Thomas seems to suggest a further use of this principle. It is necessary that every effect be necessary or contingent. Evidently this does not imply the necessity of every effect, but it does, in any case, imply the necessity that everything be predisposed in a determinate way by providence according to the *lex necessitatis vel contigentiae* mentioned a moment ago.

Second, it is perhaps important to underscore the reason that Thomas generally invokes to explain the fact that in the universe there are different levels of necessity and contingency. The diversity of levels itself contributes to the perfection of the world. This postulate is so pervasive in Thomas that it is even used in the extremely delicate question about predestination. We will return to it in Chapter 6. Let it suffice for now to observe that, for Thomas, in relation to divine providence, the margin of indeterminacy in the universe tends toward zero: *Invenitur igitur uniuscuiusque effectus secundum quod est sub ordine providentiae necessitatem habere.*[79]

The Commentary on the *Politics* and the Role of *De bona fortuna*

We have already spoken of the different approach to the subdivision of philosophy, founded on the rational order, that is proposed in the *Sententia libri Ethicorum*. The prologue to the Commentary on the *Politics* takes its cue instead from the celebrated Aristotelian adage (taken from *Physics*, II) according to which art imitates nature. On the other hand, since natural things are the product of the divine intellect, and the human intellect has a certain likeness to it (and is itself produced by divine intellect), it is normal that in his activity (through art) man should take direction from nature. Nevertheless, nature does not by itself bring the things that belong to art to completion, but functions, rather, as a model for art and predisposes its principles. Because of this, though in the speculative domain human reason is passive with respect to nature (it is restricted to observing it), in the domain of action it is active, for it must bring to completion what nature suggests to it, so to speak. Reason, however, aims at ordering not only natural things but human beings too insofar as they permit themselves to be directed and governed by reason. And since reason always begins from what is more simple, or from parts, to realize what is more complex, or a totality, its end, in the practical sphere will be to realize growing forms of

79. *Sententia libri Metaphysicae*, VI, l. 3.

community or associated life, whose apex (and, thus, final end) is the city (in the Greek or Aristotelian sense) or state. From this general approach we can draw out the four fundamental characteristics that seem to distinguish—on the basis of the Aristotelian treatment—political science: (a) it is necessary for the completion of philosophy; (b) inasmuch as it is directed toward the organizing of human communal life, it belongs not to the speculative sciences or the productive arts but to the practical sciences; (c) in this last sphere it has the primary place and has an architectonic function, since the state is the most noble and perfect thing that man can bring about; (d) from the methodological point of view, it starts from the analysis of the principles and the parts and proceeds then to arrive at the analysis of the whole.

Thomas's commentary (which is mostly incomplete) does not permit us to gain a precise picture of his political doctrines, which can perhaps be more easily reconstructed from the *De regno* and the *Summa*.[80] Thomas's reconstruction and interpretation of Aristotle's text seem here to leave little room for more original digressions. So, if it seems entirely normal, if not taken for granted, that Thomas should follow Aristotle in describing man as a political animal (*animale sociale, animale civile, animale politicum*) and in stressing that this tendency toward communal life is founded on and realized through language, we should not be overly surprised by the fact that the commentary offers no original ideas of special prominence about what regards, for instance, natural slavery. Thomas limits himself on this point to expounding the Aristotelian thesis according to which, for those who are unable to govern themselves by reason, it is good that they be governed by the nature of another. Also in respect to the relationship between the individual and common good, Thomas does not seem to propose a particularly innovative analysis, nor does he seem to be interested in dealing with the tensions on this issue that can be found in Aristotle's text.

There is instead perhaps a last point that merits attention regarding Thomas's relationship to Aristotle in the area of practical philosophy, and it has to do with the direct role that Thomas appears to have played in the composition of the *Liber de bona fortuna*, which is a synthesis of the *Magna moralia* (1206b30–1207b19) and the *Eudemian Ethics* (1246b37–1248b11). The text, put together in Latin by William of Moerbeke, was introduced to Paris by Thomas during his second regency. He had brought it with him from Italy. This leads us to consider the age-old question about Thomas's relationship with William, who was the most celebrated translator of Greek of that time and a fellow Dominican. There are two contrary theses about this relationship that have been advanced for de-

---

80. These two texts, however, as we have seen, do not agree on certain delicate points, such as the best form of government.

cades. According to the one, William's work depended entirely on Thomas, and according to the other, Thomas had no privileged relationship with William nor privileged access to his translations of Aristotle and his commentators. Neither thesis seems completely true. It does appear plausible that Thomas and William had a special relationship,[81] and that allowed Thomas to have easy access—and, to some extent, ahead of others—to Moerbeke's work,[82] and to propose to him the translation of certain texts. The case of the *De bona fortuna* is exemplary. The title itself of the work (which, again, does not correspond to any writing conceived as such by Aristotle but belongs solely to the history of Latin translations of Aristotle) first appears in Thomas. And Thomas cites it more than once, not only to oppose any rigidly anti-providentialist interpretation of Aristotle (such as the one that formed in the Arab peripatetic tradition), but to find in Aristotle himself (in Aristotle reassembled in Latin!) the ultimate root of freedom of will, as we saw in *De malo*, q. 6: if man is subject to the celestial bodies in what regards his body, and to the higher separate substances (angels) in what regards his intellect, he answers only to God in what regards his will.

Thomas's Intention in the Commentaries on Aristotle

At the end of this all too brief overview of Thomas's commentaries on Aristotle we return to a question that we posed at its beginning but whose answer we postponed. Why did Thomas comment on Aristotle so extensively and intensely? Normally, a student or a master would deal with Aristotle in the faculty of arts, and the commentaries on Aristotle were principally (if not always, as we should note) the fruit of teaching in the faculty of arts. But this is not the case for Thomas. We do not know whether Thomas studied in the faculty of arts in Paris (nor what he learned earlier in Naples), but he certainly never taught in this faculty in a strict sense. Thus, Thomas's commentaries do not respond to a professional demand. Thomas did not comment on Aristotle until the last years of his life, because of obligations to teaching statutes or programs (even though after his death his commentaries were then sought by the masters of the faculty

---

81. See C. Steel, "Guillaume de Moerbeke et Saint Thomas," in *Guillaume de Moerbeke: Recueil d'études à l'occasion du 700ème anniversaire de sa mort (1286)*, ed. J. Brams and W. Vanhamel (Leuven: Leuven University Press, 1989), 57–82, especially 68–69 and 81–82; V. Cordonier, "Sauver le Dieu du Philosophe: Albert le Grand, Thomas d'Aquin, Guillaume de Moerbeke et l'invention du Liber de bona fortuna comme alternative autorisée à l'interprétation averroïste de la théorie aristotélicienne de la providence divine," in *Christian Readings of Aristotle from the Middle Ages to the Renaissance*, ed. L. Bianchi (Turnhout: Brepols, 2011), 65–114.

82. The *Physics*, *De anima*, and *De sensu*. The Commentary on the *Metaphysics* seems to have been done using principally the *Media* (an anonymous translation of Aristotle's work) and then revised using Moerbeke's first translation of the *Metaphysics* and his revision.

of arts, which bears witness to the undisputed prestige he had earned as an Aristotle commentator among those who were professionally bound to read and comment on Aristotle).

We can, thus, hypothesize, as we have already said, that Thomas read and commented on Aristotle's work to prepare himself adequately for the drafting of certain parts of his own theological works, and above all (or almost exclusively) for the *Summa theologiae*. This is almost certainly true for the *De anima* and the *Nicomachean Ethics*, which are connected to the psychological and practical parts of the *Summa*. But the same cannot be said of the commentaries on Aristotle's other works: the *Politics*, the logical works, the *Physics*, the *Metaphysics*, and even less the *De sensu*, the *De generatione*, and the *Meteorologica*. When Thomas worked on the commentaries on the *Physics* and the *Metaphysics*, the speculative part of the *Summa* was already finished. And, after all, why should he interest himself from a theological point of view in phenomena like the composition of mixed bodies, meteors, and earthquakes? So, the connection between his activity as commentator and theologian is valid and established, but only up to a certain point, and not in general.

We can only appeal, then, to what we said earlier. Thomas's interest in Aristotle's works is not simply instrumental, that is, it is not directed only at drawing from the well of Aristotelian knowledge what is useful or necessary for building the new scientific edifice of Christian knowledge. His interest is, rather, an essential feature of his overall attitude. Thomas sought, until his very last years, to engage with the complete system of the sciences (seeking to keep himself up-to-date even in regard to texts whose translation had only just become available in those last years). Perhaps the knowledge of lightning and earthquakes was not of immediate use in his theological writings, but Thomas remained convinced (by his personal formation, by his apprenticeship with Albert the Great, by his extraordinary intellectual curiosity) that a good theologian must be, in the first place, a person of science in general, and hold to the duty of never neglecting engagement with the profane sciences, even if he does not take up each one in an analytic way.

TWO NON-ARISTOTELIAN COMMENTARIES
Beyond Forms: The Commentary on the *Liber de causis*

Two other commentaries of the second period in Paris can be placed together with the commentaries on Aristotle: The Commentary on the *Liber de causis* and the Commentary on Boethius's *De ebdomadibus*.[83] In regard to the former we

---

83. As already indicated, following the Leonine editors, we adopt the spelling of Boethius's work that omits the initial "h."

should first of all say a word about the nature of the *Liber de causis*, whose origin can probably be traced back to the circle of al-Kindi (c. 795–865). Known in the Arabic world by the name the *Discourse on the Exposition of the Pure Good*, it was subsequently circulated in the Latin world as the *Liber de causis*, thanks to a translation by Gerard of Cremona (c. 1114–87) in the second half of the twelfth century. The *De causis* is, in fact, a collection of 31 propositions (32 in the Latin version) taken from Proclus's *Elementatio theologica* and placed in a different order that manifests the influence of Plotinus.

There are explicitly present in the *De causis* syncretistic characteristics that are typical of the beginnings of Arab philosophy, and of the circle of al-Kindi in particular, such as the creationistic interpretation of the action of the first cause and its identification with pure being. As such, the first cause is the cause of being, which is the first of created things. Some basic themes are present in the *De causis* that constitute a kind of common patrimony of medieval Neo-Platonism. Among these are, for example, the primacy of the most remote cause over the proximate causes and the doctrine that the cause is in the effect in the mode proper to the effect and the effect is in the cause in the mode proper to the cause. To this is linked, as a consequence, the principle according to which everything that is produced or bestowed by a higher cause is received according to the mode and measure of the recipient. In the Latin world the *De causis* had initially been thought to be an Aristotelian work about separate substances and, so, in a certain way at the apex of the Aristotelian corpus. It is no accident that the *De causis* figures in the Paris faculty of arts' statutes (which we have already mentioned several times) as a text that it was obligatory to teach, and in some compendia for the use of students it appears coupled with the *Metaphysics*. The *De causis* had been the object of an attentive paraphrase by Albert the Great in Book II of the *De causis et processu universitatis*,[84] and Thomas already knew and cited it (almost 70 times) when he was composing the Commentary on the *Sentences* (while it was still believed by many to be an Aristotelian work).[85] But already

84. Given the form of the work, which is composed of axioms or propositions accompanied by comments, Albert hypothesized that the text was a collection made by David Iudaeus (Avendauth) of sayings of Avicenna and al-Fārābī related to a letter of Aristotle, "On the Principle of the Totality of Being."

85. On the presence of *De causis* in the whole of Thomas's work, see C. Vansteenkiste, "Il *Liber de causis* negli scritti di San Tommaso," *Angelicum* 35 (1958): 325–74. For a critical assessment of the studies on this question, see C. D'Ancona Costa, "Saint Thomas lecteur du *Liber de causis*: Bilan des recherches contemporaines concernant le *De causis* et analyse de l'interprétation thomiste," *Revue Thomiste* 92 (1992): 611–49. D'Ancona also has a lovely introduction to her own Italian translation of Thomas's commentary, Tommaso d' Aquino, *Commento al Libro delle cause* (Milan: Rusconi, 1986): especially at 78–120.

here—as has been very ably noted—Thomas manifests some perplexity, so much so that he occasionally thinks that the author of the *De causis* might be someone else, an authority comparable to Aristotle and Avicenna. Above all, Thomas had immediately understood the decidedly Neo-Platonic background that characterizes the work and the proximity to some themes of Pseudo-Dionysius, to whom we will return shortly. This is an obvious proof of Thomas's uncommon and particularly sophisticated philosophical sensibility, able to grasp the significance and doctrinal place of the texts beyond their presumed origin and standard interpretation. Thomas would have his intuition confirmed some years later, and precisely after William of Moerbeke had produced his translation of Proclus's *Elementatio theologica*, which he concluded in March 1268 at the papal curia in Viterbo. Having acquired Proclus's text, Thomas realized that the *De causis* was only a compilation, reduced and in some cases reworked, of the *Elementatio*. In the prologue to his commentary Thomas notes the real provenance of the text:

Thus, there are some writings on the first principles, divided into different propositions, in a way similar to the procedure of those examining certain truths one at a time. A book of this sort exists in Greek, written by the Platonist Proclus. It contains 211 propositions and is entitled *Elementatio theologica*. The book [upon which we are about to comment] exists in Arabic and is called *De causis* among Latins. We know that it was translated from Arabic and does not exist at all in Greek. Thus, it seems that one of the Arab philosophers excerpted it from Proclus's book, since everything in it is contained much more completely and extensively in Proclus's book.[86]

The commentary dates from 1272 and so is subsequent not only to the *prima* and *secunda pars* of the *Summa* but also probably to the Commentary on the *Metaphysics* itself, and, therefore, is Thomas's last work on metaphysical questions, and perhaps the one that more than any other reflects the final development of his thought in this area. On the basis of his discovery of its dependency on Proclus, in his Commentary on the *De causis* Thomas always seeks to compare its propositions with those of the *Elementatio*. Because of this comparative work Thomas has no problem in seeing that Proclus's text is not only more complete but in general more clear and articulate. Thomas thereby reveals that the compiler of the *De causis* has betrayed his source on certain points that are of no small importance. But, on the other hand, Thomas appreciates the work of integrating monotheism within a Neo-Platonic horizon, with the rejection, for example, of the world of ideas. On account of his philosophical penetration Thomas recognized, as we previously observed, that the *De causis* had some affinity, from this point of view, with the work of Pseudo-Dionysius. This is worth noting in itself. Thomas could

---

86. Commentary on the *Liber de causis*, prol.

in no way imagine that Dionysius was not the man converted by Paul at the Areopagus or, in any case, one of the first Fathers of the Church, but, in all probability, a much later direct disciple of Proclus. The link that, for us, connects the *De causis* to the work of Pseudo-Dionysius—the common dependency on Proclus—was, thus, intuited by Thomas on a purely philosophical, doctrinal level. There are many elements that Thomas assimilates from the *De causis*. The first is its doctrine of causality, that is, the already-mentioned primacy of remote causes over proximate causes, and, above all, the circular interpretation of causal processes, which takes the cause to be present in the effect but according to the mode of the effect (and, thus, in a weakened way), while the effect is pre-contained in the cause in the mode of the cause (and, thus, in a nobler way). It is precisely this circularity of the causal relationship that founds the dynamic of participation and, *de facto*, ensures the continuity and, indeed, the unitariness of the universe—a unitariness that has its manifestation in the order of the world, that is, in the providential governance that rules it. And, nevertheless, Thomas notes that what in the "Platonists" is understood solely in reference to formal causality, must in reality also include, if not first of all, efficient causality. In short, the relationship of the causes should be understood not only as a process that leads from the first and most universal forms to those that are more determinate and numerous, but also as the creation of being. The most remote cause is first because it gives being. This is the way that Thomas reinterprets the great novelty of the *De causis* that is contained in prop. 4 (*prima rerum creatarum est esse*). Being is what is first created, in the sense that it is the first effect of God's efficient causality. (The author of the *De causis*, as Thomas points out, refers not to *esse commune* but to the being of the first effect, namely, Intelligence.) Nevertheless, this very production of being presupposes that God himself is being, indeed, pure being.

Although the monotheistic (Islamic) concern recognized by Thomas is effectively present in the *De causis*, it is also true that the Neo-Platonic hierarchical structure, with various grades of mediation, is far from abolished or suppressed. Thomas does not intend to deny the existence of intermediate realities (the intelligences, which are identified with the angels of Judeo-Christian revelation), but he introduces some decisive corrections: the elimination of the souls of celestial bodies (the souls of which the *De causis* speaks are more generically identified with human souls); the radical rejection (that we already considered in the *De potentia*) of the thesis according to which the intelligences are delegated a causal role vis-à-vis lower beings, souls in particular;[87] a more careful distinction be-

---

87. For Thomas, the intelligences do mediate in some way but not as efficient causes. Instead, he holds that they produce intelligible forms that they convey to souls.

tween angelic supertemporality (aeveternity or *aevum* in the Scholastic lexicon) and divine eternity.[88]

This last point leads us to another that is, in fact, the crucial point of Thomas's commentary, namely, the way in which Thomas interprets and employs proposition 9 of the *De causis*: *Cause prime non est yliathim*.[89] The term *yliathim* may appear mysterious, inasmuch as the translator was unable to find a Latin equivalent of the Arabic term and simply transliterates it. Since *yliathim* seems to echo the Greek *hylē* (matter), the thesis of proposition 9 lends itself to being interpreted in the sense of the universal hylomorphism of Avicebron: God alone is absolutely simple, whereas the intelligences possess a spiritual matter. But Thomas proceeds differently, understanding that here *yliathim* does not designate matter but exactly the contrary, that is, form. This interpretive choice is not only historically more correct (once again Thomas, although he does not have the necessary philological instruments at his disposal, intuits the authentic philosophical meaning of the thesis in question), nor does it merely represent another occasion to reject universal hylomorphism (as he had already done in the *De ente*). It expresses in the most complete way one of the fundamental theses—or perhaps *the* fundamental thesis—of Thomas's metaphysics: the basic composition is not matter-form (the composition that constitutes the essence of sensible realities) but that between essence and existence. Even the most elevated of intelligences, although it is totally free of matter, possesses an essence that is different from its existence. Only in God do essence and existence coincide. The consequences of this position can be easily grasped. The real metaphysical difference that characterizes Thomas's universe is not between what is material and immaterial (a classical, Platonic distinction but also, at bottom, an Aristotelian distinction, if we consider the doctrine of separation proposed in Book I of the *Metaphysics*), but between what possesses form (a form) and that which is above every form. What truly distinguishes God, or the first cause, is not the simple fact that he is above matter; it is that he is above every form. Being beyond forms means being unthinkable, unrepresentable, unobjectifiable. God is not a possible object of thought, and cannot be thought in objective terms. That Thomas expressed this fundamental thesis—which is also already present in some way even in his early writings (the *De ente* comes to mind)—in

---

88. According to Thomas, the angels too are atemporal, but their duration is not characterized by the fullness of being, that is, by the absolute identity of being and essence, which distinguishes God, but by a certain form of potentiality in the measure in which the essence of each angel is distinct from its being and in potency to it.

89. C. D'Ancona, "'*Cause prime non est yliathim*': *Liber de causis*, prop. 8(9): le fonti e la dottrina," *Documenti e studi sulla tradizione filosofica medieval* 1 (1990): 327–51.

the Commentary on the *Liber de causis* is not at all surprising. The superiority of the One over the forms is an exquisitely Neo-Platonic thesis, systematized precisely by Proclus. Thomas's originality is not only in transferring this approach to the Neo-Platonic One to the Christian God, but in making it an interpretive key of the whole of reality. Having an essence that is distinct from existence, and, hence, possessing a form (even one that is very noble, perfect), and so being thinkable in objective terms, is what characterizes every creature and distinguishes it from God. But it should also be noted that there is nothing truly negative, nothing unworthy, in possessing an essence or form: the form is (in an Aristotelian manner), indeed, the actuality of each thing, its perfection. The topic of the distinction between being and essence, and of the superiority of pure being over what is also form, thus, permits Thomas to mark in the clearest way the distance between God and creatures and, at the same time, fully to safeguard the dignity and even the (relative) perfection of creatures. Each creature is such because it has a form (an actuality) to which a further actuality is added (existence). Therefore, the limit of each creature is not in some grave imperfection or ontological deficiency but in the fact that these two actualities do not coincide, as they do in God.

Good and Participation: The Commentary
on Boethius's *De ebdomadibus*

Unlike the Commentary on the *De Trinitate* (which we discussed in Chapter 2), the Commentary on the *De ebdomadibus* is only a literal exposition of Boethius's text. What is striking in this case is precisely the very strict adherence to the text commented on. Apart from Aristotle, no other philosophical authority is cited in this commentary, and the biblical citations are confined to the introductive lines, which develop a series of considerations based on a verse of Ecclesiasticus chosen as the epigraph.

The lack of elements of external criticism make it quite difficult to determine the date of this work, which is very uncertain. For a long time it was supposed that it was possible to situate the Commentary on the *De ebdomdibus* in 1257–58, but the sole apparent justification for this dating was the desire to place it in proximity (also chronologically) to the Commentary on the *De Trinitate*. But certain circumstances render this conjecture rather implausible, beginning with the fact that, as the Leonine Commission editors have observed, in the autograph of the Commentary on the *De Trinitate*, the *De ebdomadibus* is indicated by the abbreviation *epd.* (thus, *De epdomadibus*), while in the commentary on it, it is referred to—quite unusually—as *De ekdomatibus*. We cannot appeal in this case to some paleographic accident, for Thomas—as we will soon see—

uses this seemingly aberrant spelling in an entirely conscious way, proposing a different interpretation of the title's meaning (and, above all, of its origin). However, the Leonine Commission editors did not formulate other hypotheses about the commentary's dating. Gauthier, for his part, had suggested situating it between 1271 and 1272, and, thus, during the period of the second Paris regency that we are now discussing. From the point of view of internal criticism there also seem to be no elements that would justify a more precise dating. It is, at any rate, a fact worth noting that whereas in other works Thomas confidently uses the conceptual pair *quo est/quod est*—introduced by Gilbert de la Porrée to express the Boethian distinction between *esse* and *quod est*—he does not even mention it here, that is, in what should be the natural place to employ it.

Regarding the interpretation of Boethius's title, the most noteworthy aspect is that Thomas ends up aligning himself with an already well-established tradition, but he gets there by a rather unusual route. The original title of the opuscule, as it is opportune to recall, is *Quomodo substantiae in eo quod sint bonae sint cum non sint substantialia bona*. But since Boethius observes in the opening lines that this question is taken precisely from the "hebdomads," the treatise began gradually to circulate under the title *De ebdomadibus*, a title that had the obvious advantage of much greater brevity. Yet, even today it is still not clear what the term "hebdomads" is supposed to mean. Is it a series of writings collected in groups of seven, a mixed composition of prose and verse, or even the *Consolation of Philosophy* itself, as has also been suggested?[90] The medieval reception of the work too manifests a diversity of opinions on this topic. The author of the *Fragmentum admuntense* edited by Nikolaus Häring holds, for example, that the term must be interpreted in its literal sense as "week," adducing as the explanation—suggestive in itself—that the wise men of antiquity would set aside seven or eight days to dedicate themselves to reflection on particularly difficult questions.[91] Remigius of Auxerre, Thierry of Chartres, Gilbert de la Porrée, Clarembald of Arras, Alain de Lille, Albert the Great—with different nuances—hold, on the other hand, that the term *ebdomades* must be understood as deriving from the (fictitious) Greek word *ebdo* (*concipio*), and indicates conceptions of the mind.[92] Reading *ekdomates* in the place of *ebdomades*,

---

90. See, for example, the hypothesis suggested by Obertello in the introductory note to his own translation of the theological tractates: Boezio, *La consolazione della filosofia—Gli opuscoli teologici*, ed. Obertello (Milan: Rusconi, 1979), 379–80.

91. *Commentum super Boethii librum De hebdomadius (Fragmentum admuntense)*, in *Commentaries on Boethius by Thierry of Chartres and His School*, ed. N. M. Häring (Toronto: Pontifical Institute of Mediaeval Studies, 1971), 119.

92. A synthetic picture of these different interpretations can be found in the introduction of Bataillon and Grassi to the commentary *De ebdomadibus* in vol. 1 of the Leonine edition, 20–63.

Thomas connects the meaning of the word with Greek word *ekdídōmi*, corresponding with the Latin *edere*. According to Thomas, then, *ekdomates* stands for *editiones*, not in the sense of editions or publications (the sense that is probably most immediate for us) but in the sense of mental products, of conceptions. *Edere*, in its most pregnant sense, means the same as *concipere*. So, *editiones* must be understood along the lines of *conceptiones*, and, in fact, at least once in the course of the commentary, the two terms are used synonymously (*editiones seu conceptiones*). Moreover, Thomas's choice for the epigraph (*Precurre prior in domum tuam, et illic aduocare, et illic lude et age conceptiones tuas*)[93] should perhaps be understood in this light.

What are the "conceptions" meant here? Certainly those that Boethius considers in himself (*Ebdomadas vero ego michi ipse commentor*), as Thomas explains in the commentary, but also—perhaps—the *communes animi conceptiones* that represent the group of fundamental axioms or rules that Boethius himself introduces in the text as the solution to the problem in question, that is, about how things can be considered good insofar as they exist. If this the case, then the sense in which Thomas understands the current title of Boethius's opuscule is not as far from the views of Thierry of Chartres and the tradition following Gilbert de la Porrée as is commonly thought.

Apart from its reference to the content of the work, the epigraph chosen by Thomas provides insight into what is, honestly, one of the most winsome passages in all of Thomas's writings. The passage that compares wisdom and play, activities that have in common not only pleasure but, above all, the fact of being gratuitous, ends in themselves.

The Distinction between *esse* and *id quod est* The real starting point of Thomas's commentary on the *De ebdomadibus* is the celebrated Boethian distinction between *esse*, "being," and *id quod est*, "that which is."[94] Thomas very carefully

---

93. Sir. 32:11–12; *Vulgate*, Eccl. 32:15–16.

94. The proper way to understand this conceptual pair is ever a subject of debate. For a review of the positions on this topic, see R. M. McInerny, *Boethius and Aquinas* (Washington, D.C.: The Catholic University of America Press, 1991), 161–98. The fundamental thesis of McInerny's volume—already anticipated in his article "Boethius and Saint Thomas Aquinas," *Rivista di Filosofia neoscolastica* 66 (1974): 219–45—is that Boethius intends to speak exactly as Thomas explains, especially in reference to the thesis according to which there is just one being beyond every composite. On Thomas's interpretation, see V. Clare, "Whether Everything That Is, Is Good: Marginal Notes on St. Thomas's Exposition of Boethius' De hebdomadibus," *Laval Théologique et Philosophique* 3 (1947): 66–76 and 177–94; 5 (1949): 119–40; E. Trepanier, "Saint Thomas et le De hebdomadibus de Boèce," *Laval Théologique et Philosophique* 6 (1950): 131–44; C. Fabro, *Partecipazione e causalità secondo s. Tommaso d'Aquino* (Turin: SEI, 1960), especially 204–13; G. Schrimpf, *Die Axiomenschrift des Boethius* (De Hebdomadibus) *als philosophisches Lehrbuch des Mittelalters* (Leiden: Brill, 1966), 119–38; G. Casey, "An Explication of the *De hebdomadibus* of Boethius in the Light of St. Thomas's Commentary," *The Thomist* 51 (1987): 419–34.

points out that, initially at least, this is not a distinction between things but between intentions, that is, between concepts (which makes it such that, initially, this part of the text can be read very differently by those who hold that Thomas posits a very sharp real distinction between being and essence and by those who reject this interpretation). In fact, at this level of the discussion, "being" and "that which is" relate to each other as abstract and concrete. This allows us, nevertheless, to identify some fundamental differences. The first is that "to be"—as an abstract term—cannot be its own subject (just as "to run" is not the subject of "running"), whereas "that which is" indicates the subject that possesses being, or better: that which subsists precisely because it receives the form of being. The latter expression (*forma essendi*) has an unequivocally Neo-Platonic background, which Pierre Hadot has well demonstrated.[95] Thomas does not appear to devote much attention to it, identifying the assumption of the *forma essendi* with that of act of being (*scilicet suscipiendo ipsum actum essendi*). But later it will be explicitly qualified as the *principium essendi*, that is, as that which determines the exercise of the act of being in each individual being. And from this point of view Thomas is not very distant from that line of Neo-Platonism that has its roots in Porphyry and develops through Pseudo-Dionysius and the *De causis* (despite the direct origin of this work in Proclus's *Elementatio theologica*)—a line that takes the difference between the first cause and every other being (including immaterial beings) to reside in the fact that the former is pure, indeterminate and undeterminable being, while everything else is being and form, that is, formally determined being (*ens habens yliathim*, to use the pregnant expression that we encountered in the *De causis*).

The second principal difference between being and "that which is" is that the latter can participate in something.[96] But to clarify this point Thomas dis-

95. See P. Hadot, "*Forma essendi*: Interprétation philologique et interpretation philosophique d'une formule de Boèce," *Les Etudes Classiques* 38 (1970): 143–56. Hadot suggests interpreting the Boethian conceptual pair (probably through the influence of Marius Victorinus) starting with the superiority of the *einai* over *on* (at the hypostatic level) postulated by Porphyry. The principle that subtends this ordering is that pure being, in the measure in which it is received in beings, is contracted and determined, and what permits such determination is, precisely, the form. The expression *forma essendi* would, therefore, signify that a being *is* when it receives its form of being—when, that is, it assumes its particular manner of exercising the act of being. See, also, the previous contribution of Hadot, "La distinction de l'être et de l'étant dans le De hebdomadibus de Boèce," in *Die Metaphysik im Mittelalter*, Miscellanea Mediaevalia 2, ed. P. Wilpert (Berlin: de Gruyter, 1963), 147–53.

96. On the concept of "participation" in Thomas, besides the classic volume of Fabro cited in n. 94, see N. Clarke, "The Meaning of Participation in St. Thomas Aquinas," *Proceedings of the American Catholic Philosophical Association* 26 (1952): 147–57; the imposing volume of L.-B. Geiger, *La participation dans la philosophie de S. Thomas d'Aquin* (Paris: Vrin, 1953); and the more recent contribution of R. A. Te Velde, *Participation and Substantiality in Thomas Aquinas*, Studien und Texte zur Geistesgeschichte des Mittelalters 46 (Leiden: Brill, 1995), especially 8–20.

tinguishes between three modalities of participation: (a) that in which the particular participates in the universal; (b) that in which the subject participates in the accident or matter in form; (c) that (more generic) in which the effect participates in the form.

This last acceptation is, in fact, immediately set aside. What Thomas is interested in is showing how it is impossible for being to participate in something in the first two ways. With the second way, being is still understood abstractly, so it cannot be assimilated to the subject that participates in accidents or to the matter that participates in form. The participation indicated by the first way can occur in abstract terms (whiteness, for example, can participate in color). But because being is the term that is absolutely most universal, there is nothing more universal above it and so it cannot participate in a more encompassing term. It could be objected that "that which is" is just as universal. Precisely because of this, however, it participates in being, not as that which is less universal participates in what is more universal, but as that which is concrete participates in what is abstract (even though Thomas does not go on to explain, at least in this case, how this type of participation relates to the three modalities he has distinguished; on the other hand, still dealing with intentions, this relationship does not yet constitute anything real).

And from this a third difference can be identified. Unlike concrete terms, abstract ones (including, in this instance, being) can have nothing added to them. "Humanity," for example, indicates solely what man as such is, excluding everything that does not enter into its essential concept. But if we take "man" in concrete, nothing prevents many other characteristics being added beyond that of being a man.

This permits us, following the path of Boethius's text itself, to move on to the subsequent further distinction between *esse simpliciter* and *esse aliquid*. From what we have already seen, it is only within *id quod est* that this distinction that can have a place. *Esse simpliciter* is what derives from the substantial form of each thing (from that form that is identical with the essence itself of the thing). *Esse aliquid* is what derives from the accidental forms of the thing (those forms that are not a part of the essence of a thing in a strict sense). To receive its *esse simpliciter*, "that which is" must participate in being according to its substantial form. And when it is thus constituted it can participate in something extrinsic to the essence and so have *esse aliquid*. This is, indeed, an ambiguous formulation, for (at least from one perspective) "that which is" already is something determinate through its substantial form.

It is only when Boethius comes to treat of the axioms related to what is simple and what is composite that Thomas moves in his commentary from the logical order to the real order. In composite things *esse* and *quod est* differ not only *secundum intentiones* but *realiter*. And this is one of the few occasions in which this adverb is explicitly employed by Thomas in reference to the relationship that obtains between the ontological principles of a thing. Because being itself is not composite, as is evident from what has already been said, it follows, inversely, that no composite thing is *its* being (and much less is it being in general). In simple beings, however, being and "that which is" are really identical. But this does not mean that such realities are absolutely simple. Reprising the essentials of the argumentation already developed in this regard in the *De ente et essentia*, Thomas undertakes to show that even simple forms (insofar as they lack matter) are composite in another sense. Every form is, in fact, "determinative of its being (*determinativa ipsius esse*)," that is, it is not pure being but qualified, determinate being, endowed with an objective content—which is, precisely, its form. Only that which does not participate being, that which is subsistent being, is simple in an absolute sense. And that which is such—as was already shown in the *De ente*—cannot but be one, since it is intrinsically lacking in any principle of plurification or differentiation.

We return, thus, to what we saw earlier. Joining the suggestions from Boethius with what he was able to draw in another way from the *De causis* and Avicenna, Thomas identifies the fundamental caesura of his metaphysical universe with the opposition between what is only being—and, as such, unobjectifiable, inexpressible, indeterminable—and what is formally determinate. If the distinction between being and essence plays a precise role in Thomas's thought, it is exactly here that it makes all of its weight felt, and not in relation to the problem of creaturely contingency or the centrality of the act of being in finite things. With respect to the question about whether this distinction can be understood as "real," it continues to appear wrongly formulated from the start,[97] because it does not seem to be what Thomas is truly concerned with (despite the centuries-long debate between Thomists and Suarezians—or, if one prefers—between Dominicans and Jesuits). The same passage that we have just considered from the Commentary on the *De ebdomadibus* confirms this in a certain way. A real distinction is spoken of in regard to composite beings (*sicut esse et quod est differunt secundum intentiones, ita in compositis differunt realiter*) but not in regard to simple things (*in simplicibus ... necesse est quod ipsum esse et id quod est sit unum et idem realiter*). And yet it is precisely in regard to simple beings that the distinction has the most sense and value, to the extent that it

---

97. On this subject see P. Porro, "Qualche riferimento storiografico sulla distinzione di essere ed essenza," in Tommaso d'Aquino, *L'ente e l'essenza*, trans. and ed. P. Porro (Milan: Bompiani, 2002), 183–215.

allows us to separate subsistent being from all other forms, however eternal, necessary, and immaterial (and we will recall that these are all characteristics that in other works Thomas attributes to separate substances) they may be.

The Goodness of Things   After this long ontological introduction, which is perfectly justified by the axiomatic position taken by Boethius, Thomas's commentary faithfully follows the course of the opuscule, taking up its specific topic—ascertaining whether finite things are good in their own substance or by participation. If we opt for the second hypothesis, it seems necessary to admit thereby that things are not good in themselves. But if they are not good in themselves, they cannot even tend toward the good, since everything tends toward what is like itself. It is evident, however, that everything desires its good and its perfection. On the other hand, if things are good by their own substance, their being itself would be good. Being and goodness would be identical exactly as they are in the first good itself. Consequently, everything would be God.

Perhaps the most relevant aspect of Thomas's commentary on this point is his elucidation of the manner in which Boethius contrasts being something by participation with being something substantially. According to Thomas, this antithesis makes sense only if participation is understood in the second of the three ways we saw before, namely, the mode by which a subject participates in accidents and matter in form. In effect, accidents are extrinsic to the substance of the subject and the form is extrinsic to the substance of the matter. Thus, in these cases what a thing has on account of its substance can stand in opposition to what it receives by participation (or through its substantial form or accidental forms). If participation is understood in the first way—the participation of the particular in the universal—this sort of opposition becomes not only unjustified but dangerous because it runs the risk of creating a form of radical Platonism. If species and genera were really extrinsic to each other as accidents are to their subject and form is to matter, they would be separately existing ideas. But Aristotle is perfectly correct to hold that genera do not exist outside of species and that all species are already implicitly contained in genera. It is pointless to say that Thomas adopts the more charitable reading of Boethius, suggesting that, with respect to the alternative posed a moment ago, he had intended to refer to the participation that we find in the relationships between the subject and accidents and matter and form. In any event, it is a fact that, starting with the *De ente*, the correct use of logical predicables as a means toward a preliminary purification in every metaphysical inquiry is a constant concern for Thomas.

An exigency of the same type can be found in another clarification Thomas makes regarding Boethius's way of distinguishing between what belongs to a thing by participation and what belongs to it "*per se.*" This is a true distinction if "*per se*" is understood to indicate what enters into the definition of a thing. But it is a false distinction if "*per se*" is understood to indicate the way that the subject enters into the definition of the predicate. In this latter case the accident, although it inheres in the subject "*per se,*" can be predicated of it by participation.

Boethius's own answer to the question about the provenance of the goodness of things seems not to pose any special problem. The being of finite things is good since it comes from that which is essentially good. However, Thomas—with Aristotle's help—makes an observation in the conclusion of his commentary on the fourth chapter that dilutes the Platonizing tendency of Boethius's approach. There is, in fact, a twofold goodness in things: that which derives from their relationship to the first good itself and that which they possess in themselves, and not according to being, but according to their own virtue. In other words, the ontological goodness of things is a relative goodness, whereas the goodness that things possess in an absolute sense is eminently practical.

Thomas's commentary concludes with the analysis of two possible objections that Boethius himself poses against his own solution. The first appears rather intricate at first: if all things are good in their being, since they come from the one who willed that they be good, then white things should be white in their being, since they come from the one who willed that they be white. In this way the being of things would be not only good but also white and everything else. The answer, however, is relatively simple: God is essentially good but he is not essentially white. Thus, that which receives its being from God will be good in its very being, but this does not hold for all dispositions or properties. The second objection is not very different: since God is not only essentially good but also essentially just, all things must be not only good but also just. But neither is this necessary, for justice properly regards operation whereas goodness regards being. And although in God being and operation form a unity, this is not true for us. On the other hand, justice is a kind of good, and as such has a more narrow extension. The genus is found in all the species, but the contrary does not hold. Here too (where he follows Boethius's text quite closely) Thomas is concerned to keep open the possibility of considering more than the ontological goodness of things; he also wants to consider the capacity of things (their virtue) to seek their own perfection. Thomas's cosmos, in a certain sense, possesses a greater autonomy than Boethius's.

Thomas seems more interested in the metaphysical presuppositions of the

De ebdomadibus than its specific topic. And from this point of view the general purpose of Thomas's engagement with Boethius seems, in fact, to have to do with a parallel inquiry into the methodological structures (the Commentary on the *De Trinitate*) and certain fundamental concepts (the Commentary on the *De ebdomadibus*) of first philosophy.

THOMAS AND THE "JEWISH QUESTION":
THE LETTER TO THE COUNTESS OF FLANDERS

Among the many responses and opinions that Thomas furnishes various interlocutors appears a text that is traditionally called the *Epistola ad Ducissam Brabantiae* (*Letter to the Duchess of Brabant*), a title that it also bears in the Leonine edition. The identity of this mysterious duchess has been at the center of a long debate, which has seen the following candidates proposed: Adelaide (or Alice) of Burgundy, wife (and then widow) of Henry III of Flanders; Margaret of France, daughter of Louis IX and wife of Duke John; Margaret of Constantinople, daughter of Baldwin I and Countess of Flanders between 1245 and 1278. The last candidate, proposed by Leonard Boyle, seems the most plausible, since the same countess seems to have addressed more or less the same questions to both the Franciscan John Peckham (a great adversary of Thomas) and (as Gilbert Dahan subsequently noted) a secular master (who might have been Gerard of Abbeville). Evidence suggests that the text can be dated to 1271.

Assuming that Margaret of Constantinople is the addressee, the letter is more properly titled *Epistola ad comitissam Flandriae* (*Letter to the Countess of Flanders*), a title that does appear in Tolomeo of Lucca's catalogue and in at least one Paris manuscript. But in the tradition (in the Prague Catalogue, Bartholomew of Capua's catalogue, and Bernardo Gui's catalogue) the same text appears under other names, as *De regimine Iudaeorum* (on the manner of governing the Jews) or simply as *De Iudeis*. And, in fact, although the questions do not all concern the relations with Jews in the territory, it would be clearly disingenuous to deny that this is beyond a shadow of a doubt the most important aspect of the text. The *Letter*, then, is the principal place in which Thomas deals with the Jewish question.[98]

The content is a little disappointing, and this impression is also confirmed when it is compared just to the responses of John Peckham. Thomas confesses

---

98. See J. Y. B. Hood, *Aquinas and the Jews* (Philadelphia: University of Pennsylvania Press, 1995). The basic thesis is that Thomas did not directly contribute to the strengthening of a climate of hostility against the Hebrews, with the exception, perhaps, of what concerns the severe condemnation of usury (see, especially, 108).

very honestly at the beginning that answering the questions was truly difficult for him because of duties connected with teaching and because of the limits of his competence (and the *Letter* concludes with the invitation to inquire of people more expert in the area). It is also possible—at least it is comforting to think (even though there is no objective indication about it)—that Thomas was uncomfortable about what he was asked. The first and most important questions have to do with how to treat the Jews. This is one of the cases in which Thomas does not manage to question the customs of the time. To the countess's first question about whether it is legitimate to impose financial burdens on the Jewish community, Thomas answers with an appeal to the distressing general principle according to which the Jews, being the bearers of an inexcusable historical fault, can even be legitimately deprived of all their goods save for those necessary for survival. This principle is qualified in two ways. The first qualification is set down only to avoid creating scandals. New tributes beyond those already in force should not be exacted, since every novelty creates confusion and disorder. The second is more relevant. If the only thing possessed by the Jews derives from usury (which seems to be the specific case that the countess mentions to Thomas), it should not be kept by the rulers, lest the latter be stained indirectly by the same sin of usury. This does not mean that this money should not be taken from the Jews by taxation. If it is taken from the Jews, it should be returned to those from whom it was extorted (to use Thomas's own language), redistributed by the bishops or by the rulers for the common good. For this same reason Thomas has no trouble in granting that the Jews can—indeed should—be fined for the practice of usury, so long as the money from these fines is then handled in the ways just indicated and other sanctions are added to these fines "so that it not be thought that the guilty party is sufficiently punished when he ceases to possess the money taken from others." The obligation to restore or redistribute goods collected from the Jews certainly does do economic harm to the rulers, but it is a harm that, in the final analysis, stems from the negligence of the rulers themselves, as Thomas observes quite dryly:

But if it be said that the princes of countries suffer loss from this, this loss should be imputed to them as coming from their own negligence, for it would be better if they compelled Jews to work for their own living, as they do in parts of Italy, than that, living without occupation they grow rich by usury, and thus their rulers be defrauded of revenue. In the same way, and through their own fault, princes are defrauded of their proper revenues if they permit their subjects to enrich themselves by theft and robbery alone, for they would be bound to restore [to the real owner] whatever they had exacted from them [the thieves].

Thomas uses the same model for dealing with sums that exceed what is collected through normal taxes. Both the money taken from the Jews and the excess from taxes should be dealt with in the ways mentioned earlier, that is, they should be returned to those from whom they were extracted by usury, or redistributed, or used for purposes of public benefit.

Connected with this are other questions raised by the countess about the selling of public offices (which Thomas regards as legitimate but discourages, suggesting that the offices be entrusted to competent persons), the possible deposit that the office holders should make for their position (which Thomas sees as an implicit case of usury and, as such, absolutely unacceptable), the licitness of taxing Christian subjects (which Thomas concedes, since the rulers have a right to live at the community's expense and to procure what is necessary for its defense, but specifies that it is "absolutely immoral for the rulers to demand taxes beyond the established limits out of greed or to give themselves over to excessive spending, that is, without justification"), and what should be done when functionaries collect more taxes than it is right to ask. (For Thomas, in these cases, the prince is obliged to return the sums that were wrongly taken or, when that is impossible, to use the money for the common good.)

The last question has again to do with the Jews. The countess asks whether it is appropriate to make them outwardly distinguish themselves in some manner from Christians. Unfortunately, Thomas's response is again disappointing, because he simply refers the question to the decisions of advisors and customary practices:

The reply to this is plain and corresponds to the statute of the general Council: Jews of each sex in all Christian provinces, and all the time, should be distinguished from other people by some clothing. This is also mandated to them by their own law, namely that they make for themselves fringes on the four corners of their cloaks, through which they are distinguished from others.

It would, of course, be anachronistic and unjust to pretend that Thomas has the ability to depart from the social norms and conventions of his time. Nevertheless, it is true that in this area Thomas does not display the intellectual courage that he does with respect to many other questions (and in his general approach to philosophy). On the other hand, it would likewise be unjust to accuse Thomas of an irrational and extreme anti-Semitism. To cite but one example, Thomas strongly opposes the practice of the forced baptism of Jewish children. Baptizing children against the will of their parents not only constitutes a danger to the faith but is in itself repugnant to natural justice (*Quodlibet* II, q. 4, a. 2).

NATURE, THE INFLUENCE OF THE STARS, AND
DIVINATION: TREATISES AND OPUSCULES
De occultibus operationibus naturae

During the last years of his teaching, between Paris and Naples, Thomas composed various other opuscules on the most disparate topics in reply to requests from confreres, friends, or other interlocutors. We can locate the *De occultibus operationibus naturae*, for example, in the area of natural philosophy. Its addressee is simply referred to as a transalpine knight or soldier (*miles ultramontanus*). The expression "transalpine" itself does not tell us much, since it is a relative term. If Thomas wrote the piece in France—as seems most likely—then the addressee would be an Italian soldier, and if it were written in Italy, then it would be a French soldier. It is, in any case, worth noting that people of different extractions, not strictly or professionally interested in philosophy, turned to Thomas, who was a theologian, for an authoritative opinion on questions that were not always strictly theological. Thomas's fame as a scholar and expert *also* in philosophy must have been well established, and the esteem that he continued to enjoy among the masters of the Paris faculty of arts is proof. The basic concern of *De occultibus operationibus naturae* is stated early on: there are natural phenomena, such as tides and magnetism, that appear to be without explanation; they do not seem to be traceable to the principal qualities of mixed bodies (which depend—as we will see in the *De mixtione elementorum*—on the proportion of elements that enter into their composition). This means that such phenomena do not depend on the action of the bodies themselves, but on external and higher principles. These superior agents can be identified as the celestial bodies and separate substances (angels or intelligences, wicked spirits, or even God himself), bearing in mind that, in the general structure of the universe, the celestial bodies are always in turn subject to the separate substances. We must, however, note that some of the apparently unexplainable phenomena regard all the individual bodies of the same species (all magnets as such, for instance, attract iron), others regard the majority or a conspicuous number of them, and still others are exceptional cases. If the phenomenon is such that it regards all the individuals of a species, as is the case with magnets (or rhubarb, which always has the property of being able to help with certain physical ailments), it is necessary to suppose that this derives from a specific form immanent in these bodies, impressed on them by the movements of celestial bodies (movements that, on the other hand, always obey separate substances). In other words, phenomena of this type are "occult" only in appearance, because they can be explained in the same way that all other natural processes can. Sublunary bodies act in virtue of natural forms impressed by the movements of celestial bodies, and these movements, since they are regulated by separate substances, express the order and regularity of the course of nature:

We find the influence of separate intellectual substances in the operations of nature that proceed along fixed paths to determined ends—with order and in a most fitting way—like those things which are made by art; so that the whole work of nature seems to be the achievement of a wise agent. Thus nature is said to act with wisdom.

Amid this ordered concatenation of nature—which, as such, is potentially deterministic— only the human soul is an exception, inasmuch as it is produced not by the celestial bodies but directly by an immaterial agent (God); thus it retains its freedom with respect to the material world:

All powers and activities of things that exceed the virtues of the elements, arise from their proper forms, and are traced back to higher principles, to the powers of celestial bodies, and still further to separated substances. For from these principles the forms of inferior bodies are derived, the rational soul alone excepted, which so proceeds from an immaterial cause, that is, from God, that it is in no way the product of the power of celestial bodies. Otherwise it could not have intellectual power and activity wholly free of the body.

However, when (to return to the second of the cases mentioned earlier) the operation is not proper to all of the individuals of a given species, we must suppose that the phenomenon is produced not by a form immanent to the natural bodies, impressed on them by the celestial bodies, but by the movement itself of the celestial bodies. In other words, in this case the movement of the celestial bodies is purely mechanical (as the action of a saw depends on the motion of the person sawing) and is not mediated by a form immanent to the natural bodies. This is what happens with tides. It is not proper to water to produce this kind of movement in virtue of its own immanent natural form. It is, rather, the moon that moves the water with its own movement.

As far as singular or exceptional cases are concerned, the phenomena do not depend on celestial bodies but directly on separate substances, which can act on both natural and artificial bodies. Necromantic images produce their effects—according to the example used by Thomas—by the action of demons that act in them, just as, in an opposite case, the miraculous efficacy of certain relics depends on the action of God, who uses them to produce certain effects. It is obvious that this cannot be caused by celestial bodies, because they always act in a natural way, always producing the same effects. What changes in the things subject to their influence is the greater or lesser propensity to receive their influence.

De judiciis astrorum

During the second Paris period Thomas wrote another brief opuscule devoted to the influence of celestial bodies on sublunary events with the title *De judiciis astrorum*. It seems to be dedicated to his *socius* and friend Reginald of Piperno. Precisely because the natural influence of celestial bodies (themselves moved by the angelic intelligences) on the sublunary world is undeniable, it is not an evil thing to consult the stars, that is, to interpret the natural effects that can be deduced from their movements, and it is not opposed to the scientific consideration of reality. Farmers do their work during determinate times of the year, being aware that the change of seasons depends upon celestial forces. Sailors determine navigation according to the movement of the stars, and, finally, physicians take account of "critical days," which are determined by the position of the stars. But it is completely illicit and erroneous to think that human actions are also subject to the stars:

> But one thing must be absolutely certain, namely, that the human will is not subject to the necessity of the stars. If this were so, free will would disappear, and without it we could not attribute merit to good deeds or fault to bad deeds. And so every Christian must hold quite firmly that the things that depend on the human will—that is, all human operations—are not subject to the necessity of the stars.

It can occur, however, that demons interfere with astrological consultations. The prophecies that result from this are, then, the product of an implicit or explicit pact with demons, which is even more execrable.

So, Thomas again is firm in rejecting every form of astral (or astrological) determinism, but always with the qualification that we have seen on other occasions. The will is not subject to the necessity of the stars because it is immaterial and directly produced (as a faculty of the rational soul) by an absolutely immaterial agent, namely, God. Nevertheless, if we do not cultivate our rationality, and are dominated by our bodily nature, the natural conditioning produced by the movements of the stars will become, to some extent, inevitable. This is why (as we already mentioned in commenting on *Summa theologiae*, Ia, q. 115, a. 4, ad 3) Thomas explains that only the wise man is truly free and immune from every influence of the celestial bodies. This same thesis reappears, in a still more clear way, as we will now see, in the *De sortibus*.

De sortibus

Related to the *De judiciis astrorum* is one of Thomas's more unique opuscules, the *De sortibus*, written in Paris presumably—according to the editors of the

Leonine Commission—during the summer of 1270 or 1271. It seems that we can identify the addressee as James of Tonegno (near Vercelli), the chaplain of Urban IV, who might have known Thomas from his stay in Orvieto. If this is, in fact, the addressee (the manuscripts do not all agree on this), the opuscule—as Antoine Dondaine and J. Peters suggest—could have originated in very special circumstances.[99] James of Tonego was elected bishop of Vercelli, but only by a faction of the chapter. The other group supported and elected another candidate. The problem could not be promptly resolved by the Holy See because of a long period of vacancy (from November 1268 to September 1271). Consequently, it was decided to settle the matter by drawing lots. James's request of the master would then have had personal relevance. He wishes to know how far it is permissible to have recourse to lots. Gauthier, however, while he also believes that James is the opuscule's addressee, has proposed dating the text to the Orvieto period (1263–65).[100] In this case there would be no connection with the contested election of James as bishop of Vercelli. Whatever the case may be, Thomas took the occasion of his interlocutor's request to write a veritable treatise, however small, on everything related to lots:[101] the proper place of lots, their purpose, how information is sought through them, their effectiveness, and whether the Christian religion allows them. With regard to the first point, it is obvious to Thomas that it is senseless to consult lots about things that are necessary and are always the case. Thus, it is senseless to consult them when it is a question of whether God exists, whether $2 + 3 = 5$, or whether the sun will rise. It would be ridiculous to have recourse to lots, says Thomas, regarding mathematical truths. But it also makes little sense to have recourse to them in the case of natural events that usually occur, unless these events are connected with human affairs. According to Thomas, there is a point to using lots to inquire, for instance, about whether a river might overflow and flood our house and fields, or whether the rain might be plentiful during the summer. But it seems pointless to use lots to determine whether a river will overflow in a desert. Thus, lots have a proper place only in human matters. And since everyone is concerned for himself, for his loved ones, and for the people he knows, this sphere can be

99. A. Dondaine and J. Peters, "Jacques de Tonengo et Giffredus d'Anagni auditeurs de saint Thomas," *Archivum Fratrum Praedicatorum* 29 (1959): 52–72.

100. In a note in the apparatus of the edition of q. 22, a. 1 [36] of *Quodlibet* XII (on the question: *Utrum liceat uti sortibus, maxime in apertionibus librorum*), Gauthier, in effect, dismantles, at least in part, the very captivating construction of Dondaine and Peters, pointing to the fact that during the Orvieto period James and Thomas were both at the curia (Thomas de Aquino, *Quaestiones de quolibet*, ed. R.-A. Gauthier (Rome-Paris: Commissio Leonina-Cerf, 1996), 428. See also the proposed date in *Index nominum et operum* of the same volume, 488).

101. It parallels in part what he had already written in *Summa theologiae* IIa-IIae, q. 95.

even further restricted. No one who lives in France consults lots about what affects people living in India whom he does not know (an example that seems to tell in favor of the text's Parisian origin). Lastly, no one consults lots about things that are in his power or that he can know on his own. No one consults lots to know whether he will eat or whether what stands before him is a man or a horse. So, lots exclusively regard human affairs that are relevant to us and that we cannot effectuate or know by ourselves.

What could be the purpose of consulting lots? They would be useful to distribute goods when a consensual and voluntary distribution becomes impracticable, or to distribute titles or offices when there is no agreement about who should receive them, or to distribute punishments when it is not known who should be punished (as is the case in reprisals in which the victims are chosen at random). This is the domain of the *sors divisoria* ("distributive lot"), which is appropriate whenever we do not know how distribute something equitably. But there is also the domain of the *sors consultoria* ("advisory lot"), which has to do with decisions about courses of action. Here lots are a substitute for practical deliberation (*consilium*). Finally, there is the *sors divinatoria* ("divinatory lot"), which is consulted to know the future.

Regarding how information is sought from lots, Thomas makes three general divisions. In the first are people who directly call upon God or demons, as is the case with, respectively, prophets and necromancers. In the second division are people who seek signs or indications about certain things that interest them. In this group we find several different kinds of people. There are astrologers, who consider celestial movements,[102] and augurs, who interpret the movements and sounds of animals and even human sneezes. But there are also people who seek knowledge through omens—that is, by taking what some people say and do to be an indication about something else—and people who seek knowledge in the figures that appear in certain bodies—for example, by chiromancy, which considers the lines on a human hand, or spatulamancy, which examines the shoulder blades of animals.

In the third division are people who seek knowledge of hidden things from evaluating the outcome of actions that they themselves perform. The principal example that Thomas points to is geomancy, which interprets the figures that are created by points made on the ground or on some other material. But Thomas also mentions the practices of hiding pieces of paper (some with writing, some blank) and discerning what must happen to the people who take them, of doing the same thing with straws of different lengths, and of rolling

---

102. To speak of astrologers Thomas uses the traditional terms *astronomi*, *mathematici*, and *geneatici*.

dice (whether to know how to divide something or to evaluate the future). Duels could also be placed in this division (as long as one of the contestants is not far superior to the other) along with other trials and ordeals, with the qualification that the outcome is not indifferent for people who subject themselves to the trial and invoke divine judgment in some way. The term "lots"—which suggests the attempt to know the unknown through some event—seems to belong most properly to this division even though Thomas notes that the three divisions can sometimes overlap.

We might be surprised by Thomas's meticulous classification of lots and by his detailed knowledge of divinatory techniques. But it should be noted that in the thirteenth century the disciplinary boundaries were much less taken for granted, as they seem to be today, and that to William of Moerbeke, the translator of Aristotle and other philosophical and scientific works, there is also attributed a treatise on geomancy.

In discussing the effectiveness of divinatory techniques, Thomas first considers various opinions regarding the course of human events. The first opinion is held by those people who do not admit any government higher than human reason and who consider any events that escape its control to be entirely fortuitous. People of this view regard divinatory and advisory lots as useless since, for them, whatever happens is fortuitous. Thomas finds this position unacceptable because it excludes divine providence from human affairs. Other people hold that all human actions are necessitated by celestial influences, that is, by the movement of the stars. On this view, each of the three kinds of lots mentioned earlier (distributive, advisory, and divinatory) would be of use. Thomas observes that this position has an element of falsity, since it posits that celestial bodies can influence incorporeal things—in this case, the human reason and will. But bodies are inferior to non-bodily things. And yet, Thomas will add a qualification to this similar to the one we saw in *De judiciis astrorum*:

Because in human acts not only are the intellect and will involved, which are not subject to the impression of the stars, but also the sensitive part of the soul, which, because it uses a corporeal organ, is necessarily subject to the heavenly bodies, one can say that from the disposition of the heavenly bodies, some inclination exists in us to do this or that, insofar, that is, as we are lead to this through the apprehension of the imagination and through the passions of the sensitive appetite, namely, anger, fear, and others of this type, to which man is more or less disposed according to bodily make-up, which is subject to the disposition of the stars.... And because, according to Solomon, "the number of fools is infinite," reason rules perfectly in but a few. The inclinations of the heavenly bodies, thus, decide the outcome in many men. And for this reason astrologers sometimes foretell true things from an examination of the stars, especially about common occurrences, although in particular occurrences they frequently fail, on account of reason, which is not subject to the heavenly bodies.[103]

The passage is clear enough: only a few, the wise, can consider themselves to be truly immune to the influence of the stars. This does not imply a *de facto* recognition of astral determinism. What the celestial forces produce, as we have seen, is an inclination, which is not, of itself, necessitating. What is more, the influence of the stars, being natural, regards what tends only in a single direction, whereas the human intellect—because of the plurality of the forms that it conceives and has at its disposal—is never determined toward only one thing. In other words, the stars can contribute toward producing everything that belongs to the regularity of nature, but they do not explain individual events, which, as such, remain accidental and fortuitous. The influence of celestial bodies, for example, could never explain why a person, digging a hole, would find a treasure, even if they could separately explain why a person has an inclination to dig a hole to look for a treasure. What appears fortuitous from a human perspective could, in fact, have been directed by a higher intellect.[104] All human events, even those that escape human foresight, are, thus, subject to divine ordination, and here too—as in the *De malo* and the *Summa contra Gentiles*—Thomas appeals to the *De bona fortuna*. The principle or cause of reason is not reason itself but something higher, and nothing is higher than human science and intellect if not God. The synthesis of Aristotelian texts in the *De bona fortuna* permitted Thomas to make Aristotle (contrary, in this case, to the traditional peripatetic—above all Arab—interpretation of him) a firm proponent of divine providence. Because from this point of view nothing is truly random or fortuitous, consulting lots can in this sense be worthwhile, that is, since external events and human acts are subject to divine governance. In the final analysis, the divine governance of the world is in this way the basis for any use of lots (whether distributive, advisory, or divinatory). It can, however, happen that demons (who are also subject to divine providence and function, despite themselves, as its instruments) interfere and deceive people who consult lots inappropriately. In this case *De sortibus* does not depart from what we saw in *De iudiciis astrorum*. But how can we know whether the use of lots is legitimate or an execrable pact with demons? Thomas answers this question in the fifth chapter of the opuscule, which is devoted to the licitness of divinatory techniques. We should avoid the superstitious or vain use of lots, and that can be ascertained by considering what the lots are about. Since, as we have seen, the

103. *De sortibus*, c. 4.

104. Thomas's example in this case is rather bizarre. The fact, he says, that a person trips over a stone on the road may appear entirely fortuitous, but it appears much less so if it is known that another person had placed the stone there and sent the first person down the road to run into it.

influence of the stars extends to bodies and does not hinder free will, it is not vain or superstitious to consult the stars about natural phenomena. An astrologer, then, is not committing the sin of superstition if he tries to determine from the movements of the celestial bodies whether the next summer will be rainy or dry (here the astrologer is simply acting like a meteorologist), but he would sin in this way if he pretended to know from the stars whether he would find a treasure by digging a hole. It is vain and superstitious to consult lots about what does not have a natural or human cause, but it is not vain and superstitious to consult lots if there is such a cause. And because what does not have a natural or human cause surely has a remote cause in God, it is not absolutely wrong to use lots about what is brought about by divine assistance. But four conditions must be respected in this regard: (a) we should not seek divine judgment through lots without any real necessity, for this would be to put God to the test (*tentare Deum*); (b) recourse to divine judgment, even in cases of necessity, must be accompanied by the requisite reverence and devotion; (c) divine oracles should not be forced into the service of human and worldly matters; (d) we should not have recourse to lots, understood as an expression of divine judgment, in place of divine inspiration manifested by the Holy Spirit. Supposing that James of Tonengo is the interlocutor (and, therefore, that the hypothesis of Dondaine and Peters is correct), this is exactly the case that would be relevant. Thomas's answer is, thus, that it is not permissible to draw lots for the election of someone as bishop, or some other ecclesiastical office, because in this case the divine inspiration manifests itself through the agreement of the electors. Drawing lots in these circumstances would constitute a veritable sin against the Holy Spirit. But consulting lots in secular affairs is a different matter, and in these cases it would be, for Thomas, legitimate in principle, should there arise disagreements and the divisions threaten to destabilize the community. So, the use of distributive lots is permissible with regard to secular offices but not with regard to religious ones. With respect to divinatory lots, the requirement of necessity (the first of the conditions just listed) would seem not to present itself very often. The permissibility of recourse to divine judgment is limited more in regard to fact than in principle.

De mixtione elementorum

The *De mixtione elementorum* is dedicated to Filippo di Castrocielo, who was a master of the faculty of medicine at the University of Bologna and was called to Naples by Charles of Anjou. He may have been a classmate of Thomas during the latter's studies in Naples as a young man. All of this could suggest that the text was composed by Thomas during his time in Naples after the second regency in Paris. But the absence of any reference to the unity of substantial form has led some scholars (Gauthier among them) to suppose that it was written in Paris prior to 1270 (and so in 1269). The issue that Thomas deals with in this work has to do with how the composition of mixed bodies is to be understood or, more precisely, the persistence of the substantial forms of the elements (water, air, fire, and earth) in the mixed bodies that they constitute. Thomas holds that it is impossible for these substantial forms as such to continue in such bodies, for then in each of these bodies there would be more than one substantial form. The human body, for example, would have not only its proper specific substantial form, the soul, but, together with it, the forms of earth, water, etc.). On the other hand, to be able to "host" the different forms of different elements, the matter should be divisible (that is, receive the forms in portions different from itself); but matter is divisible only on the basis of quantity, as we already know. Every body is constituted by the composition of matter subject to quantity and the form that unites itself to it. If the forms of elements remain as substantial forms in act, since more than one body cannot exist in the same place, we would not have one mixed body but the aggregation of many distinct bodies. In other words, the composition of any substance would be purely apparent, because it would be a mere aggregation (and so no substance would be united in itself). But Thomas also rejects the contrary thesis, according to which the forms of the elements remain in mixed bodies, not in their fullness and actuality, but in an attenuated way, in an intermediate state. Mixed bodies would in this case be a kind of reciprocal attenuation of the elements. For Thomas, this thesis explicitly contradicts the principles of Aristotelian philosophy, which exclude substantial forms having a more or less, that is, different grades of intensity, and it also excludes the existence of something in between substantial forms and accidental forms. Therefore, the forms of the elements persist either as substantial forms (which is what the first position holds) or as merely accidental forms (which is what the first position does not accept). Thomas's solution is to posit that the forms of the elements remain in mixed bodies, not as forms but through their qualities, and so only partially, through the power that produces these qualities. Fire, for example, remains in a determinate mixed body, not through its substantial form (and so as pure fire), but through the quality of heat, which is a product of the power of fire. And since qualities, unlike substances, admit of different grades of intensity, and can attenuate and condition each other, every mixed or composite body will have its proper disposition that will depend on the different proportions of the qualities of the elements in the composite itself.[105]

105. See A. Maier, "La struttura della sostanza materiale," in Maier, *Scienza e filosofia nel Medioevo. Saggi sui secoli XIII e XIV*, trans. and intro. M. Parodi and A. Zoerle (Milan: Jaca Book, 1983),

De motu cordis

The *De motu cordis* is likewise dedicated to Filippo di Castrocielo. In this case it is more probable that the work was composed during the last years in Naples (and so after the spring of 1272). In any case, we will try not to isolate it from the other works we have discussed in this chapter. It seems to have a strictly medical (or physiological) question in view. What is the cause of the heart's movement? It does not seem that we are dealing with a voluntary movement here, since it does not seem to depend on the vegetative or nutritive soul (plants, which also have the nutritive soul, do not have a heart), nor on the sensitive soul or the rational or intellective soul, since the heart does not seem to correspond to any sensitive or intellectual appetite. But, on the other hand, the heart's movement does not seem to be natural either, because every natural movement is directed toward a determinate place (its natural place, as rocks move toward the center of the earth and fire toward the sky); the heart, though, moves in opposite directions through expansion and contraction. Neither is it a violent movement, for no movement of this sort preserves a thing's nature; rather, it is opposed to it. But the heart's movement is what permits something to continue in life, and it is not in conflict with the nature of living things. It cannot come from the outside (from universal nature or from an intelligence), because it appears to be what is most proper, and, thus, intrinsic, to every living thing. It cannot be produced by heat, because it would appear that the heart's movement produces an alteration like heat and not vice-versa. What is more, locomotion is always more basic than any movement of alteration. Thomas's response is that the heart's movement is natural, not in the sense that inanimate bodies move toward their natural place, but in the sense in which, as Aristotle says, in Book VIII of the *Physics*, the movement of things that have the principle of movement in themselves—living beings or animals—is equally natural. The movement of the heart, although it does not come from the sense or appetite, is caused by the sensitive soul as the form and nature of a living body (since the soul can move and sustain the whole body in life through a specific organ, namely, the heart). Put differently, the heart's movement does not correspond to a determinate appetite, but depends on the soul since the soul is the form that gives being to animals. However, since the sensitive soul not only is the principle of the body's movement but also is moved by perceptions or passions, it is clear why the soul's movements influence the heart's. Organic phenomena do not determine the soul's movements but vice-versa:

15–152, especially 41–45 (German edition: "Die Struktur der materiellen Substanz," in *An der Grenze von Scholastik und Naturwissenschaft* [Rome: Edizioni di Storia e Letteratura, 1952], 3–140).

The sensations of the soul are not caused by changes in the heart, but just the opposite is the case. This is why in the passions of the soul, such as anger, there is a formal part that pertains to a feeling, which in this example would be the desire for vengeance. And there is a material part that pertains to the heart's motion, which in the example would be the blood enkindled around the heart. But in the things of nature, the form is not the result of the matter, but on the contrary, as is evident in Book II of the *Physics*, matter has a disposition for form. Therefore, although someone does not desire revenge because his blood is burning around the heart, he is more prone to become angry because of it. But actually being angry is from the desire for vengeance.

THEOLOGICAL OPINIONS AND RESPONSES
De forma absolutionis

Among the writings of the second Parisian regency, alongside the true opuscules, there are also some "opinions" of a strictly theological nature, beginning with the *De absolutionis*, which is another response to a request by John of Vercelli, perhaps written February 11, 1269.[106] The opinion regards a small anonymous book on a sacramental problem: the use of the formula *Ego te absolvo* in confessions. It is, in fact, a question that is a little strange, which has more specifically to do with the option between two formulas of absolution, a "deprecative" one (*Misereatur tui* ...: "May the Lord have mercy ...") and an "indicative" one (*Ego te absolvo* ...: "I absolve you ..."), which gradually came into use along with the first formula in the first half of the eleventh century and became the more common one. Through the first formula the confessor limits himself, so to speak, to interceding for the sinner, while the remission of sins is worked directly by God. The confessor's intercession, nevertheless, transforms the penitent's attrition (imperfect sorrow for sins) into perfect contrition and guarantees divine pardon for the sins committed. With the second, indicative, formula, the priest exercises the "power of the keys" more directly, personally absolving the sinner. Perhaps the most curious aspect of the book, for us, is that the author (who is entirely unknown) defends a previous theological custom (all of the theological authorities cited are rather old and, in fact, Peter Lombard is the axis of the position) and holds that the indicative formula is too presumptuous (for it seems to attribute too much authority to the priest). Thomas, citing passages from the Gospels, holds, on the contrary, that the author's position is the presumptuous one. It is the indicative formula that is essential for the validity of the sacrament.

This small work offers us an idea of the opinions that might be requested

---

106. The uncertainty is paradoxically about the year and not the day, which is clearly indicated: *In festo cathedrae Petri*, which is February 22.

of a master of theology such as Thomas, but the possible philosophical implications of his sacramental theology are, however, to be found not in it, nor, obviously, in the decision about the correct form of absolution, but in the general
theory about the causality of the sacraments, which, moreover, is one of the
points about which Thomas seems to have changed his mind over the course of
his career. In the Commentary on the *Sentences* Thomas substantially adheres,
in effect, to a *dispositive* interpretation of the causality of the sacraments.[107]
Since God alone can be the efficient cause, in the strict sense, of grace, the
sacraments are efficient causes only of the created character or ornament of the
soul and they are the material and dispositive causes of sanctifying grace. In
other words, the sacraments produce grace only indirectly, that is, they cause
a disposition that requires the presence of grace. Later, in the *tertia pars* of the
Summa theologiae, Thomas opts for a more directly instrumental interpretation
of the sacraments: the sacraments are the "means" (the instrumental causes)
through which God produces grace.[108] In this sense, the sacraments indeed produce grace directly and not a disposition for it, but only as instruments and not
as the principal cause. Thomas does not seem to have sympathy for the more
original thesis—the conventional one—developed at Oxford by other Dominican masters like Richard Fishacre and Robert Kilwardby. According to this
view, the causal efficacity of the sacraments derives not from an inherent power
but from a pact between God and the Church. It is not by chance that Fishacre
says of causality that it is *sine qua non, a voluntate Dei, ex divina pactione*.[109]

Ad lectorem Venetum de 36 articulis and
Ad magistrum ordinis de 43 articulis

There are also two series of related *responsiones* ("responses") that we should
touch on that date from 1271: *Ad lectorem Venetum de 36 articulis* and *Ad magistrum ordinis de 43 articulis*. In the manuscripts there is also a third series of
responses to a list of 30 articles (*de 30 articulis*), which is, in fact, merely a first
draft of the responses to Bassiano da Lodi, the *lector* of the priory in Venice.
Thomas revised some of the text (combining some responses and adding others),
perhaps also because during Wednesday Mass of Holy Week in 1271 (April 1) he
had received another list of questions, from John of Vercelli. Many of the ques-

107. *In IV Sent.*, d. 1, q. 1, a. 4, qc. 1.
108. *Summa theologiae* IIIa, q. 60, aa. 1 and 3–5.
109. For the general coordinates of the debate on the causality of the sacraments, see I. Rosier-
Catach, *La parole efficace: signe, rituel, sacré* (Paris: Editions du Seuil, 2004), especially 135–39 for the
treatment of Thomas. Thomas's doubts concerning the *sine qua non* or *per pactionem* model of causality
are formulated (already) in the *Sentences* (*In IV Sent.*, d. 1, q. 1, a. 4, qc. 1).

tions on this other list (27 to 43) are similar (and sometimes identical) to those of Bassiano, and this helped Thomas better to understand some of the questions put to him by the latter, questions to which he had initially given a hasty or inappropriate answer. John's questions had been sent not only to Thomas but to two other prestigious masters of the order, Albert the Great and Robert Kilwardby. We have their responses too and are, thus, able to make a comparison among the three that often aids in seeing the differences in their respective positions. Thomas's responses have an additional value. He is careful to note that John has asked him in each question to clarify the opinion of the "saints" (the Fathers of the Church) and his own and to explain—in the event of differences—their compatibility.

The questions do not have a precise order, but it is not hard to observe certain dominant themes (leaving aside the more theological topics). Two such themes are the cosmological role of the angels or intelligences and the connection between higher and lower causes. To Bassiano's first question, about whether the angels are the movers of the celestial bodies, Thomas answers that not only has this been proved in many ways by philosophers, but it is also affirmed with evidence by the "sacred doctors." Thomas seems here to postulate complete identity between the angels of the Scriptures and the movers or intelligences of the philosophers—an identity that is again stated in the second response ("It seems to me that it is possible to prove demonstrably that the celestial bodies are moved by some intellect."), and still more explicitly in the responses to John of Vercelli (ad 3: "I do not ever recall having read that the fact that the celestial bodies are moved by spiritual creatures has been denied by the saints or philosophers."). But this is not an identification or superimposition that is entirely innocuous, as Kilwardby and Albert appear to think. (Albert notoriously changed his mind about it.) Thomas stresses in the *Responsiones* that if all the natural processes of the sublunary world depend on celestial movements, and the latter depend on the intelligences, then the intelligences play an essential role in the administration of the universe, presiding over all the processes of generation and corruption. One question that seems nearly the same in the two lists (question 8 on John's list and question 10 on Bassiano's) asks whether the blacksmith would be able to move his hand toward the hammer if the angels did not move the celestial bodies. Thomas says that if the question is intended to deal with human free will, the answer is obvious: the blacksmith's will is not subject to the celestial bodies, nor to the angels, but only to God. But if we consider the corporeal side of things, we must say that, if the motion of the heavens ceased, organic life on earth would also cease, and so the soul would no longer have a body to move, unless, apart from the order of nature (*praeter ordinem naturae*), God were to keep the body alive even without the causes on which it naturally depends. The reference to what God could accomplish in the absence of the natural order removes the suspicion, at least in part, that the condemnation of 1277 could have indirectly implicated Thomas on this point. However, in his answer to Bassiano, Thomas adds a sarcastic note that might have irritated some people. Certainly the divine wisdom, in the absence of the celestial movements, should be able not only to keep the blacksmith's body and hand alive but to maintain the material structure of the hammer too—*quod tamen probabile non videtur*.

Without a doubt other questions could appear more bizarre. John asks in one of his questions whether it would be possible for an angel to lift the entire earthly globe up to the sphere of the moon even if, in fact, he does not do it or never will do it. It is, therefore, a conjectural question, *de potentia absoluta*, about what angels could do and not about what they actually do in the normal (ordained) course of events. Thomas responds that the problem has nothing to do with the weight since, as is evident, the weight does not constitute any problem for an angel. The difficulty instead has to do with the ordained course of events:

It seems to me that it must be said that the [angel] could not do it in virtue of his natural power because no power of nature can change the order of the principal parts of the universe, to which it belongs that the earth be at the center.[110]

Because the *responsiones* of 1271 often raise the question, implicitly at any rate, of the alternatives of the ordered course of nature and what separate substances could do *de potentia absoluta*, they have a special importance, for they show how Thomas comes down entirely on the side of the first way of understanding the universe.

Sometimes the intersection of different series of questions permits us better to see how Thomas proceeded in drafting his responses. In the initial list of 30 questions from Bassiano, there is one that asks whether the bodies of the saints shine more brightly than the sun after the day of judgment. Thomas's answer seems quite out of place: "I see no danger in holding that after the resurrection the moon will be as bright as the sun, and the sun seven times brighter than it is now." This might seem to be a joke, but things become clearer when we read a similar question from John (37): "Will the glorified bodies shine brighter than the sun, and the moon shine as brightly as the sun, and the sun seven times more brightly than now, and the bodies of the saints seven times more brightly than the sun?" This is the same formulation that we find in the *Responsio de 36 articulis*.

110. *Ad magistrum ordinis de 43 articulis*, a. 17.

Or consider this: a. 14 of the *Responsio de 30 articulis* asks whether it is possible to know the distance between the earth's surface and its center. Thomas's answer is laconic: *Dico quod potest* ("It is possible"). Only later does Thomas realize that the question regards the location of hell, as is suggested by a. 31 of John's list. This is, in Thomas's view, a useless question and of no real pertinence to the doctrine of the faith. Thus, in the revised responses to Bassiano, the answer is more developed: "I hold that it is possible to know the distance between the surface of the earth and its center but not the distance to hell, because I do not believe that man can know where hell is located."[111] This same attitude of rational sobriety leads Thomas to express his perplexity about the notion that the names of the saints and the damned are written by the hand of God in heaven and on earth (*Videtur michi hoc non esse verum*).[112] It might at first surprise us that in the *Reponsiones* Thomas seems to admit that fire really afflicts the damned, contrary to what he holds in other places. But this apparent contradiction is easily resolved if we notice that here Thomas is referring to the bodies of the damned and so to the state after the final judgment rather than to the separated souls in the prior state.[113]

In his response to John (in the prologue) and in his response to Bassiano (in the conclusion to the *Responsio de 36 articulis*) Thomas complains that the questions have been posed to him without arguments *pro et contra*—arguments that would have allowed him to understand better (especially the *contra*) the sense of the questions. This is an interesting remark, because it unequivocally shows that the structure of the Scholastic *quaestio* was not merely a literary genre or a stereotyped way of organizing the material to be treated, but a veritable *forma mentis* that allowed one better to grasp the nature of each problem precisely through the contrary rational arguments.

The final element worth considering in these texts is in the response to John of Vercelli. It is Thomas's respectful but clear positioning of himself at the beginning:

I must first of all complain that many of these articles do not regard the doctrine of the faith but rather philosophical dogmas. It is, in fact, very detrimental to affirm or deny such things that do not pertain to the doctrine of piety as if they regarded sacred doctrine.... Thus, with respect to the things that the philosophers said that are not repugnant to the faith, it seems to me better not to affirm it as a dogma of the faith—even if it is sometimes introduced under the name of the philosophers—nor to deny it as contrary to the faith, so that it does not offer an occasion to the wise of this world to scorn the doctrine of the faith.

111. *Ad lectorem Venetum de 36 articulis*, a. 25.
112. *Responsio de 43 articulis*, aa. 30–31.
113. *Responsio de 30 articulis*, a. 28; *Responsio de 43 articulis*, a. 27; *Responsio de 36 articulis*, a. 21.

These *Responsiones*, far from being occasional writings of marginal importance, propose once more with great clarity two essential characteristics of Thomas's thought: the great confidence in the ordained course of nature, which links Thomas to the Greco-Arab peripatetic tradition and leaves little room to what the separate substances could do apart from this course of things; and the full and rigorous independence of the doctrine of the faith and philosophy from each other—an independence to be maintained not only to protect philosophy but even more to protect the interests of the faith itself.[114]

INTERVENTIONS IN CONTEMPORARY
DEBATES: *DE UNITATE INTELLECTUS* AND
DE AETERNITATE MUNDI

While it is very likely that Thomas was recalled to Paris because of ecclesiological debates and not for purely theological reasons—as we said at the beginning of this chapter—there is no doubt that in these same years he found himself involved in contemporary debates of a strictly philosophical nature. His attitude is, however, much less unilateral and predictable than is often supposed. On the one hand, Thomas takes a decisive position against some of the theses held by those masters of the Paris faculty of arts who were more aware of the autonomy of their role (those who have been called "radical Aristotelians" or "Latin Averroists"—ambiguous but now much-used labels—such as Boethius of Dacia and Siger of Brabant). On the other hand, Thomas also seeks to distance himself from the theses of many of his colleagues in the faculty of the-

---

114. The *responsiones* of Thomas must, then, be numbered with all probability among the *Responsio ad lectorem bisuntinum de 6 articulis*, which Mandonnet situated similarly (but without any real proof) in 1271. The addressee, the lector Gerard of Besançon, is not otherwise known. The questions do not have much philosophical relevance: the first three, for example, deal with the form of the star that appeared to the magi, the fourth and fifth treat of the permissibility of certain expressions in preaching (for example, "the stars were created by baby Jesus's little hands"), the sixth treats of the practice of confession (if one is required to confess the circumstances that could aggravate a sin, even if such circumstances would then allow the person with whom the sin was committed to be identified). Thomas's attitude in this case (especially in the response to the fourth and fifth articles) is rather curt: "I do not hold that such frivolities should be preached when preaching ought to refer to such an abundance of most certain truth." Finally, the so-called *De secreto* could be placed in this genre of writing. This work contains the responses provided by a few masters (among whom are Thomas and Peter Tarentaise)—on the occasion of a general chapter that was held in Paris in 1269—to six questions about the possibility that a religious superior could force a friar to tell the truth about a hidden fault of which he is accused or about the knowledge that he has about another's misdeed. In general, the masters deny such a possibility, but the most interesting aspect (bear in mind that the text is a kind of report of the meeting) is that in his response to the final two questions, Thomas distances himself from some answers of the others, admitting that the superior, when the case has juridical relevance, can order the friar to speak the truth.

ology, and especially from the Franciscans. This does not mean that Thomas situated himself in the "center" between the Aristotelian "left" of the masters of arts and the Neo-Augustinian "right" of the Franciscan masters of theology (according to Van Steenberghen's celebrated image), but that he unhesitatingly chooses to follow an entirely personal theological path, established and perfected by his intense engagement with the philosophical tradition. The uniqueness of his choices (to avoid the term "originality," which is also irreducibly ambiguous) is confirmed, on the one hand, by the bewilderment they produced not only among the Franciscans but among some colleagues in his own order (as we will see in the concluding chapter), and, on the other hand, by the fact that he almost immediately stands out as a model for the "Aristotelians" of the faculty of arts (who are traditionally considered his adversaries). In other words, Thomas does not go after the *artistae* on their own terrain. On the contrary, he himself is the one to determine the terrain, becoming an almost indispensable point of reference in his approach to Aristotle. It is enough to consider the panorama of Parisian commentaries on Aristotle from the last decades of the thirteenth century to see how great their debt is to the Dominican master, and the fact itself that the masters of arts asked the order for Thomas's commentaries after his death. Thomas's interventions in the debates occurring in Paris in 1270 show a complex plurality of levels of reading, which regard both questions intrinsic to philosophy and its extrinsic relationship to theological doctrines. In the first case Thomas denounces the errors that conflict with the correct interpretation of Aristotle and the peripatetic tradition and those that conflict with general principles of philosophy itself (as with the thesis of the unicity of the potential intellect). In the second case he rejects the pretense to demonstrate what cannot be demonstrated with natural principles alone (the thesis about the world's temporal beginning) and the worry about certain philosophical doctrines (the unicity of the substantial form in the human composite) that leads to even more dangerous anthropological and theological positions. Two opuscules manifest this particular complexity above all: *De unitate intellectus* and *De aeternitate mundi*.

In regard to the first text (probably composed in 1270), the target is the doctrine of the unicity of the potential or possible intellect, already rejected by Thomas on several occasions but here in an unusually harsh and even violent tone.[115] We will consider only a few essential elements of the question. In his

---

115. See, above all, the precise analysis of A. de Libera, *L'unité de l'intellect. Commentaire du* De unitate intellectus contra averroistas *de Thomas d'Aquin* (Paris: Vrin, 2004). See also A. Petagine, *Aristotelismo difficile. L'intelletto umano nella prospettiva di Alberto Magno, Tommaso d'Aquino e Sigieri di Brabante* (Milan: Vita e Pensiero, 2004), especially 167–210.

Great Commentary on the *De anima* (departing from what he had said in the *Compendium* and the Middle Commentary), Averroes holds that not only must the agent intellect be posited as one and separate for all humanity (a doctrine that Leibniz would later call "monopsychism" because it posits a single soul for all human beings) but the potential intellect (that which actually thinks) must be too. Averroes was led to such an extreme—and in a certain sense counterintuitive—thesis not only by the ambiguities present in Aristotle's *De anima* (in which the potential intellect, like the agent intellect, is described as impassible and unmixed) but by specific theoretical problems. If the intellect is a form that is immanent in the human composite, it would be similar to all the other naturally immanent forms, and, therefore, a possible object of knowledge more than a cognitive faculty. Moreover, if each of us thinks through his own intellect, everyone will have his own intelligible species and concepts. In this way, however, no knowledge could be held to be truly universal (and, thus, properly scientific) and, in the end, it would become impossible to explain the communication of knowledge. How can we be certain that two men are really thinking the same thing if they are thinking with different intellects? And how can we be certain that the master and the disciples are truly understanding the same intelligible content? Averroes's complex solution substantially separates sensible knowledge from intellectual knowledge. What individuals can produce in the cognitive process are phantasms, that is, sensible images or species derived from sensations. The action of the agent intellect (which is also a separate substance) is exerted upon these phantasms to bring about the abstraction of the intelligible species. This species is impressed upon the one and separate possible intellect, which, thus, is actualized, uniting with the agent intellect. In this process, human beings are not strictly excluded from thought, but they participate in it *only through the phantasms*. It is through the phantasms that we are able to join ourselves, in knowledge, to the possible intellect, and, thus—mediately—to the agent intellect. Thought is, therefore, understood by Averroes as an activity that, on the one hand, requires content (and this is assured by the phantasms that we provide), and, on the other hand, a principle that guarantees the universality and immateriality of these contents (and this is the role of the potential intellect). The later distinction between the "objective reality" (objective content) and "formal reality" of a content (its being a content, independently of its content) has its roots here. We need show only two consequences of this position. First, for Averroes, man is not always provided with a rational soul as his substantial form. On the contrary, each human being is joined to this form only indirectly, through phantasms, and only during the actual exercise of thought. What is proper to every human being in every condition is, thus, the sensitive soul. The more sophisticated internal sense of this soul—the cogitative power—represents, then, the highest individual faculty. Second, that which actually thinks is never the individual in a strict sense but the potential intellect (as the specific intellect of humanity). Human individuals participate in the activity of thought, offering only potentially intelligible content (phantasms), which will become actually intelligible.

In the *De unitate intellectus*, Thomas immediately declares that his intention is not to show that the unicity thesis contradicts the Catholic faith (which, for Thomas, is obvious), but rather that it is opposed to the original doctrine of Aristotle (Averroes, the commentator on Aristotle *par excellence,* is here called the "perverter" of Aristotle) and the whole peripatetic tradition:

There is no need now to show that the foregoing position is erroneous because it is repugnant to Christian faith: a moment's reflection makes this clear to anyone. Take away from men diversity of intellect, which alone among the soul's parts seems incorruptible and immortal, and it follows that nothing of the souls of men would remain after death except a single intellectual substance, with the result that reward and punishment and their difference disappear. We intend to show that the foregoing position is opposed to the principles of philosophy every bit as much as it is to the teaching of faith. And, Latin writers on this matter not being to the taste of some, who tell us they prefer to follow the words of the peripatetics, though of them they have seen only the works of Aristotle, the founder of the school, we will first show the foregoing position to be in every way repugnant to his words and judgments.[116]

In the opuscule Thomas examines at length the positions of Aristotle and his commentators (Themistius, whose paraphrases Thomas knows directly through William of Moerbeke's translation; Theophrastus, whom he knows through Themistius; Alexander of Aphrodisias, whom he knows though Averroes himself). We note that Thomas reproaches his adversaries (the *artistae* and perhaps Siger of Brabant in particular) for not knowing the texts of the peripatetic tradition besides those of Aristotle, and, thus, for not adequately knowing that philosophy of which they intend to be the spokesmen. However, we should also note that Thomas reads the authors he mentions from a very particular angle. Thomas's Aristotle seems to admit, without any hesitation, that even the agent intellect is a part of the soul and Thomas's Themistius becomes a proponent of the thesis according to which the agent intellect and potential intellect are two distinct faculties and not two aspects of a single faculty.

Still, the thesis of the unicity of the potential intellect conflicts not only with the Aristotelian tradition but with experience itself. Each one of us can,

116. *De unitate intellectus*, proem.

in fact, perceive with evidence that it is he himself who is thinking—and not something separate from him, something that would think *through* him:

Whoever wishes to disagree on this point necessarily says what is absurd. That this individual man understands is manifest (*Manifestum est enim quod hic homo singularis intelligit*), for we would never ask about intellect unless we understood, nor when we ask about intellect are we asking about anything other than that whereby we understand.[117]

Thomas's fundamental strategy is mostly based on what we have already observed: in Averroes's doctrine, *the individual human being is not the one who thinks* (the subject of thought), but *what is thought* (the object of thought) since we enter into the process of thought only through the phantasms, through, that is, the content of thought. This is also how Thomas makes his case against those who have reprised and developed Averroes's doctrine in the Latin world, Siger of Brabant first of all, who had tried to reinterpret the separate potential intellect not as *form* but as the *motor* of our cognitive activity.

Thomas proposes three principal arguments against the possibility that each man thinks by joining himself to the separate possible intellect by means of phantasms:

1. There would be no link between us and the intellect when we are generated (that is, we would not be rational or intellectual beings by our natural form) but it would only be established by sense activity. To make the point of this objection more explicit we could say that, from the Averroist perspective, we are human beings in the strict sense—*rational* animals—not when we are born, or by nature, but only when the conjunction between the separate potential intellect and the phantasms elaborated by our internal senses is realized.

2. In the entire Aristotelian tradition, actually thinking something is nothing but the potential intellect being informed by the intelligible species of the thing being thought. Now, the intelligible species that informs the intellect is abstracted from phantasms since the phantasms themselves are potentially and not actually intelligible. But since potency is obviously not identical with act, the intelligible species (the true content of thought) *in itself* (in act) is not the same as the intelligible species *in the phantasms*, and so the intelligible species is not what unites the one and separate intellect with our phantasms, but what separates it from them. The unbridgeable gap between potency (phantasms) and act (the intelligible species as effectively "thought") interrupts the continuity hypothesized by Averroes between individual sense knowledge and superindividual intellectual knowledge. Put differently, we cannot say, as Averroes

117. *De unitate intellectus*, c. 2.

pretends to, that man takes part in thought through his phantasms, because phantasms are *not yet* thought, but only that which is in potency to thought. (To use Thomas's own example: when a person is reflected in a mirror, the action of reflecting belongs to the mirror, not to the person; analogously, the action of thinking—in the Averroist doctrine—belongs solely to the one potential intellect, and not to the person who contributes the sensible images.)

3. Even if we admit that the intelligible species in themselves (in act) and in the phantasms (in potency) are identical, this does not change matters. The intelligible species is *that through which* something is known, whereas the intellect is *that which* knows. Thomas's example is, in this case, more easily understood. The relationship between the potential intellect and individual people, as Averroes describes it, is similar to that between someone who has the power of sight and a colored wall. The wall does not see but its color is seen. Analogously, in Averroes's doctrine, the human being does not think but his phantasms are thought.

With respect to the theoretical exigency at the basis of the Averroist solution—that of assuring the universality of knowledge—we already know Thomas's solution, having encountered it in the *De ente et essentia*. It implicitly appeals to Avicenna's position. The sameness of the content of thought among different people is guaranteed by the identity of the content itself (that is, the identity of the essence known) and does not require the unicity of the thinking subject. Because, in other words, the object of our thought is the essence of the material thing, it is the latter that remains always identical with itself, prescinding from the various subjects that think it: "Therefore, there is one thing that is understood by me and you, but it is understood by means of one thing by me and by means of another by you, that is, by different intelligible species, and my understanding differs from yours and my intellect differs from yours."[118] The Averroist error, in this regard, is to confuse the role of the intelligible species—which is that *through which* the intellect thinks—with the *object* of thought, which is, rather, the quiddity itself of the thing. The Averroists, thus, come dangerously close to Platonism:

But it remains to ask what is the understood itself. For if they say that the thing understood is one immaterial species existing in the intellect, in a way they unwittingly slide into the teaching of Plato, who taught that there can be no science of sensible things, but every science is of one separate form.[119]

---

118. *De unitate intellectus*, c. 5.
119. *De unitate intellectus*, c. 5.

As Thomas interprets them, Averroes and his followers, far from being "radical Aristotelians," hold a dualist anthropology of a basically Platonic sort:

They think that the possible intellect is devoid of every sensible nature and that it is not present in the body, because it is a certain substance which exists in separation from the body and is in potency to all intelligible forms.[120]

If this is how things are, we can perhaps better understand why in the opuscule Thomas continues intensely to battle every form of anthropological dualism and to defend his own thesis of the unicity of the substantial form of the human composite. Ultimately, the Averroist position could be understood as a limit case of the doctrine of the plurality of substantial forms in human beings: individual human beings have a sensitive soul, to which is added (in virtue of the "continuation" through phantasms) a further intellectual form, which, in itself, is separate. This view is not so dissimilar to that of those Franciscans, who, in order to defend the substantiality of the human soul (the fact that it is a substance complete in itself, capable of autonomous subsistence), end up separating it *de facto* from the lower functions of the body and breaking up the essential unity of the human composite. The *De unitate intellectus* undeniably closes with a rather strident denunciation of the masters of arts (perhaps Siger of Brabant in particular),[121] but we must stress—on the basis of that complexity of levels that we mentioned earlier—that in this same opuscule Thomas continues to distance himself from many of his theological colleagues, especially the Franciscans. As Thomas sees things, Averroes and the Franciscans—who, according to contemporary historiography, stand opposed to each other—belong

---

120. *Quaestiones disputatae de anima*, a. 2

121. "It is yet more puzzling, indeed worthy of indignation, that anyone professing himself to be a Christian should presume to speak so irreverently of the Christian faith as to say that 'the Latins do not accept this as a principle,' namely, that there is only one intellect, 'perhaps because their law is contrary to it.'" Thomas follows this by attributing to his adversary (Siger?) what today is usually called "the doctrine of two truths," and, in fact, this is probably one of the places in which the doctrine was "invented" (at that time neither Siger nor Boethius of Dacia seems ever to have held any such doctrine, having limited themselves to holding to the epistemological autonomy of the respective spheres of natural philosophy and theology): "Even more serious is this subsequent remark: 'Through reason I conclude necessarily that intellect is numerically one, but I firmly hold the opposite by faith.' Therefore, he thinks faith is of things whose contrary can be necessarily concluded. " Later taken up by Bishop Tempier in the celebrated prologue of the condemnation of 1277, this invention testifies to the condemnation's capacity to function, according to the happy expression of A. de Libera (*Penser au Moyen Âge* [Paris: Editions du Seuil, 1991], 193), as an *opérateur historique*, that is, the condemnation of 1277 is one of the most obvious cases of the "heuristic" function of censures: the censurers create an "error" and attribute it to those censured. From this moment forward, the error—now given life as a golem—will have an autonomous existence. For an account of the vicissitudes of the "two truth theory" and clarifications in regard to the more common interpretations of it, see L. Bianchi, *Pour une histoire de la "double vérité,"* Conférences Pierre Abélard (Paris: Vrin, Paris 2008).

in this instance, in fact, to the same vast horizon of "Platonic dualism" that denies the *natural* and essential unity of the human composite.

Thomas's attitude in the *De aeternitate mundi*, which was probably composed in 1271 and so can be situated in more or less the same period—despite appearances and traditional interpretations—is not very different. For Thomas, if we consider revelation, it is impossible to deny that the world was created in time. Nevertheless, it is always possible to ask ourselves whether it is rationally contradictory to suppose (along with the philosophers) an eternal creation. Like Averroes and Maimonides, Thomas explicitly denies that this possibility is contradictory in itself. To say that things were created from nothing is not necessarily to say that things were created *after* nothing. It could also be to say that they are eternally drawn from nothing (*ex nihilo*): *ex* (from) indicates the origin (indeed, in this case, it indicates the lack of origin: things have been drawn from absolute non-being) and not temporal succession.[122] Rationally speaking, there are no arguments to defend the temporality of creation. God could have easily created the world from eternity:

First, we should show that it is not necessary that an agent cause, in this case God, precede in time that which he causes, if he should so will. [And this can be done in several ways.] First, no cause instantaneously producing its effect necessarily precedes the effect in time. God, however, is a cause that produces effects not through motion but instantaneously. Therefore, it is not necessary that he precede his effects in time.

In this case the target of the opuscule would seem, then, to be more the Franciscan theologians (according to whom it would be possible to demonstrate rationally the impossibility of an eternal creation) than the masters of the faculty of arts, with whom Thomas would appear to be in partial agreement—although he does not accept their view that the eternity of the world is the only thesis that is "philosophically" defensible (see pp. 150–55 above). Unlike the conclusion of the *De unitate intellectus*, here the conclusion is directed against the theologians, who attack the philosophers on this point:

There are other arguments adduced as well, but I refrain from answering them at present, either because they have been suitably answered elsewhere, or because they are so weak that their very weakness lends probability to the opposing view.

---

122. See Aquinas's *De aeternitate mundi*: "Now, whatever naturally pertains to something in itself is prior to what that thing receives only from another. A creature does not have being, however, except from another, for, considered in itself, every creature is nothing, and thus, with respect to the creature, non-being is prior to being by nature. Nor does it follow from the creature's always having existed that its being and non-being are ever simultaneous, as if the creature always existed but at some time nothing existed, for the priority is not one of time. Rather, the argument merely requires that the nature of the creature is such that, if the creature were left to itself, it would be nothing."

DE SUBSTANTIIS SEPARATIS

The *terminus ad quo* of the *De substantiis separatis* can be determined by the fact that in this opuscule Thomas cites Book Lambda as Book XII of Aristotle's *Metaphysics*. So, its composition is certainly after the middle of 1271 (that is, after Moerbeke's translation of the *Metaphysics* began to be circulated in Paris).[123] However, this is not sufficient to allow us to date it with certainty to the last part of the second Paris regency or to the period of his subsequent return to Naples. In any case, we can say that this is one of Thomas's last writings, and, thus, it has a special value. The structure itself of the work—perhaps addressed to Reginald of Piperno and left unfinished—is significant. The first section, which takes up almost the entirety of what was actually completed (cc. 1–17), is devoted to the analysis of philosophical positions on separate substances, whereas the chapters that follow—to c. 20—deal with the treatment of angels from the point of view of the Catholic faith.

Aimed at exclusively considering separate substances ("we ought to begin with the earliest human conjectures about the angels so that we will be in a position to accept whatever we find that agrees with faith, and refute whatever is opposed to Catholic teaching"), the first chapters offer a particularly effective synthesis of the way Thomas understood the different philosophical traditions, especially Platonism and Aristotelianism. After having recapitulated certain basic presuppositions of the Pre-Socratics and, above all, of Plato (always based on the summaries of Aristotle, since the Platonic *corpus* as such was not available in the Latin Middle Ages), Thomas reprises the essentials of Aristotle's critique of Platonism, namely, his rejection of the isomorphism between mental operations and divisions of reality:

It is by no means necessary that what the intellect understands separately should have a separate existence in reality. Hence, neither should we posit separate universals subsisting outside individuals nor likewise mathematicals outside sensible things, for universals are the essences of particular things themselves and mathematicals are certain limits of sensible bodies.[124]

Rejecting the Platonic characterization of the supersensible world, Aristotle subsequently chose "a more certain and evident path" in his own inquiry into separate substances. This path is that of motion, which, not by chance, is what supports the first of Thomas's five ways in the *Summa*. Thomas, however, em-

---

123. Moerbeke reintroduces Book Kappa and this moves Book Lambda ahead one. Previously, Book Lambda had been regarded as Book XI.

124. *De substantiis separatis*, c. 2.

phasizes two principal limits of the Aristotelian position: the substantial denial of demons (that is, of the possible negative influence of separate substances) and the postulation of a strict identity between the number of separate substances and the celestial movements.[125] The topic of the separate substances becomes, thus, for Thomas, the occasion to expound in summary form the points of agreement and disagreement between the most famous philosophers of antiquity. In Thomas's reconstruction (cc. 3–4), Plato and Aristotle agree on the following:

- the mode of existence of the separate substances (they participate in something that is one and good in itself—at least according to the way Thomas interprets the Aristotelian principle of the causality of the maximal as it is presented in Book II of the *Metaphysics*: what is maximally being and true is the cause of the being and truth of all other beings);

- the nature of separate substances, that is, their immateriality (which does not entail the complete absence of potentiality);

- the conception of providence, even if Thomas seems to grant to Plato, and still more to Aristotle, much more than can be explicitly found in this regard in their texts.

Thomas sees Plato and Aristotle disagreeing on the following:

- whereas Plato posits a double order of spiritual substances (intellects and gods, that is, separate ideas or universals) beyond the souls of the celestial regions, Aristotle posits only the intelligences, among whom is the supreme God (this order is both intellectual and intelligible, that is, thinking and thought: which could, in fact, be quite easily applied to the Neo-Platonic forms);

- Plato does not limit the number of separate substances to the number of celestial movements;

- Aristotle, as we noted, does not posit demons, whereas Neo-Platonism does.

The chapters that follow are devoted to a new engagement with Avicebron, who has accompanied Thomas since the *De ente et essentia*. From his youthful work to his more mature work, Thomas has never really changed his mind. Here Thomas once again explains, first, that Avicebron erroneously identifies

125. This was a topic of much debate. It turns up decades later in Dante's *Convivio*, to cite just one example. *See P. Porro*, "Intelligenze oziose e angeli attivi: note in margine a un capitolo del Convivio dantesco (II, IV)," in *Studies in Honour of Alfonso Maierù*, Textes et etudes du Moyen Âge 38, ed. S. Caroti, R. Imbach, Z. Kaluza, G. Stabile, and L. Sturlese (Louvain-la-Neuve: FIDEM, 2006), 303–51.

the logical order and the real order, holding that logical composition (that according to which every species is composed of genus and difference) must be understood as a real composition (in which the genus is effectively identical with matter and difference with form). Avicebron's second error, linked with the first, is to hold that the expressions "being in potency," "being subject," and "being receptive" all mean the same thing. For Thomas, as we know, something can be in potency without necessarily being material and without being an already constituted subject with respect to an added perfection or actuality. (In separated substances, the forms themselves—independently of matter—are in potency to being and do not themselves preexist being as subjects.) Thomas notes further problems with Avicebron. Avicebron inverts the correct path of thought, pretending to ascend from lower beings to higher beings through the analysis of material principles. He is in danger of returning to the monism of the first naturalists (who posited matter as the substance of all things). In this way Avicebron destroys the very principles of first philosophy, taking away oneness and being from individual things.[126] Violating the Aristotelian interdict, he proceeds to infinity in the series of material causes without the possibility of ever reaching prime matter.[127] Thomas can repropose, then, as an alternative to universal hylomorphism, the basic thesis of his Commentary on the *De causis*:

Material substances are finite in two senses, namely, on the part of the form which is received in matter and on the part of being itself, in which it shares according to its own mode, as being finite from below and from above. A spiritual substance, however, is finite from above, inasmuch as it receives being from the first principle according to its proper mode; it is infinite from below, since it is not received in a subject. But the first principle, God, is infinite in every way.[128]

Among the other opinions that are rejected in the opuscule is one that holds that separate substances are not created;[129] also rejected is one that holds that some separate substances do not derive immediately from God.[130] Thomas refutes the latter thesis in a particularly dense chapter (c. 10), observing that if

126. Universal hylomorphism presupposes the plurality of forms: each thing should possess the form of corporeity and its specific form, but anything that has two forms or acts is not one in itself and, as such, is not truly one being.

127. To explain the difference between the matter of separate substances and that of corporeal substances, Avicebron must posit a further common substrate, and, therefore, another matter that receives these differences, and so on *ad infinitum* according to the same argumentative mechanism as the "third man."

128. *De substantiis separatis*, c. 8.

129. Thomas attributes a creationist thesis to both Plato and Aristotle. The error of both is to have held the creation of these substances to have been eternal.

130. This is the thesis of creation through intermediaries as it is developed in the *De causis* and Avicenna.

this were the case, the order of the world would result more from a necessary process than from the intention of an agent. We could nevertheless object, with Avicenna himself, that the whole emanative process could have been arranged from the beginning by the intention of the first agent. However, Thomas notes, we must distinguish between the productions that occur through changes and movements and those that occur without change and movement (a distinction that we have already encountered in the *De potentia*). In the first case, it is normal that what proceeds from the first principle also proceeds through secondary causes. But this is not true of the second case, that is, in creation properly understood ("that mode of production which takes place without motion—and is called creation—is reduced to God alone as its author").[131]

Analogously, the thesis that some perfections of separate substances do not come directly from God should also be rejected. Thomas appears to be aiming at the Neo-Platonic (and especially Proclean) doctrine according to which the lower forms receive being from the form of Being, life from the form of Life, and intelligence from the form of Intelligence. In this case too Thomas makes use of Aristotelian principles in his refutation. Thus, he argues that a unitary effect cannot be reduced to several first principles and this for the simple reason that an effect cannot be more simple than its cause (c. 11). Among the other erroneous opinions that Thomas refutes are the thesis (attributed to Origen) according to which spiritual substances were created equal by God (c. 12) and the thesis according to which they do not possess a knowledge of individual realities and so do not exercise any providential action (c. 13; in c. 14 this is discussed in reference to God). In this connection it is interesting how Thomas excludes Aristotle from the proponents of the latter thesis, denying that he had actually held that God does not think what is other than him:

It is, therefore, apparent to anyone who considers carefully the above words of the Philosopher, that it is not his intention to exclude absolutely from God a knowledge of other things, but rather, that God does not understand other things through themselves as participating in them in order that he then may become understanding through them— as happens in the case of any intellect whose substance is not its understanding. He rather understands all things other than himself by understanding himself, inasmuch as his being is the universal and fontal source of all being and his understanding is the universal root of understanding encompassing all understanding.[132]

This occasion permits Thomas to explain once more the distinct modes of knowledge belonging to God, simple substances, and human beings (c. 16). God

---

131. *De substantiis separatis*, c. 10.
132. *De substantiis separatis*, c. 14.

knows all things through his essence, and this knowledge is universal, not in the (Avicennian) sense that he is limited to knowing the universal nature of things, but because it extends to *all* things, including individual things. Angelic intellects know all things (universally and as individuals) participating in the divine intellect, that is, through the intelligible species that are connatural to them from the moment of their creation or contemplating the same things in the Word.[133] Human beings, however, acquire intelligible species (by which they can know things by universals) from the images of sensible things through the action of the agent intellect. Insofar as he knows all things, God is provident, but his providence, as we already know, does not nullify or compromise (at least in Thomas's view) the contingency of creation:

Just as [God's] providence disposes that such effects be, so it likewise disposes that certain of these effects be necessary for which it has ordained necessarily acting proper causes, while certain others should be contingent for which it has ordained proper contingent causes.[134]

After having refuted the dualistic Manichaean theses about co-original principles of evil and good (c. 17), Thomas expounds the fundamental points of the Catholic faith on spiritual substances, appealing above all to Pseudo-Dionysius:

- Like every other creature, the separate substances have been created directly by God.
- *They all began to exist after they had not existed*, that is, from non-being. (However, Thomas does not take a clear position on *when* they were created, whether together with corporeal creatures—according to the Augustinian doctrine of the simultaneous creation—or before them—according to the view that Thomas attributes to Gregory Nazianzen, Jerome, and John Damascene).

---

133. Thomas, in effect, distinguishes two modes of angelic knowledge. According to this distinction, angels know either by means of the intelligible species connatural to the angels themselves (what is placed in them at the moment of creation and not obtained through abstraction, as happens instead in humans) or by means of direct vision in the Word. To this Thomas adds the distinction between morning and evening knowledge: the former understands things according to the being that they have in the Word; the latter considers the being of created things in their own natures (*Summa theologiae* Ia, q. 58, a. 6). Whereas the first distinction regards the *mode* of knowledge (through the innate species or by means of the ideas that are in the Word), the second regards the *object* itself (precisely according to the being that they have in the Word or according to the being that they have in their own natures). An evening knowledge is, therefore, possible in the Word or by means of an innate species (*Summa theologiae* Ia, q. 58, a. 7). See B. Faes de Mottoni, "Tommaso d'Aquino e la conoscenza mattutina e vespertina degli angeli," *Medioevo* 18 (1992): 169–202.

134. *De substantiis separatis*, c. 16.

- *They are incorporeal and immaterial* (beyond the corporeal similitudes sometimes suggested by the Scriptures).

- They are in place *only through virtual contact*, that is, *not on the basis of their substance* (which is incorporeal), but *in virtue of their operations*, that is, of the actions of understanding and willing—another thesis condemned by Tempier in 1277.

- *The do not move in a corporeal way.* Their movement is nothing but the succession of their applications to different points of space.[135]

- They are divided up between good and evil, even if the latter are not evil by nature (having been created good like the others), but because of a choice of their will.

The *De substantiis separatis* concludes, thus, with a long reflection on the topic of the sin of the angels, a topic Thomas himself takes to be an extremely difficult one ("it seems impossible that an incorporeal and intellectual substance could become evil with its own appetite").[136] For a "moderate intellectualist" (as we have defined that) like Thomas—for whom every error of the appetite and will presupposes an error of judgment and the apprehension of a false good—it is very hard to explain how purely intellectual substances can be mistaken in the apprehension of the true good. The part of the opuscule that was completed ends, in effect, with the question left open.[137]

135. As we have already seen in the discussion of the *Quodlibeta*, angels can choose to move in a discrete or continuous manner, and, consequently, they can choose to pass through all the space included between two points (continuous movement) or to move themselves from one point to another without passing through the intermediate space (discrete movement). See above, n53.

136. *De substantiis separatis,* c. 20.

137. One brief final observation to offer further justification for the length of this chapter: the years of the second Parisian regency are, for Thomas, without a doubt, his most intense years from the point of view of productivity. It is hard to imagine anyone doing this. It was, in fact, calculated that in this period Thomas wrote the equivalent of more that four thousand large printed and formatted pages of dense text, an average of four to five pages each day—a striking pace that makes it less unlikely that, as the biographical and hagiographical tradition maintain, Thomas was able to dictate four different works to four different secretaries at once.

6

THE LAST NEAPOLITAN
PERIOD AND A COMPLEX
LEGACY

———•:•:•———

After four years, Thomas left Paris again in the spring of 1272, during a period
in which the university was again disturbed by tensions and strikes. In June
of 1272 the chapter of the Roman Dominican province, meeting in Florence,
had put Thomas in charge of founding a new *studium* of theology, allowing
Thomas to decide on its location. It is possible that Thomas was already in Italy
at this point, since the masters of arts in Paris sent their request to this chapter
to have Thomas return to Paris (and it is worth noting here that it is the *artistae*—that is, the philosophers, and not the theologians—who were particularly
attached to him).[1] Thomas decided on Naples—where he had received his first
university education—as the site of the new *studium*. This decision is perfectly understandable, subjective motivations aside, and perfectly in line with the
general demands of the order, if we keep in mind that Naples, as the capital
of the Angevin Kingdom, was at the time one of the most important cities, if
not the most important city, in Italy, and could already boast of an antecedent
university tradition (that of the *studium* founded by Frederick II). Charles I of
Anjou himself could, in fact, have played a role, at least indirectly, in the event.
In a famous letter of July 31, 1272, the Angevin sovereign did not hesitate to in-
vite the masters and students of Paris—who, as we just noted, were in the midst
of another round of strikes—to transfer to Naples to continue their studies in
peace, praising the city's amenities and advantages.[2] We also know that Thom-

---

1. The request is noted in a subsequent letter of the masters of the arts dating from May 1274. We
will come back to this shortly. In the subsequent letter the masters ask for the relics of him whom they
were unable to make return to Paris while he was alive (*quem vivum non potuimus rehabere*), see CUP,
I, no. 447, pp. 504–5.

2. Ibid., no. 443, pp. 501–2.

as's teaching salary was an ounce of gold per month—an emolument that, nevertheless, went directly to the order, and in the circumstances, to the priory in Naples (but the order took care of the expenses of Thomas connected with his activities, such as those related to his secretaries).

As we have already noted, in Naples Thomas continued much of the work started during the second Paris regency or before. Regarding the *Summa theologiae*, this last return to Italy coincides with the drafting of the *tertia pars*. Some scholars (Eschmann, Glorieux, and Torrell himself, at least initially) hypothesized that Thomas could have already composed in Paris 20 or 25 questions of the *tertia pars* on Christological topics. In Naples Thomas would then have completed this section and started the one on sacraments, interrupting it at q. 90.[3] According to Gauthier, on the contrary, the *tertia pars* would have been started in Naples. Regarding the Aristotelian commentaries, it is probable that in Naples Thomas finished the ones on the *Metaphysics* (up to Book XII) and the *Posterior Analytics*, and started the commentaries on the *De caelo et mundo* and the *De generatione et corruptione*. Among his opuscules, the *De motu cordis* and perhaps (the tentativeness is necessary) the *De mixtione elementorum*. It is possible that Thomas returned to the old project of the *Compendium theologiae*, started in Rome between 1265 and 1267, working on the part on hope, which would remain incomplete. As far as the biblical commentaries go, it is thought that Thomas gave a course on the Psalms (up to Psalm 54) in the fall of 1273. We have already commented on the discussions about the chronology of the Pauline commentaries in Chapter 4. Finally, Thomas obviously continued his activity as a preacher, apparently commenting on the *Pater noster* during Lent in 1273.[4]

3. The *tertia pars* was completed by Thomas's collaborators and students (and perhaps, chiefly, Reginald of Piperno) on the basis of the youthful Commentary on the *Sentences*.

4. The dating of the sermons is rather complicated: on this topic one can refer to L.-J. Bataillon, "Les sermons attribués à Saint Thomas. Questions d'authenticité," in *Thomas von Aquin. Werk und Wirkung im Licht neuerer Forschungen*, ed. A. Zimmerman, Miscellanea Mediaevalia 19 (Berlin: de Gruyter, 1988), 325–41. The testimonies collected in the canonization process confirm that the sermons on the Our Father (*Collationes in Orationem Dominicam*), transcribed by Reginald of Piperno, were given in the vernacular, as were the sermons on the Ten Commandments (*Collationes in Decem Praecepta*), collected by Pietro d'Andria. However, it is not easy to situate them with precision. They could date from 1273, or, more likely, from the Italian period between the two Parisian regencies. Cf. J.-P. Torrell, "Les *Collationes in Decem Praeceptis* de Saint Thomas d'Aquin. Édition critique avec introduction et notes," *Revue des Sciences Philosophiques et Théologiques* 69 (1985): 5–40 and 227–63. Reginald also transcribed the sermons on the Creed (*Collationes in Symbolum Apostolorum*), but it is difficult to situate them in the final period in Naples. The sermons on the Ave Maria (*Collationes in Salutationem Angelicam*) must be traced back to the period of the second Parsian regency. Fr. Bataillon—who, unfortunately, passed away bfore he could finish his meticulous edition of the sermons—surveyed 21 other sermons of probable (even if not always unquestionable) authenticity, which are available at the

The more relevant philosophical aspects of this last phase of Thomas's work have already been noted in Chapter 5, above all those that regard the Aristotelian commentaries, and it is not necessary to return to them here. Moreover, without denying that the Christology and theory of the sacraments developed in the *tertia pars* present different interesting doctrinal implications,[5] the topics that dominate this last phase are more strictly theological.

EPISTOLA AD BERNARDUM ABBATEM CASINENSEM: FOREKNOWLEDGE AND FREEDOM

From the end of 1273 onward Thomas interrupted his activity, indeed, he even got rid of his writing instruments, perhaps in response to an experience that he had around December 6, 1273 (the feast of St. Nicholas), that has been interpreted by some as mystical ecstasy and by others as an ischemic attack. It is after this "transformation" that Reginald—who inherited his autograph manuscripts[6]—reported the famous phrase "Everything that I have written seems like straw" (*Omnia quae scripsi videntur michi palee*).

After a brief period of rest with his sister Theodora at the Castle of San Severino at the beginning of 1274 (around the end of January and the beginning of February), Thomas set out for the Council of Lyon, convoked by Gregory X in view of a possible agreement with the Greeks. Thomas's health was already weak and it was further compromised on the trip because of a rather ordinary accident: he struck his head violently against a branch and remained dazed for a long time (*fere stupefactus*, William of Tocco would write). He therefore declined the invitation of the monks of Montecassino who had asked him to make a small deviation from his route to explain a difficult passage of Gregory the Great to them, preferring to send his reply in writing.[7] The *Epistola ad*

---

moment in Tommaso d'Aquino, *I Sermoni (Sermones) e le due lezioni inaugurali (Principia)*, ed. and trans. C. Pandolfi and G. M. Carbone (Bologna: ESD, 2003). On Thomas's preaching activity, see J.-P. Torrell, "La pratique pastorale d'un théologien du XIIIe siècle: Thomas d'Aquin prédicateur," *Revue Thomiste* 82 (1982): 213–45. (See also Torrell's large-scale introduction to the fundamental themes of Thomas's spirituality in *Thomas Aquinas*, vol. 2, *Spiritual Master*.)

5. One noteworthy question is dealt with in, for example, *Summa theologiae* IIIa, q. 18, which, discussing Christ's will in relation to the Father, contributes to clarifying some of the points of Thomas's general position on the will and freedom of the will, and, above all, the distinction between *voluntas ut natura* or *voluntas absoluta considerata* (which directs itself "naturally" toward those things that are intrinsically good, rejecting ends that are evil in themselves) and *voluntas ut ratio*, or *per modum rationis*, which can also choose an end that is immediately less good, in view of a final superior end. On this question, see A. A. Robiglio, *L'impossibile volere: Tommaso d'Aquino, i tomisti e la volontà* (Milan: Vita e Pensiero, 2002), especially 3–42.

6. But as a member of the Dominican Order, Reginald evidently could not regard this material as his private possession.

7. So, at least something was written by Thomas after his famous decision—so much emphasized

Bernardum abbatem Casinensem has to do with the problem of the compatibility between divine foreknowledge and human freedom, which the monks of the abbey—through their abbot Bernard Ayglier—raised again in connection with a passage in Gregory the Great's *Moralia in Iob*. Thomas merely reprises the model borrowed from Boethius, which we have already seen several times. Considered in themselves, or absolutely, human actions are not necessary. Considered in relation to divine foreknowledge, they are foreknown with necessity, but always taking into account the fact that the necessity of divine foreknowledge is not absolute but hypothetical or conditional (if God knows what will happen, it will happen) and so such as not to determine the intrinsic modal status of the events known. To use Thomas's own example: if I see Peter while he is seated, it is necessary for me to see him seated, but the fact that Peter is seated certainly does not depend on the fact that I am seeing him (and what holds for our vision or knowledge of the present also holds for God even for past and future events, since divine knowledge is atemporal).

A CLARIFICATION OF THE CAUSES
OF PREDESTINATION AND THE MORAL
ORDER OF THE WORLD

It is perhaps appropriate at this point to stress—almost in conclusion—that whereas Thomas follows the Boethian model on divine foreknowledge and future contingents, he follows the Augustinian model on *the cause of predestination* in the strict sense (if, that is, the foreknowledge of human merits can be the cause of predestination). This is, in fact, one of the points on which Thomas changed his mind (at least in part) over the course of his work. In the Commentary on the *Sentences* (*In I Sent.*, d. 41, q. 1, a. 3) he had recognized that the foreknowledge of human merits and deeds could not be the cause of predestination in its entirety (otherwise the bestowal of grace would be something owed rather than something, indeed, gratuitous), but he had conceded that some effect of

---

in the hagiographies—not to write again. The "straw," we might say, retained its value. And it is also possible that Thomas wrote on his deathbed. We refer to the possibility, defended by many learned Thomist authorities (including Gauthier), that the hymn *Adoro Te devote* (which is included in its entirety in the fourth version of William of Tocco's *Ystoria*) may have been composed by Thomas himself on his death bed, at Fossanova, between March 4 and 5, 1274. On the other hand, the authenticity of the hymn has frequently been called into question (by, for example, Wilmart, Hugueny, and Gy), but was defended recently by R. Wielockx: see R. Wielockx, "Poetry and Theology in the *Adoro Te deuote*: Thomas Aquinas on the Eucharist and Christ's Uniqueness," in *Christ among the Medieval Dominicans: Representations of Christ in the Texts and Images of the Order of Preachers*, ed. K. Emery Jr. and J. Wawrykow (Notre Dame, Ind.: University of Notre Dame Press, 1998), 157–74; "*Adoro te devote*: Zur Lösung einer alten Crux," *Annales Theologici* 21 (2007): 101–40.

predestination could have its cause in our actions. In other words, the young Thomas did not deny that the final end of the divine will, in predestining a person to salvation, could only be the goodness itself of God, but he admitted in men who are predestined a *merit for glory* in reference to the creaturely will already informed by grace, and a merit consistent at least in *disposition to grace* prior to the temporal apposition of the latter. Beginning with the *De veritate*, and perhaps still more in the *Summa theologiae*, Thomas assumes a much more rigid position in which—along the lines of the Augustinian doctrine of irresistible grace—human merit no longer appears to play any decisive role.[8] The exposition of the *Summa* (Ia, q. 25, a. 5) is particularly significant in this regard. Asking about predestination essentially means asking about the possible motivations of the divine will. But here it is necessary to distinguish, first of all, between the cause of an act of the will *ex parte actus volendi* (in reference to the act itself by which something is willed) and *ex parte volitorum* (in reference to what is willed). No one has ever been so temerarious—according to Thomas—as to hold that the merits could be the cause of divine predestination in the first sense, that is, *ex parte volendi*, or, in the circumstance, *ex parte actus praedestinatis*. The problem, instead, is in determining whether predestination has some foundation in the effects. Setting aside the Origenian position (according to which the effects of predestination in this life depend on the merits acquired in the previous, purely spiritual, life) and the Pelagian position (according to which the effects of predestination depend on the merits acquired in this life), Thomas concerns himself more particularly with the thesis that we could call Semipelagian: the merits that follow the effect of predestination are the cause of predestination itself, that is, God grants grace to those people that he knows will make good use of it. For Thomas, the error of this thesis is in its artificial separation of what must be attributed to grace and what must be attributed to free will. What belongs to grace is, in fact, an effect of predestination and cannot thereby be considered a cause of it. If, therefore, there is a basis on our side for predestination, it must be in something that is in our power without being also an effect of predestination. But this is impossible, since our free will is also among the effects of predestination. Just as the action of secondary causes is not distinct from that of the primary cause, so also the operation of our free will

8. See the careful reconstruction of this question by M. Paluch, *La profondeur de l'amour divin: La prédestination dans l'oeuvre de Saint Thomas d'Aquin*, Bibliothèque thomiste 55 (Paris: Vrin, 2004). The change is (correctly) detected by Paluch already in the transition from the position in the Commentary on the *Sentences* to the *De veritate* q. 6, a. 2, which signals a change of interest from the question of the intelligibility of human merit (and, therefore, from a concern with the temporal causes of the effects of predestination) to the question—more markedly Augustinian— of the intelligibility of the divine choice (and, namely, to a concern with the eternal cause of predestination).

can never be considered independently or apart from divine predestination. Of course, Thomas concedes, in the particular circumstance an individual effect of predestination (grace, glory) can be considered the cause of another (according to the twofold order of efficient and final causality), and in this sense we can say, for example, that God foresees elevating someone to glory for his merits inasmuch as he foresees granting him the grace to acquire those merits. But on the whole, the totality of the effects of predestination has no foundation in the person predestined (*impossibile est quod totus praedestinationis effectus in communi habeat aliquam causam ex parte nostra*).

We have lingered over a topic that could be considered exclusively theological, not so much because of its obvious implications for human action as because of the "cosmological" thesis that it advances. For Thomas, the general reason why some are saved and others condemned is to be found only in the manifestation of divine goodness. Since it is impossible that this goodness be manifested in creation with the same unity and simplicity that it has in God, it is necessary that it reveal itself in the world and in humanity according to different levels. Because of this, goodness is manifested in the elect under the form of mercy and in the reprobate under the form of justice, and this is the only real reason why people are destined to different fates:

The reason for the predestination of some, and reprobation of others, must be sought for in the goodness of God. Thus, he is said to have made all things through his goodness, so that the divine goodness might be represented in all things. Now it is necessary that God's goodness, which in itself is one and undivided, should be manifested in many ways in his creation; because creatures in themselves cannot attain to the simplicity of God. Thus it is that for the completion of the universe there are required different grades of being; some of which hold a high and some a low place in the universe. That this multiformity of grades may be preserved in things, God allows some evils, lest many good things should never happen.... Let us then consider the whole of the human race, as we consider the whole universe. God wills to manifest his goodness in men: in respect to those whom he predestines, he does this by means of his mercy, as sparing them; in respect to others, whom he reprobates, he does this by means of his justice, in punishing them. This is the reason why God elects some and rejects others.

We note the peculiar—and, frankly, disconcerting—turn that theodicy takes here in Thomas: God permits certain evils to happen to preserve the multiplicity of levels in the universe and this holds for both the metaphysical order and the (much more delicate) moral order. The same conclusion is repeated by Thomas, without hesitation, in his Commentary on the Epistle to the Romans:

The excellence of the divine goodness is so great that it cannot be manifested in one way or in one creature. Consequently, he created diverse creatures in which he is manifested in diverse ways. This is particularly true in rational creatures in whom his justice is manifested with regard to those he punishes according to their deserts and his mercy in those he delivers by his grace. Therefore, to manifest both of these in man he mercifully delivers some, but not all.[9]

But if we specifically ask why certain people are the object of divine mercy and others the object of condemnation, this interrogative can only be referred to the unfathomability of the divine will. It is no accident that Thomas explicitly appeals here to Augustine (*Quare illum trahat et illum non trahat, noli velle iudicare, si non vis errare*).[10] What we have is an ultimate limit that resists any attempt at explanation. As Thomas observes in the *Summa*, moreover, the same thing is encountered in physics: a general reason can be given for why prime matter, which is uniform and indeterminate in itself, is divided and distinguished by four elementary forms, namely, the necessity of the differentiation of the species. But precisely why a determinate part of matter itself is found under the form of fire and another, for instance, under the form of earth, simply depends, without any other reason, on the divine will. In the same way, in the construction of the walls of a house, certain rocks are found in a determinate position and others are found in another position; but why a particular rock is put in the place it is depends on the will of the builder.

According to Thomas, this does not permit us to accuse God of injustice. Justice and injustice have a place only where something is owed, and each person must be given what is his. But God owes nothing to creatures: what God gives depends entirely on his liberality, and no one has a right to claim as his what was never owed to him. In this case too the *Super Romanos* simply explains the same thesis:

It is clear that distributive justice has its place in things given as due. If, for example, some persons have earned a wage, more should be given to those who have done more work. But this has no place in things given spontaneously and out of mercy. If, for example, a person meets two beggars and gives one an alms, he is not unjust but merciful. Similarly, if a person has been offended equally by two people and he forgives one but not the other, he is merciful to the one, just to the other, but unjust to neither.[11]

The different treatment that God metes out to people in the same circumstances is, in Thomas's judgment, humanly inexplicable but legitimate. Ultimately, the inequality does not, in itself, imply injustice (*Summa theologiae*, Ia, q. 23, a. 5, ad 3: *Neque tamen propter hoc est iniquitas apud Deum, si inaequalia non*

9. *Super Epistolas ad Romanos*, IX, l. 4.
10. Aurelius Augustinus (Augustine of Hippo), *In Iohannis evangelium tractatus*, tr. 26, 2, CCSL 36, ed. R. Willems (Turnhout: Brepols, 1990), 260 (ll. 7–8).
11. *Super Epistolas ad Romanos*, IX, l. 3.

inaequalibus praeparat: "Nor is there injustice in God on this account, if he treats unequally people who are not unequal").

Apart from the fact, then, that in what is basically his last truly doctrinal writing (the *Epistola ad Bernardum abbatem Casinensem*) Thomas makes reference to a strictly rational model such as that of Boethius (that is itself based on the Aristotelian distinction between absolute necessity and hypothetical necessity) to explain the compatibility of foreknowledge and free will, Thomas's position on predestination suggests two conclusions that—as we know—many other interpreters abstain from drawing.

1. In the first place, Thomas shows that in this regard he is quite faithful to the mature position of Augustine, which substantially excludes human merit from the causes of predestination. Since this is both a theme that is absolutely central in Augustine and one on which the Franciscan masters, to a certain extent, part company with the Bishop of Hippo, it is easy to see how the presumed opposition between Thomas and the "Neo-Augustinianism" of the Franciscans becomes merely a matter of labels. Doctrinal agreement and disagreement in thirteenth- and fourteenth-century Scholasticism must always be verified case by case, question by question.

2. In the second place, the idea that the only real divine motive for the division between the elect and the damned resides (evidently together with the exigency of the manifestation of divine goodness) in the necessity that the ordering of the universe include different "moral" states is, indeed, one of Thomas's least comprehensible—and, frankly, unfortunate—doctrines. The Neo-Platonic doctrine of levels of the universe is in this case transposed into a different context (that of eschatology), but it is also stripped of its original optimism. As Henry of Ghent will say some years after Thomas's death, the fact that the different ontological levels of nature contribute to the beauty of nature itself can be agreed, but that the division between the elect and the reprobate contribute to the "moral" beauty of the universe is very difficult to accept and hold.

AFTER THOMAS: SOME REMARKS ON HIS LEGACY

Having declined the invitation, as we noted, to take a detour to Montecassino on his way to the Council of Lyon, Thomas instead decided to stay with his niece Francesca at the castle of Maenza. But his condition worsened rapidly. When he felt that he was near the end, he asked to be transferred to the nearby Cistercian abbey of Fossanova. Here he died on March 7, 1274.[12]

---

12. According to one account of Thomas's last days, he had tried without success to set out again for Rome, stopping at Fossanova. And according to another account, the monks of Fossanova had

In fact, Thomas never ceased to travel (for almost a century) even when dead, since his remains endured an incredible series of trips before finding rest in 1369 in Toulouse, where they are preserved today (after being moved during the period of the French Revolution) in the church of the Jacobins.[13] If we mention in passing the adventures of Thomas's mortal remains, it is only to recall that the masters of the Parisian faculty of arts (that is, the "philosophers" of Paris) explicitly asked the general chapter of the Dominicans meeting in Lyon (in a letter of May 2, 1274 to which we have already referred) to be able to have the relics of the man whom they were not able to keep in Paris while he was alive, together with the books on philosophical topics (*ad phylosophiam spectantia*) that Thomas had begun in Paris before his transfer to Naples and that he had promised to send (*de quibus nobis mittendis speciali pro missione fecerat mentionem*).[14] The list is rather surprising for us because it includes, along with the Commentary on the *De caelo*, a commentary *Super librum Simplicii* (presumably a commentary on Simplicius's *Categories* or his *De caelo*, translated by William of Moerbeke in 1266 and 1271 respectively), an exposition of Plato's *Timaeus*, a book only identified by its title, *De aquarum conductibus et ingeniis erigendis*, and other treatises on logic that Thomas would have been able to compose in the meantime.[15] As we have already observed, the content and tone

---

come to bring him back by horse. The hypothesis that Thomas was poisoned (and, what is more, by the order of the Angevin king) does not seem to have any foundation, but it was nevertheless held by Giovanni Villani and by Dante in the *Purgatorio*: "Charles came to Italy to make amends / and slaughtered the young Conradin—and then / dispatched Thomas to Heaven, to make amends." See Dante, *Purgatory*, trans. Anthony Esolen (New York: The Modern Library, 2004), 217 (XX, 67–69).

13. It has been calculated that—only in regard to the most important relocations (essentially those recorded here) and supposing that they all happened by land (which was not the case)—during about thirty years of his life Thomas would have traveled approximately 15,000 kilometers (about 9320 miles). See Torrell, *Saint Thomas Aquinas*, vol. 1, *The Person and the Work*, 280; P. Porro, "Tra Napoli e la rive gauche: Tommaso d'Aquino," in *I viaggi dei filosofi*, ed. M. Bettetini and S. Poggi (Milan: Raffaello Cortina, 2010), 57–71.

14. *CUP*, I, nn447, 504–5; see note 1 above.

15. Birkenmajer has suggested that the *De aquarum conductibus et ingeniis erigendis* is not a work of Thomas's but a translation by Moerbeke of Hero of Alexandria's *Pneumatica*. Cf. A. Birkenmajer, "Der Brief der Pariser Artistenfakultät über den Tod des hl. Thomas von Aquino," in *Vermischte Untersuchungen zur Geschichte der mittelalterlichen Philosophie* (Münster: Aschendorff, 1922), 1–32. Birkenmajer's paper also appears in *Études d'histoire des sciences et de la philosophie du Moyen Âge*, Studia Copernicana I (Wrocław: Zakład Narodowy im. Ossolińskich 1970), 277–311. Birkenmajer's hypothesis has been rejected by E. Grant. Cf. E. Grant, "Henricus Aristippus, William of Moerbeke, and Two Alleged Mediaeval Translations of Hero's Pneumatica, *Speculum* 46 (1971): 656–69. The treatise could, in fact, be either a partial translation of Pappus of Alexandria's *Collection* or a selection of texts of Anthemius. Cf. C. Steel, "Guillaume de Moerbeke et saint Thomas," in *Guillaume de Moerbeke. Recueil d'études à l'occasion du 700e anniversaire de sa mort (1286)*, ed. J. Brams and W. Vanhamel (Leuven: Leuven University Press, 1989), 57–82, esp. 72n39; W. Vanhamel, "Biobibliographie de Guillaume de Moerbeke," in *Guillaume de Moerbeke. Recueil d'études à l'occasion du 700e anniversaire de sa*

of the letter are particularly significant because they testify to the respect and, indeed, the devotion that the masters of arts cultivated toward Thomas (despite the fact that he has sometimes been portrayed as their principal adversary), to the point of considering him almost one of them: hence, as being a "philosopher" besides being a "theologian" (and this obviously leads us back to what we said in the introduction to this book).

Furthermore, it is also a fact that, while he was still alive and also after his death, Thomas's teachings were not unanimously accepted and were actually harshly attacked—for reasons that we will see—above all by the theologians, and Franciscan theologians in particular (while, of course, the Dominicans—with some significant exceptions—progressively attempted to close ranks around them). At any rate, the effects of the celebrated condemnation of 1277 (promulgated by Bishop Tempier on March 7, exactly three years after Thomas's death, a circumstance that to some scholars seems perhaps not purely coincidental) already began to affect the memory of Thomas Aquinas and his legacy. Whether Thomas was directly implicated by the intervention of March 7[16] or was the object of separate proceedings (an hypothesis rejected by J. M. M. H. Thijssen and by John Wippel but defended by Roland Hissette and Robert Wielockx)[17] has been the topic of much discussion, which continues today. The complex events of the first months of 1277 lend themselves to different levels of reading. It is certain—because this was the explicit purpose of the intervention—that the articles condemned by Tempier were taken from propositions taught by the Parisian faculty of arts, and from this perspective it would not have been possible for Thomas's doctrines to be directly implicated. But, on the other hand, it is likewise undeniable that some of the condemned articles are identical with theses that Thomas adopted as well: to cite only a few examples: the impossibility

---

mort (1286), ed. J. Brams and W. Vanhamel, 301–83, esp. 372–76. The reference to these works gives us the occasion to recall, on the other hand, many other smaller works that were attributed to Thomas after his death which are almost certainly inauthentic (among which, a work on alchemy is frequently cited erroneously), especially if they are not found listed in the catalogue of works by Thomas put together by Gilles Emery and included in Torrell, *Saint Thomas Aquinas*, vol. 1, *The Person and His Work*, 330–61. The authenticity in some of these cases, much as it is seriously doubted, cannot be absolutely excluded. In relation to the work on alchemy attributed to Thomas, see C. Crisciani, "Tommaso, Pseudo-Tommaso e l'alchimia: Per un'indagine su un corpus alchemico," in *Letture e interpretazioni di Tommaso d'Aquino oggi: cantieri aperti. Atti del Convegno internazionale di studio (Milano, 12–13 settembre 2005)*, ed. A. Ghisalberti, A. Petagine, R. Rizzello, Quaderni di Annali Chieresi (Turin: Istituto di filosofia S. Tommaso d'Aquino, 2006), 103–19.

16. It must be remembered that only on February 4, 1325, did the bishop of Paris Stephen of Bourret free Thomas from all suspicion on this front, voiding the condemnation promulgated by his predecessor Tempier to the extent that the condemnation might regard the Dominican theologian.

17. See pp. 159–61 above for the thesis condemning the impossibility of a numeric multiplicity of angels in the same species.

of a numeric plurality of angels within the same species,[18] the idea that angels themselves are in place only by virtue of their operations or applications,[19] the refusal to consider creation as a veritable change,[20] the conviction that there is no malice of the will without there being an error in reason,[21] the reinterpretation of the action of the fire of hell on the separated soul in coercive terms.[22] This would explain both the subsequent acquittal by Bishop Bourret (which would have been entirely superfluous, as is evident, if no one had grasped the harmony or affinity between Thomas's theses and some of the condemned articles) and the fact that, prior to acquittal, a Dominican master such as John of Naples had disputed a question related to the possibility of teaching the whole of Thomas's doctrine in Paris (*quantum ad omnes conclusiones ejus*), without his having been subject to the excommunication foreseen by the condemnation of 1277.[23] It is surprising, however, that the thesis about the unicity of the substantial form is absent from Tempier's syllabus, and all the more so since it would become real terrain of doctrinal conflict in the years after Thomas's death. We know that in the same month of March in 1277, Henry of Ghent, one of the masters of theology whom Tempier consulted in view of preparing the list of 219 condemned

18. See R. Wielockx, "Autour du procès de Thomas d'Aquin," in *Thomas von Aquin*, ed. Zimmermann, 413–38; R. Hissette, "Saint Thomas et l'intervention épiscopale du 7 mars 1277," *Studi* 2 (1995): 204–58; J. F. Wippel, "Thomas Aquinas and the Condemnation of 1277," *The Modern Schoolman* 72 (1995): 233–72; R. Hissette, "L'implication de Thomas d'Aquin dans les censures parisiennes de 1277," *Recherches de Théologie et Philosophie Médiévales* 44 (1997): 3–31; ibid., "Philosophie et théologie en conflit: Saint Thomas a-t-il été condamné par les maîtres parisiens en 1277?" *Revue Théologique de Louvain* 28 (1997): 216–26; J. M. M. H. Thijssen, "1277 Revisited: A New Interpretation of the Doctrinal Investigations of Thomas Aquinas and Giles of Rome," *Vivarium* 35 (1997): 72–101; J. F. Wippel, "Bishop Stephen Tempier and Thomas Aquinas: A Separate Process against Aquinas?" *Freiburger Zeitschrift fur Philosophie und Theologie* 44 (1997): 117–36; R. Hissette, "Thomas d'Aquin compromis avec Gilles de Rome en mars 1277?" *Revue d'Histoire Ecclésiastique* 93 (1998): 5–26; idem, "Thomas d'Aquin directement visé par la censure du 7 mars 1277? Réponse à John F. Wippel," in *Roma, Magistra Mundi: Itineraria culturae mediaevalis: Mélanges offerts au Père L. E. Boyle à l'occasion de son 75e anniversaire*, ed. J. Hamesse. Textes et etudes du Moyen Âge 10 (Louvain-la-Neuve: FIDEM, 1998) vol. I, 425–37; J. M. M. H. Thijssen, *Censure and Heresy at the University of Paris, 1200–1400* (Philadelphia: University of Pennsylvania Press, 1998); R. Wielockx, "A Separate Process against Aquinas: A Response to John F. Wippel," ed. Hamesse, in *Roma, Magistra Mundi*, vol. II, 1009–30; R. Wielockx, "Procédures contre Gilles de Rome et Thomas d'Aquin: Réponse à J. M. M. H. Thijssen," *Revue des Sciences Philosophiques et Théologiques* 83 (1999): 293–313.

19. See pp. 307–10 above.

20. See pp. 210–12 above.

21. See pp. 273–77 (even though, as we have attempted to show, Thomas's intellectualism is, in reality, rather moderate).

22. See pp. 241–55 above.

23. See C. Jellouschek, "Utrum licite possit doceri Parisius doctrina fratris Thomae quantum ad omnes conclusiones eius," in *Xenia thomistica*, vol. III, ed. S. Szabo (Rome: Typis polyglottis Vaticanis, 1925), 73–104 (text 88–101). The subject is *Quodlibet* VI, q. 2, which was disputed in the Advent session of 1315 (according to the dating suggested by R. Friedman).

theses, was summoned by the bishop and by the papal legate Simon de Brion (later Pope Martin IV) and rather threateningly invited to take a more clear and univocal position on the matter. In fact, in his first *Quodlibet*, Thomas did not explicitly denounce as erroneous the thesis of the unicity of the substantial form in the human composite. We know that Tempier's intention was to extend his investigation even to the faculty of theology, after having condemned the "erroneous" theses taught in the faculty of arts. The proceedings begun against the young Augustinian bachelor Giles of Rome (who was close to some of Thomas's positions but also quite independent) is proof of this. Giles would be expelled from Paris, where he was able to return and teach as a *magister* only some years later in 1285. It is, therefore, completely plausible that a similar—but posthumous—proceeding was undertaken against Thomas, as Hissette and Wielockx suggest: but the Dominican order would have had the advantage of being able to draw out the investigation for a long time until it was finally suppressed.

But in England in the situation was more grave. Again in March of 1277 (and precisely on March 18), an important Dominican master, Robert Kilwardby—who, in the meantime, had become archbishop of Canterbury—condemned 30 theses at Oxford, some of which were clearly traceable back to Thomas (in particular those related to the unicity of the substantial form).[24] The same condemnation was then reaffirmed by Kilwardby's successor as archbishop of Canterbury, the Franciscan John of Peckham (who had already engaged in lively polemics with Thomas while the latter was still alive), first on October 29, 1284, and again, with the addition of other propositions (some of which were also connected to the unicity of the substantial form), on April 30, 1286.[25] It will be noted that the topic of the unicity of the substantial form—and, that is, Thomas's decision to make the rational soul the one form of the human composite, without considering it a subsisting substance or as form and substance together—is the topic that, in the decades immediately following Thomas's death, marks the real difference between Thomas's followers (some of whom, like Richard Knapwell, had to face first excommunication and then silencing for their fidelity) and his adversaries (such as Peckham).

24. *CUP*, I, n. 474, 558–60. See especially a. 7 (*Item quod intellectiva introducta corrumpitur sensitiva et vegetative*). In this article Thomas articulates his embryological principles, which we discussed in Chapter 3. And see aa. 12 and 13 (*Item quod vegetativa, sensitiva et intellectiva sint una forma simplex; Item quod corpus vivum et mortuum est equivoce corpus, et corpus mortuum secundum quod corpus mortuum sit corpus secundum quid*). These articles deal with the unicity of the substantial form in a human composite.

25. See D. A. Callus, *The Condemnation of St. Thomas at Oxford* (London: Blackfriars, 1955); P. Glorieux, "Comment les thèses thomistes furent proscrites à Oxford, 1284–1286," *Revue Thomiste* 32 (1927): 259–91.

But Peckham's positioning is part of a much more bitter conflict between the Franciscans and Dominicans, which had already led in 1279 to the publication of the so-called *Correctorium* of William de La Mare, a Franciscan master at Oxford. The *Correctorium* consists in a list of theses, or better, of veritable articles, taken from different works of Thomas.[26] Each thesis is first illustrated in its essential lines and then accompanied by its refutation or "correction" (from which the name *Correctorium* derives). The list is in itself significant because it presents a fairly precise image of how Thomas was perceived a few years after his death, but it also permits us quickly to recapitulate some points that uniquely characterize his doctrines: to cite only some of the perhaps more relevant doctrines: that the rational soul is the one form of the human composite; that the human intellect does not know individuals; that the soul in the present state cannot think without phantasms; that the temporal beginning of the world cannot be demonstrated; that in incorruptible substances there cannot be more than one individual within the same species; that angels do not have a hylomorphic composition; that angels are necessarily incorruptible; that separate substances are localizable in virtue of their operations; that angels are able to move from one point to another without passing through the intermediary points; that angels possess connatural (innate) cognitive species; that the human will is moved by the intellect; that reason is the principle of freedom; that the intellect is a more noble power than the will; that the essence of beatitude consists more in an act of the intellect than in an act of the will; that in the beatific vision God is seen through his essence and not through a created species; that matter and accidents do not have their idea in God; that God cannot make matter without form; that the fire of hell acts on the separated soul only by keeping it from its proper operation.

Beginning with the general chapter of 1282 the Friars Minor decided that Thomas's *Summa theologiae* would be read by students of theology (indeed, only by the more gifted) only if it was accompanied by the corrections of William de La Mare (and not as marginal notes but as an integral part of the text).

---

26. In Glorieux's edition there are 48 from the *prima pars* of the *Summa*, 12 from the *prima secundae*, 16 from the *secunda secundae*, 9 from the *De veritate*, 10 from the *Quaestiones disputatae de anima*, 1 from the *De virtutibus*, 4 from the *De potentia*, 9 from the *Quodlibeta*, and 9 from the Commentary on the *Sentences* (for a total of 118). Glorieux's edition (see p. 398n28 below) is actually an edition of the *Correctorium Corruptorii "Quare"* of Knapwell that includes the articles of William to refute them in turn. Since Knapwell sometimes pools two of William's articles together in his rebuttal (which happens on at least five occasions), the articles can be calculated differently in this way (coming out, for example, to 123 instead of 118). Besides the edition of Glorieux, see also R. Hissette, "Trois articles de la seconde rédaction du *Correctorium* de Guillaume de la Mare," *Recherches de Théologie Ancienne et Médiévale* 51 (1984): 230–41.

398 | THE LAST NEAPOLITAN PERIOD

In this paradoxical way, the *Correctorium* contributed, against its intentions, to the circulation of the *Summa*, and, above all, contributed to a first nucleus of Thomas's doctrines that his followers had to begin to concern themselves with defending, and, therefore, to make their own. To use the language of Jacques Lacan (if this is appropriate in the history of philosophy), we might say that William and the first Franciscan critics restored to the Dominicans the first truly definite image of "Thomism" that the members of Thomas's order wished to advocate.

It did not take long for the Dominicans to respond, and these responses initially consisted in "corrections" of the "corruption" (*correctoria corruptorii*) produced by William de La Mare.[27] To this genre of "counter-corrections" belongs the *Quare* attributed to Richard Knapwell (ca. 1282–83);[28] the *Sciendum* attributed to Robert Orford (ca. 1283);[29] the *Circa* (60 articles) composed by John of Paris around 1282–84;[30] the *Quaestione* (31 articles), of English origin, attributable perhaps to William of Macclesfield;[31] the *Apologeticum veritatis contra corruptorium* (also in 31 articles) by Rambert de' Primadizzi, written in Paris around 1286–87.[32] Along with this counteroffensive, the order began to protect the memory of Thomas from an institutional perspective as well. In the general chapter of 1279 in Paris it was set down that no one would be permitted to express himself in irreverent or disrespectful terms in regard to his writings, even if they did not agree with their content. In a subsequent general chapter in 1286, also held in Paris, it was prescribed that every Dominican friar should

27. On the polemic of the *correctoria* see P. Glorieux, "Les correctoires: Essai de mise au point," *Recherches de Théologie Ancienne et Médiévale* 14 (1947): 287–304; M. D. Jordan, "The Controversy of the *Correctoria* and the Limits of Metaphysics," *Speculum* 57 (1982): 292–314. For an overall look at the reception of Thomas's teaching in the first 50 years see: P. Glorieux, "*Pro et contra Thomam*: Un survol de cinquante années," in *Sapientiae procerum amore: Mélanges médiévistes offerts à dom Jean-Pierre Müller OSB à l'occasion de son 70ème anniversaire*, ed. T. W. Kohler, Studia Anselmiana 63 (Rome: Editrice Anselmiana, 1974), 255–87. It should also be remembered that the Franciscan opposition to Thomas was not limited to questions of a speculative or doctrinal nature: Pietro di Giovanni, to cite just one example, strongly attacks Thomas's understanding of poverty. See M.-T. d'Alverny, "Un adversaire de Saint Thomas: Petrus Iohannis Olivi," in *St. Thomas Aquinas 1274–1974: Commemorative Studies*, vol. 2, ed. A. Maurer et al. (Toronto: Pontifical Institute of Mediaeval Studies, 1974), 179–218.

28. See P. Glorieux, *Les premières polémiques thomistes. I: Le* Correctorium Corruptorii "Quare," Bibliothèque thomiste 9 (Le Saulchoir-Kain: Revue des Sciences Philosophiques et Théologiques, 1927).

29. See P. Glorieux, *Les premières polémiques thomistes. II: Le* Correctorium Corruptorii "Sciendum," Bibliothèque thomiste 31 (Paris: Vrin, 1956).

30. See J.-P. Müller, *Le* Correctorium Corruptorii "Circa" *de Jean Quidort de Paris*, Studia Anselmiana 12–13 (Rome: Herder, 1941).

31. See also Müller's *Le* Correctorium Corruptorii "Quaestione." *Texte anonyme du ms. Merton 267*, Studia Anselmiana 35 (Rome: Herder, 1974).

32. See Rambertus de Primadizzi, *Apologeticum veritatis contra Corruptorium*, Studi e testi 108, ed. J.-P. Müller (Città del Vaticano: Biblioteca Apostolica Vaticana, 1943).

strive to promote Thomas's doctrines, at least as legitimately defensible opinions, and whoever (masters, bachelors, lectors, priors) taught avowedly contrary theses would be suspended from his duties and from the privileges of the order. The general chapter at Saragossa in 1309, besides reprising the same directives, added that, even in cases of necessity, the friars were not permitted to sell the Bible or the works of Thomas—an unequivocal recognition of the value that was already attributed to his works.[33]

The first period of the formation of a "Thomist" school (and using the term "Thomist" with great caution) is, thus, characterized by an essentially defensive strategy in which we see in the front lines Dominicans of primarily English (William Hothun, Richard Knapwell, Robert Orford, Thomas Sutton, William of Macclesfield) and French (Giles of Lessines, Bernard of Trilia, Peter of Auvergne, John of Paris, Bernard of Auvergne, Hervé Nédellec, Armand de Belvézer, Guillaume Pierre Godin, Pierre de La Palude) origins.[34] We should also place alongside these groups, at least in Italy, figures such as Rambert de' Primadizzi, John of Naples, Tolomeo of Lucca, Remigio de' Girolami, and, in the Germanic realm, John of Fribourg, John and Gerard of Sterngasse, Henry of Lübeck, and, above all, John Picardi of Lichtenberg.[35]

But we should not think that all of the Dominican intellectuals immediately allied themselves with Thomas's positions. The most well known and obvious cases are those of James of Metz, Durando di San Porziano, and Dietrich of Freiberg.[36] The last of these three openly distanced himself from Thomas on

33. On this topic, see M. Burbach, "Early Dominican and Franciscan Legislation Regarding St. Thomas," *Mediaeval Studies* 4 (1942): 139–58; L. Bianchi, "Ordini mendicanti e controllo 'ideologico': il caso delle province domenicane," in *Studio e studia: le scuole degli ordini mendicanti tra xiii e xiv secolo. Atti del xxix Convegno internazionale. Assisi, 11–13 ottobre 2001* (Spoleto: CISAM, 2002), 326–34; Torrell, *Thomas Aquinas*, vol. 1, 308–10; Robiglio, *La sopravvivenza e la gloria*, 33–49. Important observations on the "institutional" role of the Dominican Order in the development of Thomism (and on the fact that the recommendations of the chapters do not seem to make reference to any particular doctrine or to any particular work, but only to the necessity of faithfully following Thomas as a model) is found is M. J. F. M. Hoenen, "Thomas von Aquin und der Dominikanerorden. Lehrtradition bei den Mendikanten des späten Mittelalters," *Freiburger Zeitschrift für Philosophie und Theologie* 57 (2010): 260–85.

34. For the first generations of English and French Thomists see, above all, F. J. Roensch, *Early Thomistic School* (Dubuque, Iowa: The Priory Press, 1964).

35. See the historiographical evaluation proposed in *Deutsche Thomisten des 14. Jahrhunderts: Lektüren, Aneignungsstrategien, Divergenzen—Thomistes allemands du XIVe siècle: lectures, stratégies d'appropriation, divergences. Akten des Kolloquiums an der Universität Freiburg im Breisgau vom 28.–30. Januar 2010)*, ed. Hoenen, Imbach, Konig-Pralong, 227–430.

36. On James of Metz, see B. Decker, *Die Gotteslehre des Jakob von Metz. Untersuchungen zur Dominikanertheologie zu Beginn des 14. Jahrhunderts* (Münster: Aschendorff, 1967). On Durandus of Saint-Pourcain, see J. Koch, *Durandus de S. Porciano op. Forschungen zum Streit um Thomas von Aquin zu Beginn des 14. Jahrhunderts* (Münster, Aschendorff, 1927); E. Lowe, *The Contested Theological*

such crucial points as transubstantiation, angelology, the theory of the intellect, and the distinction between being and essence. The case of Meister Eckhart is more complex. His differences with Thomas have often been excessively emphasized, but we see in his Parisian debate with the Franciscans (and with Gonsalves of Spain in particular) that he is not too far from the moderate intellectualism specific to Thomas. To this day it is still a matter of controversy whether it is possible to speak of a veritable "anti-Thomism" between the end of the thirteenth century and the beginning of the fourteenth century, and this is all the more so since it also appears difficult to speak of a real established "Thomism" at this same time. It has been suggested that the decisive step in this matter was taken as a consequence of the canonization process that occurred under John XXII.[37] This process consisted principally of an investigation in Naples from June 21 to September 18, 1319, a second in Fossanova, November 10–20, 1321, and lastly the proclamation of July 18, 1323. The hypothesis that Thomism first emerged from this process is quite plausible, but, on the other hand, it cannot be denied that a certain "Thomist identity" had already constituted itself before this, as an effect of William de La Mare's *Correctorium* and the responses to it, and, above all, around the fundamental doctrine of the unicity of the substantial form, as the interventions of Peckham and the condemnation of Knapwell show. And it is, moreover, significant that the doctrine that posits the rational or intellectual soul as the *forma corporis humani per se et essentialiter* was already definitively affirmed—after having been so strongly suspected of heresy—by the Council of Vienne (1312),[38] and, therefore, well before the canonization. What is unques-

---

Authority of Thomas Aquinas: The Controversies between Hervaeus Natalis and Durandus of St. Pourçain (New York: Routledge, 2003); I. Iribarren, *Durandus of St Pourçain: A Dominican Theologian in the Shadow of Aquinas* (Oxford: Oxford University Press, 2005). On the divergences between Dietrich of Freiberg and Thomas, see A. Maurer, "The *De quidditatibus entium* of Dietrich of Freiberg and Its Criticism of Thomistic Metaphysics," *Mediaeval Studies* 18 (1956): 173–203; and especially R. Imbach, "'*Gravis iactura verae doctrinae*': Prolegomena zu einer Interpretation der Schrift *De ente et essentia* Dietrichs von Freiberg OP," in *Freiburger Zeitschrift für Philosophie und Theologie* 26 (1979): 369–425; idem, "Prétendue primauté de l'être sur le connaître. Perspectives cavalières sur Thomas d'Aquin et l'école dominicaine allemande," in Lectionum varietates: *Hommage à Paul Vignaux (1904–1987)*, ed. J. Jolivet, Z. Kaluza, and A. de Libera (Paris: Vrin, 1991): 121–32; idem, "L'antithomisme de Thierry de Freiberg," *Revue Thomiste* 97 (1997): 245–58; A.-S. Robin, "L'antithomisme de Dietrich de Freiberg dans le *De visione beatifica*," in *Recherches sur Dietrich de Freiberg*, ed. J. Biard, D. Calma, R. Imbach, Studia Artistarum 19 (Turnhout: Brepols, 2009), 165–69. But on these authors see also the new overviews mentioned in n. 39 below.

37. Robiglio, *La sopravvivenza e la gloria*, 53–54; See also Robiglio's "Tommaso d'Aquino tra morte e canonizzazione (1274–1323)," in *Letture e interpretazioni*, ed. Ghisalberti, Petagine, 197–216.

38. It is, in fact, one of the errors imputed (*post mortem*) to Peter John Olivi, but it is significant that the thesis opposed to Thomas is now described as heretical. See the *constitutitio Fidei catholicae*: "Furthermore, with the approoval of the holy council We reject as erroneous and contrary to the truth of the Catholic faith any doctrine or opinion that rashly asserts that the substance of the

tionable is that Thomas's doctrines truly changed the setting of Scholastic debates between the thirteenth and fourteenth centuries (as much in the sphere of theology as in that of the *artistae*, if we consider Thomas's enormous influence on the interpretation of Aristotelian works), standing out early on as a doctrinal whole with which it was inevitably necessary to engage positively or negatively. The new historiographical approaches to the philosophy of the fourteenth century, free of the Neo-Scholastic ideology that had conditioned previous approaches, continue to offer us an increasingly complex, variegated picture, that concretely depicts the creation of a Thomist tradition through a plurality of internal approaches and an intense confrontation with many objections from without.[39]

It is, furthermore, worth mentioning that Thomas's works reached the cultural boundaries of the Latin world in a short time. With regard to the Jewish world, already at the end of the thirteenth century (probably between 1288 and 1291), Hillel of Verona (Hillel ben Samuel) included a translation of the first chapter of Thomas's *De unitate intellectus* (without mentioning Thomas's name) in the last part of his *Tagmulē ha-Nefesh* (*The Rewards of the Soul*). At the beginning of the fourteenth century, Judah ben Moses Romano translated selections of the *Summa contra Gentiles*, selections of the Commentary on the *De causis* (incorporated in his own translation of the *De causis*), and, above all, the *De ente et essentia*, accompanied by some notes of commentary. Other translations would be carried out in the fourteenth century by Eli ben Joseph Chabillo (*Quaestiones disputatae de anima*) and Abraham Nehemiah ben Joseph (Commentary on the *Metaphysics*).[40]

---

rational and intellectual soul is not truly and of itself the form of the human body or that calls this into doubt. In order that the truth of the pure faith may be known to all and the path to error barred, We define that from now on whoever presumes to assert, defend, or obstinately hold that the rational and intellectual soul is not of itself and essentially the form of the human body is to be censured as heretic." Heinrich Denzinger, *Enchiridion symbolorum definitionum et declarationum de rebus fidei et morum-Compendium of Creeds, Definitions, and Declarations on Matters of Faith and Morals*, Latin-English, 43rd Edition, ed. Peter Hünermann (San Francisco: Ignatius Press, 2012), 290 (§902).

39. The colloquia organized at Tolouse by the *Revue Thomiste* are particularly informative on this topic, especially "Saint Thomas au XIV siècle. Actes du colloque de Toulouse, juin 1996," *Revue Thomiste* 97 (1997); "Antithomisme: Histoire, thèmes et figures, i. L'antithomisme dans la pensée médiévale et moderne. Actes du colloque de Toulouse, mai 2007," *Revue Thomiste* 108 (2008); Also, C. Viola, "L'École thomiste au Moyen Âge," in *La philosophie contemporaine. Chroniques nouvelles*, vol. VI/I, *Philosophie et science au Moyen Âge*, ed. G. Floistad (Dordrecht: Nijhoff, 1990), 345–77; and now currently in progress, the project ANR-DFG *Thomisme et antithomisme au Moyen Âge (XIIIe–XVe siècles)*, coordinated by R. Imbach and M. Hoenen.

40. On the reception of Thomas in Jewish circles, see G. Sermoneta, "Pour une histoire du thomisme juif," in *Aquinas and the Problems of His Time*, ed. G. Verbeke and D. Verhelst, Mediaevalia Lovaniensia I/5, (Leuven–The Hague: Leuven University Press–Martinus Nijhoff, 1976), 130–35; idem, "Per una storia del tomismo ebraico," in *Tommaso d'Aquino nel suo settimo centenario. Atti del Congresso internazionale (Roma-Napoli, 17–24 aprile 1974)*, vol. II (Naples: Edizioni Domenicane Italiane, 1976),

In the Byzantine world, the brothers Demetrios and Prochorus Kydones had, in the second half of the fourteenth century, a massive (and controversial) project of translating Thomas's principal works, which included the *Summa contra Gentiles*, the *Summa theologiae* (Ia, Ia-IIa, IIa-IIae, and some questions of the *tertia pars* and the *Supplementum*); the *Quaestiones disputatae De potentia* and *De spiritualibus creaturis*, the *De rationibus fidei*, the *De articulis fidei* and *De aeternitate mundi*. Later, Georgios Scholarios translated the *De ente et essentia* (with the commentary of Armand de Belvézer) and the commentaries on the *De interpretatione*, the *Physics*, and the *De anima*, along with the prologue to the Commentary on the *Metaphysics* and the opuscule (whose authorship by Thomas is doubtful) *De fallaciis*. There were also selections from the major works made available in *florilegia*, and the versions (attributed to Maximus Planudes) of the *Expositio super Symbolum Apostolorum* and the *Sermo de festo corporis Christi*.[41]

Finally, it should certainly also be noted that at least one of Thomas's texts seems to have been copied and circulated in the Muslim world, although in Greek and not Arabic. A copy of Demetrios Kydones's translation of the *Summa contra Gentiles* was among the manuscripts that Mehmed II had reproduced in his *scriptorium* after the conquest of Constantinople.[42]

Coming back to the Latin world, it was the reception of Thomas's work after the canonization that led to the birth of Thomism proper. We are not able (and perhaps, in any event, it would be pointless in this book) to trace the history of this phenomenon and so will only mention some of its more important stages: the vigorous institutional reappropriation and teaching of Thomas's doctrines in the fourteenth century at the University of Cologne, especially on account of the *bursa Montana*;[43] the period of the great Renaissance commen-

---

354–59; idem, "Jehudah ben Moseh ben Daniel Romano, traducteur de Saint Thomas," in *Hommage à George Vajda. Études d'histoire et de pensée juives*, ed. G. Nahon and C. Touati (Louvain: Peeters, 1980), 235–62; C. Rigo, "Yehudah ben Mosheh Romano traduttore degli Scolastici latini," *Henoch* 17 (1995): 141–70; M. Zonta, *Hebrew Scholasticism in the Fifteenth Century: A History and Source Book* (Dordrecht: Springer, 2006). The translation of the *De ente* must have been complete before 1320.

41. On the reception of Thomas in Byzantium, see S. Papadopoulos, "Thomas in Byzanz: Thomas-Rezeption und Thomas-Kritik in Byzanz zwischen 1354 und 1435," *Theologie und Philosophie* 49 (1974): 274–304.

42. The codex is actually preserved in the Vatican Library (Vat. Gr. 613). On the *scriptorium* of Mehmet, see J. Raby, "Mehmed the Conqueror's Greek *scriptorium*," *Dumbarton Oaks Papers* 37 (1983): 15–34, especially at 20.

43. The *bursae* were colleges (mainly private foundations) in which masters and students led a common life under the leadership of a regent. The *bursa Montana* was founded by one of the champions of the Thomistic rennaisance in Colgne, Henry of Gorkum, but derived its name from the second regent (Gerard de Monte). The recovery of Thomism here takes place within two distinct but related contexts: on the one hand, within the so-called *Wegestreit*, the conflict between the *via antiqua* and the *via moderna*, and, on the other hand, within the conflict between the Thomists and the Albertines

tators: Jean Cabrol's (Capreolus) commentary on the Commentary on the *Sentences*, Thomas de Vio's (Cajetan) commentaries on the *Summa theologiae* and the *De ente et essentia*, Sylvester of Ferrara's (Ferrariensis) commentary on the *Summa contra Gentiles*;[44] the rooting of Thomas's doctrines in the Spanish universities, especially through the work first of Francisco de Vitoria and then of the *Salmaticenses*; the conflict with the new Jesuit Scholasticism, above all in regard to grace (the *congregatio de auxiliis*).[45] The salient point of the development of Thomism in the Renaissance and early modernity occurred in 1567, when (on April 15) Thomas was declared a Doctor of the Church by Pope Pius V at a time when, among the Latins, only Ambrose, Jerome, Augustine, and Gregory the Great enjoyed this dignity.[46] From this moment onward, Thomas's destiny would be ever more intimately linked with that of the Church or Rome, and so with the Catholic tradition, making Thomas the polemical target not only of the Reformers,[47] within the Christian confessions, but also of all philosophers outside the Roman Church.

It is not surprising, then, that the other fundamental turning point in the reception of Thomas is the decision at the end of the nineteenth century explicitly to make him the official reference point for Catholic thought and the champion of the *philosophia perennis*, in contrast both with modern philosophy (later within the Church itself) and with "modernism." It was, above all, Leo XIII's encyclical *Aeterni Patris*, promulgated on August 4, 1879, that sanctioned this decision in an unequivocal way.[48] The pontiff proposed a new conjunction of philosophy

---

among proponents of the *prima via*. The other basic characteristic of the Cologne Thomism of the fifthteenth century is the decision to focus, above all, on teaching in the faculty of arts. On this topic, see H. Goris, "Thomism in Fifteenth-Century Germany," in *Aquinas as Authority*, ed. P. van Geest, H. Goris, and C. Leget (Leuven: Peeters, 2002), 1–24.

44. On the Thomism of the Renaissance see C. Giacon, *La seconda scolastica*, vol. 1, *I grandi commentatori di san Tommaso* (Milan: Bocca, 1944) and republished by Nino Aragno (Turin: 2001). Giacon's volume is perhaps still the best introduction to sixteenth-century Thomism's internal debates and to the figures of Cajetan and Sylvester of Ferrera in particular. See also P. O. Kristeller, "Thomism and the Italian Thought of the Renaissance," in *Medieval Aspects of Renaissance Learning*, ed. E. Mahoney (Durham: Duke University Press, 1974), 29–91; P. Conforti, "La tradizione scolastica tomista fra Umanesimo e Rinascimento. Trecento e Quattrocento," *Studi* 2 (1995): 259–81. The commentaries of Cajetan and Sylvester of Ferrera are reproduced in the Leonine editions of the two *Summae*.

45. For a synthetic placement of these various stages of Thomism, see R. Cessario, *A Short History of Thomism* (Washington, D.C.: The Catholic University of America Press, 2005).

46. It was also Pius V who extended this title to the Greek Fathers, in particular to Athanasius, Basil, Gregory Nazianzen, and John Chrysostom.

47. Starting evidently with Luther: see D. Janz, *Luther and Late Medieval Thomism: A Study in Theological Anthropology* (Waterloo, Ont.: Wilfrid Laurier University Press, 1983); K.-H. zur Muhlen, "On the Critical Reception of the Thought of Thomas Aquinas in the Theology of Martin Luther," in *Aquinas as Authority*, 65–86.

48. Heinrich Denzinger, *Enchiridion symbolorum definitionum et declarationum de rebus fidei et*

and theology (and between reason and faith), one that he held had already been achieved by the Scholastic masters, especially Thomas, who is "leader and master of all" and, thus, "worthy of being esteemed the special bulwark and honor of the Catholic Church." Catholic teachers should, therefore, strive to make the Thomist doctrine "penetrate the souls of their students" in "preference to all others" in light of its "depth and excellence." The pontiff, thus, established a precise perspective for the whole Catholic tradition: all of the essentials of Christian philosophy are brought back to the Middle Ages, and the whole of the Middle Ages are centered on Thomas, assuming everything that preceded him to be a kind of preparation and everything that followed a kind of crisis and decline.

The encyclical's posititive effects were the revival of the study of medieval philosophy, the launching of projects of editions of works of the great Scholastic masters, beginning, of course, with Thomas (the Leonine edition),[49] and the founding of important centers for the spread of Scholastic thought and Thomism, such as the Higher Institute of Philosophy at Louvain in Belgium, started by Cardinal Désiré Mercier in 1887.

Some years later, in the encyclical *Pascendi* (September 8, 1907),[50] Pope Pius X reproposed the program of his predecessor in a more binding manner: "In the first place, with regard to studies, we will and ordain that Scholastic philosophy be made the basis of the sacred sciences.... And let it be clearly understood above all things that the Scholastic philosophy we prescribe is that which the Angelic Doctor bequeathed to us." And in a *motu proprio* of June 29, 1914, entitled *Doctoris Angelici*, Pius X further explained that there is no need to follow the other Scholastic doctors, but *only* Thomas Aquinas.

To this end the Congregation of Studies published a kind of vademecum of Thomist thought (July 27, 1914) that listed 24 theses of Thomas (or attributed to him) to which it was necessary to adhere more or less strictly. In this case too, a quick glance at the list helps us to understand what Thomas had become at the beginning of the twentieth century.[51] The first and principal place is given to the

morum-Compendium of Creeds, Definitions, and Declarations on Matters of Faith and Morals, 625–26 (§3135–3140).

49. See L.-J. Bataillon, "Le edizioni di *Opera Omnia* degli scolastici e l'Edizione Leonina," in *Gli studi di filosofia medievale fra Otto e Novecento. Contributo a un bilancio storiografico. Atti del Convegno internazionale, Roma, 21–23 settembre 1989*, Storia e letteratura 179, ed. R. Imbach and A. Maierù (Rome: Edizioni di Storia e Letteratura, 1991), 141–54; See also "La Commission Léonine. Philologie et histoire au service de la pensée," ed. R. Imbach and A. Oliva, *Revue des Sciences Philosophiques et Théologiques* 89 (2005): 5–110.

50. Heinrich Denzinger, *Enchiridion symbolorum definitionum et declarationum de rebus fidei et morum—Compendium of Creeds, Definitions, and Declarations on Matters of Faith and Morals*, 695–704 (§3472–3500).

51. Ibid., 720–23 (§3601–3624).

theses about the composition of potency and act and being and essence (insisting in a very clear way on the real distinction between the two principles, thesis 3). There follow (to mention only a few) the theses on matter as principle of individuation, the unicity of substantial form, the connection between immateriality and intellectuality, the modalities of knowledge, the primacy of the intellect over the will, and the necessity of knowing God's existence only *a posteriori*. As we see, the theses as a whole correspond to what Thomas actually taught. But some of them (such as the one on the real distinction between being and essence) have taken on a life that goes beyond their original context. The identity of being and God has itself taken on a different character. It no longer has an apophatic tone (God's non-objectifiability as pure being beyond all forms) but almost becomes a thesis of positive theology. (Thesis 23: "The Divine Essence is well proposed to us as constituted in its metaphysical concept by its identity with the exercised actuality of its existence, or, in other terms, as the very subsisting being; and by the same token it exhibits to us the reason of its infinity in perfection.") This reconstruction of the identity of God and being in positive terms—now detached from its vital reference to the Neo-Platonic tradition of the *De causis* and from certain presuppositions of Avicennian metaphysics—will cement the centrality that the act of being, as "act of all acts," will have across all of Neo-Thomism in the first half of the twentieth century (and beyond).[52]

The promulgation of the 24 theses also provoked quite harsh reactions as well, especially from the Jesuits (despite the fact that a Jesuit of the Gregorian University, Guido Mattiussi, contributed to the formulation of the theses). The doctrines of Francisco Suarez (not always compatible with those of Thomism) continued to play an important part in the order's program of formation, and the passionate debate between Neo-Thomists and Neo-Suarezians about the correct way to understand the composition of being and essence is clear evidence of this.[53] The *exclusive* privileging of Thomas was somewhat attenuated under Benedict XV, but his undisputed primacy in Catholic thought was not impaired. This primacy has been reaffirmed in more recent documents (such as John Paul II's encyclical *Fides et ratio*).

52. We should, however, mention Anthony Kenny's celebrated contribution, according to which Thomas's concept of being, which is so central for the Neo-Scholastics, is intrinsically confused (*Aquinas on Being* [Oxford: Clarendon Press, 2002]). In Kenny's view, Thomas used the term "being" in many different ways (as many as 12, see 189–82) without ever integrating these different senses into a systematic and coherent whole. Kenny even argues that Thomas's identification of God and being is an obstacle for his project of natural theology.

53. On this question see P. Porro, "Qualche riferimento storiografico sulla distinzione di essere ed essenza, in Tommaso d'Aquino," in *L'ente e l'essenza*, trans. and ed. P. Porro (Milan: Bompiani, 2002), 183–215.

It should be acknowledged, however, that this primacy has not produced, as was to be feared, a flattening and homogenization. Twentieth-century Thomism is, rather, a whole that is complex and diverse. The positions of a Gilson cannot, for example, be grouped together with those of a Garrigou-Lagrange (and it is not by chance that the two disagree about the possibility of progress in philosophy), even within a common acceptance of the privileged reference to Thomas.[54] On the other hand, the reception of Thomas in the twentieth century is not an entirely Neo-Thomist and Neo-Scholastic affair. We should also point out the intersection of Thomism with transcendental philosophy, phenomenology (Edith Stein), Heideggerian "fundamental ontology" and "history of being," Protestant theology,[55] and, finally, analytic philosophy.[56] All of this involves, above all, "theoretical" Thomism, so speak. Along with this, historical and philological research has made enormous strides forward on account, above all, of the Leonine edition, which quite early on stood out as a veritable model for every project of a critical edition of medieval texts.[57] Each new volume of the Leonine Commission offers us not only a much more trustworthy text than the numerous previous editions but also a better understanding of the context, the specific interlocutors, and sources of the Thomas's works. What was

54. For an evaluation of the bearing of Neo-Scholasticism on medieval studies at the end of the eighteenth and the beginning of the nineteenth centuries in France, see J. Jolivet "Les études de philosophie médiévale en France de Victor Cousin à Etienne Gilson," and A. de Libera, "Les études de philosophie médiévale en France d'Étienne Gilson à nos jours." For Germany see A. Zimmermann, "Die gegenwärtige Diskussion von Lehren des Thomas von Aquin in Deutschland." For Italy see C. Vasoli, "La neoscolastica in Italia." These essays can be found in *Gli studi di filosofia medievale*, ed. Imbach and Maierù, 1–20, 21–50, 155–66, 167–89. The volume also contains contributions on other national traditions. For Géry Prouvost (who gives special consideration to the differences between Gilson and Maritain), the multiplicity of approaches of Neo-Thomism is rooted, in some way, in the ambiguity already present in Thomas's work itself. See G. Prouvost, *Thomas d'Aquin et les thomismes* (Paris: Cerf, 1996).

55. J. Bowlin, "Contemporary Protestant Thomism," in *Aquinas as Authority*, 235–51.

56. For some "historiographic" indications on this question, see M. Micheletti, *Tomismo analitico* (Brescia: Morcelliana, 2007); P. Müller, "Il tomismo analitico. Prospettive e contributi," in *Letture e interpretazioni*, 177–86. For an appraisal of the principal interpretive lines on Thomas in English-language philosophy in recent decades (an appraisal that, it should be noted, does not adopt the perspective of a "militant"—so to speak—analytical Thomism), see F. Kerr, *After Aquinas: Versions of Thomism* (Oxford: Blackwell, 2002). The presence of Thomas in the philosophy of the twentieth century is so varied and vast that a brief account of it is impossible. On this subject, some monographic issues of the *Revue Thomiste* are helpful. In particular see "Saint Thomas au XX siècle. Actes du colloque du Centenaire de la "Revue thomiste," *Revue Thomiste* 93 (1993); "Saint Thomas d'Aquin et l'onto-théologie. Actes du colloque de Toulouse, juin 1994," *Revue Thomiste* 95 (1995); "Antithomisme: Histoire, thèmes et figures, II: L'antithomisme dans la pensée contemporaine. Actes du colloque de Toulouse, mai 2007," *Revue Thomiste* 108 (2008): 2.

57. See C. Luna, "L'Édition Léonine de Saint Thomas d'Aquin: vers une méthode de critique textuelle et d'ecdotique," in *La Commission Léonine*, 31–110.

really missing in a large part of twentieth-century Thomism was precisely the necessary attention to the way Thomas arrived at particular conclusions, as he engaged not with abstract traditions of thought (Aristotelianism, Platonism, Averroism, etc.), but with texts that can be definitely identified—those texts that Thomas always sought out right up to the end of his life and that should each time be used and evaluated in different ways according to the problem in question.

It has been said that it is ultimately necessary to free medieval philosophy from the burden of Thomas. This is perhaps an overly ambitious project, but it is, above all, sterile, because although it may be right to part with the Thomas-centrism that dominated the study of medieval thought at least up until the 1970s, it would be an obvious methodological ingenuousness to ignore the actual role that Thomas played historically in the developments of medieval and subsequent thought. It is perhaps simpler, or at least more profitable, to try to separate definitively the direct engagement with Thomas's writings from the vicissitudes of Thomism and, above all, twentieth-century Thomism, as the research of recent decades has extensively begun to do.

It would, however, be too much to attempt to attribute this second and more circumscribed purpose to our present work. With much more modest intentions, it would achieve a goal greater than we had expected if it succeeded in offering even some idea of the complex stratification of Thomas's work and in doing justice, at least in part, to the uncommon intellectual curiosity that always animated Thomas's activity.

BIBLIOGRAPHY

PRINCIPAL EDITIONS OF THOMAS'S WORKS

The critical edition of Thomas's complete works edited by the Leonine Commission (which is the commission instituted, or at least made possible, for such an end, by Pope Leo XIII in 1880) is to this day in progress: Sancti Thomae de Aquino doctoris angelici *Opera Omnia*, iussu impensaque Leonis XIII P.M. edita, cura et studio fratrum praedicatorum, 1882 ss. The commission has changed locations over the course of the years, moving from Rome-Grottaferrata to Paris. The locations are as different as the publishers that have collaborated with the project. So far, the following volumes have appeared (we indicate—when actually available—the names of the editors of the editions of the individual texts):

1/1   *Expositio libri Peryermenias, editio altera retractata.* Edited by R.-A. Gauthier, Leonine Commission. Rome-Paris: Vrin, 1989.

1/2   *Expositio libri Posteriorum, editio altera retractata.* Edited by R.-A. Gauthier, Leonine Commission. Rome-Paris: Vrin, 1989.

2   *Commentaria in octo libros Physicorum Aristotelis.* Rome: Ex Typographia Polyglotta S. C. de Propaganda Fide, 1884.

3   *In libros Aristotelis De caelo et mundo expositio. In librum primum Aristotelis De generatione et corruptione expositio. In libros Aristotelis Meteorologicorum exposition.* Rome: Ex Typographia Polyglotta S. C. de Propaganda Fide, 1886.

4–12 *Summa theologiae cum Supplemento et commentariis Caietani.* Rome: Ex Typographia Polyglotta S. C. de Propaganda Fide, 1888–1906.

13–15 *Summa contra Gentiles cum commentariis Ferrariensis.* Rome: Typis Riccardi Garroni, 1918–30.

16   *Indices in tomos 4–15.* Apud Sedem Commissionis Leoninae. Rome: S. Sabina-Aventino, 1948.

22   *Quaestiones disputatae de veritate.* 3 vols. Edited by A. Dondaine. Rome: Editori di San Tommaso, 1970–76.

23   *Quaestiones disputatae de malo.* Edited by P.-M. Gils, Leonine Commission. Rome-Paris: Vrin, 1982.

24/1 *Quaestiones disputatae de anima.* Edited by B.-C. Bazán, Leonine Commission. Rome-Paris: Cerf, 1996.

24/2 *Quaestio disputata De spiritualibus creaturis.* Edited by J. Cos, Leonine Commission. Rome-Paris: Cerf, 2000.

25   *Quaestiones de quolibet.* Edited by R.-A. Gauthier, Leonine Commission. Rome-Paris: Cerf, 1996.

26   *Expositio super Iob ad litteram.* Edited by A. Dondaine. Rome: Ad Sanctae Sabinae, 1965.

28   *Expositio super Isaiam ad litteram.* Edited by H.-F. Dondaine and L. Reid. Rome: Editori di San Tommaso Ad Sanctae Sabinae, 1974.

40   *Contra errores Graecorum ad Urbanum papam. De rationibus fidei ad Cantorem Antiochenum. De forma absolutionis paenitentiae sacramentalis ad Magistrum Ordinis. De substantiis separatis ad fratrem Raynaldum de Piperno. Expositio super primam et secundam Decretalem ad archidiaconum Tudertinum.* Edited by H.-F. Dondaine. Rome: Ad Sanctae Sabinae, 1969.

41   *Contra impugnantes Dei cultum et religionem. De perfectione spiritualis vitae. Contra doctrinam retrahentium a religion.* Edited by H.-F. Dondaine. Rome: Ad Sanctae Sabinae, 1969.

42   *Compendium theologiae,* pars I: *De fide.* Edited by H.-F. Dondaine; pars II: *De spe.* Edited by G. de Grandpré; *De articulis fidei.* Edited by H.-F. Dondaine; *Responsio ad magistrum Ioannem de Vercellis de 108 articulis.* Edited by H.-F. Dondaine; *Responsio ad magistrum Ioannem de Vercellis de 43 articulis.* Edited by H.-F. Dondaine; *Responsio ad lectorem Venetum de 36 articulis.* Edited by H.-F. Dondaine; *Responsio ad lectorem Bisuntinum de 6 articulis.* Edited by H.-F. Dondaine; *Epistola ad ducissam Brabantiae.* Edited by H.-F. Dondaine; *De emptione et venditione ad tempus.* Edited by H.-F. Dondaine; *Epistola ad Bernardum abbatem Casinensem.* Edited by A. Dondaine; *De regno ad regem Cypri.* Edited by H.-F. Dondaine; *De secreto.* Edited by H.-F. Dondaine. Rome: Editori di San Tommaso, 1979.

43   *De principiis naturae ad fratrem Sylvestrum. De aeternitate mundi. De motu cordis ad magistrum Philippum de Castro Caeli. De mixtione elementorum ad magistrum Philippum de Castro Caeli. De operationibus occultis naturae ad quendam militem ultramontanum. De iudiciis astrorum. De sortibus ad dominum Iacobum de Tonengo. De unitate intellectus contra Averroistas. De ente et essentia.* [attributed] *De fallaciis.* [attributed] *De propositionibus modalibus.* Edited by H.-F. Dondaine. Rome: Editori di San Tommaso, 1976.

44/1   *Sermones.* Edited by L. J. Bataillon. Paris: Cerf, 2014.

45/1   *Sentencia libri De anima.* Edited by R.-A. Gauthier, Leonine Commission. Rome-Paris: Vrin, 1984.

45/2   *Sentencia libri De sensu et sensato cuius secundus tractatus est De memoria et reminiscencia.* Edited by R.-A. Gauthier, Leonine Commission. Rome-Paris: Vrin, 1985.

47   *Sententia libri Ethicorum.* 2 vols. Edited by R.-A. Gauthier. Rome: Ad Sanctae Sabinae, 1969.

48   *Sententia libri Politicorum.* Edited by H.-F. Dondaine and L-J. Bataillon; *Tabula libri Ethicorum.* Edited by R.-A. Gauthier. Rome: Ad Sanctae Sabinae, 1971.

50   *Super Boetium De Trinitate.* Edited by P.-M. J. Gils; *Expositio libri Boetii De ebdomadibus.* Edited by L.-J. Bataillon and C. A. Grassi, Leonine Commision. Rome-Paris: Cerf, 1992.

From a methodological perspective, the Leonine edition is gradually gaining respect as a genuine point of reference in the sphere of ecdotic and critical textual work, inasmuch as it examines the medieval editions of theological and philosophical texts (the kind characterized by the academic traditions). For an evaluation of the work in this sense, see C. Luna,

"L'édition léonine de Saint Thomas d'Aquin: vers une méthode de critique textuelle et d'ecdotique," in *La Commission Léonine. Philologie et histoire au service de la pensée*, edited by R. Imbach and A. Oliva, *Revue des Sciences Philosophiques et Théologiques* 89 (2005): 31–110. See also the entire issue (available also as a small, self-contained volume, Vrin: Paris, 2005) of the same *Revue des Sciences Philosophiques et Théologiques* (R. Imbach and A. Oliva, "Présentation," 5–7; G. Dahan, "Les éditions des commentaires bibliques de saint Thomas d'Aquin," 9–15; O. Weijers, "La Commission Léonine et l'histoire intellectuelle du XIIIᵉ siècle," 17–21; P. Bermon, "Le renouvellement de la lecture et de la diffusion de l'oeuvre de Saint Thomas d'Aquin," 23–30).

Among the prior complete editions worthy of mention, at least for their historico-documentary worth, are:

Parma: *Sancti Thomae Aquinatis Doctoris Angelici Ordinis Praedicatorum Opera Omnia ad fidem optimarum editionum accurate recognita.* 25 vols. Parma: Typis P. Fiaccadori, 1852–73. Reprint: New York: Musurgia, 1948–50.

Piana: *Divi Thomae Aquinatis Opera Omnia.* 15 vols. Gratiis privilegiisque Pii V, Pont. Max., excusa. Rome: 1570.

Vivès: *Doctoris Angelici divi Thomae Aquinatis sacri Ordinis F. F. Praedicatorum Opera Omnia sive antehac excusa, sive etiam anecdota . . . , studio ac labore Stanislai Eduardi Fretté et Pauli Maré sacerdotum, Scholaeque thomisticae Alumnorum.* 34 vols. Paris: apud Ludovicum Vivès, 1871–72.

Another complete edition of wide circulation is the so-called *editio taurinensis manualis* in 33 volumes (Rome-Turin: Marietti), which takes up in a more maneagable format the text of some of the first volumes of the Leonine edition, now and then with some small corrections. It is, for example, a widespread custom, at least in Italy, to cite Thomas's two *Summae* in this edition:

Liber de veritate catholicae Fidei contra errores infidelium seu Summa contra Gentiles. Textus Leoninus diligenter recognitus, cura et studio P. Marc, coadiuv. C. Pera et P. Caramello, t. I: introductio; t. II-III: textus. Turin-Rome: Marietti, 1961–67.

Summa theologiae, cum textu ex recensione Leonina, cura et studio P. Caramello, 5 vols. Turin-Rome: Marietti, 1952.

For the *Summa theologiae* alone the distinguished edition is—based completely on the Leonine text and with corrections proposed by the Leonine Commission itself—published in a single volume by San Paolo Edizioni (Cinisello Balsamo, 1999).

The Marietti edition, moreover, includes Thomas's other fundamental works that are not yet available in the Leonine edition or in a critical edition, among which the following stand out:

Catena aurea in quattuor evangelia, vol. 1, *Expositio in Matthaeum et Marcum*; vol. 2, *Expositio in Lucam et Ioannem.* Edited by A. Guarienti. Turin-Rome: Marietti, 1953.

In duodecim libros Metaphysicorum Aristotelis exposition. Edited by M.-R. Cathala and R. M. Spiazzi. Turin-Rome: Marietti, 1950; 3rd ed., 1977.

In librum Beati Dionysii De divinis nominibus exposition. Edited by C. Pera, with historical introduction and doctrinal synthesis by P. Caramello and C. Mazzantini. Turin-Rome: Marietti, 1950.

Quaestiones disputatae de potentia. In S. Thomae Aquinatis, *Quaestiones disputatae.* 2 vols. Edited by P. M. Pession. Turin-Rome: Marietti, 1965, 1–276.

For the *Scriptum super Sententiis,* however, one must still refer to the edition edited by P. Mandonnet (Books I–II, 2 vols. [Paris: Lethielleux, 1929]) and M. F. Moos (from Book III to distinction 22 of Book IV, 2 vols. [Paris: Lethielleux, 1922–37]); for the remaining distinctions of Book IV (23–50), refer to the edition of Fiaccadori or to the Vivès edition cited above. The Prologue, at least, is available in a new accurate edition by the current president of the Leonine Commission, Adriano Oliva: see A. Oliva, *Les débuts de l'enseignement de Thomas d'Aquin et sa conception de la* sacra doctrina. *Avec l'édition du prologue de son commentaire des* Sentences, Bibliothèque thomiste 58 (Paris: Vrin, 2006). Also in 2006 some fragments attributed to the hypothetical *alia lectura* on the *Sentences* that Thomas may have conducted at Rome were published: see Thomas Aquinas, *Lectura romana in primum Sententiarum Petri Lombardi,* Edited by L. E. Boyle and J. F. Boyle, Studies and Texts 152 (Toronto: Pontifical Institute of Mediaeval Studies, 2006). For some reservations about this edition, see A. Oliva, "La questione dell'*alia lectura* di Tommaso d'Aquino. A proposito dell'edizione delle note marginali del ms. Oxford, Lincoln College Lat. 95," *Quaestio* 6 (2006): 516–21 (the article is in French notwithstanding the Italian title, attributable to the editoral authorities). On the problems of the *alia lectura,* see above in the section "The Foundation of the *Studium* in Rome and the Problem of the *alia lectura*" at the beginning of Chapter 4. Two isolated questions on self-knowledge and the immortality of the soul, the authenticity of which is doubtful, were edited by L. A. Kennedy: indications relative to these questions can be found in the section below, "Contributions on Specific Themes and Aspects," in this bibliography.

For the critical edition of the commentary on the *Liber de causis,* see Thomas d'Aquin, *Super librum de causis expositio,* edited by H.-D. Saffrey, Textes philosophiques du Moyen Âge (Paris: Vrin, 2002).

Finally, there is the edition of Thomas's works directed by R. Busa in conjunction with the production of the *Index Thomisticus: S. Thomae Aquinatis Opera Omnia ut sunt in Indice Thomistico,* 7 vols, edited by Robert Busa (Stuttgart: Bad Cannstatt, 1980).

For a complete and updated list of the available editions of each of Thomas's most important works, as well as the primary French, Italian, and English translations, see "Brief Catalogue of the Works of Saint Thomas Aquinas" by G. Emery, OP, the appendix to J.-P. Torrell's *Saint Thomas Aquinas,* vol. 1, *The Person and His Work.* A concise index of the editions referred to is also included in Tommaso d'Aquino, *L'ente e l'essenza,* edited by P. Porro, 2nd ed. (Milan: Bompiani, 2006), 225–33.

PRINCIPAL ENGLISH TRANSLATIONS

The only comprehensive project to translate Thomas's entire *Opera Omnia* into English is being directed and published by the Aquinas Institute for the Study of Sacred Doctrine in Lander, Wyoming.[1] To date, the entire *Summa theologiae* and many of Thomas's commen-

---

1. The preparation of this bibliography of English translations of Thomas benefitted from the work of Gilles Emery in Torrell's *Thomas Aquinas,* vol. 1, noted above. It was also greatly helped by the work of Thérèse Bonin, whose running catalog, 1998–present, is perhaps the most complete list of Thomas's English-language works. It can be found at: http://www.home.duq.edu/~bonin/thomasbibliography .html. For the most part, partial translations of larger works contained in readers, source books, in-

taries on the New Testament are available. The volumes are hardbound and include the
Latin text with the English translation on facing pages.

We should also mention here the large (although not complete) collection of Thomas's
works in English translation presently available online at http://dhspriory.org/thomas/. At
the moment there are 71 works on this site.

Theological Syntheses

On Love and Charity: Readings from the "Commentary on the Sentences *of Peter Lombard."*
Translated by Peter A. Kwasniewski, Thomas Bolin, OSB, and Joseph Bolin. Washington, D.C.: The Catholic University of America Press, 2008.

Summa contra Gentiles. 5 vols. Translated and edited by A. C. Pegis, J. F. Anderson, V. J.
Bourke, C. J. O' Neil. Notre Dame, Ind.: University of Notre Dame Press, 1975.

Summa theologica. 5 vols. Translated by the Fathers of the English Dominican Province.
Westminster, Md.: Christian Classics, 1981.

Summa theologiae. Complete set, Latin-English. Lander, Wy.: The Aquinas Institute, 2012.
———. 60 vols, Latin-English. Edited by T. Gilby and T. C. O'Brien. Cambridge: Cambridge University Press, 1964–73.

Thomas Aquinas's Earliest Treatment of the Divine Essence: Scriptum super libros Senten-
tiarum, *Book I Distinction 8.* Translated by E. M. Macierowski and Joseph Owens.
Medieval Studies Worldwide. Center for Medieval and Renaissance Studies. Albany:
State University of New York Press, 1997.

Biblical Commentaries

Catena Aurea: *Commentary on the Four Gospels Collected out of the Works of the Father
by S. Thomas Aquinas.* 4 vols. Translated by John Henry Newman. Oil City, Penn.:
Baronius Press, 2009.

Commentary on St. Paul's Epistle to the Ephesians. Translated by Matthew L. Lamb. Aquinas Scripture Commentaries 2. Albany: Magi Books, 1966.

Commentary on St. Paul's Epistle to the Galatians. Translated by Fabian R. Larcher. Aquinas
Scripture Commentaries 1.Albany: Magi Books, 1966.

Commentary on St. Paul's Epistles to Timothy, Titus, and Philemon. Translated by
Chrysostom Baer. South Bend, Ind.: St. Augustine's Press, 2006.

Commentary on the Epistle to the Hebrews. Translated by Chrysostom Baer. South Bend,
Ind.: St. Augustine's Press, 2006.

Commentary on the Gospel of John. 3 vols. Translated by James A. Weisheipl and Fabian
R. Larcher. Edited by Daniel Keating and Matthew Levering. Thomas Aquinas in
Translation. Washington, D.C.: The Catholic University of America Press, 2010. Also
published in 2 vols. (Latin-English, includes the Greek text of the Gospel) by the
Aquinas Institute for the Study of Sacred Doctrine, 2013.

---

troductions, and collections are not included in this bibliography. Among these types of works, the
following are especially helpful: *An Introduction to the Metaphysics of St. Thomas Aquinas,* trans. and
ed. by James F. Anderson (Washington, D.C.: Regnery Publishing, 1953); *Thomas Aquinas, Selected
Writings,* trans. and ed. by Ralph McInerny (Harmondsworth: Penguin Classsics, 1998); *Thomas Aquinas, Selected Philosophical Writings,* trans. and ed. by Timothy McDermott, World's Classics (Oxford:
Oxford University Press, 1993).

Commentary on the Gospel of Matthew. 2 vols. Translated by Jeremy Holmes and Beth Mortensen. Lander, Wy: The Aquinas Institute, 2013.

Commentary on the Letters of Saint Paul: Complete Set. Latin-English edition, includes Greek text of the epistles. 5 vols. Edited by John Mortensen. Lander, Wy.: The Aquinas Institute, 2012.

The Literal Exposition on Job: A Scriptural Commentary Concerning Providence. Translated by Anthony Damico. Classics in Religious Studies 7. Atlanta, Ga.: Scholars Press, 1989.

St. Thomas Aquinas Commentary on Colossians. Naples, Fla.: Sapientia Press of Ave Maria University, 2006.

Commentaries on Aristotle

Commentaries on Aristotle's On Sense and What Is Sensed and On Memory and Recollection. Translated by Edward Macierowski. Thomas Aquinas in Translation. Washington, D.C.: The Catholic University of America Press, 2005.

Commentary on Aristotle's De Anima. Translated by Kenelm Foster and Silvester Humphries. Aristotelian Commentary Series. Notre Dame, Ind.: Dumb Ox Books, 1994.

Commentary on Aristotle's De anima. Translated by Robert C. Pasnau. New Haven, Conn.: Yale University Press, 1999.

Commentary on Aristotle's Metaphysics. Translated by John P. Rowan. Aristotelian Commentary Series. Notre Dame, Ind.: Dumb Ox Books, 1995.

Commentary on Aristotle's Nicomachean Ethics. Translated by C. I. Litzinger. Aristotelian Commentary Series. Notre Dame, Ind.: Dumb Ox Books, 1993.

Commentary on Aristotle's On Interpretation. Translated by Jean Oesterle. Notre Dame, Ind.: Dumb Ox Books, 2004.

Commentary on Aristotle's Physics. Translated by Richard J. Blackwell, Richard J. Spath, and W. Edmund Thirlkel. Aristotelian Commentary Series. Notre Dame, Ind.: Dumb Ox Books, 1999.

Commentary on Aristotle's Posterior Analytics. Translated by Richard Berquist. South Bend, Ind.: St. Augustine's Press, 2007.

Commentary on the Politics. Translated by Richard Regan. Indianapolis: Hackett, 2007.

Commentary on the Posterior Analytics of Aristotle. Translated by F. R. Larcher. Albany: Magi Books, 1970.

Exposition on Aristotle's Treatise on the Heavens. 2 vols. Translated by Fabian R. Larcher and Pierre H. Conway. Columbus: College of St. Mary of the Springs, 1964.

On Memory and Recollection. Translated by John Burchill. Dover, Mass.: Dominican House of Philosophy, 1963.

St. Thomas Aquinas on Aristotle's Love and Friendship: Ethics, Books VIII–IX. Translated by Pierre Conway. Providence, R.I.: Providence College Press, 1951.

Other Commentaries

Commentary on the Book of Causes. Translated by Vincent A. Guagliardo, Charles R. Hess, and Richard C. Taylor. Thomas Aquinas in Translation. Washington, D.C.: The Catholic University of America Press, 1996.

The Division and Methods of the Sciences: Questions V and VI of His Commentary on the

De Trinitate *of Boethius*. Translated by Armand Maurer. Mediaeval Sources in Translation 3. 4th ed. Toronto: Pontifical Institute of Mediaeval Studies, 1986.

An Exposition of the On the Hebdomads *of Boethius*. Latin-English. Translated by Janice Schultz and Edward Synan. Thomas Aquinas in Translation. Washington, D.C.: The Catholic University of America Press, 2001.

Faith, Reason and Theology: Questions I–IV of His Commentary on the De Trinitate *of Boethius*. Translated by Armand Maurer. Mediaeval Sources in Translation 32. Toronto: Pontifical Institute of Mediaeval Studies, 1987.

The Trinity *and* The Unicity of the Intellect. Translated by Rose W. Brennan. St. Louis: B. Herder, 1946.

Disputed Questions

The De malo *of Thomas Aquinas*. Latin-English. Translated by Richard Regan. Oxford: Oxford University Press, 2002.

De unione verbi incarnati. Latin-English. Dallas Medieval Texts and Translations 21. Translation, introduction, and notes by Roger W. Nutt. Latin Text by Walter Senner, OP, Barbara Bartocci, and Klaus Obenauer. Louvain: Peeters Press, 2014.

Disputed Questions on Virtue. Translated by Ralph McInerny. South Bend, Ind.: St. Augustine's Press, 1998.

Disputed Questions on Virtue. Translated by Jeffrey Hause and Claudia Eisen. Indianapolis: Hackett, 2010. (Includes *On the Virtues in General, On Fraternal Correction, On Hope,* and *On the Cardinal Virtues.*)

On Charity. Translated by Lottie H. Kendzierski. Mediaeval Philosophical Texts in Translation 10. Milwaukee: Marquette University Press, 1960.

On Creation: Quaestiones Disputatae de Potentia Dei, *Q. 3*. Thomas Aquinas in Translation. Translated by Susan C. Selner-Wright. Washington, D.C.: The Catholic University of America Press, 2010.

On Evil. Translated by John A. and Jean T. Oesterle. Notre Dame, Ind.: University of Notre Dame Press, 1995.

On Evil. English only. Translated by Richard Regan and edited by Brian Davies. Oxford: Oxford University Press, 2003.

On Spiritual Creatures. Translated by Mary C. Fitzpatrick and John J. Wellmuth. Mediaeval Philosophical Texts in Translation 5. Milwaukee: Marquette University Press, 1949.

On the Power of God. Translated by Laurence Shapcote. Reprint: Eugene, Ore.: Wipf and Stock, 2004.

On the Virtues (in General). Translated by John Patrick Reid. Providence: Providence College Press, 1951.

The Power of God. Translated by Richard Regan. Oxford: Oxford University Press, 2012. (Abridged.)

Questions on the Soul. Translated by James H. Robb. Mediaeval Philosophical Texts in Translation 27. Milwaukee: Marquette University Press, 1984.

The Soul. Translated by J. P. Rowan. St. Louis: B. Herder, 1949.

Truth. 3 vols. Translated by Robert W. Mulligan, James V. McGlynn, and Robert Schmidt. Library of Living Catholic Thought. Chicago: Regnery, 1952–54. Reprint: Indianapolis: Hackett, 1994.

Quodlibetal Questions

"Faith, Metaphysics, and the Contemplation of Christ's Corporeal Presence in the Eucharist: Translation of St. Thomas Aquinas' Seventh *Quodlibetal Dispute*, Q. 4, A. 1 with an Introductory Essay." Translation and Introduction by Roger W. Nutt. *Antiphon: A Journal of Liturgical Renewal* 15 (2011, 2): 151–71.

Quodlibetal Questions 1 and 2. Translated by Sandra Edwards. Mediaeval Sources in Translation 27. Toronto: Pontifical Institute of Mediaeval Studies, 1983.

Other Writings

An Apology for the Religious Orders. Translated by John Procter. London: Sands, 1902. Reprint: Westminster, Md.: Newman, 1950.

Aquinas against the Averroists: On There Being Only One Intellect. Translated by Ralph M. McInerny. Purdue University Series in the History of Philosophy. West Lafayette, Ind.: Purdue University Press, 1993.

The Aquinas Catechism: A Simple Explanation of the Catholic Faith by the Church's Greatest Theologian. Manchester, N.H.: Sophia Institute Press, 2000. (Includes *Collationes de decem praeceptis, Collationes super Pater Noster, Collationes super Ave Maria, De articulis fidei et Ecclesiae sacramentis,* and *Collationes super Credo in Deum.*)

Aquinas on Being and Essence: A Translation and Interpretation. Translation by Joseph Bobik. Notre Dame, Ind.: University of Notre Dame Press, 1965.

Aquinas on Matter and Form and the Elements: A Translation and Interpretation of the De Principiis Naturae *and the* De Mixtione Elementorum *of St. Thomas Aquinas.* Latin-English. Translated by Joseph Bobik. Notre Dame, Ind.: University of Notre Dame Press, 1998.

The Aquinas Prayer Book: The Prayers and Hymns of Saint Thomas Aquinas. Translated by Robert Anderson and Johann Moser. Sophia Institute, 2000. (Includes *Officium de festo Corporis Christi* and many of the prayers composed by St. Thomas, such as *Adoro te devote* and *Pange lingua.*)

Compendium of Theology. Translated by Lawrence Lynch. New York: McMullen, 1947.

The Compendium of Theology. Translated by Cyril Vollert. St. Louis: B. Herder, 1947. Reprint: *Light of Faith: The Compendium of Theology.* Manchester, N.H.: Sophia Institute, 1993.

Compendium of Theology. Translated by Richard Regan. Oxford: Oxford University Press, 2009.

Concerning Being and Essence. Translated by G. G. Leckie. New York: Appleton-Century-Crofts, 1937.

Ending the Byzantine Greek Schism: Containing the 14th c. Apologia *of Demetrios Kydones for Unity with Rome and St. Thomas Aquinas' "Contra Errores Graecorum."* Translated by Peter Damian Fehlner and edited by James Likoudis. 2nd ed. New Rochelle, N.Y.: Catholics United for the Faith, 1992.

How to Study: Being the Letter of St. Thomas Aquinas to Brother John, De modo studendi. Latin-English. Translated by Victor White. London: Blackfriars, 1953.

The Letter of Saint Thomas Aquinas De Occultis Operibus Naturae ad Quemdam Militem Ultramontanum. Translated by J. B. McAllister. Washington, D.C.: The Catholic University of America, 1939.

On Being and Essence. Translated by Armand Maurer. Mediaeval Sources in Translation 1. Toronto: Pontifical Institute of Mediaeval Studies, 1968.

"On Kingship, or, The Governance of Rulers." Translated by Paul E. Sigmund. In Sigmund, *St. Thomas Aquinas on Politics and Ethics: A New Translation, Backgrounds, Interpretations.* Norton Critical Edition. New York: W. W. Norton, 1988.

On Kingship to the King of Cyprus. Translated by Gerald Phelan and I. T. Eschmann. Mediaeval Sources in Translation 2. Toronto: Pontifical Institute of Mediaeval Studies, 1949.

On Reasons for Our Faith against the Muslims, Greeks and Armenians. Translated by Peter Damian Fehlner. New Bedford, Mass.: Franciscans of the Immaculate, 2002.

On the Eternity of the World (De aeternitate mundi). In *St. Thomas, Siger de Brabant, and St. Bonaventure, On the Eternity of the World.* Translated by Cyril Vollert, Lottie Kenzierski, and Paul M. Byrne. Mediaeval Philosophical Texts in Translation 16. Milwaukee: Marquette University Press, 1964, 19–25.

On the Unity of the Intellect against the Averroists (De Unitate Intellectus Contra Averroistas). Translated by Beatrice H. Zedler. Mediaeval Philosophical Texts in Translation 19. Milwaukee: Marquette University Press, 1968.

The Principles of Nature. Translated by Pierre Conway. Columbus: College of St. Mary of the Springs, 1963.

The Religious State, The Episcopate and the Priestly Office: A Translation of the Minor Work of the Saint on the Perfection of the Spiritual Life. Translated by John Procter. St. Louis: B. Herder, 1902. Reprint: Westminster, Md.: Newman, 1950.

"Saint Thomas Aquinas on the Movement of the Heart." Translated by Vincent R. Larkin. *Journal of the History of Medicine* 15 (1960): 22–30. (*De motu cordis.*)

The Sermon-Conferences of St. Thomas Aquinas on the Apostles' Creed. Translated by Nicholas Ayo. Notre Dame, Ind.: University of Notre Dame Press, 1988. Reprint: Eugene, Ore: Wipf and Stock, 2005.

Thomas Aquinas: The Academic Sermons. Translated by Mark-Robin Hoogland. The Fathers of the Church, Mediaeval Continuation 11. Washington, D.C.: The Catholic University of America Press, 2010.

Treatise on Separate Substances. Translated by Francs Lescoe. West Hartford, Conn.: Saint Joseph College, 1959.

LIFE AND WORK

The volume by Torrell cited above (*Thomas Aquinas*, vol. 1, *The Person and His Work*) also offers, at present, the most reliable reconstruction of the life and chronology of the works of Thomas and, de facto, replaces the work, however meritorious, of J. A. Weisheipl, *Friar Thomas d'Aquino: His Life, Thought, and Work* (Washington, D.C.: The Catholic University of America Press, 1983); the Weisheipl volume too includes a catalog of Thomas's authentic works. Another compelling biographical reconstruction is that of Simon Tugwell, "The Life and Works of Thomas Aquinas," in Tugwell's *Albert and Thomas: Selected Writings* (New York: Paulist Press, 1988), especially 201–67.

The principal sources on the life of St. Thomas are collected in D. Prümmer and M. H. Laurent, eds., *Fontes vitae S. Thomae Aquinatis notis historicis et criticis illustrate* (Toulouse: Saint-Maximin, 1937), and A. Ferrua, ed., *S. Thomae Aquinatis vitae fontes praecipuae* [rectius: praecipui] (Alba: Edizioni Domenicane, 1968). The biography of Thomas prepared by William of Tocco in view of the canonization process is now available in a critical edition:

Guillelmus de Tocco, *Ystoria sancti Thomae de Aquino*, ed. C. Le Brun-Gouanvic, Studies and Texts 127 (Toronto: Pontifical Institute of Mediaeval Studies, 1996).

LEXICONS, DICTIONARIES, AND RESEARCH TOOLS

Busa, R., ed. *Index Thomisticus.* Sancti Thomae Aquinatis operum omnium indices et concordantiae in quibus verborum omnium et singulorum formae et lemmata cum suis frequentiis et contextibus variis modis referuntur, quaeque auspice Paulo vi Summo Pontifice, consociata plurium opera atque electronico ibm automato usus, digessit Robertus Busa si in Gallaratensi Facultate Philosophica Aloisiani Collegii professor. 56 vols. Stuttgart-Bad Cannstatt: Frommann-Holzboog, 1974–80. (Available online at Corpus Thomisticum: http://www.corpusthomisticum.org/it/index.age.)

Deferrari, R., and M. J. Barry. *A Lexicon of St. Thomas Aquinas Based on the* Summa theologica *and Selected Passages of His Other Works.* Washington, D.C.: The Catholic University of America Press, 1948–49.

———. *Complete Index of the* Summa theologica *of St. Thomas Aquinas.* 2 vols. Baltimore: The Catholic University of America Press, 1956.

Mondin, B. *Dizionario enciclopedico del pensiero di San Tommaso d'Aquino.* 2nd ed. Bologna: ESD, 2000.

Petri de Bergomo. *In Opera Sancti Thomae Aquinatis Index seu Tabula Aurea.* Rome: Edizioni Paoline, 1960.

Schütz, L. *Thomas-Lexikon.* Paderborn: Schöningh, 1881. Reprint: Frommann-Holzboog, Stuttgart-Bad Cannstatt, 1958; 2nd ed., 1983.

Stockhammer, M. *Thomas Aquinas Dictionary.* New York: Philosophical Library, 1965.

BIBLIOGRAPHIC RESOURCES

Bourke, V. J. "Thomistic Bibliography, 1920–1940." *The Modern Schoolman* 21, Supplement (1945).

Ingardia R. *Thomas Aquinas. International Bibliography, 1977–1990.* Bowling Green, Ohio: Philosophy Documentation Center, 1993.

Mandonnet, P., and J. Destrez. *Bibliographie thomiste, Bibliothèque thomiste* 1. Kain: Le Saulchoir, 1921. 2nd ed. revised and completed by M.-D. Chenu, Paris: Vrin, 1960.

Miethe, T. L., and V. J. Bourke. *Thomistic Bibliography, 1940–1978.* London: Greenwood Press, 1980.

Wyser, P. *Thomas von Aquin,* Bibliographische Einführungen in das Studium der Philosophie. Bern: Francke, 1950.

The volumes of the *Bulletin Thomiste* (42 volumes between 1924 and 1965) must be added to the resources already mentioned, and the *Rassegna di Letteratura tomistica,* which was an undertaking energetically willed and carried forward by C. Vansteenkiste (29 volumes between 1966 and 1993). Recently Enrique Alarcón has inaugurated a new bibliographic project, whose first number has appeared: *Thomistica 2006. An International Yearbook of Thomistic Bibliography* (Bonn: Nova et Vetera, 2007). Above all, however, Alarcón is responsible for the most rich and ambitious online project relating to Thomas: *Corpus Thomisticum* (http://www.corpusthomisticum.org). The project includes five parts: the complete edition of Thomas's *Opera Omnia* (even though the origin of the available text is not always clear); an ample and up-to-date bibliographic catalog of all of the works on Thomas and his thought; an index of the primary extant Thomistic research tools (with the republication online of some of these, such as the *Index Thomisticus* and the *Thomas-Lexikon*); a search engine for locating and sorting terms, phrases, and citations through the whole of Thomas's work, with the possibility of obtaining correlations and statistical data; the digital reproduction of some of the principal manuscripts of the works of Thomas.

PRIMARY TEXTS BY AUTHORS OTHER THAN AQUINAS

The primary texts referred to in this book by authors other than Aquinas are not included in the bibliography. Complete information on these can be found in the footnotes.

STUDIES
Some General Presentations of Thomas's Thought

Among the classic introduction to the thought of Thomas it is necessary to recall at least:

Aertsen, Jan A. *Nature and Creatures: Thomas Aquinas's Way of Thought.* Studien und Texte zur Geistesgeschichte des Mittelalters 21. Leiden: Brill, 1988.

Chenu, Marie-Dominique. *Toward Understanding St. Thomas.* Translated by A. M. Landry and D. Hughes. Chicago: H. Regnery, 1964.

Davies, Brian, and Eleonore Stump, eds. *The Oxford Handbook of Aquinas.* Oxford: Oxford University Press, 2012.

Fabro, Cornelio. *Introduzione a San Tommaso.* Milan: Ares, 1983.

Gardeil, H.-D. *Introduction to the Philosophy of St. Thomas Aquinas.* 3 vols. Translated by John A. Otto. Reprint: Eugene, Ore.: Wipf and Stock, 2009–12. Gardeil's original project, *Initiation à la Philosophie de S. Thomas d'Aquin*, was composed of four vols: logic, cosmology, psychology, and metaphysics. This English translation includes only the latter three.

Gilson, Etienne. *Thomism: The Philosophy of Thomas Aquinas.* Translated by Laurence K. Shook and Armand Maurer. Toronto: Pontifical Institute of Mediaeval Studies, 2002.

Imbach, Ruedi, and Adriano Oliva. *La philosophie de Thomas d'Aquin.* Repères Philosophiques. Paris: Vrin, 2009.

Kretzmann, Norman, and Eleonore Stump, eds. *The Cambridge Companion to Aquinas.* Cambridge: Cambridge University Press, 1993.

Leppin, Volker. *Thomas von Aquin.* Zugänge zum Denken des Mittelalters 5. Münster: Aschendorff, 2009.

Rosemann, Philipp W. Omne ens est aliquid. *Introduction à la lecture du "système" philosophique de saint Thomas d'Aquin.* Louvain: Peeters, 1996.

Schönberger, Rolf. *Thomas von Aquin zur Einführung.* Hamburg: Junius, 1998.

Stump, Eleonore. *Aquinas.* Arguments of the Philosophers. London: Routledge, 2003.

Vanni Rovighi, Sofia. *Introduzione a Tommaso d'Aquino.* 13th ed. Tome-Bari: Laterza, 2007.

Zimmermann, Albert. *Thomas lesen.* Legenda 2. Stuttgart: Frommann-Holzboog, 2000.

All of John Wippel's studies noted in the following section, while not representing systematic introductions to the whole of Thomas's thought, offer an often irreplaceable point of entry to many of the fundamental aspects of his philosophy.

Contributions on Specific Themes and Aspects
Only the works actually cited in the notes of this volume are included here.

Abate, G. "Intorno alla cronologia di San Tommaso." *Miscellanea Franciscana* 50 (1950): 231–47.

Aertsen, Jan A. "Method and Metaphysics. The *via resolutionis* in Thomas Aquinas." In *Knowledge and the Sciences in Medieval Philosophy. Proceedings of the Eighth International Congress of Medieval Philosophy*, vol. 3, *Annals of the Finnish Society for Missiology and Ecumenics*. Edited by R. Työrinoja, A. Inkeri Lehtinen, and D. Føllesdall, 3–12. Helsinki, 1990.

———. "Was heißt Metaphysik bei Thomas von Aquin?" In *Scientia und ars in Hoch- und Spätmittelalter*. Edited by I. Craemer-Rügenberg and A. Speer, 217–39. Miscellanea Mediaevalia 22. Berlin: de Gruyter, 1994.

———. *Medieval Philosophy and the Transcendentals: The Case of Thomas Aquinas.* Studien und Texte zur Geistesgeschichte des Mittelalters 52. Leiden: Brill, 1996.

———. "The Triad 'True-Good-Beautiful': The Place of Beauty in the Middle Ages." In *Intellect et imagination dans la philosophie médiévale / Intellect and Imagination in Medieval Philosophy / Intelecto e imaginação na filosofia medieval. Actes du XIe Congrès International de Philosophie Médiévale de la Société Internationale pour l'Étude de la Philosophie Médiévale (SIEPM), Porto, du 26 au 31 août 2002*, vol. 1. Edited by M. C. Pacheco and J. F. Meirinhos, 415–35. Rencontres de Philosophie Médiévale 11. Turnhout: Brepols, 2006.

Amerini, Fabrizio. *Tommaso d'Aquino. Origine e fine della vita umana.* Pisa: ETS, 2009.

Antithomisme. Histoire, thèmes et figures, I. L'antithomisme dans la pensée médiévale et moderne. Actes du colloque de Toulouse, mai 2007. Revue Thomiste 108, no. 1 (2008).

Antithomisme. Histoire, thèmes et figures, II. L'antithomisme dans la pensée contemporaine. Actes du colloque de Toulouse, mai 2007. Revue Thomiste 108, no. 2 (2008).

Ashworth, E. Jennifer. *Les théories de l'analogie du XII au XVI siècle.* Paris: Vrin, 2008.

Bataillon, L.-J. "Les sermons attribués à Saint Thomas. Questions d'authenticité." In *Thomas von Aquin. Werk und Wirkung im Licht neuerer Forschungen*. Edited by A. Zimmermann, 325–41. Miscellanea Mediaevalia 19. Berlin: New York, 1988.

———. "Le edizioni di *Opera Omnia* degli scolastici e l'Edizione Leonina." In *Gli studi di filosofia medievale fra Otto e Novecento. Contributo a un bilancio storiografico. Atti del Convegno internazionale, Roma, 21–23 settembre 1989*. Edited by R. Imbach and A. Maierù, 141–54. Storia e Letteratura 179. Rome: Edizioni di Storia e Letteratura, 1991.

———. "Saint Thomas et les Pères. De la *Catena* à la *Tertia pars*." In *Ordo sapientiae et amoris. Image et message de saint Thomas d'Aquin à travers les récentes études historiques herméneutiques et doctrinales. Hommage au Professeur Jean-Pierre Torrell op à l'occasion de son 65e anniversaire*. Edited by C. J. Pinto de Oliveira, 15–36. Studia Friburgensia 78. Fribourg: Éditions Universitaires de Fribourg, 1993.

Bazán, B. C. "Les questions disputées, principalement dans les facultés de théologie." In *Les questions disputées et les questions quodlibétiques dans la faculté de théologie, de droit et de médecine*. Edited by B. C. Bazán, G. Fransen, J. F. Wippel and D. Jacquart, 13–149. Turnhout: Brepols, 1985.

————. "The Human Soul: Form and Substance? Thomas Aquinas' Critique of Eclectic Aristotelianism." *Archives d'Histoire Doctrinale et Littéraire du Moyen Âge* 64 (1997): 95–126.

————. "Thomas d'Aquin et les transcendantaux." *Revue de Sciences Philosophiques et Théologiques* 84 (2000): 93–104.

Bernardi, Brenno. *Studio sul significato di* esse forma essentia *nel primo libro dello* Scriptum in libros Sententiarum *di San Tommaso d'Aquino*. Bern-Frankfurt am Main-New York-Nancy: Peter Lang, 1984.

Bernath, K. Anima forma corporis: *Eine Untersuchung über die ontologischen Grundlagen der Anthropologie des Thomas von Aquin*. Bonn: Bouvier, 1969.

Bianchi, Luca. *L'errore di Aristotele. La polemica contro l'eternità del mondo nel XIII secolo*. Pubblicazioni della Facoltà di Lettere e Filosofia—Università di Milano 104. Florence: La Nuova Italia, 1984.

————. "Ordini mendicanti e controllo 'ideologico': il caso delle province domenicane." In *Studio e studia: le scuole degli ordini mendicanti tra XIII e XIV secolo. Atti del XXIX Convegno internazionale. Assisi, 11–13 ottobre 2001*, 303–38. Spoleto: CISAM, 2002.

————. *Pour une histoire de la "double vérité."* Conférences Pierre Abélard. Paris: Vrin, 2008.

Birkenmajer, A. "Der Brief der Pariser Artistenfakultät über den Tod des hl. Thomas von Aquino." In *Vermischte Untersuchungen zur Geschichte der mittelalterlichen Philosophie*, 1–32. Münster: Aschendorff, 1922.

Black, D. B. "Mental Existence in Thomas Aquinas and Avicenna." *Mediaeval Studies* 61 (1999): 45–79.

Blythe J. M. *Le gouvernement idéal et la constitution mixte au Moyen Âge*, Vestigia 32. Fribourg-Paris: Academic Press–Cerf, 2005.

Boland V. *Ideas in God according to Saint Thomas Aquinas: Sources and Synthesis*. Studies in the History of Christian Thought 69. Leiden: Brill, 1996.

Bowlin J. "Contemporary Protestant Thomism." In *Aquinas as Authority*. Edited by P. van Geest, H. Goris, C. Leget, 235–51. Leuven: Peeters, 2002.

Boyle L. E. "The Quodlibets of St. Thomas and Pastoral Care." *The Thomist* 38 (1974): 232–56. (Republished in *Facing History: A Different Thomas Aquinas*, 13–35. Louvain: FIDEM, 2000.)

————. "Alia lectura fratris Thome." *Mediaeval Studies* 45 (1983): 418–29. (Republished in *Facing History: A Different Thomas Aquinas*, 93–106.)

————. "The De regno and the Two Powers." In *Essays in Honour of Anton Charles Pegis*. Edited by J. R. O'Donnell, 237–44. Toronto: Pontifical Institute of Mediaeval Studies, 1974. (Republished in *Facing History: A Different Thomas Aquinas*, 1–12.)

————. "The Setting of the *Summa theologiae* of Saint Thomas." In *Facing History: A Different Thomas Aquinas*, 65–91. Louvain-la-Neuve: FIDEM, 2000.

Brams, J., and W. Vanhamel, "Biobibliographie de Guillaume de Moerbeke." In *Guillaume de Moerbeke. Recueil d'études à l'occasion du 700ème anniversaire de sa mort (1286)*. Edited by J. Brams and W. Vanhamel, 301–83. Leuven: Leuven University Press, 1989.

Brungs, A. *Metaphysik der Sinnlichkeit. Das System der* passiones animae *bei Thomas von Aquin*. Halle an der Saale: Hallescher, 2002.

Burbach, M. "Early Dominican and Franciscan Legislation Regarding St. Thomas." *Mediaeval Studies* 4 (1942): 139–58.

Callus, D. A. *The Condemnation of St. Thomas at Oxford.* 2nd ed. London: Blackfriars, 1955.

Casey, G. "An Explication of the *De hebdomadibus* of Boethius in the Light of St. Thomas's Commentary." *The Thomist* 51 (1987): 419–34.

Cessario, R. *A Short History of Thomism.* Washington, D.C.: The Catholic University of America Press, 2005.

Chardonnens, D. *L'homme sous le regard de la Providence. Providence de Dieu et condition humaine selon* l'Exposition littérale sur le Livre de Job *de Thomas d'Aquin.* Bibliothèque thomiste 50. Paris: Vrin, 1997.

Chenu, M.-D. "Notes de lexicographie philosophique médiévale: *Disciplina.*" *Revue des Sciences Philosophiques et Théologiques* 25 (1936): 686–92.

———. "La date du commentaire de s. Thomas sur le De *Trinitate* de Boèce." *Revue des Sciences Philosophiques et Théologiques* 30 (1941–42): 432–34.

———. *Is Theology a Science?* Translated by Adrian Howell North Green-Arnytage. Twentieth Century Encyclopedia of Catholicism, vol. 2. New York: Hawthorn Books, 1959.

———. *Toward Understanding St. Thomas.* Translated by A.-M. Landry, OP, and D. Hughes, OP Chicago: Henry Regnery Company, 1964.

Clare, V. "'Whether Everything That Is, Is Good': Marginal Notes on St. Thomas Exposition of Boethius' *De hebdomadibus.*" *Laval Théologique et Philosophique* 3 (1947): 66–76, 177–94; 5 (1949): 119–40.

Clarke, N. "The Meaning of Participation in St. Thomas Aquinas." *Proceedings of the American Catholic Philosophical Association* 26 (1952): 147–57.

Conforti, P. "La tradizione scolastica tomista fra Umanesimo e Rinascimento. Trecento e Quattrocento." *Studi* 2 (1995): 259–81.

Congar, Y. "Aspects ecclésiologiques de la querelle entre Mendiants et Séculiers dans la seconde moitié du XIIIe siècle et le début du XIVe." *Archives d'Histoire Doctrinale et Littéraire du Moyen Âge* 28 (1961): 35–161.

Corbini, A. *La teoria della scienza nel XIII secolo. I commenti agli Analitici secondi. Unione Accademica Nazionale.* Testi e studi 20. Florence: SISMEL-Edizioni del Galluzzo, 2006.

Cordonier, V. "Sauver le Dieu du Philosophe: Albert le Grand, Thomas d'Aquin, Guillaume de Moerbeke et l'invention du Liber de bona fortuna comme alternative autorisée à l'interprétation averroïste de la théorie aristotélicienne de la providence divine." In *Christian Readings of Aristotle from the Middle Ages to the Renaissance.* Edited by L. Bianchi, 65–114. Turnhout: Brepols, 2011.

Costa, J. "Il problema dell'omonimia del bene in alcuni commenti scolastici all'*Etica Nicomachea.*" *Documenti e studi sulla tradizione filosofica medievale* 17 (2006): 157–230.

Courtenay, W. J. *Capacity and Volition. A History of the Distinction of Absolute and Ordained Power.* Quodlibet 8. Bergamo: Lubrina, 1990.

Courtine, J. F. *Inventio analogiae. Métaphysique et ontothéologie.* Paris: Vrin, 2005.

Crisciani, C. Tommaso, "Pseudo-Tommaso e l'alchimia. Per un'indagine su un *corpus alchemico.*" In *Letture e interpretazioni di Tommaso d'Aquino oggi: cantieri aperti. Atti del Convegno internazionale di studio (Milano, 12–13 settembre 2005).* Edited by A. Ghisalberti, A. Petagine, and R. Rizzello, 103–19. Quaderni di Annali Chieresi. Turin: Istituto di filosofia S. Tommaso d'Aquino, 2006.

Cunningham, F. A. "A Theory of Abstraction in St. Thomas." *The Modern Schoolman* 35 (1958): 249–70.

Dales, R. C. *Medieval Discussions of the Eternity of the World.* Brill's Studies in Intellectual History 18. Leiden: Brill, 1990.

d'Alverny, M. T. "Un adversaire de Saint Thomas: Petrus Iohannis Olivi." In *St. Thomas Aquinas 1274–1974. Commemorative Studies*, vol. 2. Edited by A. Mauer et al., 179–218. Toronto: Pontifical Institute of Mediaeval Studies, 1974.

D'Ancona Costa, C. "'*Cause prime non est yliathim.*' Liber de causis, prop. 8(9): le fonti e la dottrina." *Documenti e studi sulla tradizione filosofica medievale* 1 (1990): 327–51. (In French, in a volume of essays: *Recherches sur le* Liber de causis, 97–119; see below.)

———. "Saint Thomas lecteur du *Liber de causis*. Bilan des recherches contemporaines concernant le *De causis* et analyse de l'interprétation thomiste." *Revue Thomiste* 92 (1992): 611–49 (Also in *Recherches sur le* Liber de causis, 229–58; see below.)

———. *Recherches sur le* Liber de causis. Études de philosophie médiévale 72. Paris: Vrin, 1995.

Dauphinais, M., and M. Levering, eds. *Reading John with Saint Thomas Aquinas: Theological Exegesis and Speculative Theology.* Washington, D.C.: The Catholic University of America Press, 2005.

Davies, B., ed. *Aquinas's* Summa theologiae. Critical Essays on the Classics. Lanham, Md.: Rowman and Littlefield, 2005.

Decker, B. *Die Gotteslehre des Jakob von Metz. Untersuchungen zur Dominikanertheologie zu Beginn des 14.* Münster: Jahrhunderts, Aschendorff, 1967.

Delle Donne, F. "Per scientiarum haustum et seminarium doctrinarum: storia dello *Studium* di Napoli in età sveva." *Quaderni del Centro di studi normanno-svevi* 3. Bari: Adda, 2010.

Denifle, H. "Die Constitutionen des Predigerordens in der Redaction Raimunds von Peñafort." *Archiv für Literatur- und Kirchengeschichte des Mittelalters* 5 (1889): 530–64.

Denifle H., and É. Châtelain, eds. *Chartularium Universitatis Parisiensis* [CUP]. Paris: Delalain, 1889–97. Reprint: Bruxelles: Culture et Civilisation, 1964.

Denzinger, Heinrich. *Compendium of Creeds, Definitions, and Declarations on Matters of Faith and Morals,* Latin-English. Edited by Peter Hünermann. 43rd ed. San Francisco: Ignatius Press, 2012.

Di Martino, C. Ratio particularis: *la doctrine des sens internes d'Avicenne à Thomas d'Aquin. Contribution à l'étude de la tradition arabo-latine de la psychologie d'Aristote.* Études de philosophie médiévale 94. Paris: Vrin, 2008.

Doig, J. C. *Aquinas on Metaphysics. A Historico-Doctrinal Study of the Commentary on Metaphysics.* The Hague: Martinus Nijhoff, 1972.

Dolan, E. "Resolution and Composition in Speculative and Practical Discourse." *Laval Théologique et Philosophique* 6 (1950): 9–62.

Domanyi, T. *Der Römerbriefkommentar des Thomas von Aquin. Ein Beitrag zur Untersuchung seiner Auslegungsmethoden.* Basler und Berner Studien zur historischen und systematischen Thoelogie 39. Bern: Lang, 1979.

Donati, S. "La dottrina delle dimensioni indeterminate in Egidio Romano." *Medioevo* 14 (1988): 149–233.

———. "Materia e dimensioni tra XIII e XIV secolo: la dottrina delle dimensiones indeterminatae." *Quaestio* 7 (2007): 361–93.

Dondaine, A. *Secrétaires de saint Thomas*. Rome: Editori di S. Tommaso (Leonine Commission), 1956.

———. "Les *Opuscula fratris Thomae* chez Ptolémée de Lucques." *Archivum Fratrum Praedicatorum* 31 (1961): 142–203.

Dondaine, A., and J. Peters, eds. "Jacques de Tonengo et Giffredus d'Anagni auditeurs de saint Thomas." *Archivum Fratrum Praedicatorum* 29 (1959): 52–72.

Dondaine, H.-F. "*Alia lectura fratris Thome?* (Super I Sent.)." *Mediaeval Studies* 42 (1980): 308–36.

Donneaud, H. *Théologie et intelligence de la foi au XIII siècle*. Paris: Parole et Silence, 2006.

Doolan, G. T. *Aquinas on the Divine Ideas as Exemplar Causes*. Washington, D.C.: The Catholic University of America Press, 2008.

Doucet, V. *Commentaires sur les Sentences. Supplément au Répertoire de M. Frédéric Stegmüller*. Quaracchi-Florence: Typ. Collegii S. Bonaventurae, 1954.

Dunne, M. "Concerning 'Neapolitan Gold': William of Tocco and Peter of Ireland: A Response to Andrea Robiglio." *Bulletin de Philosophie Médiévale* 45 (2003): 61–5.

Elders, L. J., ed. Quinque sunt viae. *Actes du Symposium sur les 5 voies de la Somme théologique (Rolduc 1979)*. Studi tomistici 9. Vatican City: Libreria Editrice Vaticana, 1980.

Eschmann, I. T. "St. Thomas Aquinas on the Two Powers." *Mediaeval Studies* 20 (1958): 177–205.

Evans, G. R., ed. *Medieval Commentaries on the Sentences of Peter Lombard: Current Research*, vol. 1. Leiden: Brill, 2002.

Ewbank, M. B. "Diverse Orderings of Dionysius's *triplex via* by Saint Thomas Aquinas." *Mediaeval Studies* 52 (1990): 82–109.

Fabro, C. "Sviluppo, significato e valore della 'IV via.'" *Doctor Communis* 1–2 (1954): 71–109.

———. *Partecipazione e causalità secondo s. Tommaso d'Aquino*. Turin: SEI, 1960.

Faes de Mottoni, B. "*Enuntiatores divini silentii*: Tommaso d'Aquino e il linguaggio degli angeli." *Medioevo* 12 (1986): 199–228.

———. "Tommaso d'Aquino e la conoscenza mattutina e vespertina degli angeli." *Medioevo* 18 (1992): 169–202.

Finnis, J. *Natural Law and Natural Right*. 2nd ed. Oxford: Clarendon Press, 2011.

Flüeler, C. *Rezeption und Interpretation der Aristotelischen Politica im späten Mittelalter*, 2 vols. Bochumer Studien zur Philosophie 19. Amsterdam: Grüner, 1992.

Galluzzo, G. "Aquinas on Common Nature and Universals." *Recherches de Théologie et Philosophie Médiévales* 71 (2004): 131–71.

———. "Aquinas on the Structure of Aristotle's Metaphysics." *Documenti e studi sulla tradizione filosofica medievale* 15 (2004): 353–86.

———. "Aquinas's Interpretation of *Metaphysics* Book Beta." *Quaestio* 5 (2005): 413–27.

García Cuadrado, J. Á. "Existence et vérité: nome et verbe dans l'*Expositio libri Peri hermeneias* de Thomas d'Aquin." *Revue Thomiste* 106 (2006): 355–92.

Gauthier, R.-A. "Les *Articuli in quibus frater Thomas melius in Summa quam in Scriptis*." *Recherches de Théologie Ancienne et Médiévale* 19 (1952): 271–326.

———. *Introduction à Saint Thomas d'Aquin*, Somme contre les Gentils. Paris: Éditions Universitaires, 1993.

Geenen, C. G. "Saint Thomas et les Pères." In *Dictionnaire de théologie catholique*, vol. 15/1. Edited by A. Vacant, J.-E. Mangenot, and É. Amann, coll. 738–61. Paris: Letouzey et Ané, 1946.

Geiger, L.-B. "Abstraction et séparation d'après S. Thomas *In De Trinitate* q. 5, a. 3." *Revue des Sciences Philosophiques et Théologiques* 31 (1947): 3–40. (Republished in *Philosophie et spiritualité*, vol. 1, 87–124. Paris: Cerf, 1963; and *Penser avec Thomas d'Aquin*. études thomistes présentées par R. Imbach, 139–83. Fribourg-Paris: Éditions Universitaires-Cerf, 2000.)

———. *La participation dans la philosophie de S. Thomas d'Aquin*. 2nd ed. Paris: Vrin, 1953.

———. "Les rédactions successives de *Contra Gentiles* I, 53 d'après l'autographe." In *Saint Thomas d'Aquin aujourd'hui*. Edited by J. Y. Jolif et al., 221–40. Recherches de philosophie 6. Bruges Paris: Desclée de Brouwer, 1963.

———. "Les idées divines dans l'oeuvre de Saint Thomas." In *St. Thomas Aquinas, 1274–1974: Commemorative Studies*, vol. 1. Edited by A. Maurer, 175–209. Toronto: Pontifical Institute of Mediaeval Studies, 1974. (Republished in *Penser avec Thomas d'Aquin, études tho*mistes présentées par R. Imbach, 63–110. Fribourg-Paris: *Éditions Universitaires-Cerf, 2000*.)

Gevaert, J. *Contingent en noodzakelijk bestaan volgens Thomas van Aquino*. Brussels: Paleis der Academiën, 1965.

Ghisalberti, A., A. Petagine, and R. Rizzello, eds. *Letture e interpretazioni di Tommaso d'Aquino oggi: cantieri aperti. Atti del Convegno internazionale di studio (Milano, 12–13 settembre 2005)*. Quaderni di Annali Chieresi. Turin: Istituto di filosofia S. Tommaso d'Aquino, 2006.

Giacon, C. *La seconda scolastica*, vol. 1, *I grandi commentatori di san Tommaso*. Milan: Bocca, 1944. Reprint: Turin: Nino Aragno, 2001.

Gibson, S., ed. *Statuta antiqua Universitatis Oxoniensis*. Oxford: Clarendon Press, 1931.

Gils, P.-M. "Les *Collationes marginales* dans l'autographe du Commentaire de S. Thomas sur Isaïe." *Revue des Sciences Philosophiques et Théologiques* 42 (1958): 254–64.

———. "Textes inédits de S. Thomas: les premières rédactions du *Scriptum super Tertio Sententiarum*." *Revue des Sciences Philosophiques et Théologiques* 45 (1961): 201–28; 46 (1962): 445–62, 609–28.

Gilson, É. *The Spirit of Mediaeval Philosophy*. Translated by A. H. C. Downes. Notre Dame, Ind.: University of Notre Dame Press, 1991.

Glorieux, P. "Comment les thèses thomistes furent proscrites à Oxford, 1284–1286." *Revue Thomiste* 32 (1927): 259–91.

———. *Les premières polémiques thomistes*, vol. 1, Le Correctorium Corruptorii "Quare." Bibliothèque thomiste 9. Le Saulchoir-Kain: Revue des Sciences Philosophiques et Théologiques, 1927.

———. "Les correctoires. Essai de mise au point." *Recherches de Théologie Ancienne et Médiévale* 14 (1947): 287–304.

———. *Les premières polémiques thomistes, volume II: Le Correctorium Corruptorii "Sciendum."* Bibliothèque thomiste 31. Paris: Vrin, 1956.

———. "Pro et contra Thomam. Un survol de cinquante années." In *Mélanges médiévistes offerts à dom Jean-Pierre Müller, OSB à l'occasion de son 70ème anniversaire*. Edited by T. W. Köhler, 255–87. Studia Anselmiana 63. Rome: Editrice Anselmiana, 1974.

Goris, H. "Thomism in Fifteenth-Century Germany." In *Aquinas as Authority*. Edited by P. van Geest, H. Goris, C. Leget, 1–24. Leuven: Peeters, 2002.

Grabmann, M. *Die theologische Erkenntnis- und Einleitungslehre des hl. Thomas von Aquin auf Grund seiner Schrift* In Boethium De Trinitate. Freiburg: Paulusverlag, 1948.

Grant, E. "Henricus Aristippus, William of Moerbeke, and Two Alleged Mediaeval Translations of Hero's *Pneumatica*." *Speculum* 46 (1971): 656–69.

Hall, D. C. *The Trinity: An Analysis of St. Thomas Aquinas'* Expositio *of the* De Trinitate *of Boethius.* Studien und Texte zur Geistesgeschichte des Mittelalters 33. Leiden: Brill, 1992.

Hamesse, J. "Theological *Quaestiones Quodlibetales*." In *Theological* Quodlibeta *in the Middle Ages. The Thirteenth Century.* Edited by C. Schabel, 17–48. Leiden: Brill, 2006.

Hankey, W. J. "Aquinas and the Platonists." In *The Platonic Tradition in the Middle Ages: A Doxographic Approach.* Edited by S. Gersh and M. J. F. M. Hoenen, 279–324. Berlin: de Gruyter, 2002.

Häring, N. M., ed. *Commentaries on Boethius by Thierry of Chartres and His School.* Toronto: Pontifical Institute of Mediaeval Studies, 1971.

Hasse, D. N. *Avicenna's* De anima *in the Latin West: The Formation of a Peripatetic Philosophy of the Soul 1160–1300.* Warburg Institute Studies and Texts. Turin: Nino Aragno, 2000.

Henle, R. J. *Saint Thomas and Platonism: A Study of the* Plato *and* Platonici *Texts in the Writings of Saint Thomas.* Den Haag: Martinus Nijhoff, 1956.

Hissette, R. *Enquête sur les 219 articles condamnés à Paris le 7 mars 1277.* Louvain: Publications Universitaires; Paris: Vander-Oyez, 1977.

———. "Trois articles de la seconde rédaction du *Correctorium* de Guillaume de la Mare." *Recherches de Théologie Ancienne et Médiévale* 51 (1984): 230–41.

———. "Saint Thomas et l'intervention épiscopale du 7 mars 1277." *Studi* 2 (1995): 204–58.

———. "L'implication de Thomas d'Aquin dans les censures parisiennes de 1277." *Recherches de Théologie et Philosophie Médiévales* 44 (1997): 3–31.

———. "Philosophie et théologie en conflit: Saint Thomas a-t-il été condamné par les maîtres parisiens en 1277?" *Revue Théologique de Louvain* 28 (1997): 216–26.

———. "Thomas d'Aquin compromis avec Gilles de Rome en mars 1277?" *Revue d'Histoire Ecclésiastique* 93 (1998): 5–26.

———. "Thomas d'Aquin directement visé par la censure du 7 mars 1277? Réponse à John F. Wippel." In Roma, Magistra Mundi. Itineraria culturae mediaevalis. *Mélanges offerts au Père L. E. Boyle à l'occasion de son 75e anniversaire*, vol. 1. Edited by J. Hamesse, 425–37. Textes et études du Moyen Âge 10. Louvain-la-Neuve: FIDEM, 1998.

Hoenen, M. J. F. M. "Thomas von Aquin und der Dominikanerorden. Lehrtradition bei den Mendikanten des späten Mittelalters." In *Deutsche Thomisten des 14. Jahrhunderts: Lektüren, Aneignungsstrategien, Divergenzen—Thomistes allemands du XIV siècle: lectures, strategies d'appropriation, divergences. Akten des Kolloquiums an der Universität Freiburg im Breisgau vom 28.-30. Januar 2010.* Edited by M. J. F. M. Hoenen and R. Imbach. *Freiburger Zeitschrift für Philosophie und Theologie* 57 (2010): 260–85.

Hoenen, M. J. F. M., R. Imbach, and C. König-Pralong, eds. *Deutsche Thomisten des 14.*

Jahrhunderts: Lektüren, Aneignungsstrategien, Divergenzen—Thomistes allemands du xive siècle: lectures, stratégies d'appropriation, divergences. Akten des Kolloquiums an der Universität Freiburg im Breisgau vom 28.-30. Januar 2010. Freiburger Zeitschrift für Philosophie und Theologie 57 (2010): 227–430.

Hood, J. Y. B. *Aquinas and the Jews.* Philadelphia: University of Pennsylvania Press, 1995.

Humbrecht, T. D. *Théologie négative et noms divins chez Saint Thomas d'Aquin.* Bibliothèque thomiste 57. Paris: Vrin, 2005.

Imbach, R. *"Gravis iactura verae doctrinae.* Prolegomena zu einer Interpretation der Schrift *De ente et essentia* Dietrichs von Freiberg OP." *Freiburger Zeitschrift für Philosophie und Theologie* 26 (1979): 369–425.

———. "'Ut ait Rabbi Moyses.' Maimonidische Philosopheme bei Thomas von Aquin und Meister Eckhart." *Collectanea Franciscana* 60 (1990): 99–115.

———. "Prétendue primauté de l'être sur le connaître. Perspectives cavalières sur Thomas d'Aquin et l'école dominicaine allemande." In *Hommage à Paul Vignaux (1904–1987).* Edited by J. Jolivet, Z. Kaluza, and A. de Libera, 121–32. Paris: Vrin, 1991.

———. "Alcune precisazioni sulla presenza di Maimonide in Tommaso d'Aquino." *Studi* 2 (1995): 48–63.

———. Quodlibeta. *Ausgewählte Artikel/Articles choisis.* Edited by von F. Cheneval, T. Ricklin, C. Pottier, S. Maspoli, and M. Mösch. Freiburg: Universitätsverlag, 1996.

———. "L'antithomisme de Thierry de Freiberg." *Revue Thomiste* 97 (1997): 245–58.

Imbach, R., and A. Maierù, eds. *Gli studi di filosofia medievale fra Otto e Novecento. Contributo a un bilancio storiografico. Atti del Convegno internazionale, Roma, 21–23 settembre 1989.* Storia e letteratura 179. Rome: Edizioni di Storia e Letteratura, 1991.

Iribarren, I. *Durandus of St Pourçain: A Dominican Theologian in the Shadow of Aquinas.* Oxford: Oxford University Press, 2005.

Janz, D. *Luther and Late Medieval Thomism: A Study in Theological Anthropology.* Waterloo Ont.: Wilfrid Laurier University Press, 1983.

Jellouschek, C. *"Utrum licite possit doceri Parisius doctrina fratris Thomae quantum ad omnes conclusiones eius."* In *Xenia thomistica,* vol. 3. Edited by S. Szabó, 73–104. Rome: Typis Polyglottis Vaticanis, 1925.

Jenkins, J. "Expositions of the Text: Aquinas's Aristotelian Commentaries." *Medieval Philosophy and Theology* 5 (1996): 36–62.

Johnson, M. F. *"Alia lectura fratris Thome*: A List of the New Texts Found in Lincoln College, Oxford, Ms. Lat. 95." *Recherches de Théologie Ancienne et Médiévale* 57 (1990): 34–61.

Jolivet, J. "Les études de philosophie médiévale en France de Victor Cousin à Étienne Gilson." In *Gli studi di filosofia medievale fra Otto e Novecento. Contributo a un bilancio storiografico. Atti del Convegno internazionale, Roma, 21–23 settembre 1989.* Edited by R. Imbach and A. Maierù, 1–20. Storia e Letteratura 179. Rome: Edizioni di Storia e Letteratura, 1991.

Jordan, M. D. "The Controversy of the Correctoria and the Limits of Metaphysics." *Speculum* 57 (1982): 292–314.

———. "Aquinas's Construction of a Moral Account of the Passions." *Freiburger Zeitschrift für Philosophie und Theologie* 33 (1986): 71–97.

———. "Thomas Aquinas' Disclaimers in the Aristotelian Commentaries." In *Philoso-*

phy and the God of Abraham: Essays in Memory of J. A. Weisheipl, OP. Edited by R. J. Long, 99–112. Toronto: Pontifical Institute of Mediaeval Studies, 1991.

Kane, W. "Abstraction and the Distinction of the Sciences." *The Thomist* 17 (1954): 43–68.

Kennedy, L. A. "The Soul's Knowledge of Itself: An Unpublished Work Attributed to St. Thomas Aquinas." *Vivarium* 15 (1977): 31–45.

————. "A New Disputed Question of St. Thomas Aquinas on the Immortality of the Soul." *Archives d'Histoire Doctrinale et Littéraire du Moyen Âge* 45 (1978): 205–23.

Kenny, A. *Aquinas on Mind.* London: Routledge, 1993.

————. *Aquinas on Being.* Oxford: Clarendon Press, 2002.

Kerr, F. *After Aquinas: Versions of Thomism.* Oxford: Blackwell, 2002.

Klima, G. "Aquinas' Theory of the Copula and the Analogy of Being." *Logical Analysis and History of Philosophy* 5 (2002): 159–76.

Kluxen, W. *Philosophische Ethik bei Thomas von Aquin.* 3rd ed. Hamburg: Felix Meiner, 1998.

Koch, J. *Durandus de S. Porciano op. Forschungen zum Streit um Thomas von Aquin zu Beginn des 14. Jahrhunderts.* Münster: Aschendorff, 1927.

Kockelmans, J. J. *The Metaphysics of Aquinas: A Systematic Presentation.* Leuven: Bibliotheek van de Faculteit Godgeleerdheid, 2001.

Kretzmann, N. *The Metaphysics of Theism: Aquinas's Natural Theology in* Summa contra Gentiles *I.* Oxford: Clarendon Press, 1997.

————. *The Metaphysics of Creation: Aquinas's Natural Theology in* Summa contra Gentiles *II.* Oxford: Clarendon Press, 1999.

Kristeller, P. O. "Thomism and the Italian Thought of the Renaissance." In *Medieval Aspects of Renaissance Learning.* Edited by E. Mahoney, 29–91. Durham, N.C.: Duke University Press, 1974.

Künzle, P. *Das Verhältnis der Seele zu ihren Potenzen. Problemgeschichtliche Untersuchungen von Augustin bis und mit Thomas von Aquin.* Freiburg: Universitätsverlag, 1956.

Lafont, G. *Structures et méthode dans la* Somme théologique *de saint Thomas d'Aquin.* Paris-Bruges: Desclée de Brouwer, 1961.

Lenzi, M. "Alberto e Tommaso sullo statuto dell'anima umana." *Archives d'Histoire Doctrinale et Littéraire du Moyen Âge* 74 (2007): 27–58.

————. *Anima, forma e sostanza: filosofia e teologia nel dibattito antropologico del XIII secolo.* Uomini e mondi medievali 28. Spoleto: CISAM, 2011.

Leroy, M. V. "Le savoir spéculatif." *Revue Thomiste* 48 (1948): 236–339.

Libera, A. de. "Les études de philosophie médiévale en France d'Étienne Gilson à nos jours." In *Gli studi di filosofia medievale fra Otto e Novecento. Contributo a un bilancio storiografico. Atti del Convegno internazionale, Roma, 21–23 settembre 1989.* Edited by R. Imbach and A. Maierù, 21–50. Storia e Letteratura 179. Rome: Edizioni di Storia e Letteratura, 1991.

————. *Penser au Moyen Âge.* Paris: Éditions du Seuil, 1991.

————. *L'unité de l'intellect. Commentaire du* De unitate intellectus contra averroistas *de Thomas d'Aquin.* Paris: Vrin, 2004.

————. *Archéologie du sujet,* vol. 1: *Naissance du sujet.* Bibliothèque d'histoire de la philosophie. Paris: Vrin, 2007.

Lisska, A. J. *Aquinas's Theory of Natural Law: An Analytic Reconstruction.* Oxford: Clarendon Press, 1996.

Lohr, C. St. *Thomas Aquinas* Scriptum super Sententiis: *An Index of Authorities Cited.* Avebury: Amersham, 1980.

Lonfat, J. "Archéologie de la notion d'analogie d'Aristote à saint Thomas d'Aquin." *Archives d'Histoire Doctrinale et Littéraire du Moyen Âge* 71 (2004): 35–107.

Lowe, E. *The Contested Theological Authority of Thomas Aquinas: The Controversies between Hervaeus Natalis and Durandus of St. Pourçain.* London: Routledge, 2003.

Lutz-Bachmann, N. "Praktisches Wissen und 'Praktische Wissenschaft': Zur Epistemologie der Moralphilosophie bei Thomas von Aquin." In *Handlung und Wissenschaft— Action and Science. Die Epistemologie der praktischen Wissenschaft im 13. und 14. Jahrhundert—The Epistemology of the Practical Sciences in the 13th and 14th Centuries.* Edited by M. Lutz-Bachmann and A. Fidora, 89–96. Berlin: Akademie Verlag, 2008.

Macdonald, S. "The *Esse/Essentia* Argument in Aquinas's *De ente et essentia.*" *Journal of the History of Philosophy* 22 (1984): 157–72.

Maier, A. "Die Struktur der materiellen Substanz." In *An der Grenze von Scholastik und Naturwissenschaft,* 3–140. 2nd ed. Rome: Edizioni di Storia e Letteratura, 1952.

Maierù, A. "Formazione culturale e tecniche d'insegnamento nelle scuole degli Ordini Mendicanti." In *Studio e studia: le scuole degli ordini mendicanti tra XIII e XIV secolo. Atti del XXIX Convegno internazionale. Assisi, 11–13 ottobre 2001,* 3–31. Spoleto: CISAM, 2002.

Mandonnet, P. "Chronologie des questions disputées de Saint Thomas d'Aquin." *Revue Thomiste* 23 (1918): 266–87 and 340–71.

Manzanedo, M. F. "La antropología filosófica en el commentario tomista al libro de Job." *Angelicum* 62 (1985): 419–71.

———. "La antropología teológica en el commentario tomista al libro de Job." *Angelicum* 64 (1987): 301–31.

Marenbon, J. *Le temps, l'éternité et la prescience de Boèce à Thomas d'Aquin.* Conférences Pierre Abelard. Paris: Vrin, 2005.

Marion, J.-L. *Dieu sans l'être.* Paris: Presses Universitaires de France, 1982.

———. "Saint Thomas d'Aquin et l'onto-théo-logie." *Revue Thomiste* 95 (1995): 31–66.

Marmursztejn, E. *L'autorité des maîtres. Scolastique, normes et société au XIII siècles.* Paris: Belles Lettres, 2007.

Maurer, A. "The *De quidditatibus entium* of Dietrich of Freiberg and its Criticism of Thomistic Metaphysics." *Mediaeval Studies* 18 (1956): 173–203.

McInerny, R. M. "Boethius and Saint Thomas Aquinas." *Rivista di Filosofia neoscolastica* 66 (1974): 219–45.

———. *Boethius and Aquinas.* Washington, D.C.: The Catholic University of America Press, 1991.

———. *Aquinas and Analogy.* Washington, D.C.: The Catholic University of America Press, 1996.

Meersseman, G. G. "In *libris gentilium non studeant.* L'étude des classiques interdite aux clercs au moyen âge?" *Italia medievale e umanistica* 1 (1958): 1–13.

Merlan, P. "Abstraction and Metaphysics in St. Thomas' *Summa.*" *Journal of the History of Ideas* 14 (1953): 284–91.

Micheletti, M. *Tomismo analitico.* Brescia: Morcelliana, 2007.

Montagnes, B. *The Doctrine of the Analogy of Being According to Thomas Aquinas.* Translated by E. M. Macierowski. Marquette Studies in Philosophy. Milwaukee: Marquette University Press, 2004.

Muckle, J. T. "Isaak Israeli's Definition of Truth." *Archives d'Histoire Doctrinale et Littéraire du Moyen Âge* 8 (1933): 5–8.

Mühlen, K. H., Zur. "On the Critical Reception of the Thought of Thomas Aquinas in the Theology of Martin Luther." In *Aquinas as Authority*. Edited by P. van Geest, H. Goris, and C. Leget, 65–86. Leuven: Peeters, 2002.

Mulchahey, M. M. *"First the Bow Is Bent in Study . . .": Dominican Education before 1350.* Studies and Texts 132. Toronto: Pontifical Institute of Mediaeval Studies, 1998.

Müller, J. P. Le Correctorium Corruptorii *"Circa" de Jean Quidort de Paris.* Studia Anselmiana 12–13. Rome: Herder, 1941.

———. Le Correctorium Corruptorii *"Quaestione". Texte anonyme du ms. Merton 267.* Studia Anselmiana 35. Rome: Herder, 1974.

Müller, P. "Il tomismo analitico. Prospettive e contribute." In *Letture e interpretazioni di Tommaso d'Aquino oggi: cantieri aperti. Atti del Convegno internazionale di studio (Milano, 12–13 settembre 2005).* Edited by A. Ghisalberti, A. Petagine, and R. Rizzello, 177–86. Quaderni di Annali Chieresi. Turin: Istituto di filosofia S. Tommaso d'Aquino, 2006.

Neumann, S. *Gegenstand und Methode der theoretischen Wissenschaften nach Thomas von Aquin auf Grund der* Expositio super librum Boethii De Trinitate. Münster: Aschendorff, 1965.

Nuchelmans, G. *Secundum/tertium adiacens.* Amsterdam: Koniglijke Akademie van Wetenschappen, 1992.

Oeing-Hanhoff, L. "Wesen und Formen der Abstraktion nach Thomas von Aquin." *Philosophisches Jahrbuch* 71 (1963): 14–137.

Oliva, A. *Les débuts de l'enseignement de Thomas d'Aquin et sa conception de la* Sacra Doctrina. *Avec l'édition du prologue de son Commentaire des* Sentences. Bibliothèque Thomiste 58. Paris: Vrin, 2006.

———. "La questione dell'*alia lectura* di Tommaso d'Aquino. A proposito dell'edizione delle note marginali del ms. Oxford, Lincoln College Lat. 95." *Quaestio* 6 (2006): 516–21.

———. "Quelques éléments de la doctrina theologie selon Thomas d'Aquin." In *What Is Theology in the Middle Ages? Religious Cultures of Europe (11th–15th Centuries) as Reflected in Their Self-Understanding.* Edited by M. Olszewski, 167–93. Archa verbi. Subsidia 1. Münster: Aschendorff, 2007.

———. "La *Somme de théologie* de Thomas d'Aquin: Introduction historique et littéraire." *Chôra* 7–8 (2009–10): 217–53.

———. "L'enseignement des *Sentences* dans les *Studia* dominicains italiens au XIII siècle: l'*Alia lectura* de Thomas d'Aquin et le *Scriptum* de Bombolognus de Bologne." In *Philosophy and Theology in the* Studia *of the Religious Orders and at the Papal Court.* Edited by K. Emery Jr. and W. J. Courtenay, 49–73. Rencontres de Philosophie Médiévale 15. Turnhout: Brepols, 2012.

O'Rourke, F. *Pseudo-Dionysius and the Metaphysics of Aquinas.* Studien und Texte zur Geistesgeschichte des Mittelalters 32. Leiden: Brill, 1992.

Owens, J. "Metaphysical Separation in Aquinas." *Mediaeval Studies* 34 (1972): 212–18.

———. "Stages and Distinction in De ente: A Rejoinder." *The Thomist* 45 (1981): 99–123.

————. "Aquinas' Distinction at *De ente et essentia* 4: 119–23." *Mediaeval Studies* 48 (1986): 264–87.

Paluch, M. *La profondeur de l'amour divin. La prédestination dans l'oeuvre de Saint Thomas d'Aquin.* Bibliothèque thomiste 55. Paris: Vrin, 2004.

Panella, E. "Jacopo di Rinuccio da Castelbuono op testimone dell'*alia lectura fratris Thome.*" *Memorie domenicane* 19 (1988): 369–85.

Papadopoulos, S. "Thomas in Byzanz. Thomas-Rezeption und Thomas-Kritik in Byzanz zwischen 1354 und 1435." *Theologie und Philosophie* 49 (1974): 274–304.

Pasnau, R. *Thomas Aquinas on Human Nature. A Philosophical Study of* Summa theologiae, *Ia 75–89.* Cambridge: Cambridge University Press, 2002.

Patfoort, A. "*Sacra doctrina.* Théologie et unité de la *Iᵃ Pars.*" *Angelicum* 62 (1985): 306–15.

————. "La place de l'analogie dans la pensée de S. Thomas d'Aquin. Analogie, noms divins et 'perfections.'" *Revue des Sciences Philosophiques et Théologiques* 76 (1992): 235–54.

Petagine, A. *Aristotelismo difficile. L'intelletto umano nella prospettiva di Alberto Magno, Tommaso d'Aquino e Sigieri di Brabante.* Milan: Vita e Pensiero, 2004.

Philippe, P. "Le plan des *Sentences* de Pierre Lombard d'après S. Thomas." *Bulletin Thomiste* 3 (1930–33): 131–54.

Piché, D., ed. *La condamnation parisienne de 1277.* Paris: Vrin, 1999.

Pini, G. "Henry of Ghent's Doctrine of *Verbum* in Its Theological Context." In *Henry of Ghent and the Transformation of Scholastic Thought. Studies in Memory of Jos Decorte.* Edited by G. Gulden-Tops and C. Steel, 307–26. Ancient and Medieval Philosophy I/31. Leuven: Leuven University Press, 2003.

————. "*Absoluta consideratio naturae*: Tommaso d'Aquino e la dottrina avicenniana dell'essenza." *Documenti e studi sulla tradizione filosofica medievale* 15 (2004): 387–438.

Porro, P. "*Possibile ex se, necessarium ab alio*: Tommaso d'Aquino e Enrico di Gand." *Medioevo* 18 (1992): 231–73.

————. *Forme e modelli di durata nel pensiero medievale. L'*aevum, *il tempo discreto, la categoria "quando."* Ancient and Medieval Philosophy I/16. Leuven: Leuven University Press, 1996.

————. "Heidegger, la filosofia medievale, la medievistica contemporanea." *Quaestio* 1 (2001): 431–61.

————. "Qualche riferimento storiografico sulla distinzione di essere ed essenza." In *Tommaso d'Aquino, L'ente e l'essenza.* Translation, introduction, and notes by P. Porro, 183–215. Milan: Bompiani, 2002.

————. "Tommaso d'Aquino, Avicenna e la struttura della metafisica." In *Tommaso d'Aquino e l'oggetto della metafisica.* Edited by S. L. Brock, 65–87. Rome: Armando, 2004.

————. "Intelligenze oziose e angeli attivi: note in margine a un capitolo del *Convivio* dantesco (II, IV)." In *"Ad ingenii acuitionem". Studies in Honour of Alfonso Maierù.* Edited by S. Caroti, R. Imbach, Z. Kaluza, G. Stabile, and L. Sturlese, 303–51. Textes et études du Moyen Âge 38. Louvain-la Neuve: FIDEM, 2006.

————. "Astrazione e separazione: Tommaso d'Aquino e la tradizione greco-araba." In *Tommaso d'Aquino, Commenti a Boezio* (Super Boetium De Trinitate. Expositio libri Boetii De ebdomadibus). Translation, notes, and introduction by P. Porro, 527–80. Testi a fronte 107. Milan: Bompiani, 2007.

———. "Metafisica e teologia nella divisione delle scienze speculative del *Super Boetium De Trinitate.*" In *Tommaso d'Aquino, Commenti a Boezio* (Super Boetium De Trinitate. Expositio libri Boetii De ebdomadibus). Translation, notes, and introduction by P. Porro, 467–526. Testi a fronte 107. Milan: Bompiani, 2007.

———. "La (parziale) rivincita di Marta. Vita attiva e vita contemplativa in Enrico di Gand." In *Vie active et vie contemplative au Moyen Âge et au seuil de la Renaissance.* Edited by C. Trottmann, 155–72. Collection de l'École Française de Rome 423. Rome: École Française de Rome, 2009.

———. "Individual Rights and Common Good: Henry of Ghent and the Scholastic Origins of Human Rights." In *The European Image of God and Man: A Contribution to the Debate on Human Rights.* Edited by H. C. Günther and A. A. Robiglio, 245–58. Leiden: Brill, 2010.

———. "Tra Napoli e la rive gauche: Tommaso d'Aquino." In *I viaggi dei filosofi.* Edited by M. Bettetini and S. Poggi, 57–71. Milan: Raffaello Cortina, 2010.

———. "Antiplatonisme et néoplatonisme chez Avicenne (*Ilāhiyyāt*, livre VII)." In *Adorare caelestia, gubernare terrena.* Edited by P. Arfè, I. Caiazzo, and A. Sannino, 113–45. Turnhout: Brepols, 2011.

———. "Immateriality and Separation in Avicenna and Thomas Aquinas." *In The Arabic, Hebrew and Latin Reception of Avicenna's "Metaphysics."* Edited by A. Bertolacci and D. N. Hasse, 275–307. Berlin: de Gruyter, 2012.

Porter, J. *Nature as Reason: A Thomistic Theory of the Natural Law.* Grand Rapids, Mich.: Eerdmans, 2005.

Proclus. *Elementatio theologica.* Greek text edited by E. R. Dodds. Oxford: Clarendon Press, 1963.

———. *Elementatio theologica.* Latin text of the Moerbeke translation: *Ancient and Medieval Philosophy,* I/15. Edited by H. Boese. Leuven: Leuven University Press, 1987.

———. *Proclus' Elements of Theology.* Translated by Thomas Taylor. Frome: The Prometheus Trust, 1998.

Prouvost, G. *Thomas d'Aquin et les thomismes.* Paris: Cerf, 1996.

Putallaz, F. X. *Le sens de la réflexion chez Thomas d'Aquin.* Preface by R. Imbach. Paris: Vrin, 1991.

Raby, J. "Mehmed the Conqueror's Greek *scriptorium.*" *Dumbarton Oaks Papers* 37 (1983): 15–34.

Rigo, C. "Yehudah ben Mosheh Romano traduttore degli Scolastici latini." *Henoch* 17 (1995): 141–70.

Robert, J.-D. "La métaphysique, science distincte de toute autre discipline philosophique, selon saint Thomas d'Aquin." *Divus Thomas* 50 (1947): 206–22.

Robiglio, A. A. *L'impossibile volere. Tommaso d'Aquino, i tomisti e la volontà.* Milan: Vita e Pensiero, 2002.

———. "'Neapolitan Gold': A Note on William of Tocco and Peter of Ireland." *Bulletin de Philosophie Médiévale* 44 (2002): 107–11.

———. "*Et Petrus in insulam deportatur:* Concerning Michael Dunne's Opinion on Peter of Ireland." *Bulletin de Philosophie Médiévale* 46 (2004): 191–94.

———. "Tommaso d'Aquino tra morte e canonizzazione (1274–1323)." *In Letture e interpretazioni di Tommaso d'Aquino oggi: cantieri aperti. Atti del Convegno internazionale di studio (Milano, 12–13 settembre 2005).* Edited by A. Ghisalberti, A. Petagine, and R. Rizzello, 197–216. Quaderni di Annali Chieresi. Turin: Istituto di filosofia S. Tommaso d'Aquino, 2006.

———. *La sopravvivenza e la gloria. Appunti sulla formazione della prima scuola tomista (sec. XIV).* Sacra doctrina. Bibliotheca 53. Bologna: ESD, 2008.

Robin, A. S. "L'antithomisme de Dietrich de Freiberg dans le De visione beatifica." In *Recherches sur Dietrich de Freiberg.* Edited by J. Biard, D. Calma, and R. Imbach, 165–91. Studia Artistarum 19. Turnhout: Brepols, 2009.

Roensch, F. J. *Early Thomistic School.* Dubuque, Iowa: The Priory Press, 1964.

Roland-Gosselin, M.-D. *Le De ente et essentia de S. Thomas d'Aquin, introduction, notes et études historiques.* 2nd ed. Kain: Le Saulchoir, 1948.

Roling, B. Locutio angelica. *Die Diskussion der Engelsprache als Antizipation einer Sprechakttheorie in Mittelalter und früher Neuzeit.* Studien und Texte zur Geistesgeschichte des Mittelalters 97. Leiden: Brill, 2008.

Rosemann, P. W. *Omne agens agit sibi simile. A "Repetition" of Scholastic Metaphysics.* Leuven: Leuven University Press, 1996.

———, ed. *Medieval Commentaries on the Sentences of Peter Lombard,* vol. 2. Leiden: Brill, 2010.

Rosier-Catach, I. *La parole efficace: signe, rituel, sacré.* Paris: Éditions du Seuil, 2004.

Roverselli, C. "Linee di antropologia nel *Contra impugnantes* di Tommaso d'Aquino." *Sapienza* 41 (1988): 429–45.

Russell, J. D. *Lucifer: The Devil in the Middle Ages.* Ithaca: Cornell University Press, 1984.

"Saint Thomas au XIVe siècle. Actes du colloque de Toulouse, juin 1996." *Revue Thomiste* 97 (1997).

"Saint Thomas au XXe siècle. Actes du colloque du Centenaire de la 'Revue thomiste'." *Revue Thomiste* 93 (1993).

"Saint Thomas d'Aquin et l'onto-théologie. Actes du colloque de Toulouse, juin 1994." *Revue Thomiste* 95 (1995).

Schmidt, R. "L'emploi de la séparation en métaphysique." *Revue Philosophique de Louvain* 58 (1960): 373–93.

Schrimpf, G. *Die Axiomenschrift des Boethius* (De hebdomadibus) *als philosophisches Lehrbuch des Mittelalters.* Leiden: Brill, 1966.

Schulz, G. Veritas est adaequatio intellectus et rei. *Untersuchungen zur Wahrheitslehre des Thomas von Aquin und zur Kritik Kants an einem überlieferten Wahrheitsbegriff.* Studien und Texte zur Geistesgeschichte des Mittelalters 36. Leiden: Brill, 1993.

———. "Die Struktur mathematischer Urteile nach Thomas von Aquin, *Expositio super librum Boethii De Trinitate,* q. 5 a. 3 und q. 6 a. 1." In Scientia *und ars in Hoch- und Spätmittelalter.* Edited by I. Craemer-Rügenberg and A. Speer, 354–65. Miscellanea Mediaevalia 22. Berlin: de Gruyter, 1994.

Sermoneta, G. "Per una storia del tomismo ebraico." In *Tommaso d'Aquino nel suo settimo centenario. Atti del Congresso internazionale (Roma-Napoli, 17–24 aprile 1974),* vol. 2, 354–59. Naples: Edizioni Domenicane Italiane, 1976.

———. "Pour une histoire du thomisme juif." In *Aquinas and the Problems of His Time.* Edited by G. Verbeke and D. Verhelst, 130–35. Mediaevalia Lovaniensia I/5. Leuven: Leuven University Press, 1976.

———. "Jehudah ben Moseh ben Daniel Romano, traducteur de Saint Thomas." In

Hommage à George Vajda. Études d'histoire et de pensée juives. Edited by G. Nahon and C. Touati, 235–62. Louvain: Peeters, 1980.

Speer, A., ed. *Thomas von Aquin: Die* Summa theologiae: *Werkinterpretationen.* Berlin: de Gruyter, 2005.

Steel, C. "Guillaume de Moerbeke et Saint Thomas." In *Guillaume de Moerbeke. Recueil d'études à l'occasion du 700ème anniversaire de sa mort (1286).* Edited by J. Brams and W. Vanhamel, 57–82. Leuven: Leuven University Press, 1989.

———. *Der Adler und die Nachteule. Thomas und Albert über die Möglichkeit der Metaphysik.* Lectio Albertina 4. Münster: Aschendorff, 2001.

———. "Avicenna and Thomas Aquinas on Evil." In *Avicenna and His Heritage. Acts of the International Colloquium, Leuven-Louvain-la-Neuve, September 8–September 11, 1999.* Edited by J. Janssens and D. De Smet, 171–96. Leuven: Leuven University Press, 2002.

Stegmüller, F. *Repertorium Commentariorum in Sententias Petri Lombardi.* 2 vols. Würzburg: Schöningh, 1947. Reprint: 2007.

Stump, E. "Biblical Commentary and Philosophy." In *The Cambridge Companion to Aquinas.* Edited by N. Kretzmann and E. Stump, 252–68. Cambridge: Cambridge University Press, 1993.

———. "Aquinas on the Suffering of Job." In *The Evidential Argument from Evil.* Edited by D. Howard Snyder, 49–68. Bloomington: Indiana University Press, 1996.

Suarez-Nani, T. *Les anges et la philosophie. Subjectivité et fonction cosmologique des substances séparées à la fin du XIIIe siècle.* Études de philosophie médiévale 82. Paris: Vrin, 2002.

———. *Connaissance et langage des anges selon Thomas d'Aquin et Gilles de Rome.* Études de philosophie médiévale 85. Paris: Vrin, 2003.

———. "Tommaso d'Aquino e l'angelologia: ipotesi sul suo significato storico e la sua rilevanza filosofica." In *Letture e interpretazioni di Tommaso d'Aquino oggi: cantieri aperti. Atti del Convegno internazionale di studio (Milano, 12–13 settembre 2005).* Edited by A. Ghisalberti, A. Petagine, and R. Rizzello, 11–30. Quaderni di Annali Chieresi. Turin: Istituto di filosofia S. Tommaso d'Aquino, 2006.

Tavuzzi, M. "Aquinas on Resolution in Metaphysics." *The Thomist* 55 (1991): 199–227.

Te Velde, R. A. *Participation and Substantiality in Thomas Aquinas.* Studien und Texte zur Geistesgeschichte des Mittelalters 46. Leiden: Brill, 1995.

Thijssen, J. M. M. H. "1277 Revisited: A New Interpretation of the Doctrinal Investigations of Thomas Aquinas and Giles of Rome." *Vivarium* 35 (1997): 72–101.

———. *Censure and Heresy at the University of Paris, 1200–1400.* Philadelphia: University of Pennsylvania Press, 1998.

Tolomeo of Lucca. *Historia ecclesiastica nova* XXIII (15). In A. Dondaine, "Les *Opuscula fratris Thomae* chez Ptolémée de Lucques." *Archivum Fratrum Praedicatorum* 31 (1961): 142–203.

Torraca, F. "Le Origini. L'età sveva." In *Storia della Università di Napoli.* Edited by F. Torraca et al., 1–16. Naples: Ricciardi, 1924. Reprint: Istituto italiano per gli studi storici. Ristampe anastatiche. Bologna: il Mulino, 1993.

Torrell, J.-P. "La pratique pastorale d'un théologien du XIIIe siècle: Thomas d'Aquin Prédicateur." *Revue Thomiste* 82 (1982): 213–45.

———. "Les *Collationes in Decem Praeceptis* de Saint Thomas d'Aquin. Édition critique avec introduction et notes." *Revue des Sciences Philosophiques et Théologiques* 69 (1985): 5–40 and 227–63.

———. "Le savoir théologique chez Saint Thomas." *Revue Thomiste* 96 (1996): 355–96. (Republished in *Recherches thomasiennes. Études revues et augmentées*, 158–76. Bibliothèque thomiste 52. Paris: Vrin, 2000.)

———. *Thomas Aquinas*, vol. 1, *The Person and His Work*. Translated by Robert Royal. Washington, D.C.: The Catholic University of America Press, 1996.

———. *Thomas Aquinas*, vol. 2, *Spiritual Master*. Translated by Robert Royal. Washington, D.C.: The Catholic University of America Press, 2003.

———. *Aquinas's Summa: Background, Structure, and Reception*. Translated by B. M. Guevin. Washington, D.C.: The Catholic University of America Press, 2005.

Torrell, J.-P., and D. Bouthillier. "Quand saint Thomas méditait sur le prophète Isaïe." *Revue Thomiste* 90 (1990): 5–47.

Trépanier, É. "Saint Thomas et le *De hebdomadibus* de Boèce." *Laval Théologique et Philosophique* 6 (1950): 131–44.

Trottmann, C. "La syndérèse: heurese faute?" In *Mots médiévaux offerts à Ruedi Imbach*. Edited by I. Atucha, D. Calma, C. König-Pralong, and I. Zavattero, 717–27. Textes et études du Moyen Âge 57. Porto: FIDEM, 2011.

Van Geest, P., H. Goris, and C. Leget, eds. *Aquinas as Authority*. Leuven: Peeters, 2002.

Van Riet, G. "La théorie thomiste de l'abstraction." *Revue Philosophique de Louvain* 50 (1952): 353–93.

Van Steenberghen, F. *Le problème de l'existence de Dieu dans les écrits de S. Thomas d'Aquin*. Philosophes médiévaux 23. Louvain-la-Neuve: Éditions de l'Institut Supérieur de Philosophie, 1980.

Vansteenkiste, C. "Avicenna citaten bij S. Thomas." *Tijdschrift voor Filosofie* 15 (1953): 437–507.

———. "Il *Liber de causis* negli scritti di San Tommaso." *Angelicum* 35 (1958): 325–74.

Vasoli, C. "La neoscolastica in Italia." *In Gli studi di filosofia medievale fra Otto e Novecento. Contributo a un bilancio storiografico. Atti del Convegno internazionale, Roma, 21–23 settembre 1989*. Edited by R. Imbach and A. Maierù, 167–89. Storia e Letteratura 179. Rome: Edizioni di Storia e Letteratura, 1991.

Viola, C. "L'École thomiste au Moyen Âge." In *La philosophie contemporaine. Chroniques nouvelles, vol. VI/1, Philosophie et science au Moyen Âge*. Edited by G. Fløistad, 345–77. Dordrecht: Nijhoff, 1990.

Weisheipl, J. A. "The Meaning of *sacra doctrina* in the *Summa theologiae*, I, q. 1." *The Thomist* 38 (1974): 49–80.

White, K. "Three Previously Unpublished Chapters from St. Thomas Aquinas' Commentary on Aristotle's *Meteora*: *Sentencia super Meteora* 2, 13–15." *Mediaeval Studies* 54 (1992): 49–93.

———. "The *Quodlibeta* of Thomas Aquinas in the Context of His Work." In *Theological Quodlibeta in the Middle Ages: The Thirteenth Century*. Edited by C. Schabel, 49–119. Brill's Companions to the Christian Tradition 1. Leiden: Brill, 2006.

Wielockx, R. "Autour du procès de Thomas d'Aquin." In *Thomas von Aquin. Werk und Wirkung im Licht neuerer Forschungen*. Edited by A. Zimmermann, 413–38. Miscellanea Mediaevalia 19. Berlin: de Gruyter, 1988.

———. "Poetry and Theology in the *Adoro Te deuote*: Thomas Aquinas on the Eucharist and Christ's Uniqueness." In *Christ among the Medieval Dominicans: Representations of Christ in the Texts and Images of the Order of Preachers*. Edited by K. Emery Jr. and J. Wawrykow, 157–74. Notre Dame, Ind.: University of Notre Dame Press, 1998.

———. "A Separate Process against Aquinas. A Response to John F. Wippel." In *Magistra Mundi. Itineraria culturae mediaevalis. Mélanges offerts au Père L. E. Boyle à l'occasion de son 75ᵉ anniversaire*. Edited by J. Hamesse, 1009–30. Textes et études du Moyen Âge 10. Louvain-la Neuve: FIDEM, 1998.

———. "Procédures contre Gilles de Rome et Thomas d'Aquin. Réponse à J. M. M. H. Thijssen." *Revue des Sciences Philosophiques et Théologiques* 83 (1999): 293–313.

———. "*Adoro te devote*: Zur Lösung einer alten Crux." *Annales Theologici* 21 (2007): 101–40.

———. "Au sujet du commentaire de Saint Thomas sur le *Corpus Paulinum*: critique littéraire." In *Doctor communis. L'interpretazione di San Tommaso delle dottrine di San Paolo. Atti della IX Sessione plenaria, 19–21 giugno 2009*, 150–84. Città del Vaticano: Pontificia Academia Sancti Thomae Aquinatis, 2009.

Wilhelmsen, F. D. "A Note: The Absolute Consideration of Nature in Quaestiones Quodlibetales, VIII." *The New Scholasticism* 57 (1983): 352–61.

Wippel, J. F. "Thomas Aquinas and Avicenna on the Relationship between First Philosophy and the Other Theoretical Sciences: A Note on Thomas's Commentary on Boethius's *De Trinitate*, Q. 5, article 1, ad 9." *The Thomist* 37 (1973): 133–54.

———. "The Title 'First Philosophy' according to Thomas Aquinas and His Different Justifications for the Same." *The Review of Metaphysics* 27 (1974): 585–600.

———. "Metaphysics and *Separatio* according to Thomas Aquinas." *The Review of Metaphysics* 31 (1978): 431–70.

———. "Aquinas' Route to the Real Distinction: A Note on *De ente et essentia*, c. 4." *The Thomist* 43 (1979): 279–95.

———. "Quidditative Knowledge of God according to Thomas Aquinas." In *Graceful Reason: Essays in Ancient and Medieval Philosophy Presented to Joseph Owens CSSSR on the Occasion of his 75th Birthday*. Edited by L. Gerson, 273–99. Toronto: Pontifical Institute of Mediaeval Studies, 1983.

———. *Metaphysical Themes in Thomas Aquinas*. Studies in Philosophy and the History of Philosophy 10. Washington, D.C.: The Catholic University of America Press, 1984.

———. "Truth in Thomas Aquinas." *The Review of Metaphysics* 43 (1989): 295–326, 543–67.

———. "The Latin Avicenna as a Source for Thomas Aquinas's Metaphysics." *Freiburger Zeitschrift für Philosophie und Theologie* 37 (1990): 51–90.

———. "Thomas Aquinas and the Condemnation of 1277." *The Modern Schoolman* 72 (1995): 233–72.

———. "Bishop Stephen Tempier and Thomas Aquinas: A Separate Process against Aquinas?" *Freiburger Zeitschrift für Philosophie und Theologie* 44 (1997): 117–36.

———. "Thomas Aquinas and the Axiom 'What Is Received Is Received according to the Mode of the Receiver.'" In *A Straight Path: Studies in Medieval Philosophy and Culture. Essays in Honor of Arthur Hyman*. Edited by R. Link-Salinger et al., 279–89. Washington, D.C.: The Catholic University of America Press, 1998.

———. *The Metaphysical Thought of Thomas Aquinas. From Finite Being to Uncreated*

Being. Monographs of the Society for Medieval and Renaissance Philosophy 1. Washington, D.C.: The Catholic University of America Press, 2000.

―――. "Thomas Aquinas on Creatures as Causes of *esse.*" *International Philosophical Quarterly* 50, "A Festschrift in Honor of W. Norris Clarke, SJ" (2000): 197–213.

―――. "Thomas Aquinas on Our Knowledge of God and the Axiom that Every Agent Produces Something like Itself." *Proceedings of the American Catholic Philosophical Association* 74 (2000): 81–101.

―――. "Thomas Aquinas' Commentary on Aristotle's Metaphysics." In *Uses and Abuses of the Classics: Western Interpretations of Greek Philosophy*. Edited by J. J. E. Gracia and J. Yu, 137–64. Aldershot-Burlington: Ashgate, 2004.

―――. *Metaphysical Themes in Thomas Aquinas II*. Studies in Philosophy and the History of Philosophy 47. Washington, D.C.: The Catholic University of America Press, 2007.

Wisnovsky, R. "Final and Efficient Causality in Avicenna's Cosmology and Theology." *Quaestio* 2 (2002): 97–123.

Wissink, J., ed. *The Eternity of the World in the Thought of Thomas Aquinas and His Contemporaries*. Studien und Texte zur Geistesgeschichte des Mittelalters 27. Leiden: Brill, 1990.

Wohlman, A. *Thomas d'Aquin et Maïmonide. Un dialogue exemplaire*. Paris: Cerf, 1988.

Zimmermann, A. *"Ipsum enim [<est>] nihil est (Aristoteles, Peri hermeneias* I, c. 3): Thomas von Aquin und die Bedeutung der Kopula." In *Der Begriff der repraesentatio im Mittelalter. Stellvertretung, Symbol, Zeichen, Bild*. Edited by A. Zimmermann, 282–95. Miscellanea Mediaevalia 8. Berlin: de Gruyter, 1971.

―――. *Thomas von Aquin. Werk und Wirkung im Licht neuerer Forschungen*. Miscellanea Mediaevalia 19. Berlin: de Gruyter, 1988.

―――. "Die gegenwärtige Diskussion von Lehren des Thomas von Aquin in Deutschland." In *Gli studi di filosofia medievale fra Otto e Novecento. Contributo a un bilancio storiografico. Atti del Convegno internazionale, Roma, 21–23 settembre 1989. Storia e Letteratura 179*. Edited by R. Imbach and A. Maierù, 155–66. Rome: Edizioni di Storia e Letteratura, 1991.

Zonta, M. *Hebrew Scholasticism in the Fifteenth Century. A History and Source Book*. Dordrecht: Springer, 2006.

CHRONOLOGY

ca. 1224/1225: Born at Roccasecca (near Naples)

Thomas's date of birth has traditionally been retrospectively reconstructed from the date of his death (March 7, 1274). According to William of Tocco and Bernard Gui, Thomas was 49 when he died. So, the date of his birth has been determined by counting backward from the date of his death. On the other hand, Tolomeo of Lucca refers to Thomas's death at 48 or 50 years of age, an indication that suggests 1226 as possibly the year of Thomas's birth. Some studies (see pp. 3–6) also propose 1220 or 1221 as a possible year of birth. At that time Roccasecca was located in the countship of Aquino, and it is probable that Thomas would have derived his toponymic from a branch of his family tree that, until the preceding century, had held the countship.

ca. 1230–30: Stay at the Benedictine Abbey of Montecassino

As the youngest son, Thomas was destined, according to the customs of the age, for an ecclesiastical career. Therefore, between June 1230 and May 1239 Thomas was an oblate of his parents, Theodora and Landolfo, at the Benedictine Abbey of Montecassino, with the hope that he would one day become the abbot.

1239–44: Studies in Naples

Thomas began to attend the *studium generale* of Naples (founded by Frederick II) probably in the autumn of 1239. It is believed—on the basis of what William of Tocco reports—that Peter of Ireland would have been among Thomas's teachers (even though the information has recently been held in doubt). It is also probable that Thomas would have had his first acquaintance with the texts of Aristotle at Naples.

1244 (April): Entry into the Dominican Order

The circumstances in which Thomas first came into contact with the Friars Preachers (Dominicans) are not entirely clear. Although a Dominican priory was established in Naples in 1231, in 1239 there were only two friars there: John of San Giuliano and Thomas of Lentini (Frederick II had expelled the medicant orders from the city but permitted these two friars to remain). Most likely, Thomas was won over to the new order by them and received the habit.

1244–45: Forced Stay in Roccasecca

The entry of Thomas into the order was strongly opposed by his family, especially by his mother; seeing the plan for a possible career at Montecassino vanish, she personally went to Naples with the intention of dissuading her son. Thomas, however, had already departed for Rome and from there, with the Master General of the order, John the Teuton, set out for Bologna. Theodora, then charged one or more of Thomas's brothers—who were at that time engaged in one of Frederick II's military campaigns in northern Lazio—to intercept the Dominican brothers. Peter of Vigne was, perhaps, one of the members of the group that carried out the task. Thomas was then brought back to Roccasecca, where he was prevented from traveling for about a year.

1245 (summer): Short Stay in Naples

Having overcome his family's resistance, Thomas returned to Dominicans in Naples in the summer of 1245. In the fall of the same year he then left for Paris, again in the company of John the Teuton.

1245–48: Studies in Paris

In all probability, Thomas continued his philosophical formation in Paris under the guidance of Albert the Great (but the possible relationships with the faculty of arts are still difficult to determine), and he perhaps also began his theological formation at the same time.

1248–52: Student and Assistant to Albert the Great in Cologne

In June 1248 the general chapter of the Dominicans in Paris decided to establish a *studium generale* in Cologne, the organization of which was entrusted to Albert the Great. Albert probably left for Cologne in the summer of 1248, bringing Thomas with him. The latter was already, in a certain way, acting as assistant, having the responsibility of transcribing the notes of the master's courses (such as the courses on Dionysius's *Divinis nominibus* and Aristotle's *Nicomachean Ethics*). On the other hand, it is probable, as Adriano Oliva has recently demonstrated, that the cursory lectures on the Bible (especially Jeremiah and Isaiah), traditionally placed in the Cologne period, were conducted after the return to Paris.

1252–56: First Period of Teaching in Paris
as a Bachelor of the *Sentences*

The appointment was entrusted to Thomas probably through the influence of Albert the Great, to whom John the Teuton turned for the name of an young theologian able to carry out the function of bachelor in Paris. In fact, according to the standard account Thomas perhaps did not meet the minimum age requirement (29 years old) for the appointment (but the question depends, of course, on the exact date of his birth). Thomas read and commented on Peter Lombard's *Sentences* over a two-year course, between 1252 and 1253 or between 1253 and 1254, even though the material redaction of the commentary most likely continued for two more years. In addition to the Commentary on the *Sentences*, the *De ente et essentia* and the *De principiis naturae* must be located in this period.

1256–59: Regent-Master in Paris

Thomas received the *licentia docendi* in February 1256 (in this case too according to the tradition, before the age required by the statutes for masters of theology, which was 35— again, everything depends on the exact year of his birth). In the spring of the same year (between March and June, but the precise date is uncertain) Thomas held his inaugural lecture (the so-called *principium*) on Psalm 103:13 (104:13 in the Hebrew enumeration): "He who waters the hills from his high dwelling" (*Rigans montes de superioribus suis*). In the autumn of 1256 (October or November) Thomas took part in the controversy between secular clergy and the mendicant orders with the tract *Contra impugnantes Dei cultum et religionem,* in which he refutes the theses against the friars set forth by the secular William of St. Amour in his *De periculis novissimorum temporum.* Following upon the developments of this controversy, Thomas and Bonaventure were admitted into the *consortium magistrorum* on August 15, 1257. The *Quaestiones disputatae de veritate,* the *Quodlibeta* VII–XI, and, presumably, the *Super Boetium De Trinitate* belong to this first period of teaching in Paris.

1259: Return to Italy

In the spring of 1259 Thomas was made part of a commission charged with reforming the organization of studies within order. The commission's proposals—which attributed great importance to philosophical preparation—were ratified at the general chapter held in Valenciennes in the same year. Moreover, the politics of the order were such as to insure a rapid rotation of the regent-masters at Paris, both to free the posts so that others could attain the rank and to guarantee an effective dissemination of the ideas to the various provinces. Thomas, therefore, concluded his first period of regency in Paris in 1259, but it is not certain whether he was back in Italy already at the end of 1259 or at the beginning of 1260. Most likely, Thomas made an initial return to his priory in Naples before transferring to Orvieto in 1261. It is not out of the question that in this period of transition Thomas could have worked on *Summa contra Gentiles,* which he had started in Paris (where he had composed the first 53 chapters of Book I, which were revised later in Italty). The first draft of the work continued at Orvieto until 1264–65.

1261–65: Conventual Lector in Orvieto

By September 1261 Thomas was occupied as lector at the Dominican convent of Orvieto (and not, as is often erroneously held, at the *studium* attached to the papal curia), with the primary task of looking after the pastoral formation of the friars. Besides the completion of the *Summa contra Gentiles,* the *Super Job,* the first part of *Catena aurea* (Matthew), the *Expositio super primam et secundam decretalem,* and some smaller works: the *De emptione et venditione ad tempus,* the *De articulis fidei et ecclesiae sacramentis,* the *Contra errores Graecorum* (at the request of Urban IV), and the *De rationibus fidei* all belong to this period.

1265–68: Regent-Master in Rome

Following the provincial chapter held in Anagni in September 1265, Thomas was invited to establish a *studium* at Santa Sabina. From what we know, it seems that the *studium* was entirely linked, for all practical purposes, to the person of Thomas. This is suggested by two facts, namely, that there is no information about other bachelors or masters connected to the *studium* and that it appears to have ceased operating after Thomas's departure. According to Tolomeo of Lucca, Thomas may have begun work on a new version of his Commentary on the *Sentences* (on the question of the *alia lectura* or the *lectura romana,* see pp. 185–88), only later to abandon this attempt in favor of the project of the *Summa theologiae,* of which the *prima pars* was surely composed during this period. During this same period, it is possible that he returned to the *Catena aurea* (Mark, Luke, and John); the commentaries on Paul's epistles (*Expositio et lectura super Epistolas Pauli Apostoli*)—but the editorial sequence of the commentaries on Paul's epistles is especially complex and it is still an object of discussion whether Thomas might have held a second course on Paul's epistles Naples (see pp. 188–90); the *Super librum Dionysii De divinis nominibus*, the *De potentia*, the *De anima*, the *De spiritualibus creaturis*, the *Responsio ad magistrum Ioannem de Vercellis de 108 articulis*, the *Sentencia libri de anima*, and also the *Compendium theologiae*—at least the first part, *De fide* (the second part, *De spe*, which was never completed, probably belongs to the last period in Naples). The treatise *De regno, ad regem Cypri*, could have been composed during these years, although a later date has been hypothesized (the authentic portion stops at II, 8; the other 62 chapters were authored by Tolomeo of Lucca).

1268–72: Second Regency in Paris

Thomas left Rome after the summer of 1268, probably in September. The motives for his return to Paris are not clear: a decisive role seems to have been played by a new wave of conflict between the seculars and the mendicants. Thomas returns to this debate in these years with two polemical treatises: the *De perfectione spiritualis vitae* and the *Contra doctrinam retrahentium a religion*. Also belonging to this period, besides the *secunda pars* of the *Summa theologiae* (and also, perhaps, the beginning of the *tertia pars*), are: the *Lectura super Ioannem* (a *reportatio*, perhaps by Reginald of Piperno), the *Lectura super Matthaeum* (recorded by Peter of Andria and Léger di Besançon), the *Quaestiones disputatae De malo*, *De virtutibus*, and *De unione Verbi incarnati*, and the *Quodlibeta* I–VI and XII. The chronology of the commentaries on Aristotle's work is very complicated: *Sententia libri Ethicorum* can be firmly placed in the period of the second Parisian regency (to which the *Tabula libri Ethicorum* needs to be affixed; it is a work cataloging the contents of the *Ethics*). The *Sentencia libri de sensu et sensate* could have been started in Rome and finished in Paris before 1270. The *Expositio super Physicam* and the *Sententia super Meteora* both come from the second stint in Paris (1268–70), before 1270. The *Expositio Libri Peryermeneias* can be situated between December 1270 and October 1271. The *Expositio Libri Posteriorum* was begun in conjunction with *Expositio Libri Peryermeneias* or immediately after and was finished in Naples, presumably before 1272, using the new translation of Aristotle by Moerbeke. The *Sententia Libri Politicorum* must have been composed entirely in Paris. The *Sententia super Metaphysicam* has a more uncertain dating: the first six books could have been composed around 1270–71 (even if Books II and III were subsequently revised or corrected) and the commentary on the later books starts at the middle of 1271, but it is possible that the work was completed in Naples. Two commentaries that do not treat Aristotle's works need to be added: the *Super librum De causis* and the *Expositio libri Boetii de ebdomadibus* (the dating of this commentary is, in truth, very uncertain). A number of opuscula, treatises, and opinions can be located in this period, which we note without suggesting their relative chronology: the *De forma absolutionis*, the *Ad lectorem Venetum de 36 articulis*, the *Ad magistrum ordinis de 43 articulis*, the *De secreto*, the *Epistola ad comitissam Flandriae* (also known as *Epistola ad ducissam Brabantiae*), the *De occultibus operationibus naturae*, the *De iudiciis astrorum*, the *De sortibus*, the *De mixtione elementorum* (which also could have been completed in Naples), the *De unitate intellectus*, the *De aeternitate mundi*, and the *De substantiis separatis*.

1272–73: Regent-Master in Naples

At the start of the summer of 1272, the chapter of the Roman Province, gathered in Florence, entrusted to Thomas the work of organizing a new *studium* of theology, leaving to him the possibility of selecting the location. Thomas, who had probably already returned to Italy, opted for Naples, where he held the final courses on the Psalms (the *Lectura* or *Postilla super Psalmos*). Besides the continuation of the *tertia pars* of the *Summa theologiae* (perhaps already underway at Paris and halted in Naples with q. 90), some preaching, and most likely the *De motu cordis,* there presumably belong to this period the incomplete commentaries on the *De caelo et mundo* and the *De generatione et corruption*. It is also very likely, as we have said, that there were some commentaries started in Paris that were completed here.

1274 (March 7): Death at Fossanova

Following a mysterious experience during the course of the celebration of Mass in December 1273, Thomas stopped writing and appeared profoundly changed. After a brief period of rest at the home of his sister Theodora in the castle of San Severino at the beginning of February 1274, he departed for the Council of Lyon convoked by Gregory X. He declined an invitation from the abbot of Montecassino to stop at the abbey to explain a difficult passage of Gregory the Great on the relationship between divine foreknowledge and human freedom, sending instead a written response (*Epistola ad Bernardum abbatem Casinensem*). During the journey Thomas's condition worsened. He stopped at Maenza, at the castle of his niece Francesca and later was transferred to the abbey of Fossanova (near Rome), where he died on March 7, 1274.

1277 (March 7): Condemnation by Bishop Stephen Tempier of
219 propositions considered heterodox and dangerous

The censure (preceded by a brief consultation with a commission of theologians gathered together for that purpose) was aimed at the faculty of arts, but some of the theses seem to point also—at least indirectly—to Thomas. (Even the date of the intervention, exactly three years after Thomas's death, has seemed to some not wholly accidental.) Also in March 1277 the investigation appeared to expand to the faculty of theology as well, with the condemnation and (temporary) removal from Paris of Giles of Rome (considered to some degree to be very near to certain of Thomas's positions). A posthumous procedure—destined to remain without result—was probably launched directly against Thomas's doctrines too.

1277 (March 18)

Condemnation in Oxford by Robert Kilwardby, Dominican archbishop of Canterbury, of some propositions that, at least, can be traced back to Thomas's doctrines (and above all to the unicity of substantial form).

1284 (October 29)

John of Peckham, new Franciscan archbishop of Canterbury, confirms the condemnations of his predessesor, adding to them 8 other articles. Peckham had already clashed with Thomas, while he was still alive, on the problem of the possibility of the eternity of the world and the unicity of substantial form.

1319: First Canonization Process (Naples, June 21–September 18)

1321: Second Canonization Process (Fossanova, November 10–20)

1323 (July 18): Canonization in Avignon

1325 (February 14)

The bishop of Paris, Stephen Bourret, revokes the condemnation of 1277 to the extent to which it could have concerned Thomas.

1567 (April 15): Thomas Aquinas Proclaimed
Doctor Ecclesiae by Pope Pius V

1879 (August 4): The Encyclical *Aeterni Patris*
Promulgated by Pope Leo XIII

The encyclical makes Thomas Aquinas the principal point of reference for Catholic thought, marking a renewal of studies, but also causing a certain dogmatic rigidity at the level of interpretation. With a *motu proprio* on 18 January 1880, Leo XIII initiated the so-called *editio Leonina* of the works of Thomas Aquinas, which has gradually established itself as a scientific model for the critical edition of medieval texts and is still in progress.

INDEX OF MANUSCRIPTS
CITED

INDEX OF NAMES

I thank Marienza Benedetto and Francesco Marrone for their help in the preparation of the first two indexes.

SUBJECT INDEX

absolution, 366–67

abstraction, 107–8, 113–14

accidents: essence, possession of, 13, 24–25; God as cause of, 335–36; God distinguished from, 138, 206; ideas of, 78; subject that participates in, 349–51; substance and, 108

actual infinite, the, 95–97

Ad lectorem Venetum de 36 articulis, 367

Ad magistrum ordinis de 43 articulis, 367

Adoro Te devote, 388n

analogy, 10–12, 33–40, 138–39

angels/angelology: angelic knowledge, modes of, 383n133; as atemporal and characterized by a form of potentiality, 344n88; as composite of essence and being, 308–9; cosmological role of, 368–69; the human soul and, 246; language of, 310–11n; as mixed topic, 309–10; sin of, 384; species and, 19, 159–61, 256–57

beauty, 203–5

being: as actuality of every act and perfection of every perfection, 212–13; convertibility with one, 218–19; definition of, 13; the doctrine of analogy and, 33–40; essence and, 12–13, 20–23, 148–49, 155–59, 212–13, 350–51; general modes of, 61–62; God and, 48–51; the good and, 83, 199n29; the One/Good and, 198–202; reality, in the different levels of, 23–26; substantial and accidental, distinction between, 6–7; "that which is" and, distinction between, 347–51

Bible, the: *Catena aurea in quatuor Evangelia*, 173, 175–77; commentaries on the epistles of Paul, 188–90; Commentary on the Book of Job, 173–75; Commentary on the Epistle to the Romans, 390–91; Commentary on the Gospel of John, 264–67; "cursory" lectures on, 5–6

birthdate of Thomas, 3, 56n5

birthplace of Thomas, 3–4

Catena aurea in quatuor Evangelia, 173, 175–77

cause/causality: Aristotelian principle of, 30; determinism and, 333–36; effects and, relationship between, 101; efficient, existence of

God derived from, 225–26; of evil, 269–70; hierarchical order of, 334–35; Neo-Platonists on, 192–93, 343; of the sacraments, 367; secondary, 215–17

celestial bodies: actions of, 335; each as a species in itself, 255–56; as immutable in substance, 266; incorruptibility of, 318; influence of, 245, 327, 358, 361–63; as intrinsically necessary, 147; separate substances and, 160, 356; sublunary bodies and, 35

Christ, commentary on, 265

Christian Neo-Platonism, 142–43

Christian theology. *See* theology

commentary on Aristotle: approach to, 313–15; Averroes, agreement with and dissent from, 317–20; commentatorial tradition, engagement with, 316–20; on the *De anima*, 258–61, 313, 321; *De memoria et reminiscentia*, 322; on determinism, fate, and providence, 333–37; *Expositio libri Peryermenias* (Commentary on the *De interpretatione*), 312–13, 322–27; *Expositio libri Posteriorum* (Commentary on the *Posterior Analytics*), 312–13, 322–23, 327–29; *Expositio super Physicam*, 312; framework of, 312–13; *Liber de bona fortuna* and, 338–39; on the *Metaphysics*, 329–37; natural philosophy, the works of, 320–22; on the *Nichomachean Ethics*, 304–5, 313; on the *Physics*, 317, 320–21; on the *Politics*, 337–38; rational philosophy, 322–29; reasons for, 339–40; *Sentencia libri de sensu et sensato*, 312–13, 322; *Sentencia libri Metaphysicae*, 313; *Sentencia libri Politicorum*, 313; *Sententia libri Ethicorum*, 304–5; *Sententia super libros De generatione et corruptione*, 313, 320–21; *Sententia super librum De caelo et mundo*, 313–14, 316–17, 320–21; *Sententia super Meteora*, 312–13, 321; *Tabula libri Ethicorum*, 304

Commentary on *Liber de causis*, 341–45

Commentary on the Book of Job, 173–75

Commentary on the *De anima*, 258–61, 313, 321

Commentary on the *De divinis nominibus* of Pseudo-Dionysius: beauty, 203–5; the One/Good and being, relationship of, 198–202; Platonic tradition, occasion to deal with,

human action: conscience cannot be mistaken, 308; divine foreknowledge and, 388; external principles of and the law, 293–99; intrinsic principles of, 288–91; the passions, 283–88; virtues and vices, specific points regarding, 299–302; voluntary, moral value from, 282–83. *See also* will, the
human law, 294–95
human life, beginning of, 164, 175n77

ideas: abandonment of doctrine of, 141–43; Avicenna and Thomas's position on, 76–78; definition of, 75–76; revisions of Thomas's thought on, 78–79
ignorance, 271–72
immateriality, intellective capacity and, 19
impossibility, divine omnipotence and, 207–8
individuation. *See* difference/individuation
infinite, the actual, 95–97
intellect, the: agent, 100–101, 232–34, 244–46, 258; beatitude and, 95; divine and human, the Word and the way of relating, 140–45; possible/potential, 233, 243–44, 246, 257–58, 372–77; the soul and, 161–62, 243–46; truth and, 324; the will and, 84–86, 95, 165–66, 273–77

Jewish question, the, 353–55
justice, 299–300, 391–92
just war, 299–300

knowledge: angelic, modes of, 383n133; Aristotelian epistemology, Thomas's, 79–80; characterizations of human, 230–34; cognitive process, 234–35; of creatures, 150–55; curiosity, vice of, 301–2; demonstration, types of, 223–24; divine, 68–71, 73–75; of God, 44–47, 99–102; of God as man's final end, 164–72; God's will and, 146; of the individual by human and divine intellect, 71–73; learning, 80–82; modes belonging to God, simple substances, and human beings, 382–83; self-evident, 223; sense and intellectual, difference between, 234; senses, origin in the, 13–14; separated soul, capacity of, 250–51, 253–54. *See also* science(s)

law: basic features of, 293–94; rationality and natural law, 296–99; types of, 294–96
legacy, Thomas's: canonization and birth of Thomism, 402–3; Catholic thought, official

reference point for, xii, 403–4; condemnation and "corrections," 394–98; Dominican "counter-corrections," 398–99; in the Jewish, Byzantine, and Muslim worlds, 401–2; masters of arts, respect and devotion by, 394; mortal remains, travels of, 393–94; Thomists and anti-Thomists among the Dominicans, 399–401; twentieth-century Thomism, 404–7
Liber de veritate catholicae fidei contra errores infidelium, 121–24. See also *Summa contra Gentiles*
literal sense, principle of the priority of, 5–6
lots, consultation of, 358–63
love, 284, 286–88

magister of theology, duties of, 310–12
matter: immateriality, 19; individuation and dimension in, 15–16; as principle for Aristotle, 8–10; substantial or accidental being and, 7
mendicant orders: Franciscans and Dominicans, conflict between, 397; secular clergy, conflict with, 53–59, 263–64, 303. *See also* Dominicans
metaphysics: duality of Aristotelian, 110–11; separation as cornerstone of, 113; theology and, 111–15; twofold process of resolution, 110
Metaphysics (Aristotle), 329–37. See also *Sentencia libri Metaphysicae*
metaphysics of Exodus, 157
miracles: associated with Thomas, 217–18n71; characteristics of, 217
moral philosophy, 305
motion: existence of God derived from, 224–26; sempiternity of, 318–19
Muslims: reason in arguments responding to, 183; Thomas's legacy among, 402

natural law, 294, 296–99
natural philosophy: apparently unexplainable phenomena, 356–57; commentary on Aristotle's works of, 320–22; influence of celestial bodies on sublunary events, 358
nature: conditions/principles for understanding, 9–12; processes in, 7–10; reality, structure of, 6–9
Neapolitan *studium* period: *Epistola ad Bernardum abbatem Casinensem*, 387–88, 392; establishment of the *studium*, 385–86; sermons during, 386n4; writing undertaken during, 386–87
Nichomachean Ethics (Aristotle), 304–5, 313. See also *Sentencia libri Ethicorum*